RETAIL STRATEGY

RETAIL STRATEGY

PLANNING AND CONTROL

David Walters and Jack Hanrahan

First published 2000 by
MACMILLAN PRESS LTD
Houndmills, Basingstoke, Hampshire RG21 6XS
and London
Companies and representatives
throughout the world

ISBN 0–333–75234–1 hardback

ISBN 0–333–75235–X paperback

A catalogue record for this book is available
from the British Library.

This book is printed on paper suitable for recycling and made from fully managed and sustained forest sources.

10 9 8 7 6 5 4 3 2 1

09 08 07 06 05 04 03 02 01 00

Typeset by Ian Kingston Editorial Services, Nottingham, UK

Printed & bound in Great Britain by Antony Rowe Ltd,
Chippenham, Wiltshire

DEDICATION

This book is dedicated to Mike Smith, who died in October 1998. Mike Smith was one of a few retailers who understood and practised strategic management. It was a privilege to have known him and to have worked with him. His contributions to Argos are well known. His contributions to retailing as an academic subject are less well known, but will leave a lasting impact on those who knew him well.

David Walters

CONTENTS

ACKNOWLEDGEMENTS

We owe a number of thanks to those who contributed considerable effort to produce this book.

Jane Oldroyd, who has processed numerous versions of each chapter and diagram, is owed a particular mention. Without her help we would probably still be at chapter three, with two very sore fingers.

The Board of Freedom Furniture is also thanked for their cooperation. They provided us with a considerable amount of data and time during a particularly busy period in the Company's activities.

We should also thank a pedantic reviewer whose attention to detail brought about changes that we (and s/he) hope made the book a more effective teaching text.

David Walters
Jack Hanrahan

THE ENVIRONMENT OF RETAIL STRATEGY

LEARNING OBJECTIVES

This chapter considers the environment within which retailing operates. A number of issues are discussed. The primary objectives of the chapter are:

- To identify the major influences that are occurring in retailing and to give examples of their impact on a number of major companies.
- To establish the fact that the rate of change is increasing as is its impact on a number of major companies.
- To establish that large and financially sound companies, often considered as part of the retail establishment, are vulnerable if they ignore the changes in the environment.
- To identify the need for retailing companies to be more prospective about planning and control and to consider alternatives to the planning activity.

INTRODUCTION

The retail environment has shown some uniform trends in recent years. Any attempt at discussing strategy and implementation decisions should be made against a review of ongoing events and issues. The difficulties confronting retailing early in 1999 (in the UK) were portrayed by comment in *The Independent* (23 January 1999). It identified 'winners and losers' among a number of retail merchandise groups. Given that a number of major retailing companies reported poor results (not just over a season notable for its characteristic high spending), *The Independent* commented:

> The slump is so severe that many retail experts are at a loss to explain it. The regular refrain from the high street is that sales are weak because of slumping consumer confidence. That seems obvious, but economists point out that employment is growing, real wages are rising and that the savings ratio is far higher now than it was at the start of the last recession, when consumers had built up huge credit card bills.

A number of UK-specific factors were cited. For example, 1997 saw a number of one-off benefits such as consumers benefiting from building society bonuses subsequent to share flotations and a similar effect following a stock market flotation of the National Grid. A survey of consumer confidence at the time showed an increase since the Christmas period. So what or where was the problem?

Answers were offered. One contributor suggested that:

> In some ways British retailers have contributed to their own problems by a lack of innovation, inefficiency and over expansion.

It was suggested that some sectors did do well, but these were new products which caught the public's imagination (e.g. mobile telephones, personal computers and digital cameras). These increases could be explained in part by a sharp fall in purchase prices. But for other sectors there were no encouraging growth signs.

Other reasons were sought. Service is poor, many retailers having reduced the number of sales staff to respond to falling sales and rising costs. Consumer awareness, or discernment, has increased. The value/benefit equation has a different emphasis. Value does include price, but it also includes service, choice and quality. Furthermore, *The Independent*'s Nigel Cope comments that during the 1980s boom, new and interesting, even exciting, offers appeared as companies such as Next, Habitat and the Ratners jewellery chain generated theatre and excitement. They over-extended themselves and ran into financial difficulties during the recession which followed. As Cope suggests:

> Now many retailers groups are run, by safe, sound accountants. They make fewer mistakes but they take fewer risks. The result, some say, is a lack of inspiration – too many shops looking too similar and selling indistinguishable goods at uncompetitive prices.

And there are longer-term trends. One is a gradual shift towards buying fewer consumer goods and more services instead. Foreign holidays, health clubs and 'eating out' are increasingly popular. Add to this a reverse of the view that an immediate purchase will save money as prices can only increase: in all likelihood the price will be reduced; hence consumers delay purchases.

Clearly a number of organizations had not forecast these events, or if they had, did not have the appropriate strategies in place to cope with the dynamic environment. Examples of 'winners and losers', together with a 'recipe for success' by sector were suggested.

The *apparel* sector had Next and The Gap reporting strong sales, with strong brands and attractive store designs. Marks & Spencer, for many years a category leader was quoted as reporting:

> Plunging sales and profits, poor ranges, inadequate stocking and staffing levels so low it has affected customer service. The spring fashion range... was given a pasting by fashion experts.

Department stores also had sector 'winners and losers'. The John Lewis Partnership and Debenham were seen as winners; both have strong own brands and exclusive designer labels. The House of Fraser (specifically Dickins and Jones) was the sector loser. Success was suggested to be based upon knowledgeable and helpful staff in sufficient numbers, together with the JLP 'never knowingly undersold' price guarantee.

Electricals (brown and white goods and *small electricals*) had Dixons as a sector winner. Comet, the loser despite considerable efforts and expenditure in a repositioning exercise, was held back by its dependence on white goods and poor store portfolio (which presumably is being addressed in the repositioning exercise). Success for Dixons was due to its assortment of innovative products priced to make sales. Dixons were early to offer customers free access to the Internet by introducing Freeserve.

The *DIY* sector has B&Q as a clear winner. Do-It-All, with a weak brand and store portfolio, was suggested as the sector loser. The recipe for success is size, assortment and price.

The *music and video* sector has two winners; Virgin and Woolworths. W. H. Smith has lost out and has been reducing its music and video presence in-store. Success is again about size and assortment. Virgin's megastore format, offering a huge assortment of titles together with augmentation (T-shirts, books and magazines) has been one approach. Woolworths, with its huge market share, uses its volume and lower operating costs to offer lower prices on its successful 'chart range'.

Furnishings, always a difficult sector, was led by IKEA. The loser was suggested to be MFI. The recipe for success for IKEA has been style, assortment and price, with a clear target customer. MFI would appear to have abandoned the furnishings sector and is concentrating on kitchens and bathrooms.

The need for a strategy which has clear focus and direction is essential. Such an approach must be able to identify core competencies *as well as* environmental trends which will modify the opportunities confronting the organization. Given both of these, an approach which identifies an appropriate strategic response *and* a plan for its implementation can be developed.

Effective strategy is developed first by identifying and understanding the implications of the changing events in the business environment. Many of the events occurring currently have a wide international impact, and they may be seen to be influencing the results and responses of large retailers. The remainder of this chapter offers a review of those issues that have been (and remain) significant on an international basis. The changes, or issues, that we see as important from a strategic planning perspective are:

- The growth of global companies
- Changing customer characteristics
- Innovation, format changes, spin-offs and unrelated diversification
- Customer loyalty
- People
- Legends run into trouble too!

INDUSTRY ISSUES

The growth of global companies

Possibly the largest retailer in the world, Wal-Mart, has begun to make itself a world brand. Having 'conquered Canada, Mexico, Latin America, Asia and Germany, [Wal-Mart] is rumoured to be seeking entry into the UK. The Wal-Mart formula: "...a ruthlessly efficient computerized inventory and distribution system, no-frills marketing, and prices to beat anyone"' (Cornwell, 1999) is well known. Cornwell argues that such a formula, which has resulted in global sales of US$137 billion from 2700 stores in the USA alone, should be attractive in the UK (where prices are among the highest in Europe for packaged grocery items, electrical products etc.).

Cornwell also argues that Wal-Mart needs a 'strategic fit' to be available for a successful geographical diversification. He cites Wal-Mart's move into Germany as an example. A recent change in shopping laws (removing the opening hours constraints) made the fit possible. Wal-Mart acquired WertKauf and Interspar, who together operated 95 hypermarkets. The WertKauf store format is similar to Wal-Mart SuperCenters (200 000 sq ft (20 000 sq metres), which now sell food).

The UK has problems for Wal-Mart. Roads are busy and land is scarce and high-priced. Planning permission is increasingly difficult to obtain, as Government declared policy is to maintain the viability of existing retailers. Furthermore, there is an assumption that a recession may not be far away. Wal-Mart eventually acquired Asda stores after Asda had announced a merger agreement with Kingfisher PLC. Certainly Wal-Mart's entry into the UK has been made easier (if not possible), by the acquisition. There is an obvious 'fit' in terms of philosophy – both are price-led companies and the UK Government's policy of competition will have been enhanced by the move.

The Kingfisher organization is one of the United Kingdom's largest retailing organizations, with a large and successful overseas component. Sir Geoffrey Mulcahy, CEO, outlined the case for scale and cross-border considerations amongst European retailers. Kingfisher, with major brands B&Q, Darty, Comet, Woolworth and Superdrug, serves over 11 million customers weekly, and each brand has a significant position in their markets.

Mulcahy argued the point for cross-border retailing, giving a clear perspective of Kingfisher's views. A point relevant to the growth of global companies concerns attitudes: '...the buying advantages and operational efficiencies realized by US retailers because of their scale and passed on to customers in better value are beginning to raise legitimate questions in the minds of sophisticated European shoppers'. Mulcahy suggested that manufacturers also have a major issue to face; gross margins are similar in the USA and the UK, with product prices much lower in the USA.

For Kingfisher there are some strategic issues: 'Our philosophy is to capitalise on the advantages of size and transferable know-how in management expertise and trading principles without diluting established domestic brand values or strengths'. Hence they have Darty, a well-established brand in France, and Comet, similarly established in the UK. Both are strong and well-known electrical retailers in these markets, but both recognize local market differences. It is only when and where centralization can be used as a point of exchange for best practice and joint sourcing that it is considered. The Kingfisher strategic goal is: '...to have leading market positions wherever we operate. In the European community we believe that this can be achieved most effectively by accomplishing the trick of bringing together strong domestic brands. The key is to find a compatible partner.... Being big in chosen and related markets is what matters.... Kingfisher is a strategic coherence of retail brands which centres on value for customers in home and family mass markets. This separates the different businesses around a series of common brand values which makes exchange of experience relevant and increasingly allows us to explore opportunities for joint sourcing across the group as a whole'.

In the Asia–Pacific region Australian retailers in the food/supermarket sector have shifted their focus to potential acquisition targets in Asia and the US following the attention of the ACCC Australian Competition and Consumer Commission's expressed concern about the decreasing number of independents in Australia. Coles Myer has been reported as making a bid for Dairy Farm International, which owns retail chains in Hong Kong, China, India, Indonesia, Japan, Malaysia and Singapore, as well as Franklins in Australia.

The issue of size and scale is one for concern domestically as well as on an international scale. The US food market has had no major national dominant multiple. Recently Wal-Mart has entered the sector (Cornwell, 1999) and Kroger acquired Meyer, which, according to reports, has resulted in a $US43 billion chain with 2200 supermarkets in 31 states and convenience stores in six states (*Australian Financial Review*, 1998).

Aldi is also showing interest in the Asia–Pacific region. The Aldi formula of between 500 and 1000 product lines is unknown in Australia (where the company has been conducting research) and has started recruiting (Mitchell, (1999). While there are mixed views concerning Aldi's likely potential, one analyst suggested that a gap had appeared due to the move by the major food retailers towards fresh foods.

Changing consumer characteristics

A universal characteristic of consumer classification is the decline in importance of demographics and socio-economics and the use of psychographics or social–cultural characteristics. This does not suggest that the former have no role in customer segmentation and profiling; rather, they now form the first measure among a number of others aimed at refining the process and, on the way, reducing the commercial risk. Field (1997) shows that retailers can no longer depend on traditional methods of stereotyping consumers. The new consumer behaves erratically and is well informed, sophisticated, a demanding fickle individual, non-conformist and intolerant of poor service. Field uses the 'traditional' variables to explore UK consumer behaviour. He suggests that women comprise a higher proportion of the labour force than men, often better educated and better equipped to contribute to the service economy. The trend to single status continues. Men have become 'house husbands' and their dominance in decision making has declined. Another international trend is the expanding importance of the 'grey market' – those who are retired or nearing retirement. This group has significant spending power and is becoming the target of a number of media vehicles. Fry (1997) reports there are some 18 million people over 50 in the UK, and this represents 32% of the population. Typically they have no mortgage, no commitment to offspring and live in relative comfort thanks to inherited wealth *and* private pensions. Both Field and Fry comment on the mistaken image the media often present of the 'greys'. Far from being stereotyped in their interests and expenditure patterns, they are large purchasers of training shoes and sports clothing, 'adventure' holidays and health club/gymnasium subscriptions.

Salmon (1996) suggests five attributes that consumers have always required: good assortments of quality merchandise, convenience, service, reassurance and competitive prices. Salmon argues that a number of consumer-led changes are resulting in demands that small independent and non-specialist retailers will be unable to meet. For example, working dress codes have been relaxed, resulting in employees dressing in other socially acceptable ways. It follows that *wider merchandise assortment* requirements are likely to limit the ability of small stores to compete. Stores with limited assortments become inconvenient places to shop because consumers cannot purchase all of their (or their families') requirements.

Convenience has become an important feature of the shopping mission decision. It considers accessibility, ease of transaction and possibly home delivery. *Reassurance* has become reliance on manufacturer and retailer brands. Products and service have been designed to eliminate the need for sales personnel, who explain application details and warranties; these have also become less essential as product and process technology combine to deliver both performance and reliability. Hence the stronger the brand, the more *reliable* the product and the less need for *reassurance*. *Service* is closely allied to reassurance. The easier the product (or the service) is to use, the less need there is for service or sales personnel. *But* as we commented earlier, some retailing companies have misread this situation and have reduced service such that transactions support has been reduced to a level causing considerable customer dissatisfaction. Salmon suggests that there is evidence of *heightened price consciousness* among consumers. While basing his argument partially on the decreased need for reassurance, he does add two other valid points. The first is that consumers' interests have expanded and these, if they wish to pursue them, can exceed their resources. He argues that if economies are made it is by substituting low-price versions of FMCG (fast-moving consumer goods), largely food and household products, such as the ranges offered by Aldi. He also suggests that in many parts of the world consumer income has been decreasing. This suggestion may be based upon the fact that inflation in the developed countries of the world has been very low as governments monitor economies closely and pass the control of interest rates to central banks.

Cornell (1999) reports an interesting response in Japan to the 1998 recession. Escapism and self-analysis were common factors in consumer responses. Dentsu Inc. (a social analysis group) suggests the key words: 'tentative innovation groping for an exit'.

Dentsu identifies four determining desires for Japanese consumers as they cope with a domestic economic crisis and a lesser role in the world:

- The desire to indulge in fantasy
- The desire to spend on products of real value
- The desire to enjoy being unconventional
- The desire to deal positively with uncertainty

Sport, convenience stores, books about failure, price-based propositions and the film *Titanic* were dominant product/services sales during 1998. This point is taken up by Laurance and Ryle (1999). The authors describe a number of factors which have resulted in deflation across a number of consumer goods. Technology (lowering costs), commodity prices in decline, and inexpensive imports have lowered prices at the point of sale. Many of the commodity price reductions, such as oil by some 58% (January 1999), have international impact, and prices for many consumer goods have fallen. The authors demonstrate the impact of deflation by using time and an average wage to illustrate the price deflation effect. The impact of deflation, together with the fact that many durables markets (other than the computer and mobile telephone markets) are largely saturated and the increased interest in service markets, has reduced the prosperity of the traditional high street retailers – internationally.

Kaletsky (1999) had, a few weeks earlier, made similar comments, but with a reference to the fact that a hitherto 'major' of UK retailing, Marks & Spencer, had seen its share price fall 'to half their value of a few months ago'. Kalestky expressed some surprise that: '...Britain's biggest retailer and the company believed to have its finger most reliably on the pulse of the solid middle classes, announced its worst trading results in memory...' The company's problems, he suggests, were due to misreading consumer fashions, but above all it got its pricing strategy wrong: it assumed that consumers were prepared to continue to pay a premium for quality and service. Consumers deserted M&S for competitors who offer similar quality but with prices that were falling rather than increasing. The argument is extended to other sectors. Kaletsky suggests that it is retailer confidence, not consumer confidence that has collapsed: '...not because the demand for their products and service has suddenly weakened, but because raising prices has become very hard'. He continues with: '...the gloom in British industry is largely a consequence of 'money illusion', which is due to the fact that inflationary expectations in British industry and commerce are still very firmly entrenched'. Kalestky adds a view suggesting that City analysts 'make matters worse' by assuming that their role; '...is to predict corporate profits, rather than real economic activity'. He adds that Japanese and American business assumes that profit growth is achieved through cost efficiencies, product innovations and market expansion rather than built on rising prices. The financial press offers incredulous and dismissive comments concerning volume growth achieved by 'aggressive discounting'. Kaletsky concludes with two comments. Falling prices are compatible with healthy economic growth and rising corporate profits and that anyone who doubts this should consider the success of the electronics industry and of Wal-Mart, the world's largest retailer!

The inference to be drawn is that a number of influences are operating to change the relationship between customer and retailer. These are both *external* to the relationship (such as commodity prices and the technology effect) and *internal*, as the range of products and services available to the consumer are expanded by an innovative and competitive market-place.

Another perspective of consumers and consumer trends is proposed by authors with a science/technology perspective. Farrar (1999) reports that scientists have forecast that; '...in 50 years people will save an hour a day as a result of new technology, but that the resultant inactivity could take its toll on their waistline and threaten their health. The British man will become 20 lb heavier and the average woman's weight will increase by 17 lb'. Their argument is based upon the fact that technology and robotics will see almost all physical activities replaced or augmented by computers and machinery. The product/service forecasts for the not too distant future include:

- The intelligent cleaning droid which will clean the home when it 'senses' it is necessary *and* will do so discerningly.
- A washing machine that will rapidly clean and dry clothes made from non-iron fabrics.
- A smart kitchen, in which the cooker, refrigerator, bin and cupboards interact, determining *what* food you have, *how* to cook it, and *when* to order more.
- Intelligent furniture that can adjust light levels, select music, relay messages and pay bills.
- Holographic conferencing: virtual reality equipment that facilitates active working from home.
- Home-help droids for heavy lifting, security and gardening.
- Sentient networks that tell you how best to use public transport to avoid delay, and automatic car convoys which travel safely on key routes.

A problem may emerge: 'By 2050 we're going to have a small number of hard working rich and a vast majority of idle poor', a view expressed to Farrar by Kevin Warwick (Professor of Cybernetics at Reading University). Scase (University of Kent) suggests that the social changes that labour-saving devices will bring could also strain personal relationships, lead to unemployment and spark an anti-technology backlash. He (Scase) also suggests the possibility of the UK becoming an impersonal society, preoccupied with technology but with many low paid jobs and with a number of people who will receive no benefits of more time.

The topic of middle class wealth was cause for a comment from Smith (1999). Smith identifies the growth of middle class affluence in Britain due to decreases in inflation and interest rates. He also suggests that the introduction of self-assessment taxation has encouraged an assessment and update of many taxpayers' taxable situations; many have found that this has increased their tax payments. But despite this Smith quotes research by Morgan Stanley which suggests; '...an average middle-class family with annual earnings of £25000 and a mortgage of £50000 will enjoy an 11% rise in spending power this year compared with 1998. Disposable income for these households is 50% greater than at the height of the 1980s boom.... For families with bigger mortgages the gains are even greater. A household with a £75000 mortgage will see a 19% gain in spending power this year (1999)'. Smith was commenting on the debate to adjust welfare payments and taxation in the UK, the major issue being one of taxing child benefit. While there is concern for prosperity to continue, and for the acceptance of a tax/welfare payment trade-off, the fact remains that the middle classes are important politically and it would be difficult to reduce this new-found affluence.

Returning to the topic of consumer classification and the emergence of lifestyle profiles to augment socio-economics and demographics, the new social classification system proposed by David Rose (University of Essex) was unveiled in late 1998. Rose claims that his classification system; '...isn't designed to try to divide society up by consumption, nor to segment it by markets. It is a similar guideline to ABC1 in the sense that it uses numbers'. Upton (1998) reports views and reactions to the Rose proposals: 'Rose's system interests marketers and market researchers because it is a more accurate tool with which to draw distinctions between purchasing habits. Details like including self-employed and small employers are seen as a big improvement'.

The response of the 'industry' is guarded. The Chairman of the Census Interest Group at the Market Research Society sees an opportunity for an alternative to the ABC1 model, but suggests it needs evaluation, and adds: 'The old system is ingrained among media buyers and advertisers'. Melanie Howard identified a major problem confronting *all* classification systems: the dynamism of consumer change. There are rapid changes of social class, marital status and large changes occurring in values and attitudes. She comments: 'It's a question of how marketing can catch up with reality. We need to understand the differences. We've moved away from grouping people together to explain their similarities. We are all becoming individualised and sophisticated. Companies are going to have to do more sophisticated marketing, which has already started with the direct marketing industry through vehicles such as loyalty programs.'

The Henley Centre has a not dissimilar view: 'Instead of looking at consumer identity, we look at modes of acting and behaving at different times.... We segment people according to occasions instead of what you think their identity is all the time. The question is not what are their backgrounds, but when will they be in this mode? When will they want to chill out? When will they want to splash out?' (Stokes Jones). Jones also suggests a problem in persuading the media owners to change and to move away from social grades; they back the current system, despite the fact that they are aware of its shortcomings.

Thus we seem to have a consensus of opinion favouring lifestyle/ sociocultural profiles of consumers. The consensus also appears to be that the consumer is dynamic in two senses. Who and what they are 'fits' a specific situation, and attitudes to situations are not permanent.

Innovation, format changes, spin-offs and unrelated diversification

Recent years have witnessed significant developments in retail format design and size. At a 'macro' level, malls, out-of-town shopping centres and retail warehouses have changed the landscape, and in a number of countries have met with government responses to control growth. At a 'micro' level, retailers are increasing profitability, productivity and cash flow through the use of information which identifies, evaluates and subsequently controls format and in-store environment opportunities.

In the UK, Tesco and Asda have increased space productivity and profitability by adjusting the merchandise mix to include high-margin non-food items. In another response to market-based opportunities, the major multiples have developed smaller formats or entered 'partnership arrangements' with small, local, independent retailers to sell their merchandise. Small-scale formats such as Metro (Tesco) and Local (Sainsbury) have been very successful and have been used as 'models' elsewhere. For example, Woolworths (Australia) has introduced the Metro concept, with Coles Myer offering a similar concept.

The multiples have also seized the opportunity to participate in the growth available from forecourt retailing. In the UK Tesco has joined with Esso, Safeway with BP and Somerfield with Elf.

Field (1997) discusses the growth of leisure-related retailing and cites Centre O in Germany as an example of a large leisure unit/large retail complex combination. Within the UK, Freeport Leisure, a factory outlet operator, has adopted a similar, if not as large, approach to the leisure-based retail opportunity. Book retailing has flirted with format innovation for sometime. Its recent response has been to accelerate the coffee shop/browser format approach as a response to Amazon's expansion of Internet selling.

The increasingly successful involvement of retailers in unrelated product markets has been a significant trend. Williams (1999) refers to this concept as *convergence*. Reasons for convergence given by Williams are:

- Electronic commerce encourages new relationships between suppliers and customers, with new possibilities for alliances within the value chain to deliver value benefits cost-effectively to customers.

- Digital technology means that a greater effective bandwidth is available on any communications infrastructure. It also allows new product combinations such as PC/TVs or home entertainment centres.
- Consumer database technology permits customized approaches to customers, thereby improving the intimacy of supplier/customer relationships and transactions.

Events that are influencing the search outside traditional markets are:

- Deregulation, especially in utilities and telecommunications markets, has already witnessed a number of new entrants. For example, UK retailers now sell gas and electricity.
- Domestic and core markets are approaching saturation, and this motivates the search for alternative sources of growth.
- Customer dissatisfaction in some sectors (notably financial services) is prompting a number of new entrants.
- In a number of instances businesses have leveraged strong brands (and their customer relationships) into complementary (and new) areas.

To be successful with convergence strategies, six core capabilities appear necessary:

- Brand building and management
- Alliance (partnership) identification and management
- Customer information management
- Customer relationship management
- Innovation management
- Developing and managing enabling technology

A number of examples are available. Both Tesco and Marks & Spencer have made notable progress with unrelated diversification based upon strong brands and customer relationship management. The moves have been responsible for retaining customers and expanding the customer transactions with each company. Tesco has even launched a range of books for children and cooks.

Spinoffs, or related diversification, has been equally popular. Barmash (1998) comments on US activities and suggests a reverse argument to that made for synergy: that: '...often important pieces of the company have as great or greater a value than the whole company, at least in terms of investor sentiment'. Examples of recent successful *spinoffs* are Limited (Brylane, Inc. and Intimate Brands), Kmart (Sports Authority and Borders Group) and one from Melville Corporation (Footstar Inc.). Bamash reports on the subsequent success of the share prices.

There has been significant growth of manufacturer stores. These include Polo, Mont Blanc, Levi, Rockport, Nike and other leisure clothes brands, which have opened stores in prime locations. Rockport's marketing manager gave what appears to be the primary motivation: 'Many consumers don't want white athletics shoes.... We're really approaching the adventure travel segment. Sport is becoming fashion now'. Given such arguments it is necessary for control at the point of sale if consumer fashion trends are to be monitored closely and responses made quickly. Clearly the margins are available in these exclusive merchandise areas.

Specialist retailing has shown an international increase. This reflects consumer indulgence *and* retailer innovative responses. Examples of recent specialist developments are Lush, E'Spa (in health and beauty) and Qii, an international herbalist offering remedies for hangovers and smoking and solutions for sudden 'stresses such as moving house'. Carr (1999) reports the success of Lush in an interview with its Australian co-licensee, Sarah Paykel, who mentions its handmade products, with their simple packaging and the avoidance of advertising promoting beautiful women!

E'Spa is a spa treatment service that: '...in one of eight specialized rooms can include "marine mud envelopment" with sea salts from Northern Brittany and special soothing mud from Canada, or a hydrotherapy bath that massages your entire body with 170 air-and-water jet holes'.

Established retailers have responded. In Australia, the Coles Myer group, well established in accepted categories, is looking to expand with specialist (imitative) responses to the successful innovators. They plan health and beauty outlets, books, and arts and craft specialisms. One particularly innovative format from Coles Myer is Let's Eat: '...where you can pick up fresh groceries, or a cooked meal to take home, or eat in house with wine by the glass or the bottle'.

The impact of information sciences and technology

Retailing has been among the most innovative of sectors with its applications of information sciences and technology. Information management applications extend throughout planning and control activities.

McKinnon (1996) identified the role of information technology in the development of retail logistics. The reduction of large areas of cost, the decrease of lead times, and the increase in accuracy throughout the supply chain, have been based upon IT developments, such as EDI (electronic data interchange) and EPOS (electronic point of sale) systems, and applications such as SCM (supply chain management), ECR (efficient consumer response), QR (quick response), CMI (co-managed inventory) and many other systems. These have been largely based upon cooperation within the supply chain with suppliers, and this in itself has resulted in a significant improvement in supplier/distributor relationships. Waller and Yeomans (1999) discuss yet further developments, suggesting that network economics will challenge:

- The nature of the firm – it will become more networked and flexible.
- The organization of the firm – consumers will benefit from direct access to information.
- The origin of competition – global competitors across all sectors.

- The size of the firm – becomes smaller as transaction costs no longer carry scale benefits.
- Traditional performance measures, such as return on assets or capital employed, may no longer be appropriate.
- The valuation of the firm 'value' may change with the rules of engagement.

These challenges raise some interesting issues for the future. Currently the 'glamour' applications are those of internet commerce. In another PricewaterhouseCoopers publication a number of questions are raised: What are the Internet growth drivers? What are potential sales? What are the opportunities and challenges?

The PricewaterhouseCoopers report identifies the drivers as new users, new technology and new attitudes, and considers these issues and their impact on the growth of Internet use. Of particular interest to this review are the perceived opportunities and challenges.

Opportunities are based upon assumptions concerning consumer acceptance. But assuming shoppers take up the advantages offered, retailing can benefit from:

- Increased sales and lower inventories.
- Management and staff can devote time saved from less inventory management to merchandising and sales generation.
- Increased customer visits.
- A reduction of markdowns.
- Access to new customer segments.

But there are challenges:

- First-time order management and delivery fulfilment through cost-effective distribution systems is essential.
- Online ordering systems must be linked with inventory management systems, replenishment, pricing and customer tracking.
- Systems and procedures must be developed to support customer bi-format purchasing.
- Customer ordering and pickup/delivery requirements will require flexible systems.
- The task of customer traffic flow management will take on new dimensions to meet new customer expectations

An Ernst & Young (1998) study 'Internet Shopping' produced for the National Retail Federation makes some interesting revelations: '...nearly one-third of consumers (32%) with online access have purchased products or services on the Internet. Yet only four percent make more than 10 purchases a year. Sixty four percent of those with Internet access research products online and later buy them through traditional channels – double the percentage of consumers who research and buy the same products online. Overall,

90 percent of consumer respondents said their online research is valuable to future purchasing decisions'. However, the report continues by suggesting there to be evidence that: 'The Internet is much more than a passive advertising vehicle... research shows that the Internet appears to be accelerating purchase decisions'.

This view is endorsed by Ody (1997), who argues that forecasts of Internet sales are largely speculative and points out that an increase in Web-enabled homes does not necessarily mean that they go online to shop. The top-selling items on the Web (travel, insurance, software, books and music) indicate a very slow shift into conventional high street products. Experiments by retailers are more notable for their failure or low profitability than for their success.

Another interesting projection concerns the take-up of digital TV services for interactive shopping. Existing customers with satellite dishes are being targeted with promotional offers. There is a large proportion of C2s, Ds and Es rather than As, Bs and C1s, (the Internet segment). Ody suggests that market projections of market size for interactive TV retailing are even more speculative than for Internet retailing! Ody concludes that most electronic shopping schemes have not survived over the past 10/15 years, suggesting that they were technology- rather than consumer-driven.

Ody's views are reflected in the activities (or lack of) of two of Australia's largest food multiples. Coles Myer's deal with Peapod (a US Internet Company) have been delayed, with no trials planned, and Woolworths' trial in the northern and western suburbs of Sydney continues. A spokesman said: '...although it hadn't been swamped with offers, it was still relatively pleased with how the trial was going and would decide this month (March 1999) on the future of the service' (Mellish, 1999).

Davidson (1999) presents an interesting perspective of e-commerce. He considers the initial view that the intermediary would become unnecessary and that 'brick and mortar' retailers would become redundant. Recent experience has proven this not to be the case: the Internet has brought back the intermediary, albeit one of a different nature. The new intermediaries locate suppliers and link them with enquiring customers. The comments of de Leon (Andersen Consulting) suggest that there will no longer be specific industries: '...rather as power shifts from industry to consumer companies with move from industrial groupings to clusters of companies servicing particular types of customer desires or intentions'. De Leon is suggesting a completely new way of conducting business, resulting in quite different and new ways of thinking about R&D, with marketing acquiring new customers and converting prospects into customers: 'What we find interesting about the e-economy is the fact that Internet companies are able to bundle products and services – either their own, or those of a trading partner who is just one click away – to create holistic solutions targeted at customers' life intentions'. Historical analogies exist; the 'market' concept, which stretches back hundreds of years, and the more modern shopping mall share with e-commerce the fact that they were (and are) successful because they were able to offer a value proposition to customers – it was (is) cheaper and more time-effective to trade within their walls than outside them.

E-commerce has identified one core competence. Companies that are successful are those that know the most about their customers, and so are able to customize a relevant package of goods and services individual to the customer and delivered at a single point that is both time- and cost-effective.

Information for decision making is just as important. In Australia, Betta Electrical, a chain of electrical goods retailers, has announced a program of data development aimed at improving operating efficiency. Store data will be combined with demographic and census data from ABS, together with motivational research data and product information data, to create a sophisticated management resource available to the stores via the Internet. Betta are using the Cor Vu Executive Information System data mining tool to profile potential and actual store performance. This system is one of a number now available. These systems also improve space layout and utilization. Davidson (1999) recounts an anecdote concerning Wal-Mart, who used data mining software to explore the fact that one store sold: '...anomalous quantities of nappies on Friday afternoons.... Wal-Mart discovered that the increased nappy sales were accompanied by increased beer sales, so it placed premium beer next to the nappies and impulse sales of beer rocketed (Apparently young men in suits entering the stores on their way home from work to buy nappies for the weekend bought a weekend supply of beer while they were at it)'.

Other applications of data mining and modeling illustrate how customization can be based upon predicted customer buying behaviour. Burbury (1999), interviewing Stan Rapp, chairman of McCann Relationship Marketing Worldwide, was told of examples of how companies with strong customer databases could use the information for customization of products and services. Rapp gave two examples. The first was Levi's offer of a personalized service for tailored jeans; the process resulted in a detailed customer database through which it identified that retention of these customers was triple that of people who buy ordinary jeans. Tesco, the other example, goes well beyond this. Loyalty club members are offered pension plans, wine clubs, travel, financial services, mail order, apparel, automotive sales, a mother and baby club and student cards. Rapp also refers to 'new intermediaries' – the companies with the databases – and suggests that; '...Tesco is what I think is the business model of the future.... If everyone is getting so much better at keeping customers it's going to be more difficult to acquire customers, since the value of the business is the aggregate of the value of the customer relationship'.

Customer loyalty

The previous section offers an ideal opportunity to discuss developments in customer loyalty and customer retention methods. O'Connor (1996) (like Rapp) suggests that it is the growth in computer memory capacity that has resulted in the facility to identify, track and respond to customer purchase behaviour. Given computer capacity *and* sophistication, retailers can implement reward strategies which reflect merchandise, service and format strategies.

An interesting view from O'Connor is the combination of *customer-specific marketing* and *category management*. This matrix approach is suggested in a (1996) book by Woolf. The interesting issue here is the notion that customer loyalty data is used to plan more effective category management and, through this, efficient consumer response systems (Note: both category management and efficient consumer response are discussed in detail later). Customer loyalty programs may extend back into the supply chain to provide facilities to manufacturers to test specific communication campaigns.

Superquinn (the Eire food multiple) operates an effective loyalty club through a subsidiary STM (SuperClub Target Marketing). An extensive range of services is offered (details are discussed later). An interesting point made by the company is that it has a clear view concerning the mission for SuperClub. The company distinguishes clearly the difference between incentive and loyalty. Incentive schemes are short-term methods to encourage customer interest in and trial of a particular product/service by offering special benefit/value offers. Loyalty schemes seek to build lasting relationships with customers by providing targeted benefit/value offers on a long-term basis. Loyalty schemes typically require a much greater financial and time investment by the organization.

A review of customer loyalty programs' effectiveness and their impact on customer relationship management has been the subject of a Pricewaterhouse Coopers publication. Potter (1998) suggests that because the top 5% of most retailers' customers account for 20% of total transactions and 30% of profits generated, they warrant special treatment. Potter also identifies six forces driving retailing towards customer relationship management:

- Technology provides accurate customer profiling.
- Mass media fragmentation necessitates the use of a variety of communication methods.
- Mass market fragmentation leads towards increased segmentation.
- Retail saturation restricts growth opportunities.
- Continued price competition has squeezed profitability.
- Dynamic consumer behaviour creates challenges for maximizing customer satisfaction.

An interesting view concerns the changes required in company culture to succeed in the modern retail environment. Potter suggests some essential shifts:

From	*To*
Products	Customers
Selling	Fulfilling needs
Transactions	Relationships
Product margin	Lifetime value
Mass marketing	Relationship marketing
Meet existing demand	Create new demand
Share of category	Share of customer

While we may not agree with all of these, there is sufficient to begin to explore customer/retailer relationships and even the viability of the supply chain to meet the demands that such changes will require. We intend discussing these issues.

People

> Retail is both customer intensive and labor intensive. If your employees are good with customers, customers come back to the store. Some become loyal customers, and loyal customers are your most valuable asset. If you do not develop loyal customers, you are locked into a perpetual round of costly price promotions that usually attract, but rarely hold, customers. (O'Connor, 1996)

O'Connor identifies the role of people as employees *and* customers and concludes that the role of senior management includes regular customer contact; without customer familiarity it becomes difficult, if not impossible, to be effective in retailing. But equally senior management need to have regular contact with staff at all levels. Staff: '...have their own ideas of what is right or wrong. They have ambitions that may or may not be ambitions we think are right or even moral'. O'Connor's point is that staff are integral to success and as such should be involved in the planning and running of the business. The Sears 'case study' discussed in this book gives an excellent example of both the importance *and* the contribution to be made by staff.

The importance of staff and staff development has become an international concern. The Australian Retailers' Association has become active in promoting the contribution of people to profitable retailing. Retailers themselves are becoming aware of the need for attention to detail and for specialist interests among staff. Myers-Grace, prior to opening a refurbished department store in the Sydney CDB sought: 'musicians to work in the music section and staff with library skills and indepth knowledge of publishers, titles and authors for the book section' (Vincent, 1998). The focus on staff development has caused both the industry and the NSW Government to become involved in training (and funding) at all levels of recruitment and development.

Legends run into trouble too!

The fragile structure of retailing, particularly that of small independent specialists is a well-known problem. However, when the legends announce profit forecast reductions some concerns are necessary. The problems of Sears and its subsequent recovery is a classic case study and is referred to later.

In the UK, two 'high street giants', Marks & Spencer and Sainsbury have experienced difficulties. Murphy (1998) suggests that M&S suffers from a: '...dangerous complacency that stops it looking over its shoulder at advancing competition'. Murphy cites M&S's food operation. Hitherto seen as a 'treat' with some exclusivity, the company has overlooked the growth of competition into the upmarket segment and the erosion of its competitive advantage. The M&S problem has been exacerbated by the company's expansion plans, which were expected to double its investment spend to £800 million, much of which has been put on hold.

'Sainsbury once had the recipe for success. The official grocer to the middle classes, its stores had a social cachet Tesco and Asda could only watch with envy' (Rushe, 1999). Focus on Sainsbury increased as commentators suggested that the *Value to Shout About* advertising campaign (discussed later) had not been successful. Competition, particularly from Tesco, has been intense, as Tesco stores increased in both number and size and product ranges increased to offer similar if not wider choice. Sainsbury's expansion plans are behind those of their competitors and those for large units are hampered by government planning restrictions. Sainsbury's edited CBD stores, *Local,* are behind those of Tesco in terms of numbers. The problem for Sainsbury is how to communicate its strong reputation for quality *and* that it is no more expensive than its competitors.

Following senior appointments at Marks & Spencer, City commentators were not slow to make suggestions for recovery. Michael Baws (1999) had eight suggestions:

- Cut prices. Customers no longer share the value/price view. Competitors are offering improved benefit/value.
- Listen to the customer. M&S, it is claimed, misunderstood customers, underestimated competition and made serious mistakes with its inventory management.
- Improve store layout. Coordination and ideas are part of the current benefit/value equation.
- Improve communications with the outside world.
- Improve supply chain management, particularly inventory planning and management.
- Recruit from outside into senior management roles.
- Sell through the 'new media'.

Changes have been made and plans announced for catalogue developments, a customer loyalty program and increased advertising for food ranges. However, a number of redundancies were implemented.

In June 1999 further consolidation was announced with the closure of unprofitable stores throughout Europe. This, following on from the poor reception of the company's spring/summer fashion ranges, has given a number of lessons to M&S, the industry, and investors.

Clearly M&S and Sainsbury have received press attention because of their size and because of their importance. However, the 'charges' are similar for both companies: complacency and a lack of contact with customers, exacerbated by dynamic competition, can undermine the largest of companies. Perhaps a well thought through strategy would help?

SUMMARY

In this chapter we have identified and commented upon a number of trends and issues that have been responsible for influencing retailing. Our conclusion is that, unless management is aware of external environmental events and reviews their impact on the company's strategic direction regularly, it is unlikely that the company can be successful. What follows is a structured approach to retail strategy and its implementation. We have reviewed current thinking and application in developing this text. We commenced the project with the intention of using new approaches to the strategy problem. Our review of retailing issues convinces us that this is a relevant approach to take.

QUESTIONS, ACTIVITIES AND CONSIDERATIONS

- Given the Wal-Mart/Asda development consider the following:
  - Tesco's policy announcement that they intend to increase margin yield by increasing non-food revenues.
  - The Kingfisher response. Would a UK acquisition strengthen its competitive position?
- Are there limitations to customer loyalty programs? If so, what are they?
- Is 'e-commerce' an opportunity or a threat to conventional store-based retailing?
- Project the likely impact of technology on retailing.
- Considerable diversification has occurred in retailing. This has been made manifest by both related and unrelated diversification and extensive globalization by retailers and consumer goods manufacturers. What developments are we yet to see?

REFERENCES

Australian Financial Review (1998) Supermarket merger in US. *The Australian Financial Review*, 20 October, Sydney.

Barmash, I. (1998) *The Emporium*, Net column.

Baws, M. (1999) Plain way for Salisbury to put sparks back into Marks. *Daily Mail*, 6 March, London.

Burbury, R. (1999) Revolutionary rap on marketing is to dig your data. *The Australian Financial Review*, 16 February, Sydney.

Carr, M. (1998) Coles gets crafty with retailing. *The Australian Financial Review*, 16–27 November, Sydney.

Carr, M. (1999) Big retailers rethink supermarket plans. *The Australian Financial Review*, 3 March, Sydney.

Carr, M. (1999) Retail Therapy in perspective. *The Australian Financial Review*, 16–17 January, Sydney.

Cope, N. (1999) Canny consumers outsmart the stores as high streets run into hard times. *The Independent*, 23 January, London.

Cornell, A. (1999) Crippled Japan learns to shop all over again. *The Australian Financial Review*, 16–17 January, Sydney.

Cornwell, R. (1999) Wal-Mart set to conquer Britain. *The Independent*, 17 February, London.

Cowe, R. (1999) A do-it-yourself America. *The Guardian*, 17 April, London.

Davidson, J. (1999) Evolving e-economy shifts the balance of power. *Special Report: Internet and E-Commerce, The Australian Financial Review*, 9 March, Sydney.

Davidson, J. (1999) Retailer finds a better way to employ data. *The Australian Financial Review*, 14 January, Sydney.

Eldridge, J. D. (1998) Food for Thought: Internet. *Retail and Consumer Worlds*, Issue 27, PricewaterhouseCoopers.

Farrar, S. (1999) Millennium man will be a 14 stone sloth. *The Sunday Times*, 21 February, London.

Field, C. (1997) Consumer Trends, in *The Future for UK Retailing* (ed. J. Fernie). Financial Times Retail and Consumer, Financial Times Business Limited, London.

Fox, C. (1998) Rockport Australia lands on its feet. *The Australian Financial Review*, 3 November, Sydney.

Fry, A. (1997) Shades of grey *and* Why we are not spending. *The Observer*, 7 February, London.

Kaletsky, A. (1999) Why business must get used to falling prices. *The Times*, 19 January, London.

McKinnon, A. C. (1996) The development of retail logistics in the UK: a position paper. Paper prepared for Technology foresight and available at http://www.21st.centuryretailing.org.uk/ukretail.htm.

Mellish, M. (1999) Online supermarket shopping hype cools. *Sydney Morning Herald*, 1 March, Sydney.

Mitchell, S. (1999) Grocers brace for German rival. *The Australian Financial Review*, 1–5 April, Sydney.

Mulcahy, Sir Geoffrey (1998) Paper given at Goldman Sachs International Retailing Conference.

Murphy, C. (1998) How can Marks and Spencer prevent the sales slump? *Marketing*, 29 October, London.

National Retail Federation/Ernst & Young Study (1998) Internet's tremendous power in driving consumer sales in other channels of distribution is overlooked.

O'Connor, M. J. (1996) People. *International Trends in Retailing*, Andersen Consulting, **13**: 2.

O'Connor, M. J. (1996) The Profitable Importance of Loyalty. *International Trends in Retailing*, Andersen Consulting, **13**: 1.

Ody, P. (1997) Home Shopping, in *The Future for UK Retailing* (ed. J. Fernie). Financial Times Retail and Consumer, Financial Times Business Limited, London.

Potter, G. (1998) Where have customer loyalty schemes led us? *Retail and Consumer Worlds*, Issue 27, PricewaterhouseCoopers.

Rushe, D. (1999) Sainsbury has little to shout about *The Sunday Times*, 14 February, London.

Salmon, W. J. (1996) Retailing at the Millenium: how changes in consumer buying behaviour are driving concentration. *International Trends in Retailing*, **13**(1), June.

Smith, D. (1999) All aboard the money-go-round. *The Sunday Times*, 14 February, London.

Superquinn Website, Support Office, Dublin.

Vincent, P. (1998) Reinventing retail. *The Sydney Morning Herald*, 17 October.

Waller, A. and Yeomans (1999) Food for thought: making technology pay: a vision for tomorrow's supply chain. *Supply Chain Management*, Issue 28, PricewaterhouseCoopers.

Waples, J. (1998) Wal-Mart take over talk boosts Asda shares. *The Sunday Times*, 20 December, London.

Williams, R. P. (1999) Food for thought: convergence. *Retail and Consumer Words*, Issue 28, PricewaterhouseCoopers.

2 BACKGROUND TO STRATEGY: A REVIEW OF RECENT AND CURRENT APPROACHES

LEARNING OBJECTIVES

This chapter will identify and explore a number of relevant issues concerning retail strategy formulation.

- A top/down–bottom/up approach which considers *both* customer satisfaction *and* the need to meet shareholder value objectives.
- The importance and the influence of a thoroughly researched business definition.
- A review of recent approaches to strategy formulation, with particular reference to Porter (1996) and the options offered for developing a *value-based* approach.
- An approach to retail strategy (using the top/down–bottom/up methodology) which uses the business definition to evolve functional strategies (i.e. merchandise, customer service, format and environment, and communications) which are integrated and from which the implementation tasks (attributes and activities) may be readily distilled.
- The application of the model through discussion of the stages and components of the model by using an extended example.

INTRODUCTION

As we have seen in the opening chapter, retailing has experienced a number of changes during recent years. These have brought about an increasing sophistication in management approach. Successful retail businesses are both effective and efficient in their management of strategic and operational activities.

The competitiveness of the majority of retail product markets has led successful companies closer to their target markets, using information to deliver greater value with closely controlled merchandise, format, customer service and directed communications decisions.

Observation of these companies suggests that they share a basic approach to managing their activities. In this chapter we introduce a generic version of this approach with comments suggesting how it may be applied.

In Figure 2.1 we illustrate the generic model. It has six specific but interrelated activities. It represents a 'top/down–bottom/up' approach. The top/down influence is the need for the business to satisfy shareholder return requirements. The bottom/up influence commences with defining the scope of the mission of the business within the context of a customer focus and then interpreting this as a strategic position. These two components represent the long-term view of the business. It is within these parameters that merchandise, customer service, store format and environment and the customer

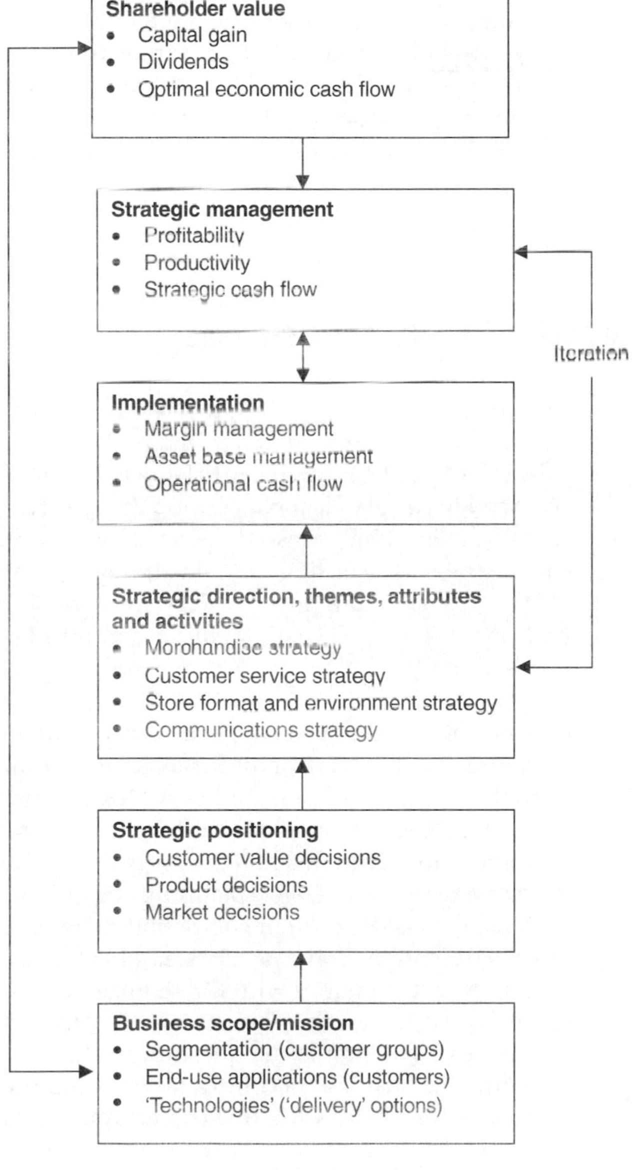

Figure 2.1 A retail planning model.

communications strategy are developed. We will consider the detail of this activity in this chapter.

Given strategic direction, two activities remain: these are concerned with the strategic and operational allocation and management of resources. Strategic management requires *effective decisions*: ensuring that the organization is making the right decisions. Implementation is the process of doing the right things right! To ensure that both occur satisfactorily, performance measures relative to the authority and responsibility profiles of management at each level are devised. As we describe later, these need to be flexible to reflect short-term opportunities and requirements that occur. In other words, we are suggesting that management effectiveness is increased if managers have prescribed performance ranges rather than single point targets. Flexibility offers opportunities to be different – a strategic necessity!

This chapter discusses the background to the model and provides examples of decision-making and performance options. Chapter 3 will deal with the performance criteria in detail.

THE PROBLEMS IN DEFINING THE BUSINESS

The starting point for any strategic planning is a clear view of what the business actually is. As long ago as the early 1960s there was no dispute about this. Levitt's (1960) seminal article focused the attention of management on the need to be very clear concerning the question: 'what business are we in?'. Equally, Tilles (1969) stressed the need for a correct and 'explicit' definition of the business as a starting point in strategic planning.

We suggest that in time it will be the contribution of Abell (1980) that has had most impact. Abell identified a number of significant issues for management:

- *Strategic issues*: any change in the product–market portfolio implies a change in the nature of the business definition. It is the business definition that is the key to assessing the strategic impact of change.
- *Organizational issues*: given the business definition, the question should be asked: 'how does this reflect in the organization structure?'
- *Planning process issues*: planning techniques are often used without explicit consideration of compatibility between the process and the business definition. Robinson (1982a,b, 1983) discussed the implications of *not* matching techniques with the requirements of the business unit.
- *Conceptual issues*: these are fundamental to the problem of defining the business. The first is the question of the number of dimensions used to define the business. Secondly, how should the business definition change over time? Third is the role of multiple factors, i.e. when should several factors be used to identify niche opportunities or relaxed to extend the opportunity to a broad market definition? Fourth come the questions of

definition and organization levels and product–market strategies. Fifth are the definitions of market boundaries: are competitors' definitions similar? Finally, how do the market boundary definitions change over time?

An effective business definition requires consideration of corporate capabilities and capacities: in essence the core competencies of the organization. Prahalad and Hamel (1990) describe *core competencies* comprehensively:

> Core competencies are the collective learning in the organization, especially how to coordinate diverse production skills and integrate multiple streams of technologies... [core competence] is also about the organization of work and delivery of value, communication, involvement, and a deep commitment to working across organization, boundaries. It involves many levels of people and all functions.... Core competence does not diminish with use. Unlike physical assets, which do deteriorate over time competencies are enhanced as they are applied and shared... need to be nurtured and protected.... Core competencies are the glue that binds existing businesses. They are also the engine for new business development. Patterns of diversification and market entry may be guided by them, not just by the attractiveness of markets.

Johnson and Scholes (1996) emphasize the need to understand the relationship between strategic capability and competencies which exist to undertake the various separate activities of the business. They argue: 'It is an understanding of the competence in performing various *value activities* and managing the *linkages* between activities which is crucial when assessing strategic capability'. They offer a structured audit approach to facilitate this process

Implications for retail strategy

Within the context of both Levitt and Tilles (the clear view of the nature of the business), retailers have made both implicit and explicit statements. For all large multiple retailers, the positioning of their retail offer (i.e. merchandise, format and trading environment, customer service and customer communication) conforms to annual report mission statements. Activities reinforce both these statements as merchandise, format and service strategies are honed into standardized reflections of effective marketing activities. Retail outlets are designed and planned to meet requirements for efficient customer and merchandise handling, resulting in planned sales volumes and budgeted costs by servicing clearly defined target customer segments. As and when customer requirements shift, so we see responses which meet the changed needs. The example of Tesco in the UK is noteworthy. During the 1980s the company moved from its operations-led approach to become a prominent retail marketing company. Merchandise ranges reflected consumer expectations for variety and quality at competitive prices. Both format and service decisions reflected the growing expectations of consumers for convenience. Communications shifted away from a price emphasis towards the promotion of the benefits available to the customer from the new strategy.

These activities also reflect the strategic, organizational, planning process and conceptual issues explored by Abell. The shift from an operations-led business and the merging of buying and marketing were organizational changes that were necessary and proved to be very successful. The introduction of the Metro store concept (copied by Woolworths in Australia) is an example of a structured response to changes within the target product market.

Abell (1980) proposed a three-dimensional matrix for the purpose of defining the business: customer functions served, customer groups and technology. Day (1990) extended this by adding activities in the value-added chain. He argued that a multidimensional business definition '...helps an organization break away from an internal orientation, that emphasizes the characteristics of the products or services being offered, to reveal what the business does for its chosen customers'.

Abell's three-dimensional business definition matrix can be applied to retail strategy. Figure 2.2 illustrates the expansion seen by food retailers. The example given fits Tesco PLC subsequent to the announcements of their move into banking and financial services and the trial (addition) of home deliveries.

Many retailers are finding advantages from *brand leverage*, a process in which related products and services may be introduced using the strength of

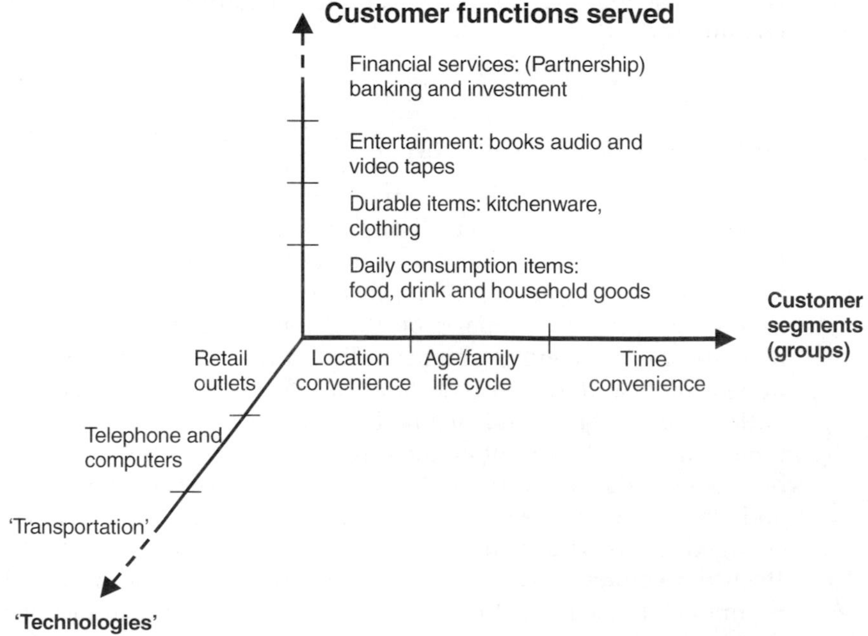

Figure 2.2 Abell's business definition matrix applied to multiple food retailing.

the existing brand to facilitate introduction. In the UK, Tesco and Sainsbury have used brand leverage to extend their activities, initially into petrol retailing and subsequently into financial services. Woolworths (Australia) have also used the concept to move into forecourt activities and Internet retailing. Both Tesco and Woolworths re-entered the 'High Street' with branded Metro convenience stores.

DETERMINING STRATEGIC DIRECTION

Ansoff (1965) introduced the product–market matrix, which laid a firm foundation for thinking through *alternative directions*: market penetration, product development, market development and diversification. Withdrawal and consolidation were added subsequently. Ansoff used the concept of *common thread* to provide direction.

Porter's (1980) contributions to the strategy debate have been considerable. Porter's generic strategies have become common vocabulary in management. While the options are widely used – or discussed – they are not without problems. Johnson and Scholes have identified these problems.

Porter's generic strategies were aimed at achieving *sustainable competitive advantage*. *Cost leadership strategies* are typified by a firm setting out to become *the* low-cost producer in its industry. The emphasis of the low-cost producer is on a standard product–market offer based upon scale and other cost advantages.

A *differentiation strategy* involves an organization in seeking to be unique within its product market, offering features valued by customers and rewarded by a lack of price sensitivity. The logic of the strategy is that the firm selects attributes which deliver value to buyers *but* are different from its rivals' offers.

Focus strategies are based upon identifying a narrow competitive scope (target product-market) which it addresses exclusively. Focus strategies may be cost-based or differentiation-based.

Porter argued that for long-term profitability a clear generic strategy is necessary: failure to articulate a clear strategic direction results in being 'stuck in the middle'.

Johnson and Scholes (and others) have identified problems with Porter's generic strategies. While they offer a structure for the strategy debate they have proven difficult to implement. Issues raised concern lack of clarification and interpretation.

Day (1990) extends Abell's contribution. The inclusion of value chain considerations reflects the contributions of Porter (1980, 1985) and expands the model. However, it could be argued that this dimension could be accommodated by viewing the customer functions served in a broad context. This might be approached by comparing *existing* customer functions served against those that could *potentially* be served. This particular component of

Abell's work is fundamental to the proposed retail strategy model which features in the next chapter.

For example, organizations pursuing cost-based strategies are vulnerable to competition and it is highly unlikely that *sustainable competitive advantage* is a realistic objective. Johnson and Scholes argue that Porter's view of differentiation implies that the uniqueness of the differentiation will eliminate price sensitivity: it is possible to offer a differentiated product–market offer at the same (or similar) price to competitors with the objective of increasing market share. They also use the example of Sainsbury to contest the claim that being 'stuck in the middle' leads to profitability problems. Cronshaw *et al.* (1994) explored the strategic implications of being 'stuck in the middle', using Sainsbury as an example and concluded that: '...(it) is best employed as a classification scheme of strategic outcomes – it says that firms which fail in both cost and quality dimensions perform poorly'. Clearly the long-term success of Sainsbury casts doubt on this conclusion. The company's recent problems (1998/99) are a reflection of competitive response. Its choice of target market segment remains correct. We conclude from this that provided the value expectations of the target market segment are known and understood, a successful response results in a viable value positioning. We shall return to this topic at a later point in this chapter.

A VALUE-BASED APPROACH TO STRATEGY

An interesting, but more recent, contribution from Porter (1996) suggests that an inability by companies to distinguish between operational effectiveness and strategy is 'a problem for many'. Porter claims: 'The quest for productivity, quality and speed has spawned a remarkable number of management tools and techniques.... Although the resulting operational improvements have often been dramatic, many companies have been frustrated by their inability to translate those gains into sustainable profitability. And bit by bit, almost imperceptibly, management tools have taken the place of strategy'.

Porter argues that confusion exists between *operational effectiveness* and *strategic positioning.* He contends: 'Operational effectiveness means performing similar activities *better* than rivals perform them... (it) includes but is not limited to efficiency. It refers to any number of practices that allow a company to better utilize its inputs.... In contrast, strategic positioning means performing *different* activities from rivals' or performing similar activities in different ways'.

Operational effectiveness, claims Porter, is insufficient for long-term competitive success. However, competitive strategy; 'is about being different... the essence of strategy is in the activities – choosing to perform activities differently or to perform different activities than rivals'. In essence, strategic effectiveness is doing the right things; operational effectiveness is doing the right things right.

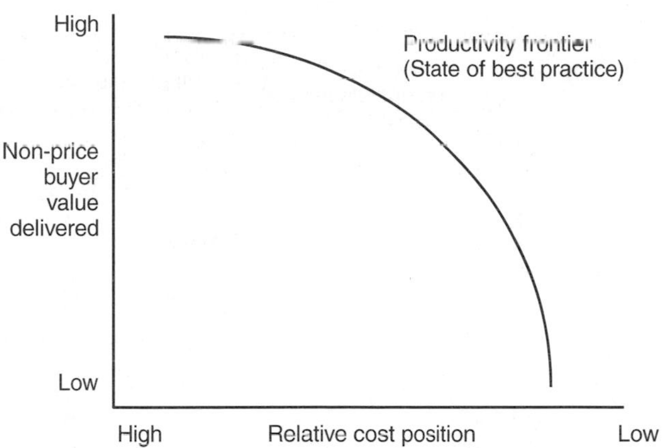

Figure 2.3 The productivity frontier. (Source: Porter, M. (1996) What is strategy? *Harvard Business Review*, Nov/Dec.)

Porter's model of a productivity frontier does not identify the entire situation. The productivity frontier, rather than being; '...the sum of all existing best practices at any given time... the maximum value that a company delivering a particular product or service can create at a given cost...' may be better viewed as a coordinated value-creating process in which delivered customer value is *optimized* within a set of constraints imposed by the necessity to deliver long-term shareholder value (including 'sustainable profitability'). Operational effectiveness is achieved by extending value creation into the implementation of the customer value delivery; see Figure 2.3.

The productivity frontier is constantly shifting outwards: '...as new technologies and management approaches are developed and as new inputs become available'. The point that Porter makes is that management has the facility: '...to improve on multiple dimensions of performance at the same time'. In other words they can lower cost and improve differentiation simultaneously. Clearly this requires some thought. Rather than attempt to move the frontier outwards in an indiscriminate way, a planned response to market-defined opportunity can result in achieving a position of advantage. The strategic response, one which will offer extended advantage, is one based upon developing operational effectiveness which can be targeted to meet a specific opportunity.

Porter's approach can be used to explore this proposition. In Figure 2.4 we suggest a market-based value response. Rather than expand the productivity frontier indiscriminately, a targeted approach is more realistic. By matching competencies (actual or developed skills and resources) with market segment expectations a stronger response, which is ultimately more profitable, may be made.

Figure 2.4 suggests three segments in the UK food market and also suggests the locations of current competitors. Waitrose presents a problem. Many of its outlets are small (in comparison with competitors), in locations of current competitors and in locations in which catchment profiles have changed.

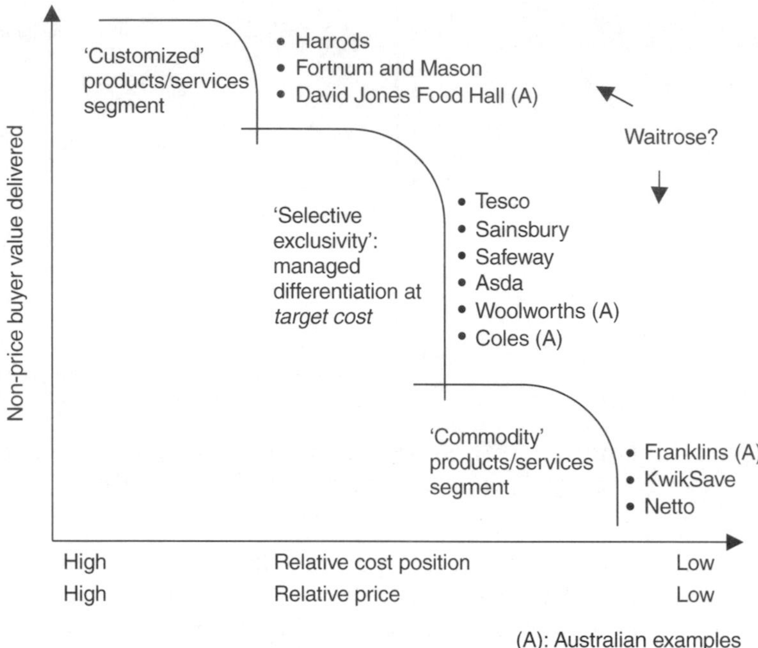

Figure 2.4 Applying Porter's productivity frontier to UK food retailing.

Given a strategic direction, management then focuses on cost-effective implementation by developing operating efficiencies in those activities that will result in increased customer response *and* possibly lowered costs.

Alternatively, Best (1997) suggests that value is benefits/price- (customer cost) based and coordinates the value creation process. He explains: 'The process starts with the customer (customer needs and use situations) and ends with the customer (the customer's level of satisfaction). The job of the marketing team is to create a set of delivered customer benefits at a total cost of purchase that leads to a superior customer value'. Figure 2.5 is based upon Best's customer analysis, value creation and customer satisfaction model. The notion of value drivers has been added, and this addition reinforces the view (Webster, 1994; Shenkman, 1992) that customers formulate criteria upon which their value requirements are based and which also serve as evaluative criteria when choosing among competitive offers. Best's process is probably best described by describing marketing's activity as a deductive role. From this input, the response (i.e. the shape of the productivity frontier) is then managed such that the best possible match may be obtained leading to customer satisfaction and loyalty *and* corporate profitability. The US department store group Nordstrom pursues this approach.

Porter appears to be using his approach to value strategy to reinforce his views on generic strategy: 'Competitive strategy is about being different. It means deliberately choosing a different set of activities to deliver a unique mix of activities... the essence of strategy is in the activities – choosing to perform activities differently or to perform different activities than rivals.

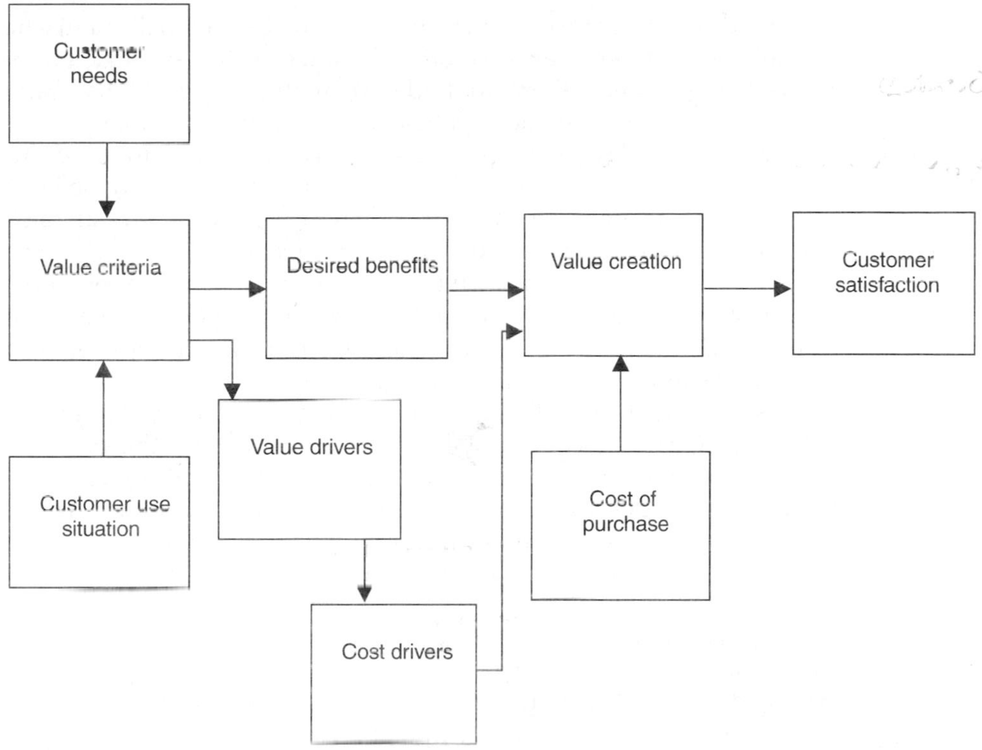

Figure 2.5 Customer analysis, value creation and customer satisfaction. (Adapted from Best, R. J. (1997) *Market Based Management*. Prentice Hall, Englewood Cliffs, New Jersey.)

Otherwise, a strategy is nothing more than a marketing slogan that will not withstand competition'.

Porter argues that strategic positions emerge from three sources, not mutually exclusive and often overlapping. *Variety-based positioning*; '...is based on a choice of product or service varieties rather than customer segments... (it) makes economic sense when a company can best produce particular products or services using distinctive sets of activities' (for example, specialist retailers). *Needs-based positioning* focuses on the needs of a particular group of customers: '...which comes closer to traditional thinking about targeting customers' (department stores). *Access-based positioning* is based upon: '...segmenting customers who are accessible in different ways... needs are similar to those of other customers... the best configuration of activities to reach them is different' (food retailing: supermarkets). Porter suggests customer geography or scale but clearly this includes technology. Porter's strategic positioning alternatives have a strong similarity with Abell's three-dimensional business definition matrix: the variety-based option (product/service characteristics) reflects the thinking upon which end-use or needs are based; needs-based positioning reflects traditional segmentation, while access-based positioning compares closely to technology or delivery options.

Porter continues his argument by introducing the notion that a sustainable strategic position requires trade-offs. He suggests: '...a strategic position is not sustainable unless there are trade-offs with other positions. Trade-offs occur when activities are incompatible... a trade-off means that more of one thing necessitates less of another'. A retailer can offer a customized product or service or it can offer a 'never knowingly undersold' pricing policy. To do both leads to an untenable margin situation. Porter's trade-offs arise for three reasons. The first is potential *inconsistencies in image or reputation*: given a reputation for offering classic styled ladies wear, a change to contemporary fashion styles undermines an established positioning (a problem shared by Wallis (1980s), Laura Ashley (1990s) and Country Road (1990s)). Different positions require *different resource configurations and skills*; the IKEA example typifies this situation. IKEA has structured its activities to lower costs by having customers effect their own delivery and assembly; the format would be unable to meet the needs of customers requiring high levels of service. Trade-offs are suggested to be characterized by *optimal features*; to staff a store with over-trained sales personnel (providing them with skills not called upon) is value-destroying. Furthermore, Porter argues, productivity is improved when the skills and resources are fully utilized; efficiencies of learning and scale are often achieved. Trade-offs also arise from *limits on internal coordination and control*. By choosing to compete in a specific way and making this explicit, management makes the priorities, direction and characteristics of its offer very clear. Companies, particularly retailing companies, cannot be 'all things to all customers'. Porter concludes that trade-offs are an essential feature of strategy: 'They create the need for choice and purposefully limit what a company offers. They deter straddling or repositioning [by this we assume that Porter implies short-term expedient repositioning], because competitors that engage in those approaches undermine their strategies and degrade the value of their existing activities'.

Activities are an important element within Porter's new approach. He considers them to be component of a strategy, designed to implement it: the components of strategic themes. He uses activity system maps to illustrate strategy. The 'higher-order strategic themes' are implemented through closely linked activities. We shall suggest how these may be used to develop costs and cost savings in a later chapter by using attribute (or functional cost) analysis.

Porter suggests the importance of activities by his statement: 'Positioning choices determine not only which activities a company will perform and how it will configure individual activities but also how activities relate to one another. While operational effectiveness is about achieving excellence in individual activities, or functions, strategy is about *combining* activities'. Furthermore, it is important to ensure that 'fit' between activities occurs: '...competitive advantage comes from the way... activities fit and reinforce one another'. Fit is described as *simple consistency* between each activity and the overall strategy. It ensures that competitive advantage compounds activities rather than them cancelling each other out. Secondary fit occurs when *activities are reinforcing*. This differs from consistency in that the activities are programmed to implement strategy at various stages of its 'roll out'. Third-order fit, or *optimization of effort*, is a process of coordination of those activities which are critical elements of the organization's strategy.

Implications for retail strategy

There can be little doubt that retailing has been prominent in: 'The quest for productivity, quality and speed and has spawned a remarkable number of management tools and techniques'. In other words, as an industry retailing has a well-developed operational effectiveness. However, this should come as no surprise, as many sectors of retailing operate on very low margins, and for organizations in highly competitive low-growth markets profits can only be increased by improving operational effectiveness. This has been noticeable with UK food multiples, where operating margin percentage increases have been responsible for significant growth in contribution. The extent to which operational effectiveness has been focused towards target market segments is difficult to identify. Some successes may be assumed: for example, Tesco (in the UK), Woolworths (Australia) and Wal-Mart (USA) have clearly added operational effectiveness to their recent success. There are examples of some organizations where perhaps some attention to this aspect may offer benefits. Franklins (Australia) and Laura Ashley (UK) are two companies that have been given publicity suggesting this could be so.

Positioning is an interesting topic. Given the close similarity between the Abell and Porter models and the earlier discussion we will not be repetitive, but some examples will serve to validate the approach. Variety-based positioning typifies specialist retailing, where merchandise width, depth and availability attract a strong customer base. Dick Smith's electronics offer would satisfy this classification. Needs-based positioning, the focus on a specific segment, is what David Jones (Australian department store group) is attempting by moving back towards the affluent socio-economy/demographic groups. Access-based positioning may be applied to companies such as Tesco and Woolworths, who have identified customer needs for a basic product but which can be 'delivered' either through off-centre superstores or CBD limited size outlets.

Trade-off examples were given earlier. What is useful concerning the principle of trade-offs is the extent to which they may be applied to other management decisions; this will be explored in depth. Suffice it to say at this point that trade-off considerations across margins, asset base productivity and cash flow and, on a macro basis, between profitability, productivity and strategic (or economic) cash flow are extensions of strategic management.

RETAIL STRATEGY: A BASIC MODEL

Before we can discuss a strategy model in detail we will establish some basic concepts which will be used to expand the detailed model forming the theme of this chapter and clarify some terms introduced in the previous chapter.

Themes, attributes and activities

Porter (1996) introduced *mapping activity systems* (activity-system maps) to: '...show how a company's strategic position is contained in a set of tailored activities designed to deliver it'. They have a number of components. Porter argues that: 'Activity system maps can be useful for examining and strengthening strategic fit' by asking basic questions concerning the consistency of each activity with the overall positioning and whether there are ways in which the activities may be reinforced (and may reinforce each other). Activity analysis may also identify duplication of effort and, therefore, the unnecessary use of resources.

With some modification Porter's activity system maps can be used within the strategy planning process. In Figure 2.6(a) and (b) we illustrate the scheme proposed by Porter.

Decision making is based upon strategic themes and attributes which interpret the strategy. 'Strategy is the creation of a unique and valuable position, involving a different set of activities.... The essence of strategic positioning is to choose activities that are different from rivals' Porter (1996). Our model modifies Porter's approach. Between 'higher-order strategic themes' and 'tightly linked activities' we have introduced 'attributes' which are derived from customer expectations and which form the basis of the planning process. Attributes facilitate the process of identifying the component activities and of the potential trade-offs.

To make it more relevant for our purpose we have introduced some small modifications. *Strategic themes* are based upon explicit statements of the organization's mission and business scope (which together identify the strategic positioning of the business). These are fundamental to the strategy process, because not only do they make clear statements to the stakeholders, they also direct the four retail strategy components (merchandise, customer service, format and environment, and communications). They achieve this through the *attributes* and *activities* which relate to each strategic theme. For example, a specialist retailer would identify as one strategic theme a *focused merchandise assortment*. From this a *primary attribute* would be derived: merchandise characteristics (extensive width, depth and availability); visual merchandising and merchandise augmentation attributes are likely.

The attributes, in turn, are associated with *activities* which ensure the delivery of the attribute value or benefit to the customer. Continuing with the example, activities related to merchandise assortment are likely to include assortment profiling, sourcing, design and quality specifications (and quality control). Identifying themes, attributes and activities offers a number of benefits. The first is a comprehensive analysis of 'fit' (the response to customer expectations and the integration of attributes and activities). Secondly, we can identify linkages between attributes which are not necessarily based upon the same theme. Thirdly, we can, through analysis of the activities, build a view of the costs necessary for the implementation of the overall strategy.

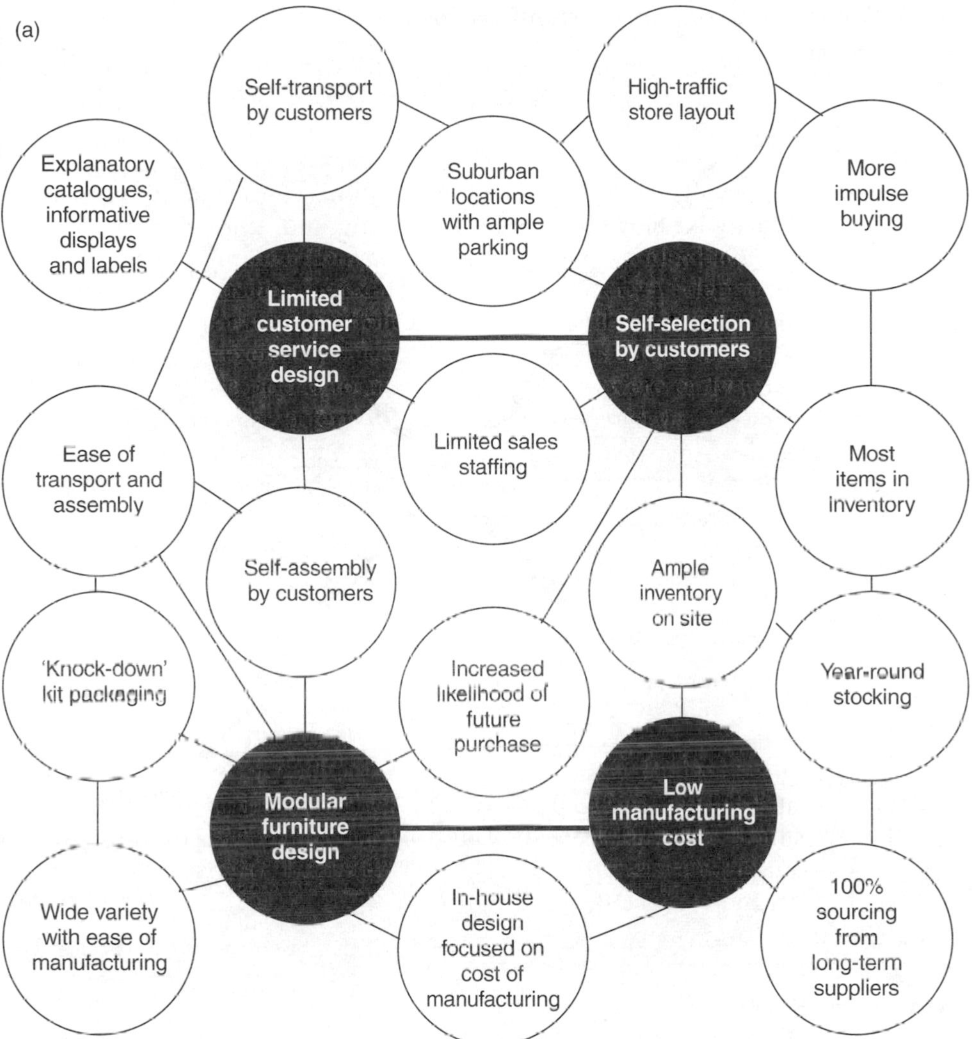

Figure 2.6 (a) Mapping activity systems. Activity system maps, such as this one for IKEA, show how a company's strategic position is contained in a set of tailored activities designed to deliver it. In companies with a clear strategic position, a number of higher-order strategic themes (in the dark areas) can be identified and implemented through clusters of tightly linked activities. (Source: Porter, M. (1996) What is strategy? *Harvard Business Review*, Nov/Dec.) (b) Using activity mapping to develop a strategy model.

Trade-off analysis

Porter suggests trade-offs as a means by which alternative strategic directions may be identified and resolved: 'Trade-offs create the need for choice and protect against repositioners and straddlers'. Porter uses the concept in a marketing context (i.e. to resolve, or to clarify, positioning in the market and its management). We extend the use into performance alternatives.

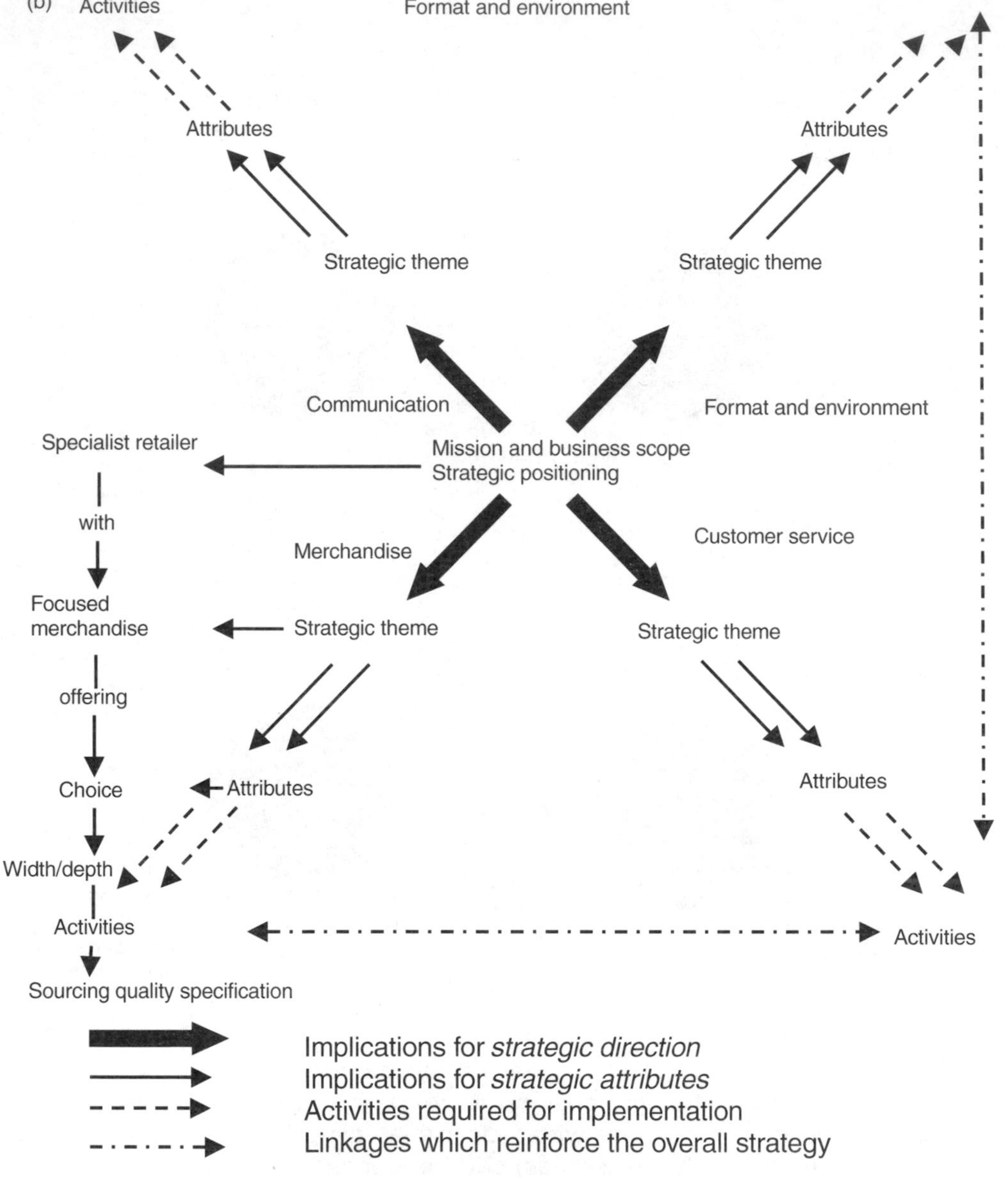

Figure 2.6 (continued)

The trade-off options between margins and asset productivity (the du Pont model) are well known by retailing management using the GMROI control (gross margin return on inventory investment) i.e.

$$\frac{\text{Revenues} - \text{COGS}}{\text{Sales}} \times \frac{\text{Sales}}{\text{Assets (Inventory)}} = \text{GMROI}$$

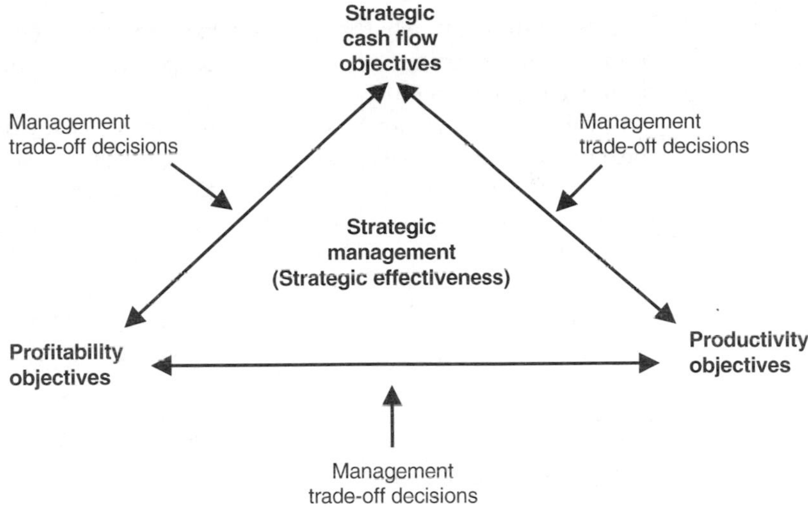

Figure 2.7 Strategic management decisions: strategic effectiveness.

The principle of performance trade-offs may be extended. Management trade-offs occur at two levels. At a **strategic level** the role of management is to plan (and monitor) the *effective* allocation of resources. At an **operational level** the role becomes one of ensuring *operating efficiency*. Having made resource allocation decisions, the operating managers' task is to ensure that dedicated resources are utilized efficiently to implement strategy.

Strategic management decisions (Figure 2.7) focus on profitability, productivity and cash flow decisions. Given the expectations of the shareholders, these may be translated into quantitative objectives and the implications for resource allocation; see Walters and Hanrahan (1997).

Recent work in shareholder value-based planning (and management) has provided an effective linkage between investment performance, strategic and operational management. In Figure 2.7 we see that management trade-off decisions arise from the fact that there are alternatives. For example, a strategic choice can exist between operating with a wide choice, high service, luxurious ambience offer or, of course, the reverse. The implications for investment decisions in both fixed and current assets will be significantly different: the profitability, productivity and cash flow performance expectations will be equally different. Given the decision to pursue an opportunity, these issues must be addressed. Part of the process involves identifying and evaluating alternative combinations of assets and funding that will optimize performance. Leasing fixed assets is an alternative to ownership: it requires less investment funding but does require high margins (profitability) from which lease payment commitments may be met. Trade-off decisions can be used to explore (and resolve) the profitability/cash flow options. For example, the decision to adopt an 'up-market' option introduces the trade-off situation between profitability and cash flow. Not only will occupancy and staff costs be high (relative to the down-market option) but it is possible that additional working capital will be needed to extend the supply chain in order to offer exclusive merchandise.

Within the components identified in Figure 2.7 a number of options for measuring objectives are used by retailers. Often the selection reflects organizational issues of control and delegation, and typically a number of performance metrics are used to reflect specific performance expectations. The issue for the 'executive' is to adopt workable objectives which will reflect the *shareholder value* expectations.

Thus we would expect to see specific objectives for the components of *strategic cashflow*:

- Profit +
- Depreciation =
- *Operational cash flow*

  \+
- Changes (+/–) working capital +
- Changes (+/–) fixed assets +
- Changes (+/–) capital employed (equity and or/debt) =
  Strategic cash flow

Profitability objectives are various:

- Gross profit ($/%): reflects overall buying effectiveness.
- Operating profit ($/%): reflects effectiveness in distribution and store operations.
- EBIT% (earnings before interest and tax): identifies effectiveness of the management of the business and *before* financial management decisions are considered.
- Net profit %: is a measure of interest to investors indicating overall profitability.
- ROI (return on investment), ROAM (return on assets managed) (%) is a measure of specific managerial effectiveness. It indicates management's effectiveness in generating profits from the asset base.
- ROCE % (return on capital employed) is also an investor measurement indicating managerial effectiveness.
- GMROI/CMROI (%) are often used to monitor buyer performance being a combination of stock turn and gross and/or contribution margins.

Productivity objectives identify the expected utilization of fixed and current assets:

- Asset turnover: is measured by sales/total assets and indicates the effectiveness of the use of organizations' assets (buildings, inventory etc.).
- Space productivity: is measured by sales/sales area or 'profit'/sales area. Both measure the effectiveness of the use of selling area and are used to make internal and external comparisons.

- Inventory productivity is a critical measure: stock turn indicates a number of effectiveness and efficiency performance issues related to buying and merchandising.
- HRM productivity: indicates the effectiveness and efficiency of personnel within the organization. Typically it is measured by sales/number of personnel or 'profit'/number of personnel.
- GMROI/CMROI have been mentioned above.

Clearly not all of the measures are relevant, or possibly they vary with the nature of the business, with particular emphasis placed on some ratios more so than others. The notion of trade-off analysis is also important here. The return on investment/return on assets managed indicates the choices available to management in the task of generating a profitable return on the asset base available. In order that an acceptable return be realized (and customer satisfaction objectives be met) management must decide upon an *optimal* performance for both profitability and productivity. For example, a strategic intention to provide nationwide after-sales service will require extensive service facilities and inventories. The extent to which this investment will *increase* profitability (customers' responses) but *decrease* the overall return on investment (due to the increased investment) is a management decision.

Similarly the choices between cash flow and profitability and cash flow and productivity require judgement-based decisions. Both operational and strategic cash flow may be increased by adjusting either profitability or productivity. Revenue increases resulting in increased profitability will boost operational cash flow, as will a reduction in working capital and fixed assets for strategic cash flow. Both will have an impact on the profitability and productivity of the business.

It follows that profitability, productivity and strategic cash flow objectives should be optimized during the trade-off process. The management issue is to resolve these concerns by identifying key decision areas and working through the relative sensitivity issues occurring as alternative trade-off situations are explored.

Operating efficiency decisions are shown in Figure 2.8.

At the operational level management is concerned with *implementing* the strategic direction. Trade-off decisions comprise both performance optimization and positioning classification or definition (the Porter context). Given the profitability, productivity and cash flow decisions, operating management is to develop a retail strategy which delivers the customer value (or satisfaction) proposed by the positioning statement, *and produce* the planned financial performance.

Given a required profitability, productivity and cash flow performance, the implementation process interprets these by developing and implementing a 'mix' of merchandise, customer service, format and store environment, and communications decisions that interpret the strategic positioning and deliver satisfactory returns.

We have discussed operational cash flow, but at the strategy implementation level its importance is crucial; negative values result in business failure. Consequently an objective for strong positive cash flow is essential.

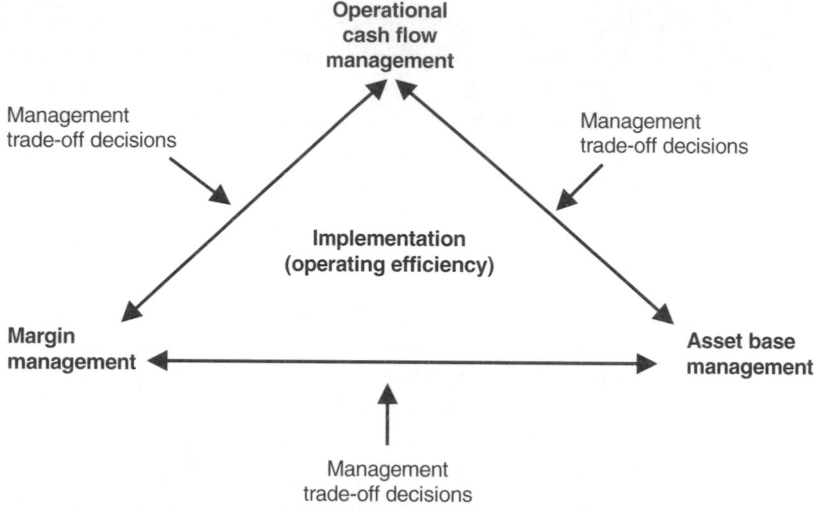

Figure 2.8 Implementing strategic direction: *operating efficiency* decisions.

Margin management performance is influenced by:

- The merchandise assortment profile: wide and deep assortments require extensive inventory and are often prone to markdowns.
- Merchandise augmentation: increases the inventory levels in each product category. It *should* increase sales of high margin accessories and therefore profitability through its impact on margins.
- Visual merchandising: also increases the transactions per customer by promoting add-on sales.
- Service characteristics: the services offered to customers have an impact on revenues. They are cost items. Services should be added with profit enhancement through customer satisfaction (added value) in mind.
- Supplier relations policy: large retailer have identified the benefits of improved working relationships with their suppliers. An exchange of information has increased cooperation and thus, together with some rationalization, has had a significant impact on margins.

Asset base management has a number of components:

- Again the merchandise profile is important: an increase (decrease) in width, depth or availability reduces (increases) asset base productivity.
- Merchandise augmentation: similar influences occur as with assortment decisions.
- Service characteristics: any service offer which requires fixed assets will impact upon asset base performance. High service offers should be aware of the impact this may have.

- Service augmentation: while there may be implications for fixed asset investment they are not likely to be of the same magnitude as for the initial service characteristics decision. However, the addition of personnel to the service offer may be regarded as an increase in fixed intangible assets
- Information systems: data generation analysis and allocation require considerable fixed asset investment.

The trade-off principle is the same as that discussed earlier. An obvious trade-off confronting many retailers concerns the investment in information systems and the anticipated improvement in revenues and profitability that will result from improved knowledge concerning customer behaviour and operating characteristics.

Components and process

There are a number of components and processes involved in developing retailing strategy. These are:

- Determining a *mission*, or the scope of the business
- Deciding upon *strategic positioning*
- Developing a *strategic direction* and its themes, attributes and activities
- Deciding performance criteria for *strategic management effectiveness*
- Planning the *operational implementation*

Determining the mission: the mission or business scope should reflect the expectations of the target customer group. Abell's business definition matrix (Figure 2.2) is a useful model for this purpose. It identifies a customer segment, their product–service expectations (applications) and also determines the 'technologies' available to deliver the offer. Recent developments in FMCG food retailing are examples of movements within the matrix to address emerging opportunities, e.g. Tesco's Metro Stores for time-short customers and home shopping offers for mobility restricted customers. Figure 2.9 identifies the options.

The components of the business scope/mission have been discussed in an earlier example (see Figure 2.2). Here we identify the generic components.

Customer end-use/applications decisions are influenced by:

- The customer shopping mission: this will be discussed in detail subsequently, but at this juncture it is sufficient to identify the fact that individuals demonstrate different shopping behaviours depending much on need and time availability; these in turn influence the choice of store type *and* products purchased.
- Expected 'value': value also has differing criteria (see Figure 2.5 and the discussion on customer analysis, value creation and customer satisfaction).

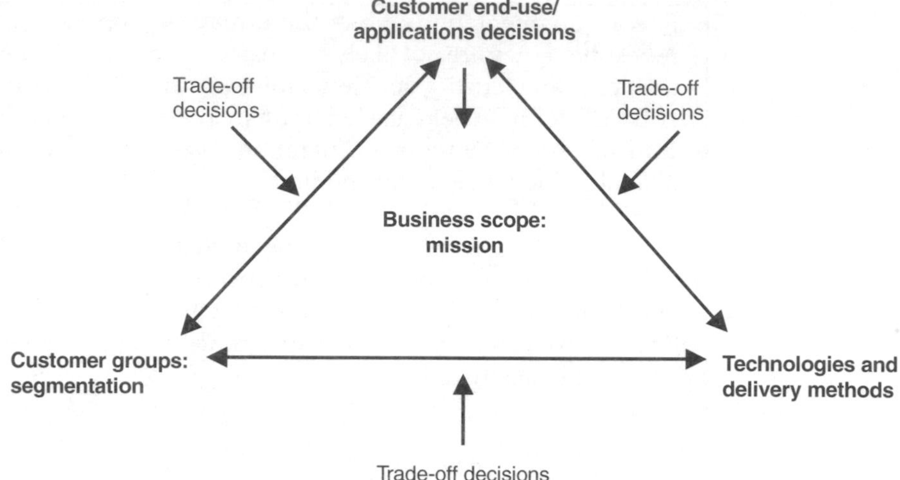

Figure 2.9 Defining the business scope/mission.

- Relevant 'added value' characteristics: 'added value' has a close association with expected value. It is often expressed in expectations of variety, exclusivity or perhaps service.

Customer groups (segmentation) are clearly based in the marketing literature and comprise:

- Demographics
- Socio-economics
- Lifestyle compositions/aggregations
- Customer behaviour responses

Technologies and delivery methods were also described by Figure 2.2. Their generic components are:

- Value communication: the use of 'media' to communicate with and inform customers of the value content, availability etc. of the offer.
- The method of transacting value exchange with customers.
- Value delivery: the methods available to customers for them to receive purchases and subsequent services.

The business scope/mission eventually adopted by a retail organization is reached through a series of trade-off decisions. Not all customer groups respond to end-use offers, nor do they accept the same delivery methods. The business scope/mission adopted should identify a specific customer offer and match each of the components with the needs of customers.

Exhibit 2.1 provides an example of a business scope/mission.

Exhibit 2.1

Mission statement
To develop a strong customer identity within our target customer segment by identifying and monitoring their preferences for merchandise and shopping experience and to enjoy a long ongoing relationship with customers. To provide long-term, mutually profitable opportunities for suppliers. To ensure full and satisfying employment opportunities through profitable growth. To provide consistent shareholder value.

Objectives
- To meet quantitative financial performance criteria
- To meet quantitative and qualitative market/customer based criteria
- To be our customers' first choice store
- To be a destination purchase retailer

Business scope

Customer end-use/applications
- Customer shopping missions
  - First choice supplier
  - Destination purchasing visits
  - Regular browsing visits
- Expected 'value'
  - Exclusivity
  - Choice (width, depth, continuity)
  - Quality merchandise
  - Quality service(s)
  - Compatible pricing levels
- Relevant 'added value' characteristics
  - Merchandise augmentation
  - Visual merchandising
  - Service augmentation

Customer groups: segmentation variables
- Demographics
  - Age
  - Life cycle
  - Social class
  - Education
  - Residential area
  - Type and ownership of residence
- Socio-economics
  - Occupation
  - Income

Exhibit 2.1 *(continued)*

- Lifestyle groups (psychographics)
  - Strivers
  - Adapters
  - Pressured
  - Achievers
  - Traditionals
- Behaviour(s)
  - Occasions
  - User status
  - Loyalty
  - Benefits
  - Usage rate
  - Readiness to buy

Technologies and delivery methods

- 'Value' communication media
  - Print media
  - Broadcast media
  - Database management
  - Electronic media (computer-based)
- Transaction processing
  - Personal
  - Telephone
  - Electronic media
- Value delivery
  - Direct (store to customers)

Strategic positioning is the long-term position sought by the organization and reflects a combination of customer value and product and market decisions. The objective of strategic positioning is to create an identity which is distinctive and sustainable.

Strategic positioning has two functions. The first is to make a statement to the target customer concerning the value proposition, or retail offer, that is being made. The second function is to make very clear to operating management, employees and suppliers the contributions expected of them by the executive. Figure 2.10 suggests that strategic positioning is a composite of customer service, product and market-based decisions. The skill in strategic positioning is the managerial judgement which identifies the essential features of the positioning statement, those of less importance and the eventual position reached through trade-off decisions. The components of the 'decision areas' and the trade-off possibilities will help to understand this vital decision. These are:

- *Customer service decisions.* These fall into three main categories: the facilities and information available to the customer (customer services) and the

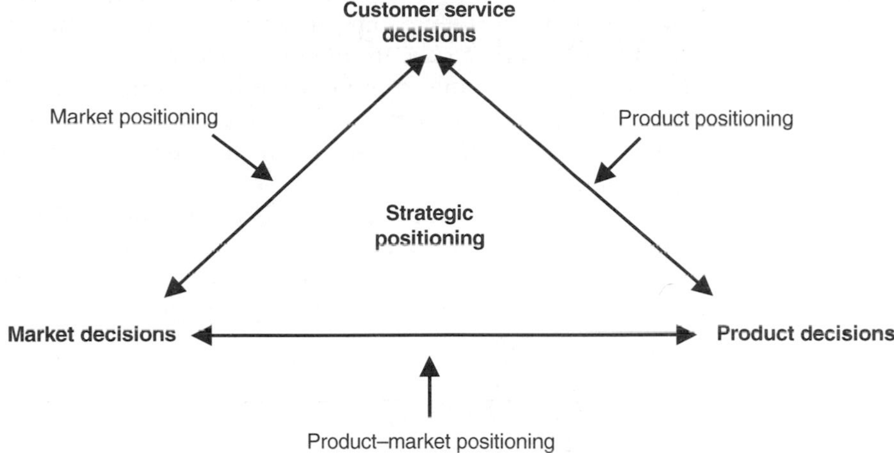

Figure 2.10 Developing the strategic positioning.

shopping service facility characteristics (the extent of self-service/advice to be made available to customers). The inclusion of merchandise attributes reflects the choice and convenience aspects of service.

- *Product decisions.* These reflect the assortment profile strategy (core products and supporting ranges); augmentation decisions (the range of accessories for both core and supporting product ranges); and the important decision on branding policy (the role of retail *and* supplier brands).
- *Market decisions.* There are three important decision areas here. The first is the intended coverage of the activity (i.e. the regional, national, and possibly international coverage objectives) and the structure of the coverage (such as company-owned and operated stores, franchise operations or Internet facilities). A location/catchment strategy identifies the precise characteristics of required markets (such as demographics and socio-economic profiles). The third consideration concerns the actual store environment characteristics, and includes store layout, internal signage and directioning.

Trade-off decisions occur between each of the three main decision topics. *Market positioning* emerges as a combination of location and customer service factors (such as siting, catchment profile and non-store retailing, together with the accompanying package of product and service attributes (by offer and location) and pricing policy details (i.e. uniform pricing or specific location pricing reflecting service aspects, such as convenience). *Product positioning* details merchandise assortment dimensions, specific core merchandise policy and a style/design statement. It should also specify in some detail the roles of retail and supplier/manufacturer brands within core and support merchandise groups. Finally *product–market positioning* details the merchandise range cover objectives by store type/location and ownership types.

Included in product–market positioning are details concerning the response offer to customers, such as its intentions to become a first-choice store within specific target customer/core merchandise groups. The nature of customer communications should also be clarified for both store and non-store retail offers. Exhibit 2.2 continues with a detailed example typical of department store offers.

Strategic direction comprises a number of themes which form the basis on which the strategy is implemented. *Attributes* specify components such as merchandise, customer service, format and environment, and customer communications strategies. *Activities* specify the tasks required to implement the strategy.

Exhibit 2.2

Strategic positioning
To be identified as the country's primary department store group on measures of customers' perceptions of value (satisfaction) and shareholder value. To be acknowledged world wide as a centre of excellence and innovation in retailing by competitors and customers.

Customer service decisions

- Merchandise ranges to meet the choice, style, quality and exclusivity expectation of our target customer group. Monitor both customer expectations and supply markets to ensure maximum customer satisfaction.
- A level of customer service which offers unobtrusive help and assistance. Provide the level of product knowledge that helps customers make purchasing decisions and instills confidence in their decisions. Provide service facilities which increase the satisfaction of purchases.
- Stores and home shopping facilities will meet the needs of customers for access and time convenience, currently and in the future.
- Personal communication with customers providing information relevant to their buying needs and interests.

Market decisions

- Planned opening of stores in catchment areas identified by a predominance of target customers.
- Store environment which provides comfortable and convenient shopping with informative merchandise presentation. Signage and way finders will add to in-store convenience.
- Home shopping facilities through catalogue and Internet computer services are available for time-constrained customers.

Exhibit 2.2 *(continued)*

Product decisions

- A balanced stock assortment will meet the variety and lifestyle needs of customers
- Product quality and performance will be assured by buying only from major international suppliers
- Brand and labelling policy will be to feature dominant national and international 'names'. Where no merchandise offers can be found with congruent specification to our profile, store brand ranges will be developed.

Market positioning

- A 'full range store' aiming to meet the majority of customers' needs in apparel, furniture, homeware, leisure and gifts.
- Customer service and service facilities will be helpful but not forcefully persuasive.
- Our pricing policy is to be competitive, offering to match competitor prices for similar items.

Location

- The company will have a presence in the CBD areas of capital cities
- Locations will be maintained and expanded in suburban areas which match the target customer profile.
- For 'time-constrained' customers, home shopping facilities will continue to be expanded using the most suitable and available technology.

Product positioning

- The company will maintain the necessary width, depth, availability, exclusivity and continuity profiles of its assortment that its customers expect.
- A 100% in stock position will be maintained on core product merchandise ranges.
- Price points will reflect the incremental added value expected by customers.

Product–market positioning

- The company's objective is to be the first choice/destination purchase store for its target customer group.
- Core merchandise ranges will reflect the first choice/destination purchases of the target customer with market competitive prices.
- Customer service is to be a planned response to customer in-store and home-based needs.
- Relevant and specific information will be shared with customers.

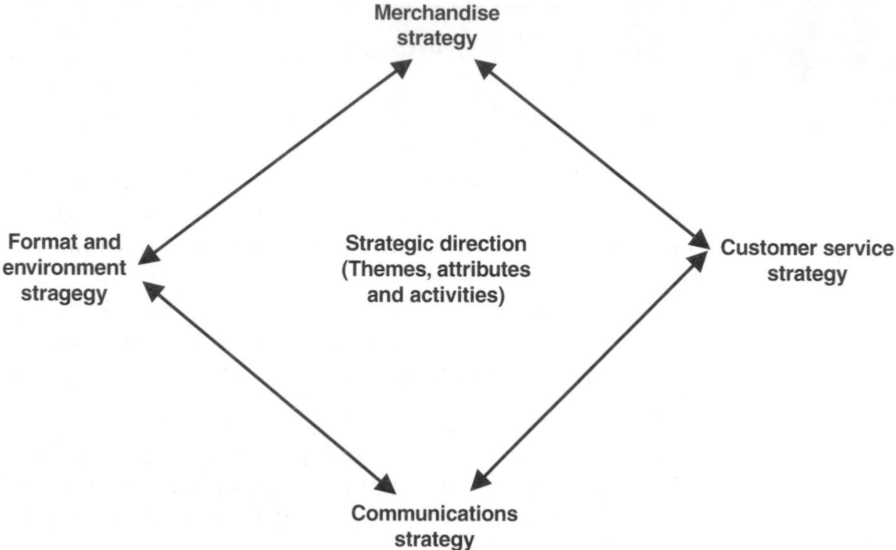

Figure 2.11 Converting strategic direction into implementable strategy. Strategies reflect attributes (e.g. merchandise strategy); activities are the strategy components (e.g. assortment characteristics).

The strategic positioning exercise resulted in a retail offer proposition which requires both strategic direction and the mechanism for implementation. By this stage in the planning process there should be no doubts concerning the viability and acceptability of the retail offer. The customer will find the offer acceptable and the company can deliver the offer.

Strategic direction is a four-component strategy statement (see Figure 2.11). It identifies *merchandise strategy* (i.e. assortment characteristics, merchandise augmentation and visual merchandising) in detail for all core and support merchandise ranges. A *customer service strategy* will identify the service characteristics on a similar basis (i.e. the element of the service offer, additional service augmentation features, the role of service staff (service intensity) and the extent of service facilities within the store environment (i.e. the service density)). A *format and environment strategy* details the number of stores, the number of formats, precise locations, store size and format design features. The *customer communications strategy* will specify the role of communications, the extent of the media to be used and the database requirements necessary for it to be effective.

Implementation is effected by identifying the attribute components and activities required by the strategic themes established in the plan. Exhibit 2.3 offers a detailed explanation of themes, attributes and activities by continuing with the department store example.

Strategic management effectiveness: if the strategy is to deliver shareholder value (i.e. to meet the investors' expectations for profitability, productivity and cashflow), objectives for these should be determined. Again the notion of trade-off possibilities exists, and these are suggested in Figure 2.12.

For any strategy to be effective it must be managed. Effective management requires planning and control through a series of performance metrics.

Figure 2.12 identifies three primary areas for setting performance objectives: strategic cash flow, profitability and productivity. Each of these is important and contributes to creating shareholder value. However, we cannot reach decisions concerning their individual performance criteria; the impact of each on the others is an important consideration. Figure 2.12 identifies these impacts. For example, strategic cash flow should consider the merchandise profile (the impact of width, depth and availability) on working capital (cash flow) and on profitability (a profit margin issue). Sourcing also has an impact. Single versus multiple sourcing influences buying margins (profitability) and inventory and storage requirements also have impacts on working capital and fixed asset requirements (strategic cash flow). A value-added (augmentation) policy will have similar implications, putting pressures on both profitability and cash flow. Co-production (the involvement of the customer in 'manufacturing' and 'distribution', as done by IKEA and in other 'flat pack' offers) is one way of improving both profitability and strategic cash flow. While price is an important issue (and is part of the positioning

Exhibit 2.3

Strategic direction (themes, attributes and activities)

Strategic themes

Targeted merchandise assortment. An exclusive range of merchandise, which through customer research, fits customers' expectations for core merchandise groups with core characteristics, i.e. width, depth, availability and continuity. Expectations of style, fabric colours and brand labels are all components within the merchandise decision.

Extensive customer service. All aspects of service are identified. These cover support service activities, customer transaction management, service products and activities internal to the store. External services such as product-support activities (delivery and installation) and home-based service activities are components of the service offer.

Spacious, comfortable and informative, shopping environment. The predominant retailing format is to provide customers with an environment in which they feel free to purchase and browse at a leisurely pace, with no pressure from sales staff. It should also be entertaining and informative.

Relevant information flows. Emphasis is on two aspects of information: information telling customers about the company's offer and information contributing towards the decision-making processes and maximizing its performance for shareholders.

Exhibit 2.3 *(continued)*

Attributes and activities

Attribute	*Attribute components*	*Activities*
▪ Merchandise characteristics (specific merchandise features)	▪ Assortment profile and core ranges ▪ Variety: width depth availability continuity ▪ Style/design ▪ Quality ▪ Exclusivity ▪ Pricing (price point) ▪ Seasons/themes ▪ Stock items/price point levels	▪ Merchandise profile ▪ Merchandise specification (design, quality etc) ▪ Supplier identification and management (number of suppliers, items supplied, terms) ▪ Merchandise systems (inventory control, buying and replenishment, assortment mix management, local marketing requirements) ▪ Logistics systems (maintaining instore availability/instock, replenishment activities ▪ Concessions (how many? which? terms of agreement)
▪ Merchandise augmentation (merchandise related products and accessories)	▪ Core ranges ▪ Variety ▪ Congruence	▪ Specification ▪ Supplier identification and management ▪ Merchandise systems ▪ Logistics systems ▪ Concessions
▪ Visual merchandising (coordinated, in formative displays; ambience)	▪ Store design	▪ Core ranges ▪ Themes and seasons ▪ Liaison with customer information ▪ Liaison with buying/ merchandising

Exhibit 2.3 *(continued)*

Attribute	*Attribute components*	*Activities*
■ Service characteristics (Range of services offered)	■ Internal	■ Customer handling and transaction processes – Process type – POS equipment ■ Credit system alternatives – database system ■ Wardrobe services ■ Wedding lists
	■ External	■ After sales warranties and servicing ■ Delivery and installation ■ 'Home-based' services
■ Service intensity ■ (Number, duties and deployment of service dedicated staff)	■ Staff resources	■ Skills ■ Number ■ Recruitment ■ Training
	■ Deployment	■ Job specifications ■ Labour scheduling
■ Service augmentation: *information* (Product offer and availability. Uses, maintenance and care)	■ Internal	■ Displays and demonstration areas
	■ External	■ Catalogues and mailings ■ Web sites ■ Cooperative advertising
■ Service augmentation: *facilities* (Service related 'accessories, changing rooms, design services)	■ Internal	■ Store information centres ■ Changing rooms ■ Child care facilities: crèche and baby care ■ Shopping items deposit centre ■ Interior design
	■ External	■ On-site design services ■ Catering ■ Equipment hire

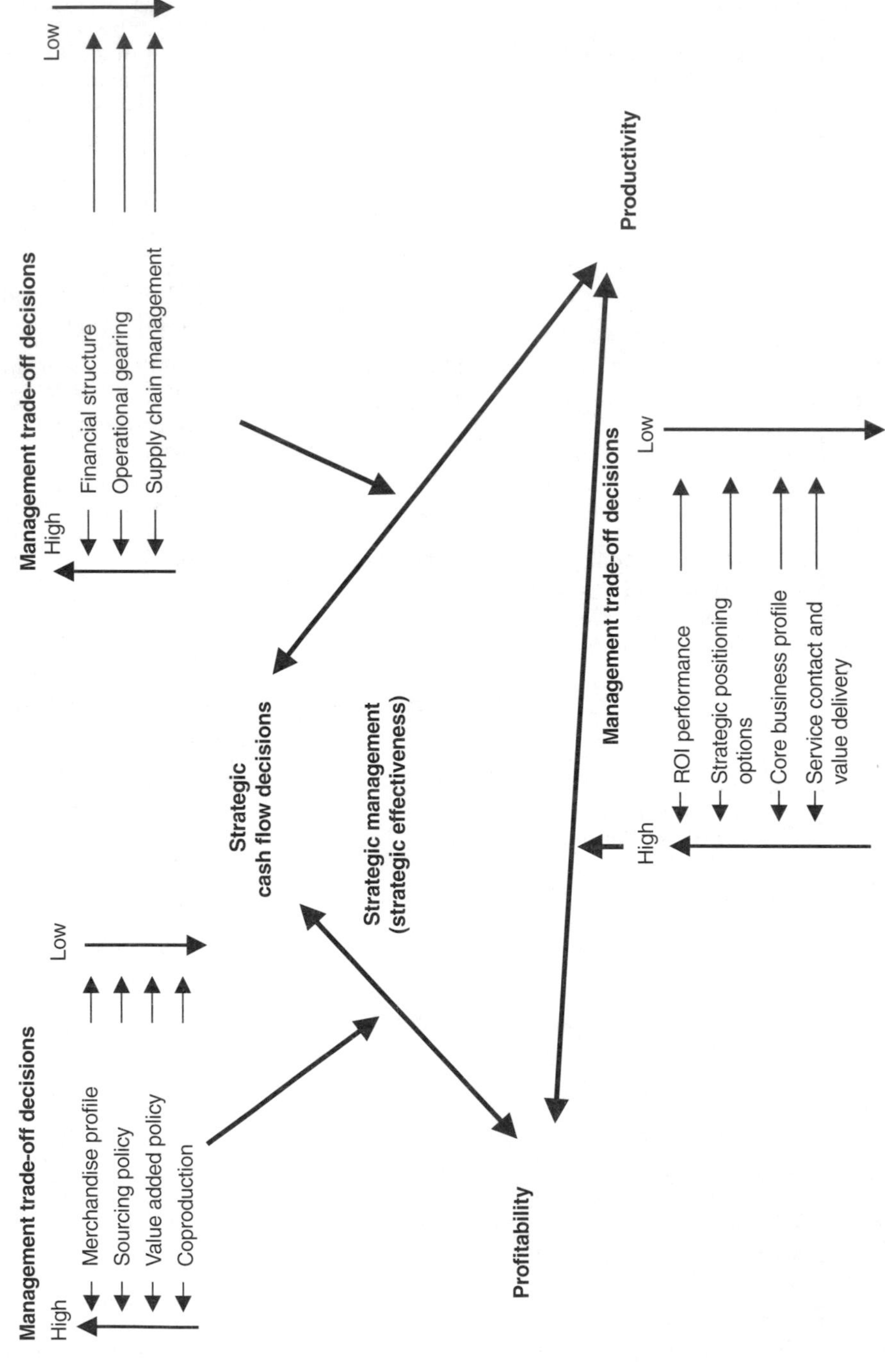

Figure 2.12 Trade-off decisions and strategic management.

offer), the cost reductions for both the product and the logistics infrastructure components of storage and delivery are clearly worthwhile. The issue for management is to identify competitive advantage profile *and* costs. Can customers' value expectations be met such that the organization's performance requirements are also met? Again, the issues of compromise are apparent and should be resolved using the trade-off model to identify 'what if?' scenarios.

The decision situations arising from the profitability/productivity and productivity/strategic cash flow interfaces are resolved in a similar manner. The reader is encouraged to use Figure 2.12 to consider these.

It is at this stage of the process that iteration should occur. Questions should be asked concerning the compatibility of customer satisfaction and shareholder value expectations. Figure 2.1 (p. 23) suggests this as an essential part of the planning process. The trade-off exercise described earlier does help to bridge this situation and should be conducted with both objectives in mind. Clearly, the ideal situation is one in which customer and shareholder value expectations are met by a unique (or exclusive) strategic direction which offers competitive advantage. What is more likely is that a 'fit' is difficult to obtain, and as a result some compromise should be considered. It is for this reason that a number of retailers have identified *strategic imperatives* (customer value expectations that are critical to the success of the initiative) and *strategic desirables* (those aspects of customer expectations that, while they add to the competitiveness of the positioning, are not essential). The result of iteration should be a strategic direction (comprising themes, attributes and activities) that meets customer expectations *and* profitability, productivity and cash flow performance expectations for capital gain, dividends and optimal economic cash flow.

Operational implementation, or the operational interpretation of the strategy, requires us to meet both customer satisfaction and corporate performance objectives. It is likely that some iteration between strategic management effectiveness (meeting investor expectations) and operational feasibility will be necessary. For most retail organizations this becomes an inevitable (and expected) part of the process. The decisions confronting management concern the modifications they are prepared to make to *all* of the objectives.

The managerial implications for operational management (whose task is to implement the plan) are described in Figure 2.13. Essentially their task is to work within the profitability, productivity and cash flow parameters that result from the 'strategic management' process and the subsequent iteration. The implementation task is one of working within the constraints of an operational budget and delivering the features of the themes, attributes, activities and positioning. These are identified in Figure 2.13. Again, a process in which trade-off analysis is prominent becomes necessary. Figure 2.14 identifies the issues confronting operational management: the compromises between profitability/productivity/cash flow performance. Figure 2.14 suggests the performance options available. Further consideration may help.

The options available between margin management and asset base management will all relate to the operational return on investment eventually

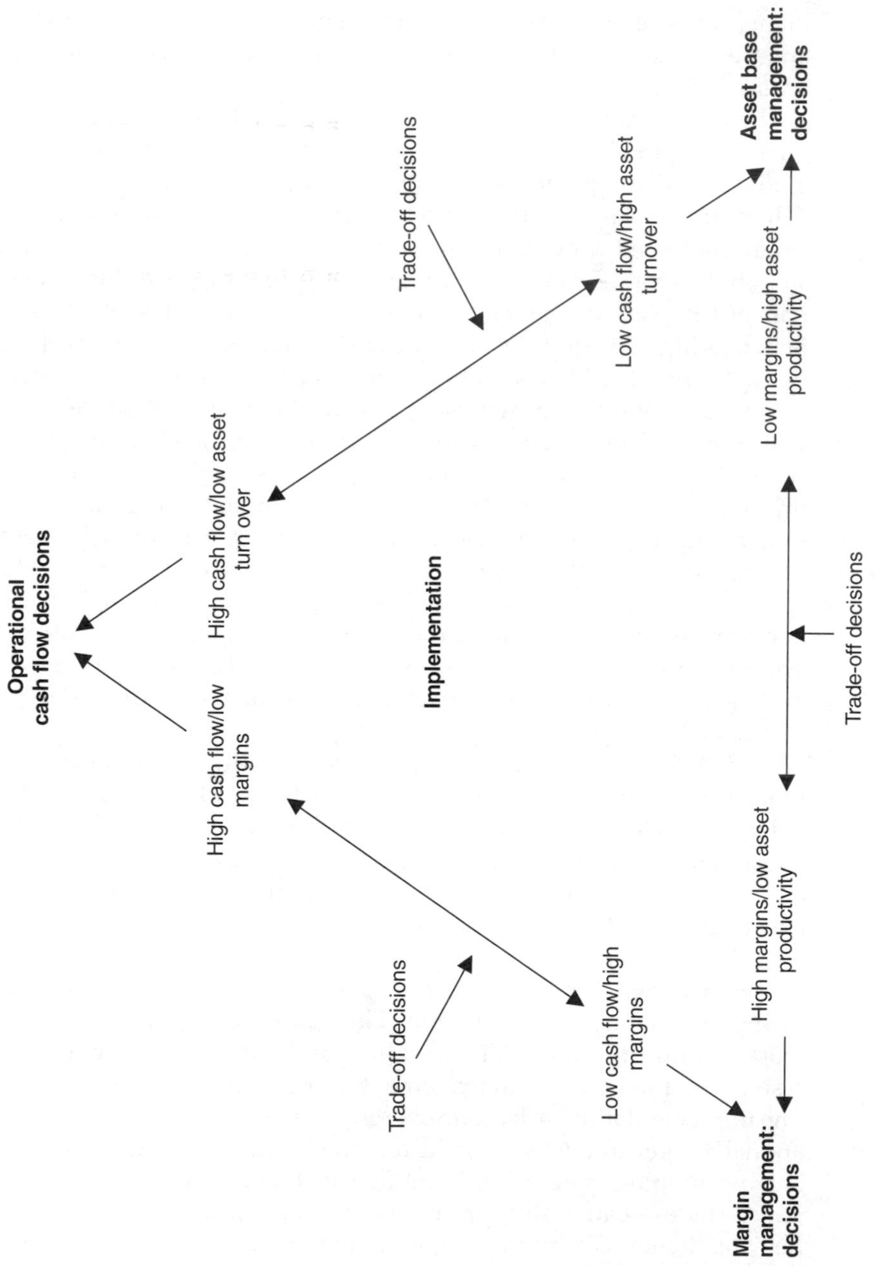

Figure 2.13 Implementing operational management decisions: evaluating trade-offs.

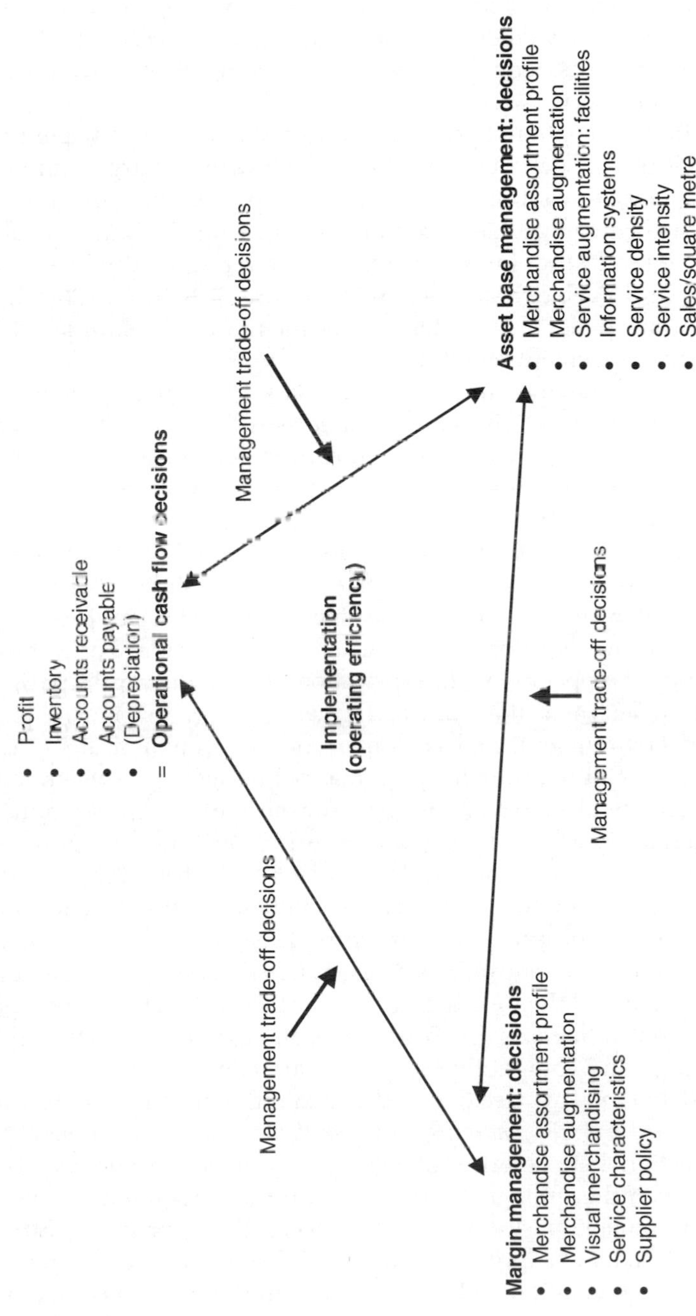

Figure 2.14 Operational management decisions: managing the activities.

achieved. (The margin management [EQ] asset base management 'arithmetic' will determine this: see the discussion on trade-off analysis earlier in this chapter.) It follows that the options between high margins/low asset productivity and low margins/high asset productivity concern positioning decisions (now fixed), core merchandise groups (and the width, depth and availability characteristics demanded by the positioning decision) and the extent of services and service delivery.

Trade-off options between margin management and operational cash flow decisions are described by a low cash flow/high margins and high cash flow/low margins continuum. The task for operational managers is to determine an assortment profile (a combination of width, depth, availability *and* price point ranges), an inventory management program (which determines location and levels of inventory and therefore stock turn profiles), and a supplier relations policy (which determines the number of suppliers and the buying margins/payment schedules).

Finally the operational cash flow/asset base management trade-off decisions identify options which influence the high cash flow/low asset turnover and low cash flow/high asset turnover decision range. Within this continuum operational managers are left to decide upon pricing, promotions (purpose and number) and working capital management performance (such as changes in inventory levels, accounts receivable and accounts payable).

The strategy process is completed by establishing a business plan in which performance expectations (objectives) and the strategic process (strategic positioning and direction) are detailed and which leads to operational implementation (the operational interpretation of attributes and, specifically, activities which determine the shape of the merchandise, customer service, store format and environment, and customer communication strategies). The business plan should not only include financial budgets for the strategic and operational activities but should show how the marketing, operational and financial interfaces are to be managed. Figure 2.15 illustrates this principle.

So far we have explored the process by which strategy is derived. Our concluding task in this chapter is to provide some structure for the process, and Figure 2.16 proposes this structure. It is a formal approach very like most planning and control processes. *External influences* reflect current *customer behaviour* and their likely future expectations and behaviour. Similarly, other external influences (such as political, economic, social and technological change and competitive response) are considered when *mission*, *objectives* and *strategies* are decided and which influence the organization's views on *projected revenues*, *margins* and *cash flows*. These, together with the strategic direction, help determine the *resource requirements* and *allocation decisions*.

Given the strategic themes and attributes required to create: '...a unique and valuable position...' (Porter, 1996), 'the appropriate attributes may be identified and expressed in terms of merchandise characteristics, merchandise augmentation and the other activities discussed earlier. It is this unique (or perhaps exclusive) combination of activities which determines the detail of the *retail strategy*. Implicit in the process is a review of cost effectiveness at both strategic and operational levels.

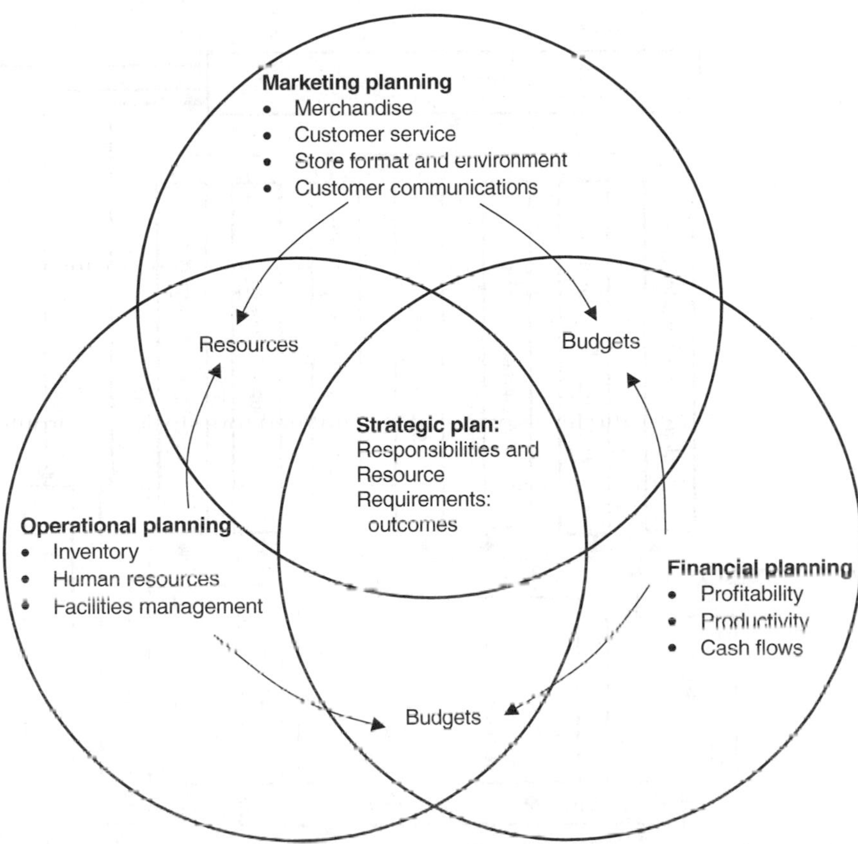

Figure 2.15 An integrated approach to strategic planning.

SUMMARY

This chapter has introduced a model for strategy analysis, development, evaluation and implementation. It has used concepts that are well established in the literature and some more recent contributions, and has introduced some new thoughts and approaches.

By introducing shareholder value expectations the approach includes the increasingly important issues for management: the overall performance of the business such that investor satisfaction together with customer satisfaction are, together, considered in the planning process. This necessitates a combination of top/down–bottom/up procedures to ensure optimal performance.

The introduction of strategic themes, attributes and activities ensures the inclusion of customer expectations and identifies the external and internal characteristics of the strategy such that the target customer, suppliers, employees and shareholders understand the value proposition which emerges. It is considering the interests of all stakeholders.

The chapter has also established a model upon which the book will build an approach to planning and controlling retailing strategy.

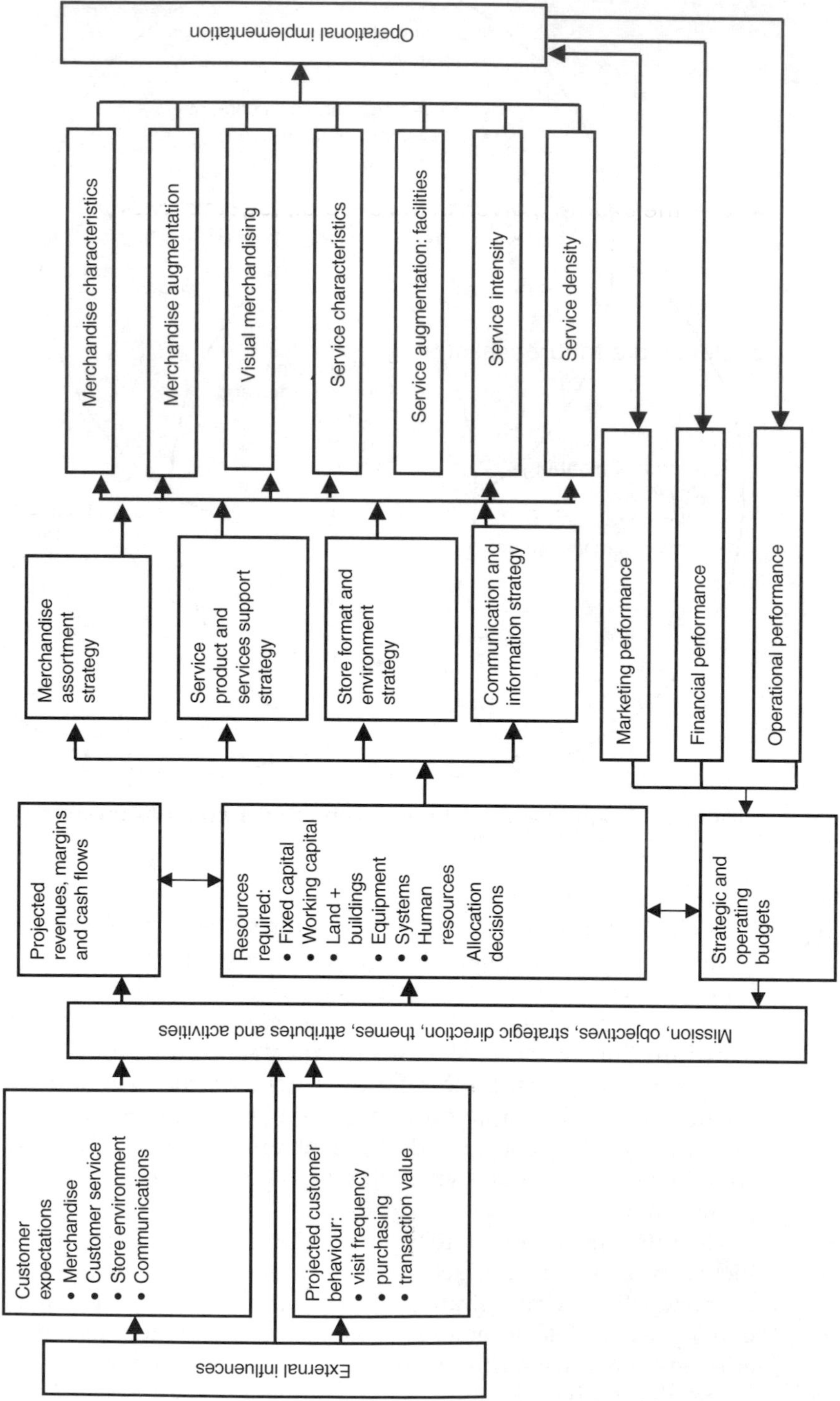

Figure 2.16 Retail strategy: planning and control.

QUESTIONS, ACTIVITIES AND CONSIDERATIONS

- Identify the areas for potential conflict between:
  - business scope/mission and strategic positioning
  - strategic direction and implementation, and business scope/mission and shareholder value
- Use the example given in the chapter, together with published material for a department store, to develop a possible strategic plan. Visit the organization to develop an understanding of operational implementation issues.
- Develop a theoretical strategic plan for:
  - a fast-moving consumer goods retail company
  - a consumer durable retailer
  - a non-store retailer
- What will be the planning concerns for the WalMart/Asda senior management group?

REFERENCES

Abell, D. F. (1980) *Defining the Business: The Starting Point of Strategic Planning*. Prentice Hall, Englewood Cliffs, NJ.

Ansoff, H. I. (1965) *Corporate Strategy*. McGraw-Hill, New York.

Best, R. J. (1997) *Market Based Management*. Prentice Hall, Englewood Cliffs, NJ.

Cronshaw (1994) [Please complete].

Day (1990) [Please complete].

Grant, R. (1995) *Contemporary Strategy Analysis*, 2nd edn. Blackwell Business, Oxford.

Harris, D. and Walters, D. (1992) *Retail Operations Management*. Prentice Hall, Hemel Hempstead.

Hofer, C. W. and Schendel, D. E. (1978) *Strategy Formulation: Analytical Concepts*. West Publishing, New York.

Johnson, G. and Scholes, K. (1996) *Exploring Corporate Strategy*. Prentice Hall, Hemel Hempstead.

Levitt, T. (1960) Marketing myopia. *Harvard Business Review*, July/August.

Luck, D. J. and Ferrell, O. C. (1979) *Marketing Strategy and Plans*. Prentice Hall, Englewood Cliffs, New Jersey.

Norman, R. and Ramirez, R. (1993) From Value Chain to Value Constellation: Designing Interactive Strategy. *Harvard Business Review*, July/August.

Porter, M. E. (1980) *Competitive Strategy*. The Free Press, New York.

Porter, M. E. (1985) *Competitive Advantage*. The Free Press, New York.

Porter, M. (1996) What is strategy? *Harvard Business Review*, Nov/Dec.

Prahalad, C. K. and Hamel, G. (1990) The core competence of the corporation. *Harvard Business Review*, May/June.

Rappaport, A. (1986) *Creating Shareholder Value*. The Free Press, New York.

Robinson, C. G. (1982a) *Portfolio Planning Techniques: The Boston Consulting Group's Approach*. [Publisher?].

Robinson, C. G. (1982b) *A Plethora of Portfolio Planning Techniques*. School of Business Leadership, University of South Africa, Pretoria.

Robinson, C. G. (1982c) Experience curves as a planning tool, Part 2. Pyrrhic victories and practical problems. *South African Journal of Business Management* **13**: 159–168.

Robinson, C. G. (1983) *PIMS as a Strategic Planning Tool*. School of Business Leadership, University of South Africa, Pretoria.

Robinson, C. G. (1986) *Strategic Management Techniques*. Butterworth Publishers (Pty) Ltd, Durban.

Rumelt, R. (1988) The evaluation of business strategy, in *The Strategy Process: Concepts, Contexts and Cases* (eds. Quinn, J. B., Mintzberg, H. and James, R.M.). Prentice Hall, New York.

Shenkman (1992) [Please complete].

Tilles, S. (1969) Making strategy explicit, in *Business Strategy* (ed. Ansoff, H.I.). Penguin Books, New York.

Walters, D. and Hanrahan, J. (1997) Value based planning and operational implementation: considerations for retailing strategy. *Macquarie Economics Research Papers*, Number 12/97, September.

Webster, F.E. (1994) *Market Driven Management*. John Wiley, New York.

OPERATIONAL MANAGEMENT AND STRATEGY

LEARNING OBJECTIVES

In this chapter we consider the role of operations management in implementing strategy. The chapter will provide:

- An introduction to key success factors and their importance in strategy implementation.
- A review of process design and management and the controversial topic of business process re-engineering.
- An application of process management design to retail operations management.
- A retail operations management model.

INTRODUCTION

If strategic objectives are to be met it follows that some clear direction should be set for operations management. Furthermore, if the strategy is to be successful the operations activity should be capable of its implementation.

An approach that has proved to be successful is one which identifies critical (key) success factors for successful strategy implementation. Key success factors have been variously defined. Hofer and Shendel (1977) offer a definition which has stood the test of time:

> ...those variables which management can influence through its decisions and which can affect significantly the overall competitive positions of firms in an industry...

Grant (1995) develops this definition by suggesting:

> ...by analysing competition and demand, we can identify the potential for competitive advantage in a particular industry in terms of the factors that are important in determining a firm's ability to survive and prosper.

He argues that the approach be 'straightforward and commonsensical'. The suggestion is that to survive and prosper in an industry there are two criteria to be met: one is to meet customer satisfaction expectations and the other is to survive competition. From these questions, key success factors can be derived.

Grant gives an example based upon retailing. He starts with a simplified notion that:

Profit = Revenue – Costs

Expanded this becomes:

Profit = (Sales per square metre)×selling area×gross margin
–(costs of administration, selling, inventory etc.)

When these are examined more closely they suggest:

- The importance of store location in determining sales per square metre.
- Buying power is a major influence in determining gross margins and in permitting competitive pricing that generates high sales per square metre.
- The influence of merchandise mix on sales and margins.
- The role of inventory management systems on inventory costs and sales.

In a more structured approach a specific example is given using fashion retailing as a subject industry; see Figure 3.1.

This suggests that not only should there be *strategic fit* but there should also be *operational fit* such that there should be compatibility between resources and capabilities, organization and systems, and values and management style. Grant offers four strategic fit criteria, two of which are suited for assessing organizational fit:

- *Consistency with resources and capabilities* is (for Grant) concerned with matching resources and capabilities with strategic decisions. Clearly strategic decisions requiring long-term commitment of resources require such analysis, but so too do operational decisions; without the skills and resources which relate to tasks of *implementing* a market-led strategy its success is unlikely.
- *Consistency with organization and systems* may similarly be considered. Unless the organization is in a position to administer its supply chain and customer relationships it is unlikely to make its strategies successful.

Survival in an industry has a number of basic requirements. If it is to survive *and* prosper it requires not simply strategic and operational fit, but congruence between them. Furthermore, for success to be ensured key success factors should be identified and form the basis of an operations management plan.

	What do customers want? (Analysis of demand)	+	How does a firm survive? (Analysis of competition)	=	Key success factors
Fashion retailing	■ Demand fragmented by garment, style, quality, colour ■ Customers willing to pay price premium for style, quality and exclusivity ■ Retailers seek reliability and speed of supply		■ Low entry barriers ■ Low seller concentration ■ Few scale economies ■ Medium/high retailer concentration ■ Retail buying power strong ■ Price and non-price competition strong		■ Need to combine selective differentiation with low cost operations ■ Key differentiation variables and rapid response to style and fashion change ■ Strong customer franchise ■ Low overhead and labour costs exception less price sensitive segments ■ Space utilization
Superstore activities: ■ food ■ home improvement	■ Low prices ■ convenient location ■ Wide range of products		■ Local dense catchments ■ Customers are price sensitive: price competitiveness a requirement ■ Uses bargaining power to influence merchancise and other input costs		■ Low-cost operation requires operational efficiency, scale efficient stress ■ Large purchasing volumes to maximize buying power ■ Wide merchandise ranges ■ Large sales areas ■ Convenient access (drive time) ■ Easy parking ■ High levels of space productivity

Figure 3.1 Identifying key success factors.

STRATEGIC AND OPERATIONAL FIT

Rumelt (1988) suggests four criteria that should be applied to assessing strategic fit:

- *Consistency*: the strategy must not present mutually inconsistent goals and policies.
- *Consonance*: the strategy must represent an adaptative response to the external environment and to the critical changes occurring within it.
- *Advantage*: the strategy must provide for the creation and/or maintenance of competitive advantage in the selected area.
- *Feasibility*: the strategy must neither overtax available resources nor create unsolvable sub-problems.

Each of these criteria has implications for the implementation process. If we assume that the strategic direction adopted by the organization has market relevance (discussed earlier in this chapter) it follows that if it is to be successful it should have *organizational fit*, or as Rumelt suggests, 'feasibility'.

Given that the consistency issues discussed above have been resolved we can move on to consider how critical success factors may be derived. An acceptable assumption for any retailing business is that objectives will be seeking similar performance outcomes, and thus there will be similar performance monitors to indicate growth and successful implementation of strategies, which will optimize the primary objectives for profitability, productivity and cashflow. The performance monitors will include targets to:

- Increase sales revenue in real terms
- Increase the number of purchasing customers
- Increase the size of average customer purchase
- Increase contribution at store/operational unit level
- Increase the gross margin yield in real terms
- Increase the 'value' delivered to customers

There may be others, but these are sufficient to identify five generic critical success factors which have application to all conventional retailing organizations:

- Increasing sales revenue in real terms by increasing customer visit frequencies and average customer transactions
- Increasing gross margin in real terms by improved margin management
- Increasing contribution by managing operating costs
- Increasing the productivity of physical and human assets
- Increasing customer satisfaction by increasing the value expected by customers

It follows that there are a number of variables which support the operations management critical support factors. Some examples of key support variables for each critical success factor are:

- *Increase sales revenue by*:
  - Improving local catchment appeal of merchandise and service by applying *local marketing* techniques to identify *local* merchandise and service preferences.
  - Improving/maintaining merchandise availability.
  - Database management: EPOS applications.
  - Increasing customer visiting frequencies by creating points of interest within retail outlets.
  - Using visual merchandising and merchandise augmentation (explained in detail in Chapter 6) to encourage wider and larger expenditures.
  - Customer loyalty scheme management.
- *Increase gross margin/profit by*:
  - Improving merchandise profiles, thereby reducing markdowns.
  - Improve shrinkage control.
  - Reduce damage.
  - Optimizing sales/inventory holding ratios.
- *Increasing contribution by*:
  - Reviewing job structures and tasks.
  - Reallocating and rescheduling labour and tasks.
  - Reviewing full-time/part-time ratios.
  - Increasing the quality of staff training.
  - Controlling costs for utilities.
  - Using sales and inventory data to optimize replenishment.
  - Ensuring that promotions and in-store customer communication are managed to give cost effective results.
- *Increasing productivity by*:
  - Ensuring that space management systems and planning recommendations are implemented.
  - Using labour scheduling systems.
  - Ensuring that ambience and visual merchandising enhance merchandise offers.
  - Ensuring that credit sales controls are applied to minimize bad debts and maximize cash flow.
  - Ensuring replenishment accuracy.
- *Add value to the offer by ensuring that*:
  - Sales staff are trained, knowledgeable and helpful.
  - Merchandise and service augmentation offer advice and information to customers.
  - Store ambience is perceived to be comfortable, exciting etc. (as determined by the positioning strategy) and is an environment in which customers wish to shop frequently and regularly.

Given the critical success factors together with the key variables developed to facilitate the strategy we can turn to measuring the success of the implementation activity. Figure 3.2 is used to bring together the operations

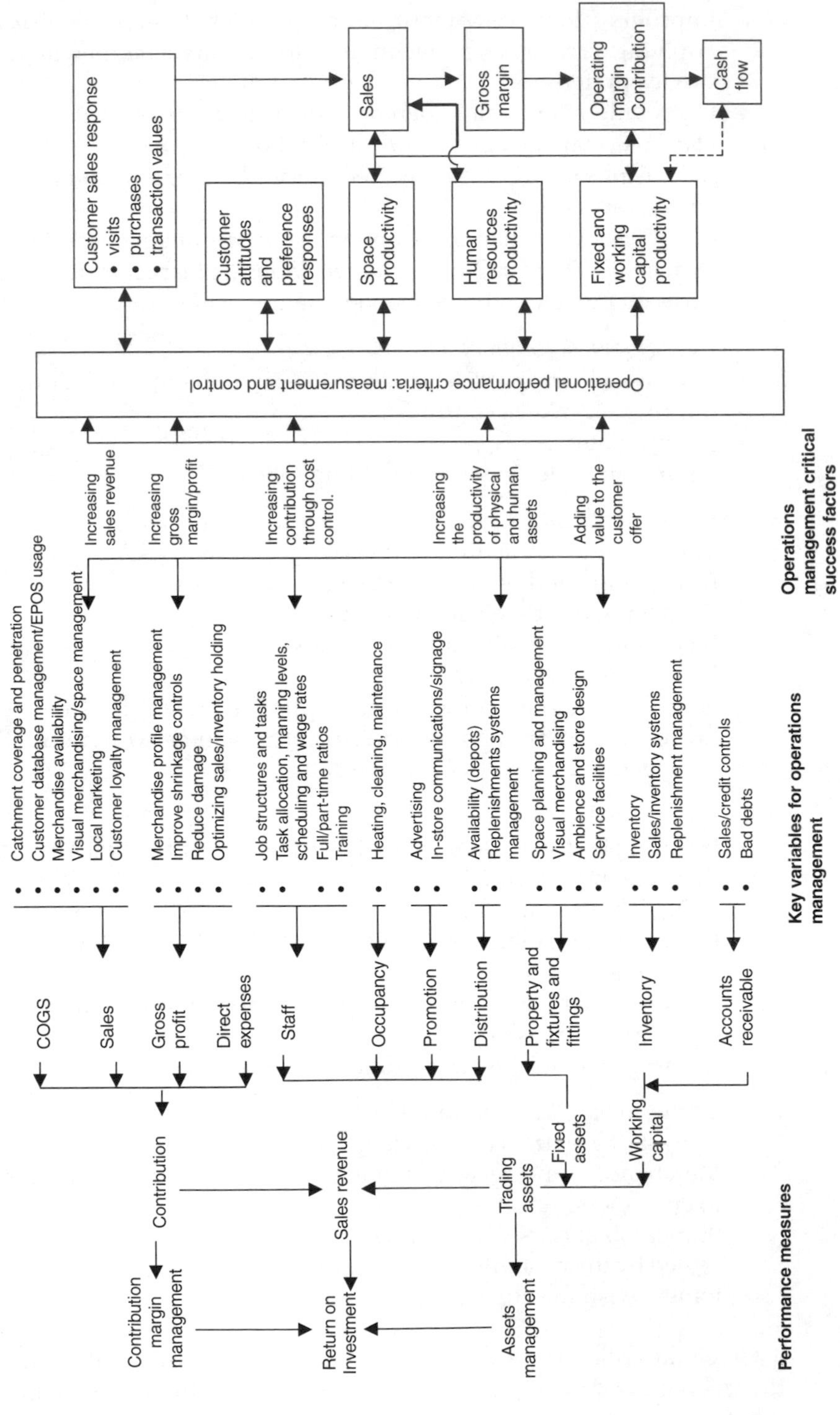

Figure 3.2 Retail operations: planning and controlling strategy implementation.

management activity and involvement in implementing strategy. The critical success factors and key variables are the central feature, and Figure 3.2 proposes that the performance of the operations management activity is measured by allocating costs in the conventional manner, resulting in a Du Pont ratio appraisal *and* by monitoring the impact of management's decisions on the profitability, productivity and cash flow performance of the business through the media of space used, human resources and the relevant aspects of fixed and working capital.

For store-based retailers space allocation and management are critical activities. Sales and contribution from selling area are important performance measures and are used as primary control metrics. The application of space management technology to implement merchandise and format and environment objectives is now common practice. Software packages of varying sophistication are now available. Retailers can quite easily plan space revenue and contribution optimization at one level and, at another, use CAD/CAM systems to initiate and modify format design on a three-dimensional basis.

However, a link is required between critical success factors and operations management key variables. Process design and management offers such a means.

PROCESS DESIGN AND MANAGEMENT: IMPLICATIONS FOR OPERATIONS MANAGEMENT

In Chapter 1 we discussed a number of developments within the business environment. It will be recalled that the dominance of a customer-focused approach to business is clearly apparent in a wide range of organizations. A number of authors have identified the need for fundamental changes to marketing as a concept and as a business discipline. Murray and O'Driscoll (1996) discuss the role of marketing within macro- and micro-business systems, while Webster (1994) and Kotler (1994) compare the traditional transaction process with the increasingly favoured view of marketing being based upon value creation and delivery, resulting from long-term relationships with suppliers and customers. Webster suggests:

> Our definition of marketing is built around the concept of the value chain. Marketing is the process of defining, developing and delivering value.

Kotler and Webster feature a model developed by Anterasian and Phillips (1988); see Figure 3.3. The *value approach* suggests that it is the attributes (customer expectations) and activities that are important, not necessarily organizational functions. This is a fundamental issue, and one which influenced the development of process design and management and their subsequent application.

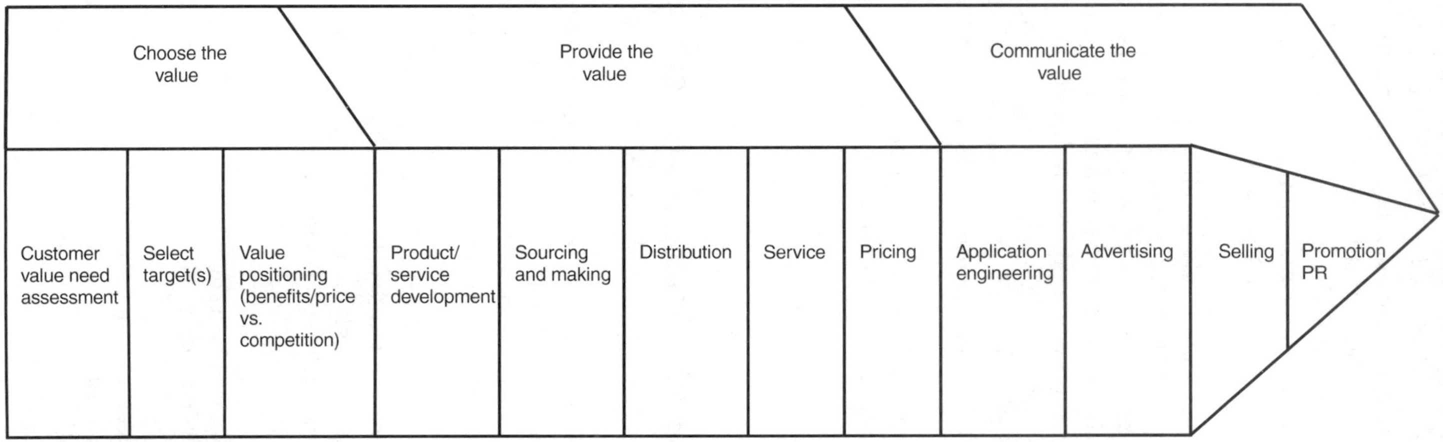

Choose the value			Provide the value					Communicate the value			
Customer value need assessment	Select target(s)	Value positioning (benefits/price vs. competition)	Product/ service development	Sourcing and making	Distribution	Service	Pricing	Application engineering	Advertising	Selling	Promotion PR

Notes:
Value = Benefit – price.
Benefit = Attribute(s) desirable to customer (in customer's eyes).
Price = Total costs to customer (as perceived by customer).
Superior perceived value = Customer believes buying/using the product or service gives a net value superior (more positive) than alternative's value.

Figure 3.3 The marketing value chain. (Source: Anterasian, C. and Phillips, L. W. (1988) *Discontinuities, Value Delivery, and the Share-Returns Association: A re-examination of the 'Share-Causes-Profits' Controversy*. Research Program Monograph, Report No. 88-109. The Marketing Science Institute, Cambridge, MA, p. 8. Reproduced with permission.)

Business process re-engineering is an approach that found favour as a successful approach to cost reduction in the early/mid-1990s. Hammer and Champy (1993) defined it as:

> the fundamental rethinking and radical redesign of business processes to achieve dramatic improvements in critical contemporary measures of performance, such as cost, quality, service and speed.

The proposal was to redesign business processes in ways that increase their efficiency in fundamental ways. If we assume that strategy seeks the *effective* use of resources, then its implementation (by operations management) seeks to do so using the most *efficient* use of resources allocated. Hammer and Champy suggested that to be effective the approach questions the way in which a process is organized and managed: 'If we were starting afresh, how would we design this process?'

There has been doubt expressed concerning the technique. It has been suggested that the result of the majority of 're-engineering' projects has been to reduce overall costs through redundancies, but the long-run effect has been damaging to the organization. Micklethwait and Wooldridge (1996) offer an account of the 'rise and fall' of business process re-engineering.

On the plus side it was seen as a means by which an organization could be broken down into its component parts and then reassembled using only those that were necessary to result in an efficient operation. Process was seen as more important than product: good products resulted from good processes. Fuelled by information technology the disciples of business process re-engineering argued that many inefficiencies could be removed in a move towards a more efficient and leaner organization. Events suggest that the concept resulted in short-term cost savings accompanied by irreparable damage to morale subsequent to the very large number of middle management redundancies which resulted. Charles Handy (1994), quoted in Micklethwait and Wooldridge, joined the criticism of re-engineering:

> blowing organizations apart is not conducive to a statement of commitment and euphoria.... The trouble with re-engineering when it is done badly – which it mostly is – is that it leaves people shattered, even the people left behind.

Hamel and Prahalad (1994) argued along a similar line, to the effect that re-engineering has:

> more to do with shoring up today's businesses than creating tomorrow's industries. Any company that succeeds at restructuring and re-engineering, but fails to create the markets of the future will find itself on a treadmill, trying to keep one step ahead of the steadily declining margins and profits of yesterday's businesses.

However, as Micklethwait and Woolridge suggest:

> In other words, re-engineering is less than it was originally cracked up to be. But that does not mean that it is useless. Re-engineering tends to work

> particularly well in things such as logistics and order fulfilment, because it forces a company to concentrate on speed and service – the two things which most interest customers.

This is very much the approach we take. Retailing *is* concerned with margins but it is also concerned with 'speed and service'. Commercial research suggests that customers of food multiples do not enjoy shopping; they find the experience less than satisfying. Efficient customer handling and campaigns such as Tesco's 'one ahead' have met with success. To make these effective strategy components requires 'going back to basics', not necessarily to reduce staff but rather to offer improved service and possibly to develop multi-skilling skills.

While essentially a cost reduction approach, the concept offers operations managers a useful model with which to consider their role and tasks when implementing strategy decisions. Knox and Maklan (1998) make a useful contribution by arguing for the use of process engineering as an approach to the resource transformation. They propose an interesting model for the management of adding customer value. Their UOVP (unique organization value proposition) follows a similar argument to that of Webster (1994), in which a *value proposition* (an explicit statement of what it is the organization intends to deliver to the customer) is used both internally and externally as a platform for resource allocation, planning and control.

The authors (Knox and Maklan) pursue an argument that essentially follows a line that suggests:

> The traditional approach to transforming resources into goods and services is too sequential and functionally driven to create value commensurate with that demanded by the market place today.

Their thesis is that the traditional, functionally oriented transformation functions, such as procurement manufacturing, logistics, marketing and sales, complicate and often delay accurate and rapid response to customers:

> Rapid and interactive customer problem solving is complicated by the functional divisions between each stage of the process.

The recent emphasis on cost reduction and market competitiveness process-centred management techniques (such as TQ, Kaizen, JIT and Best Practice) was welcomed by Western managements. The resulting flatter structures replaced functional organizations and, while some adjustments and modifications have been made, there has been a general move towards process management solutions.

The process management approach typically cuts across an organization's existing functions. The competitive company understands that market-place advantage is derived by assuming a customer perspective of value and taking a process management-led approach to solutions rather than a functional perspective:

> Therefore, organizations have restructured around business processes rather than functions. Someone (usually the process owner) needs to be accountable to the customer for the entire process and measured on their perceptions of performance (Knox and Maklan).

A *service culture* has replaced the marketing (and before that the sales-led) approach:

> We have moved from an economy of 'make and sell' to one of 'listen and serve' (Knox and Maklan).

Process design

A process is essentially: 'a method of doing things' Garvin (1988). Its primary purpose is to create a set of predetermined *outputs* from a set of *inputs* and to add value to the inputs. Outputs result from a transformation process (or set of processes). A simple transformation process is shown as Figure 3.4.

Customer value (and its precise meaning to the customer) is crucial because without an understanding of this it is not possible to begin to understand the processes which are best able to deliver the value and create customer satisfaction. Grant (1995) addressed the issue of Key Success Factors (see pp. 61–7), and these suggest areas which influence customer value. We can extend this to consider a *customer value equation*; see Figure 3.5. By analysing customer demand characteristics (Figure 3.1) we can identify *what it is that customers want*, and these become the customer value and value delivery service characteristics. Other issues which will influence customer value expectations are price and acquisition costs.

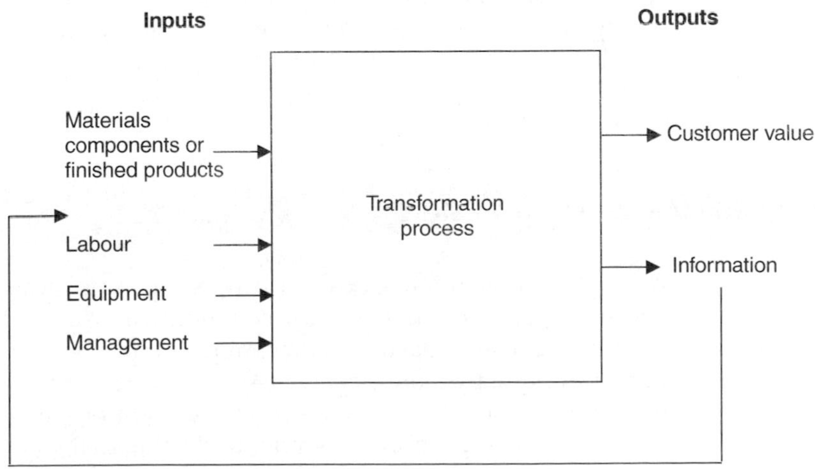

Figure 3.4 A transformation model.

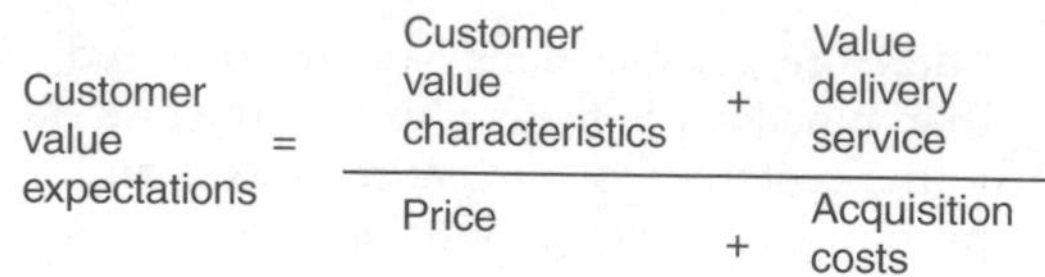

Figure 3.5 The customer value equation.

Customer value characteristics are the results or benefits delivered. It follows then that apparel retailers may be delivering a range of value characteristics ranging from status through to basic utility requirements of protection from environmental concerns: cold and wet weather, hazards of the work environment etc.

Value delivery service has a number of generic or universal characteristics. Parasuraman *et al.* (1988) have identified five 'universal dimensions'. They are:

- Dependability (the match between expectations and perceptions)
- Responsiveness ('time' performance)
- Authority (credibility)
- Empathy (the customer perspective)
- Tangible evidence (can the results be verified?)

Price and acquisition costs are important and should be measured not only in terms of price but also in terms of access convenience, time convenience and form utility. It follows that the value equation identifies the customer's trade-off potential between price and acquisition costs. This feature is used to segment retail markets.

Thus the customer value equation may be used to identify not simply what the customer wants *but also* the activities or the processes that are necessary to deliver the customer value. From this exercise process design can be developed.

PROCESS MANAGEMENT DESIGN

A number of techniques exist for process analysis, design, implementation and management. Three of those commonly in use are described below:

Service/attribute mapping is a technique similar to flow charting and has been developed by Shostack (1984). The purposes of service or attribute mapping are: to chart activities from the point of view of the customer; to ensure that all aspects of the service add value to the customers' experience of the service; and to identify the points at which the service system could fail to produce the intended value for customers. Map constructs have a formula. The customers and service participant(s) are identified *down* the chart (map) and the service process steps which contribute towards each activity are identified *across* the chart. The maps also identify a 'line of visibility' which delineates activities visible to the customer from those which take place elsewhere within the organization. Two issues are exposed. Employees who have customer contact must be trained to ensure that customer acceptability is ensured. Another concern is that processes with customer involvement are supported either by staff, systems or equipment. Points at which failure may occur are usually: steps in the process that add no value for the customer; steps that have had insufficient support where customers' expectations are being conditioned in advance of service delivery; steps that result in ambiguity and confusion, particularly where customer involvement and cooperation are essential; steps involving employee judgement; and points within the service delivery system which are vulnerable because of design weakness, low reliability, or excessive system throughput. A more complex approach can include time and costs. See Figure 3.6 for an example of service/attribute mapping.

A further issue is that the customer can be an additional force for value improvement in those aspects which have high visibility (IKEA). Those activities with most steps visible to the customer are typically those with high customer involvement, suggesting that customers are assuming responsibility for successful outcomes. The 'self-checkout' systems introduced by Sainsbury and Safeway are vulnerable to such concern.

Pareto analysis identifies the relative importance of problem causes. The *Pareto concept* is well known. Pareto was one of many who observed the relationship between inputs and outputs such that typically 20% of products, customers, orders etc. account for 80% of revenues, profits etc.

Heskett *et al.* (1997) cite the case of a power supply company using Pareto analysis to identify the relative importance of problem causes. It is an approach which may be applied effectively to customer service problems: once a hierarchy of problems has been established management may tackle them. While an effective approach, it is *reactive* in its application and is preferred as a means of control. However, if used *during* research *expectations* can also be established in a rank-ordered structure, and this would facilitate a proactive approach; see Figure 3.7.

Cause and Effect' (fishbone) charting is shown in Figure 3.8. The problem/issue to be explored is the 'head' of the fish and the 'bones' identify primary components of the topic under review. Secondary components are shown as subsidiary bones.

A detailed explanation of the approach by Ishikawa can be read in Hammer and Champy (1993). The technique identifies the primary influencing factors and then continues the analysis to identify the factors which influence these.

For each of these techniques one comment is common to each. The techniques themselves *do not* provide solutions. Rather, they should be used to identify the issues to be examined in detail.

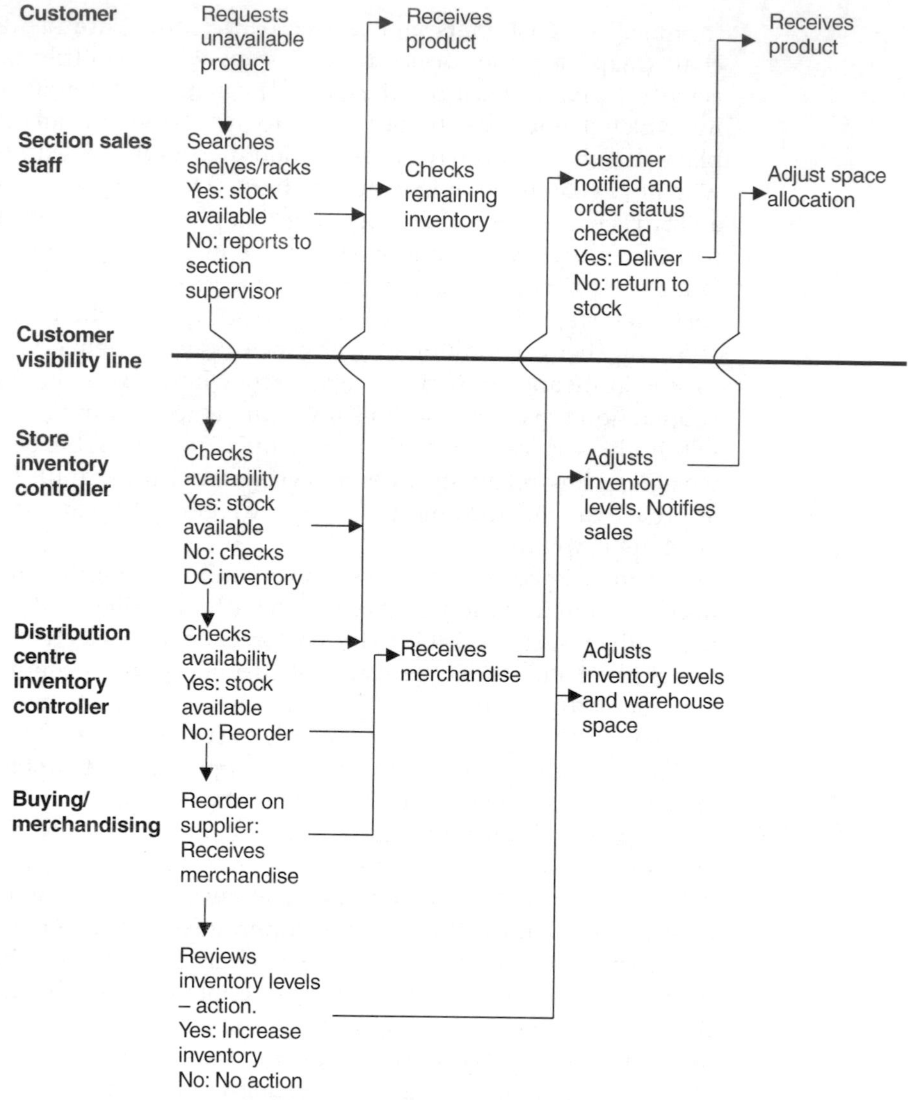

Figure 3.6 Developing a service map for customer product availability.

Techniques into results

It will be recalled that process design and management move the organization away from a functional management base towards identifying key processes. Knox and Maklan (1998) use five core processes:

- *Supply partnerships* – the ways in which an organization develops its 'inputs' from suppliers.
- *Asset management* – the use of assets to add value to the inputs. This assumes assets to be tangible and intangible.

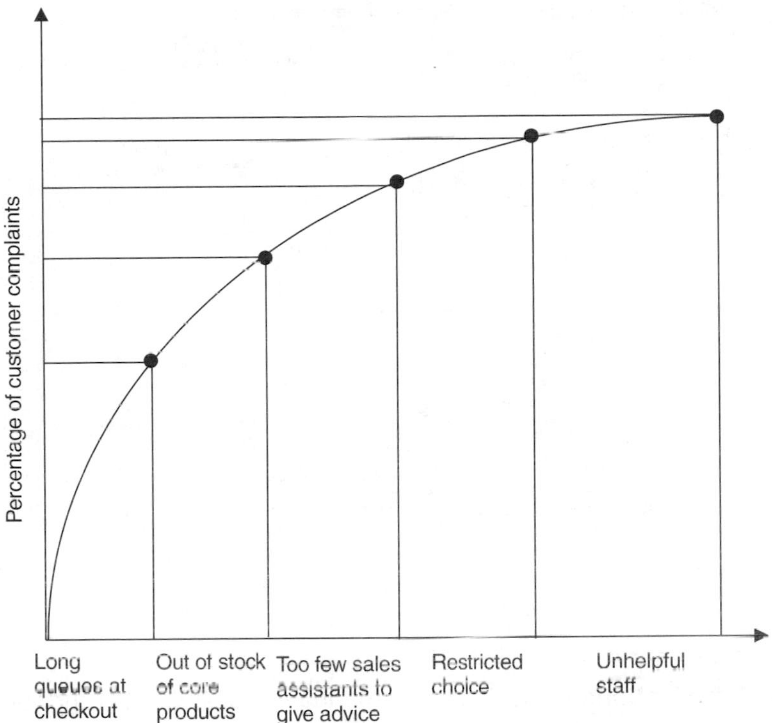

Figure 3.7 Using Pareto analysis to establish customers' service preferences.

- *Resource transformation* – the deployment of assets against inputs to create goods and services for sale to the next level in the value chain.
- *Customer development* – the process which addresses the balance between customer acquisition and retention from a detailed knowledge of customer motivation and behaviour.
- *Marketing planning* – a coordinating use of the marketing mix through the business processes to deliver customer value. Knox and Maklan propose their UOVP (unique organization value proposition) to this. The UOVP comprises these five core processes together with reputation, product and service performance, product brand and customer portfolio, and networks.

These should possibly be regarded as *generic processes*. While they, or processes very similar to them, are common to most organizations, different emphases may be applied. For example, in repeat purchase businesses, such as food multiples, the *customer development* process is very much concerned with retaining customers – hence the intensive interest in customer loyalty programs. However, there are organizations for which customer attraction is far more important (for example, matrimonial apparel), and for these customer development focuses upon customer attraction. We shall return to this topic.

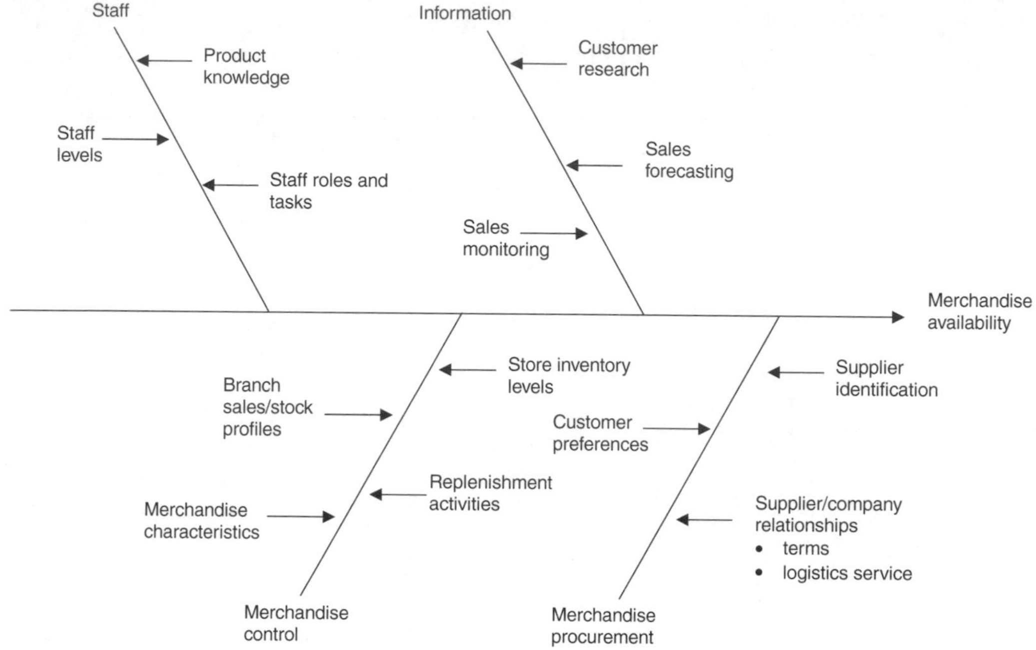

Figure 3.8 Fishbone analysis of merchandise availability components.

Before considering this topic in more detail we will consider the issues of implementation. Heskett *et al.* (1997) identify eight important considerations:

- Encouraging leadership commitment by calibrating the potential results from value improvements by benchmarking performance against the 'best in the world' as opposed to merely the best in the industry.
- Involving middle management in value improvement rather than marginalizing them. Often their contributions are based upon current day-to-day experience.
- Maintaining both a customers' and an employees' perspective in the design process, particularly for product services for which there is a high level of perceived risk.
- Involving customers to develop ownership.
- Measuring activities and performance at every step of the value improvement process.
- Shielding employees from the potential effects of a value improvement process (i.e. job losses or major shifts in roles and tasks which decrease job satisfaction).
- Creating a 'habit' of continuing value improvement such that it becomes second nature to everyone within the organization.
- Expecting and seeking basic changes in organization culture as it embraces such initiatives.

These issues can have a major impact on an organization, such that fundamental changes are required. Johansson *et al.* (1993) suggest these to be: culture, structure, performance measurement, incentive systems and management style. They have found *culture* the most difficult because it requires fundamental changes in the behaviour of all employees as the organization moves from the 'command and control of functions to a delayered environment that emphasizes process excellence through teamwork'.

Structure requires a balance to be developed between functional expertise and process involvement. Mobility and flexibility become major issues. *Performance measurement* will focus on a team approach to contribution to enhance competitiveness through improvements in cost, quality, time and service (major components in the *customer value equation*). *Incentive systems* that are individual-based need to be de-emphasized and then removed completely. *Management style* changes may be required. They should emphasize: 'shared values and a vision of excellence through empowerment of all members of the workforce and investment to enable continuous process improvement'.

Johansson *et al.* conclude that the general framework used is very similar to that used for *change management*, suggesting both share common needs if the move from a functional orientation towards being process led is to be successful.

Process design: a retail operations management model

A conclusion that may be reached from the process design/management literature is that it offers management an opportunity to be more flexible in its approach to the task of implementing strategy. A risk for many organizations is that a functional approach may be responsible for myopic solutions. Instead of being creative in the response to an opportunity the solution offered may be constrained by limitations imposed by staying *within* the confines of functional capabilities and capacities rather than exploring the benefits of looking *outwith* the existing functional organizational structure and benefiting from external resource contributions.

The inclusion of *key variables for operations management* and *critical success factors* focuses management's attention on the essential factors for success. By identifying these characteristics the *core processes* are more clearly defined and managed.

An approach using this proposal is featured as Figure 3.9. We have modified Knox and Maklan's five core processes and suggest four: customer perspectives, supplier partnerships, asset management and resource transformation, and coordination and management.

We prefer customer perspectives, as this implies a more extensive understanding of customer motivation and behaviour within the context of the customer value equation. We combine asset management and resource transformation because we consider them to be interrelated such that trade-off situations exist and should be explored with a view to achieving

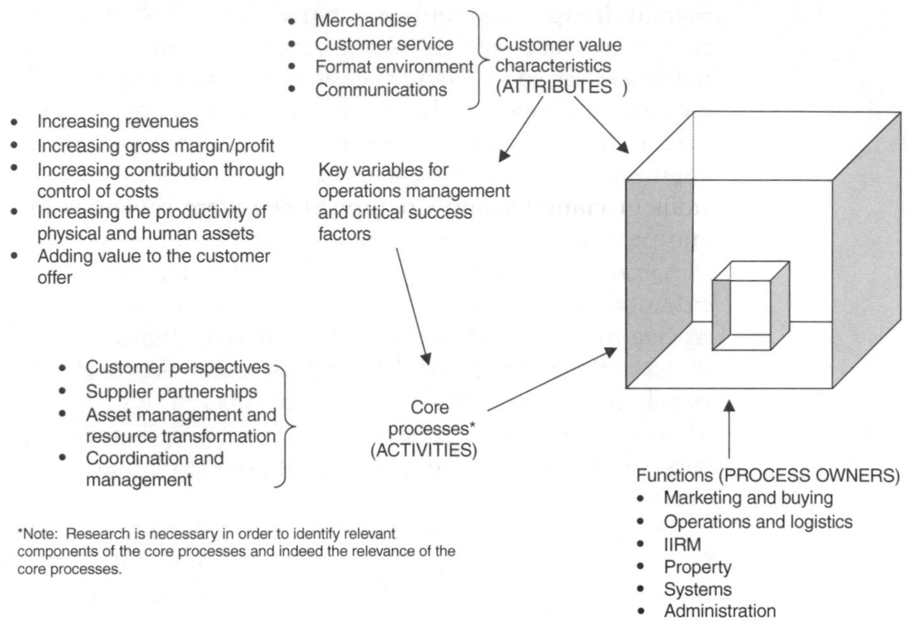

Figure 3.9 A process-led model for operations management.

cost-efficient solutions. We have replaced marketing planning with coordination and management in an attempt to broaden the planning activity such that it reaches and considers all possible stakeholders within the value chain. Within the context of our retail strategy model (Figure 2.7 (a) and (b)), the *processes* are the activities which combine to produce attributes.

Attributes are shown in Figure 3.9 as outputs, customer value characteristics, and the components of the strategic theme. Functions are those typically seen in retailing organization structures.

SUMMARY

The implementation of strategy tasks operating managers with ensuring that an efficient operational interpretation is made of the organization's strategy. This chapter has taken the reader through this process and has identified and explored processes and techniques useful to the task.

The role of key success factors in both strategic and operational management is helpful, even essential, because they identify issues which are significant to the competitive position of the firm and which require operational management to address when interpreting the strategic positioning of the firm. Two imperatives appear. Failure to consider the factors will put the position of the firm at risk in the long term. However, the long term may be of inconsequential significance if the key success factors and the operational components are not managed within budget.

The chapter introduced business process design and management as a useful technique for managing strategy implementation. The early contributions of Hammer and Champy (1993) were reviewed (as were comments concerning the efficacy of the concept). Despite the criticisms made of 're-engineering', it does have much to offer retail management. One of its primary benefits is that it forces an appraisal of both outputs and inputs. Micklethwait and Woolridge (1996) suggest that activities which are often close to the customer and impact on customer service can benefit from a review of processes.

The chapter was concluded by developing a model, based on process design and management, for strategy implementation in retail operations activities.

QUESTIONS, ACTIVITIES AND CONSIDERATIONS

- Identify the key success factors of the following types of retailing organization:
  - A department store
  - A specialist children's wear chain
  - An Internet-based specialist (e.g. books and recorded music)
- For a successful prominent retailing company:
  - Identify its strategic direction, theme, attributes and activities.
  - Identify its key success factors
  - Identify the processes which are important for successful implementation of its strategy.

The processes used by IKEA follow. They have ascertained a 'willingness' on the customers' part to be involved in the selling, logistics and manufacturing processes. Given IKEA's understanding of this it has identified suppliers capable of adding value to the product such that the customer involvement in the manufacturing process continues on from a specified point. The company has balanced its investment in fixed assets (i.e. equipment and HR) and operational assets: there is very little fixed capital but there is a preponderance of supervisory and quality control staff. HR concerns are reflected by the role of staff in the stores: sufficient numbers to meet medium/heavy customer traffic flows with skills capable of undertaking prescribed roles and tasks. Coordination and management activities are designed to ensure that the suppliers are 'trained' to meet

IKEA product design and quality specifications. Inventory is managed across a range of manufacturing locations, distribution centres, and retail outlets on an international basis. It is the role of the *process owners*, functional management, to meet commitments to each process.

- What are the likely implications of information science developments for operations management?

REFERENCES

Anterasian, C. and Phillips, L. W. (1988) *Discontinuities, Value Delivery and the Share Return Association: A re-examination of the 'Share-Causes-Profits' Controversy.* Research Program Monograph, Report No 88-109. The Marketing Science Institute, Cambridge, MA.

Fortune (1994) Charles Handy sees the future. *Fortune*, 31 October.

Garvin, D. A. (1988) *Managing Quality*. The Free Press, New York.

Grant, R. M. (1995) *Contemporary Strategy Analysis*. Blackwell Business, Oxford.

Hamel, G. and Prahalad, C. K. (1994) *Competing for the Future*. Harvard Business School Press, Boston, MA.

Hammer, M. and Champy, J. (1993) *Re-engineering the Corporation*. Nicholas Braeley Publishing, London.

Heskett, J. L., Sasser, W. E. Jr and Schlesinger, L. A. (1997) *The Service Profit Chain*. The Free Press, New York.

Hofer, C. W. and Schendel, D. E. (1978) *Strategy Formulation: Analytical concepts*. West Publishing, New York.

Johansson, H. J., McHugh M., Pendlebury, A. J., Wheeler, W. A. III (1993) *Business Process Re-engineering*. Wiley, Chichester.

Knox, S. and Maklan, S. (1998) *Competing on Value*. Financial Times/Pitman, London.

Kotler, P. (1994) *Marketing Management: Analysis, Planning and Control*. Prentice Hall, New York.

Murray, J. W. and O'Driscoll, A. (1996) *Strategy and Process in Marketing*, Prentice Hall, Hemel Hempstead.

Micklethwait, J. and Woolridge, A. (1996) *The Witch Doctor's*. Heinemann, London.

Parasuraman, A., Zeithaml, V. A. and Berry, L. (1988) SERVQUAL: a multiple-item scale for measuring customer perceptions of service quality. *Journal of Retailing*, Spring.

Rumelt R. (1988) The evaluation of business strategy, in *The Strategy Process: Concepts, Contexts and Cases* (Quinn, J.B. *et al.* eds.). Prentice Hall, Englewood Cliffs, NJ.

Shostack, G. L. (1984) Designing services that deliver. *Harvard Business Review*, Jan/Feb.

Webster, F. (1994) *Market Driven Management*. Wiley, New York.

PERFORMANCE EVALUATION: APPRAISING STRATEGIC INVESTMENT ALTERNATIVES AND DEVELOPING OPERATING BUDGETS

LEARNING OBJECTIVES

This chapter deals with the financial evaluation of proposed retail strategy options. We do this by first identifying the components of the retail exchange environment that the strategy will develop. This process encourages a level of detailed attributes and activities that may then be reviewed from a financial perspective.

- The Du Pont/Strategic Profit Model (SPM) is used to evaluate the role of margin management, asset management, and gearing on shareholder value return. The roles of these relationships and interrelationships are explored within the context of the evaluation process.
- In addition to evaluating potential strategy options, we consider the ongoing concern and introduce strategic ratios which enable the manager to monitor original objectives and intentions.
- The concept of the strategic profit model is extended to map strategic decisions. The extended SPM thus encourages 'what if?' approaches to be made and evaluated.
- Investment appraisal is reviewed and is specifically applied to retail strategy evaluation by including the strategic and operating expenses necessary for evaluations.
- Strategic decisions are concerned with balancing risk and return. In the strategic investment appraisal process the cost of capital is an important issue. Accordingly, we introduce the capital asset pricing model to explore strategic portfolio considerations and their impact on the cost of capital.
- The investment evaluation process is developed into a planning/budgeting model which identifies with key resource issues and performance criteria.
- An appendix offers an example which illustrates the use of financial data to identify key performance issues.

INTRODUCTION

Before any strategy can be decided upon and subsequently implemented it is essential that its financial viability, as well as its marketing effectiveness, be established. During the identification process the marketing effectiveness will have been explored; without this having been established and accepted there is no point in proceeding as the major issue to establish is the fact that the option offers an acceptable sales volume.

For any retail strategy development and evaluation process a procedure such as that suggested by Figure 4.1 is usual. We are in effect creating a retail

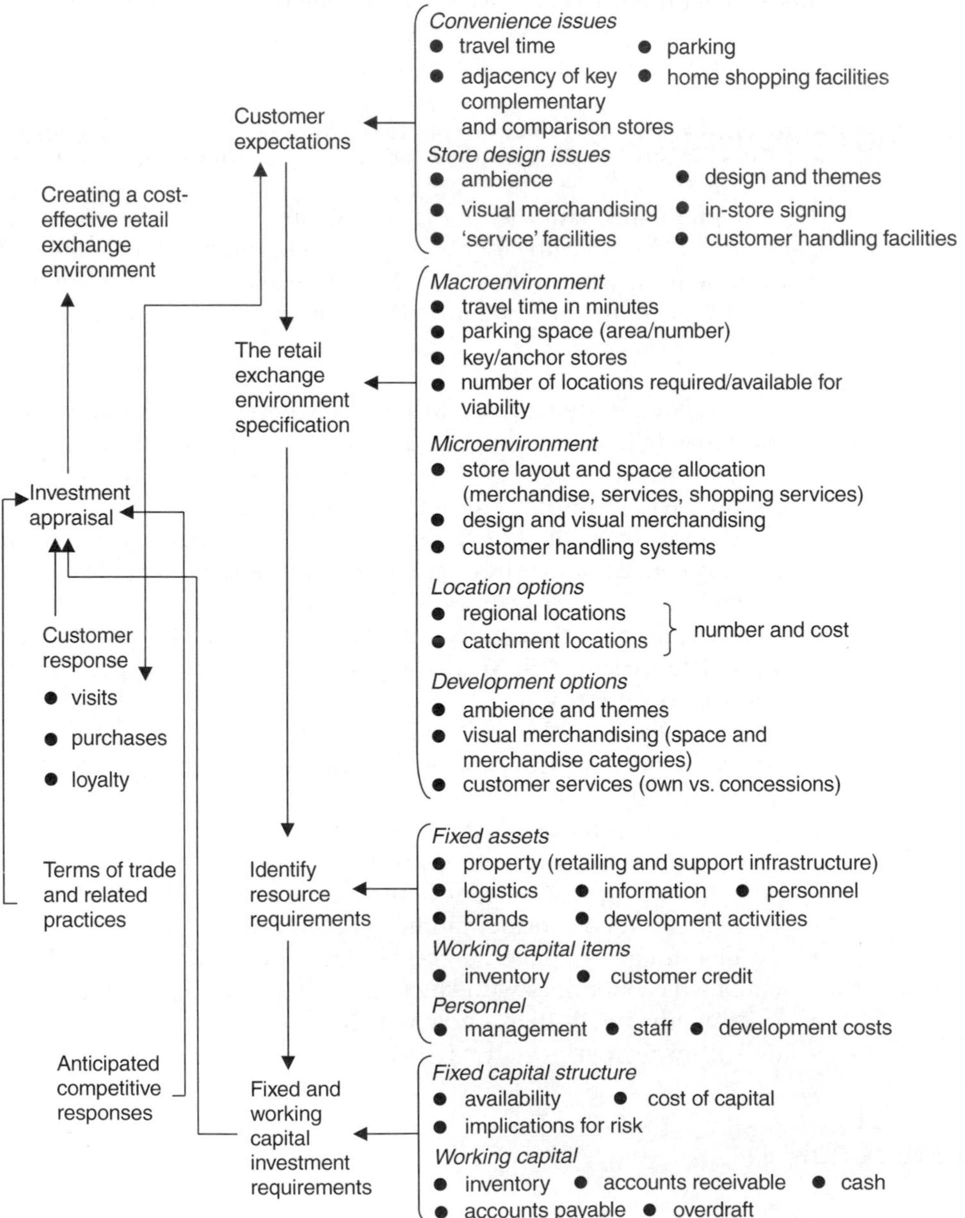

Figure 4.1 Evaluating strategic options.

exchange environment and the purpose of the financial evaluation is to establish whether or not the revenues generated will cover the capital costs *and* operating expenses *and* return a satisfactory return to the shareholders at an acceptable level of risk.

It follows that for each alternative the *customer expectations* are first identified and their expected *customer response* in terms of visits, purchases and loyalty (and estimated life span) established. Given a satisfactory answer to this a *retail exchange environment specification* is then established. Figure 4.1 suggests an approach in which macro- and micro-environments are established together with the number of outlets required for market viability (i.e. credible market presence) *and* the number of suitable locations that are available. Clearly it is essential that the number of available locations which meet the specification is established early; this will identify problems that may exist when looking for locations as and when the project is commissioned.

The specification will enable management to *identify resource requirements* and their cost together with the financial implications for *fixed and working capital investment*. A large part of this activity will be devoted to considering how the projects may be funded and the cost of the capital required to launch the project *and* fund the initial operating expenses.

To evaluate the project from a financial perspective a number of *investment appraisal* methods are available (these are discussed below). It is important to consider an estimate of the impact of *terms of trade and related practices* in the analysis. Not to do so may result in some unexpected problems: for example, a firm used to working on 60 day payment cycles with suppliers may find difficulties in a 'market' with concentrated supply sources who operate on 30 day cycles.

Similarly, it is essential that *anticipated competitive responses* are considered: specifically, who may make them and their relative marketing and financial strengths and weaknesses. These may have a significant impact on opportunities and threats and, therefore, the success of the strategy.

Effective strategies are those for which the financial implications of implementation can be understood by all levels of management. A number of methods are available for this purpose. The most frequently used method is to project the income statement (profit and loss accounts), balance sheets and cash flow statements. The purpose of this approach is to present the financial implications of a strategy in terms that are understood by managers used to working with that form of presentation. A disadvantage of this presentation is that the interrelationships between profitability, productivity and cash flow are not particularly well identified.

To some extent this problem is resolved by using the system of ratio analysis introduced by Du Pont in the 1920s. The principle of the Du Pont approach (and its subsequent interpretations) is to demonstrate the *interrelationships* of decisions:

$$\frac{\text{Profit}}{\text{Sales}} * \frac{\text{Sales}}{\text{Assets}} * \frac{\text{Assets}}{\text{Equity}} = \frac{\text{Profit}}{\text{Equity}}$$

$$\begin{pmatrix}\text{Margin}\\\text{management}\end{pmatrix} \begin{pmatrix}\text{Asset base}\\\text{management}\end{pmatrix} \begin{pmatrix}\text{Financial}\\\text{structure}\end{pmatrix} \begin{pmatrix}\text{Return on}\\\text{equity}\end{pmatrix}$$

McCammon and Harimer (1974) presented a model based upon the Du Pont approach, the *Strategic Profit Model*, which met some of the criticisms directed towards conventional financial measures. Stern *et al.* (1986) argue:

> No single measure of performance fully reflects the financial well-being of a firm. The financial performance of wholesalers and retailers is multidimensional, requiring an examination of (1) profitability, or return on investment, (2) liquidity, or the ability of the firm to meet its financial liabilities within a time frame, (3) capital structure, or leverage ratio (gearing), (4) growth pattern of sales and profits, and (5) growth potential of sales and profits. However, return on investment is accepted as an aggregate performance measure in the retail and wholesale trades. The *strategic profit model* (SPM) has been developed by managerial accountants to evaluate and diagnose profitability problems such as those that confront retailers and wholesalers.

Figure 4.2 illustrates the strategic profit model (SPM). The SPM identifies key decision areas for the business:

Net profit/sales: indicates management's ability to recover its variable and fixed costs. Stern *et al.* (1986) suggest this to express the cost/price effectiveness of the operation. Key cost factors for retailing are the cost of goods sold and the cost of operations (occupancy costs, staff, promotional costs at store/outlet level). Stern *et al.*'s view is that without effective management of buying and merchandising and store operations, together with the fixed costs of overheads etc., an adequate margin cannot be made. Bates (1990) emphasizes gross margin management:

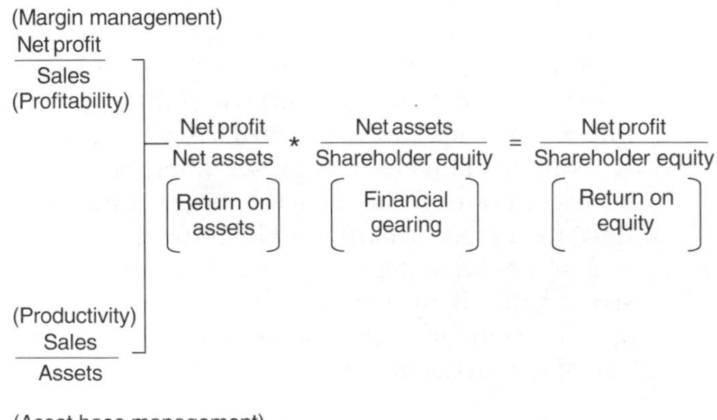

Figure 4.2 The strategic profit model.

> The key is to look beyond price and think more directly about gross margin planning. There are numerous ways to enhance gross margin.

- More effective purchasing, especially via consolidation of suppliers
- Mark-down control
- Shrinkage reduction, especially via proper measurement and control
- Merchandise mix, emphasis on higher margin items via display procedures, product adjacencies, and suggestion setting
- Price adjustments, especially via increases on non-price sensitive items.

Livingstone and Tigert (1987) considered *margin spread* as a significant issue. Their research in supermarket chains let to the conclusion that the *spread* between gross margin ratio and operating expense ratio is a critical element in determining return on investment, concluding:

> Clearly, operating profit drives return on investment for supermarkets.

These authors would disagree. A high stock turn ratio in a company operating leased outlets could have a significant impact on the overall return on assets/investment. It is this aspect of performance that the SPM is particularly helpful at highlighting in the planning stage of strategy. We shall return to this topic.

Sales/net assets: because net profit/sales ignores the utilization of assets a return on assets ratio is an essential performance measurement component. The ratio uses asset productivity data to indicate alternative methods of improving performance. Asset productivity can be increased by either increasing sales or decreasing assets, or by a combination of both. It should be said that this is *not* simply an exercise in arithmetic, but careful consideration of options. The reduction of asset value (or assets owned and employed) is becoming an important feature of strategy. Increasingly the question asked by retailers concerns the scope of the business and what comprises their *core business*. Many have resolved this by focusing on the retailing aspects of the business and divesting the support infrastructure assets and activities. Logistics was among the first activities to be outsourced, with property and information management (data collection, assembly and dissemination) being more recent candidates.

Net assets/shareholder equity: shows the dependence of an organization on borrowed funds (either short or long term). Shareholder equity (or net worth) is what remains after the organization's liabilities are subtracted from its net assets or its capital employed. The gearing ratio indicates the extent of external funding. A low ratio (more equity than debt funding) indicates a high degree of solvency and typically a preference for low-risk projects. Such companies are conservative and risk adverse. A high ratio indicates the opposite characteristics. Debt funding brings with it the advantage of expansion, unaffected control and the ability to charge interest payments against profits. It has a major disadvantage in that, regardless of sales and profitability performance, the interest payments must always be met. Because of the taxation effect debt funding is less costly than equity funds. Furthermore, the expansion of the equity base may result in a dilution of the control of the existing board of directors.

Net profit/shareholder equity: reflects the investment interest of the shareholders. Currently the return to the shareholder is a primary motivating factor, and consequently the return on equity (ROE) is an important performance characteristic. It follows that any strategic option that is recommended for consideration should, at least, offer to maintain the ROE percentage value while at the same time expanding the business. A decrease in the ROE (particularly over time) requires investigation. As the SPM demonstrates, performance changes may occur because of a number of reasons. McCammon *et al.* (1989) have suggested that the SPM offers four important managerial purposes:

- The model specifies that an organization's primary objective is to earn an adequate return on shareholders funds.
- The SPM identifies three profit paths;
  - margin management – profitability
  - asset base management – productivity
  - capital structure management – financial management
- These (above) decision areas (profit paths) are interrelated. Overall corporate performance (ROE) can be enhanced by integrated decision making, identifying and benefiting from the trade-off options that this approach offers.
- The model provides an effective means of appraising the financial implications of alternative strategies in achieving target returns on equity funds.

A useful approach to the SPM can be developed, and this is shown as Figure 4.3. However, care should be taken to ensure that the decisions input into the model are in fact strategic and not a mixture of strategic and operational decisions. This is important for a number of reasons. First, time perspectives differ, and the lead times for effectiveness between strategic and operational decisions are, as a consequence, quite different. Another concern is the temptation to 'create' an increase in return on investment or equity by simplifying the decision-making process. We suggest that a two-stage approach is more effective. Stage 1 establishes performance parameters, such as a range of acceptable ratio performances (at prescribed volume levels) *followed* by stage 2, which explores the operational aspects of the decision.

STRATEGIC AND OPERATIONAL PERFORMANCE EVALUATION: BROAD PARAMETERS

For the 'going concern', ongoing performance ratios are standards for future activities. The ratios are clustered to reflect their information role. The strategic ratios are:

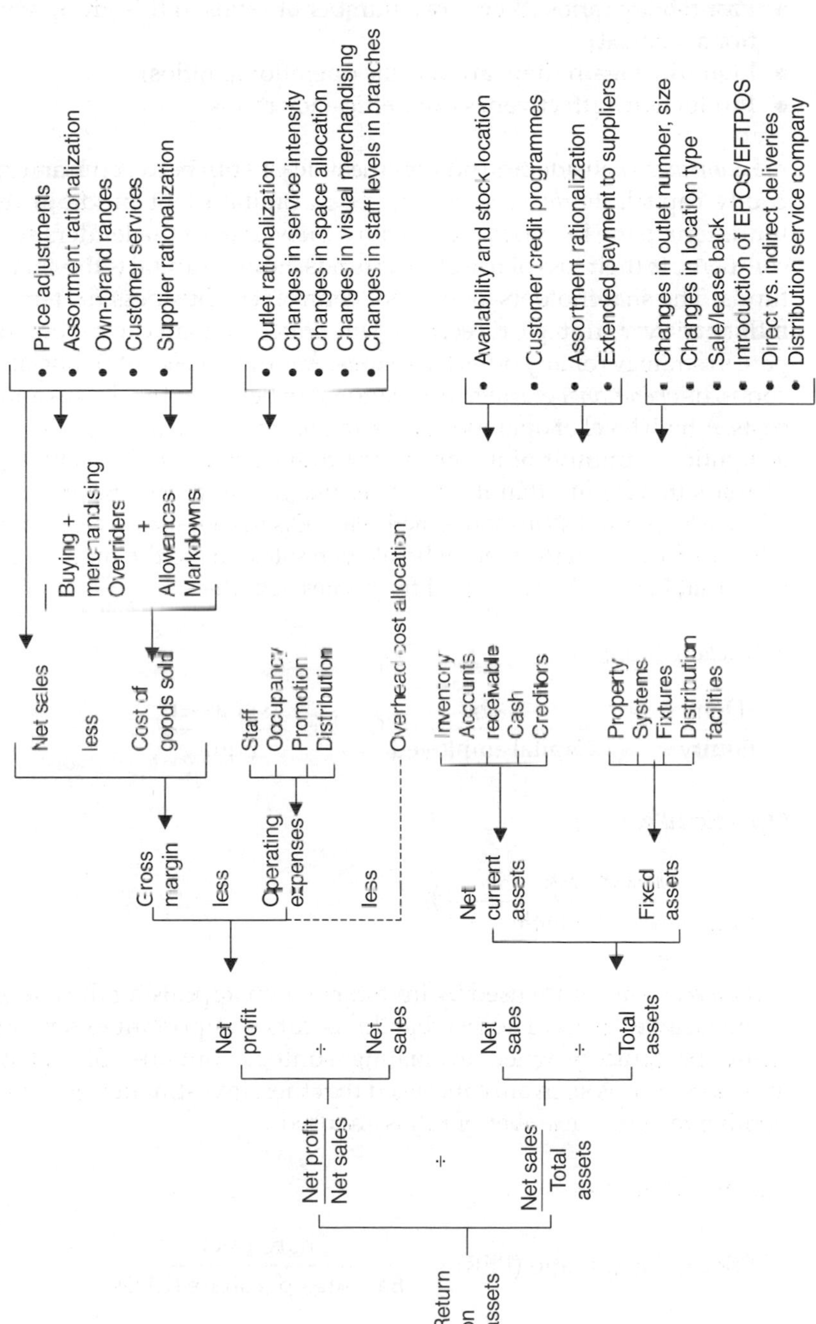

Figure 4.3 The strategic profit model, adapted to show the impact of retail management decisions.

- Financial structure ratios
- Investment ratios
- Profitability ratios (there are a number of ratios in this group with operational context)
- Liquidity (again there are specific operational ratios)
- Productivity effectiveness and efficiency ratios

Financial structure ratios indicate the relationship between loan capital and equity capital, its *financial gearing*. Loan capital (debt funding) represents funds lent to the business solely with a view to earn the lenders sufficient to compensate their loss of use of their funds. Equity capital is the shareholders' funds. The shareholders 'own' and 'control' the business (in terms of their influence over strategic direction). Subscribers of loan capital do not participate in strategy (or any other) decisions. Another aspect of financial structure concerns *operational gearing*, the relationship between fixed costs and variable costs. A high level of operational gearing occurs when an organization 'owns' a significant amount of its means of producing and delivering it products. The advantages are that it has larger margins and maximizes control over what are essentially 'in-house' activities. Disadvantages are the lack of flexibility and, often, high levels of breakeven sales due to the high levels of fixed costs that have to be recovered from sales activities.

Financial gearing

$$\frac{\text{Debt}}{\text{Equity}} \quad \text{or} \quad \frac{\text{Debt}}{\text{Capital employed}}\% \quad \text{or} \quad \frac{\text{Net assets}}{\text{Equity}}$$

Operational gearing

$$\frac{\text{Fixed costs}}{\text{Fixed costs} + \text{variable costs}}\%$$

Investment ratios are used by investors when appraising the company as a financial investment. The fact that this occurs is important to senior management, particularly when evaluating strategic options. Shareholders are investors, and as such are concerned that their investment is realizing a competitive return. A number of ratios are used.

Shareholder returns

Price earnings ratio (PER): $$\frac{\text{Share price}}{\text{Earnings per share (EPS)}}$$

Relative PER: $$\frac{\text{PER company}}{\text{PER market (or sector)}}$$

Dividend yield: $\dfrac{\text{EPS}}{\text{Net dividend per share}}$

Economic value added (EVA) = Operating profit (NOPAT) – (capital employed × cost of capital (risk adjusted)).

EVA > 0 indicates that wealth (or value) has been created for the shareholder. EVA < 0 indicates that value has been destroyed.

Market value added (MVA) = Corporate debt + market value of shares – capital invested in the business.

MVA > 0 indicates that value has been created, while MVA < 0 indicates that value has been destroyed.

Profitability ratios are primary measures of performance. They indicate the effectiveness (and efficiency of management) in generating revenues sufficient to cover the costs of merchandise, branch operations, distribution activities and interest charges *and* contribute a profit to the shareholders.

Profitability ratios

Return on sales (ROS): $\dfrac{\text{Profit}}{\text{Sales}}\%$ (carefully defined)

Gross profit (margin %): $\dfrac{\text{Sales} - \text{COGS}}{\text{Sales}}\%$

Contribution/operations profit (margin %):

$$\frac{\text{Sales} - \text{COGS} - \text{operating costs}}{\text{Sales}}\%$$

Management has both a strategic and operational interest in these ratios.

Liquidity ratios: because retailing is more of a cash business than most other businesses, liquidity is a major concern. The added value process in distribution is simpler and quicker for retailers than it is for their suppliers. Consequently it is both necessary, and useful, to be able to monitor the effectiveness and efficiency with which cash is managed. There are three major concerns. One concerns the payment of suppliers in order to obtain maximum benefit from settlement terms. The other concerns the use that can be made of suppliers' cash to develop the business (the concept of negative working capital). A third concern is the use of cash in expansion moves; this is a strategic issue, whereas the previous two concerns are primarily operational.

Liquidity ratios

Current ratio: $\dfrac{\text{Current assets}}{\text{Current liabilities}}$

Quick ratio: $\dfrac{\text{Current assets} - \text{inventory}}{\text{Current liabilities}}$

Liquidity may also be measured by calculating cash flow amounts.

Cash flow from earnings = Profit after tax + depreciation

Cash flow from operations = Cash flow from earnings
± changes in fixed capital requirements
± changes in equity funds
± changes in long-term (debt) funding

These measures are particularly useful in strategy decision making, where the organization seeks to identify sources of funds for expansion, particularly low-cost sources.

Productivity ratios (often referred to as 'efficiency' ratios) are more useful when considered from both a strategic (effectiveness) perspective and an operational (efficiency) viewpoint. Both measures are concerned with management's use of its asset base. Strategic productivity measures the *effectiveness* with which fixed assets are used. Operational productivity measures *efficiency* in the use of its working capital.

Strategic productivity ratios

Return on capital employed (net assets): $\dfrac{\text{Net profit}}{\text{Capital employed}}$

Return on equity: $\dfrac{\text{Net profit}}{\text{Equity funds}}$

Return on assets: $\dfrac{\text{Net profit}}{\text{Fixed assets}}$

Fixed asset turnover: $\dfrac{\text{Sales}}{\text{Fixed assets}}$

Operational productivity ratios

Working capital turnover: $\dfrac{\text{Sales}}{\text{Working capital}}$

Inventory turnover: $\dfrac{\text{Cost of goods sold}}{\text{Inventory}}$

Inventory cover: $\dfrac{\text{Trading period (in days)}}{\text{Inventory turnover}}$

Purchases turnover: $\dfrac{\text{Purchases per trading period}}{\text{Trade creditors (Accounts payable)}}$

Receivables (credit allowed) turnover: $\dfrac{\text{Credit sales}}{\text{Accounts receivable}}$

Days credit allowed: $\dfrac{\text{Trading period (in days)}}{\text{Accounts receivable turnover}}$

As can be seen, a number of the ratios are sales and assets based, and this fact is useful for planning purposes, as it allows management to use key ratios as broad targets to be achieved when considering alternatives. While we do not suggest that any option should be selected or rejected on this basis, past relationships between revenues, costs, profits and financial structures do offer some basic benchmarks. Using the Du Pont relationship enables basic measures to be identified and explored. The business knows better than anyone the tolerances that exist at both strategic and operational levels.

An overall approach is given by Figure 4.4, which uses the strategic profit model as a decision template. For each component, e.g. *sales revenue* or *assets*, the primary decision characteristics are identified. Management can, using experience and judgement, estimate the impact on revenues and costs (and therefore profitability) of each characteristic and consequently derive estimates of the *return on assets and equity*. Having reached an initial estimate of performance it is possible to make adjustments by review of (and adjusting the role and costs of) each characteristic, but it should be remembered that customer expectations (see Figure 4.1) have been determined and will constrain the changes that are possible.

Figure 4.4 contains all of the elements involved in evaluating and implementing strategy. What may be required is a facility for comparing options against recent performance and/or market performance (relevant for new market entrants). Two simple mechanisms are offered for this purpose. At the strategy level Figure 4.5 considers profitability and productivity options, while operational considerations are dealt with by the margin spread model in Figure 4.6.

Consider Figure 4.5, which is constructed using the relationships between profit, sales, assets and capital structure items:

Profitability × Productivity = Return on Investment

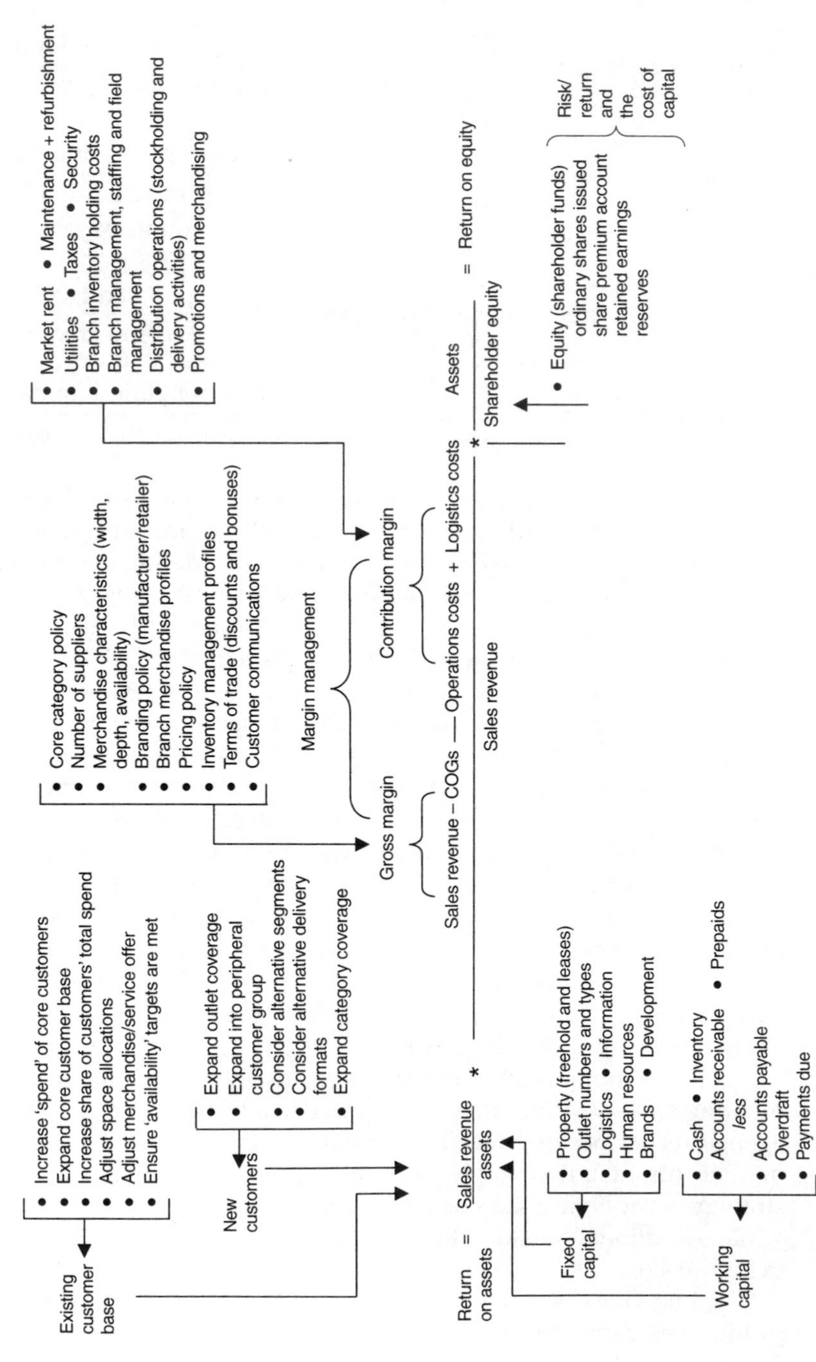

Figure 4.4 Mapping the decision issues.

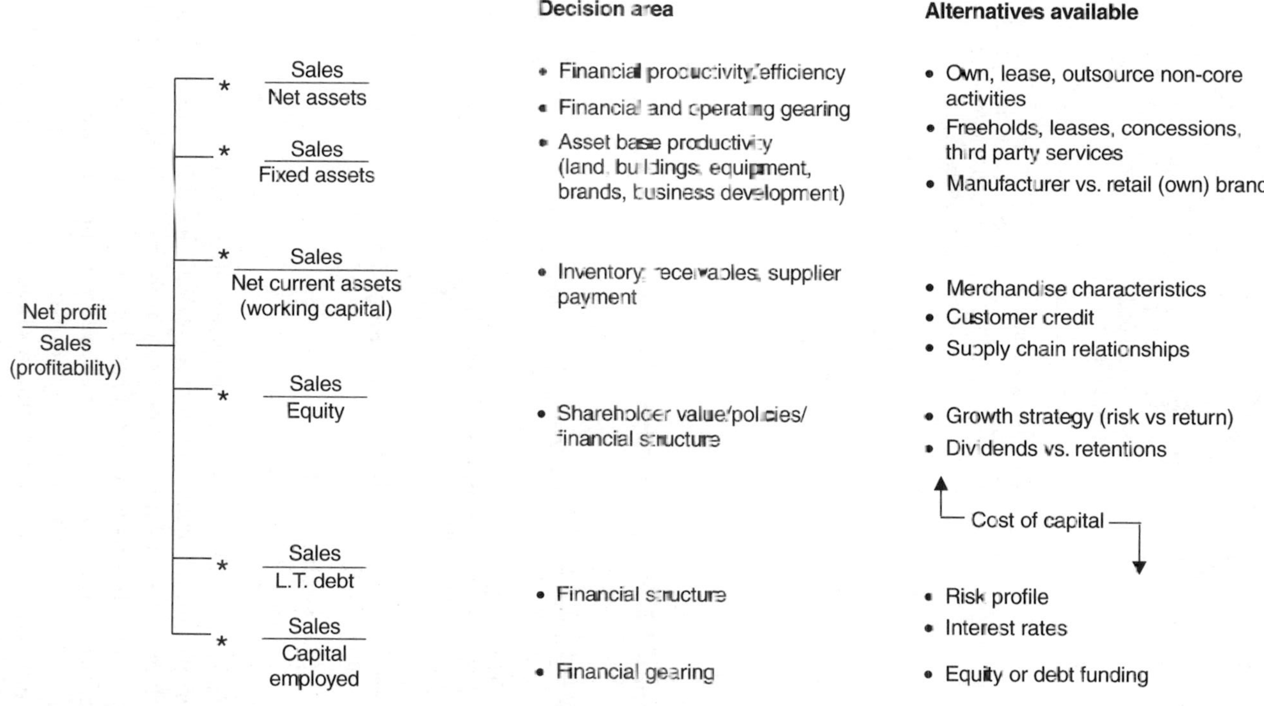

Figure 4.5 Strategic financial performance parameters (profitability and productivity): identifying decisions and options.

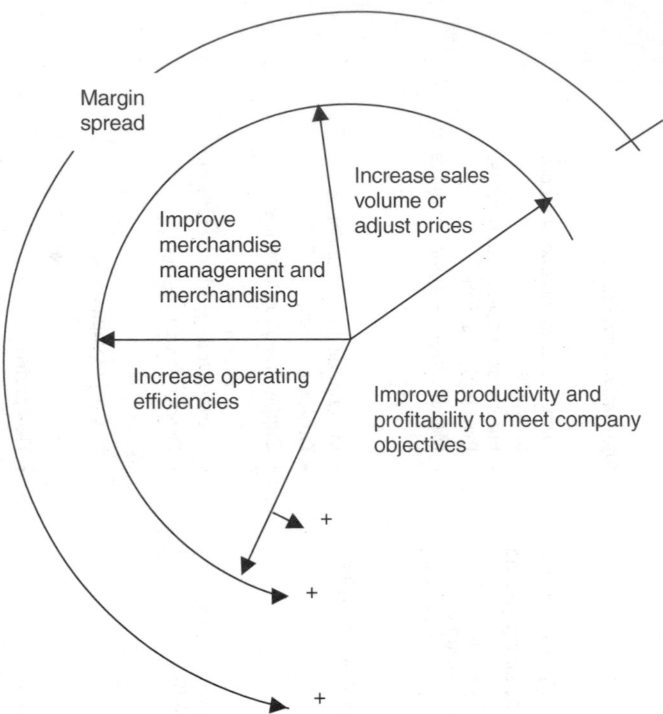

Figure 4.6 Margin management decisions.

or

$$\frac{\text{Profit}}{\text{Sales}} \times \frac{\text{Sales}}{\text{Assets}} = \text{Return on assets}$$

$$\frac{\text{Profit}}{\text{Sales}} \times \frac{\text{Sales}}{\text{Capital}} = \text{Return on capital item}$$

(i.e. equity, debt or capital employed)

Extended, Figure 4.5 can indicate alternative approaches to improving performance. For example, at a strategic level *fixed asset productivity* can be influenced in a number of ways. A high entry cost (large outlets, central locations) may be offset by leasing outlets or, possibly, by negotiating concessions with non-competing retailers already in these locations. *Working capital productivity* may be improved by adjusting merchandise characteristics/supply chain relationships to maintain choice but operate with lower inventory holding (such as the arrangements made between furniture retailers and manufacturers, discussed in detail in a subsequent chapter).

Given a broad specification of the structure of the exchange environment *and* a range of performance characteristics that are required if a project is to be successful, alternative delivery formats can be identified and evaluated.

Operational performance may be explored using the proposals of Bates and of Livingstone and Tigert. Figure 4.6 suggests three possibilities for increasing the profitability of the margin spread. For products with monopoly features (e.g. merchandise exclusivity, choice, very high quality/brand reputation) *price increases* are viable options. More effective *merchandise management* and *merchandising* are to be considered if there is no real competitive advantage. Inventory profiles based upon rates of sale can be introduced to reduce overall inventory holding levels and costs (e.g. the ABC concept) or possibly a review of in-store merchandising and promotional displays can be used to increase both inventory *and* space productivity. For example, for furniture items for which a wide variety of finishes and colours are a strong sales-motivating factor, displays may be restricted to 'one-off' colour-ways and fabric options. An increase *in operating efficiencies* is a third alternative. This may require a review of the processes involved in merchandise movements from suppliers to the point of sale; the manufacturing process might be extended to obtain benefits of economies of scale. Alternatively, solutions similar to those adopted by IKEA (customer self-delivery and assembly) may have an impact.

What has resulted is a pragmatic evaluation of the identified options. They have been reviewed against a customer-led set of market criteria *and* a set of financial performance criteria, both of which have themselves been developed from the company's experiences in its various markets/market segments.

RESOURCES PLANNING AND INVESTMENT APPRAISAL

Given the strategic options, together with forecast volumes, revenues, costs and contribution from potential retail exchange environments, we have sufficient data to evaluate the strategic value to the organization for each option. The previous analysis will have eliminated options that are unlikely to reach the profitability, productivity and cash flow performance parameters that will ultimately produce the level of return expected by shareholders.

A number of investment appraisal models are available, but the objective is to identify *the* strategic option which will maximize shareholder value *and, at the same time,* maximize customer satisfaction, creating a long-term loyal customer base.

For these reasons we propose to use the net present value (NPV) discounting method for the evaluation or investment appraisal of strategic options. At this point we should be confident that any proposal to have reached this stage of the evaluation does meet the basic profitability, productivity and cashflow performance expectations. In the real world resources are scarce and choices between options have to be made. The NPV discounting method offers the means for doing just this.

DCF methods are based upon the *present value* of future cash flows. The argument is simple: a dollar to be received in ten years from now is worth less than the dollar held today.
We can calculate future values by using compound interest given by:

$$\text{Compound value} = \text{Initial investment} \times \text{interest rate} \times \text{time in years as a multiplier}$$

or:

$$\text{CV (or TV)} = S(1+r)^t$$

where:

CV (TV) = compound or terminal value
S = sum invested
r = interest rate earned
t = time period over which S is invested

It follows that a dollar amount received immediately is worth more than the same value to be received at some future time because the sum received immediately can be invested for the intervening period and earn a return. It therefore follows that an amount promised in the future has a *present value* and this can be found by *discounting* future income values to calculate their present value:

$$\text{Present value} = \frac{\text{Future amount}}{\text{Interest} \times \text{time in years}}$$

or

$$\text{PV} = \frac{F}{(1+r)^t}$$

where:

PV = present value
F = future amount
r = interest rate/discount rate
t = time period over which value is to be calculated

The net present value (NPV) is arrived at by deducting the initial investment from the present value:

$$\text{NPV} = \sum_{t-1}^{n} \frac{F_t}{(1+r)^t} - I$$

where:

NPV	= Net present value
$\sum_{t}^{n}$	= the summation over years
t	= 1, 2, ..., n
F_t	= the forecast net cash flow arising at the end of year t. This represents the difference between operational cash receipts (revenues) and expenditures (operating costs, including capital replenishment (refurbishment costs etc.) during the life of the project.
r	= required rate of return or the discount rate
t	= time period over which valuers to be calculated
n	= project life in years
I	= the initial cost of the investment in the project

The present value is arrived at by aggregating the forecast *net cash flows* (operating revenues – operating expenses – any capital expenditures for capital replenishment and/or refurbishment) for the planned life span of the project (discounted at a rate which reflects the cost of a loan of equivalent risk on the capital market) The discount rate (discussed further below) may represent the *cost of capital* of the organization (weighted to represent the combination of debt and equity funding) or may be a *hurdle rate* (a discount rate set by management and one which considers the risk involved in a project).

It follows that an investment is *wealth creating* if its NPV is positive. All projects offering a positive NPV (NPV > 0) when discounted at the required rate of return could be accepted with the aim of maximizing the value of the shareholders' equity holding in the business.

For the evaluation of strategy options the NPV model may be used easily. Figure 4.7 identifies the data inputs required. A review of Figure 4.4 will show that the data does exist and that Figure 4.4 offers a means of exploring issues prior to entering the data into the NPV model. For example *sales revenue* (in Figure 4.4) identifies the issues that drive the *operating revenues* required by the NPV model. Similarly, for the investment (*I*) data. Again Figure 4.4 may be used for asking some 'what if?' questions prior to data entry.

The discount rate used has an obvious impact on the result. Some discussion of how the rate may be derived is essential. The *value* of the rate of interest used for discounting the forecast cash flow is influenced by the company's cost of capital. Clearly, the rate used must equal or exceed the weighted average cost of capital (WACC) *that will prevail when the project is undertaken*. The reasons for this are obvious, but will be reviewed.

Depending upon the nature of the project so the *risk* will vary. Expansion into existing markets/segments will be accompanied by lower levels of risk than that involved with new merchandise categories or market segments. *Inflation* is also to be considered. It is unlikely that a return to the levels of inflation experienced in the 1970s and 1980s/early 1990s will occur. However,

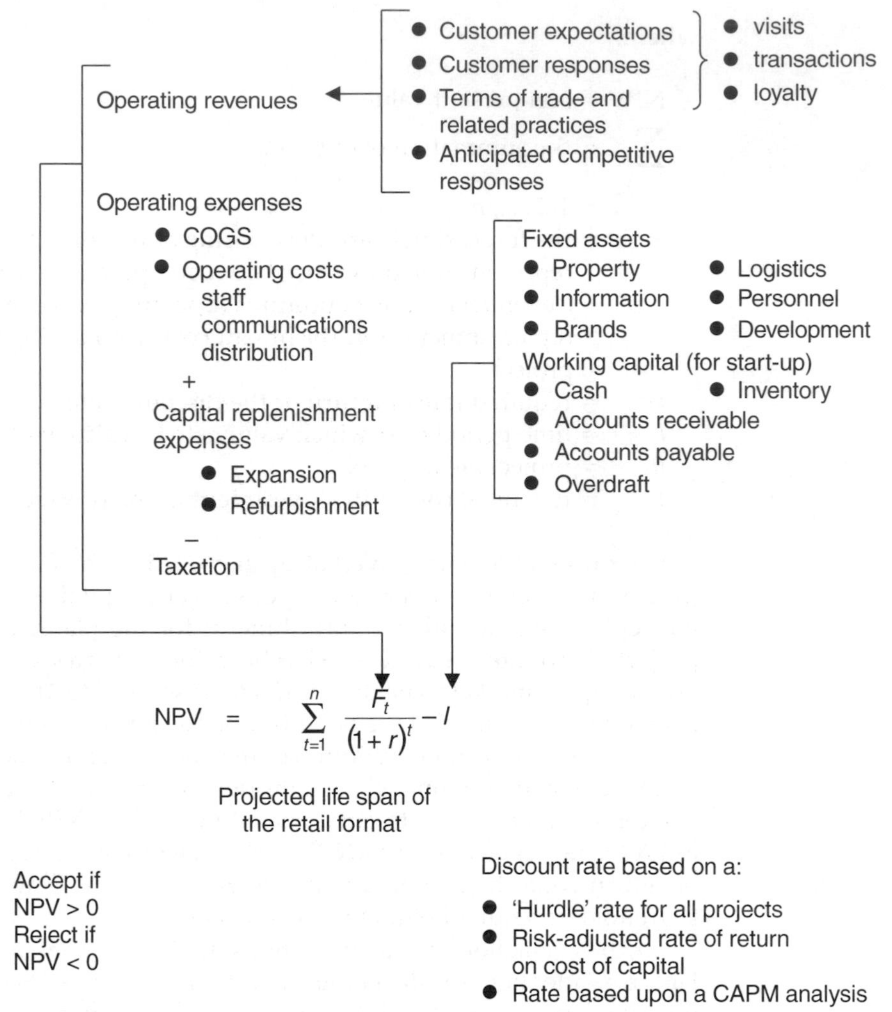

Figure 4.7 Using NPV for evaluating retail strategy options.

there are situations for which the rate of inflation of costs differs from that affecting price. For example, products sourced from countries with levels of inflation significantly different from those prevalent in the retailer's own market can be an exception. Another example concerns the influence of capacity and competition in reseller markets. Often (and particularly with durables) reseller capacity exceeds the current consumer demand, and the resultant price competition has a deflationary effect on product prices within the sector. Foreign exchange movements must also be considered. The 1998 Asian currency problems, together with strong North American and European currencies, resulted in an effective devaluation of Asian and Australasian currencies. Small decreases may be absorbed, but eventually

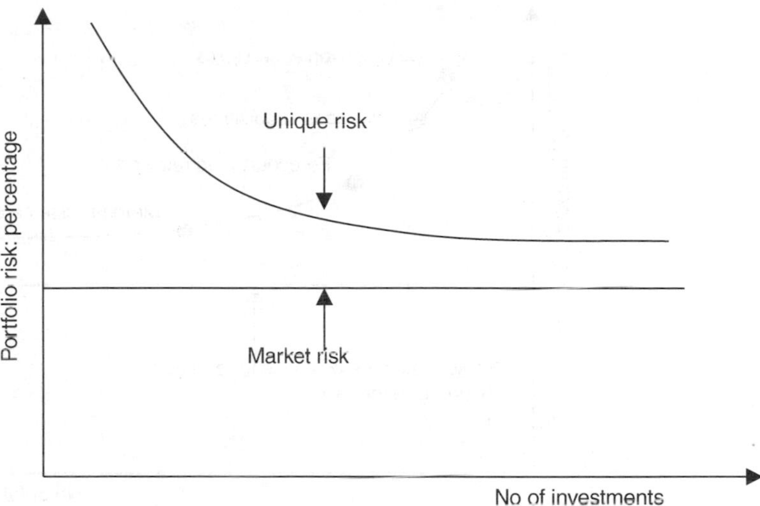

Figure 4.8 Risk/return options of investment opportunities: diversification reduces risk.

adjustments need to be made. It follows that a view must be taken prior to deciding upon the discount rate to be used. An alternative approach is to make an adjustment to the COGS figures over the lifespan of the project. Either way the analysis is far from simple.

Returning to risk; whereas inflation and foreign exchange risk are largely outwith of the control of the organization, risk can be considered quantitatively. The *capital asset pricing model* (CAPM) may be used for this purpose.

The CAPM is based upon the assumption that investors are risk-averse, and the greater the risk of a variable return on an investment, the greater will be the actual return expected by investors. The CAPM identifies the trade-off potential between market risk and expected return. The CAPM was developed to evaluate securities in the investment market. It considers risk to have two components: *market risk*, which affects all investments to much the same degree, and *unique risk*, which is specific to the particular investment and, as suggested by Figures 4.8 and 4.9, may be reduced by diversifying the investments or merchandise category and/or market activities. The underlying principle of the CAPM is that the *expected return* on an investment comprises two components – a *risk-free return* and a *risk premium*:

Expected return = Risk-free return + risk premium

For our purposes we are assuming that *market risk* affects all of the firm's activities: its core merchandise categories. *Unique risk* occurs when an additional merchandise category is added, particularly one which is new and not particularly well related to the mainstream business.

An example may help. Marks & Spencer saw an opportunity to leverage its brand across a range of categories and service products. Its expansion has

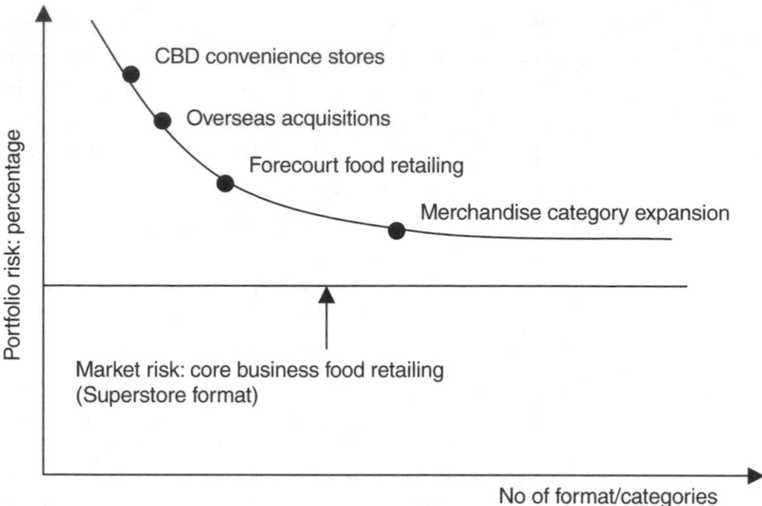

Figure 4.9 Risk/return: a hypothetical application.

been such that it has spread the risk of new activities by a planned program of diversification. The company has moved into furniture, homewares, kitchenwares and eventually into financial services, via its credit card. It follows that the *unique risk* has been progressively lowered by this planned diversification. The authors are not aware of the returns generated by these diversifications, but clearly they will have been higher than those of the core business in order to match the risk/return preferences of the shareholders.

Similarly Tesco, whose diversification has been impressive, has followed a similar strategy. Its expansion of format categories (Superstore, Metro and Tesco Express) has contained the unique risk by being related diversification activities. However, their overseas expansion, which has met with varying levels of success would appear not to have diversified the unique risk as well as might have been hoped for.

The CAPM can be expressed as a simple mathematical relationship:

$$\text{ER} = \text{Rf} + \beta(\text{Emr} - \text{Rf})$$

where:

ER = expected return
Rf = the current short term risk-free interest rate (the 'risk-free' component)
β = coefficient which measures the market risk of the individual investment (merchandise category or format expansion)
Emr = expected market return (on core business activities) for the forecast period

The Rf (risk-free rate) is usually accepted as the rate set by government bond offers and Emr is the expected return from an investment in *all* shares available on the market, i.e. the *market return*. The beta factor (β) is determined by calculating the relationship between the returns on a specific investment (activity) and those of the market. For our purposes we can consider it to reflect the relationship between a merchandise category and the overall merchandise mix of a business or the relationship between a new format and the remainder of the 'business/market'. The beta value for the 'market' as a whole is equal to 1. Investments with beta values greater than 1 are sensitive to movements of the market as a whole. If the economy expands, the investment will perform well, but if it declines these investments will reflect that lower level of performance. The beta value indicates the nature of the risk that may be involved and therefore the extent of the increase in rate of return that is to be expected.

The relationship can be expressed graphically (see Figure 4.10). The risk/return line indicates the trade-off between expected return and market risk combinations. Therefore activities at A, B and C fall on the trade-off line and the expected return compensates for their increasing levels of risk, as their NPV equals zero. In practical terms what we have is a business which has diversified its activities and in doing so has managed to increase its margins to compensate the shareholders for an increase in risk; the revenues generated less operating expenses (the cash flows) when discounted at risk/return related values meet the NPV = 0 criteria. Activities F and E have strong positive NPVs and offer a good opportunity to create shareholder value, while G and D (particularly G, with very high risk and low expected return) should not be considered.

The CAPM concept is of interest because it provides a means of forward-looking planning and evaluation in which a required rate of return (the rate used in the NPV evaluation) can be related to a level of risk as suggested by the beta value. It is important to consider the company's cost of capital, and this is calculated based upon its capital structure (the 'mix' of equity funds

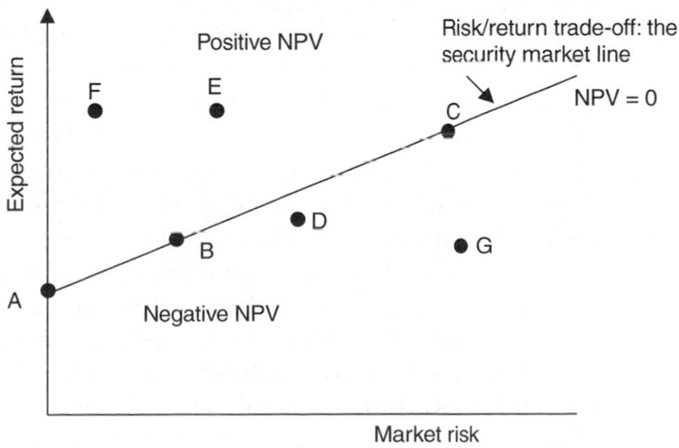

Figure 4.10 Risk/return options of alternative opportunities.

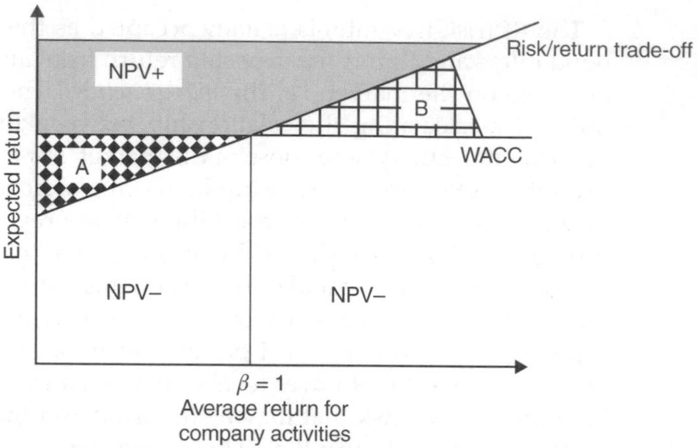

Figure 4.11 CAPM and the cost of capital.

and debt). This *weighted average cost of capital* (WACC) is a cost of capital that reflects capital structure *and* investors' perceptions of risk based upon this structure. Figure 4.11 suggests that this approach may result in the rejection of low-risk but viable projects. (the shaded area) and the acceptance of high-risk projects which fail to offer an adequate risk/return profile. The use of a beta value offers a more project/company-specific measure for evaluation. The benefits are that the approach separates marketing issues from financial structure considerations. The beta value, when applied to investor expectations, provides a value for the equity component of the WACC.

If we apply the beta concept in the context of corporate investment decisions (rather than taking the view of an investor in a stock market situation), the notion of the beta value as an indication of risk does not change: in effect, the beta used should reflect the overall investment market view of the activity (or market segment) the firm is planning to enter. Thus while the financial management literature suggests that shares with high beta values are sensitive to movements of the market (which reflect the expected performance of the economy) we can say that companies active in these sectors (with high beta values) are more exposed to the vagaries of the economy than those with low beta values. Thus we see residential property, leisure travel and services, luxury durables (high-priced brown and white goods and automobiles) and exclusive/speciality stores with higher beta values than companies offering 'commodity'-based alternatives. It is this point that should be emphasized. It follows that companies the shares of which have a beta of 1 are generally expected to perform in line with the economy. Those with low beta values are companies which may perform independently of the economy; these are likely to include food manufacturers and retailers, and energy and communications companies.

Figure 4.12 illustrates a hypothetical situation in which retailing companies in different segments of a market should expect differing rates of return,

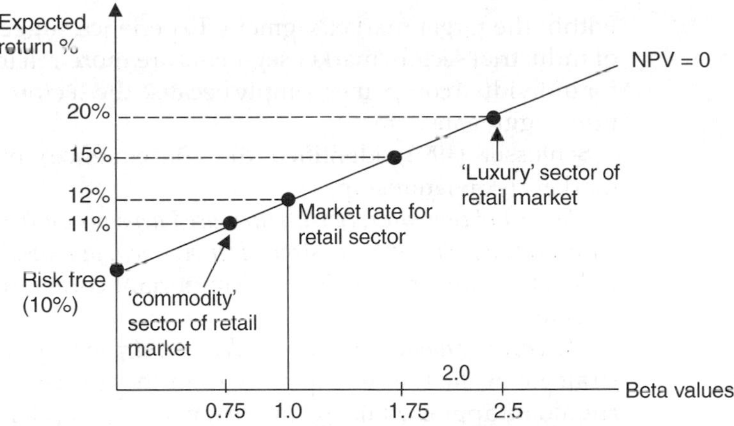

Figure 4.12 Risk/return profiles for alternative retail market offers.

these being influenced by the risk involved in opting to operate in sectors which may respond quite differently to recession and other external impacts. Clearly competition will be more intensive in the commodity sector and more selective in the luxury sector, and this may have an impact on returns generated. Figure 4.13 suggests beta alternatives for a range of retailing options. Thus the discount rate to be used for strategy investment appraisal evaluation should reflect the rate indicated by the beta value, its intersection on the security market line and the corresponding expected rate of return on the vertical axis. The first step is to estimate the 'security market line'. This is usually possible by working with a specialist financial services company which will also identify the beta values for market sectors of the economy. Typically beta values, which do not vary significantly over time, are published quarterly along with the beta values for quoted companies. The strategy evaluation should have included an identification of likely competitors

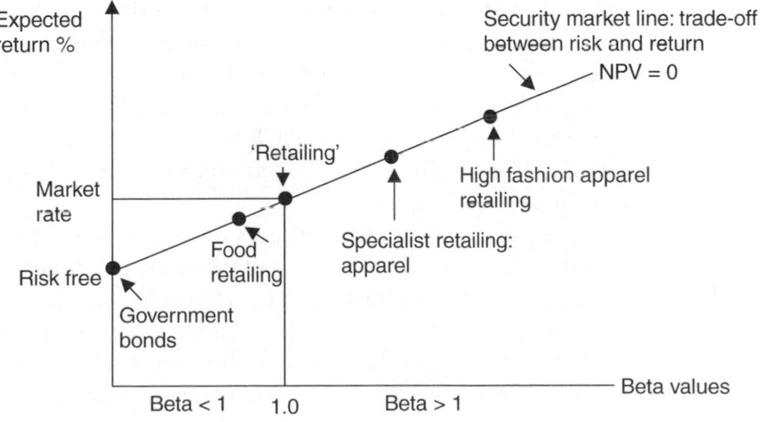

Figure 4.13 Risk/return profile.

within the target market/segment. Experience suggests that the beta values of industrial sectors/market segments are more reliable than the beta values for individual companies, simply because the sector/segment betas are based upon aggregate data.

Schlosser (1992) identified the consequences of this industry return/ market risk relationship:

The cost of capital/expected return used depends on the industry with which you are concerned when making strategic investment appraisals. The beta used should reflect the industry *and* the more important competitors within the segment targeted.

The cost of capital/discount rate does not depend a great deal on the company. A strategic evaluation to expand within the industry sector/market segment should be appraised using the current cost of capital. An alternative outwith the company's current activities/core business should be investigated using a beta value derived from the beta value of the sector, modified by dominant competitors.

Diversified (conglomerate) companies should use the beta values and therefore the cost of capital of the sectors/segments in which they are active. This approach will give a more 'realistic' answer for appraisals and therefore make resource allocation more realistic.

Resources planning and budgeting

Having decided upon the specific strategic option(s) to be implemented capital and operating budgets are required. The process by which we have reached this point provides use with the data required.

By identifying options and working through their resource requirements *and then* submitting these to an investment appraisal process we have developed both the process and the budgets. The budgets can then be passed on to the management groups responsible for implementation and operations.

Figure 4.14 summarizes the process. It will be recalled that the overall tasks are first to identify customer expectations (by specific target customer group) and then to specify the 'retail exchange environment' (the merchandise, customer service, format and environment, and communications inputs) requirements *and* the resources required if the company objectives are to be realized. An appraisal using DCF techniques follows, and provided the resultant NPV is positive (and acceptable) the overall strategy can be put into operational planning.

It proposes an iterative process by which fixed and working capital budgets are derived *out of* the overall process and, together with the *performance criteria,* may be established for *performance monitoring*. The purpose of this component of the model is to identify changes in customer and company performances and relate these to the fixed and working capital requirements with a view to making (recommending) changes. Prior to implementing the strategy two tasks remain. A review of the objectives established for *all* aspects of the retail strategy is required, together with a review of the

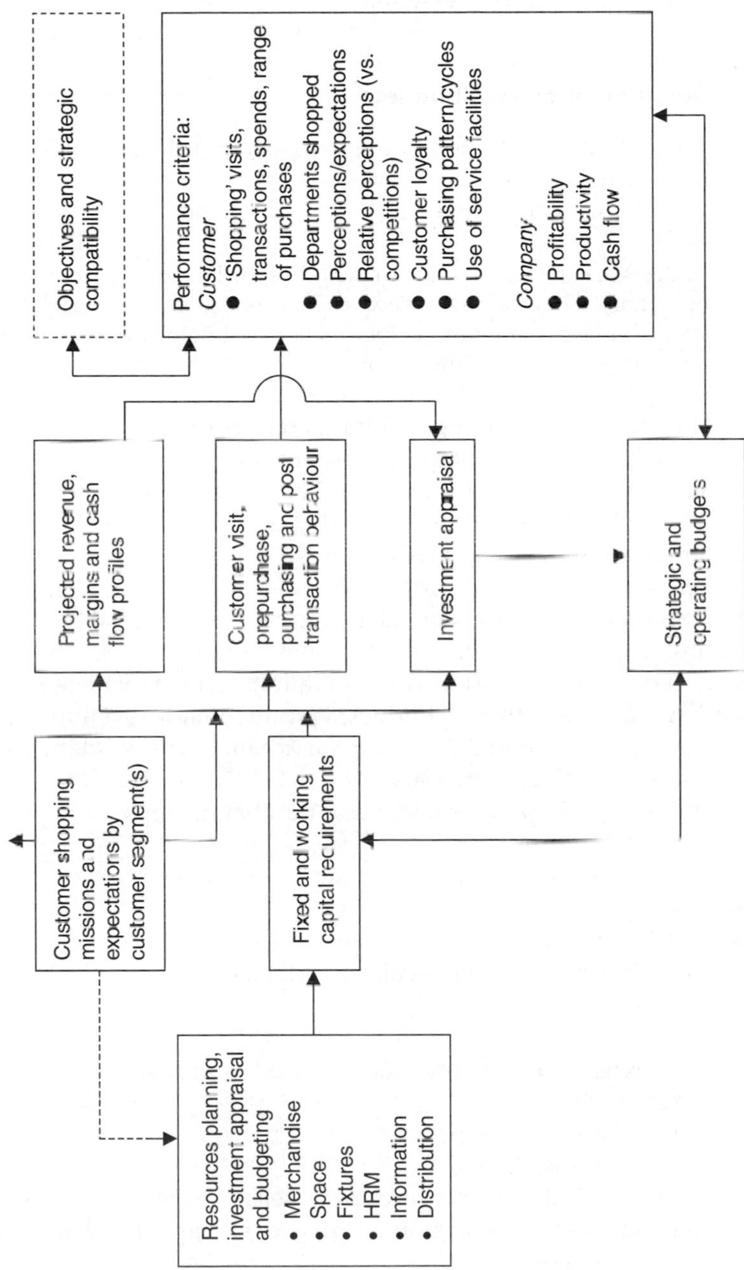

Figure 4.14 The resources, planning, investment appraisal and budgeting process.

interface areas between the strategy components, i.e. merchandise, customer service, format and environment, and customer communications. This final review will ensure that no duplication of resources has occurred, nor have there been omissions of essential features from the overall strategy.

Developing operating budgets

An important contribution to the successful implementation of any strategy is an effective operating budget.

Myddleton (1991) suggests:

> Budgets are financial plans for a period, agreed in advance for (part of) a firm's operations. They help set objectives and coordinate responsibilities. After the event, budgets communicate information and help appraise the performance of managers and of business units.

The topics of budgeting and budgetary control are extensive, and we do not intend to attempt comprehensive coverage in this chapter. However, the subject matter of the chapter would be incomplete without a discussion of relevant issues. These, in the context of the earlier content of the chapter are: revenues, resources and expenditures.

Before we discuss these topics we will consider the necessary components of a budget. Myddleton considers budgets to be formal business plans consisting of quantitative statements, usually in financial terms, covering a specific period, for (part of) a firm's operations, which managers have prepared and agreed in advance. A budget typically details revenues, resources (and their expenditure/cost details), capital expenditures, working capital requirements and profit expectations.

The budgeting process involves a number of steps:

- Forecasting general economic and industry conditions
- Stating assumptions
- Setting objectives
- Agreeing sales budgets, which are detailed by:
  - region
  - format type
  - merchandise assortment(s) (i.e. food, non-food)
  - categories
  - merchandise groups
  - merchandise items
  - time periods (i.e. in appropriate 'seasons' etc.)
- Agreeing resource inputs and expenses for capital and operating expenditures by function
- Aggregating functional budgets into a master budget

There are other aspects of the budget process that are important. One concerns *objectives*. Because operating budgets are short-term there may be a tendency for undue emphasis to be placed on short-term performance requirements and for the long term to be overlooked. An example could be to reduce price levels and/or customer service in pursuit of an annual sales objective, possibly to the detriment of a long-term positioning maintenance objective. It is not unknown for an organization to detail both long-term and short-term goals and to have a number of qualitative objectives specifying important performance aspects such as positioning, innovation leadership, and supplier and customer relationships. In this way management are reminded of the need to consider both long- and short-term objectives.

Another concern must be *responsibility*. Responsibility also has a number of considerations. The first concerns the nature of the responsibility. Responsibility centres identify the nature of the managers' responsibility and therefore the tasks of the job. *Revenue centres* are expected to generate sales and usually have low or predictable expenses which are easily controlled. Performance is measured by sales generated. *Cost centres* are activities which incur costs but do not generate substantial revenues; the performance measurements are based upon cost control. A variation of the cost centre is a cost/internal service centre which provides specific services that may be 'charged' against individual activities on the basis of utilization (e.g. computer facilities, logistics services). *Profit centres* sell their output and control both revenues and costs. Their managers' performance is measured on the excess of revenues over expenses. Care should be taken (particularly in retailing) when deciding between a profit centre and a control centre for performance measurement. Many branch/outlet managers are measured against contribution (profit generated), but in reality have little control over major expenses such as advertising. In such cases it is questionable whether such measures are applicable. *Investment centres* give management responsibility for both profit and assets (both fixed assets and working capital). Performance measurement is based upon the profit generated from the assets controlled by the manager. For each 'centre' the decision on performance expectations should be based upon achieving a balance between accountability and responsibility. It is unreasonable to expect managers to control expenses or resources (i.e. inventory) if they are not able to decide upon activity levels.

Budgets are also *communications* vehicles. They indicate intentions as well as expectations, and as such they should be easily understood by any staff member whose performance is being measured. Furthermore, the data they report should be both timely and as accurate as possible. If decisions are made daily or weekly then information cycles should respond to this need. It follows that accuracy is usually a function of time, and managers usually prefer rough figures on time rather than 'exact' data long after the event.

Motivation is another aspect of the operating budget, specifically at the time of preparation. A number of issues arise. One concerns 'fairness'. A manager will be less committed to a budget perceived as unreasonable. Similarly, commitment varies with involvement in preparing the budget; the more that managers are involved, the greater their commitment. Time is also important. If the business unit's activities produce results in a subsequent trading period, the performance expectations should reflect the 'lag' in timing. For example, a regional distribution centre's operating cycle may be quite different from that of the retail branches serviced; in such circumstances *performance appraisal* should consider the nature of the activity of the business unit. Branch activities may be set revenue objectives and cost standards for specific trading cycles. Support activities (distribution services) may be measured on their performance against service achievement *and* cost standards. Due recognition should be made of external influences over which management has no control. For example, a significant increase in interest rates may have a dramatic effect on sales. Similarly, an unexpected increase in fuel prices will change the operating costs of distribution centres. *Flexible budgeting* approaches permit these changes to be included in performance appraisal.

Budgets should help managers manage. While they prescribe desired levels of performance they should not be considered as rigid targets to be achieved at any cost! Events and circumstances change, typically after the budget has been prepared. Budgets do offer the manager the opportunity to ask a number of questions:

- What has occurred during the budget period? Have events influenced expectations? Why?
- Are there implications for future performance? If so, should the budget performance expectations be changed?
- If changes are made, how soon will they be effective? Will the changes have a significant impact on resources? Are the resources available (or can we avoid the commitment to them, i.e. cancel orders)?
- What will be the impact on overall results? Are they acceptable?

We suggest that operating budgets will be necessary for each strategy function implementation, i.e. merchandise decisions, customer service, format and environment, and communications. Each will have its own resource allocations, expenditures and impact on revenues. Clearly an overall *master budget* will be required, and this should provide two services for senior management. An indication of individual functional expectations is clearly necessary. At the same time the overall effectiveness of the resource allocation and expenditure should be considered; trade-off potential should be identified and explored. For example, visual merchandising expenditures may be more effective than advertising. Alternatively, resources allocated to aspects of customer service may be more effective in retaining existing customers than advertising expenditures aimed at attracting new customers.

We shall identify resources, revenue and expenditure considerations in the implementation chapters.

QUESTIONS, ACTIVITIES AND CONSIDERATIONS

Use the example in Exhibit 4.1 to explore a number of the following considerations:

- Would an expansion of the business using debt funding (of $100,000 at 15% interest change) be of benefit to the shareholder?
- If Ajax considered an expansion of its prices into the higher price ranges, what are the likely impact issues for:
  - inventory/stock turn?
  - margins?
  - planned growth?
  - the essential ratios?
- What would be the impact on Ajax if its suppliers *all* restricted credit periods to 60 days maximum?

Exhibit 4.1

Ajax Ltd is a floor coverings retail business. It commenced trading in 1995. By 1997 it operated 150 stores and currently (1999) it has 220 outlets. The average size of the stores is 10,000 square feet. Expansion is planned to continue for the next five years at between 30 to 40 stores per year. Staff numbered a total of 1000 in 1997 and there are now 1350 staff.

Ajax sells a range of floor coverings and emphasizes the middle price ranges. Major brands are stocked, together with some lesser known brands at the bottom end of the price ranges.

The business has been run on a 'lean' base. Outlets have been leased and capital investment tightly controlled. The early objectives of the business were to generate cash to expand the organization's outlet coverage rapidly and to return adequate profits to the investors.

Financial performance data for 1997 and 1999 are provided. The reader is encouraged to assess the performance of Ajax.

Balance Sheet		1995		1999
		$000		$000
Fixed assets		36400		48700
Current assets				
Inventory	28600		35700	
Debtors	6880		7400	
Cash at bank	35490		41300	
Prepayments	1420		1700	
	73970		86100	

Current liabilities				
Trade creditors	36400		40500	
Dividends	3900		6750	
Tax due	8320		11250	
Payments due	13130		16200	
	61750		74700	
Net current assets		12220		11400
Net assets		48620		60100
Capital and reserves				
Called up share capital	2080		2080	
Share preimum account	22490		22490	
Profit and loss account	24050		35530	
		48620		60100
Profit and loss/operating statement				
	$000			
	1997			1999
Sales	286000		343200	
Purchases	71630		84524	
Gross profit		214370		258677
Operating costs				
Salaries/wages	39000		44850	
Distribution	1170		1345	
Promotion	13000		14950	
Operating profit (contibution)		130000		161622
Administration costs	96200		1106300	
Depreciation	6500		7475	
EBIT		27300		43517
Interest	156		170	
Taxation (30%)	8143		13055	
Profit for financial period		19000		30342
Dividends	8548			13654
Profit retained	10452			16688

- Ajax operates a tight credit policy. Consider its options (and the impact of your decisions) if competitors expanded customer credit facilities and offered one year interest-free facilities.

REFERENCES

Bates, A. D. (1990) Pricing for profit, *Arthur Anderson Retailing Issues Letter,* **2**(8) September. Center for Retailing Studies, Texas A&M University.

Livingstone, J. L. and Tigert, D. J. (1987) *Financial Analysis of Business Strategy.* Babson College Working Paper, Wellesley.

Lush, R. F., CoyKendall, D. S., Kenderine, J. M. and McCammon, B. C. (1989) *Wholesaling in Transition.* University of Oklahoma Distribution Research Program, Norman, OK.

McCammon, B. C. and Hanmer, W. C. (1974) A frame of reference for improving productivity in distribution. *Atlanta Economic Review,* September/October.

Myddleton, D. (1991) *Accounting and Financial Decisions.* Longman, UK.

Scholosser, M. (1992) *Corporate Finance.* Prentice Hall, London.

Stern, L. W., El-Ansary, A. I. and Coughlan, A. T. (1996) *Marketing Channels.* Prentice Hall International, Englewood Cliffs, NJ.

5 PERFORMANCE MANAGEMENT: PLANNING AND CONTROL

LEARNING OBJECTIVES

In this chapter we will explore the relationship between the planning and control functions. A number of learning points will be introduced:

- The need for planning and control to be integrated activities and reflect both strategic and operational intentions.
- A discussion of stakeholder interests and the Kaplan and Norton, 'balanced scorecard', with an application to retailing planning and control.
- The components of an effective planning and control model are identified. These introduce an analytical infrastructure which combines qualitative and quantitative measures.
- The application of basic accounting instruments (the *pro forma* profit and loss account and the balance sheet and cash flow statements) are modified for use as planning and control instruments. They are shown as particularly useful when exploring both strategic and operational alternatives.
- The use of GMROI and Target Costing models is discussed, with a suggestion that together they can explore planning options and consider issues concerning risk and return.
- Effective planning and control occurs when both strategic and operational characteristics are considered together. The chapter concludes by developing a model to do this.
- An appendix offers a range of performance characteristics which considers qualitative and quantitative measures at the strategic and operational levels of planning and control.

INTRODUCTION

Effective strategic management relies upon a planning and control approach which embraces all interests of the business. This chapter addresses this issue together with those concerning the need for qualitative and quantitative measurement of both strategic *and* operational performance.

This chapter is concerned with market and financial performance. We would argue that both are essential features of successful strategic management. Another feature of this chapter is a stakeholder approach to planning and control. Increasingly retail businesses are considering the objectives of corporate stakeholders, such as the shareholders, suppliers and employees as well as the customer. While a strong customer focus is essential, it is necessary to combine this with an overall market perspective; in this way a 'balanced' approach results.

PLANNING AND CONTROL

Planning and control are complementary. Planning assumes objectives as outcomes, and these are of limited value without both a means by which they are to be achieved (the strategic and operational plans of the organization) and a means by which progress towards the objectives may be monitored.

But effective planning and control require more than this. Figure 5.1 suggests that planning and control comprise an overall process which tests for

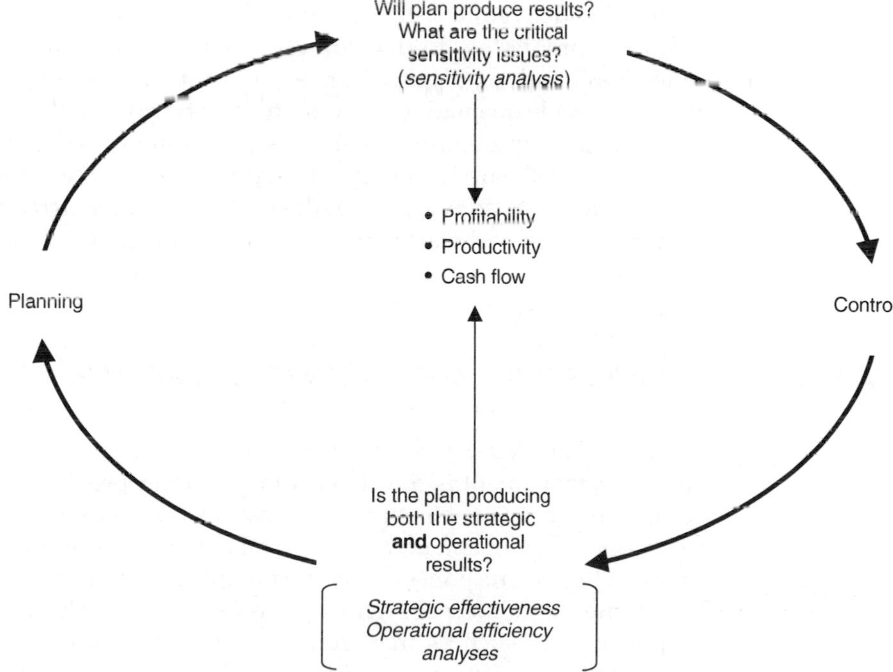

Figure 5.1 Planning *and* control: probing the future and monitoring the present.

the sensitivity of the plan on specific components of the business. It identifies three key planning and control requirements – profitability, productivity and cash flow – that should be closely monitored throughout the process. Each has a major influence on the successful outcome of the activity. Wilson *et al.* (1994) comment:

> Whilst strategy may be seen as being related to control it is usually separable. Thus it is possible for an enterprise having good strategies to fail because it has a poor control system, and vice versa... the better the formulation of the strategy the greater will be the number of feasible control alternatives and the easier their implementation is likely to be.

It follows that an insight into the likely performance of key sensitive factors, assuming certain strategic scenarios, may avoid failure *and* will identify specific control monitors for the strategy eventually selected.

A comprehensive approach to the planning process is described by Figure 5.2. Chapter 2 described and discussed a philosophy of strategic analysis and definition; here our purpose is to provide a more formal structure within which the planning and control process can take place. Thus it follows that the approach described earlier should be applied to the model in Figure 5.2. As with any planning process, attention is given to *external influences* which impact on *customer expectations* and the organization. The important activities for the business are to interpret the implications of the environment and to respond with a feasible strategy in response. The important elements of the planning process are to develop a *mission and competitive profile* with clear objectives and strategies. These in turn should be expressed in implementable qualitative and quantitative terms, which can, in turn, be formulated as market-based intentions (positioning, revenues, margins and cash flows) with supporting financial projections of fixed and working capital requirements as working budgets. *Performance criteria* in terms of customer response and market performance complete the process.

A STAKEHOLDER PERSPECTIVE: THE BALANCED SCORECARD

It has been argued that the most critical job for those concerned with performance management is to establish targets that: provide a consistent planning linkage between the organization's mission/business scope and operational management; are measurable in both content and timeliness to enable effective responses to be taken; are balanced in terms of customer, competitive and internal orientation; reflect planning horizons; and identify responsibilities such as marketing, financial and operations (Murray and O'Driscoll, 1994). The authors identify the shortcomings of financially based objectives as one-dimensional financial goals such as RONA (return on net assets). Problems identified include their narrow perspective, historical rather than future orientation emphasis, and the facility that such single

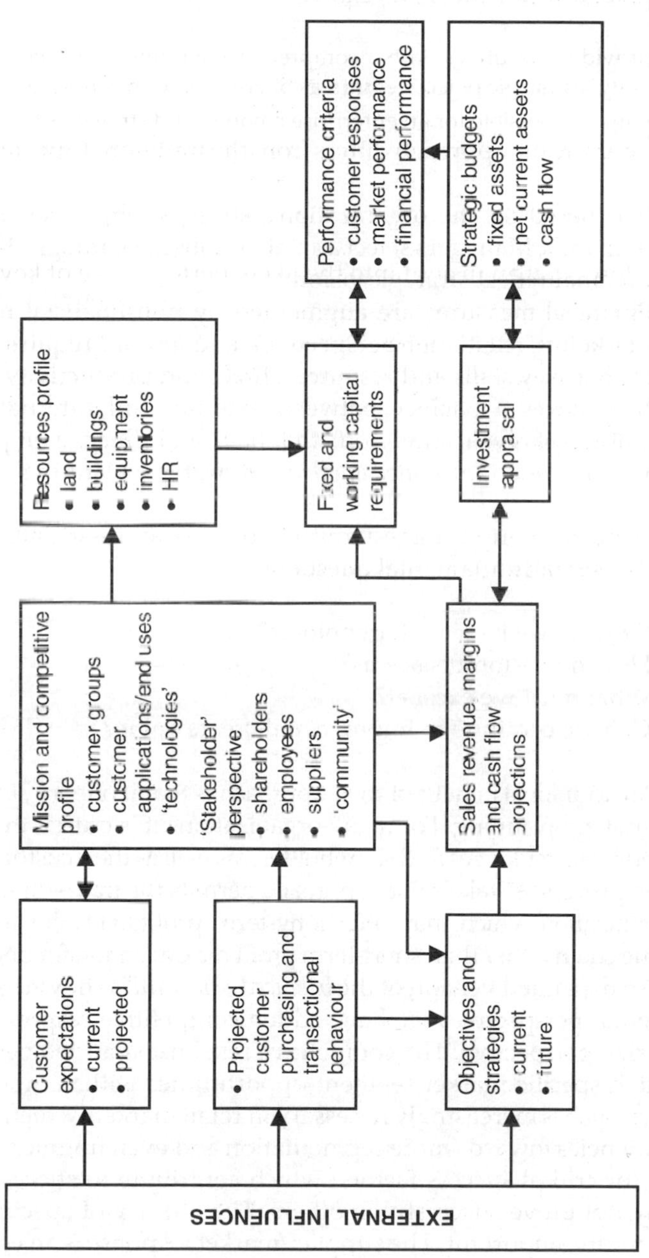

Figure 5.2 Strategic planning and control process.

objectives offer managers to improve short-term performance by manipulating either the numerator or the denominator to achieve 'success'.

The 'balanced scorecard' framework offers a range of measures which Kaplan and Norton (1992) claim:

> provides executives with a comprehensive framework that translates a company's strategic objectives into a coherent set of performance measures.

They argue the approach differs from the traditional approach in four ways:

- It is based on the organization's strategic objectives and market-based demands. Managers select a small number of strategically relevant indicators that reflect strategic vision.
- Financial measures are augmented by non-financial measures, such as marketing (customer perspective), and *forward* requirements for success such as key skills and resources, R&D and productivity requirements.
- It achieves a balance between external and internal objectives. Specifically, it reveals trade-offs that have an influence on performance.
- It provides an *integrated approach* to strategic planning.

Kaplan and Norton suggest four sets of goals and associated measures which address four fundamental questions:

- How do we look to shareholders?
- How do customers see us?
- What must we excel at?
- Can we continue to improve and create value?

An additional benefit of their approach is that it offers a *stakeholder perspective* of strategy planning. For many organizations it is crucial that they 'take' their suppliers, employees and shareholders, as well as their customers, into the planning process. A stakeholder approach permits the trade-off review and leads to optimization which may offer long-term profitability for all members of the value chain rather than short-term profit maximization for one single member.

An expanded version of the *balanced score card* is shown as Figure 5.3; to the original perspectives we have added competitive response and a supplier/market perspective. The competitive response is added because of a need to match specific market segment opportunities with competitive value drivers, which is increasingly necessary in retail markets which show evidence of tendencies towards more segmentation and even fragmentation. Value drivers (or critical success factors) which contribute to success in one segment may not prove successful in others, The efficacy of specific value drivers is therefore, important. The supplier/market response is an essential feature for any business such as retailing where the value added relies more on non-manufacturing processes.

In a subsequent article Kaplan and Norton (1996) add a planning emphasis to the balanced scorecard:

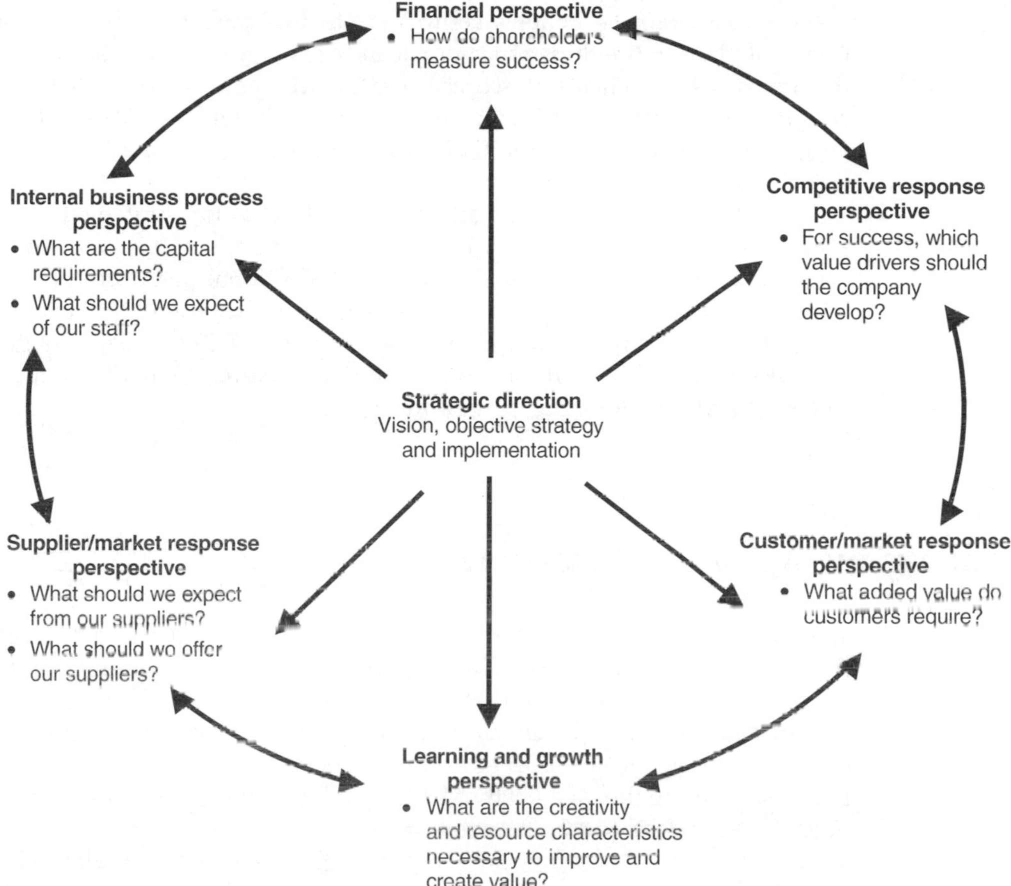

Figure 5.3 A stakeholder planning perspective. (Adapted from Kaplan, R. S. and Norton, D. P. (1992) The Balanced Scorecard – measures that drive performance. *Harvard Business Review*, Jan/Feb.)

> The scorecard lets them introduce four new management processes that, separately and in combination, contribute to linking long-term strategic objectives with short-term actions.

Translating the vision – helps managers build a consensus around the organization's vision and strategy. The authors make a valid point: for effective implementation the vision must be expressed in terms that are actionable by operational management as well as being descriptors of success to which they may agree.

Communicating and linking – facilitates vertical (up *and* down) communication, thereby ensuring that all levels of the organization understand the long-term strategy and that departmental (and individual) objectives are aligned with it.

Business planning – enables companies to integrate their business and financial plans in the third process. The authors argue that this activity uses the goals set for balanced scorecard measures as a basis for allocating resources and setting priorities, resulting in the outcome that they undertake and coordinate only those initiatives that move them towards long-term objectives.

Feedback and learning – helps organizations to develop strategic learning. Using the balanced scorecard moves management's focus *from* internal financial budget objectives *to* including the additional perspectives of customers, internal business processes and learning and growth. If we add the competitive and supplier/market responses (Figure 5.3) the claim made by the authors that 'The scorecard thus enables companies to modify strategies to reflect real-time learning' is reinforced.

PERFORMANCE: A STRATEGIC PERSPECTIVE

To make use of the stakeholder/balanced scorecard approach a 'set' of objectives for each perspective is necessary. These are shown as Figure 5.4. There are both qualitative and quantitative objectives. As suggested by Kaplan and Norton, the spread of objectives offers an opportunity to evaluate the implications of a strategic option in terms of its feasibility *and* to consider trade-off situations among the 'perspectives'. More important is the process by which objectives are derived.

Consider some hypothetical examples. An exclusive specialty retailer would, prior to taking initial steps, need to evaluate the market potential for this specific offer. Not only would it be necessary to evaluate the potential customer/market response, but the availability of equally exclusive suppliers should also form part of the initial investigation. Financial and operational performance follow. Clearly, if the offer cannot be managed profitably, producing cash flow as well as profits, then either the opportunity is unworkable or a compromise is required. The model permits the exploration of alternatives. By establishing clear performance parameters for each perspective of management through an iterative process we can arrive at a strategy that satisfies each of the stakeholders.

Another example may concern specific issues. The implications for the business of assuming the role of market leader may be evaluated using the model. The learning and growth perspective may be used to consider the impact of a number of leadership requirements on the organization, its suppliers and its competitive responses. The introduction of a new (or revised) trading format is an example. The Tesco 'Metro' format required suppliers capable of meeting both product and service characteristics (i.e. innovative convenience meals that could be 'delivered' to the customer as high-quality products) at competitive prices. The concept needed to perform profitably, producing acceptable cash flows etc., within acceptable time horizons.

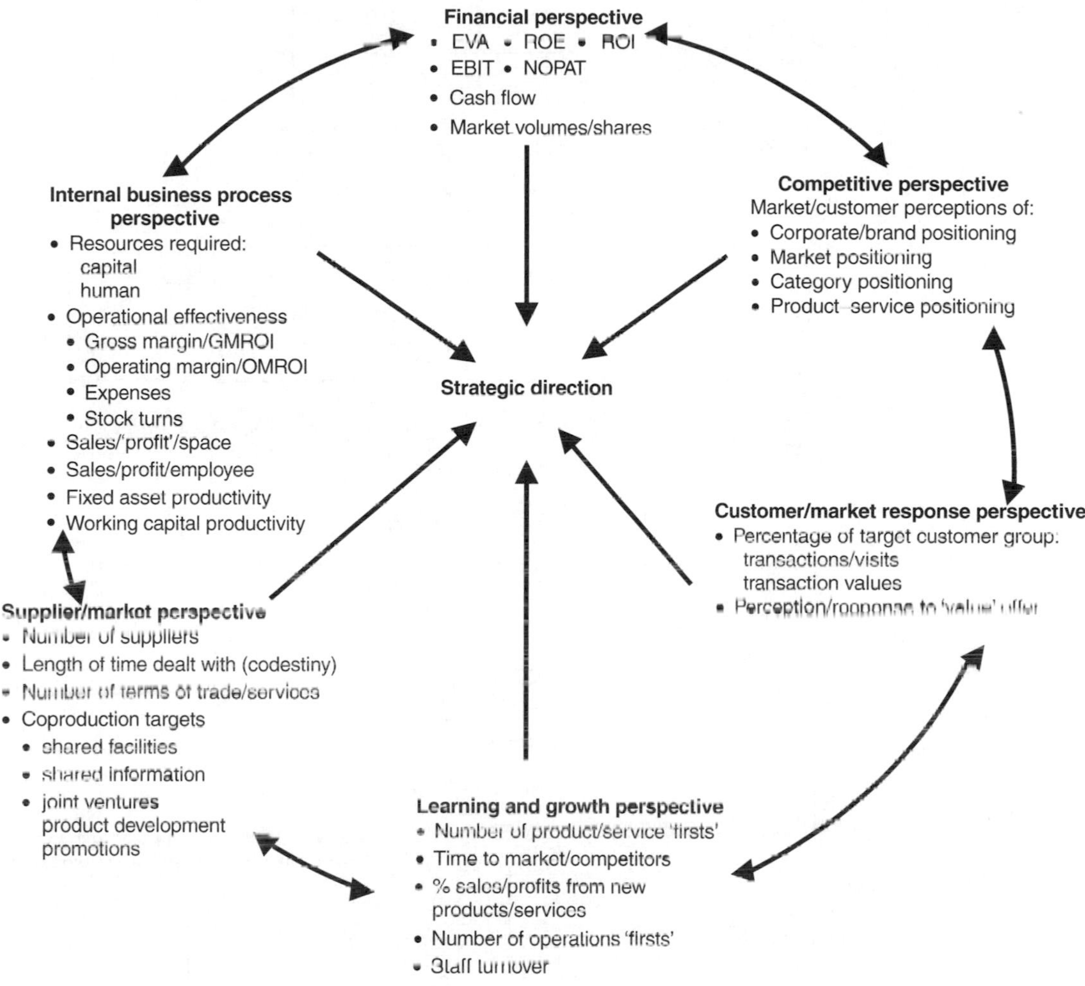

Figure 5.4 Setting stakeholder/balanced scorecard objectives.

Clearly compromise issues did arise and were resolved. The impact of adopting a market leader strategy (as opposed to evaluating one-off situations) may also be considered. This decision could have far-reaching implications for the organization and its stakeholders and would require a comprehensive evaluation of its impact and the resource requirements.

CONDUCTING BASIC ANALYSIS

To be effective the model requires an analytical infrastructure, a number of specific approaches which evaluate each of the perspectives in detail. Figure 5.5 offers an approach by which customer and competitive perspectives may

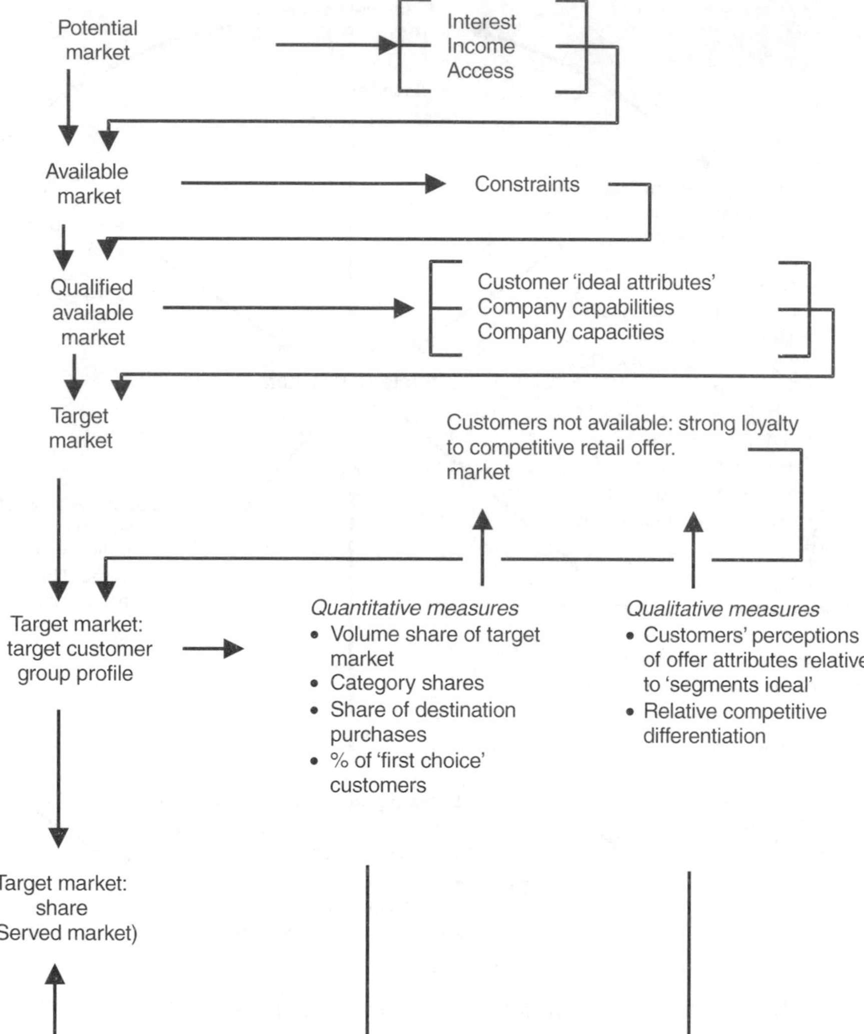

Figure 5.5 Evaluating potential and existing market performance.

be explored. It is a structured approach during which the market is realistically established in quantitative and qualitative terms. The purpose(s) of any market evaluation should be to identify economic viability and the customers' value criteria and perceptions of *all* offers, and thereby establish the criteria for success. Success is defined in volume, positioning and financial terms.

The benefit of using this, or some similar approach, is the information produced during the analysis. Not only is the market defined in terms of size, but segments (and segment characteristics) are identified together with their competitive criteria. The process identifies major competitors and the market's perceptions of relative strengths and weaknesses.

Give comprehensive market data the impact of market-based decisions on each of the perspectives may be explored. The very fact that a stakeholder approach is taken identifies the data requirements and results in a more comprehensive evaluation initially and more specific performance control criteria subsequently.

Financial performance is a critical feature of strategic planning and control. At the initial stages of planning an organization requires a projection of future patterns of profitability, productivity and cash flow. For example, a format concept which research (figure 5.5) has shown to be viable is not likely to produce either profit or cash flow for some time. Typically new ventures do not produce profits or enjoy positive cash flows until they have reached some minimum scale of effectiveness, at which point both economies of scale and scope become effective, fixed costs are covered and the venture moves into acceptable levels of profitability, productivity and cash flow.

It is necessary to be able to identify when, and at what size of business (i.e. number of outlets etc.), this will occur. A market study can identify volume potential (and the regional distribution of demand) but a financial projection of revenues and costs, together with fixed and working capital requirements, is an essential component of the stakeholder study.

We can use the basic accounting instruments for this purpose. Figure 5.6(a) illustrates a *pro forma* profit and loss account modified for use. Figure 5.6(b) is a modification used for branch/support department activities. We need to be able to examine the behaviour of those cost items which have significant impact on revenue generation.

Given this information we can ask a number of 'what if?' questions. For example, we can consider the impact of changes in the levels of staffing in retail outlets. We can evaluate alternative communications expenditure (and media) and of course the implications of adopting different pricing policies. In effect we can consider alternative positioning stances.

There are implications for investment decisions and the balance sheet. Figure 5.7 contributes to these decisions. Both the profit and loss account and the balance sheet identify the proportions of each major component (as a percentage of the total) and changes are projected by using a time trend measure. Clearly there are a number of interrelationships to be considered. An obvious issue concerns the ownership of fixed assets. These may be owned or leased; the decision is influenced not only by the availability of capital (or its opportunity cost) but also by management's view of the market's risk, its seasonality and perhaps its growth rate. The decision taken will influence operating costs – through leasing charges and their impact on profit margins, and on the fixed assets shown in the balance sheet and the return on assets generated. A number of similar considerations will arise, and these are listed in Figure 5.8.

A cash flow projection is also required. Figure 5.9 identifies the major components of sources and uses of cash and the model presented offers the facility to project overall cash flow changes together with component changes over time. Once again we make the point that it is necessary to use this in conjunction with the profit and loss projection and the balance sheet

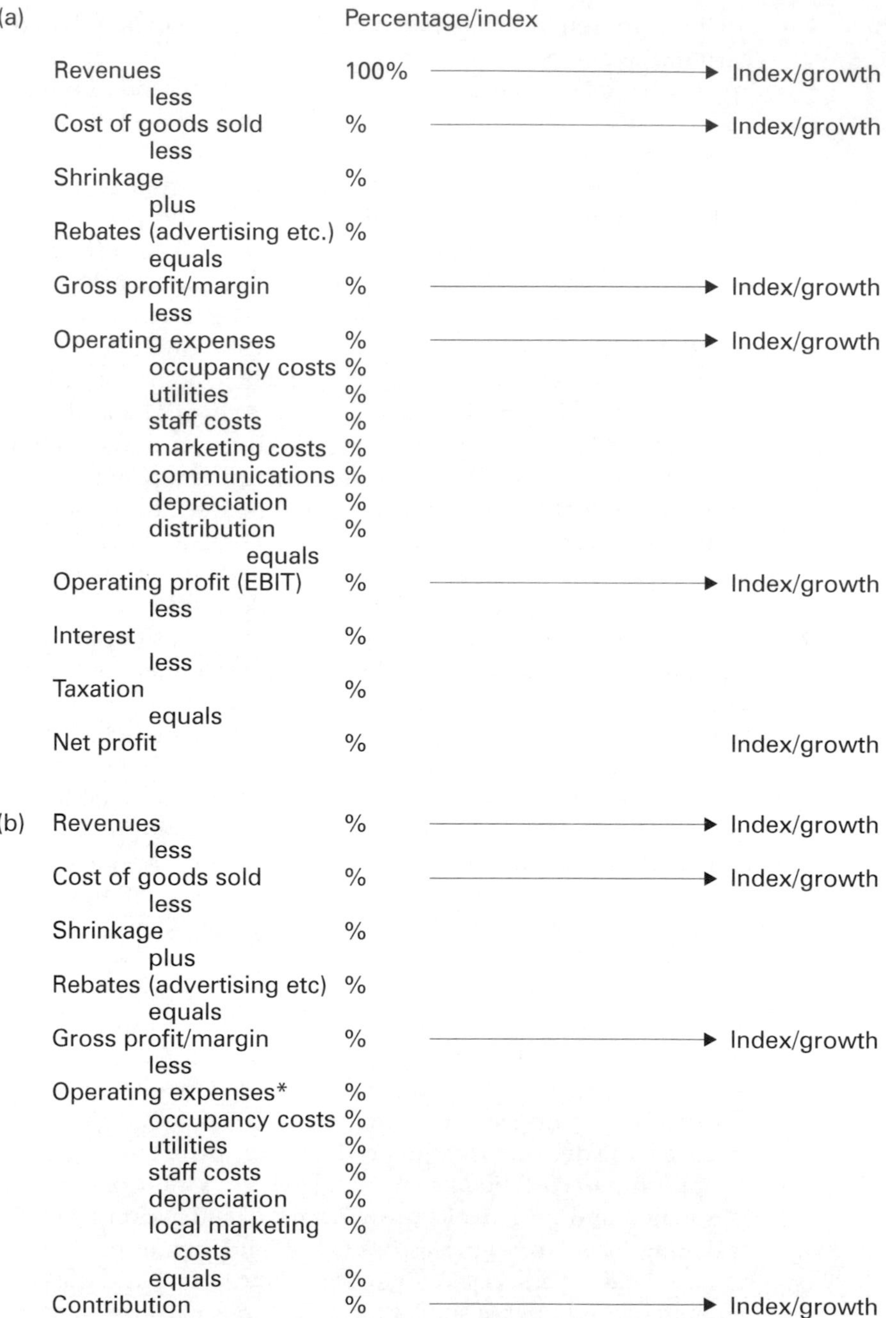

*Some companies will include a *pro rata* proportion of so-called head office costs, i.e. distribution, marketing, administration etc.

Figure 5.6 (a) Basic planning and control instruments: the profit and loss account. (b) Branch/support costs profit and loss account.

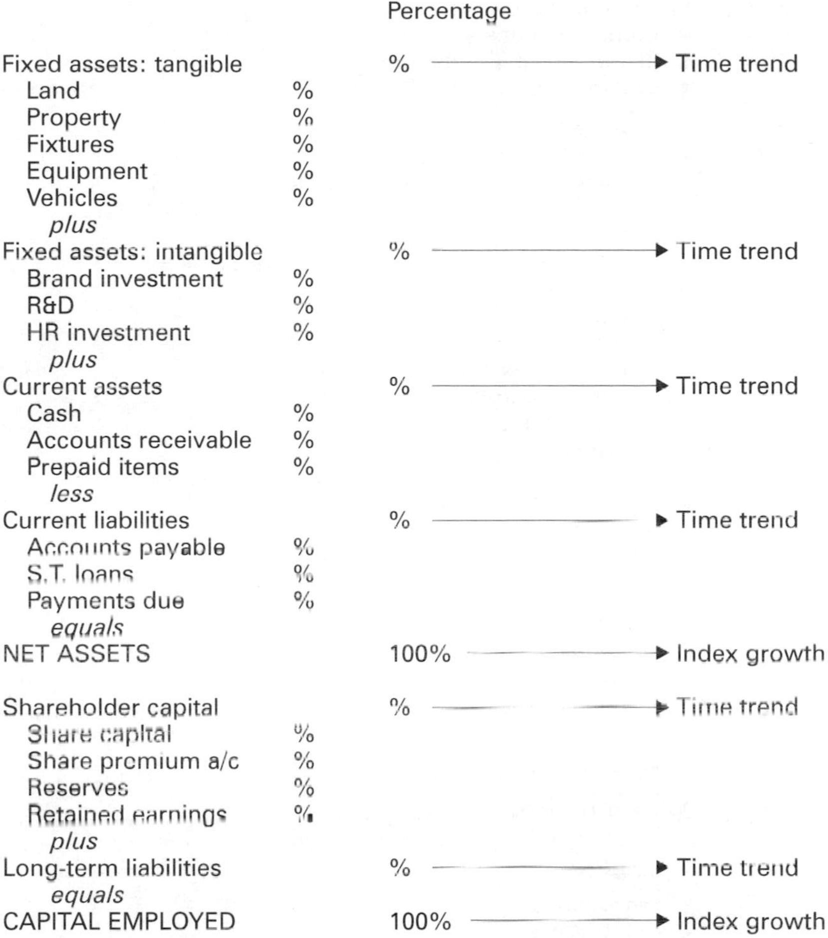

Percentage
Fixed assets: tangible
Land %
Property %
Fixtures %
Equipment %
Vehicles %
plus
Fixed assets: intangible
Brand investment %
R&D %
HR investment %
plus
Current assets
Cash %
Accounts receivable %
Prepaid items %
less
Current liabilities
Accounts payable %
S.T. loans %
Payments due %
equals
NET ASSETS
Shareholder capital
Share capital %
Share premium a/c %
Reserves %
Retained earnings %
plus
Long-term liabilities
equals
CAPITAL EMPLOYED
% Time trend
% Time trend
% Time trend
% Time trend
100% Index growth
% Time trend
% Time trend
100% Index growth

Figure 5.7 Basic planning and control instruments: the balance sheet.

documents. Changes in each of the models are seen to have an influence on each of the others. The important points to consider are the timing of the impacts, their potential significance (such as raising concerns over viability), and the fact that the approach does offer management the opportunity to consider optional solutions ahead of the events occurring.

We can introduce a time perspective. Figure 5.10 uses the Du Pont approach to identify the behaviour of revenue and cost elements over time. This can be done by projecting revenues, costs and capital requirements over the planning horizon, identifying changes that may occur in any of these items and considering the impact of the change(s) on the overall performance of the business as indicated by the ROE (return on equity). A modification can be made to include the cost of capital, which enables an NPV analysis and EVA to be calculated.

Changes in fixed assets
- number of outlets
- distribution infrastructure
- systems (software/hardware)

Changes in working capital
- inventory levels;
  - expansion of business (outlets etc)
  - growth
  - policy change (QR)
  - customer service requirements (availability)
- accounts receivable
  - expansion of business
  - growth
  - customer service (credit policy)
- accounts payable
  - expansion of business
  - growth
  - planned policy change ('negative' working capital)
- cash balances
  - transactions needs
  - contingency needs
  - speculative uses.

Changes in capital structure
- shareholder capital
  - share issues
  - bonus issues
- long term debt

Changes in operations
- lease payments

Expansion (roll out) of existing format

Change of format
- renovations
- remodelling

Franchising

Figure 5.8 Influences on performance of changes in financing methods.

PERFORMANCE: AN OPERATIONAL PERSPECTIVE

There is an obvious overlap between strategic and operational planning and control. For some organizations this can be extensive; for others there may be very little. For example, for motor vehicles and consumer durables the large investment in service facilities implies longer planning horizons than for FMCG or apparel retailers.

It follows that performance measurements may include some long-term factors, particularly the concern for fixed assets such as in a service organization and logistics networks.

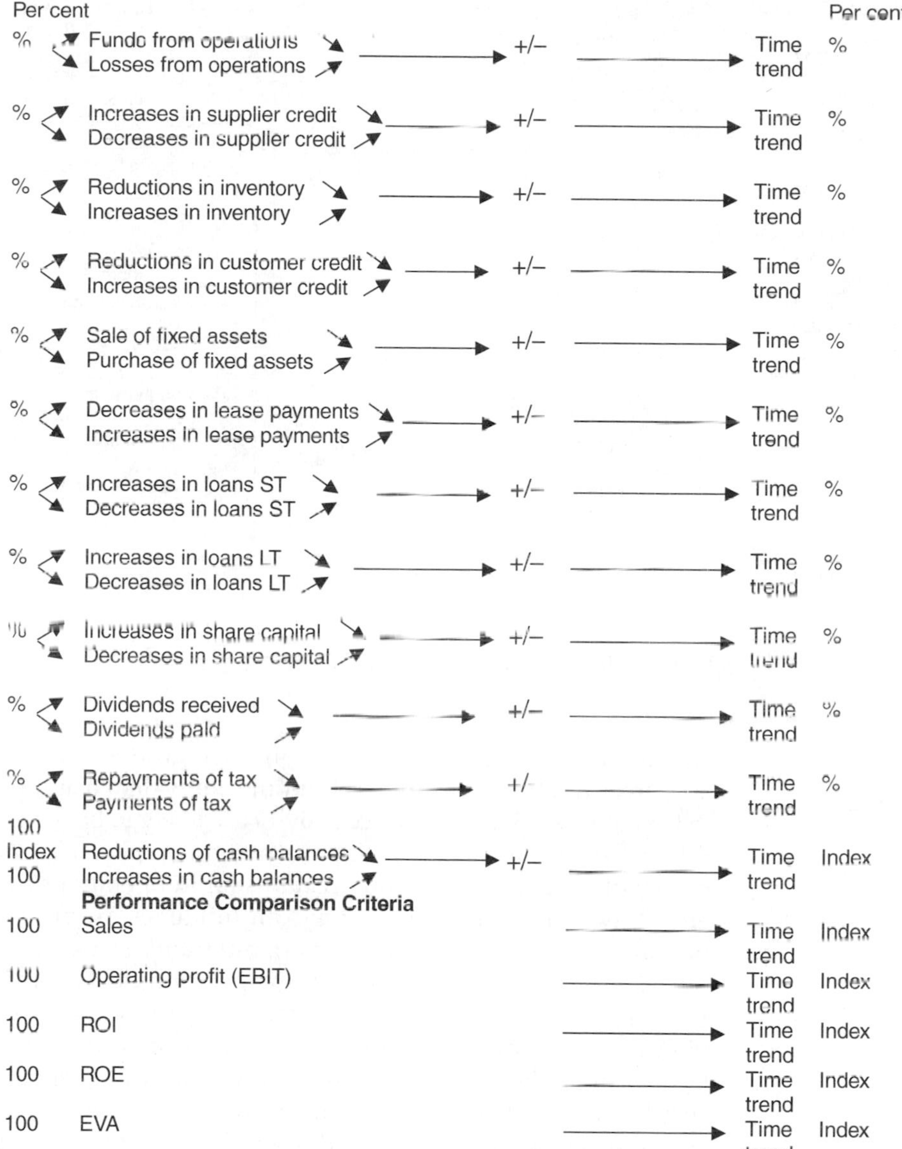

Figure 5.9 Basic planning and control instruments: sources and uses of cash.

Figure 5.11 suggests an operational control model which may be used for most retailing companies. It comprises both qualitative and quantitative data. *Customer responses* are measured by visits and sales values together with qualitative inputs which track their requirements and responses to product–service innovations. *Space and human resources productivity* measures should reflect *sales* and *gross and operating margins* per unit of space (i.e. linear or

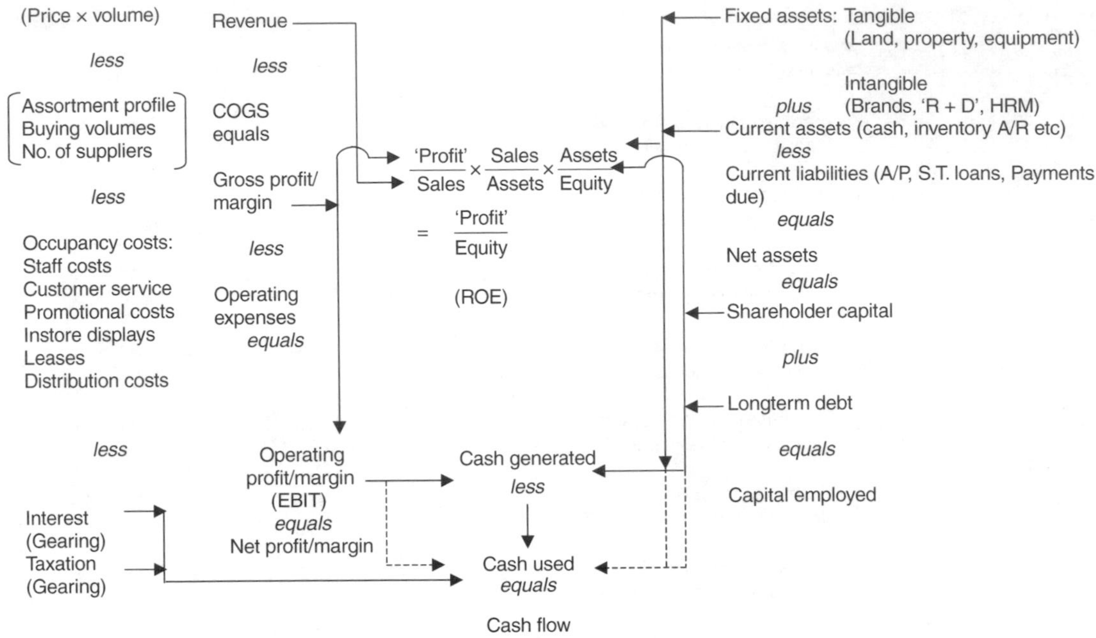

Figure 5.10 Testing for long-term sensitivity (Du Pont).

square metres) for categories or product groups. Measures for human resources (usually measured as full-time equivalents) and possibly by product category or perhaps service activity are likely to be measured in terms of *sales and operating margin*. While gross margin/employee is interesting it is not as useful as operating margin because staff in operations roles do not influence buying margins but can have an influence on markdowns. Efficient operations management can have an important impact on *fixed and working capital productivity* performance. At an operations level both are controllable. *Fixed capital productivity* may be measured by the sales/margin space performance and complemented by the performance of the distribution function by measuring branch delivery reliability and availability at predetermined cost levels. An effective overall measure of distribution performance is its cost as a percentage of sales (and operating margin) at its planned levels of service to branches. *Working capital* measures such as inventory and accounts receivable turnover data are basic measures. Inventory performance data should include turnover (and days cover) for core products and key categories; poor performance in these areas may have a major impact on revenues and profitability through the response of customers to poor availability. Similarly, customer credit allowed to key customer groups will have an influence on transaction size and frequency, and consequently this measure should also be applied to reflect selective importance. *Accounts payable* are not usually controlled by operations managers. However, it is important to relate supplier payment policy to customer credit and cash sales, as all three have an important influence on operational cash flow.

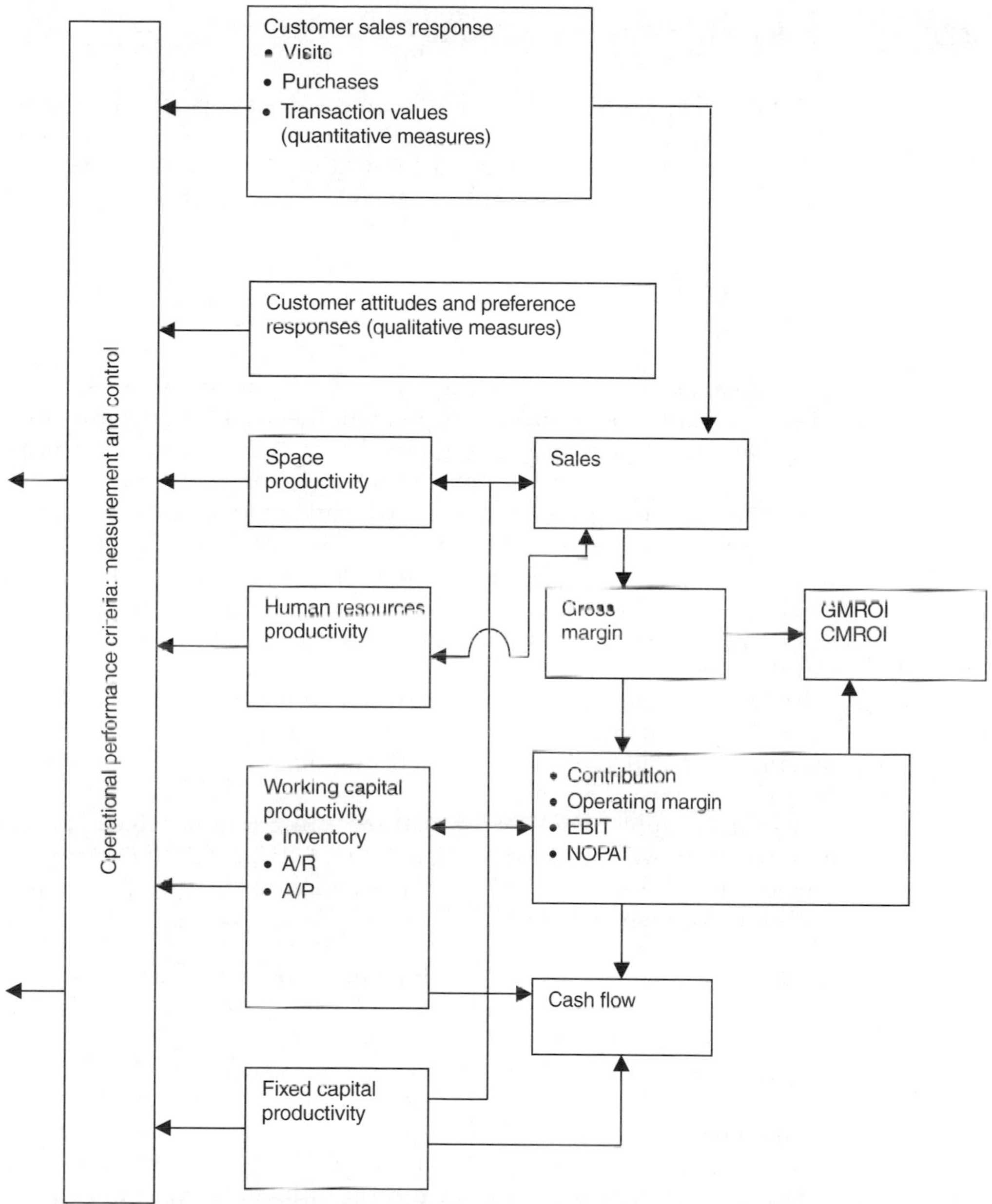

Figure 5.11 Operational performance: a basic model.

Customer credit decisions are taken by operational managers (i.e. in retail outlets), and while every effort is taken to ensure the creditworthiness of new accounts the quality cannot be guaranteed. Accordingly, it is usual practice to 'charge' branches with bad debts.

CONDUCTING BASIC ANALYSIS: OPERATIONS

GMROI and CMROI are also important measures of operational efficiency. They may need some explanation. The Du Pont method of ratio analysis/control in retailing is well documented but little understood (Walters, 1994; Walters and Laffy, 1995). It will be recalled that the Du Pont ratio hierarchy results in:

$$\text{ROI} = \frac{\text{Profit}}{\cancel{\text{Sales}}} \times \frac{\cancel{\text{Sales}}}{\text{Assets}} = \frac{\text{Profit}}{\text{Assets}}$$

This relationship may be used at any level of an organization. At a macro-level it measures the overall productivity of the assets of the business. At a micro-level (a category or product group) it may be used to measure the profitability of the inventory. A number of retail organizations use the GMROI (CMROI) approach (gross margin return on inventory investment (contribution margin)) to monitor both buying and operations activities. It is an effective measure because it allocates responsibility to relevant levels of decision making; consequently it is a measure of return on assets managed at these levels by the relevant managers. Figure 5.12(a) and (b) illustrates the GMROI/CMROI model.

Early approaches featured the GMROI application, but Lusch (1980) expanded the model to space and staff, and one of the authors (Walters) together with Laffy (1995) expanded the model further to consider margin spread and strategic applications.

A strategic application is suggested by Figure 5.13 in which *positioning options* may be evaluated and *buying objectives* (a target GMROI range) determined. Clearly the value of GMROI is identical for a range of margin and inventory turnover values:

Gross margin		**Inventory turnover**
15		10
25		6
30	GMROI	5
50	150	3
60		2.5

The margins increase as the inventory turnover values decrease. This reflects the characteristics of a number of industries in which discount offers *and* quality/service offers exist in different segments of the same industry or market.

Performance improvements can be explored. Figure 5.13 shows the principle in a broader context. Profit improvements may be realized by adjustments to the assortment profile resulting in improved gross (and operating) margins, by increasing prices of core merchandise items in categories in which a 'monopoly' may be held (e.g. strong market share), or by increasing

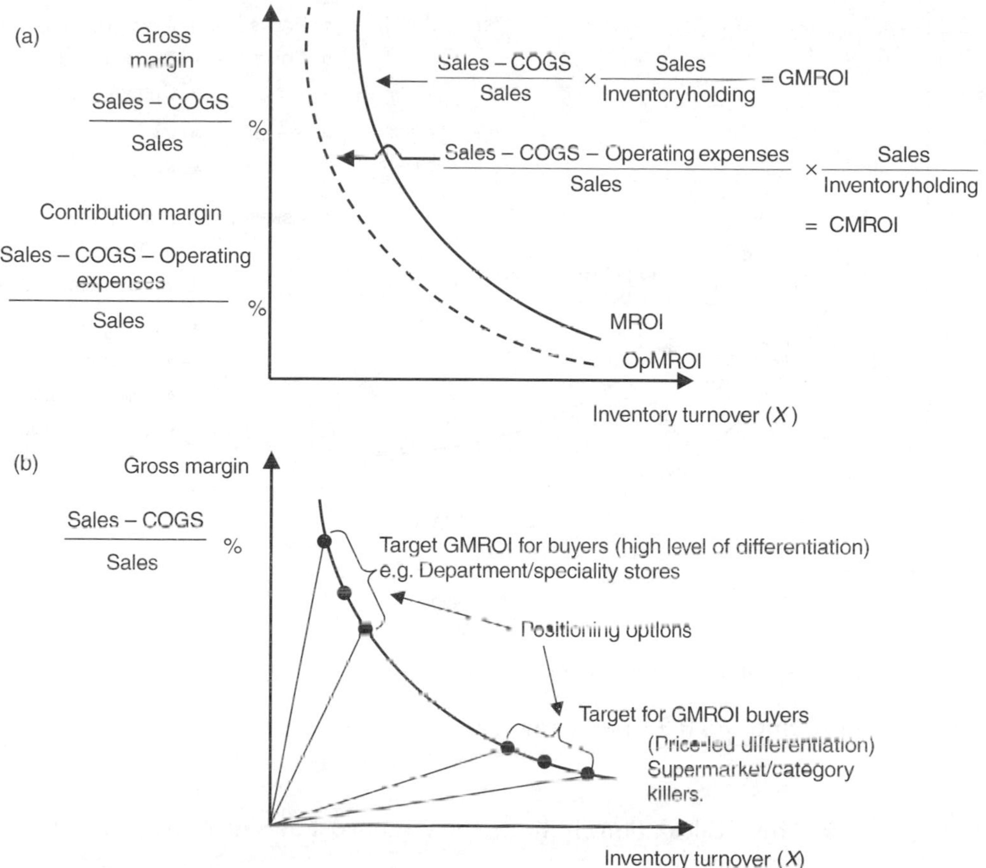

Figure 5.12 (a) The GMROI/CMROI model. (b) Using the GMROI/CMROI model to explore positioning alternatives and to set target buying GMROI values.

operational efficiencies. Alternatively, we may move towards ROA_2 from ROA_1 by increasing sales revenues (either by volume increases or price increases) or by lowering the asset values used to produce the current revenue and profit.

At an operational level the organization requires detailed information if decisions are to be made with consistency and reliability. For many companies a version of *target costing* (as developed by Toyota) is used. The basis of the process is:

- Let the market-place determine selling prices: the company identifies its target positioning and target market share, and from this a volume and target price is deduced.
- An estimate of fixed and variable costs associated with the product category (and product) is determined together with an estimate of the profit expected.

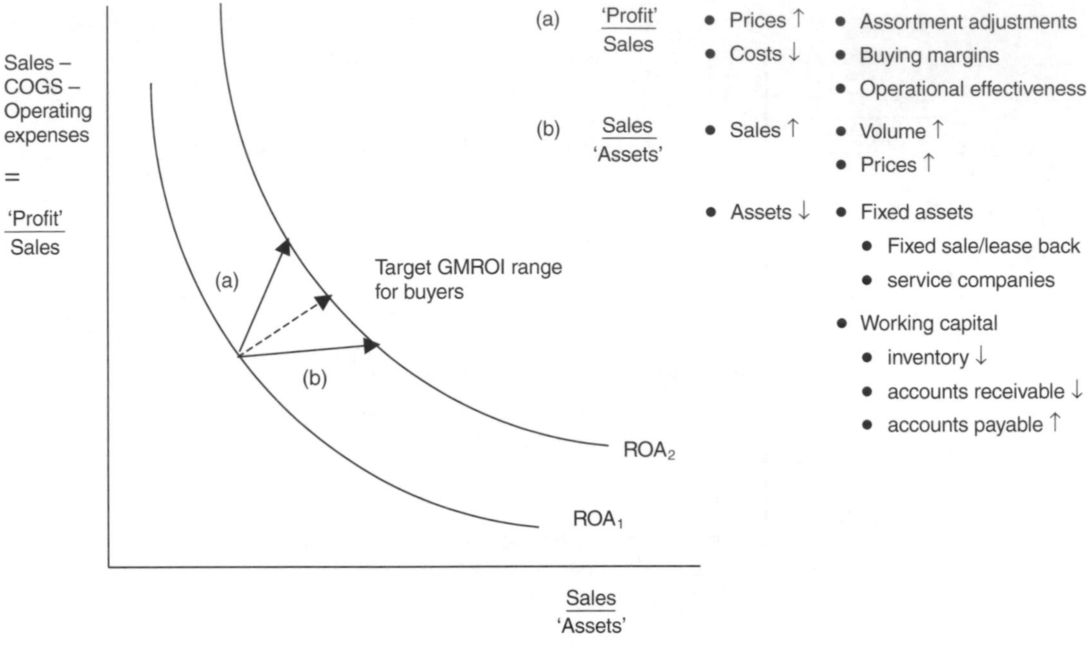

Figure 5.13 Improving the ROA performance.

- These calculations indicate the target cost at which the product must be purchased.
- A component of the negotiation process is the value of rebates and discounts given by suppliers for volume purchases and promotional allowances.

In target costing models, the cost of the product is not an outcome of the product design and delivery process. Rather, it is an input into developing an optimal retail offer. Target costing (a Japanese approach) extends beyond direct costs to include supplier, distribution and (in the case of companies such as IKEA) customer relationships, and of course includes competitor pricing policies. It has been argued that target costing has an inherent danger in that the existing required margin may become 'fixed' in the minds of management rather than be one of the variables involved in deriving an optimal retail offer: that is a combination of merchandise, customer service, format and customer communications which *optimizes* customer value satisfaction *and* corporate value expectations.

Target costing models should be combined with the GMROI models when evaluating risk and return. Typically, high margins (and low stock turns) reflect a degree of risk inherent in the product market. For example, a number of retailing categories carry extensive inventories of high value, high fashion or specialist category merchandise. Clearly there is a larger measure of the risk of markdown with these merchandise categories than there is for FMCG products. The buying margins negotiated should compensate for this risk. The GMROI model may be used to evaluate the return on investment and the target costing model may use both target price and target gross margin to identify target buying costs. If these cannot be resolved to the satisfaction of either the buyer or the vendor a number of options emerge. An alternative source is an obvious alternative: perhaps a retailer own-brand within the category may be considered, or alternatively we might consider range adjustments (i.e. reduce width, depth or availability). Clearly these options are not mutually exclusive. At a strategic level GMROI can be replaced by space and other assets, i.e. ROAM (return on assets managed).

The buying process, if it operates effectively, uses target costing models to allocate accurately the costs of procurement, distribution, merchandising and marketing a product to the product category, and, where feasible, to the product. Target costing has replaced Direct Product Profitability (costing) models in a number of companies. The reason for this is concern over the accuracy of many of the cost components *and* the lack of a market-based parameter. However, DPP/DPC was used successfully by Boots, the UK pharmacy and housewares multiple, to evaluate their pet food offer, for which they found a combination of excessively high costs and a fiercely competitive market made the category unprofitable. Similarly, Woolworths (Kingfisher, UK) came to much the same conclusion concerning the 'grobag' garden product (a bulky low-price product) which accumulated huge costs between the manufacturer, the retailer's distribution facility and the stores.

The target cost approach is outlined in Figure 5.14. It is used for both planning and control. As a process it commences with a marketing view of its role within the product category, and from this analysis volumes, prices and margins are projected. A target price is derived by evaluating the eventual delivered cost into the retail outlet (or point of sale). Once the target cost is established, performance criteria may be established at specific points within the external and internal supply chain processes. It suggests these, and also suggests that the costs and margins are measured as a percentage of selling price.

Details of the target costing approach will be discussed in Chapter 7.

SUMMARY

To conclude this chapter strategic and operational performance characteristics are brought together. Figure 5.15 considers aspects of strategic performance and Figure 5.16 reviews operational performance issues. Both use a similar framework.

Strategic performance (Figure 5.15) considers the revenue, operating and net margin performances of fixed assets, working capital, net assets and shareholder equity. *Fixed asset performance* is influenced by the size and

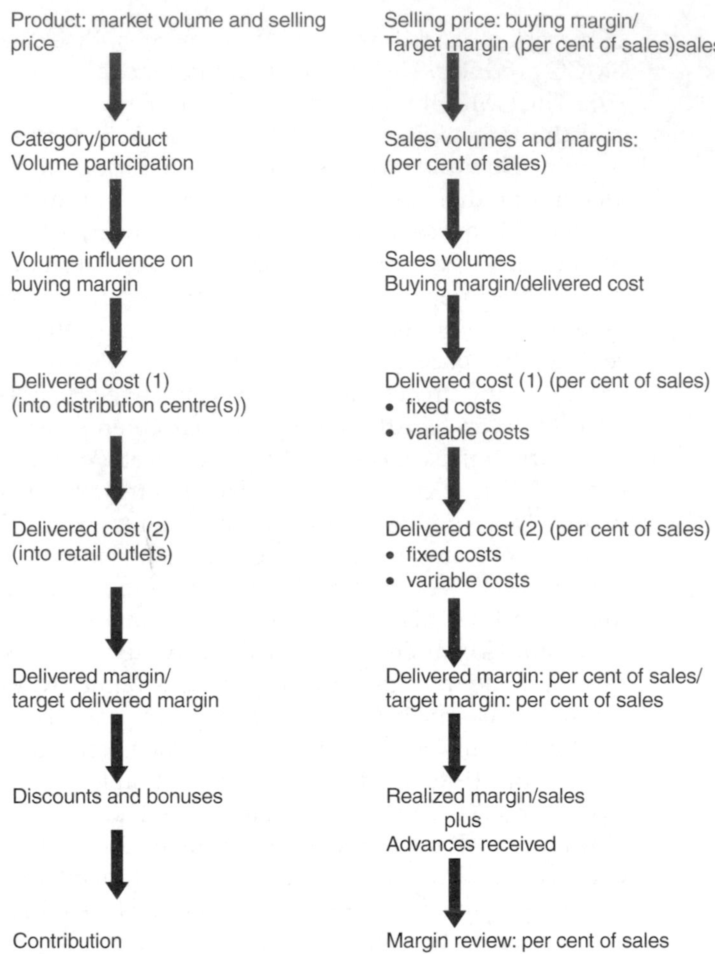

Figure 5.14 Target costing: a model for planning and controlling the buying activity.

positioning of the organization and its branding policy, which will determine the margins required if the strategy is to be effective. Similarly, the size and scope of the organization will have an impact on its strategic effectiveness and financial performance. The systems infrastructure refers to the entire support systems required to make the strategy effective. This has implications for costs, performance and effectiveness.

Working capital performance is influenced by the width, depth, availability and other relevant characteristics of the assortment strategy. Customer credit allowed (including bad debts) and supplier credit given (or taken) will also have an important impact on the effectiveness of working capital strategy and management. Cash flow performance will be influenced by changes in working capital components, as will be the return generated on working capital investment.

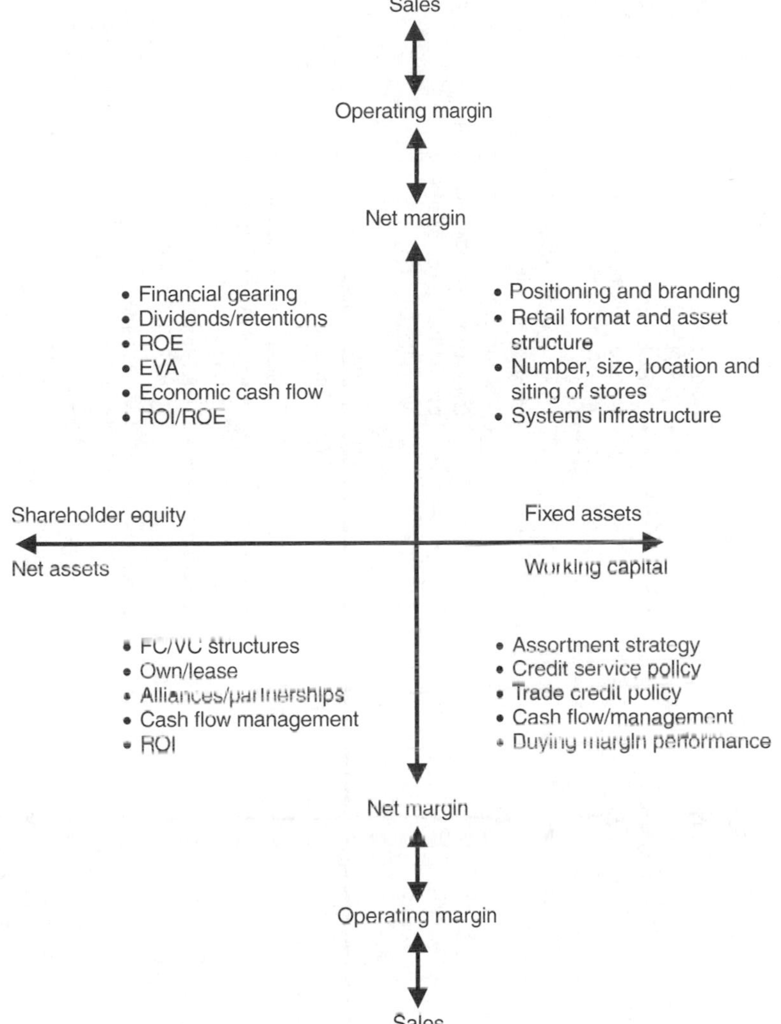

Figure 5.15 Strategic profitability, productivity and cash flow performance.

An overall view of *net asset performance* is necessary because of the trade-off possibilities which exist within and between fixed assets and working capital; hence the effectiveness of alternatives offered by alternative operational gearing options, own/lease alternatives and alliances and partnerships. Again there are implications for both cash flow management and return on investment.

The overall objective of the business is to generate an acceptable return for the *shareholders*. It follows that profitability, productivity and cash flow will be influenced by decisions concerning financial gearing (the debt/equity structure) and decisions taken on retaining profit for expansion. The

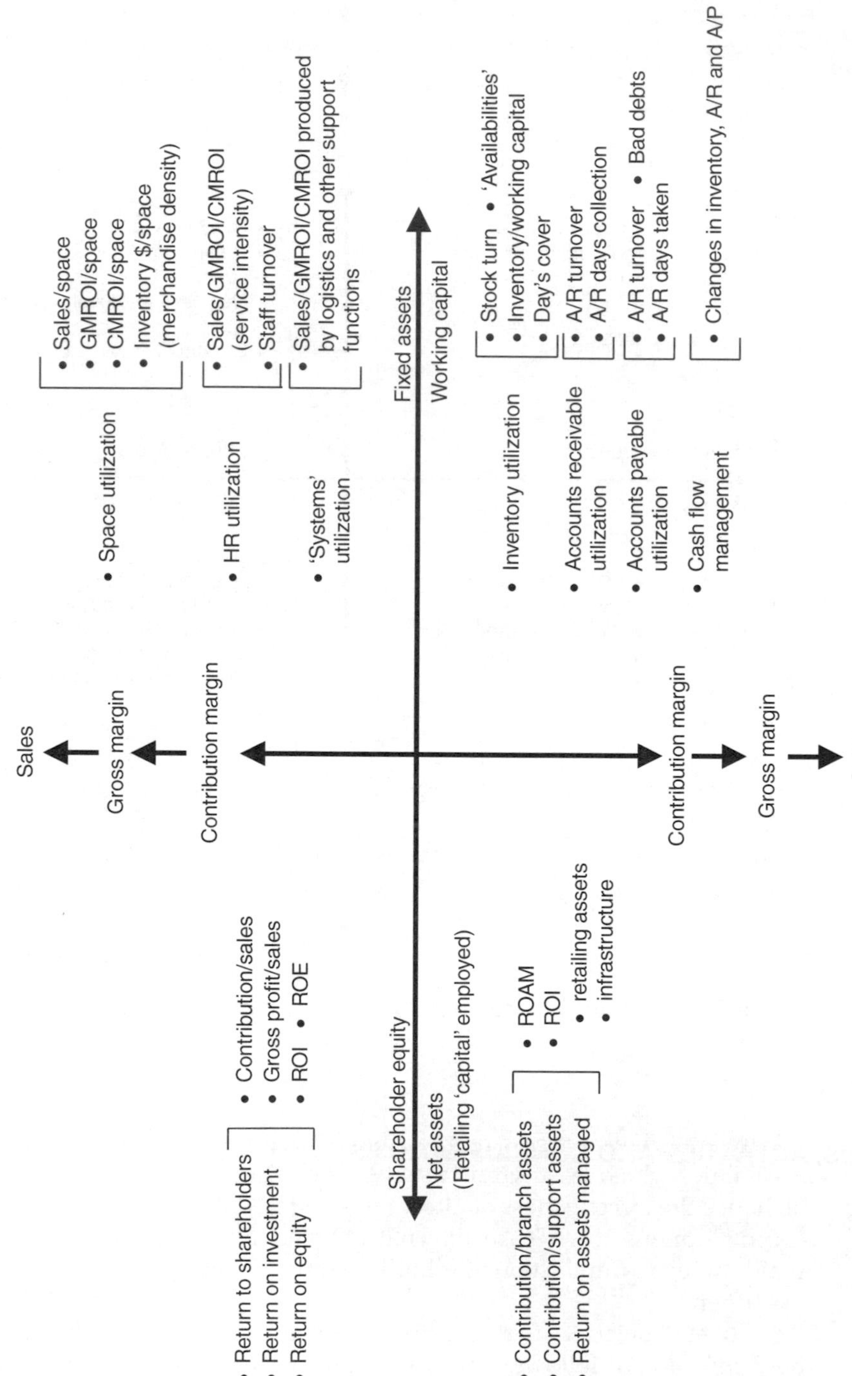

Figure 5.16 Operational profitability, productivity and cashflow.

eventual return on equity (ROE)) and the comparison of ROI/ROE (showing the effectiveness of the gearing) and the EVA generated will all be influenced by the decisions taken concerning capital structures and strategic positioning. Figure 5.15 suggests the process to be iterative, one which seeks to optimize, rather than compromise, decisions concerning fixed assets, working capital and their potential performance.

Operational performance (Figure 5.16) takes place within the parameters of the objectives and strategy determined. *Fixed asset performance* is concerned with the utilization of space together with the systems resources investment.

Human resources have become a variable cost for many retailers. Legislation aimed at increasing job security (in many countries) has caused retail employers to review the terms of employment offered such that hours worked are below that required for full benefits (vacation pay and welfare contributions by employers). This has resulted in what were once a high proportion of retail fixed costs becoming variable costs.

Working capital performance is concerned with the efficient management of inventory (to achieve the customer value required), accounts receivable (to augment customer delivered value) and accounts payable (to ensure the maximum benefits from supplier services and the use of negative cash flow) resulting in optimal working capital and cash flow performances.

Given the fixed assets and working capital resource investment, operating management's task is to ensure the target returns on the *net assets* invested in the business are achieved. Of particular importance is a comparison of performance outcomes achieved for the core business activities and from the support functions. Also useful is the return on assets managed (ROAM) at various levels of the business or by key management activities.

The contribution by operating management to *shareholder investment* is measured by the return generated on sales and on the investment in specific aspects of the business. The notion of SBUs (strategic business units) is relevant here, as it may be desirable (and necessary) to measure and compare the performance of different formats, regions, or some other organizational features of the business.

QUESTIONS, ACTIVITIES AND CONSIDERATIONS

- Recently the emphasis on business performance has been directed towards shareholder value planning and management. How does this affect the notion of stakeholder returns? Are there compromises to be made concerning employees, suppliers and, of course, customers?
- Using the performance criteria discussed in the Appendix and the balanced scorecard model discussed in the chapter, design a planning and control model for the following types of retail business:

- An FMCG retail chain
- A department store
- A specialist ladies chain
- An Internet-based vendor of books and music
- A fast food chain

Consider both qualitative and quantitative issues.

APPENDIX: PERFORMANCE CRITERIA

The balanced scorecard/stakeholder perspective of performance offers the opportunity for objectives to be set which enhance the performances of suppliers, customers and employees as well as that of the company.

An approach to determining strategic stakeholder objectives is illustrated in Figure 5A.1, which is based upon Figures 5.3 and 5.4. For each of the stakeholder topics additional, supporting, objectives are necessary. These will be qualitative and quantitative as well as strategic and operational.

Qualitative objectives

Corporate positioning

- 'Expected value'
  - quality
  - availability
  - choice
  - service
- 'Added value'
  - exclusivity
  - style/design
- 'Innovator'
  - new products
  - new processes
  - applied technology

Market positioning

- Location
  - number and size of outlets
  - convenience (siting)
- Customer services
  - facilities (physical)
  - facilities (activities)
  - facilities (information)
- Merchandise characteristics
  - assortment profile (width, depth, availability)
  - price points

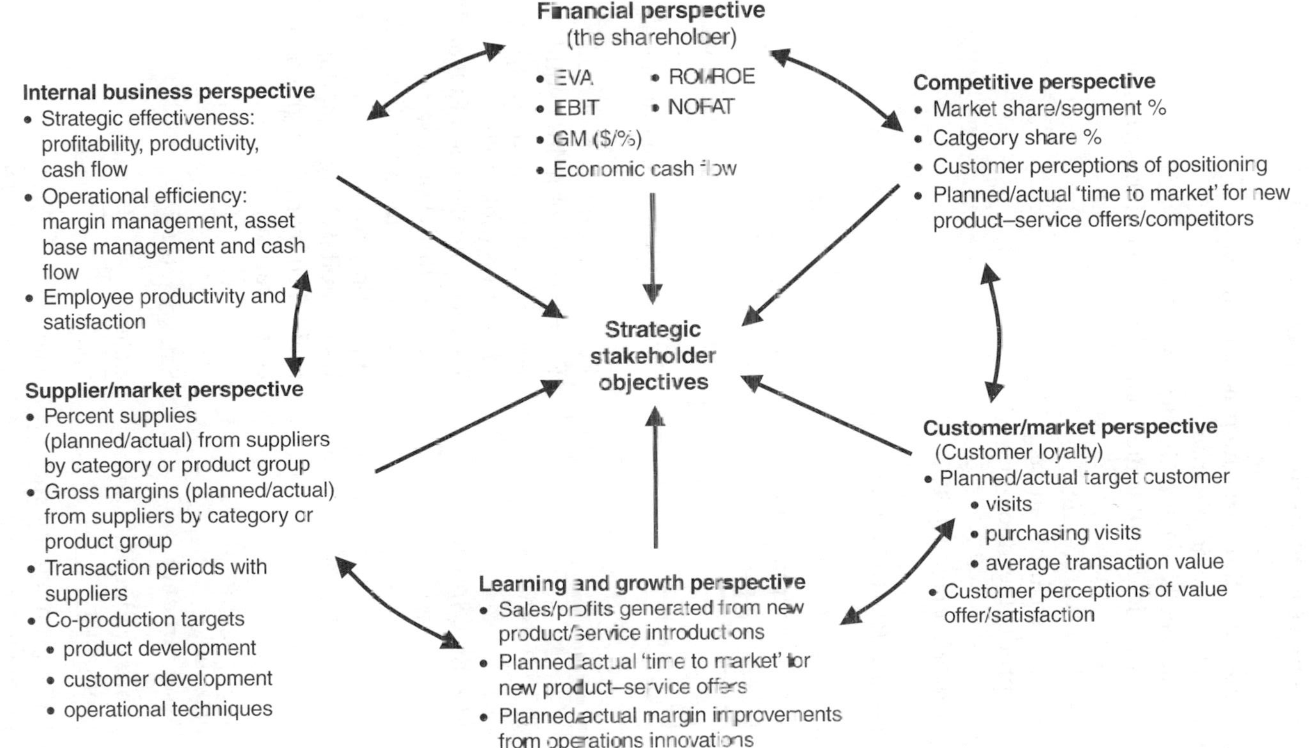

Figure 5A.1 Developing stakeholder objectives.

- Format characteristics
  - visual merchandising/merchandise density
  - service density (number of services)
  - service intensity (number of staff)

Category positioning: core product groups

- Merchandise dominance
  - market leadership characteristics
  - customer identification of destination purchase/first choice supplier
  - market share(s)
- Product positioning
  - product applications
  - product technology

Quantitative objectives

Strategic effectiveness

Profitability

• Gross profit/margin	Sales – COGS/Sales (%)
• Operating profit/margin • EBIT	Sales – COGS – operating expenses/Sales (%)
• NOPAT	Sales – COGS – Operating expenses – tax
• ROCE	Return on capital employed
• ROE	Return on shareholder equity
• ROI/RONA	Return on total capital employed or total assets (net assets)
• ROI/ROE spread	Relationship between ROI and ROE (i.e. the impact of gearing)
• EVA	Economic value added: NOPAT (operating profit – depreciation – tax) less a capital charge (capital employed multiplied by the weighted average cost of capital)

Productivity

• Asset turnover	Sales/assets (×)
• Space productivity and profitability	$\frac{\text{Sales}}{\text{Space}}$ $\frac{\text{'Profit'}}{\text{Space}}$
• HRM productivity and profitability	$\frac{\text{Sales}}{\text{FTE}}$ $\frac{\text{'Profit'}}{\text{FTE}}$
• Inventory productivity	$\frac{\text{COGS}}{\text{Inventory holding}}$

• Inventory profitability	Operating profit / Inventory holding
• Strategic cash flow	Operating profit + depreciation ± changes in working and fixed capital together with changes in equity and LT debt required for expansion
• Asset intensity	Assets/sales (%)
• Asset utilization	Per cent capacity utilized

Productivity/time profiles

Space HRM Inventory	Sales GM OPM	• 'season' • 'time': week day hour

Profitability/productivity

• ROAM	Return on assets managed: (Operating profit/SBU assets)
• GMROI	Gross margin return on inventory investment
• MROI	Continuation margin return on inventory investment
• Economic cash flow	NPV of future cash flows

Operational effectiveness

Profitability

• Gross profit/margin by: • Operating profit/margin	• categories • product groups • products • suppliers	• regions • locations • formats

Productivity

• Inventory – categories – product groups – product type – location/format	sales (COGS)/inventory holding (×) inventory/net assets (%) days cover	trends
• Accounts receivable (customer credit allowed) – customer group – categories – product groups – product type	A/R turnover collection days bad debts/sales	trends

  - location/format
- Operational cash flow — Operating profit + depreciation ± changes in working capital ± changes in fixed capital and equity and debt funding required for current operations
- Cash flow (sources)

		%
– total assortment – categories – product groups – product groups – products – suppliers – locations/formats – payments due (ST)	– operating profit – depreciation – cash balances – inventory – accounts receivables – prepaid items – accounts payable	
		100

Productivity/profitability

- GMROI
- OpMROI

} expressed for space and employees

- ROAM by:
  - categories
  - product groups
  - products
  - outlets
  - formats (divisions)
  - regions structures

} reflects levels of responsibility and organization

Stakeholder measures

Suppliers

- Relationship longevity
- Number of coproduction agreements
- Supplier costs and profits
- Supplier share of total category/product group business
- Number of suppliers

Customers

- Relationship longevity(ies) (by customer groups, location, format etc.) (life cycle)

• Visit frequencies • Average transactions • Purchases/visits • NPV estimate of business per customer/customer group over customer life cycle	• customer segment • location • format	by: • season • category • brand

Learning and Growth

• Sales and profits (%) generated from new product-service introductions over past (three) years	• Per cent of total sales/profits: planned/actual
• Time-to-market for new product-service	• Planned/actual time
• Margin improvements from operations innovations	• Planned/actual per cent • Planned/actual time for effectiveness
• 'R and D' budget	• Per cent of sales • Growth percent/growth per cent sales.

COMMENT

The performance criteria suggested here are generic in as much as they suggest topics (and measures) rather than claiming to be necessary for success. As is always the situation, the performance criteria selected should be those essential to plan and monitor strategic activities.

It will be recalled that Kaplan and Norton's balanced scorecard offered a range of measures which provide a comprehensive framework within which to translate the organization's strategic objectives into a coherent set of performance measures. We have added another perspective: the facility to consider a range of objectives which enables the 'executive' to optimize the strategic objectives in order that the stakeholders' objectives may also be realized. This approach is another use of the trade-offs in the context of customer and value delivery alternatives. Here the issue is more one of asking: if we choose to position the organization in a particular target market, will the decision prove to be profitable not only for us but also for our suppliers? We might also choose to address internal trade-offs. For example: what will be the impact on financial performance of an increase in the R&D budget? Furthermore, will planned product–service introductions be sufficiently profitable to recover R&D expenditures? And given planned operations innovations, can our suppliers accommodate the changes operationally *and* financially?

It follows that, to be effective, performance measurement should consider both the internal and external aspects of strategy planning and control. The abilities (and financial interests) of the organization are clearly important, but so too are those of the stakeholders, without whose contributions the strategic plan cannot succeed.

6 PLANNING AND CONTROL: FINANCIAL AND MARKETING PERSPECTIVES

LEARNING OBJECTIVES

Given a strategic direction, together with the attributes and activities which will be required for its implementation, the broad aspects of the plan should be evaluated for its financial and marketing effectiveness. This chapter presents a procedure for reviewing the planning and control perspectives of both the financial and marketing decisions that comprise the strategy. The chapter discusses shareholder value management and its growing importance for corporate management. Topics introduced and developed are:

- Managing for shareholder and customer value.
- The importance of profitability, productivity and cash flow to shareholder value.
- The use of the Du Pont/strategic profit model for strategic planning and control and its use in operational/implementation decisions.
- The marketing strategy considerations for retailing strategy development: strategic positioning, target customer groups and value expectations.
- Customer expectations and the implications for strategic context: attributes and activities.
- An exploration of the implications of customer shopping missions.
- Strategy, shopping missions, attributes and resource allocation decisions are discussed within the context of planning and are related to the strategy model developed in Chapter 2.

INTRODUCTION

Before moving into the details of determining merchandise, customer service, format and communications strategies (and their implementation) a discussion of some of the surrounding issues and considerations is worthwhile.

Increasingly the concerns of shareholder expectations are becoming prominent in retailing managements' decision making. The authors have presented views concerning the impact on shareholder value management elsewhere (1997, 1998) and we review only the significant issues here. Clearly shareholder expectations for return on investment have an important influence on strategy decisions. However, it is equally important to remember that any business is only in business for as long as it delivers value to customers.

Figure 6.1 presents a basic model which integrates shareholder and customer value expectations. Figure 6.1 is a generic model in that it identifies value criteria and value driver categories only. The detailed characteristics will vary by target customer group and by organization. For example, customer value criteria will reflect *specific* value characteristics and these may

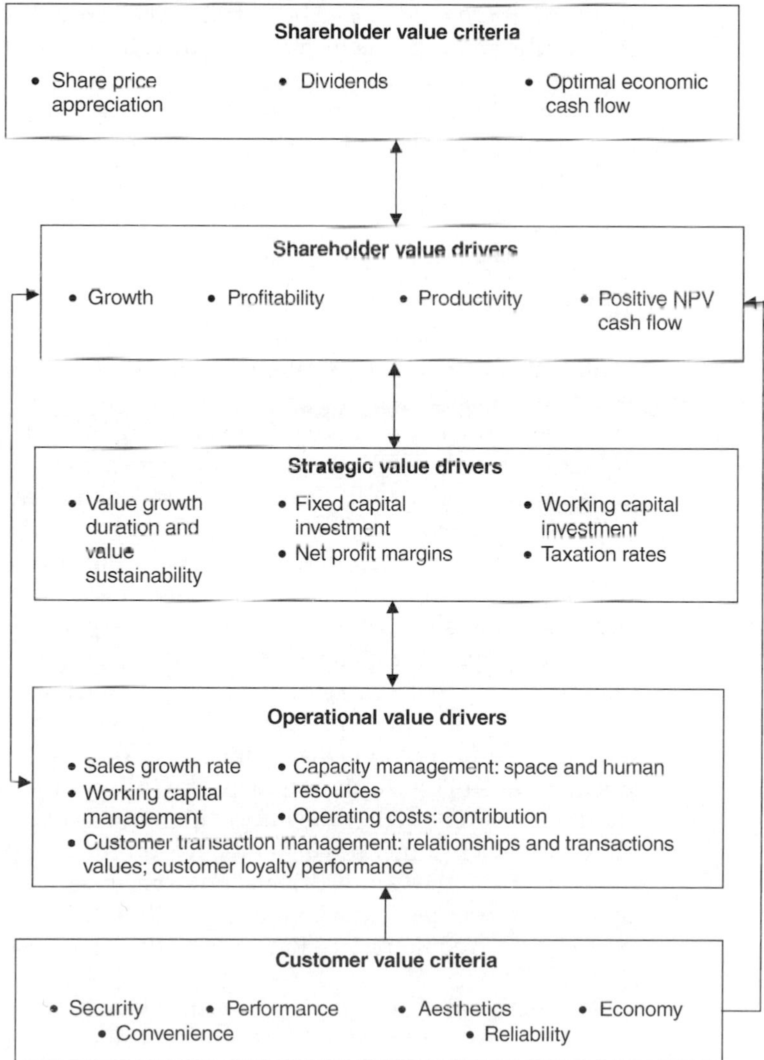

Figure 6.1 Managing for shareholder *and* customer value.

differ markedly. Customers of a specialist retailer (or department store) may see *performance* as reflected by choice and variety: the discount store customer may consider performance to be an in-stock position of a brand leader, choice being unimportant.

Shareholder value expectations (value criteria) reflect aspects of return on investments held. It is the *shareholder value drivers* that are important to management. By considering the strategic alternatives available to the organization, growth, profitability, productivity and cash flow objectives may be set. Their resultant performance will be influenced by the *strategic value drivers*, the means by which value may be delivered. For example, *value growth duration* is management's best estimate of the number of years that an investment can be expected to yield rates of return greater than the cost of capital. For Rappaport, *value sustainability* adds the sales growth rate and the threshold spread (the amount by which forecast margins exceed the threshold margin). Value growth duration and sustainability decisions within a retailing context would consider the growth potential and profitable life span of new category/product–market offers with respect to time, margin generation and productivity of dedicated fixed assets and working capital. Figure 6.1 details both strategic and operational value drivers. The implications of strategic value driver decisions for strategy implementation is reflected on the operational value drivers. An example may help here.

Often successful categories are launched as specialist retailing formats. (The reader should return to Figures 2.7(a) and (b) at this point). The issue for management to resolve is whether one specific strategic theme can, on a standalone basis, meet the growth, profitability, productivity and positive NPV requirements necessary to make a significant contribution to shareholder value. Each of the strategic and operational value drivers has implications for the merchandise, customer service, format and communications strategies that evolve.

The credibility of the specialist offer will require a number of core products with specific width, depth and availability characteristics (merchandise strategy). As a specialist offer, customers will expect a high level of product knowledge by staff capable of giving advice and 'expert' application information (customer service strategy). Another customer expectation concerns the location, size and store design adopted by the retailer (format strategy). Finally, the information concerning the product–service offer (its content, pricing, availability etc.) is a strategy issue (communications strategy) which should not simply reflect the information needs of customers but should be linked to the customer buying and decision-making process.

The role of the value drivers now becomes very clear. The strategic theme(s), attributes and activities can only be successful if they reflect key performance requirements. Rappaport (1986) suggests:

> any strategy designed to promote competitive advantage must, in the final analysis, meet the test of sustainable value creation. The value creation process in turn depends upon the translation of competitive dynamics into forecasts of value drivers.

This is the purpose (and functions) of the value drivers: the means by which value may be delivered to both customers and shareholders. Thus fixed and working capital investment value drivers comprise those elements of the investment in retail outlets, inventory, customer credit and intangible assets such as a retail fascia brand and 'R&D' activities required to research, evaluate and develop a successful offer.

The operational value drivers are the means by which strategy is implemented and monitored. Again an example may help. If we follow through with the specialist retailing example, we can see that the operational value drivers, such as working capital management and capacity management, operate to ensure that the determined product assortment meets the optimal return on inventory investment and that the revenue and contribution realized per square metre and per employee are sufficient to ensure a return on those resources. Of particular importance is the management of customer transactions. Strong customer loyalty, measured in terms of customer visit frequencies and value of transactions, is a necessary value driver if the venture is to succeed

The management of shareholder value drivers may be related to the more conventional forms of accounting and financial management. Figure 6.2 illustrates a conventional view of managing profit and loss, balance sheet and cash flow times. Possibly more useful is to use Du Pont's ratio analysis structure to explore both strategic and operational alternatives. In Figure 6.3 a strategic model is offered. The strategic profitability options of customized (highly differentiated) offers, selective exclusivity (limited differentiation) and price-leader (low price/low service) offers may be explored together with their respective asset base requirements and the subsequent return on investment options. If investment and financial management considerations are included a return on equity calculation becomes possible.

The strategic planning and control perspective is only part of the picture. It is important to be able to consider *how* the strategic options may be implemented. This is illustrated in Figure 6.4. Here the tasks of operational management (i.e. margin management and asset base management) are focused upon. At an operational level, management are concerned primarily with maintaining profitability and ensuring that the productivity of fixed and working capital meets appropriate performance levels.

The Du Pont model permits management to consider the return (and risk) profiles of alternative format/retail offers *and then continue* the exercise in detail by identifying the merchandise, customer service, format and customer communications strategies *and* their implementation activities and costs. To continue with the specialist retailing example. If we assume two format profiles are credible, these being the customized and selective exclusivity options, it is now possible to review the range of ROI (return on investment) performance outcomes by reviewing the merchandise, customer service and format options *together* with their investment requirements. If, additionally, we consider the alternative financial structures available to the organization, an initial appraisal of the alternatives can be made.

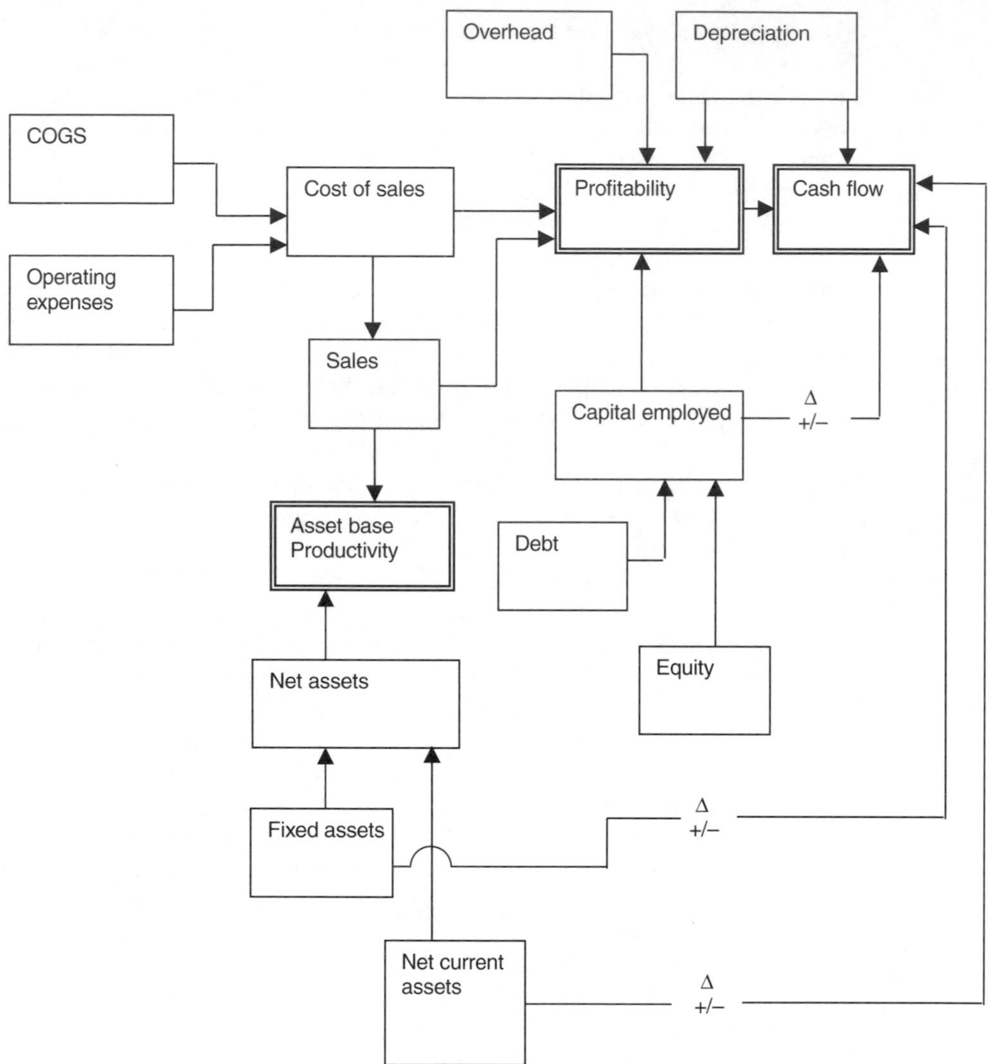

Figure 6.2 Managing shareholder value drivers.

Strategies have to be implemented. Figure 6.4 illustrates a number of the implementation decisions confronting operational managers. Returning to the example of a specialist retailing organization we suggest that margins are influenced by the dimensions of core merchandise categories (width, depth, availability etc.); product augmentation (the range of accessories made available within the core categories); and the number (and characteristics) of seasons and themes (by increasing the interest offered by the offer and therefore the visit frequency and transactions of customers).

Asset productivity issues consider both fixed and working capital decisions. Fixed capital decisions are concerned with the infrastructure

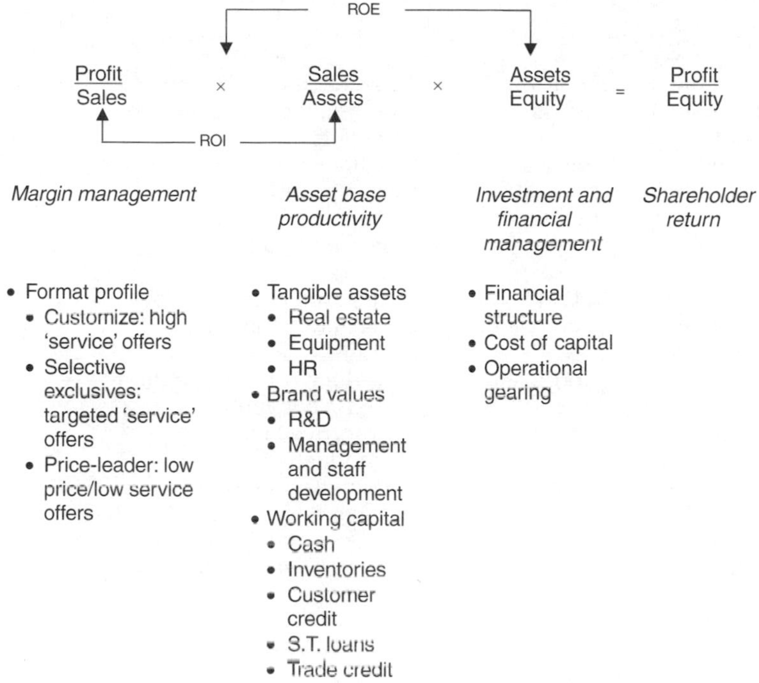

Figure 6.3 Using Du Pont for strategic planning and control.

requirements necessary to implement merchandise and service decisions. Working capital decisions relate to inventory (a merchandise consideration) and customer credit. Working capital also includes current liabilities and, therefore, trade creditors, which are an important component. For many retail companies trade creditors (accounts payable) can provide a source of interest free cash, if the supplier/retailer relationship is well managed and the retailer offers the supplier stable long-term business this source of interest-free capital extends into the long-term.

PLANNING AND CONTROL: A MARKETING PERSPECTIVE

As we have seen (Chapter 2) a central element in planning decisions concerns the strategic positioning of the organization. There are five factors that may influence the positioning decision, and these are shown as Figure 6.5. Clearly the market opportunity (a target customer group) must be identified, but other factors are important. The organization's existing positioning is one such factor. We have already discussed credibility in this context, and little need be added here. A strong identity with existing or potential customers is essential. A lack of credibility can at best slow market entry and at worst

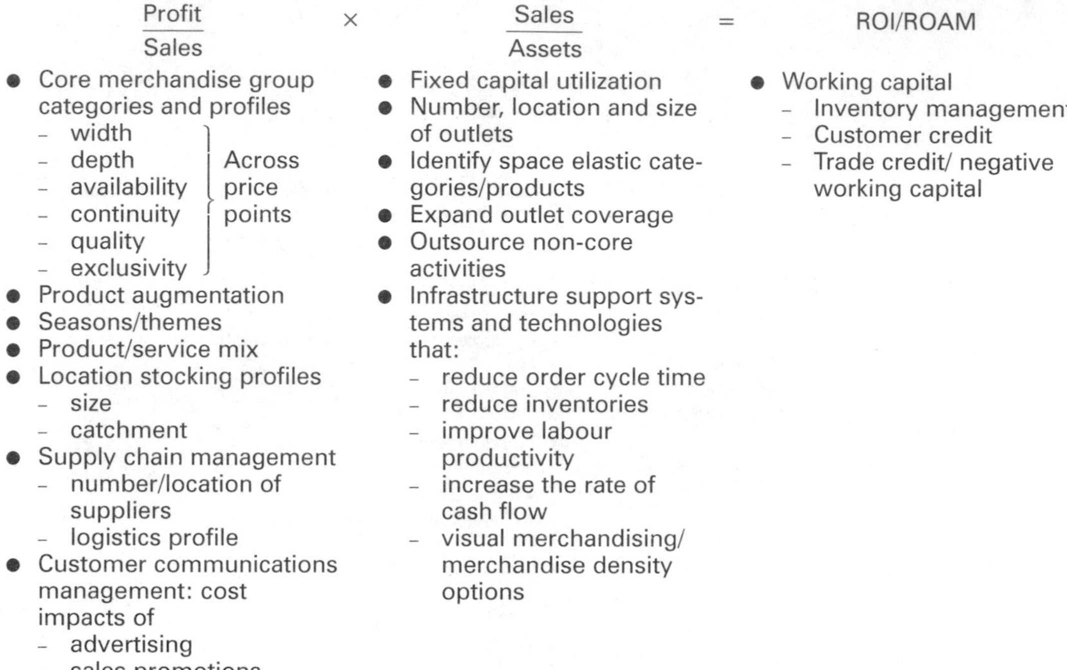

Figure 6.4 Using Du Pont for operational planning and control.

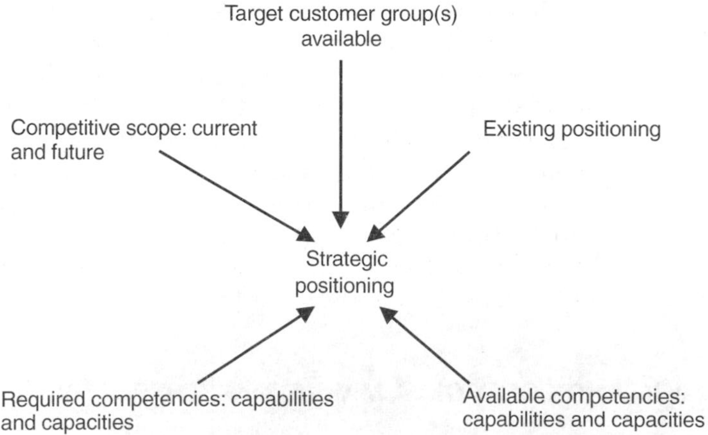

Figure 6.5 Influences on the organization's strategic positioning.

act as a major retarding influence. The response of existing and/or new competitors (new in the sense that the organization is contemplating a new venture) is another important consideration. A very strong market incumbent may be able to damage, or even prevent, market entry overtures. Two other factors are important: the competencies available and those required.

Existing competencies may be transferable, but often they are not and the gap may be considerable and impossible to bridge economically.

Returning to the target customer group. A useful approach is to identify 'customer shopping missions' through a process of customer profiling. Bucklin (1963) first proposed a product–patronage mix in which customer preferences and store types were matched. The benefits of time (35 years) together with massive strides in customer data management have enabled retailing to become more focused in customer profiling research and targeting. Changing lifestyles, the responses to social and economic change, have resulted in revised views of consumer time and expenditure budgets. Concurrently the consumer has become more discerning in the approach to when, where and what is purchased.

This has significance for strategic decisions. It suggests there are a range of shopping trips that may be taken by any individual and these will vary depending upon the circumstances of the individual. Clearly the circumstances change. A young (possibly working) mother who is accompanied by pre-school-age children while shopping for food and other similar routine needs will favour a retail offer which emphasizes convenience. On another occasion the same person may be shopping for clothes or furniture (with a partner or a friend but not with her children), and the exercise becomes more pleasure-oriented and her preferences change. Convenience may still be an element of the choice set, but choice and possibly 'education' (looking for applications ideas) and entertainment (using the occasion as a leisure activity) are much more dominant value preferences. This has obvious implications for planning and implementing retail strategy and requires detailed customer research to profile target customer groups.

Figure 6.6 suggests an approach. The research identifies the *customer group options* by defining the broad customer typology within the attractive market. Then by considering customer lifestyles *and* shopping-related lifestyles the options are narrowed. An important feature in the research is to establish customer 'qualifications', because these have important implications for store layout and display. Customer qualifications also influence the shopping missions. For example, a specialist retailer in ladies wear would expect 'qualifications' to include high levels of interest and confidence in its customers with a lesser level of knowledge (of specific products available) and levels of readiness to purchase varying from none or low to high. For a detailed discussion determining both shopping missions and customer qualifications, see Walters (1994).

Given such a profile of customer qualifications the retail organization may then reach conclusions concerning the dominant shopping missions. In this example we could expect two dominant missions: planned comparison and planned browsing. This in turn has implications for merchandise categories and assortment policy within each category, as well as for the store layout and display. If our customers' shopping missions are based primarily on collecting ideas and seeking out alternatives, then our response should be to offer categories based upon *identified* user needs (i.e. clothes for work, leisure, entertaining etc.) comprising *identified* label/brand preferences. They should

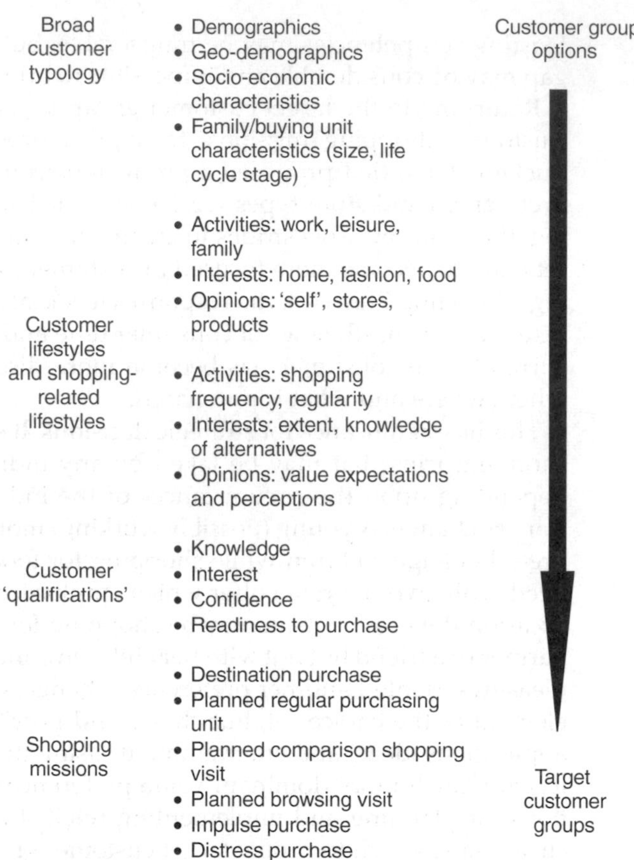

Figure 6.6 Profiling target customer groups.

be displayed to suggest coordinated combinations of products (an information service as well as a means of increasing transaction size) and be supported by product and service accessories (augmentation) that add value for the customer and revenue and contribution for the organization.

By contrast a convenience store is likely to have identified distress purchasing as the dominant shopping mission. Consequently it will be located within a minimum travel time for its customers, offer opening hours and merchandise categories that reflect the expectations of distress purchases (i.e. open early until late with a range of convenience foods and short shelf-life products (milk and bread), a delicatessen counter, news and beverages).

The importance of identifying customer value criteria has, by now, become clear. Figure 6.7 suggests generic value criteria together with detailed attributes for each of the major value criteria elements. These are an essential input into the positioning strategy, as Figure 6.8 illustrates. The diagram extends the notion developed in Chapter 2: the *positioning* decision is a response to a market opportunity and it identifies *attributes* which are in effect an interpretation of the positioning response and *activities* – management decisions – which implement the positioning decision.

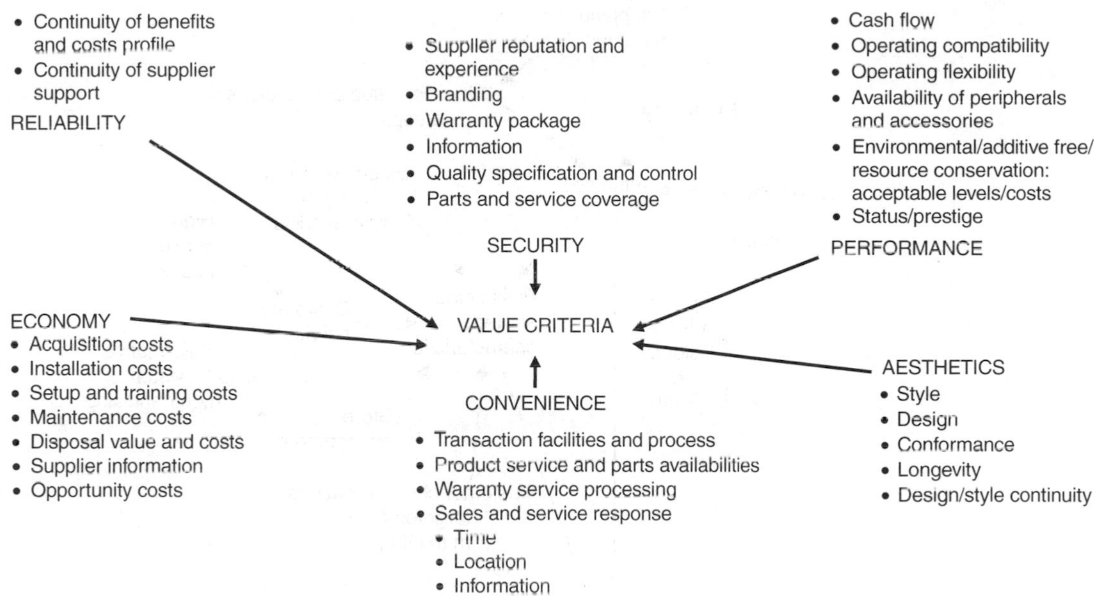

Figure 6.7 An expansion of generic value criteria.

To facilitate the process of resource allocation we suggest that the activities are allocated to specific elements of the retail offer. Figure 6.9 suggests such a process. Customer shopping missions are interpreted as a set of customer expectations based upon merchandise, customer service and store environment. These in turn are considered in terms of the resources required to deliver the attribute profile (i.e. merchandise characteristics, merchandise augmentation, visual merchandising, service characteristics, service augmentation (information and facilities) and service intensity. Figure 6.9 also identifies the detailed components (activities) of each.

However, simply to identify the value expectations (criteria), provide resources and deliver the value is not in itself sufficient. The process requires coordination, and this may be visualized as an overlapping process in which each of the attribute characteristics (and the component activities) are developed to be mutually supporting. Figure 6.10 illustrates how merchandise and customer service attributes may be coordinated to emphasize a merchandise/service-led offer such as that required in a department store or specialist retailing positioning strategy.

SUMMARY

Effective value delivery requires that both customer and shareholder satisfaction are achieved. Figure 6.11 illustrates how the financial and marketing perspectives interface in this task.

Activities

- Experienced fashion merchandisers + buyers
- Exclusive brands/labels
- Experienced and well-trained sales staff who understand style and colour coordination
- Imaginative visual displays
- Selective direct marketing to advise customers of specific merchandise using effective customer lists and relevant technology

Figure 6.8 Identifying the working linkages between shopping missions, customer expectations, attributes, positioning and activities.

Shareholder value, as described earlier, is realized by effective (strategic) management of share price, dividends and economic cash flow (positive NPV of future cash flows). Customer value is delivered by *effective management* of the positioning components, merchandise, customer service, format and communications decisions. They interface through the management of profitability, productivity and cash flow. The task confronting management is the *efficient (implementation) management* of the activities that are derived from the positioning attributes.

This chapter may be summarized by Figure 6.11, which identifies each of the topics discussed and related each of them in the planning and control process. We shall use this model to develop the following eight chapters. For each of the strategy areas, merchandise, customer service, format and environment, and communication and information, the strategy and strategy implementation processes will be discussed, together with examples of how retailing companies approach the tasks.

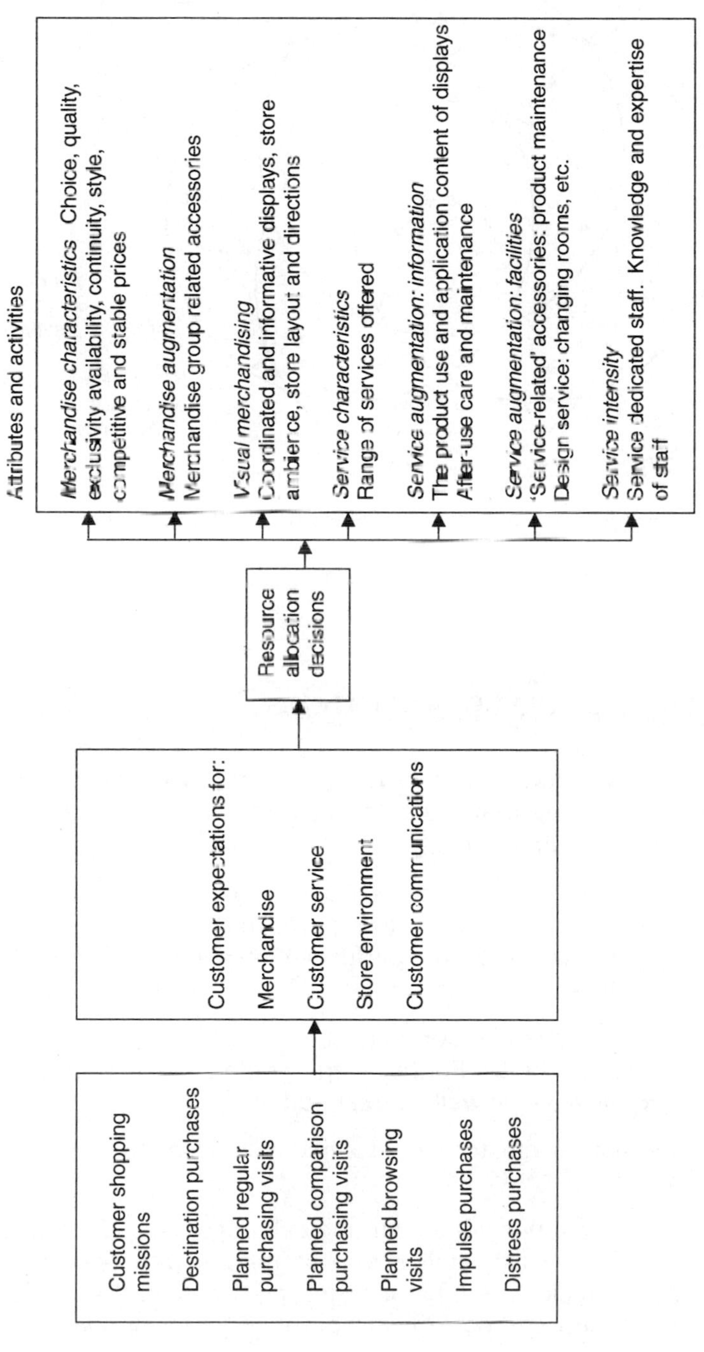

Figure 6.9 Matching customers' shopping mission expectations with the attributes of a retail offer.

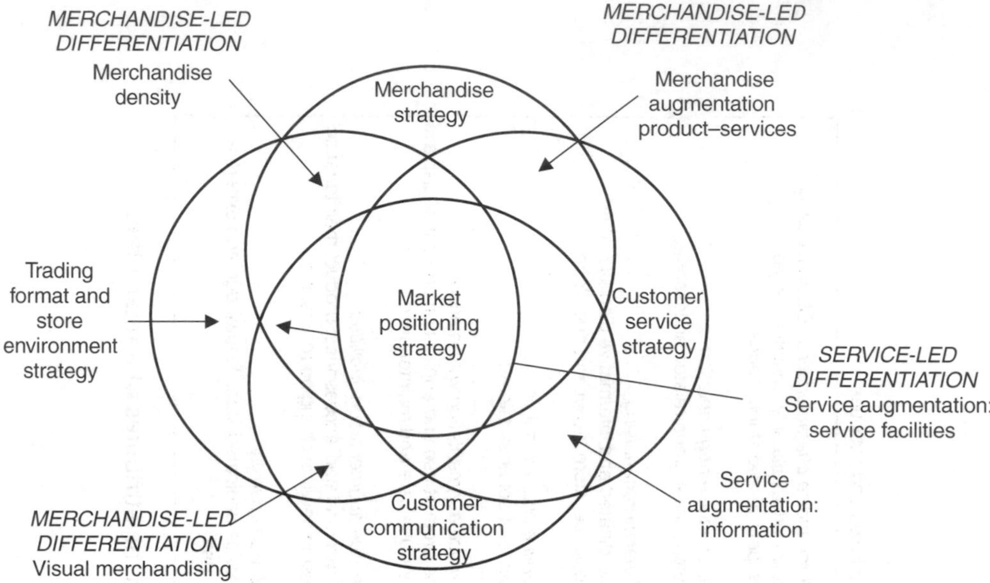

Figure 6.10 Positioning strategy and the role of merchandise and service differentiation.

QUESTIONS, ACTIVITIES AND CONSIDERATIONS

- Discuss the view that, provided an organization has identified its target customer base and meets the customers' expectations, shareholder value is maximized.
- Using the financial reports of a major multiple, calculate its profitability, productivity and cash flow performance for a period of years. Use Figure 6.2. Contrast the performance of an FMCG multiple with that of a department store group.
- Use the same two companies to analyse their performance within the context of the Du Pont/strategic profit model. Your evaluation should be qualitative as well as quantitative.
- Conduct a customer profiling exercise by observing customer activities.
- Identify the positioning strategy characteristics for a department store and a specialist retailer who competes with one of the department store's major merchandise groups. How do the interpretations (and responses) compare? Use Figure 6.8 to develop your analysis.

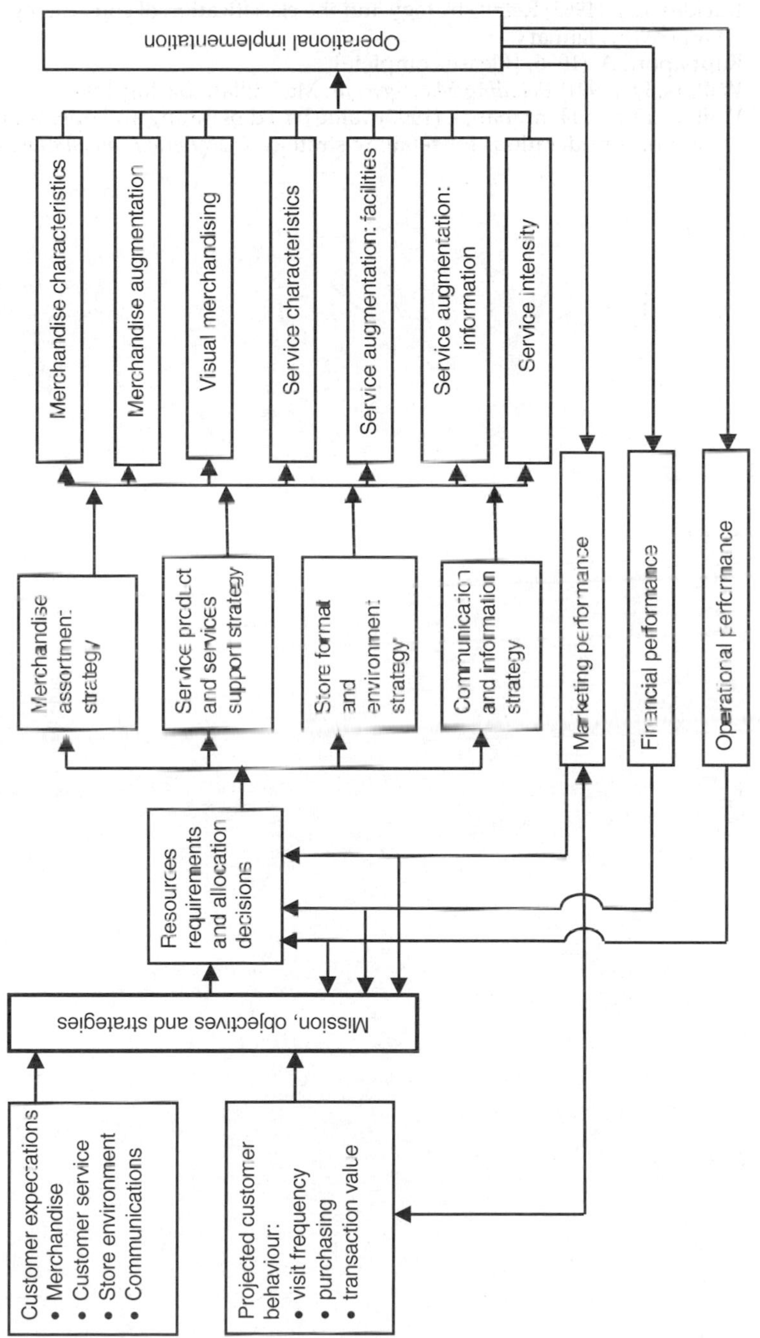

Figure 6.11 Retail planning components and process.

REFERENCES

Bucklin, L. P. (1963) Retail strategy and the classification of consumer goods. *Journal of Marketing*, January.

Rappaport, A. (1986) [Please complete].

Walters, D. (1994) *Retailing Management*. Macmillan, Basingstoke.

Walters, D. and Hanrahan, J. (1997) Value based planning and operational implementation: considerations for retailing strategy. *Macquarie Economics Research Papers*.

DEVELOPING MERCHANDISE STRATEGY

LEARNING OBJECTIVES

Merchandise strategy decisions are important in amplifying the strategic positioning of any retailer. Consequently it is important to understand the decision-making process by which this important strategy is developed. In this chapter the reader will learn:

- The role of core merchandise groups in meeting customer expectations for specific attributes such as exclusivity, variety and quality.
- The use of the merchandise strategy to reinforce and to demonstrate strategic positioning
- To understand the implications of width, depth, availability and continuity in both marketing and financial terms for the retail company.
- The role of brands in the strategy decision: the extent to which they reflect the confidence of the retailers' franchise with customers.
- The need for a merchandise strategy to respond to customer expectations for excitement and change and the implications this has for assortment changes.
- How augmentation may increase customer interest *and* transactions.
- How price communicates positioning.
- How procurement and sourcing is managed against a background of dynamic customer expectations.

INTRODUCTION

Within the space of ten years retailing has experienced a broad spectrum of consumer behaviour. The late 1980s was a period of credit-fuelled affluence and spending. The recession of the early 1990s had a severe impact on expenditure and retailing revenues and profitability. Accompanied by redundancies, house repossessions and unemployment, the result was a deep undermining of consumer confidence which has yet to be restored.

It is interesting to observe the international nature of this phenomenon and the changes in consumer behaviour. As economic prospects improve the consumer response is one of cautious optimism. Furthermore, the retailers themselves share this guarded approach. Data from a number of international sources suggest that the future will be largely dominated by 'needs' expenditure rather than by 'wants'.

This atmosphere of consumer caution is an important concern for retail merchandise strategy. What it does not suggest is a move by the market towards price-led retailing offers but rather the need for retailers to gain a much more detailed understanding of their target customers and to develop more accurate responses to their expectations.

Of the four core components of retail strategy it is merchandise which leads the overall offer. Customer tolerance thresholds towards merchandise quality, variety and exclusivity have been reduced by the increase in competition and retail capacity. International sourcing has made available the dominant brands in most merchandise categories. However, the mix of characteristics (quality, variety, etc.), the price point decisions and the creativity of the visual merchandising, together with selective merchandise augmentation, remain critical success factors in the strategy decision.

In this chapter we discuss the implications of these issues for merchandise strategy decisions. Merchandise strategy can only be successful if it is based upon a realistic assessment of the overall market-place, its recent trends and its expected developments. In particular, we need to investigate thoroughly the trends and expected developments within our specific segment, or target customer group. The proposed model is not biased towards any one set of market conditions. Rather, it is a logical and structured approach to the merchandise strategy decision; see Figure 7.1. It requires management to establish a clear set of objectives from which the strategy process then considers the key component activities.

Merchandise objectives

A set of well-defined objectives, outlining both marketing and financial goals is essential, and is the point from which merchandise strategy decisions begin. Figure 7.1 suggests suitable objects from which the marketing/buying management group can work towards building the customer merchandise offer.

Positioning

Positioning is an important issue. It is essential that the merchandise assortment reflects the positioning strategy within the context of the company and the retail offer. For a retail conglomerate, the issue is important. Often the group operates in a number of segments, and a clear positioning policy is required to ensure that each company subsidiary is identified by its target customer group and is differentiated from other offers that the group may make to other segments within the sector. An example of this issue can be

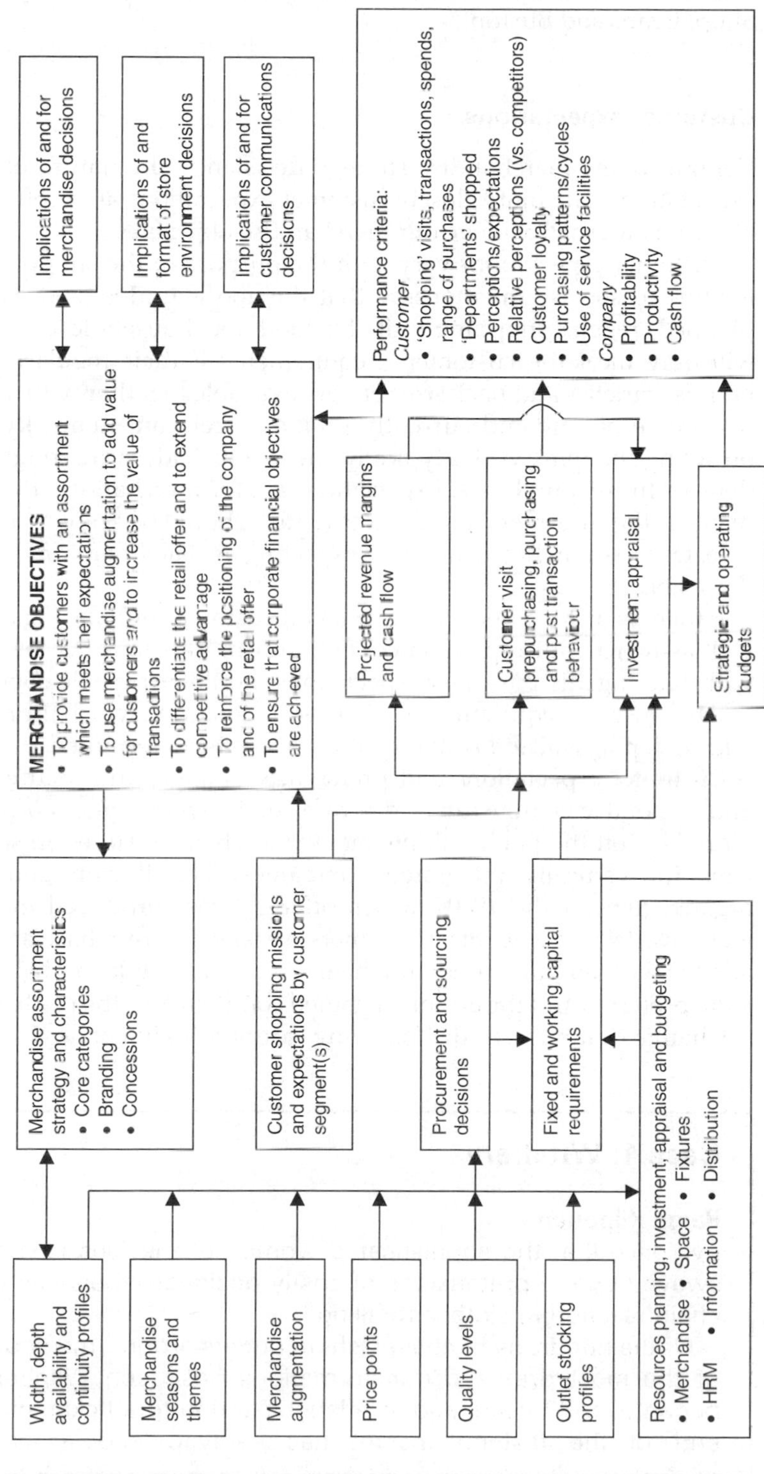

Figure 7.1 Merchandise strategy considerations.

seen with the Arcadia Group, with its Principles offers, Dorothy Perkins, Top Shop, Evans and Burton.

Customer expectations

Central to any merchandise strategy decision is the nature of customers' expectations. The more closely customer expectations are profiled the more likely it is we shall achieve our merchandise objectives.

Customer expectations vary with the purpose of the shopping visit, and for this reason we must ensure that this too is understood. For example, planned, regular shopping visits for food and household consumer items will only meet the customers' requirements if their regularly purchased brands, varieties and pack sizes etc. are available together with a representative range of new and currently promoted relevant items. By contrast, a browsing shopping visit is typically one in which ideas are sought for immediate or future purchases. Expectations are for merchandise that is current, matches the customers' preferences (which should be known) and is affordable. Distress purchases are those expecting availability foremost and brand if possible.

It follows that we need to know about customer purchasing behaviour as well as merchandise preferences before firm decisions can be made. Notwithstanding this, customer expectations should be capable of being quantified because the requirement is for information upon which the *dimensions* of width, depth, availability and continuity can be determined.

Customer expectations and preferences change, and failure to monitor and respond to change can lead to disaster. The replacement of 'bespoke tailoring' by 'off-the-peg' multiple menswear chains resulted in serious problems for vertically integrated companies. The Burton and Hepworth organizations of the 1960s, which offered 'mass produced individualism' were overtaken by events. Customers preferred to purchase at short notice and to take their purchases with them. Continental styles and manufacturers were preferred and the customer gained confidence in the ready-made suit.

Change continues, as the following case studies illustrate.

Case 1: Witchery

Paige Kilponen

Evidence that the sophisticated woman of the '90s isn't so easily swayed by the pretensions of costly designer labels has caused a chain reaction in clothes retailing.

Of the hundreds of chain fashion outlets around the country, one of the most dramatic transformations has been Witchery. What began over 30 years ago as a label catering to a fickle and faddish end of the fashion market has evolved into a classic but contemporary label. The somewhat cheap and nasty image has been replaced by a more upmarket one that has struck a chord with a burgeoning clientele.

The family-owned Witchery company, headed by retailing supremo Peter Lew, has invested a lot of time and money into turning the chain's image around. 'We're at a stage now where consumer awareness of Witchery is high', says national public relations manager Willow Michelmore. 'It's taken many years; it wasn't a sudden decision. We have achieved this new image over time; we have listened to our customers. In the last five years there have been big changes and now it's really being confirmed'.

Michelmore says the renewed interest in chain fashion arises from a preoccupation with value. 'In the '80s, people were more brand conscious and prepared to spend more money. But now people are looking for design, quality, style and which brand offers value. Witchery's vision has evolved from what the market wanted – quality, smart, simple, stylish clothes'.

Marketing, Michelmore says, has played a crucial role in Witchery's re-emergence as a desirable brand. 'It's a marketing mix, a synergy of lots of components. It's the design of the clothes but also the visual merchandising, advertising and the look of the stores themselves'.

While only a carefully selected handful of the 60-plus Witchery stores throughout Australia have been refurbished, the plan is to gradually bring each store into line with the company's new look. The flagship store in Sydney's Martin Place represents a confident move into serious designer territory. 'The position of the store has to change with the style', Michelmore says. 'We have closed stores further out of the city and opened stores in the city precinct'. Being located amid the cluster of import stores such as Chanel, Giorgio Armani, Salvatore Ferragamo and Gucci has its advantages. 'It's a benefit having those stores around the same area because the customer is looking for style and has money to spend'.

Luring customers out of the import stores and into Witchery is all part of the challenge. 'Visual merchandising is the key', Michelmore says. 'People that wouldn't normally shop at Witchery are seeing the windows and seeing the catalogues and are coming in. Advertising is the communication link to the customers. It communicates the whole lifestyle of Witchery'.

Case 2: Cue

When Cue Design first opened a handful of shops in the late '60s, it catered to a very different market. The label became known for its glitzy evening wear during the razzle-dazzle of the '70s and lagged behind the designer labels in the '80s, but has in recent years honed its product and image to fit with the '90s customer.

Owned by Rodney Levis since its inception, Cue has had more freedom to exploit and interpret an evolving market. 'We didn't do any formal research,' says general manager Gary Mathew, 'but we made a conscious effort to put out staff into the stores more frequently. There is much more communication between our retail arm and our design arm'.

That communication has led to a better understanding of one of fashion's most competitive markets. 'Retailers have become more focused on their core market', Mathew says. Dropping the word 'design' from the name in favour of a 'sharper, more modern' Cue was just a small part of repositioning the store among a crowded market of chains all pumping out very similar clothes. A sexy but subtle campaign featuring Claudia Schiffer and strategically placed advertising in fashion glossies caused a lot of women to do a double take.

While the majority of Cue stores are at home in suburban shopping malls, the opening and refurbishment of CBD stores in major cities has helped elevate the label's status. 'I believe that we more than compete with designer labels', Mathew says.

'We're doing a lot more frequent trips and there's more emphasis on quality control and we've added more people into the design area to make sure we've got what's happening now. We don't copy overseas fashion; we interpret it and Australianize it'.

That interpretation of international design trends has obviously been well received, with Cue reporting a 15% growth in sales for 1998/99. According to Mathew, the projected $55 million turnover for this year is due to a combination factors: 'We've got our product right, we're in the right retail environment and we have a strong retail team. We have an advertising coordinator and a professional visual display and merchandising team. It's like a puzzle: If all the pieces are working in unison the results are very strong'.

Cue has invested more than AUS$1 million in opening 12 new stores in the past year, bringing its total number of outlets to 63. This commitment to the chain's growth reflects a confidence that it is reading the market well. 'In the past we tended to do what we believed the market wanted; now we listen to them. We're maturing our product mix, making it more defined'.

Projected customer visit, purchasing and transactions behaviour

From research into customer expectations we would expect additional information on *how, when* and *what specifically* is purchased. This is essential input into forecasting as well as input for merchandise objectives.

A knowledge of visit frequencies, average transaction values and the range of purchases is necessary if we are to forecast revenues, margins and cash flow performance. This gives the company the information input to build financial projections of the business, and in particular gives some perspective of financial commitments for fixed and working capital.

Another vital input that this data provides is to the buying function. Armed with merchandise profile preferences *and* the size of purchases (together with frequencies) a realistic buying plan can be developed.

The *marketing objectives* should imply direction for the strategy to pursue by adding emphasis to the company mission statement. Clearly the primary objective of any retailing organization should be to build customer loyalty, and this will only be achieved by satisfying customer expectations. The ultimate measure of customer loyalty is to be the customers' first-choice store; hence the strategic positioning strategy decision should be reinforced by a statement of differentiation intentions.

The *financial objectives* make the profitability, productivity and cash flow requirements implicit. These will be reflected in the overall performance criteria (Figure 7.1) and will be expressed as stock turn, margin and 'ROI' expectations. A primary objective of the merchandise offer should be reflected in the size of customer transactions and their frequency. Customer transaction characteristics should also be featured as performance criteria and a measure by which financial and marketing objectives are linked.

The merchandise objectives should determine the *quantitative* issues of sales revenue, margins and cash flows as well as the qualitative leadership for merchandise strategy decisions.

Merchandise assortment strategy and characteristics

As Figure 7.1 suggests, merchandise strategy decisions comprise a number of component considerations. The basic formula is described by the strategic positioning statement (see Figures 2.11(a) and (b)) in which the customer value decisions, product positioning, product decisions and product–market positioning give clear guidance to the customers' requirements.

The merchandise strategy must interpret these decisions through the merchandise offer, and clearly there are a number of factors to be considered.

Core merchandise decisions

A central decision concerns *core merchandise groups*, which reflect customer expectations. The trend towards specialization in some sectors has simplified this decision, but for some retailing formats, such as department stores, the decision is not an easy one. There are some attractive growth sectors which have appeal (personal computers) with which the department store sector has had mixed success. These, and similar categories, are difficult products for non-specialists to manage, and a wise move is for customer expectations to be explored with a view to identifying the compatibility of those merchandise categories with the expectations of customers and with their perceptions of the retailer's positioning. Essentially, core merchandise groups should comprise a related, congruent range which offers 'continuity' and offers few surprises to the regular customer base.

Decisions concerning *width, depth, availability* and *continuity* are closely related to those of the core merchandise groups decision. Clearly these decisions are critical, as they involve major investment commitments. An important input is an interpretation of customer expectations, specifically customer shopping missions and shopping selection behaviour. Examples will clarify this. Chapter 5 identified a number of shopping missions. These are important inputs because they prescribe the basic merchandise profile. Customers, who may be described as making destination purchases or planned regular purchasing visits, clearly have merchandise-based reasons for doing so. It follows that they are satisfied with the brands and variety of the merchandise offer. However, a majority of comparison shoppers or perhaps browsers suggests that variety should be a major feature of the merchandise offer profile.

One other important concern is customer shopping selection behaviour. Commercial research (unpublished) suggests that consumers use a structured approach to purchasing. For routine purchases (regular food purchasing) there is evidence to suggest that a 'core purchase' of items and brands occurs, and this may be reinforced, or encouraged, by maintaining a standard store layout (a strategy followed by food multiples) and emphasized by store maps for customer use. However, apparel purchases are not made in this way. Here the customer is seeking specific attributes, often rank-ordered, and the search process follows a structured approach. The criteria comprise, brand style, colour, price range, end-use characteristics and style continuity (i.e. a purchase to match the style of a previous purchase). Clearly, it is important to know the importance of these criteria to core customers and how they may vary. Typically we can expect to find one or two key criteria, such as brand, style or end-use characteristics, and within these the others play an important but less significant role.

The extent to which an organization sees itself as a specialist retailer or seeks credibility as a supplier within a merchandise category influences the width, depth, availability and credibility offer. For department stores this may prove to be a difficult decision, because not only does it involve investment in inventory but also questions concerning the 'balance' of the offer, impact on positioning and opportunity cost are involved. Furthermore, the flexibility of the business may be influenced. Many multiple retailers operate in a varied range of catchments. Each catchment may offer quite different market opportunities, and the decision confronting the retail organization concerns the extent to which it maximizes the localized opportunities available as opposed to the decision to optimize the overall performance of the business. A favoured position is to establish a clear positioning strategy with a statement concerning the scope of the business (its customer group(s), the customer end-use applications it seeks to service and the 'technology' it will use to deliver 'value' to customers), and within this positioning and scope profile decide upon the flexibility of merchandise cover it will offer without blurring the positioning.

Branding decisions

Branding policy is an important merchandise strategy decision. Within the scope of this decision the options considered range from majoring exclusively on major supplier brands through to an exclusive own-brand offer. There are a number of influential factors. First and foremost are the customers' preferences and the way in which these may be translated into merchandise decisions. Preferences for quality may be met either by including major suppliers' brands, for which the suppliers have built a quality reputation, or alternatively, if the retailer's franchise with customers is sufficiently strong (e.g. Marks & Spencer), the merchandise offer may be completely own-label.

Typically, retailers have pursued a mixed approach to branding decisions. They assume that the strength of national and international manufacturer brands is a dominant influence in the destination purchase decision for a number of reasons. First, it is assumed that these 'labels' have distinctive value offers in terms of quality, exclusive design or some other value feature. A second assumption is that they are benchmark products, often for price/ value comparisons, and thirdly they offer the retailer credibility as a category supplier simply by their presence.

The role of own-brand merchandise then becomes one of expanding choice. This may be an extension of price ranges or quality, or a combination of these features. In almost every instance of mixed (manufacture vs. retailer brands) merchandise offers, the retailer brand is positioned as secondary to the 'leading brand'. The reason for this (as described by one retailer to the authors) is that the brand leader is the benchmark, the quality and design leader that initiates customer interest. This assumption ignores the influence of the retailer on customer loyalty. It is significant to note that a leading Australian department store group introduced a range of own-brand apparel items which were positioned below leading labels in terms of price, quality and design. The company assumed, erroneously, that customers were looking for lower prices. They were not: their response suggested they were surprised (even annoyed) that the company should consider them to be price-sensitive. It follows that an alternative strategy whereby the retail brand was positioned to be superior to the leading brands might have been met enthusiastically by store loyal customers. The point apparently overlooked (and possibly not been considered by the retailer) was that the customers were extremely store-loyal, and an exclusive, distinctive own-brand range might have enhanced both revenues *and* margins.

The issues to be resolved by the branding policy decisions relate to profitability, productivity and cash flow. Clearly the mix which maximizes the overall profit margin is the one to be adopted provided that it maximizes productivity, which is measured by stock turn, returns to space and per employee. Cash flow performance is equally important in both the short term and the long term. The attraction of leading brands is that the promotional support of the supplier will create awareness, demand, customer traffic and transactions. Theoretically profitability, productivity and cash flow follow. However, in their enthusiasm to achieve similar objectives the suppliers expand their distribution. Often what follows is fierce competition among retailers, inevitably leading to price and margin reductions. The exception to this may be seen in the (very few) large and exclusive retailers who can negotiate 'special' or 'exclusive' arrangements and can remain clear of the market mayhem.

Concessions can, to a degree, lower the risk of sub-optimal performance. By relying upon a predetermined royalty or rental agreement the host remains clear of specific competitive activities. However, the fact that the concessions are to be found in most competitors' stores, notwithstanding the concessions' own retail outlets, dulls what may have been seen as an attempt to create competitive advantage.

Branding policy should then consider two main objectives: the marketing objective of delivering value to meet target customer expectations (because if it fails to do so the customers will migrate to competitors), and secondly it should be based upon meeting financial performance requirements of profitability, productivity and cash flow. Clearly we are looking at an optimization decision process which has, as an additional consideration, the requirement to build a long-term economic profit by developing a long-term relationship with the customer base.

Seasons and themes

We have seen that customer traffic frequency and spend values are important marketing and financial objectives. By increasing the interest in the merchandise offer, customer activity may also be increased, resulting in more frequent visits and expenditure levels. Both will result in an increase in average customer visit frequencies and the size of average transactions.

Increasing the number of 'seasons' during which an organization introduces merchandise assortment changes is one option used by apparel retailers, and while it is difficult for consumer durable retailers to emulate the concept, many do 'freshen' their merchandise offers by commercializing festive seasons and other occasions, such as Mothers' and Fathers' Days.

Theme marketing meets the same objectives. It aims to maintain or to increase customer visit frequency and average transactions. Themes may be topical and linked to some festive occasion or they may reflect some individualism which creates interest and awareness. Fry's, a Californian electronics store chain, uses different themes in its stores (such as an Indiana Jones Temple theme) to add interest.

Recent years have seen the influence of Hollywood in developing merchandise ranges and in some instances complete retail themes. By extending their influence into fast food outlets and sports and toy departments, film characters are used to create interest (and revenues) in parallel outlets.

Lifestyle themes have been widely used to add interest to the point of sale and thereby generate additional sales. Japanese department stores had considerable success with this approach. Sports equipment sales were generated by creating interest in-store by demonstrating the equipment, and transactions increased by adding a range of service products, such as tuition, equipment after-care and often, where appropriate, such opportunities as golfing holidays.

Augmentation

Merchandise augmentation and related merchandise sales also meet the transaction objectives. The purchase of a major item of clothing or household equipment is used to make sales of high-margin accessories.

Successful merchandise augmentation is based upon detailed customer shopping intentions (and behaviour) knowledge. The 1980s saw widespread adoption of the coordinated merchandise displays used successfully by NEXT in the UK. Such was the impact that it caused Marks & Spencer to make changes in what was, up to that time, a very staid and traditional approach to visual merchandising.

The logic behind augmentation is simple. It is to identify opportunities to make related merchandise sales. At one point in time it was only the aggressive sales assistant who suggested a shirt and a tie to go with the suit purchase; but programmed visual merchandising is now the favoured approach, particularly now that staff are expensive and the majority of retailers have reduced sales staff. Because of this, customer information becomes essential. An understanding of what additional expenditure a customer is prepared to make is crucial: to suggest excessive amounts is seen as intrusive to the customer and is counter-productive in terms of the merchandise marketing and financial objectives.

Price pointing

Pricing decisions are an important component in the overall merchandise strategy formula for a number of reasons.

The most important is the part played in communicating the positioning strategy to the target customer. Strategic positioning comprises a coordinated mix of customer value delivery decisions, product decisions and market (competitive) decisions. Pricing decisions are both explicit and implicit in the positioning decision and its communication. For many retail offers, price takes the leading role in the customer offer.

Price performs a number of roles for the customer. It is used for quality and service perceptions. With the knowledge of this, many retailers pursue a 'good–better–best' policy, using price points as the means by which product differentiation is communicated. Consumers equate customer service expectations and location convenience with price. For example, a distress purchase is typically made with product and location availability as primary motives; price rapidly declines in importance. By contrast, a planned browsing mission may have price comparison as its primary purpose.

Leading prices offer management a means by which merchandise inventories may be allocated. Research (EPOS data) will indicate sales volumes at each range of prices. This information may be used to plan width, depth and availability profiles (and if appropriate continuity implications) for inventory planning purposes. Clearly it is expensive in terms of inventory-holding costs and markdowns to offer a complete assortment range at all price point levels. The key to achieving optimal returns on inventory investment is to identify the value/choice benefits expected by customers at specific price point breaks used to differentiate the value/attribute differentiation within the assortment.

The response to price competition is an important decision for retailers. The price/value response to discounting in FMCG markets has brought about some interesting problems. Tesco, Safeway and Sainsbury introduced 'value' lines to meet the competition of KwikSave and other price-led competitors. This can have problems. The primary concern is that the price/value characteristics are fully understood. Typically, the products are commodity-type items, and there is a risk that sales are not transferred from higher priced items with elements of differentiation to the 'basic ranges'. Furthermore, there is also the possibility that the customer response is one which purchases *only* the value lines, does not consider other aspects of the range, and maintains loyalty to their existing store. The counter argument is that these sales may be lost if no response is made.

The primary consideration should be strategic. In other words, many of the downward extensions have been operational responses to maintain volume. The implications for strategic positioning are important, and an effective merchandise strategy is one which is proactive and has a considered planned response rather than a hasty reactive response, which may have damaging long-term implications.

Quality levels

Quality has a number of perspectives for customers. One view is that it is related to price (as discussed in the preceding topic), another is its perceived relationship to performance, and a third is its link with reliability. It follows that the precise view of quality adopted by customers should be identified rather than assumed. Empirical knowledge will be useful in assortment planning and pricing.

One other aspect of quality, often neglected by management, concerns the relationship between quality and competitive advantage and the role of benchmarking in this equation. Quality shares with customer service the fact that customers assume that minimum levels of quality are built into merchandise offers. This base level is a 'qualifying level' without which the offer is not considered. It is in fact a competitive necessity. Quality offers in excess of this only translate into competitive advantage if quality is an important characteristic in the customers' value expectations set. Much depends upon the competitive situation and upon the role of the purchase. Regular purchases of commodity-type merchandise items are expected to offer a market-determined quality standard. However, purchases of differentiated products may well be determined by aspects of quality not present in competitive offers.

Customer research and benchmarking of leading competitors and merchandise items offer the means by which quality content and its importance in the purchase decision may be assessed.

Outlet stocking profiles

Multiple retail operations may be influenced to a greater or lesser degree by the extent to which local demand characteristics are important. For example, in Sydney, where there has been immigration from Europe, the Middle East and Asia, there is a strong ethnic presence, and it is important for the merchandise offer to reflect expectations and preferences. Both Coles and Woolworths offer 'relevant' product ranges which are targeted to meet cultural preferences. Regular monitoring of expectations and responses should be made within the target customer base. Often large multiple retailers have dedicated functions which consider local marketing as an important activity within the overall marketing function of the business.

Local marketing is not exclusive to markets with obvious ethnic characteristics. Within the UK, which is very small in geographical terms, there exist numerous significant differences. Such differences extend beyond food preferences and include physical characteristics and colour differences.

The use of different retail formats to meet the specific needs of individual markets has implications for merchandise decisions. In the UK, Tesco operates four different types of format: *Express* (small convenience stores on service station forecourts); *Metro* (high street/CBD branches featuring only food with a strong emphasis on convenience/ready to consume products); *Compact* (a representative range from the assortment on medium-sized, off-centre sites) and *Superstores* (fully ranged stores occupying much larger sales areas). Woolworths and Coles have followed this approach in Australia. The approach is as much a response to changing lifestyles as anything. Metro stores have been very successful with time-sensitive customers with a strong preference for convenience rather than price-sensitive customers. In the USA, Gap pursues a similar approach.

We see an important consideration for merchandise strategy decisions. As retail organizations expand their merchandise offers they are confronted with the dilemma of how to merchandise the smaller units. For multiple food operators the problem is of less concern than it is for apparel or mixed merchandise organizations, where choice may be a critical factor in the customers' choice of destination stores. The dilemma is: do we restrict the choice available in each merchandise category but offer representative assortments from each category *or* do we restrict the range of categories within each format offered? This is not an easy problem to resolve without relevant information.

Procurement and sourcing decisions

An effective procurement function is usually one that is either part of a marketing/merchandising department or one which works closely.

A number of approaches to the structure and management of procurement activities may be found.

No one solution is standard. A range of factors can be found, which have an influence on the design of the structure and on its management.

We have discussed merchandise objectives, merchandise assortment strategy and the influences on decisions that result in a strategy finally evolving. It is the role of the procurement function to source suppliers that are able to meet the merchandise specifications the strategy has developed. Following the strategy development exercise the procurement task is one in which the specification requirements are met.

Essentially, the procurement and sourcing task is one in which suppliers are sought with sufficient capacity and capabilities to meet the volume, quality, range and availability specifications required by the merchandise strategy. Procurement is not simply a process which ensures that basic specification characteristics are met at purchase prices that will ensure that target margins are realized. Rather, it is an integral part of the marketing function which, to be effective, must consider the positioning criteria the company plans to transmit.

The three roles of merchandise decisions (espoused by Hirschman and Stampfl (1980)) remain as significant factors and continue to be important in the merchandise selection/procurement strategy process. The *change agent role* is one in which judgement is used to influence customers' decisions. In this role, they influence the trial and adoption of new solutions and product applications, together with the replacement of obsolescent (and obsolete) solutions made so by technological changes or by psychological wear and tear. In some respects we can see the development of specialist assortments as an important role in developing customers' knowledge, appreciation and expanded use of such products. Customer attitudes towards innovation and their acceptance of change are important to establish.

The *gatekeeper role* is one in which the merchandise strategy process acts as a two-way source of information by using judgement on product characteristics (quality, reliability, performance etc.) and 'social acceptance', as determined by customer research and interpreted as 'product specifications' to suppliers.

Opinion leadership has similarities to the change agent role, but it is suggested by Hirschman and Stampfl to be different in that it is *passive* in its nature, having much more of an *information* aspect. They consider the creation of evaluative criteria and the covert influence of 'taste' as opinion leadership.

The procurement activity plays a role in this primary function of a merchandise strategy. Bearing these roles in mind, together with the strategy considerations two important documents are derived.

A procurement specification brief, identifying:

- Critical success factors of the value offer (security, performance, aesthetics, convenience, economy and reliability components)
- Merchandise categories comprising the core offer
- Merchandise demand centres (end-use applications, colour, style etc.)
- Branding policy
- Assortment profiles
- Price pointing, leading price ranges
- Sales volume and inventory level forecasts
- Margins, stock turns and GMROI performance forecasts.

Supplier selection and evaluation brief

- Supplier capacity/capability profiles
- Number of suppliers
- Location and country of origin
- Terms of trade, discounts etc.
- Distribution services required
- Marketing support
- Supplier performance criteria
- IT interface

Logistics and information systems structure and operations

We shall consider these later. At this juncture it should be necessary only to comment that changes in the merchandise strategy are complemented by changes in both the logistics and information systems. For example, a change in emphasis within the merchandise strategy of a multiple food retailer to expand the chilled foods content of the range could involve an investment by the company into extensive chilled storage and transportation equipment (it is more likely that this task would be outsourced) and significant investment in software to ensure that inventory management systems are updated to meet the needs of limited life span products.

Both the logistics and information systems factors may have supply chain considerations. Logistics systems should be reviewed to identify areas of compatibility requirements with those of suppliers. Similarly, the information flow requirements of short shelf-life products differ.

Finally, the location of suppliers must be taken into account. An increase in offshore suppliers (or simply an increase in the number of suppliers) can change capacity requirements profiles.

Strategic and operational budgets

There are a number of steps to be taken in developing strategic and operational budgets.

At a strategic level the organization is required to take a view on what its revenues, expenditures, margins and cash flows are likely to be at the macro (or product category) level. This is required in order to make projections for financial planning of fixed assets and working capital requirements over a forecast period. These will be used to determine levels of support necessary to make the merchandise offer effective (in-store merchandising equipment, logistics support etc.) and to fund purchasing activities.

The approach taken will vary. Large multiple retailers may consider it necessary to develop an industry forecast of sales by merchandise category and then to estimate likely market share(s) that will result from a given price and marketing expenditure level. These forecasts may then be used to produce sales and margin forecasts for the company and for whatever level of disaggregation (regions, branches etc.) that management requires.

Gross margins, contribution and net profit results may then be estimated and the estimates reviewed against the expectations or margin objectives. At this juncture decisions concerning the merchandise assortment strategy can be reviewed. It must be recognized that from the margins realized all of the company's expenses must be met, together with the profit expectations of the shareholders. The budgeting process also considers the ability of the strategy to provide adequate cash flow over both the operational and strategic time horizons.

Performance criteria

A number of topics and considerations are included under performance criteria.

Sales revenues, margins, stock turns and cash flow projections are developed into budgets and are aligned with merchandise categories and outlet formats. These then become central to the implementation tasks which follow and become major planning and control instruments.

Customer response topics are itemized and performance targets established.

Market performance expectations are established. These were discussed in Chapter 4.

Financial performance criteria comprising profitability, productivity and cash flow are established. See the discussion in Chapter 5. Of particular importance is the increase in investment requirements for both fixed and working capital.

QUESTIONS, ACTIVITIES AND CONSIDERATIONS

- What do you understand by core merchandise groups? What are their roles in merchandise strategy decisions?
- A retailing company decided to meet customer expectations for wider style/design and price variety by developing a range of concessions. What are the advantages and disadvantages of the decision?

- What considerations would a department store, with a strong 'upmarket' customer base, take into account if it was to introduce an own-label range? Which product groups (i.e. core, non-core) should feature the retail brand and where should they be positioned?
- What are the sourcing and procurement problems confronting retailers whose merchandise assortments are largely own-brand ranges?

REFERENCE

Hirschman, E. and Stampfl, R. (1980) Roles of retailing in the diffusion of popular culture: microperspectives. *Journal of Retailing*, **56**, Spring.

IMPLEMENTING AND MONITORING MERCHANDISE STRATEGY

LEARNING OBJECTIVES

Given the broad parameters of a merchandise strategy, the next activity is to translate this in a way in which positive customer response will result. The learning issues are:

- To understand the process in which a merchandise strategy is developed into an assortment profile which customers identify and respond to.
- The economics of developing an assortment which responds to customer expectations, supports the strategic positioning *and* contributes to corporate profitability.
- To understand the need for merchandise relevance using the concept of 'edited retailing'.
- To develop a merchandise profile which serves as a marketing and financial directive to buyers.
- To understand the role of pricing in influencing procurement and inventory allocation decisions.
- The sourcing and procurement tasks required in implementing merchandise strategy.

INTRODUCTION

Having decided upon the direction of a merchandise strategy it must then be put into being. The purpose of successful implementation is the realization of the merchandise objectives. Thus we need to ensure that both the marketing and financial objectives are clearly stated in qualitative and quantitative terms. Both will provide detailed planning input.

The *marketing objectives* should therefore identify customer response objectives to the positioning and loyalty decisions that reflect the merchandise role. For example, if we have decided upon the positioning stance suggested by Figure 2.11, the merchandise offer should offer exclusively, wide choice, high quality and classic styles. When asked for their perceptions these features should be prominent in customer responses. Similarly, when asked to identify their first choice for specific merchandise groups their responses should be the store for its designated core merchandise groups. In much the same way the research findings should be strong on support of branding policy.

Financial objectives should be used to guide decisions by identifying quantitative parameters for merchandise performance. These, we suggest, are stock turns, margins, GMROI and CMROI values for merchandise groups and categories.

Furthermore, detailed financial performance requirements should be explicit for suppliers. Not only are target prices (margins) useful for planning but so too accurate forecasts for additional discounts and bonuses. In addition, we should agree supplier availability, delivery frequency and delivery reliability performance parameters which will facilitate our own inventory-holding and management requirements. The overall implementation process is presented as Figure 8.1.

DEVELOPING THE MERCHANDISE PLAN

Merchandise assortment strategy and characteristics

Our positioning statement will have determined the merchandise profile. The implementation task is to deliver this with qualitative and quantitative characteristics. There are some methods available to help here.

Assortment profiles

The assortment profile identifies, for the customer (and the buyer), the positioning intent of the organization. Based upon range width and depth we can make a statement of the type of retailing offer we intend to pursue. Figure 8.2 displays assortment profiles typical of a number of retail offers. This initial statement is an indication to the customer of what is to be expected within the merchandise content of the offer and is an immediate indication to the buying function of the nature of their task. Other characteristics should be added. Availability reflects the planned 'in-stock' position, which in turn indicates service intentions to the customer. *Assortment compatibility* is the effort taken to coordinate merchandise selection into a coherent statement to the customer. It should link merchandise groups into logical buying lots and offer coordination ideas. It should also reflect the way in which the customer plans a purchase. Merchandise selection should reflect customer purchasing characteristics, and should consider their pre-purchase activities as well as actual purchasing behaviour. Customers do purchase in an organized way, and the term *demand rigidity* is used to describe the way in which customers structure their purchasing. The characteristics of the

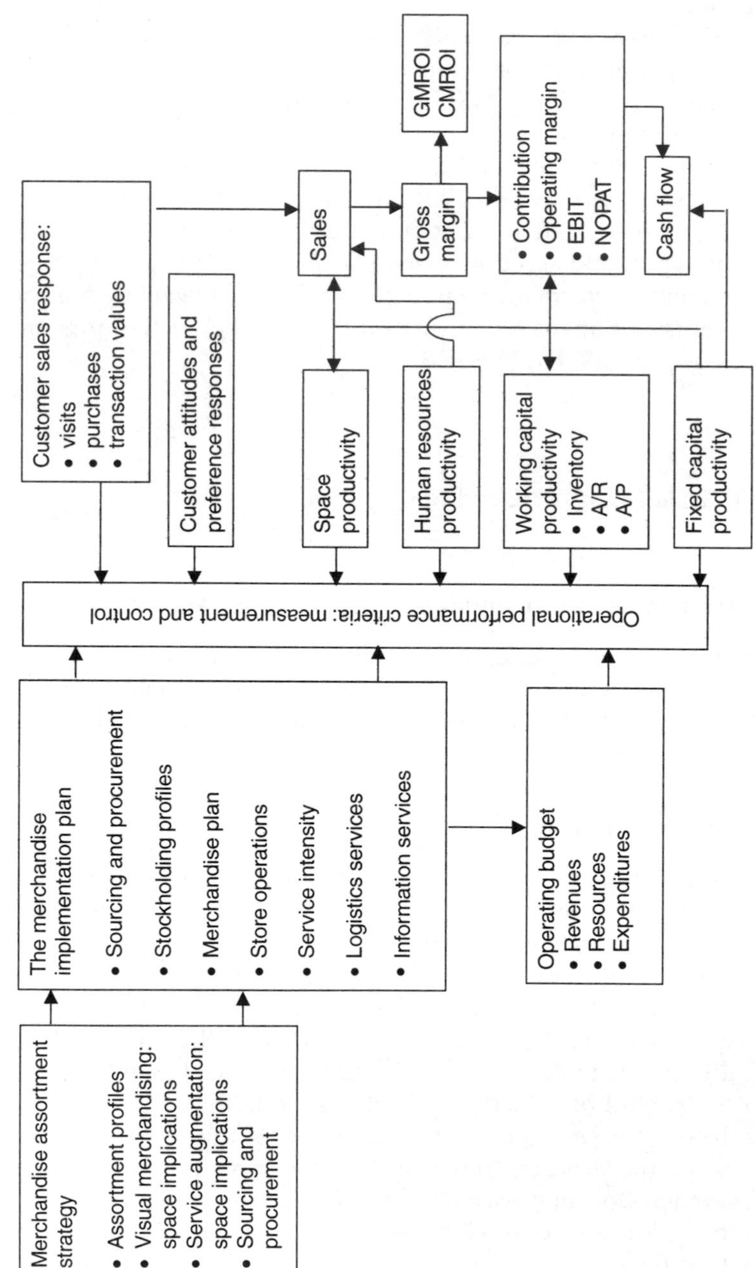

Figure 8.1 Implementing merchandise strategy.

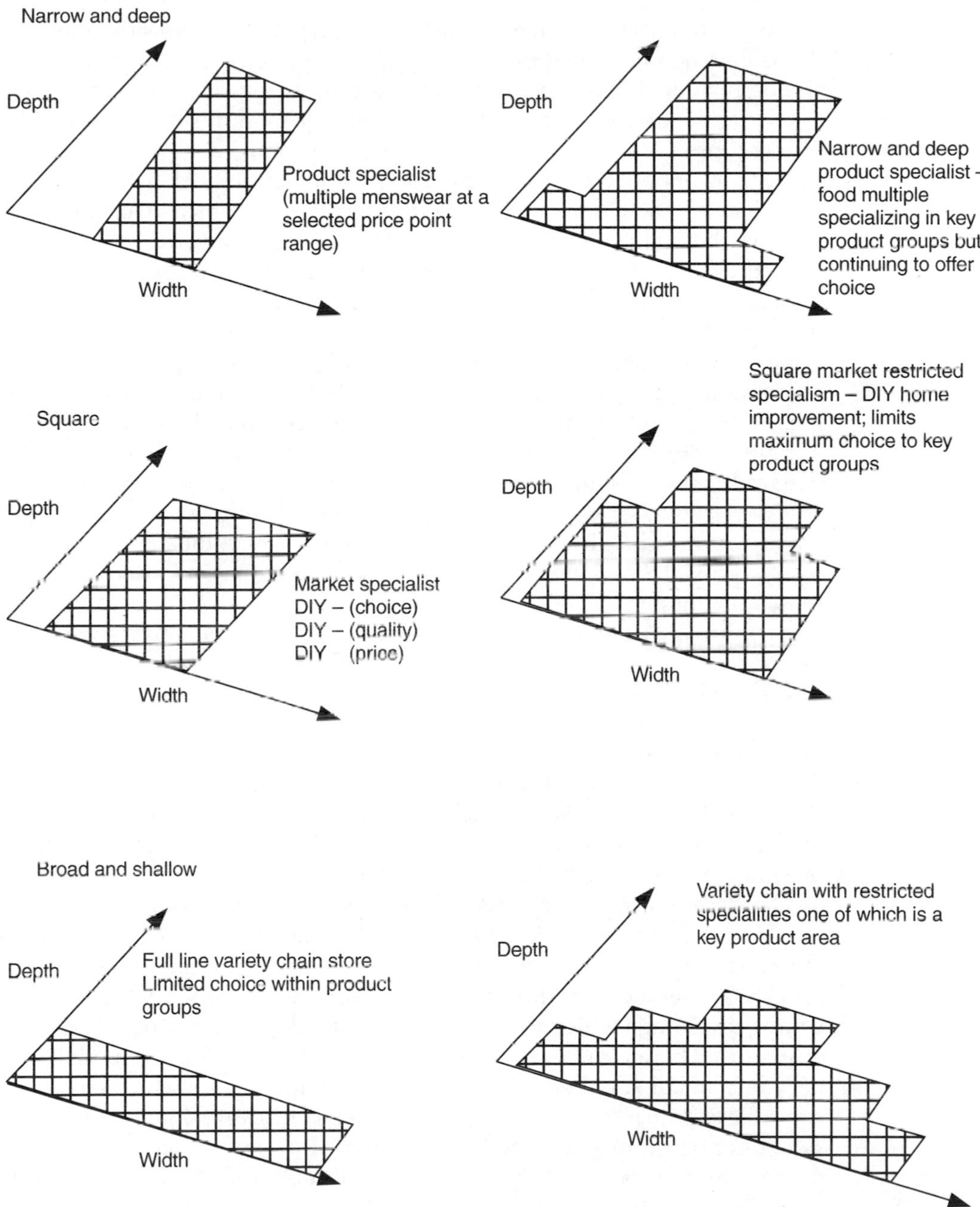

Figure 8.2 Assortment profiles for differing merchandise.

selection process may have more importance for some merchandise categories than for others, but the importance of demand rigidity is such that it may not only determine whether a purchase is made but may also influence the size of the purchase.

Continuity purchasing (china and glassware) is also a consideration. For those merchandise categories subject to this pattern the selection criteria should include the consideration of long-term supply of patterns and styles to ensure the customer the service that specialism in this type of merchandise requires.

The concept of an *ideal stock* list (comprising a *basic* stock list and a *model* stock list) is a useful approach as it offers a means by which assortment profiles may be evaluated. The approach uses the positioning decision to determine the extent of the width of the core merchandise groups. For each core merchandise group a merchandise structure is established. Within each of the core groups a hierarchy is established which is designed to reflect customer buying habits. An example will amplify the concept. For each core merchandise group a *demand centre* is identified. A demand centre identifies the major items of customer interest within the core merchandise group. For example, within a core merchandise group of menswear, the merchandise demand centres would include suits, jackets, trousers, casual wear, shirts and accessories (ties, socks, belts etc.). Within demand centres the next category would be a merchandise *class* e.g. business suits, formal suits, casual suits and travel/lightweight suits. The final group comprises *merchandise categories*, and these are grouped by styles, colours, sizes and materials. Within each group price points are used to introduce differentiation reflecting exclusivity, quality etc.

The positioning issues are determined by the dimensions of the overall ideal merchandise stock list. The overall concept is illustrated in Figure 8.3(a), in which the ideal list reflects the overall core merchandise group offer and the basic and model lists, together with the number of options within each of the demand centres, classes and categories. Again an example may help. Figure 8.3(b) describes the concept: a basic stock list is one which offers credibility and one which will offer a minimum range but one which does, nevertheless, create customer traffic and can identify the organization as having a 'qualifying' assortment. The addition of the model stock list expands the offer and suggests more than a basic range – it suggests specialization. Figure 8.3(c) suggests the assortment offer of a department store, which offers a competitive range which would cover popular demand centres, classes and categories. The specialist retailer extends the offer by using the model list to become a major supplier with a 'determining' range: one which customers consider to be a destination purchase retailer. Figure 8.4 adds a price dimension. Price points may be used to differentiate the offer on some meaningful dimension such as brand or quality. The concept of ideal, basic and model stock lists is useful when branch operation stocking decisions are being decided.

The 1980s saw the emergence and sophistication of specialization, in which the development of the 'ideal' stock list benefited from customer research. The importance of customer transaction frequency and size needs no emphasis here. However, we can manage assortment decisions to increase both during the implementation process. *Edited retailing* is a concept which extends specialist retail offers by using the knowledge of customer

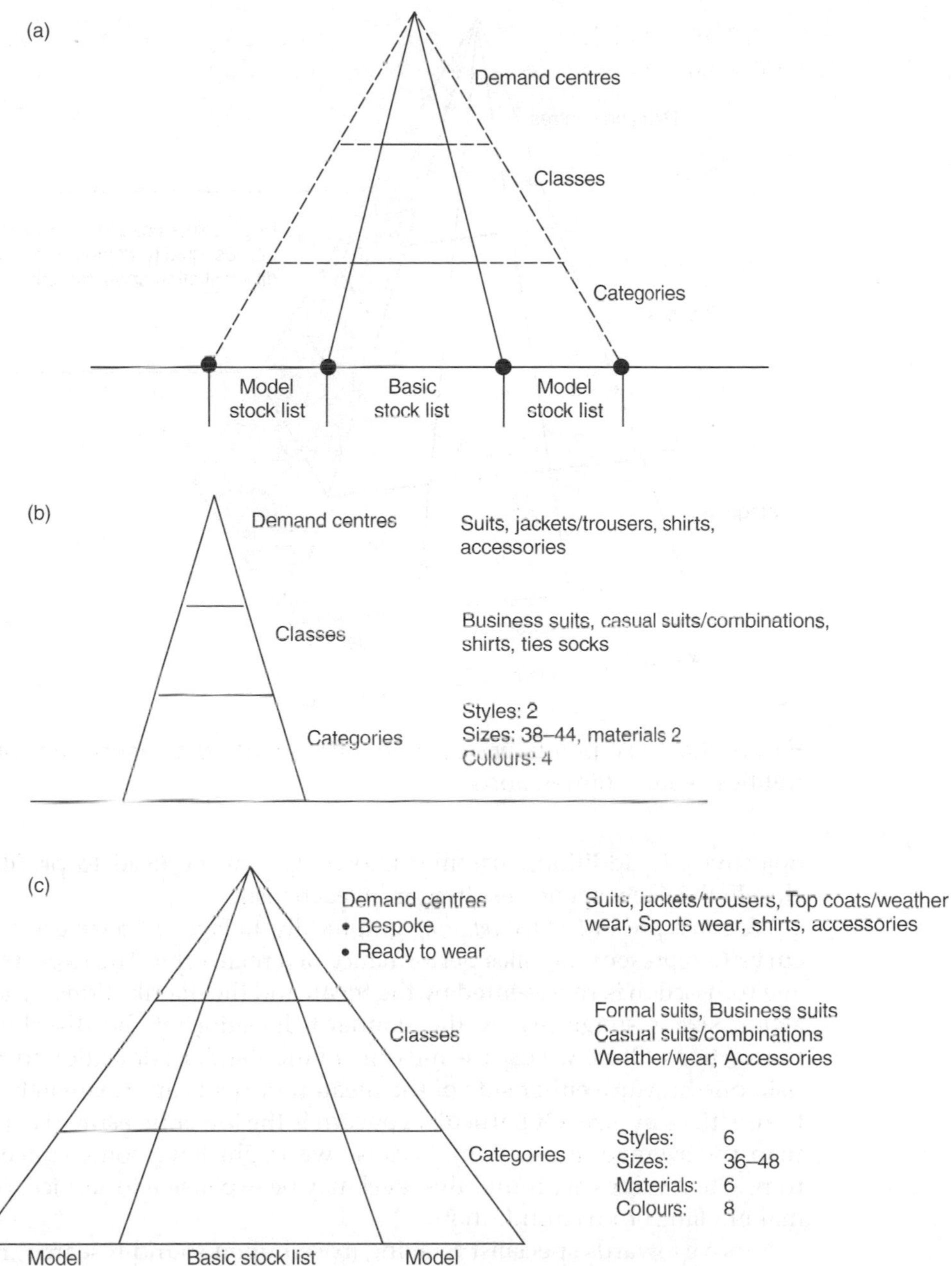

Figure 8.3 (a) The ideal stock list describes the positioning strategy. (b) The ideal stock list: basic plus model stock lists approach. (c) A basic stock list: department store.

expectations and preferences to offer more detail within the assortment. Time and effort will identify customer specifics which can determine the optimal number of seasons (merchandise offer cycles) that respond to customer expectations and which meet profitability, productivity and cash flow

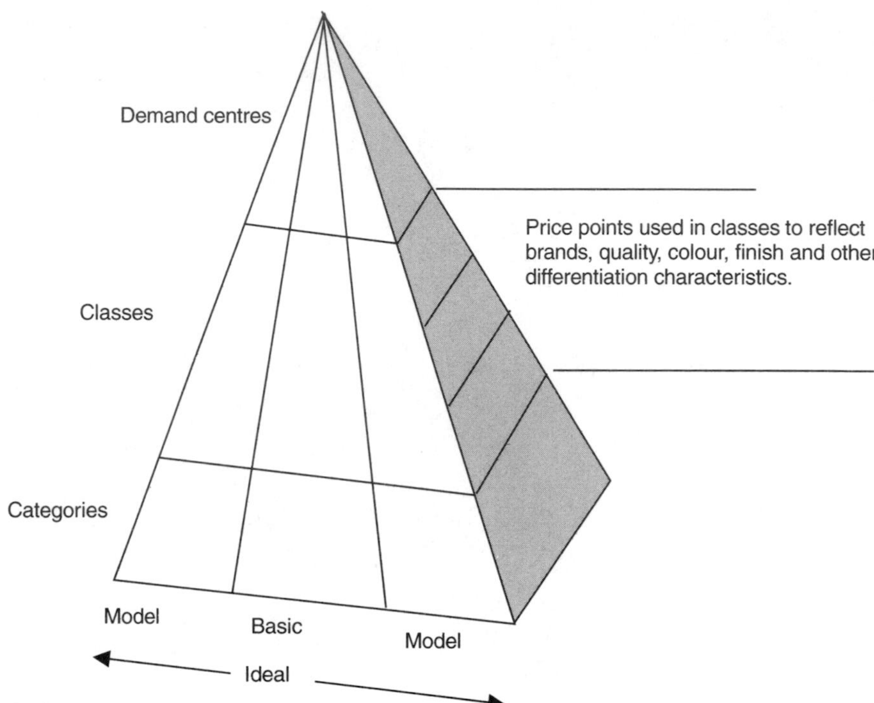

Figure 8.4 Price points are used to differentiate the assortment on competitive feature dimensions.

objectives. In addition, customer knowledge can be used to profile more closely the likely spend resulting from each visit.

We can represent *edited retailing* graphically. In Figure 8.5 we use a normal curve to represent the sales performance of a retail offer. The expected average transaction is represented by the mean and the distribution of the transaction size is suggested by the standard deviation of the distribution of transactions. Often we use the measure of the standard deviation to indicate risk: one measure either side of the mean represents approximately 70% of transactions by size. Of particular concern is the lower measure (i.e. that less than the average transaction), because we might have some concern that transaction values at around this level may be expensive to service, possibly making little or no contribution.

A move towards specialist retailing (based upon sound research) reduces this 'risk' by offering choice, but in a selected and specialist range of merchandise not only can we expect the average transaction to be increased, but it should have less dispersion. Clearly the merchandise offer is crucial. It must be relevant to the expectations of the targeted customer group; if it is not, then we can expect markdown problems. Figure 8.6 represents the likely outcomes of three alternative merchandise offers. It suggests that the average transaction will increase as the offer width is narrowed and the depth increased. Accuracy in matching the offer and customer expectations is

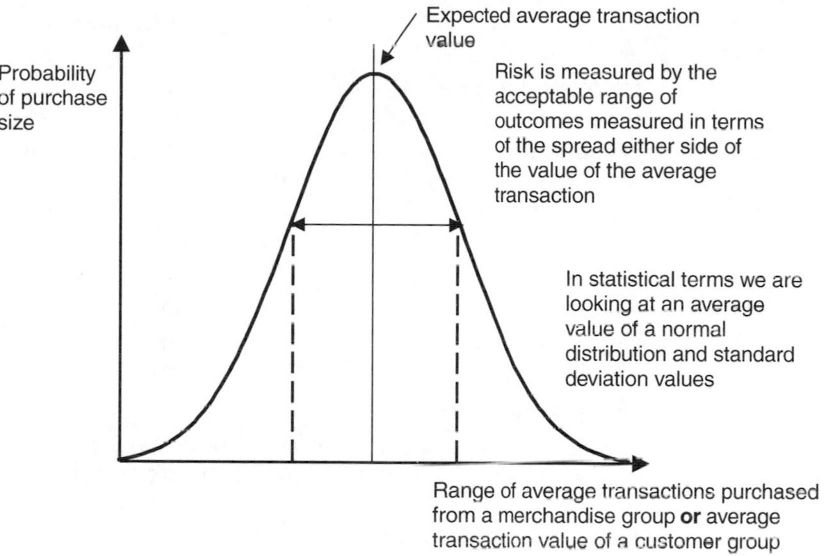

Figure 8.5 Using basic statistics to determine risk and return in merchandise decision making.

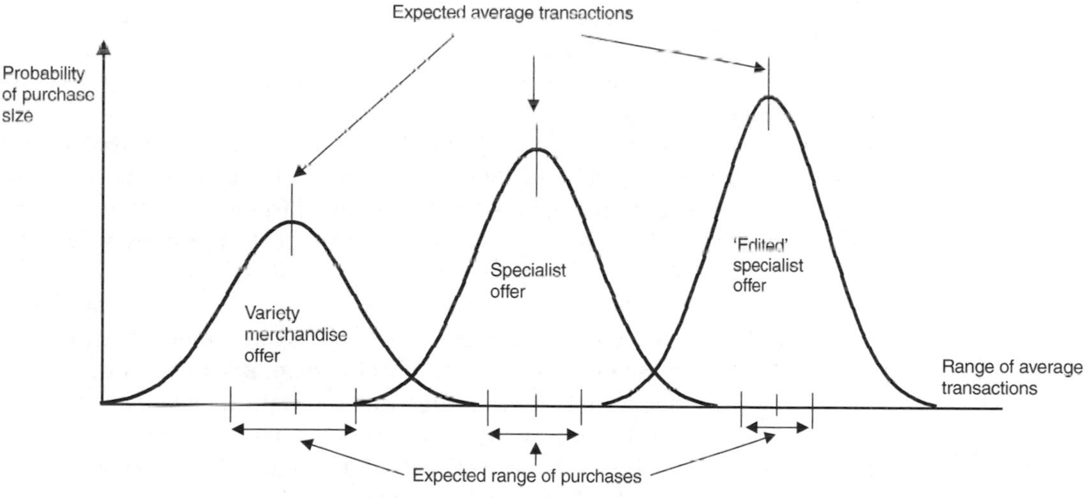

Figure 8.6 Likely outcomes of alternative merchandise offers.

essential. The risk can be offset by using the ideal stock list concept, but it will, in any event, be reduced because the inventory cover support becomes more manageable as the offer becomes more specific.

It is often useful to categorize the merchandise offer popularity (indicated by rate of sale). Within each core category of merchandise it is usual to find

	Merchandise categories		
	A	*B*	*C*
No of product groups	10	5	4
Proportion of sales (%)	75	20	5
Proportion of contribution (%)	70	20	10
Proportion of inventory holding (%)	60	30	10
Width index (%)*	100	90	80
Depth index (%)**	100	80	75
Availability %	100	90	85
Target gross margin (%)	30	25	15
Target stock turn	10	8	6
Target GMROI (GM% × stockturn)	3	2	0.9

* 'Percentage expectations' of labels, brands by customers
** 'Percentage expectations' of styles, colours and size options by customers

Figure 8.7 An assortment profile.

core product items which outsell the others. This may be based upon colour, price or style, depending upon the type of merchandise. Whatever the characteristic, it is good practice to ensure that the customer expectations influencing choice are represented and are used as an indication for establishing stocking parameters. Figure 8.7 suggests one approach commonly used by specialist retailers.

Price points (introduced earlier) may be used to maintain relevant and adequate inventory levels and avoid excesses (and the subsequent markdowns). To ensure that availability and stock turn targets are met, inventory may be allocated to the price point areas where customer activity will be focused. Figure 8.8 shows a typical approach.

Merchandise augmentation uses additional related merchandise to add both interest and to increase the customer spending within a merchandise category by displaying the item(s) together with the primary merchandise. *Merchandise augmentation* is important in the implementation task: it is used as a means of increasing the size of customer transactions and in doing so may also be considered to be an element of customer service. The role of merchandise augmentation (a third and vitally important role) in visual merchandising will be discussed below.

A majority of apparel purchases are made with an end-use occasion in mind. It follows that additional items of merchandise may be purchased to 'add finish' to an outfit etc. Merchandise augmentation is the management insight which places appropriate merchandise alongside the primary purchase merchandise. An example may help. The recorded music market uses merchandise very effectively: alongside a wide range of both audio and video recordings, books, T-shirts, calendars, magazines and other 'music'-related items *augment* the primary merchandise range.

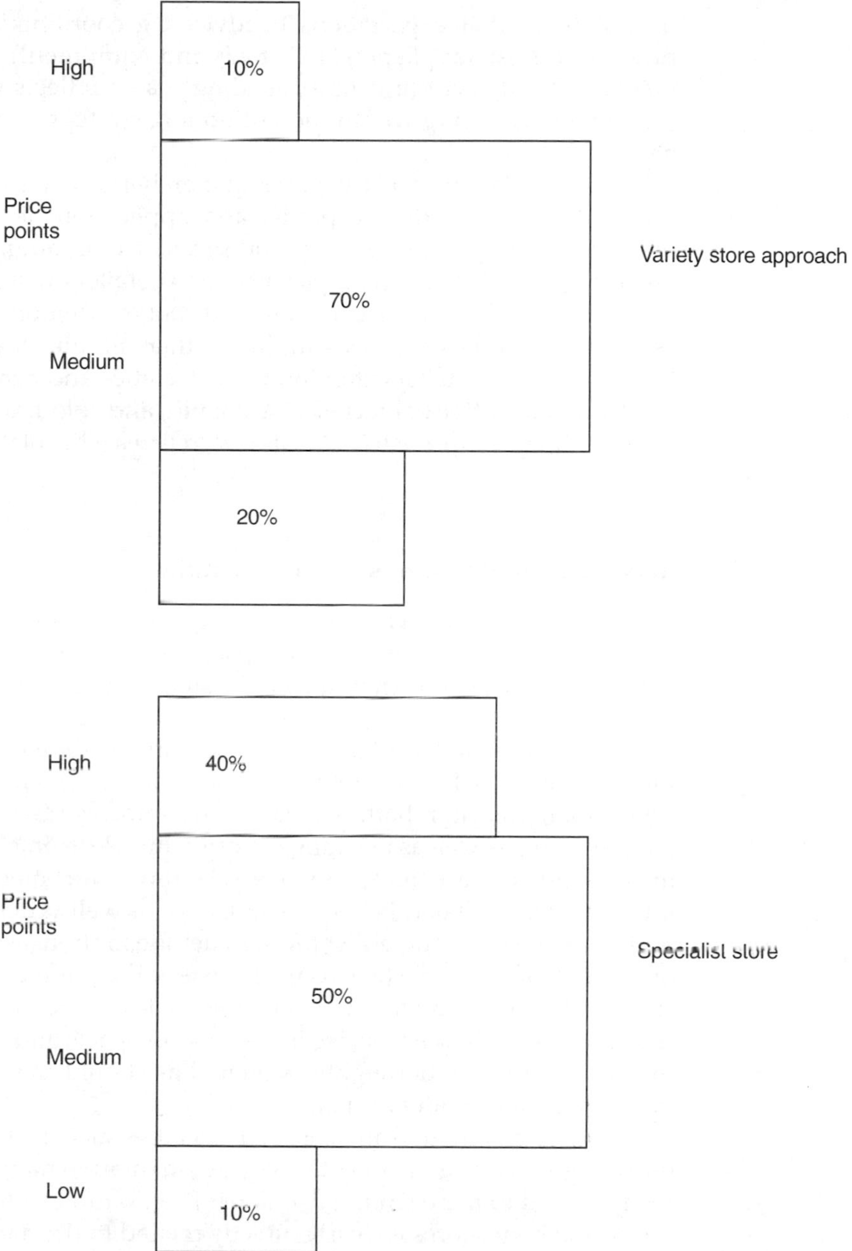

Figure 8.8 Price points are used to guide inventory allocation decisions.

Visual merchandising: space implications

Visual merchandising uses both merchandise and sales area to create persuasive and informative displays which reflect customer purchasing and end-use habits and their expectations for advice, e.g. coordination (apparel, furniture) or end-use (appliances, DIY tools and equipment). The extent of the merchandise density (inventory holding/space) reflects the importance of visual merchandising within the positioning strategy. Some examples may be useful.

Specialist retailers in all categories of merchandise use visual merchandising to demonstrate their expertise and application of their merchandise offers. Often they combine merchandise and service augmentation to create greater impact. Where space permits, food retailers will combine products into regional (country) displays and add cooking demonstrations which act as advisory facilities as well as adding further stimulus towards purchasing. Music and book retailers offer 'browser' facilities and again, where space is available, add coffee bar facilities. Aromatics and colour are used very effectively by Body Shop, Lush (soap) and Darrell Lea (chocolate) to great effect.

Service augmentation: space implications

Closely associated with merchandise augmentation and visual merchandising are service augmentation and space requirements. These will be dealt with in more detail in subsequent chapters but some mention is required here.

Service augmentation has two considerations. One concerns the role of information, which is a combination of customer service and communication. Communication both persuades and informs the customer and takes place in-store as well as in a range of print and electronic media. Clearly the in-store aspects are important considerations for merchandise strategy implementation. It may be seen as necessary, as well as desirable, to give customers use instructions, either through demonstration (as mentioned above) or through other media (e.g. recipe leaflets at the point of sale). Both require space to be allocated within merchandise sales areas. Merchandise demonstrations can be very expensive in their use of space, and thus the cost-effectiveness should be thoroughly evaluated as should their synergy with the positioning of the store format.

Service augmentation also considers facilities such as changing rooms and browsing areas. Thus aspect of service augmentation may be directly or indirectly related to merchandise decisions. The example of browser facilities in music and book stores is clearly directly related to the merchandise, and for some categories (for example popular music) can be important within the customer decision process to use one store rather than another.

Sourcing and procurement

Sourcing and procurement is the management function which is largely responsible for interpreting customer expectations for merchandise variety, quality, exclusivity and availability. In addition, the function plays a major role in achieving organizational financial objectives.

There are many activities which comprise the role of a sourcing and procurement function within the overall role of implementing the merchandise strategy. These can be considered to be both qualitative and quantitative. The merging of buying and marketing roles into one activity has resulted in an increase in effectiveness.

Qualitative aspects of sourcing and procurement are the interpretation of merchandise characteristics into delivered producing attributes; the management of supplier relationships; liaison with potential suppliers; and monitoring the supply market for new and innovative product developments.

The interpretation of merchandise characteristics is in effect interpreting the strategic positioning and value proposition of the organization. Exhibit 2.2 (Chapter 2) prescribes the product characteristics of a strategic positioning statement for a department store. Given these, sourcing and procurement have some direction for their task in identifying suppliers, and this is reinforced by the strategic direction (Exhibit 2.3), which identifies both merchandise characteristics and augmentation attribute and activity profiles. Typically this is sufficient to provide guidance for sourcing and procurement to specify a range of suppliers.

An important aspect of the process of selection is to identify the nature of company/supplier relationships that are to be sought. Among these considerations are competence bases, capacity limitations and lead times, control, flexibility and, if appropriate, political risk and the number of suppliers.

Company/supplier relationships can (and should) extend beyond the issues of control and lead times and costs and flexibility. Just as important are suppliers' core competencies with respect to their ability to meet merchandise specifications which may extend well beyond quality and price and include stringent safety factors.

Control and lead times are particularly important in the apparel sector, where quick response systems are essential if inventory-holding is to be contained but fashion opportunities are not to be missed. For retailers with predominantly staple merchandise assortments, with established product and service specifications and for whom price is an important consideration, the need for frequent and detailed control is much less urgent. However, it could be argued that even food products have an element of fashion (or perhaps fad) and the control element for response is essential. Short lead times and flexibility enable the retailer to make changes to productivity quantities if necessary and to correct quality problems.

Increasingly, offshore sourcing is a significant share of retailers' sourcing spend. Here, too, there are a number of considerations. An obvious concern is that of continuity and the risks that political developments may impose on continuity of supply. In more recent years other concerns have increased in importance. The previously made assumptions concerning the mix of skills and labour costs are no longer valid in many supply markets. Labour costs have increased and for some (for example, Singapore) their governments have decided upon an upgrading of skills and outputs as they move into the information technology markets. The result is that new sources need to be found, and the task of re-establishing and matching quality specifications and skill bases has recommenced. This is clearly so for companies sourcing from the People's Republic of China. Added to this is economic risk. Recent events in Asia have made merchandise imports less expensive. However, their currency instabilities make for uncertainty in terms of planning.

Nevertheless, offshore sourcing will remain an important feature of sourcing and procurement activities. As such, a structured approach should be taken. Given that a wide range of capacities, capabilities and cost profiles exist, sourcing decisions can be planned. Many retail companies identify specific locations on the basis of their merchandise specification criteria requirements such as:

- High volume, competitive price, low quality and technology content
- Short run, customized items
- Seasonal, speciality merchandise
- Core merchandise items, important to the organization and which require frequent supervision

Finally, the sourcing decision should also take into consideration the innovatory capabilities of suppliers. Dominant retailers, such as Tesco in food and daily requirements products, B&Q in home improvement, and Target in apparel and homewares, use their suppliers' R&D capabilities and capacities to develop their own retail brand assortment ranges.

Quantitative considerations are largely focused on realizing the margin objectives and thus are concerned with planning a product mix which meets both margin and cash flow needs. An approach to buying that is becoming popular is described in Figure 8.9. In this approach the activities and costs that are involved in moving a product into the retailer's network and to the point of sale are identified and are used to derive a target and realized margin. The method considers the volume and price targets for the product on the basis that the price is that at which it is aimed to sell the product or product range. Using this as a datum (together with the activity costs) the buying team has some clear input for negotiation purposes. At the same time, a range of performance measures are developed for use as and when the product or product range is adopted. These are particularly useful for appraising future offers from the supplier and for evaluating alternative price/delivery structures.

Cash flow planning is also important and is an important aspect of working capital management. Tully offers both reasons and examples of why and how working capital (particularly inventory) can be and is reduced (if not quite to zero then almost!). He identifies two reasons. One is that for every dollar released from inventories or receivables it 'rings up a one-time dollar to cash flow'. And second: 'the quest for zero working capital permanently raises earnings. Like all capital, working capital costs money, so reducing yields savings'. He adds that it also forces companies to produce and deliver faster than competitors. Tully's examples include food processors Campbell

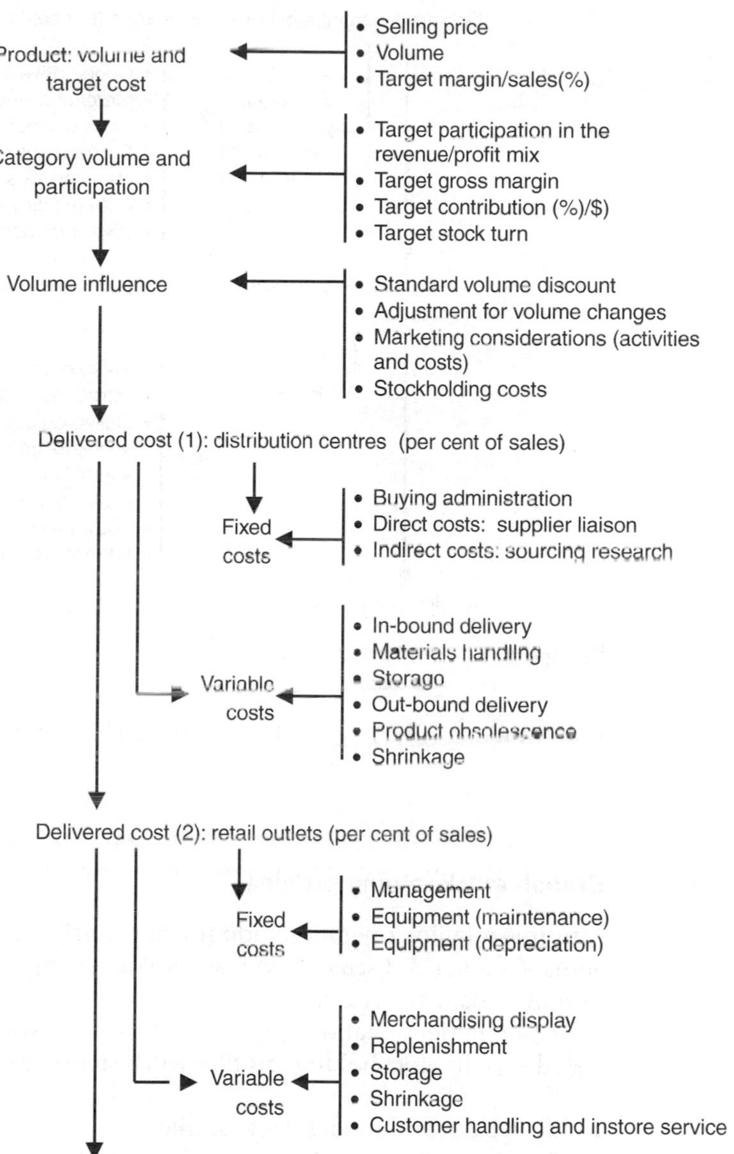

Figure 8.9 Buying: part of the implementation process *(continued overleaf)*.

and Quaker, both of which have made significant changes to their philosophies and operations systems to achieve improvements. For Quaker this resulted in reducing working capital from 13% of sales to 7.39%, freeing $200 million in cash. There is little doubt that IT enhancements, such as EDI, can produce these impressive results. Furthermore, they also reduce costs in supply chain activities. Retailers, such as Tesco in the UK, are showing similar impressive results: their 1998 Annual Report tells shareholders that some

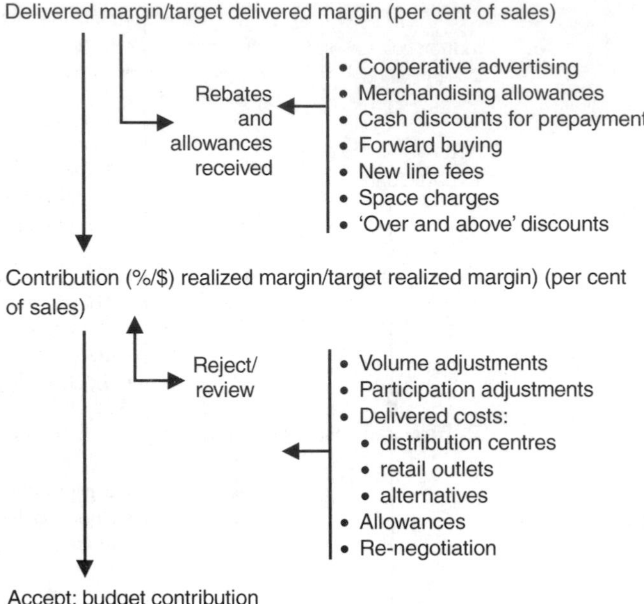

Figure 8.9 *(continued)*

£100 million will be saved from supply chain activities between 1997 and 2000.

Branch stockholding profiles

Multiple retailing operations add further considerations for assortment decisions. Chapter 3 discussed the issues concerning merchandise representation in a chain structure.

At the implementation stage some answers will already have been provided and the stockholding profiles will be based upon the following criteria:

- Ideal, basic and model stock profiles
- The elements of the strategic positioning to be addressed
- The responses to local demand characteristics
- Core merchandise characteristics to be emphasized
- The constraints of space and the responses
- The constraints of access for replenishment and implications for stock holding
- Competitive responses

In addition to these outlet considerations the overall logistics service profile and the ability to maintain in-stock performance should also be evaluated. Volumes, availability and delivery frequency, together with shelf capacities at the store/point of sale are necessary inputs in deciding upon field stock-holding profiles.

The merchandise plan

In effect, what results from all that has been discussed is the development of a planning document. A merchandise plan has five components:

- The *merchandise assortment profile* identifies the key merchandise groups specifying the positioning characteristics, key attributes and activities. This is made explicit in terms of core merchandise groups, their brand structure and their width, depth, availability etc. profiles, together with pricing decisions and price points, merchandise seasons and margin and stock turn targets. The assortment profile will specify basic and model stocks.
- The *sourcing and buying plan* will nominate the suppliers for each product category and the extent of their volume participation. Service issues will also be identified. A *buying schedule* will programme the purchasing and payment activities over a prescribed budget cycle.
- A *merchandise allocation* plan allocates merchandise ranges (and volumes and range representation) to branches based upon branch categories and branch sizes determined on the basis of sales potential, location and competitive profile. The use of 'planograms' achieves this.
- The *merchandise sales plan* identifies the sales to be achieved and inventory to be held throughout the organization. It should detail:
  - Basic and model stock lists
  - Sales forecasts (including sell-through rates and markdowns)
  - Inventory holding (locations and levels)
  - Margin details
  - Stockturn targets
  - Cashflow expectations
  - Contribution expectations
  - GMROI/CMROI
- For the buying activity the plan details *merchandise requirements* by:
  - Sales, sales seasons, regions, stores
  - Categories and products
  - Price points
  - Inventory allocation points

  It should also specify *financial aspects*:

  - Financial requirements by identifying ordering and payment periods
  - Cash flow cycles and volumes

Store operations

The role of store operations is to manage the physical aspects of the implementation activity. Given a merchandise plan, inventory and space allocation profiles, staffing budgets and logistics schedules it is up to the operations team to implement those plans. The task of implementation is crucial to the success of the merchandise plan, and the most important aspect of successful implementation is ensuring that the operations team has been involved in the development of the plan. The operations team must understand and agree with the overall merchandise strategy so as to get buy in. This commitment by the operations team is critical. If not obtained it often results in problems in executing merchandise strategy and in consistency across a chain.

When setting the merchandise plan attention to store size is important, as most stores within a chain will differ in size and shape. An exception to this is the now popular 'big box' or 'shed' format, where most of the stores have been built and developed with precise size and shape requirements. Supermarkets and DDS (discount department stores) formats have used 'Plan O Gramming' for many years now to maximize sales and profits. 'Plan O Gramming' is a quantitative tool or process that helps retailers manage the performance of PLU/SKUs (price look-up/stock-keeping units) on a given shelf or fixture in-store and across a chain. The issue of store size and shape is becoming easier to handle for most smaller retailers as a result of new software packages that can be used to develop product placement within a variety of store shapes and sizes.

The number of pieces of stock required to be carried in-store also needs to be worked out, as the decision to have a storeroom for stock that is excess to display requirements has significant cost imposts as well as staffing issues.

The store location has an impact on the nature of merchandise that is sold. The mix of the merchandise offer can also change, and this can have an impact on the gross profit that the store will achieve. An example of this would be an apparel chain that has a store in a shopping centre and one in a tourist location. Store size, shape and location also play a very important part in deciding what the stock levels in a store should be. Sales volume will also dictate what size store is required. Problems will be encountered if the store either over- or under-trades.

The type of product being sold is important and should be considered when implementing the merchandise strategy. What is the shelf life and product life cycle of the merchandise involved? Is the product a commodity item that doesn't require much selling on behalf of the staff or is it a complex product that requires input by the selling staff? Do staff just provide service or are they required to sell the product? This has particular problems when selecting training and rewarding staff. The ease of handling and replenishing the merchandise has ramifications for staff levels and shrinkage within the store.

The store fitout and visual merchandising play an important part in differentiating one store from another. The physical and intangible aspects of the store must be congruent to the overall offer and should not overpower the merchandise for sale. Visual merchandising also plays an important part in developing an ambience within the store and through good placement of product can also be a silent salesperson.

Staff requirements: service issues

Service intensity is related to the number of staff (sales- and service-dedicated) required within the store overall and departments in particular. While personnel issues are the province of the human resources management area, some are important for merchandise strategy implementation.

For a number of products it is now essential that sales staff have some level of product knowledge. It is arguable that the extent of this depends very much upon how long the product has been available. For example, personal computer customers have become very knowledgeable, and this fact is used by retailers. It is noticeable that as product categories reach maturity the spread of distribution outlet types available widens. From the introduction and growth periods of a product's life cycle, when consumers need advice and information, user knowledge and familiarity builds such that when it reaches maturity their knowledge about application and performance is often superior to that of sales personnel. Thus it follows that the introductory stages of the product require specialist retail outlets with well-trained specialist staff. Later this priority is relaxed as the customers' expectations are concerned with price and availability.

Logistics services

The move towards zero working capital in manufacturing has been picked up in distribution. The Kanban (just-in-time: JIT) concept was originally devised to eliminate waste in manufacturing: any activity or process which does not directly add value to the product is seen as a cost and therefore 'waste'. It follows that holding excess stocks is seen as wasteful. It is interesting to note that time is considered to be an expensive commodity in this regard. Not too long ago inventory was located within a supply chain to provide service to supply chain participants and the ultimate customer. JIT introduced the commitment to short consistent lead times and to minimizing or eliminating inventories while maintaining customer service levels. The rationale is simple; inventories should be planned to arrive only at the time they are actually needed. Effective cost savings become very attractive because not only are inventory levels reduced but so too are facility costs. The cost increases in transportation incurred by placing greater reliance upon improved responsiveness and flexibility are more than offset by the savings in downstream inventories and reduced facilities requirements.

The increasing application of information sciences to the concept of minimal stocks/optimum service has accelerated the feasibility of the concept. Add to this the application of the principles of materials requirements planning (MRP) to distribution inventory requirements and we have the means of cost-effective inventory management. MRP was developed in a manufacturing context as a system for forecasting materials and component requirements from an organization's master production schedule and bill of materials. The requirements for materials and components are 'time phased': in other words they are programmed for delivery when they are required for production.

DRP (distribution requirements planning) uses a different focus. Rather than a 'push' philosophy it uses a 'pull' approach, the emphasis being placed upon identifying and anticipating customer requirements at the point of sale. Thus the DRP concept relies upon forecasts of customer demand being generated and works backwards towards the replenishment and production system. DRP is a time-phased plan for distributing product from manufacturing plants through a distribution network to the point of sale.

Given increasingly sophisticated information networks an emphasis is being placed on accelerating the cost-effective flow of product through distribution networks. Tesco (1998) reported significant cost savings in their supply chain. A shift from batch replenishment methods to a continuous flow of inventory, tracked and monitored but handled as little as possible, is a major change. The company reports that 96% of merchandise lines are reordered from distribution centres using EPOS data. EDI systems at the distribution centres are working towards eliminating paper systems within the picking process.

Other cost reduction systems are based upon the implementation of ECR (efficient consumer response) methods on a partnership basis with suppliers. They give as an example a system of consolidation points where a third-party carrier collects products from several smaller suppliers for delivery to company distribution centres. This approach increases the efficiency of moving smaller more frequent orders by applying JIT replenishment philosophies. Closer collaboration with suppliers to exchange information will increase further the efficiency of the supply chain.

For these and other information-led developments to be effective, close linkages with the merchandise plan are essential. In addition to the planning and performance components of the merchandise plan, additional performance requirements are necessary.

Information systems support

The information system architecture should recognize the decision-making processes of the implementation activities. In particular the system should be capable of tracking sales for the purposes of initiating replenishment throughout the systems of both the retail organization and suppliers. It should also track customers' purchasing activities.

This latter activity is becoming an important input into customer loyalty marketing programmes. Tesco spent some £8 million on the *relaunch* of its customer loyalty programme. (*Superstore*, BBC2, February 1998). This statistic is an indication of the value of customer purchasing activity data.

In addition to revenue-producing activities, the information system should be capable of tracking key expenditure items as they occur. As competition intensifies, and trading hour extensions are used to add to competitive advantage, it becomes essential to monitor incremental costs (and revenues) with a view to evaluating the cost-effectiveness of specific strategic initiatives.

Other activities that can (and should) be monitored include staff deployment and sales patterns over time, out-of-stock profiles (items and time periods) and distribution (replenishment activities, which when matched with out-of-stock profiles can be revealing).

The operating budget

To ensure successful implementation an operating budget is prepared which will detail the revenue expectations, resources required and expenditure levels necessary to achieve the merchandise strategy objectives and the overall corporate objectives.

Clearly specific budget items will vary. A range of performance measures was identified in the appendix to Chapter 5. For the merchandise operating budget you would expect to see:

Revenues:

Sales	by	• categories	by	• regions
Gross margin		• product groups		• locations
Contribution margin		• product		• formats
GMROI		• supplier		• 'seasons'
CMROI				

Resource requirements:
Inventory by

Item		Measure
• categories	$	• sales (cogs)/inventory holding
• product groups	$	• inventory/net assets
• product	$	• days cover
• location/formats	$	• stock turn

Expenses:
Buying staff: number and salary costs
Buying administration support

SUMMARY

A sound merchandise strategy is essential for both marketing and financial objectives to be realized. The merchandise selection has, together with visual merchandising and store design, a strong visual impact which reinforces the positioning statement. An effective merchandise strategy must be customer-led, which details the space requirements and also the service expectations and response necessary by the company.

A plan for implementing the strategy should identify suppliers for each product group; stock-holding profiles (by merchandise group, price point and outlet classification); a merchandise plan (which serves to coordinate the assortment profile, sourcing and buying, merchandise allocation, and financial details, such as payment terms and cash flow performance); store operations (which detail facilities and staff requirements); the logistics services necessary to ensure merchandise availability; information systems support; and finally the operating budget, which details sources of revenues, resource requirements and expense overheads.

The effectiveness of the strategy requires a strong set of performance criteria which monitor actual against planned performance. The three performance elements of profitability (at various levels), productivity (space, staff and working capital) and cash flow are monitored against specified objectives. Successful marketing performance is indicated by customers' sales response and ongoing measurement of their attitudes and responses.

QUESTIONS, ACTIVITIES AND CONSIDERATIONS

- Using the notion of shopping missions, consider and discuss the merchandise management problems of a convenience store which identifies three clear sales patterns in its daily operations. An early morning shopping basket would typically contain milk, bread, breakfast cereals, newspapers, and occasionally tea, coffee or other beverages. During the day the typical sale comprises meat (prepacked), vegetables and fruit, canned items and personal care products. An evening sale will usually contain snack foods, alcoholic and soft drinks, rental videos and newspapers. Assume the role of a consultant to this multiple operation and offer advice on how to analyse the business.
- The 'ideal stock list' describes the positioning strategy of the organization. However, the 'basic stock list' for many organizations is required to consider choice aspects of service together with high levels of availability. How might either a furniture retailer or a specialist menswear retailer handle this problem?
- For a selected retail organization, construct its merchandise assortment strategy and identify the important features of its implemented plan.

Exhibit 8.1

Assortment rationalization to increase profitability

February 1997

Asda (a UK superstore operator) announced plans (February 1997) to remove at least 1000 lines from each store's product range to improve profitability. Both brands and variants are included in the exercise.

In a trial in three stores some 1200 items were removed. In one store up to 25% of its SKUs were removed. It is suggested that the shift is a policy move to enable the own-brand proposition (currently 46%) to increase. It also coincides with a price initiative aimed at competing with KwikSave (a food discounter) *and* to drive category growth. A large number of manufacturer brands have shown significant price decreases. Company sources suggest the rationalization across all grocery categories was to create more space for 'George' (the Asda own-brand clothing range) *and* to remove customer confusion caused by too much choice.

Other views suggest that the rationalization will result in significant cost savings and improve buying (gross) margins. Asda hopes the result will improve inventory distribution and ordering (to and for) the stores, resulting in fewer stock-outs.

The move also coincided with a period of poor performance by the superstore chains and the city view was that Asda was the most likely organization to initiate a 'price war'.

Adapted from: Richards, A. (1997) Asda axes lines in profits drive. *Marketing*, 27 February.

Instead of joining its main retailing rivals with a banking venture or a national loyalty scheme, the supermarket chain has for the moment opted to fight on different ground by concentrating on fewer key grocery brands at lower prices.

Asda reduced its assortment by 1000 lines in each of 211 stores. Brands removed were largely from the bottom 20% of sellers, with more space being given to the top two brands in the sector and to the retailer's brand. The released space has been allocated to the higher margin George clothing range.

Commentators believe that Asda is pursuing the right strategy. The Asda market segment is predominantly families outwith the more affluent A, B and C1 social groups. These customers are more likely to respond to lower prices than to banking services or perhaps a loyalty scheme. Price has always been a dominant feature of the Asda benefit/value proposition and this move is seen to reinforce the offer. It also serves to increase its differentiation in the market.

City comment suggests concern that the price reductions will adversely affect its profit growth record. They identify Sainsbury as one company that suffered the impact that range reduction can have on customer loyalty. KwikSave was also forced to react to customer demand for more brands to be stocked. The price cuts were estimated to be equivalent to 1% off gross margins.

There are suggestions of internal disagreement over the strategy. Some managers would prefer to *increase* grocery and produce ranges. At the same time previous growth performance (and developments) decreased. New store openings were to be less for 1997 and so too were the number of conversions. Asda's 'like-for-like' sales growth had dropped from 10% to 4% in early 1998. The issue at this point in time was that, despite being the consumer's champion, Asda might be unable to afford the true costs of a price war.

Adapted from: Richards, A. (1997) Can Asda afford the real cost of cuts? *Marketing*, 6 March 1997.

And later in 1998:

Research published in November 1998 suggested consumers were 'strongly in favour' of supermarkets expanding into new sectors. Some 15% would be willing to buy supermarket-branded vehicles.

The survey (1000 UK adults) conducted by CLK also found that 45% of consumers were willing to buy supermarket-branded TVs or washing machines; 32% would buy mobile phones and 29% a house or flat through a supermarket-branded estate agent. A third of consumers said they would purchase retail brand foreign package holidays.

The survey uncovered some unease concerning the strength of retailers. Fifty-four per cent agreed with the notion that supermarkets 'hit customers with inflated prices' (the UK Government has an Office of Fair Trading inquiry currently reviewing the issue).

Consumers praised the supermarkets' attempts to offer lower-priced designer goods, with 83% agreeing with the policy.

Adapted from: Darby, I. (1998) Public favours retail 'stretch'. *Marketing*, 19 November.

9 DEVELOPING CUSTOMER SERVICE STRATEGY

LEARNING OBJECTIVES

The importance afforded customer service by retailers needs no emphasis. However, the extent of a customer service offer does require considerable research. This chapter introduces the reader to the important issues.

- Customer service objectives need to reflect customer expectations. If they do not, dissatisfaction will result in the loss of customers to competitors. Excess service provision usually results in diluted profits.
- Research which identifies the relationship between service expectations and perceptions also identifies the relationship between customer service and competitive advantage.
- A structured approach to customer service is necessary if effective service delivery and the organization and management of resources is to produce customer service benefits.
- Positive employee attitudes are transmitted to customers.

INTRODUCTION

For many retailing organizations customer service has become a primary means of differentiating their offer from those of competitors. The global marketing activities of suppliers has led to broadcast availability of most international brands and labels as the suppliers compete for market share. As a consequence, brand exclusivity (from a retailers perspective) has become difficult to obtain. We made a point in Chapter 5 to the effect that a strong own-brand which captures all of the positioning benefits of a retail offer may be a successful means of making a positive and exclusive statement through the merchandise strategy.

However, even if customer service is for many retailers the method for creating exclusivity care must be taken to ensure its 'fit' with other elements of strategy. Zeithaml *et al.* (1990) suggest that as much as they may desire to provide customers with a high quality of service, many organizations continue to face the problem of a discrepancy between customer expectations and perceptions. Often the problem can be traced to the inconsistencies in the service delivery system within the organizational structure of many companies. The authors identify four major inconsistencies: the inconsistency between customer expectations and management perceptions; the inconsistency between management perceptions and service standards; the inconsistency between service standards and service delivery; and the inconsistency between service delivery and external communications to customers.

A service delivery system is the organization and management of resources into activities that produce value benefits for customers. It includes the people, facilities and performance standards required to achieve a positive service performance.

The inconsistency between *customer expectations and management perceptions of customer service requirements* is often caused by management assumptions of customer service requirements rather than a decision based upon research. Customer research (particularly ongoing research) is important if changes in customer attitudes and behaviour are to be considered in strategy decisions. The ongoing research collects and analyses data on customer perceptions of service. At the very least, informal interaction with customers would provide more positive feedback upon which to make customer service decisions.

Management perceptions and service standards: this inconsistency arises from a failure of management to translate customer expectations into better service quality standards. Often the cause is a lack of commitment by management to service quality. Typically this occurs when there is pressure on margins and cost reductions and making the short-term profit forecast occupies management's focus.

The result is failure to revise service standards as long as they meet the other performance objectives, such as productivity of fixed assets. A lack of task standardization within some organizations is another aspect identified by Zeithaml *et al.* A lack of standards often leads to a loss of customers and may prove costly due to over-service offers. Furthermore, performance monitoring becomes difficult, if not impossible.

Service standards and service delivery: even when service standards are established there is the possibility that inconsistencies will occur between the standards set and the service delivered. Zeithaml *et al.* suggest that the contributory factors are employee role ambiguity, employee role conflict, lack of perceived control and lack of teamwork. Role ambiguity occurs when employees are unsure about the expectations of their supervisors due to lack of training, limited communication and lack of performance feedback. Role conflict situations arise when employees are faced with different sets of expectations; management expects employees to sell, but customers expect an emphasis on service. A lack of perceived control takes place when employees cannot resolve customer service problems without reference to a supervisor. Insufficient commitment to the organization results in poor teamwork: a symptom of poor teamwork is the failure of distribution centre staff to recognize the retail branches as customers and to 'work to rule' when shortages due to excess demand situations occur. The authors suggest the single biggest cause may be the work culture, which does not encourage employees to feel accepted and valued as part of the organization.

Service delivery and external communications, if they are incongruent, result in the organization failing to meet its customer service promises. Typically this results as a consequence of sales 'promising' to deliver service that operations cannot possibly achieve, or if they can it will result in reduced performance returns.

If service delivery is to be effective it should be based upon a service ethic or a *customer service culture*. A service culture is an overall attitude or approach to service which is shared (rather than enforced) throughout the business. Nordstrom has approached the customer service culture issue by empowerment. It reversed the organizational structure and adopted an inverted pyramid, with the top position being occupied by customers, followed in descending order by sales people, departmental management, store management (buyers, field management etc.) and then the board of directors.

Spector and McCarthy (1995) provide a detailed account of Nordstrom's approach to developing and nurturing the 'Nordstrom Culture'. It is, in essence, a programmed structure of decentralization with its focus on customer satisfaction and the motivation of employees to ensure its maximization. They describe the Nordstrom approach:

> The Nordstrom culture sets employees free. The company believes that people will work hard when they are given the freedom to do their job the way they think it should be done, and when they can treat customers the way *they* like to be treated. Nordstrom believes that too many rules, regulations, paperwork, and strict channels of communication erode employee incentive. Without these shackles, Nordstrom people can operate like entrepreneurial shopkeepers.

A service culture must be worked at, and is only effective if senior management demonstrate their belief and commitment to a service ethic *and* in so doing get the employees onside, thereby developing both involvement and loyalty.

Customer expectations and customer perceptions

It follows that when organizations promise much and provide little customer dissatisfaction results. However, when firms promise little and exceed the promises made customer satisfaction occurs. The key to customer service strategy is to identify customer expectations and deliver service a little beyond these expectations.

More formally we suggest:

- If customer expectations > their perceptions of the service value delivered: customer dissatisfaction results

- If customer expectations = customers' perceptions of the service value delivered: customers are satisfied... just!
- If customer service perceptions > customers' service expectations: we are building competitive advantage
- If customer service perceptions (relative to competition) > customers' expectations, we are building sustainable competitive advantage

These customer service equations are an important component of the customer service strategy decision. Figure 9.1 identifies many of the considerations to be made during the development of a customer service strategy. The *customer service objectives* should clearly identify the purpose and role of customer service within the retail offer, and from this statement the extent to which customer service is proactive or reactive within the overall strategy.

These customer service equations are an important component of the customer service strategy decision. Figure 9.1 identifies many of the considerations to be made during the development of a customer service strategy. The *customer service objectives* should clearly identify the purpose and role of customer service within the retail offer and from this statement the extent to which customer service is proactive or reactive within the overall strategy.

Chapter 2 proposed a model in which the strategic positioning (a combination of the mission perspective and business scope) resulted in a strategic direction which comprises theme, attributes and activities (see Figures 2.7(a) and (b)). It is at this early stage that basic decisions concerning the purpose and role of strategy must be formulated. In the example of focused merchandise (strategic theme) the purpose and role of customer service should be made explicit. If customer service is to be an important feature of the strategy it is clearly seen as being proactive. Thus would contrast with the role of service in a discount operation, where it is a response to both customer (and competitor) expectations and is therefore reactive.

If customer service decisions are approached in this way we can make decisions concerning the role of service in the overall retail strategy, i.e. the role in which customer service will generate customer response and the implications for resource allocation. If resource allocation is to be cost-effective at the strategic level and cost-efficient at an operational level some initial research is required. From the research, management should:

- Identify and evaluate the key factors of customer satisfaction expectations: customer service value characteristics or *attributes.*
- Identify the activities which deliver the value.
- Ensure that the attributes (and activities) support the strategic positioning via the direction and theme determined in the strategic process.

The interpretation of the research into a customer service offer requires an understanding of the customers' store selection and in-store purchasing criteria and how and which customer service characteristics add value during the process. The notions of qualifying and determining levels of service are important in this regard. By identifying the levels of service that are

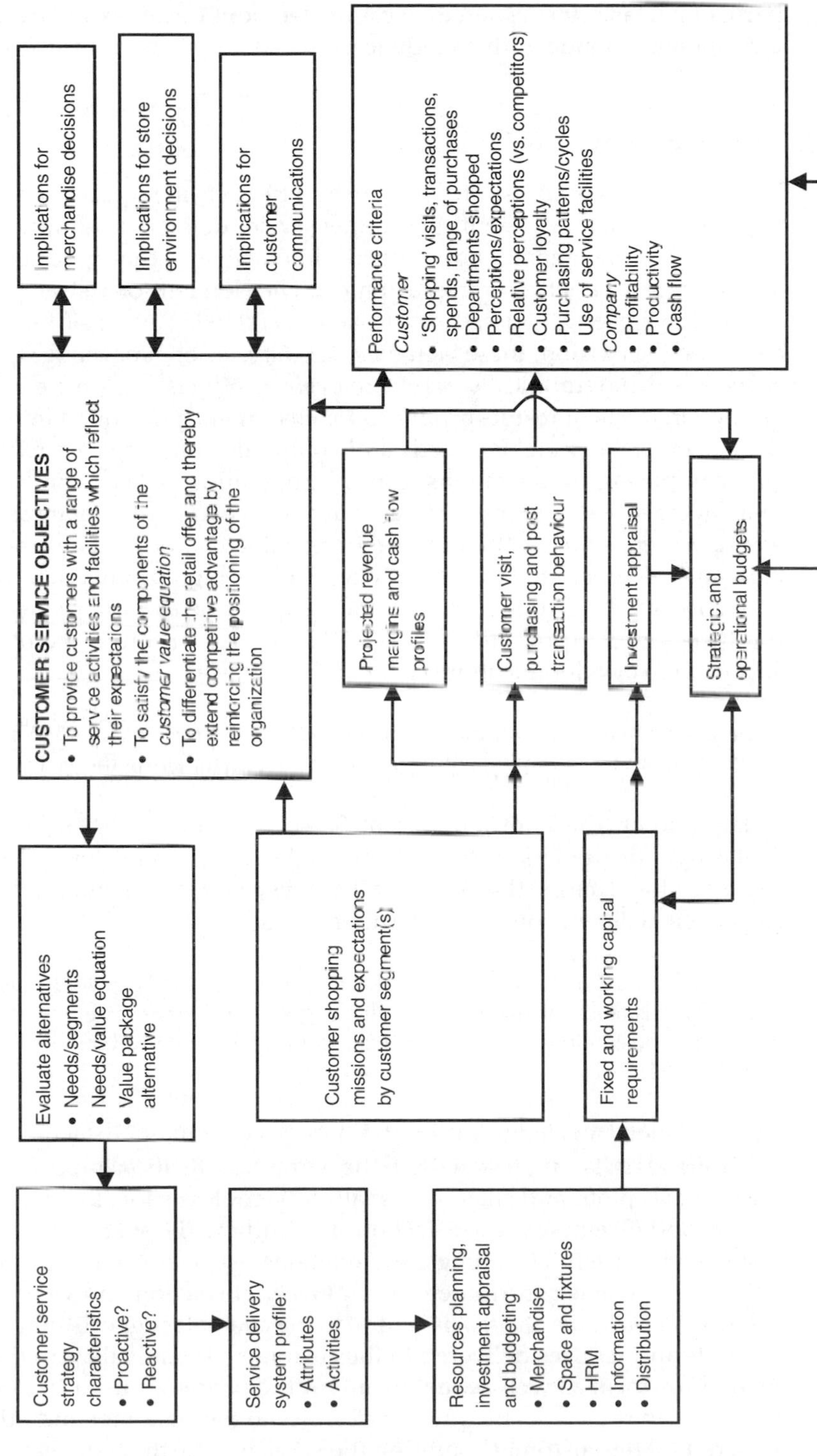

Figure 9.1 Customer service strategy considerations.

important to the critical decisions of 'consideration' and 'conviction' to use a particular retail offer, resource allocation decisions (facilities and expenditure levels) may be made with confidence.

Service delivery

If a customer service strategy is to be effective it requires a structured approach: a delivery system. A customer service delivery is, simply, the organization and management of resources into activities that produce tangible and intangible benefits for the customers. The elements of a 'strategic service vision' have been discussed by Heskett *et al.* (1997). A set of relationships comprise their vision, these being: *markets targeted* on a psychographic basis as well as demographically; *service concepts*, products and entire businesses defined in terms of results produced for customers, positioned in relation to the customers' researched needs and competitor offerings; *operating strategies*, comprising organizations, controls, operating policies, and processes that 'leverage' value to the customers over the costs to the organization; and *service delivery systems*, the physical or tangible components of the system. Heskett *et al.* concluded that companies achieve high profitability by having either *market focus* (targeted customer groups) or *operating focus* (specific product–service applications). Heskett's service vision is helpful as an approach to developing strategy, but as he suggests:

> practicing managers continued to express the need for a set of concepts that would assist them implementing strategies, not formulating them.

Based upon the contributions of Sasser and Jones (1995) and that of Schlesinger (with Heskett *et al.* (1994)) on the determinants of customer loyalty and other factors, the notion of the *service profit chain* emerged. The service profit chain, in conceptual terms, suggests:

> that there are direct and strong relationships between profit; growth; customer loyalty; customer satisfaction; the value of goods and services delivered to customers, and employee capability, satisfaction, loyalty and productivity (Heskett *et al.*, 1994).

These relationships led to the model shown as Figure 9.2.

Empirical tests suggested that the strongest relationships were those between: (1) profit and customer loyalty, (2) employee loyalty and customer loyalty, and (3) employee satisfaction. The authors (Heskett *et al.*, 1997) suggested that, in service settings, the relationships were self-reinforcing, i.e. satisfied customers contributed to employee satisfaction and vice versa.

The *customer value equation* is central to the chain. It suggests that the value of goods and services delivered to the customers is equivalent to the results created for them as well as the quality of the processes used to deliver the results, all in relation to the price of a service to the customer and other costs incurred by the customer acquiring the service. It further suggests it to be a

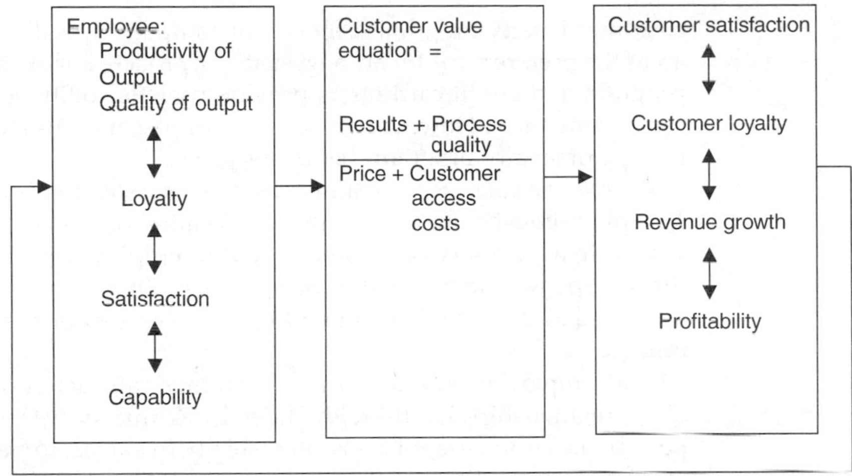

Figure 9.2 Elements of the service profit chain. (Source: Heskett, J. L., Sasser, W. E. and Schlesinger, L. A. (1997) *The Service Profit Chain*. The Free Press, New York.)

customer's perception of delivered value and becomes an influence on purchasing decisions. A detailed view of the equation is worthwhile.

Results (produced for the customer): value is attached to results. Customers buy results, not products or services. Earlier we suggested that the availability of virtually all products was a given, and it is the augmentation that creates value. In a customer service context it is likely to be the service activities delivered before, during and/or after the sale, the service facilities, or the content of the service information or perhaps the service augmentation (see Figure 9.1) that enhances customer value.

Process quality, or the delivery methods, may be as important as the product or service to the customer. Again, our comment concerning service differentiation as augmentation of a standard readily available range of merchandise is applicable. Furthermore, it would appear that customers' views of service process quality depend primarily upon the relationship between customer perceptions of the *actual* service delivered and that expected by the customer (Zeithaml *et al.*, 1990).

Price and acquisition (customer access) costs: convenience has both cost and value. The argument that marketing adds place and time utility to a 'product' and contributes to its form utility is well established. However, it is interesting to note its currency in the development of the 'Metro' and 'Express' concepts being expanded by major food retail chains. The awareness of these companies of the 'time budgets' of their customers is recognition of the price–convenience trade-off that many customers in this segment are prepared to make.

The role of customer loyalty in the service profit chain is another feature of the current service offers of many retail organizations. Customer loyalty activities are extensive in North America and Europe. In both cases the customer loyalty programs offered are company-specific, whereas in other areas the preference is for an 'aggregate' approach. For example, the Fly Buys program and credit card offers provide user flexibility across a number of retail companies. However, there are examples in both North America and Europe of loyalty programs being merged.

The role of employees in creating customer satisfaction is clearly important. The ubiquitously quoted Southwest Airlines demonstrates the extent to which delivered service value is linked to employee productivity between the company and its major competitors. This very large difference is increased by the acceptance of multi-job coverage by both employees *and* the unions.

That employee satisfaction and customer satisfaction share strong and direct relationships has been identified by Zornitsky (1995) in which a European bank demonstrated the relationship between customer satisfaction and employee perceptions of their service capability, their job satisfaction, and their intent to remain on the job.

Evaluating customer service alternatives

Heskett *et al.* refer to the 'balanced scorecard' approach of Kaplan and Norton (see Chapter 5), in which they (Kaplan and Norton) argued that performance measurement based upon financial outcomes places too much emphasis on the outcomes of past decisions and fails to identify and reward outcomes that contribute to future financial performance. It will be recalled that the 'balanced scorecard' includes non-financial outcomes such as human resource effectiveness, innovation and customer satisfaction (or loyalty), *as well as* financial outcomes.

The customer value equation imposes a number of disciplines or demands. Heskett *et al.* suggest six stages which result in service excellence:

- *Understanding customer needs*: typically determined by simple forms of marketing research (such as talking to customers). A customer/company service comment system can provide ongoing interaction; the technology for this is now effective and inexpensive.
- *Determining ways in which needs influence attitudes towards the value equation*: special needs determined by lifestyle (time and financial budgets) can influence access and spend, and therefore convenient locations and convenience products may result in strong positive responses *and* attitudes from a target customer group.
- *Establishing a return on value-enhancing investments*: again research can identify profit returns from service innovation, reduced customer defection and repeat purchases, which may be used to increase the investment level in the relevant service operations be increased.
- *Developing different value packages for various market segments*: the risk/return attitudes of customer groups differ markedly, as do the relationships between advice, installation service etc. and price. A simple but effective

approach has been used by home improvement retailers in which merchandise displays offer a range of price options. The customer has the choice of self-delivery and assembly, self-delivery and an assembly service, or delivery and assembly services. The delivery and assembly functions are outsourced by the retail company (therefore containing no fixed cost) and the customer contracts with the service provider.

- *Developing a single-minded emphasis on value*: retailers have become aware of the customer value equation and particularly that it is multifaceted. Hence the price/value equation of Wal-Mart, the exclusivity/value of Harrods and the quality/value offer of Marks & Spencer (and others) each have significance for their respective customer targets. Once the value equation has been identified it provides an opportunity for developing an organizational capability to extend the service offer to enhance profitability.
- *Ultimately, deciding whether value can be provided at a profit*: given both the costs and estimates of available returns, a decision may be made concerning the viability of a service vision by evaluating the service vision *and* the value equation; see Figure 9.3.

	Segment A	Segment B	Segment C
Common buying factors	• Very price sensitive • Buys national brands • Interested in basic products only	• Seeks 'selective exclusivity' • Price is an issue • Seeks basic elements of service	• Price is not an issue • Seeks exclusive brands only • Service-sensitive
Service factors (Customer value equation)			
Price	5	4	2
Credit	3	4	4
Advice (in-store)	2	3	4
Advisory services • new products • 'favourite brands/ labels	1	3	5
Alterations	1	3	4
Garment care service	1	2	4
Market/customer profile			
Size	$150 million	$200 mill	$75 mill
Average spend/ customer	$40	$80	$200
Average visit frequency	6 visits/year	8 visits/year	6 visits/year

Key to importance of buying factors: Least 1 2 3 4 5 Most

Figure 9.3 Segmentation by service expectations.

Essentially, the six-stage process is proposing an approach to segmentation based upon research of the importance of customer service characteristics to a range of customer segments. In Figure 9.3 a hypothetical situation is presented with the overall market represented by three quite distinct segments. The customer buying factors are indicated, together with a series of rated service factors. The diagram suggests two important considerations. One is that markets do often offer opportunities for segmentation based upon service characteristics, and the second is that, depending upon the market opportunity, competitive activities and an organization's competence profile, a decision may be reached concerning the suitability of competing in one or other segments. Returning to Figure 9.2, we can see a link between employee productivity and satisfaction and customer satisfaction. The link is the segmentation-diagnosed customer value equation.

The use of segmentation analysis incorporates the review of *service facilities, information* and *augmentation* characteristics.

An additional benefit is the *resources profile* requirements (facilities and human resources) that may be developed. Given *customer expectations, projected customer visit purchasing* and *transactions behaviour,* it is possible to decide whether value can be evaluated by estimating the *revenue, margins* and *cashflow projections* together with the *fixed and working capital* requirements implied by the resources profile. Clearly there is a need for managerial judgement at this junction; however, the segmentation profiling exercise described earlier (and by Figure 9.3) will provide an indication of the risk and return profiles of the options available.

Performance criteria

There are three aspects of performance that indicate the success of a customer service strategy: customer responses, market performance and financial performance.

Customer responses indicate the effectiveness of the service programme. Of the measures available the following are important:

Quantitative

- Visit frequency
- Average transaction/visit
- Range of departments visited
- Range of purchases
- Use of service facilities

} over time

Qualitative

- Customer perceptions/expectations
- Customer's relative perceptions of service offer

} over time

Market performance indicators of particular interest are those that are able to show positively the impact of customer service investment on market performance relative to relevant competitors. To this end we would attempt to obtain relative measures of the customer responses in comparison with competitors whose service offer is similar. In addition to these measures we suggest market share and growth performance of service-sensitive customer segments and merchandise groups.

Financial performance indicators would include the measures discussed in earlier chapters. In addition, we would suggest using customer value estimates. Estimating the value of a customer to the business is a very useful method of evaluating in *net present value* terms the effectiveness of customer service strategy and implementation decisions.

Given the customer visit and transaction data it is not difficult to project this to obtain a customer lifetime value. The success of customer loyalty programmes has made a considerable amount of data available. Most of the programmes offer an objective assessment of:

- Average length of a customer lifespan
- Purchasing patterns and values along the lifespan
- The cost of incentives to customers to maintain relevant service motivation characteristics
- Initial investment made to initiate the customer loyalty programme
- The role of specific customer service characteristics in achieving customer performance
- The merchandise/service relationships of customer segments

Given additional research the role of customer referrals can be included.

While calculations determining the lifetime value of a customer include merchandise purchases, it must be remembered that the addition of customer service facilities is an attempt to influence the amount of time spent in the 'store', the size of the transaction, the range of purchases made and the development of positive customer loyalty. It follows that a high lifetime value derives from the longevity of the customer relationship, an above average 'spend' or perhaps both, which is precisely the objective sought.

SUMMARY

This chapter has suggested that an effective customer service strategy is based upon a proactive view of customers' service expectations. It is based upon a customer value equation which, if it is to be derived with accuracy, requires a structured approach to understanding customers and the differences between customer segments.

A customer value equation has a number of alternative approaches for service delivery, such as price/value, quality/value and exclusivity/value. The role of customer service is to support the response to customers in a cost-effective manner.

The financial implications of a customer service strategy should be evaluated. Clearly, regardless of the apparent success of a specific service strategy, if it dilutes profitability, reduces productivity and impairs long-term cash flows (in the context of net present value) it cannot be deemed effective.

QUESTIONS, ACTIVITIES AND CONSIDERATIONS

- For any retail offer format, identify the components of the organization's customer value equation.
- Apply Figure 9.3 to a range of product–market sectors, such as food and related products, DIY, apparel and fast food operations.
- An FMCG retailer has identified a segment that would appear to be service- rather than price-oriented. How would you advise the company to research the opportunity?
- Which elements of customer service will require to be modified by a retailer who adds an Internet sales channel to the existing business?

APPENDIX 1

Superquinn: a customer service-led business

Feargal Quinn opened his first shop in Dundalk, Ireland, in November 1960. It was a small premises of less than 200 metres with a staff of eight. His first Dublin shop opened in Finglas in 1965. So began a progression that led to Superquinn as we know it today, incorporating 16 stores and 11 shopping centres, the market leader in grocery retailing in Ireland. Superquinn's approach was driven by a search for excellence and to be best at whatever it decided to do. Early on Superquinn focused on customer service, innovation and fresh food. Today Superquinn employs more than 3000 people.

In 1973 Superquinn pioneered the idea of in-store bakeries, where customers could actually see that the bread was fresh because it was baked before their own eyes. Over the years a whole range of specialist fresh food departments grew up around the central area of the supermarket, where packaged goods are sold. These include delicatessens, pizza kitchens, pasta kitchens, salad kitchens and even sausage kitchens, where sausages are made in the shop to traditional Irish recipes. All this is in addition to staffed departments that provide a very wide range of fresh fruit and vegetables, meat, bacon and seafood.

The company's Mission Statement is 'To be a world class company renowned for excellence in fresh food and customer service'. Another aspect of Superquinn's retailing philosophy that soon emerged was its emphasis on customer service, founded on a determination to keep close to the customer and to build an organization that would always try to see things from the customer's point of view. To remind his shop managers that their real job is the shop floor, Feargal Quinn always instructs his architect to give them a small, dingy office. People who work at Superquinn's headquarters have sometimes found that their desk disappeared while they have been away on holiday. Feargal Quinn likes to hold meetings walking around the floors of his shops, a preference that sometimes surprises those used to more conventional business encounters.

To better understand their customers' needs, Superquinn conduct feedback focus groups in each store. From there have sprung services such as playhouses for customers' children, bag packing, a rainy day umbrella service, a carry-out service to the customer's car and the removal of sweets from checkouts. Superquinn is recognized throughout Ireland as a company that understands and responds to the customer.

Such aspects of Feargal Quinn's approach to business, though they often catch the popular imagination, are in fact deeply serious in intent. Top of his priority list is the need to stay close to the customer, and Feargal Quinn feels that this is a lesson that everyone in business can learn. One of the ways he does so himself is through regular stints in each of his shops packing bags for customers, and attending fortnightly customer panels at which he listens to groups of volunteer Superquinn shoppers who will tell him how they think they could be served better. Out of such encounters with customers have come many of the innovations for which Superquinn is renowned. A customer at Superquinn is offered a range of services that is unrivalled not only in Ireland but virtually anywhere in the world.

Responsibility and authority reside with staff at the point of contact with customers. The company encourages, trains and rewards staff to serve the customer profitably with food of the highest quality and with a level of service that will generate loyalty. A notable feature of Superquinn shops, in comparison with most other supermarkets, is the number of people that they employ. Feargal Quinn has always believed that customers want a high level of human beings rather than machines. He has proved that investment in people pays off in terms of increased business that more than compensates for additional staff costs. In other markets, the perceived wisdom has been that a high level of service is something the customer has to pay for in higher prices, but in Ireland this has always been impossible because the grocery trade is so competitive.

APPENDIX 2

Brand profile and service expectations

A department store group with 30 branches operating nationwide has been successful with a merchandise range of appliances for which customers' expectations have been for a 'standard' service package typical of popular branded products in its core merchandise groups. The service offered has largely been determined by the retailer. The merchandise offer has been based upon popular models selected from those of each of the major manufacturers. After-sales and warranty services have been set by suppliers to respond to competitive minima. The retailer identified competitive prices as being the dominant feature of the overall positioning.

Some 18 months ago the company was approached by an international supplier of air-conditioning equipment with a view to stocking and selling the supplier's range. They posed no major competitive threat because their price levels were between 15 and 20% above the existing ranges stocked. An agreement was reached and initially sales were achieved at levels which satisfied both the retailer and the supplier. The product sold on its strong international reputation and its reputation for service. Service was extensive. It involved before, during and after-sales activities. The before-sales service offer involved visiting the potential customers' homes to advise on precise model requirements based upon the size of the residence and lifestyle characteristics of the potential customers. Initially the supplier provided liaison personnel for this function. Eventually (after six months) the supplier's staff moved on to other duties.

Strong promotional activity, featuring the high level of service together with recommendations from satisfied customers, generated a large number of inquiries and potential sales.

Before long problems began to occur with increasing frequency. A product fault required the return of an entire production batch. Neither the supplier nor the retailer could meet replacement demand from customers who had been given to believe that premium service was an essential feature of the offer made to customers. While this was an unfortunate 'one-off' instance, it was resolved reasonably quickly. However, another more worrying problem was beginning to emerge. A number of customers began to complain of poor product performance. The supplier was asked to investigate and found that while the products were performing to specification they were inappropriate for the circumstances in which they were operating. The retailer's staff were insufficiently experienced and/or trained for this aspect of the service function. The situation continued to deteriorate and eventually the brand was discontinued by mutual agreement.

A *post mortem* revealed the fact that neither the supplier nor retailer had sufficiently understood the strong relationship that existed between the brand's reputation and the customers' perceptions of service, as well as product performance.

This case is based upon the experience of an anonymous retail company.

REFERENCES

Heskett, J. L., Jones, T. O., Loveman, G. W., Sasser, W. E. and Schlesinger, L. A. (1994) Putting the service–profit chain to work. *Harvard Business Review*, March/April.

Heskett, J. L., Sasser, W. E. and Schlesinger, L. A. (1997) *The Service Profit Chain*. The Free Press, New York.

Kaplan, R. S. and Norton, D. P. (1992) The Balanced Scorecard – measures that drive performance. *Harvard Business Review*, Jan/Feb.

Sasser, W. E. and Jones, T. O. (1995) Why Satisfied customers defect. *Harvard Business Review*, Nov/Dec.

Spector, R. and McCarthy, P. (1995) *The Nordstrom Way*. John Wiley, New York.

Zeithaml, V., Parasuraman, A. and Berry, L. (1990) *Delivering Quality Service*. The Free Press, New York.

Zornitsky, J. J. (1995) Frontline customer capability: measuring and managing customer capability for competitive advantage. *The Conference Board*, 14 February.

10 IMPLEMENTING AND MONITORING CUSTOMER SERVICE STRATEGY

LEARNING OBJECTIVES

Having decided upon the characteristics of the customer service strategy, its implementation requires a clear set of objectives that facilitate this process. This chapter addresses these issues:

- Customer service is seen to add value to the customer offer and to do so with an accompanying increase in revenues and contribution. Unless this occurs there is doubt concerning the extent to which long-term success will be achieved.
- Customers determine service content, quality and value. They use relative measures to make comparisons. Customized service improves effectiveness.
- Customer service decisions *not* based on customer expectations typically fail.
- There is a considerable difference in service offers. Qualifying service can guarantee no more than competitive parity. Competitive advantage is based upon determining levels of service.
- Process design and management are used to identify the service attributes and activities or processes which ensure service delivery.
- Companies who project their values and corporate ethic on the service process achieve employee and customer loyalty.
- Customer service management programs using the costs (of customer service facilities etc.) for acquiring and retaining customers are used to evaluate the value of a customer to the organization.

INTRODUCTION

The important consideration for successful implementation of a customer service strategy is its overall role in the strategic positioning of the business, and therefore the retail offer. The human and physical resource requirements for a *proactive* approach to customer service are quite different from those required when being *reactive*. Similarly, the performance expectations should differ. Using the same argument made for the implementation of merchandise strategy, we suggest that there is a need to ensure that objectives are clearly stated in qualitative and quantitative terms.

Objectives should be set for customer *behaviour* responses (visit frequencies, transactions etc.) and for their *attitudes* towards services and facilities. This ensures that the role of customer service in supporting the increase in customer visits and purchases is effective. They should also be used to ensure the cost-effective use of resources in achieving the customer performance requirements. Both can be made more effective by using the approach suggested in Chapter 3. It will be remembered that we proposed a number of basic *operations management objectives* and *key variables for operations management* which can be identified with specific operations management tasks (specifically, in this context in customer service).

Thus for customer service the relevant objectives are:

- Increasing sales revenue (by increasing customer visit frequencies and customer transaction size(s) per visit)
- Adding value to the customer offer

There are a number of approaches. For example, to *increase sales revenue* we are concerned with efficient management of merchandise availability into, and within, the store. It also requires efficient implementation of visual merchandising and customer handling. Clearly there are a number of other issues, and these will be expanded upon.

Adding value to the customer offer has implications for facilities and personnel. Merchandise location and customer facilities are also important issues, as is the advice offered at the time of purchase and subsequent support.

The benefit offered by adopting such an approach is that using the format proposed by Figure 2.16 (retail operations and control) we are able to link operational performance with conventional management and financial criteria. Furthermore, the approach identifies the *activities* necessary to deliver the customer service attributes expected.

Figure 10.1 proposes an implementation process.

CUSTOMER SERVICE STRATEGY CHARACTERISTICS

Given that a customer service strategy now exists, the task here is to decide on how to deliver the service expectations of customers that will arise from the offer.

Heskett *et al.* (1997) have identified several points to be considered concerning the value content of service delivery. They are particularly relevant to customer service management design and delivery. They suggest:

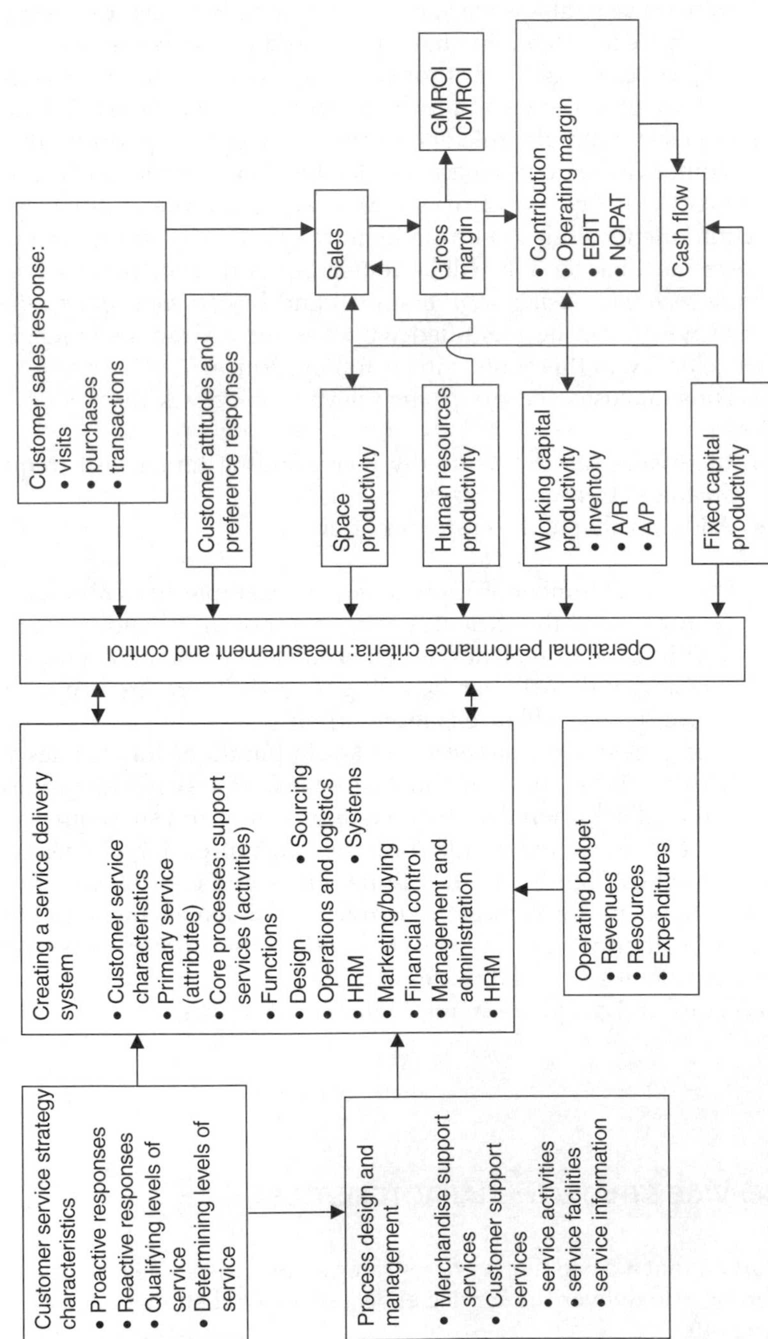

Figure 10.1 Implementing customer service strategy.

- Customers, not providers, determine and define service content, quality and value.
- Customers use relative, not absolute, measures.
- Customer evaluations are based on 'value' delivered.
- Customer expectations should be managed in an attempt to influence perceptions; in other words an organization should not communicate a service delivery package which cannot or will not be delivered.
- Because customer perceptions of delivered value are relative, customization improves delivery effectiveness.
- Delivery cost-efficiency can be increased by adapting frontline employees and support systems to meet individual customer needs.
- Value delivery decisions failing to consider customer needs are unlikely to be successful.

Because of the central role of the customer in the service decision the process requires an initial statement of the characteristics that the company sees as essential in its customer service offer; see Figure 10.1. This becomes a statement of customer service policy.

An essential component of the customer service decision concerns the service response that is to be made. Chapter 9 (Figure 9.2) explored the concept of proactive and reactive responses and their importance in interpreting the organization's response to developing competitive advantage by relating customer perceptions to customer expectations. Figure 10.2 illustrates how a furniture retail chain identifies the role of customer service. The company adopts a proactive response by ensuring that a minimum of qualifying services are available, but emphasizing the proactive responses. The competitive advantage the company seeks is seen in its proactive determining services, which were developed subsequent to extensive research among its target customer group.

The company sought to offer a number of service exclusives with which to establish a clear competitive advantage. These were identified as the involvement by customers in the design process, the extensive services available during the delivery stage, frequent follow-up visits and a 'satisfaction' offer involving a lengthy refund availability (which was rarely taken up). To date this attention to service detail has been very successful. Process management design which details merchandise and customer support services facilitates planning a service response such as that illustrated in Figure 10.2.

PROCESS DESIGN AND MANAGEMENT

The strategic direction of the organization will have determined customer service strategy: it follows that *merchandise support services* will have been determined, as will *customer support services*. Operations management is responsible for implementing these decisions. Both will be determined by

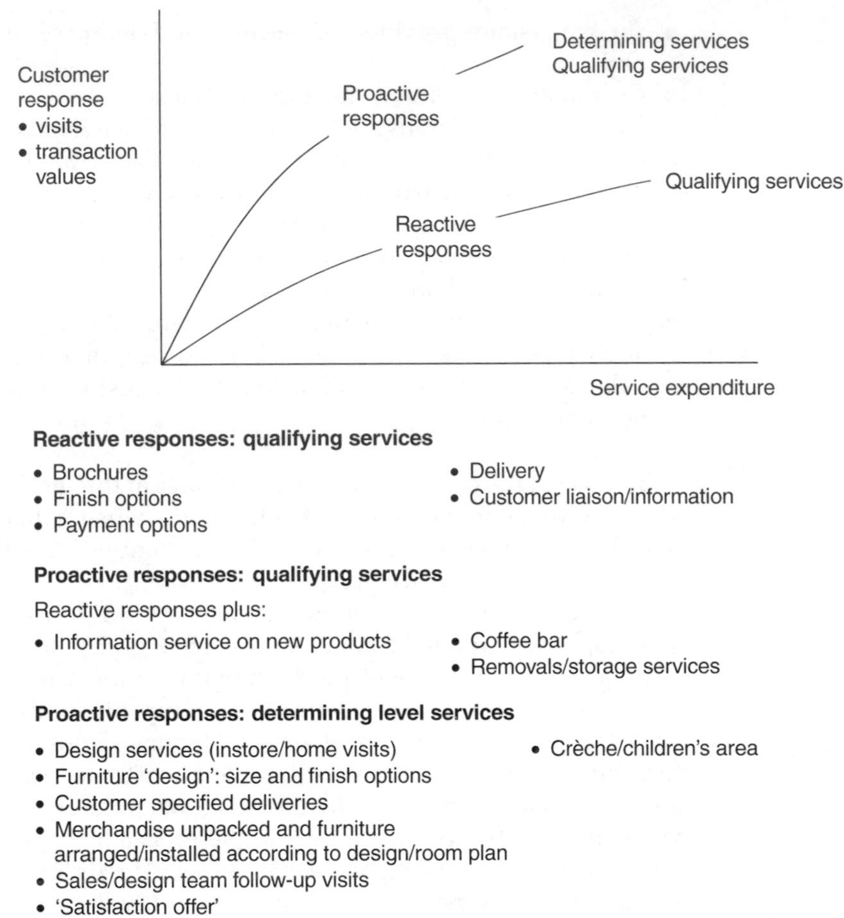

Customer
response
• visits
• transaction
values
Proactive
responses
Determining services
Qualifying services
Reactive
responses
Qualifying services
Service expenditure
Reactive responses: qualifying services
• Brochures
• Finish options
• Payment options
• Delivery
• Customer liaison/information
Proactive responses: qualifying services
Reactive responses plus:
• Information service on new products
• Coffee bar
• Removals/storage services
Proactive responses: determining level services
• Design services (instore/home visits)
• Furniture 'design': size and finish options
• Customer specified deliveries
• Merchandise unpacked and furniture
arranged/installed according to design/room plan
• Sales/design team follow-up visits
• 'Satisfaction offer'
• Crèche/children's area

Figure 10.2 Planning the service response.

the extent to which the customer service strategy is either proactive or reactive, and within this decision the extent to which they are to be resourced at qualifying or determining levels. The strategy issue is the competitive advantage that will be generated; the operations management role is to ensure that customer expectations are met. Clearly these factors will influence the content of services offered.

Some examples of merchandise support and customer support services may help. The dominance of the service content within the positioning statement is clearly the directing feature. The concern of operations management is the efficient management of resources (systems, staff, inventory, customer facilities) in ensuring successful implementation. The examples may be seen as more helpful if we first consider two 'opposite' situations: a full-service department store (whose merchandise/service offer is targeted at an affluent, self-indulgent customer group) and a price-led, limited range department store (whose merchandise/service offer has a budget-oriented customer group as its primary target). Examples of the former are Harrods, Harvey

Nichols, Neiman Marcus, Nordstrom and David Jones. The second group is represented by Debenhams, British Home Stores, Target and to a degree K-Mart.

For the full-service department store, *merchandise support services* would include product adaption (garment alteration etc.); availability of a wide range of product options (colours, sizes, alternative fixtures, power supply options, etc.); purchasing alternatives (in-store, telephone, Internet, catalogue purchasing); and a number of payment alternatives (store charge and budget accounts, EFTPOS, international credit cards etc.). A price-led store would offer a limited range of these services. Typically, product adaptation (if available at all), would be out-sourced, with a charge made to the customer. Availability and choice offers would be applicable only to the core ranges. Purchasing and payment options are likely only to cover widely accepted credit card facilities.

Customer support services would demonstrate similar differences. The full-service department store is likely to offer a range of customer-handling services (wardrobe services in apparel markets, interior design etc.); children's play areas, crèche and child care facilities; and customer lounges and restaurants (which may offer a number of alternative menus and service options). Durables purchases will be supported by delivery, installation, maintenance and service contracts; customer support may also include regular information on merchandise updates, uses and servicing offers; and customer service staff are often ascribed liaison roles with specific customers. The price-led store would offer a minimum (qualifying level) of service.

It follows that, given the decisions on which services to include in the product–service portfolio, their implementation follows. Process design and management will prove to be invaluable. By identifying the customer service attributes to be included, the necessary activities may then also be identified. Process management design techniques may be used singly or in combination. For example, Pareto analysis may be used to identify and to rank order customer service attributes. Service mapping may then be used to identify activities and the support systems, employees and other resources necessary to support service objectives.

Some of the questions to be asked include:

Customer specific:

- Who are the target customers?
- What is their estimated visit and purchase profile?
- What are their lifestyle and shopping lifestyle characteristics?
  - Lifestyles — *Activities*: work, leisure, family, shopping; *Interests*: home, fashion, food; *Opinions*: themselves, stores, products
  - Shopping-related lifestyles — *Activities*: frequency, regularity, planning, time; *Interests*: extent, knowledge of alternatives; *Opinions*: expectations, preferences, perceptions and attitudes (likes/dislikes of service offers and specific stores).
- What are the implications for customer service?

Company specific:

- How does this customer service offer differ from the existing offer?
- What are the resource requirements and what are the investment implications?
- What, specifically, are the performance criteria for both merchandise and customer support services?
- What is the expected competitive advantage and can it be achieved at the planned levels of cost?

Competitor specific:

- What is the expected competitive response from market leaders?
- Will the planned competitive advantage continue to be viable over time? If not, what adjustments are likely to be envisaged? What are their implications for resource requirements?
- What contingencies (therefore) should be considered?

From the answers to these questions the activities, facilities and information components of the service offer can be identified. Figure 10.3 is a proposal for developing a customer service planning approach. The answers reached enable a broad customer service design to be developed. From this the customer value attributes are identified, and these, in turn, identify the

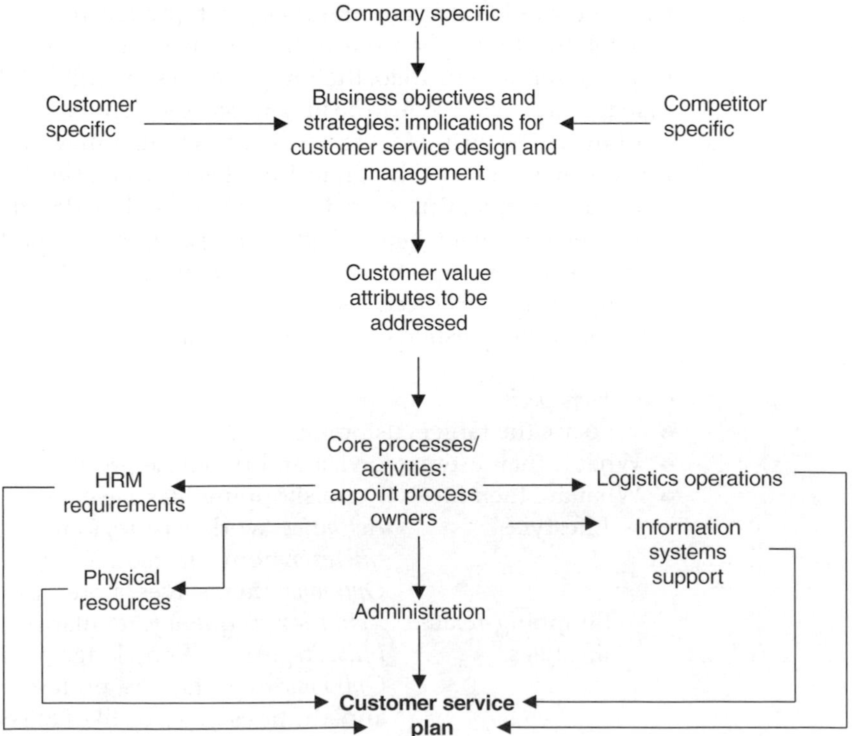

Figure 10.3 Developing a customer service planning approach.

processes which will comprise the customer service offer. The customer service plan will detail what is to be achieved and the resources required for its implementation.

The store operations plan will identify the activities and functions which together will deliver the customer service offer to the customer. Using the model developed in Chapter 3 (operational management and strategy), process design can take place. Figure 10.4 continues the example of the small chain of exclusive furniture and home furnishing stores.

The service attributes reflect an obvious customized offer, and clearly the company is a service-intensive organization with both primary and support service characteristics. It is also apparent that the majority of the service attributes are labour-intensive, requiring skills and experience, both of which will need to be managed effectively.

The activities/processes involved are next to be identified. In this example there is the suggestion that the processes are specialist and contain a large human resources input. A large specialist and human resource-biased set of processes is more difficult to manage. The task of negotiating with the process owners can prove difficult because there is likely to be joint ownership of some of the processes. For example, Design, HRM and Systems may share the ownership of the design activity, with Financial Control having more than a passing interest in asset management (the CAD equipment). The outcome is likely to be a combination of what might appear at first to be some strange alliances. The purpose of using process design (and subsequently

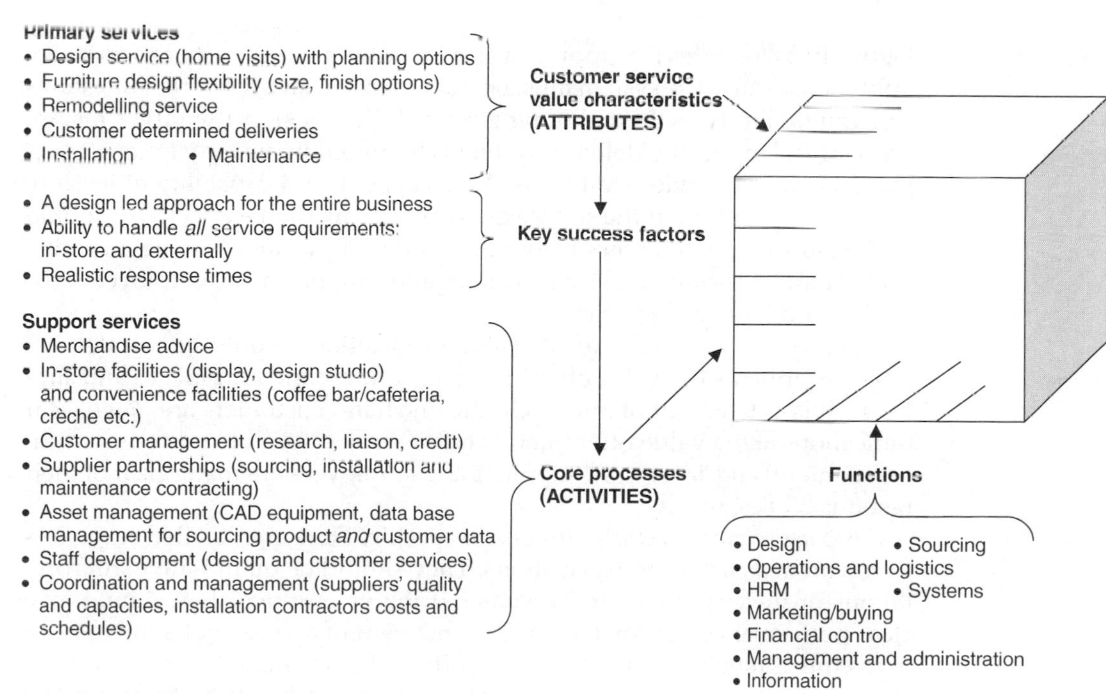

Figure 10.4 An example of process design: the customer service plan.

process management) in developing an implementation plan for customer service is simply to identify the most cost-efficient means of implementing the strategy. Hitherto, retailers have not approached the task in this way. Rather, it has been common (and remains so) in many organizations for the operations functions to undertake the obvious tasks. However, the influence of information management within many organizations has been to identify the key success factors (critical success factors) of an organization and to identify the information needs which reinforce the efficacy of the KSFs and in so doing enhance the competitive advantage of the business. The process design/management approach encourages operations directors to look at *all* the available alternatives and to resist the obvious solutions of traditional alignments in favour of structures that result in more effective service value delivery *or* more cost-efficient means of maintaining the service value currently delivered.

CREATING A SERVICE DELIVERY SYSTEM

A service delivery system is:

> the sum of information and non-information support systems, location, layout, customer management devices, décor and ambiance, and employee amenities (Heskett *et al.*, 1997).

Figure 10.5 illustrates this approach and identifies the necessity of a cohesive approach. Clearly the system must be customer-led, and the earlier questions concerning lifestyles (and shopping-related lifestyles) of the target market are a critical input: the delivery system is bounded by its target market segment, customer service strategy and the capacity and capability of its store operations planning. If the service delivery system is to be effective it should be developed with reference to four other, ongoing, influences: the corporate 'value' ethic, customer service objectives and (importantly), employee satisfaction and loyalty objectives.

The *corporate value ethic* (or its value proposition) should be a statement which represents the value offer to both customers and employees and suppliers. It is a statement of intent. On the one hand customers are given clear indications of the value offer (merchandise service, format and communication content) and 'internally' suppliers and employees are made clear of their responsibilities.

Customer service objectives are service-specific. They are detailed responses to researched customer expectations. They should be quantitative interpretations of the customer service value attributes. As such they should give clear performance parameters for each element of service. For some service items this is much easier than it is for others. For example, for merchandise characteristics (such as availability, width, depth and continuity) it is much easier to establish quantitative objectives. Others may require more thought.

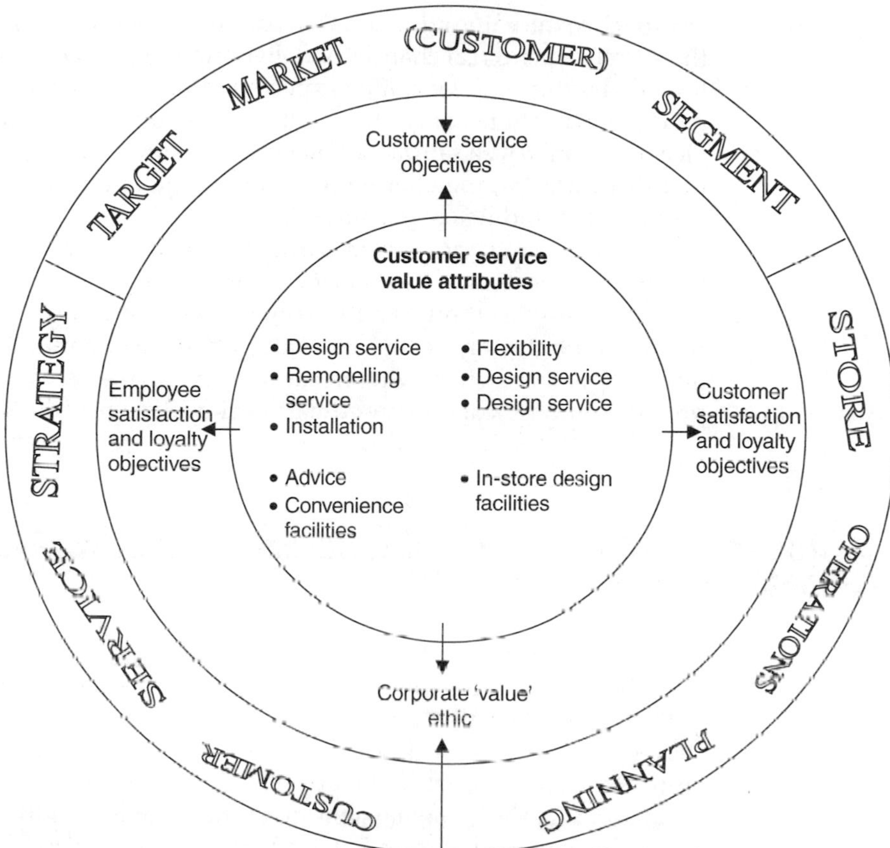

Figure 10.5 The service delivery system (developed from Figures 10.2 and 10.4.) (Adapted from Heskett *et al.* (1997).)

Delivery performance is not difficult; it can be measured by the achievement of customer-specified targets. The more qualitative aspects of service value, such as design services and advice, may be measured by regular research to monitor customer satisfaction levels.

Customer satisfaction and loyalty objectives: the purposes of a customer service offer are to support the corporate positioning of the organization *and* to develop and manage customer loyalty. It follows that customer satisfaction and loyalty objectives should be measured in terms of customer visit frequencies, customer expenditure value and profile, and the longevity of the customer relationship. Qualitative measures are also necessary, and the focus groups operated by many companies are an effective means of identifying both the strengths and weaknesses of the customer service offer.

Finally, *employee satisfaction and loyalty objectives* complete the service delivery system. The contribution by employees is an essential feature of the service offer. It can only be effective if employees are both satisfied with their roles *and* loyal to the company. The first requirement is an agreed consensual approach to the value ethic and the customer service objectives. Without this the system has no real chances of delivering the service expectations of customers. Furthermore, it can be expected to fail as disenchanted employees become reluctant to complete tasks that are central to the success of the service offer. Employee satisfaction may be measured by ongoing staff surveys and focus groups, together with more quantitative measures of staff turnover and the findings of exit interviews.

The service delivery system is an organized and cohesive approach to customer delivery service. Heskett *et al.*, (1977) provide service industry examples of its success. It offers a fundamental benefit in that it coordinates the service attributes and activities that have been identified by the process design approach. Given what needs to be done, the service delivery system provides a framework for coordinating and managing the service offer.

CUSTOMER RETENTION AND ACQUISITION: IMPLICATIONS FOR RESOURCES, PLANNING AND INVESTMENT

A customer service strategy has a large resources commitment, and consequently *all* resource requirement implications should be identified and all options and alternatives evaluated. We have established the need for the strategy to be developed around aspects of the expectations, perceptions, attitudes and behaviour of the target customer group.

An aspect of shopping missions that is necessary to address is that, regardless of the dominant mission, some attention must be directed towards developing *customer continuity*. This may result in a large program, such as the Tesco, Sainsbury and Safeway approaches, or to smaller (but effective) offers, such as those used in New Zealand, where a number of retailers offer free services etc. as an incentive for continuous patronage. The issue is one of how much should be invested in *attracting and retaining* high-value customers.

Blattberg and Deighton (1996) develop a model quantifying expenditure levels required both to attract and retain high spending customers. One example, Lands End, the catalogue casual clothes retailer, operates with very high levels of inventory to ensure high levels of availability. The authors cite a quotation of the Company's CEO, William Land:

> If we don't keep the customer for several years, we don't make money.... We need a long-term payback for the expense of coming up with a buyer.

The authors include McDonald's marketing objectives, directed towards increasing user frequency:

> The corporation's managers noted the value of what they call 'super heavy' users – typically males aged 18–34 who eat at McDonald's an average of three to five times a week and account for 77% of its sales – and they planned their marketing efforts accordingly.

A senior executive is quoted as saying:

> it is easier to get a current customer to use you more often than it is to get a new customer.

It is easier and typically less expensive, and is a marketing fact well known to the established direct marketing companies. It was (and remains) an operating necessity for catalogue businesses when they became active almost 100 years ago (earlier in the USA). It is arguable that part of the current (1998/99) success attributable to Tesco in its market share conflict with Sainsbury is due to its superior management of its customer loyalty program: stronger loyalty, larger transaction values.

Blattberg and Deighton make a significant point concerning the role of customer communications:

> As communication tools become interactive, marketing managers talk more about goals that pertain to individual relationships, such as share of customer requirements, customer contact outcomes and customer satisfaction measures

and:

> Growing a business can therefore be framed as a matter of getting customers and keeping them so as to grow the value of the customer base...

Thus a major consideration for a customer service strategy concerns how management might best determine an optimal balance between customer acquisition and retention and subsequently the allocation of resources.

Blattberg and Deighton introduce a concept of *customer equity* which is derived by first measuring each customer's expected contribution towards offsetting the company's expected fixed costs over the expected life of that customer. The expected contributions are discounted to arrive at a net present value at the company's *target rate of return* for marketing investments. The discounted expected contributions of all current customers are aggregated. It follows that the goal of maximizing customer equity (by balancing acquisition and retention activity costs) is proposed as the criterion for marketing program success.

The authors explain that while the two main determinants are the cost of acquiring customers and the future profit stream from retained customers, other factors have an influence. For retailing, these will include branding policy, product pricing strategy, customer loyalty programs and communications strategy decisions.

A simplified explanation of the approach is offered by the authors. The process is initiated by estimating the shape of the company's customer acquisition curve. Operating management is asked to provide two points on the curve: the current level of acquisition and the highest number of customers the company could (perhaps *should* is more realistic) reasonably acquire in a given time period. Managers are asked to give information concerning the customer service spend in the previous year to attract customers and the spend per prospect, and to estimate the conversion rate of prospects. They are then asked to estimate the likely conversion rate if no budget constraints had been imposed (see Figure 10.6). The $ cost per prospect, the conversion rate and the unconstrained estimate of conversion are then used to decide upon the optimum amount to spend to acquire a customer.

To establish customer retention costs, managers are asked how much they spent on retention activities in the last year, the number of customers identified at the beginning of the year, and the proportion of those customers retained. In addition they are asked to estimate the retention level if no budget constraints had been imposed.

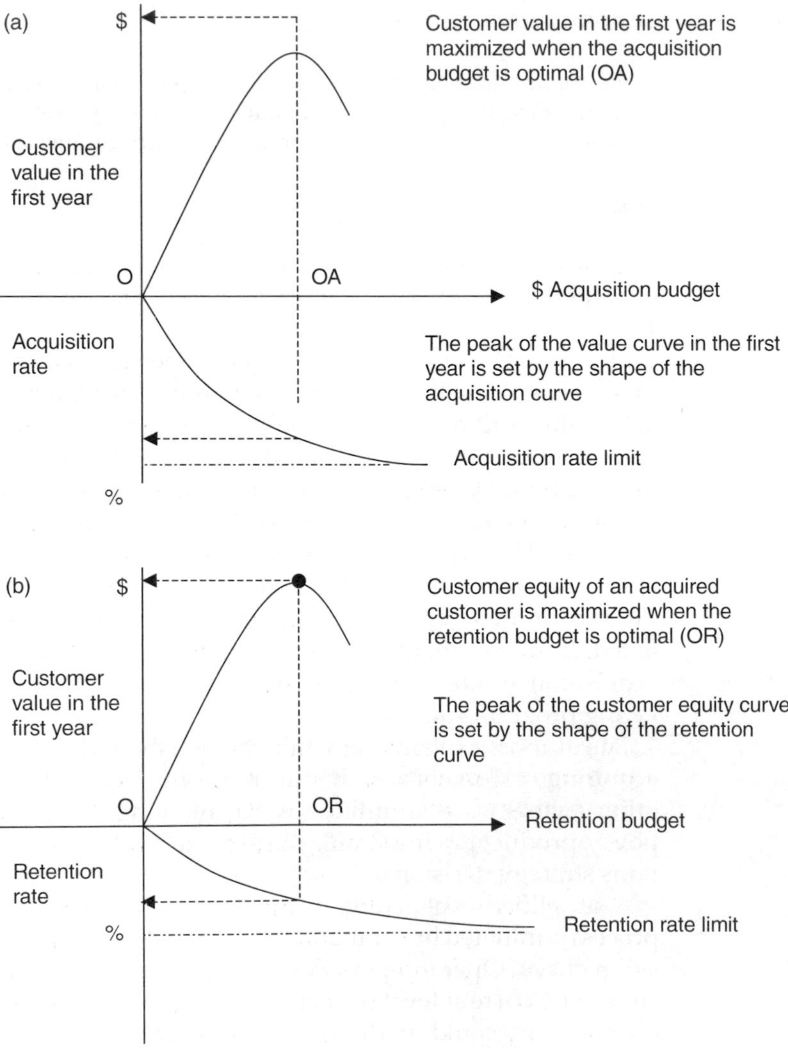

Figure 10.6 Budgeting to (a) acquire and (b) retain customers.

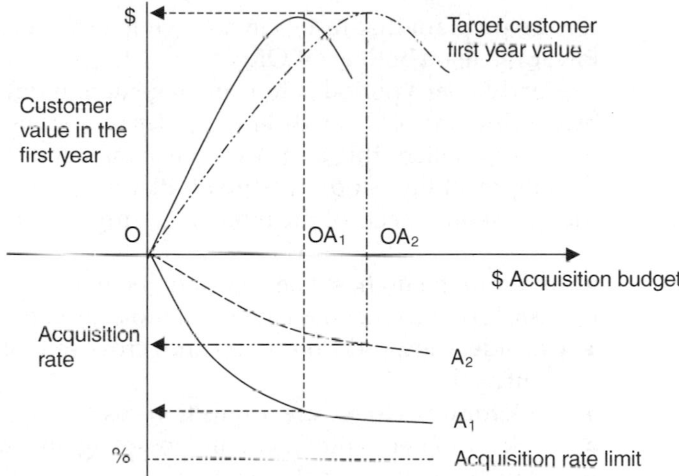

Figure 10.7 Customer acquisition spends.

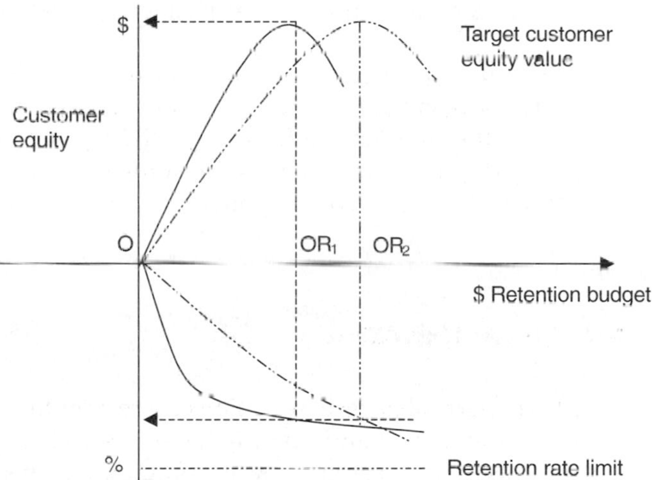

Figure 10.8 Customer retention spends.

The result of the analyses are displayed graphically. The authors discuss the method of dealing with time influence. This approach offers an opportunity to explore alternative resource allocation options. Not only can we explore the benefits of a larger allocation towards *attraction* rather than *retention* (or the reverse), but combinations of service alternatives can be explored using managerial judgemental inputs together with the modelling facility. Figures 10.7 and 10.8 illustrate this proposal.

In Figure 10.7 we suggest that an optimal acquisition budget (or combination of communication expenditure) can provide a steeper acquisition curve and in doing so achieve a target customer value at a lower overall budget (at OA_1). Similarly, in Figure 10.8 there appears an alternative retention customer service program that results in achieving a target customer equity value at a lower retention budget (at OR_2).

Clearly, over a period of time management judgement should be replaced by empirical data. Given the importance of customer retention to the success of many retailers this approach has considerable merit and is worthy of development time and investment. Blattberg and Deighton concentrate on the retention aspects of the model, offering a number of guidelines:

- Invest in the highest-value customers first.
- Transform product management into customer management.
- Consider how add-on sales and cross-selling can increase customer equity.
- Look for ways to reduce acquisition costs.
- Track customer equity gains and losses against marketing programs.
- Relate branding to customer equity.
- Monitor the intrinsic retainability of your customers.
- Consider writing separate marketing plans – or even building two marketing 'organizations' for acquisition and retention activities.

The authors discuss their model primarily in the context of manufacturing and service industries. However, none of what has been considered is exclusive to these sectors. Indeed, the activities of Tesco's customer loyalty program and its contribution to the company's success suggest that many of these factors have been considered.

PERFORMANCE MEASUREMENT

Broad performance expectations were identified in Chapter 8 and were related to market and financially based parameters. We also suggested that the success of customer loyalty programmes has increased the amount of data available. These programmes also provide investment performance data. The investment in customer loyalty programmes is such that the conventional appraisal techniques are being applied to ensure the strategic cost-effectiveness of resources.

The service delivery system approach will also provide performance data from a customer satisfaction perspective *and* from employee satisfaction and performance levels.

The operating budget

To ensure successful implementation an operating budget is prepared which will detail the revenue expectations, resources required and expenditure levels necessary to achieve the customer service strategy objectives and the overall corporate objectives.

As with other functions, specific budget items will vary. Using the performance measures identified in the Appendix to Chapter 5 we suggest the following topics:

Revenues

Sales	by:	• regions	by:	• existing customer
Gross margin		• locations		• new customer
Contribution margin		• formats		• other customer categories
		• 'seasons'		

Resource requirements

Dedicated staff
Dedicated capital equipment and materials

Expenses

Staff
Staff training
Capital equipment
Maintenance

SUMMARY

Customer service should add value to the retail offer in such a way as to create value for both the customer and the retail organization. Unless both outcomes occur there is a waste of resources. It is the customer who determines service content, quality and value. Customers make comparative evaluations of service offers, and it is during this evaluation that the contribution of customer service to competitive advantage becomes an important factor. Customer service requirements have an influence on defining market segmentation.

An effective approach to implementing customer service strategy is to use process design and management techniques which will ensure that it is customer service attributes (i.e. the elements of service required by customers), not the functional components of the business, that emerge as service features. The cost of customer service is an important consideration, and we have reviewed the concept of customer continuity in the context of customer service designed to retain, as well as acquire, customers.

QUESTIONS, ACTIVITES AND CONSIDERATIONS

- Can we consider a concept of customer service culture to be necessary if customer service strategy and implementation are to be effective?

- Undertake research on one of the major multiples (use their Web site) and use Figure 10.3 to interpret the major elements of their customer service plan.
- Apply Figure 10.4 to two quite different retailers and identify the attributes, key success factors and core processes (activities) in each of their customer service offers.
- Given the expansion of 'e-retailing', what are the likely implications for customer service for companies who plan to expand this aspect of their business?

REFERENCES

Blattberg, R. C. and Deighton, J. (1996) Manage marketing by the customer equity test. *Harvard Business Review*, Jul/Aug.

Heskett, J. L., Sasser, W. E. and Schlesinger, L. A. (1997) *The Service Profit Chain*. The Free Press, New York.

RETAIL FORMAT AND TRADING ENVIRONMENT STRATEGY DECISIONS

LEARNING OBJECTIVES

While many retailers continue to subscribe to the philosophy that retail success is primarily about location, location, location, the format and environment strategy decision is increasingly influenced by the 'purpose' expressed by consumer shopping behaviour. Customer shopping behaviour may be classified into shopping missions and expectations, which in turn may be used to create format strategies. This requires the decision maker to be able to:

- Understand the concept of shopping missions as market segments.
- Analyse customer store selection and purchasing decision processes.
- Interpret customer behaviour and expectations as input for the format and environment strategy.
- Identify significant differences in customer behaviour and to reflect these in distinctive format/environment structures.
- Match the merchandise and service offer to the format/environment design.
- Consider the relationship between characteristics of the store environment and their influence on transaction value.

INTRODUCTION

Consumer preferences for shopping environment options have changed over time:

> fewer people these days are shopping for the fun of it, and those who are shopping have indicated that they don't want to sort through hundreds of thousands of square feet of retail space to find what they're looking for. In the 1970s, 'shopping was entertainment,' said Laura Retrucci of the Marketing Corporation of America. In the 1980s, it was the guest for trendy merchandise. In the 1990s, it's a mission: find it, buy it, and get out (Spector and McCarthy, 1995).

and:

> We foolishly... treat the consumer's time as a cost-free good in the same careless way that we used to treat our precious air and water.... This omission is costly (Spector and McCarthy (1995) quoting a comment by Kemper in the *New York Times*.)

Both quotations support the view that increasingly consumer time budgets are significant in the overall shopping task. This trend has increased due to the application of technology to both customer purchasing and to order processing and handling activities. However, as Spector and McCarthy demonstrate, by understanding customer preferences other approaches are viable. The authors give considerable detail of the Nordstrom approach, which creates 'a memorable experience'. Considerable commercial research (by the retailer) supports the view that customer segments exist with strong preferences for facilities which encourage browsing and for an environment which is entertaining, comfortable and seductive in a commercial sense. Clearly there are some important issues to be considered. The Nordstrom offer is capital-intensive and requires high transaction values if a satisfactory return is to be realized. Equally, a time-efficient offer may overlook opportunities to increase customer transactions in an attempt to minimize the time spent in the shopping process. This comment obtains for both in-store shopping environments and for IT-based offers. Some years ago Argos customer research identified a strong customer preference to handle and inspect merchandise prior to committing to a purchase. It follows that an organized approach to the format and trading environment strategy is essential if the return on investment objectives are to be realized. The key to the problem is unambiguous customer research.

An overall approach to the process is shown in Figure 11.1, and this will be used to explore the process.

Customer shopping missions and expectations

A clear understanding of customer expectations is essential if workable format and trading objectives are to be developed. There are two basic objectives. One is to ensure that customer purchasing behaviour expectations are met with an environment which reflects their expectations for merchandise, customer service *and* the atmosphere and environment within which this takes place. The other objective concerns the return on investment expected by the company. The issues here include the fixed capital required and the operating expenses accompanying the format selected. It must be remembered that the ROI calculation has a number of components, and the profit margin generated has a major impact. The greater the staff costs, occupancy, maintenance and service infrastructure costs, the greater the impact on the margin generated. The GMROI/CMROI ratio relationship demonstrates the need for either high average transaction values from customer visits or a large number of transactions.

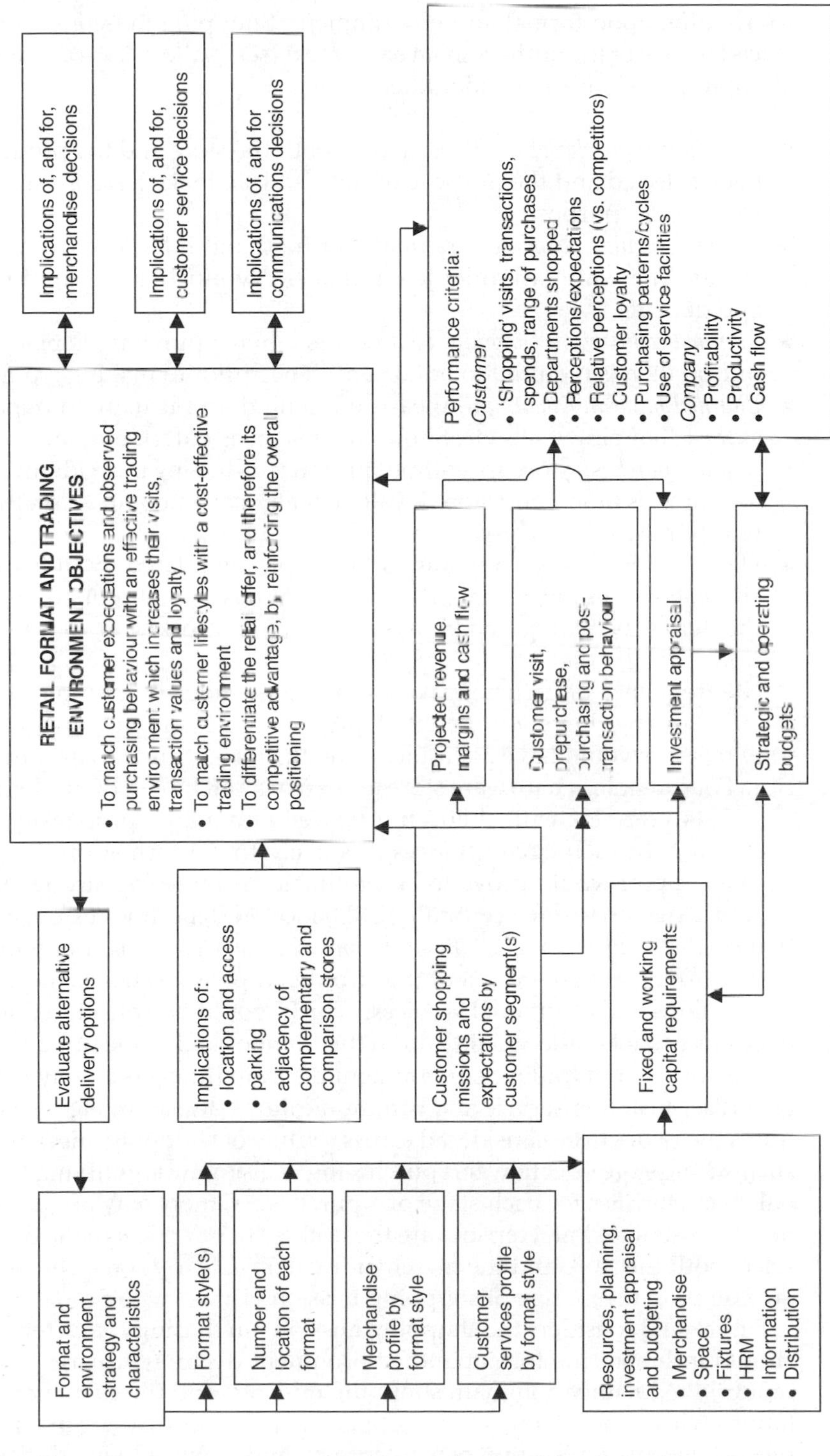

Figure 11.1 The retail format and environment strategy.

Customer shopping missions and expectations by customer segments are the key to deciding upon format and environment. Shopping missions were introduced by one of the authors in an earlier text (see Walters, 1994). A number of shopping missions can be identified:

- *Destination purchases* are those where both the store and the product have been selected and the purpose of the visit is to make a *specific* transaction for a *specific* purpose.
- *Planned regular purchases* are made for food and other everyday requirements. These are task-oriented and are very much about 'find it, buy it and get out'.
- *Planned comparison shopping visit* occurs when a purchase is planned and information is required to build confidence prior to making a purchase.
- *Planned browsing visits* are pleasure-oriented and usually to department stores, shopping malls etc. Shopping is seen as entertainment.
- *Impulse purchasing* occurs without prior needs having been identified. Factors such as brand and store loyalty usually have no impact on the resultant purchase.
- *Distress purchases* are unplanned buy typically related to an earlier purchase. For example, a vital meal ingredient has been forgotten or perhaps the item may be required because of a DIY emergency.

The frequency of occurrence of shopping missions is an important input when planning the environment. A predominance of one particular shopping mission would have an influence on the format and environment decision. For example, a hardware store located in a catchment of predominantly C2, 25–44 year-olds with children may well find a high propensity for DIY decorating. In such circumstances it is likely that a format offering 'out of hours' support would prove to be profitable and develop strong customer loyalty. By comparison a centrally (CBD) located department store may find that *planned comparison shopping* and *comparison shopping* missions would suggest a format and environment that would emphasize choice, merchandise applications and additional services, which would be considered as major decision variables and would add to the number and value of transactions.

The format and trading environment decision interacts closely with merchandise, customer service and communications decisions. Figure 11.2 illustrates the issues to be considered across a range of shopping missions at each stage of the store selection and purchasing decision by identifying the essential characteristics for each stage of a purchase. Others may augment these, but the essential characteristics are those likely to be critical to the decision to select both the store and the merchandise item. Clearly some characteristics are common to *each type* of shopping mission visit.

Figure 11.3 considers the shopping mission purchasing characteristics that should influence the format and environment decision. Clearly research is required to identify dominant shopping missions and the customers' expectations within each of the missions. Spector and McCarthy (1995) offer examples of Nordstrom's approach to format and environment decisions. To

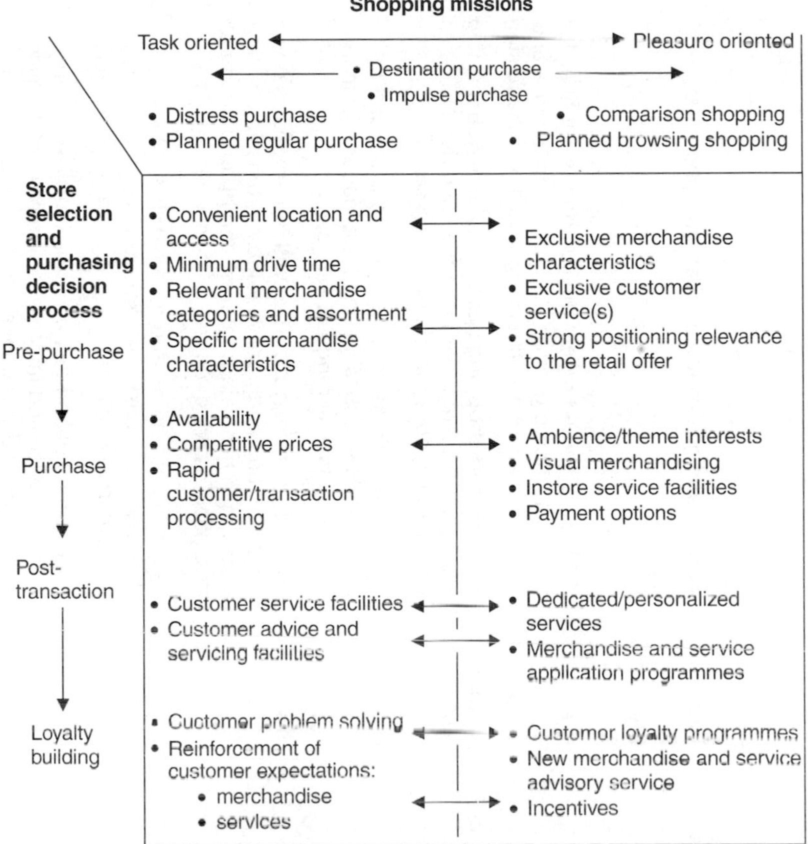

Figure 11.2 Identifying format and environment characteristics.

ensure 'a memorable experience' a coordinated approach to the merchandise and service offer is the result of both research and experience. A number of examples illustrate this approach.

Research from customer focus groups suggested that some Nordstrom customers did not shop in a cosmetics department where they felt intimidated and committed to buy. Browsing was difficult, price points were not displayed, and merchandise was 'unavailable' for testing without the assistance of a sales person. Testers have been added, pricing is very visible and both the time-short customer and the reticent customer are catered for.

Apparel, shoes and accessories are merchandised in a variety of departments depending upon the customer's age, fashion taste, personal style and price/budget range in departments which are lifestyle-led. For example, *Savvy* represents young, fun, fast, fashion. The *Collectors* department appeals to the designer customer with international labels and appeals to customers who 'invest' in their wardrobes.

Prepurchase considerations such as parking are an important consideration. During 'sales' Nordstrom offers valet parking for customers. Shopping

Shopping mission	Browsing visit frequency	Purchasing visit frequency	Average transaction value	Items purchased	Range of items purchased	Format and environment characteristics
Destination purchase	low	medium	variable by merchandise group	low	low	Ambience should reflect the customers' motives for store selection e.g. specialist/core merchandise and customer services with strong visual merchandising.
Planned regular purchases	low	high	variable by merchandise group	medium/ high	medium/ high	Responds to shopping spend. Visual merchandising 'prompts' customer with merchandise density emphasizing core merchandise ranges.
Planned comparison shopping	medium/ high	low	low	low	low	Visual merchandising is used to 'educate' and to 'persuade' by focussing on brand leader merchandise benefits. Full range of services.
Planned browsing visit	low/ medium	low	low	low	low	Focus on core merchandise with an emphasis on augmentation and application by extensive use of visual merchandising: interest and entertainment are essentials as are a full range of services
Impulse purchase visits	low	low	low	low	low	Tactically located related merchandise. Much depends upon customer attitudes (confectionary at supermarket POS) and the profit margin potential.
Distress purchase visits	low	low	low	low	low	Focus on identified distress merchandise requirements. Advice and information unlikely to be essential. Service offer is concerned with availability of critical merchandise at extended hours.

Figure 11.3 Format and environment implications of differing shopping missions.

convenience is a major concern during the *purchase* stages. Departments are designed with edited merchandise in clearly defined lifestyle categories such that the presentation is: '...instantly understood and a wardrobe can be more quickly assembled...'. Customer mobility is an essential feature, and here Nordstrom pursues a standard format with a central escalator and aisles leading to each department. Aisles are large enough for customers to both browse *and* move around (wheelchairs and baby carriages are included as important variables). An interactive computerized store plan enables customers to locate departments *and routes* them from the existing location to the desired department. Both partners and children (often non-participants in the shopping process) are catered for with lounge areas, newspapers and coffee facilities and toys, video games and other children's facilities. An obvious question emerges: how can the use of space be justified cost-effectively? The answer given by Nordstrom is that its merchandise density is high at Nordstrom:

> Nordstrom packs its selling spaces with the highest value of inventory per-square-foot of any speciality apparel retailer in the country – 20 to 30 percent more than the competition – as well as more sales people and cash registers.

To encourage customers to extend their visits to Nordstrom stores there are four restaurant concepts. Typically the stores offer at least two. The four concepts are the *Espresso Bar,* usually based outside the store entrance; *Café Nordstrom*, which serves soup, salads, pastries and beverages in a cafeteria format; the *Garden Court*, which offers full-service dining; and the *Pub*, which offers a morning coffee and sandwich service and a 'pub lunch' offer for the remainder of the day. A reservations system operates throughout the store, notifying customers that 'their table is ready'.

Returning to Figure 11.3, we suggest that Nordstrom's customers' missions comprise the first four missions. Their response is to offer an environment which encourages customers to spend time in the store *and* to increase expenditure across the range of merchandise and services. By contrast, Target and K-Mart are variety chain stores operating in the low/medium price point range, which suggests a predominance of destination and planned regular shopping mission visits.

The Target and K-Mart format and environment is functional, offers a minimum of customer services and has a very high merchandise density. Again this contrasts with Nordstrom, as there is a wider range of lower value merchandise. Customer services extend to credit facilities and deliveries. There are no restaurants. Sales assistants are (per $ sales) fewer and operate customer transaction handling and a central information centre.

Both companies use strong media campaigns to maintain customer flows. A series of planned price offers across their assortments ensure that both destination purchasing and planned regular purchases are maintained at a consistent high level.

Format and environment characteristics (see Figure 11.3) reflect this strategy. For both stores, core merchandise categories are a dominant feature of the layout and space of the stores. Visual merchandising is 'busy', focusing more on the width and depth of the category. Very few of the merchandise categories require demonstration. For example, Target's core categories of homewares (Manchester and household items) and apparel need virtually no 'advice service', as they are everyday items. Neither store group uses extensive segmentation, and therefore avoid the need to opt for significant departmentalization.

Typically, both stores locate in shopping malls and rely on the malls' other occupants to offer customer services and facilities. This location approach also has customer segmentation benefits. A typical customer for both would be a C2 customer, with a wide age spread and a family expenditure commitment. By locating in malls whose customer catchments are well represented with a viable number of such customers, financial viability is assured. The strong communications activity generates customer flows in both shopping missions.

Thus far in this chapter we have illustrated the importance of identifying *customer shopping missions by customer segment* as an initial step in the format and trading environment strategy. The importance in marketing and financial terms needs no amplification beyond emphasizing the fact that without a viable marketing concept (i.e. merchandise, format and trading environment) financial viability becomes impossible. The preceding discussion has addressed a number of the strategy decision characteristics identified in Figure 11.1. We have seen that it is necessary to *evaluate alternative delivery options* to identify a viable option for the organization. From this exercise one or more options may emerge, and at this point it becomes necessary to develop a *format and environment strategy and its characteristics*. This may result in one or more *format styles*, each of which shows marketing and financial potential.

The growth of distinctive market segments has resulted in both marketing and financial viability. For example, Tesco (in the UK) now operates four distinctive *format styles*. These have demographic and lifestyle characteristics which are sufficiently strong and economically viable for the company to maintain these distinctive offers. Clearly economies of scope expand and enhance the viability of segments hitherto lacking in potential. The expansion of a CBD convenience-based food chain (e.g. Metro) becomes attractive once the fixed costs of merchandise assortment developments are covered: modification costs (additional pack sizes, variety etc.) become minimal in the overall decision to expand and develop an additional format style.

The *number and location of each format* offers a number of issues to be resolved. A superstore/supermarket format has an 'ideal catchment profile'. Typically such a profile would comprise:

- Age group: 25–44 years
- Families: parents with '2.5 children'
- B, C1/C2 socio-economic groups
- High-density modern suburban development with some 70–80% of the catchment within a 10–15 minute drive time

- A shopping facility offering supporting stores; preferably no competitors. Specialist stores such as butchers and produce (fruit and vegetables) often enhance the overall site spend.
- A volume potential (household expenditure × number of households) sufficiently large to return a target ROI

A number of factors influence this profile. For example, it may be necessary initially to offer transportation services (scheduled bus routes and times) to reach a financially viable customer volume. Often these are maintained as they become part of customers' expectations or because of competition.

The number and location of outlets have supply chain implications. Clearly financial viability is influenced by logistics costs. Given that customer expectations include width, depth and availability characteristics, the costs of providing these expected service characteristics are vital inputs into the overall operating costs. It follows that what may appear to be an attractive location fails to be so because of the excessive costs of maintaining service expectations.

An increasing problem for food multiples is the saturation of catchment areas. Given the apparent potential of a number of high-density markets there has been rapid expansion by a number of large multiples. For some the problems are exacerbated by cannibalization. A number of companies have found that, following the opening of new, larger and improved facility stores, significant decreases in the revenues of adjacent outlets occur. The impact of the effect is influenced by local fixed costs. If the established outlet was opened during a period of expansion and competitive leases, the decline in sales revenues may have a dramatic impact on the contribution level of the store.

The introduction of customer loyalty schemes has protected local market shares on an inter-competition basis. Some retailers have found that intra-competition is significant, and in order to maintain local volumes specific loyalty/promotional offers are necessary.

The increased use of the Internet is significant. Details of the 1998 end-of-year seasonal shopping in the USA suggested expectations of a threefold increase year on year of 'online' sales. The Boston Consulting Group (BCG) and shop.org (an association of online retailers) reported that revenues tripled, growing by 230%. Their estimates were based upon 17 large Web-based retailers. The BCG estimate is that 1998 sales will reach $13 billion. An interesting fact is that sales were fuelled by a huge number of first-time shoppers:

> America Online said it has more than a million first time buyers this month (December)

The Guardian (29 December 1998) also reports:

> This holiday season marks the year that online retailing moved from an interesting consumer experiment to an accepted retail alternative (David Pecaut, senior vice-president BCG).

More significant (because in fact the estimated $13 bn is lost in the overall value of US retail sales of $2.6 trillion) is that consumers are responding to:

> The 24 hour access to Internet stores, no crowds and the convenience of shipping gifts directly have struck a chord with a growing segment of consumers (David Pecaut, BCG).

Through technology and the pressure on time budgets, combined with consumer discontent with traffic congestion and parking problems, the attraction of existing formats may decline. *The Guardian* also commented (February 1998) on a report by a property development company to the effect that changing attitudes towards food shopping (i.e. a preference for alternative formats such as telephone orders, delivered or collected) could, if sufficient numbers exist, threaten the traditional superstore/supermarket formats. Clearly an impact on both the number and location of some formats can be expected at some time in the future. This issue is significant to the format and trading environment strategy decision.

Merchandise profile(s) by format styles are important considerations. There are a number of fundamental influences:

- Customer expectations of the retail offer
- Available space
- Current merchandise categories offered and those planned
- The credibility of the organization in its current positioning situation and the potential for 'brand leverage'
- Local competition and customer loyalty to existing competitive offers

Customer expectations of the retail offer are a response to the conditioning that the positioning statement has transmitted. Consequently, merchandise characteristics should reflect the width, depth, quality, exclusivity and perhaps design continuity that the positioning statement promises. The implications for the format and environment are quite obvious with respect to visual merchandising and merchandise density. A consideration that is often overlooked is the need for consistency in what is 'offered', expected and perceived. Successful retailers are those for whom congruency exists for all three aspects. *Available space* is a factor which should be considered alongside customer expectations. Very rarely are retail outlets similar in terms of space. Indeed, growth businesses usually have a portfolio of outlets, varying in location type and size. A major factor for consideration for growth companies is how the format should be merchandised. For those organizations who have expanded their merchandise categories (as well as their width and depth profiles within each category) a dilemma can exist. The recent large new outlets are capable of carrying a complete assortment, offering both variety and availability. However, the smaller outlets present problems. Should they carry a representative assortment with *all* categories represented but with less than the full range made available, or should the offer perhaps be restricted to fast-selling items in core ranges within core categories?

There are a number of potential solutions. By offering a representative range customer expectations may not be met, particularly for those companies who have located 'flagship' stores in geographically strategic locations. Mobile customers are likely to plan purchases of items seen in the larger stores during a visit to a local but smaller branch, only to find them unavailable. By being 'specialist' in a local context the full potential of the merchandise offer may not be realized. Standard ranges supported by catalogue or store ordering services are one solution. Marks & Spencer (in the UK) have found this to be a potential answer to the problem. An alternative solution is an assortment based upon researched expectations for categories, brands and price points, and which comprises part of the overall assortment. A multiple durables chain finds this to be effective. Each location has a clear merchandise profile dependent upon the potential that its catchment has shown to exist (this is based upon research initially and reinforced by sales data as experience builds).

Local competition and customer loyalty to existing competitive offers is another important factor. Customer loyalty builds when retailers respond to customer preferences. Not only can merchandise preferences differ regionally (for geographical and ethnic reasons), but so too does shopping behaviour. For example, in Sydney the strong ethnic influence has determined both merchandise ranges *and* format and environment decisions. If strong differences are seen to exist, the solution to both merchandise and format and environment strategy is to consider a specific, localized offer rather than attempt to modify the core strategy. Typically the latter is not convincing and costs are almost as high as a dedicated offer.

Current merchandise categories offered and planned are important factors which influence the format and environment strategy decision. Supplier product development has a major influence, particularly in technology-based merchandise categories. The automotive industry has shown interesting changes in recent years. In the 1960s sales were buoyant and waiting lists existed; hence margins were secure. Supply side technology has reduced the development cycle *and* manufacturing times and costs. The product has become more sophisticated, as has the consumer. By the 1990s, supplier margins were depressed as distributors diverted the pressure of price competition back up towards manufacturers. At the same time distributor margins have been strengthened by the addition of finance services, customization and multi-franchise selling. As 2000 approaches we see both Ford and GM considering forward integration into distribution, and entry into car retailing by multiple food retailers. Clearly these developments have an impact on format and environment decisions. At the point of sale other products compete for space and visual merchandising. Vehicle design has extended product lifespans *and* service intervals. Both changes have implications for format and environment. Audi, for example, offers prospective purchasers a computer-linked package to 'design' their new vehicle. Other manufacturers have similar approaches. The consequence of such changes will be radical rethinking of the retail point of sale.

Other companies have made similar changes. Levi Strauss now offer a bespoke approach to what was once almost a commodity product. It is arguable that the strong branding of Levi, together with its equally strong promotional spend, was such that differentiation was clear and well established. However, consumer preferences and attitude shifts, together with competitive shifts (denim in Versace, Burberry and other 'prestigious' retail brands) clearly influenced this shift. The Levi POS environment has changed to include the facility for the 'bespoke tailoring' service.

Food chains moving into chilled categories (and ready meals) confront similar changes. Store format environment decisions need to consider POS equipment (both costs *and* space requirements) and often promotional methods such as cooking/preparation information areas. Customer loyalty programmes have presented retailers with detailed customer purchasing details of their customers, and this has numerous benefits. One, affecting branch merchandise profiles and space allocation, is the ability to match catchment preferences on an individual store basis. Another benefit is the use of customer data to develop in-store promotions around categories for which there is evidence of strong interest and purchasing. The third benefit is that we know who to invite!

The credibility of the organization in its current positioning situation, and the potential this offers for 'brand leverage' has important considerations. The move by Marks & Spencer and subsequently Tesco, Sainsbury and, in Australia, Woolworths and Coles into unrelated products is dependent upon customer perceptions of credibility. For financial services, format changes are important but not particularly difficult to accommodate. Clearly the method of selling such products requires dedicated staff and sales areas. Other products may require a significant review of format and environment decisions. The entry by food retailers into petrol sales was research led (which showed clearly that both task purchases occurred, for the majority of customers, on the same shopping visit); it resulted in significant changes to format and environment strategy decisions. Both space requirements *and* location decisions were important for new outlets, and a rigorous review of the capacity to handle petrol sales *as well* as potential for sales was undertaken for existing locations. Often (almost inevitably) the introduction of petrol sales was accompanied by a reduction in parking space. For an organization using convenience and easy access (parking) as a brand/positioning benefit a significant reduction in parking space may result in problems.

Customer Service profile(s) by format styles are also important considerations. Again a number of fundamental influences should be considered:

- The role of service within the retail offer
- Customer service strategy characteristics: proactive vs. reactive
- Customer service attributes and activities
- Augmentation

The role of service within the retail offer is an important issue for an aspect of retailing strategy, but it has additional significance for format environment decisions. The Nordstrom examples given earlier in this chapter suggest how important the store environment is for merchandise and service decisions.

Given a specific service strategy, the service support infrastructure follows. An organization such as Nordstrom, Harrods, David Jones or any other service-oriented company commits considerable resources to supporting the delivery of the service objectives. Clearly this must be understood at an early stage in the strategy process: to underestimate the resource requirements or to ignore the opportunity cost of their uses elsewhere will only result in a badly implemented strategy. A 'full-service' approach requires the commitment of space and dedicated staff. The implications of the cost of these (and of their impact on revenues and therefore profitability) must be explored prior to making decisions.

Customer service strategy characteristics: we have discussed the issues involved in deciding upon a customer service strategy. The implications of opting for either a proactive or reactive strategy on format and environment decisions are well illustrated by Nordstrom. Spector and McCarthy (1995) provide an excellent example of the differences between a proactive and a reactive approach to 'dressing rooms' and lounge areas:

> Comfort and ease are the guiding principles behind the design of Nordstrom's large, carpeted dressing rooms, fitting rooms and customer lounges, which are furnished with upholstered chairs and/or sofas. Fitting rooms in the stores' more fashionable ready-to-wear departments include tables, table lamps and telephones.

Spector and McCarthy quote the vice-president of planning:

> The whole point of everything we do is to make the customer happy for the long haul. If people are satisfied and excited about the experience of shopping at Nordstrom, they will come back. And if you haven't created that atmosphere, they won't come back. It's just that simple.

Being service proactive requires evidence that it is part of customers' expectations *and* that resources are available *and* will generate a return on the investment required.

Customer service attributes and activities are an integral part of the organization's strategic positioning. Figures 2.7(a) and 2.7(b) illustrate the importance of identifying the strategic theme (or direction) *and* the attributes and activities that ensure that the strategic positioning is made explicit. An example is given for a department store in Exhibit 2.3. Customer service attributes and activities together with merchandise details are given as examples of the process. Subsequently these provide input for strategic and operational costing.

Augmentation: both merchandise and service augmentation have significant implications for format and environment decisions. The more extensive each becomes, the greater the need for (and use of) selling space. Augmentation has a positive impact on average transaction value *but* there is a point at which opportunity costs increase at a greater rate than the incremental value of transactions. The decision is complicated by a number of factors, each of which requires research. For example, strong category competition from a specialist retailer will require extensive augmentation if credibility is to be established and maintained. And in less affluent catchments it is very likely that customer transactions will be restricted to primary purchases. It follows that augmentation decisions should be evaluated and monitored.

In-store motivation

Considerable expenditure is involved in creating the 'right' ambience to encourage customers to extend shopping visits and, therefore, their purchasing. We have discussed the extent to which department stores provide service facilities which are either direct (such as large changing rooms with additional features like basic personal care materials) or indirect facilities (a range of restaurants, child care etc.).

Some years ago the use of 'piped music' was used to provide a background in which a relaxed customer might respond by increasing the time spent in-store. More recently the use of in-house music has become more directed. As the exhibit explains, an audio aspect to the store environment can act as a reinforcement to the overall objective.

Case example: Shop till you bop

Jeff Buckley would be turning in his grave. Two years after his death and almost five years since the release of his debut album, *Grace*, his song *The Last Goodbuy* has found itself on high rotation at McDonald's restaurants.

And Lenny Kravitz can stop the pelvic gesturing in the name of cool right now, because he's on there as well. In-store soundtracks once blared from a dusty tape player stashed behind the counter or featured Muzak – orchestral cover versions of popular songs punctuated, in supermarkets at least, by the occasional price check or location of the latest red light special. But the next time you find yourself strolling cheerfully through a supermarket or tucking into a McMuffin and you realize they're actually playing *your* song, chances are it's no accident.

Retailers know who you are, when you shop and what's likely to be in your CD collection. And they're programming their in-house music accordingly to enhance the shopping experience and hopefully lure you back.

AEI Music-Soundcom is Australia's largest in-house music company, with 7000 clients, including Coles supermarkets, restaurants and government agencies such as Australia Post. 'What we try to do is help our clients build an identity or an image', says Soundcom's sales and marketing manager Shari Bjorn. 'Music creates experiences in a retail environment and if it's a positive experience then consumers are more likely to return, which is obviously what every retailer wants'.

Research shows that background music can influence consumer behaviour. Companies that supply in-house music can program songs that are intended to make you linger longer in a supermarket aisle, wait more patiently in a queue, or eat more quickly in a café during the lunchtime rush hour.

'Research into queuing shows that if you slow down the background music's tempo, people don't think they're queuing for as long', says Ric Solomon, managing director of Satellite Music Australia (SMA), a Sydney-based company that employs satellite technology to broadcast music to more than 2000 stores, restaurants and clubs around Australia.

Increasing the tempo also influences how we behave, says Dr Charles Areni, senior lecturer in marketing at the University of Sydney. 'By increasing the number of beats per minute, consumers move more quickly, whether they're pushing a shopping trolley through a supermarket or whether they're dining at a restaurant. If you're a restaurant and you want to increase turnover, you increase the music's tempo. Diners eat more quickly and table turnover increases. You slow the music down when you want to keep people there longer, to get them to order more wine and dessert.'

In a study of an upmarket bottle shop, Areni found people spent more on wine when they were listening to classical music. 'The interior design of the store was very elegant and there were some expensive wines there, but as long as they were playing contemporary pop music, the wines weren't selling. They switched to a classical format and dollar sales increased dramatically – people were buying more expensive bottles of wine.'

In-house music dates back to the 1920s, when Seattle company Muzak, the name of which is now synonymous with bad elevator music everywhere, began selling music to offices. 'In those days, they used adding machines which were very noisy, and Muzak was designed to mask that sound so people could have a better work environment', says SMA's Solomon. 'Getting the rights to the music was very expensive so they used to have their in-house orchestra make recordings. We don't do any of that; everything we play is by the original artist.'

SMA can program the music it broadcasts to suit different parts of the day and even different demographics. 'We know that every second Thursday is pension day, so there's more than likely going to be a predominance of older people in the supermarket and the music is tailored accordingly', says Solomon.

Nor is it only customers who are targeted. 'We know that the night stackers come in at 11 p.m. so we raise the tempo of the music so that their productivity is greater', he adds.

SMA has 10 channels that it broadcasts from its Ultimo studio. There are country, jazz, top 100, instrumental and classical channels, all running 24 hours or roughly 6000 songs a day.

'Record companies supply us each week with new releases', says Solomon. 'We're one of the better places to promote their music. When we broadcast to retailers, they can sell directly from it.'

While other retailers use satellite technology to receive their songs, David Jones still employs more traditional methods – a live pianist, which has the added benefit of allowing shoppers to make their own selections. 'You get so many requests', says Michael Hope, one of three pianists who perform at the David Jones Elizabeth Street store each week. 'People relate to the music. It puts them in a lovely frame of mind.'

Like its food, the music at McDonald's is intended for everyone, says spokesman Sarah Sammartino.

So the next time you feel like a burger ask yourself this: 'Do you want the Top 40 with that?'.

Buying to the beat - what they're playing at:

General Pants Co.
1. Words for love – Paul Van Dyk
2. Café del Mar – Energy 52
3. Flowerz – Armand Van Helden

McDonald's
1. That don't impress me much – Shania Twain
2. Honey to the bee – Billie
3. All I need – Air

David Jones
1. Someone to watch over me – George Gershwin
2. Stardust – Hoagy Carmichael
3. Time to say goodbye – Andrea Bocelli

Big W
1. Age of Reason – John Farnham
2. We rule together – The Eurogliders
3. All out of love – Air Supply

Source: Young, Victoria (1999) *Sun Herald* (Sunday Life), 4 July.

Resources planning, investment appraisal and budgeting

At this juncture the process that we described in Chapter 4 follows. The resource requirements are identified with respect to fixed and working capital inputs, which are required for startup and implementation of the format environment component of the overall strategy. These are then worked through the investment appraisal model described earlier. Once adjustments have been made strategic and operating budgets can be published.

Prior to implementing this component of the overall retail strategy two tasks remain. A review of the objectives established for *all* aspects of the retail strategy is required, together with a review of the interface areas between other strategy components, i.e. merchandise, customer service and customer communications. This final review will ensure that no duplication of resources used has occurred, nor have there been omissions of essential features from the overall strategy.

The reader is recommended to review Section 4.1, on evaluating strategic options, and particularly Figure 4.14.

SUMMARY

The ambience created by the format/environment strategy is increasingly important in persuading the customer to stay longer in-store, purchase more and return.

Central to this strategy is an understanding of the dominant shopping mission of the target customer group and the expectations that this will create for the customer. We have explored the implications not only for format and environment decisions; they are also important for merchandise and customer service and differ markedly, resulting in a specification for the format/environment strategy which will meet customer expectations more closely and result in increased customer satisfaction.

QUESTIONS, ACTIONS AND CONSIDERATIONS

- How might an FMCG multiple use shopping missions to derive format and environment options?
- 'We foolishly... treat the consumer's time as a cost-free good.... This omission is costly.' Identify recent developments that have met this admission.
- To what extent could the response to two or three shopping missions blur the focus of a strategic positioning?
- Design a research approach which could be used to:
  - identify shopping missions
  - derive customer expectations
  - develop the basis for a format/environment strategy

REFERENCES

The Guardian (1998) Americans push cyberspace stores to $13 bn boom. 29 December.
The Guardian (1998) Report on retail development. 10 February.
Spector, R. and McCarthy, P. (1995) *The Nordstrom Way*. John Wiley, New York.

12 IMPLEMENTING FORMAT AND ENVIRONMENT STRATEGY

LEARNING OBJECTIVES

An anonymous quote once suggested that the objective of any format and store environment design should be such that customers are made to feel as though they are in their own homes. While this may be difficult for a specialist sportswear and equipment retailer, the underlying point being made is that an effective strategy is one which reflects the lifestyle aspect of the customer within the product market. This chapter identifies the components of the format and environment strategy that are important to decision makers.

- Identifying the customers' needs to create an environment that meets expectations for merchandise, service *and* ambience.
- Using the target customer group's purchasing activities and transactions, together with the company's performance expectations, to arrive at store design, layout, space allocation and fixture specifications.
- Staff involvement in the format and environment strategy is essential. They have to make the format work and produce results. Their positive attitudes can be communicated to customers, with the result that positive outcomes of visit frequency and high average transactions follow.
- Merchandise stocking and replenishment systems should be matched to the customer transaction patterns.
- The use of technology to complement visual merchandising and sales staff is an important aspect of format and environment decisions. The use of customer databases in format design and modification is also an essential feature of the use of information systems support.
- Developing a store operations plan and an operating budget concludes the chapter. Without clear objectives for revenue expectations and capital and operating expenditure it is difficult to exercise control of operating activities and the longer term return on investment.

INTRODUCTION

The primary input requirements for the successful implementation of a format and environment strategy are the detailed strategy, its portfolio of format styles, the number and location of each format, the merchandise assortment each will offer, the customer service profiles, the in-store ambience and the visual merchandising program for each. The strategy will be supported by a detailed customer profile identifying qualitative/behaviour characteristics and quantitative/purchasing features. These are shown in Figure 12.1, which identifies the activities comprising the task.

Chapter 10 discussed the topics relevant to format and environment strategy decisions. Central to the overall process are *customer shopping missions and expectations* and specific issues for planning, such as *location and access, parking* and *essential complementary and comparison stores.* From these data a format strategy specification can be derived. For some businesses the process is relatively simple. Food retailing format and environment decisions have been extremely well researched by the major operators, and as a result broad specifications can be established and 'format packages' designed to meet catchment opportunities. Fast food operators and the 'pub/restaurant' subsidiaries of brewery chains can operate in a similar manner. Merchandise and customer service characteristics can be prescribed and, while some local modifications may be required, the benefits of experience can be applied to situations which do not change markedly.

For an organization confronted with the task of implementing format and environment strategy for the first time it is very much the case of starting with the basic strategy.

Format and environment strategy: the details

There are a number of essential decisions to be clarified before design and detailed work can begin. The number of *format styles* and their detailed specifications, together with the rationale for the decisions, is a primary input. Often the formats evolve over time. The Tesco store portfolio has evolved as consumer change has developed and modified shopping lifestyles. The Metro concept meets time-short customers with high disposable incomes that enable the customer to trade off time and convenience for price economies. Clearly these opportunities develop over time. However, there are influences and constraints that are much more long-term and for which a flexible approach is required.

The problem for many retailers is one of growth. Growth may be achieved through replication of an effective offer. The UK food retail multiples during the 1970s and 1980s are examples. An existing, effective 'retail formula' was expanded territorially. As suitable locations began to become difficult to find, the emphasis for growth was focused towards merchandise category expansion *and* the introduction of services. It is at this point that a flexible approach is necessary. Not all locations are suitable for the expanded ranges due to catchment profile differences, nor are they all capable of handling the entire assortment due to space constraints and often distribution access difficulties. A related example of such a problem was seen in the 1970s when Fine Fare (ultimately Somerfield) acquired a regional food chain. The geographical 'fit'

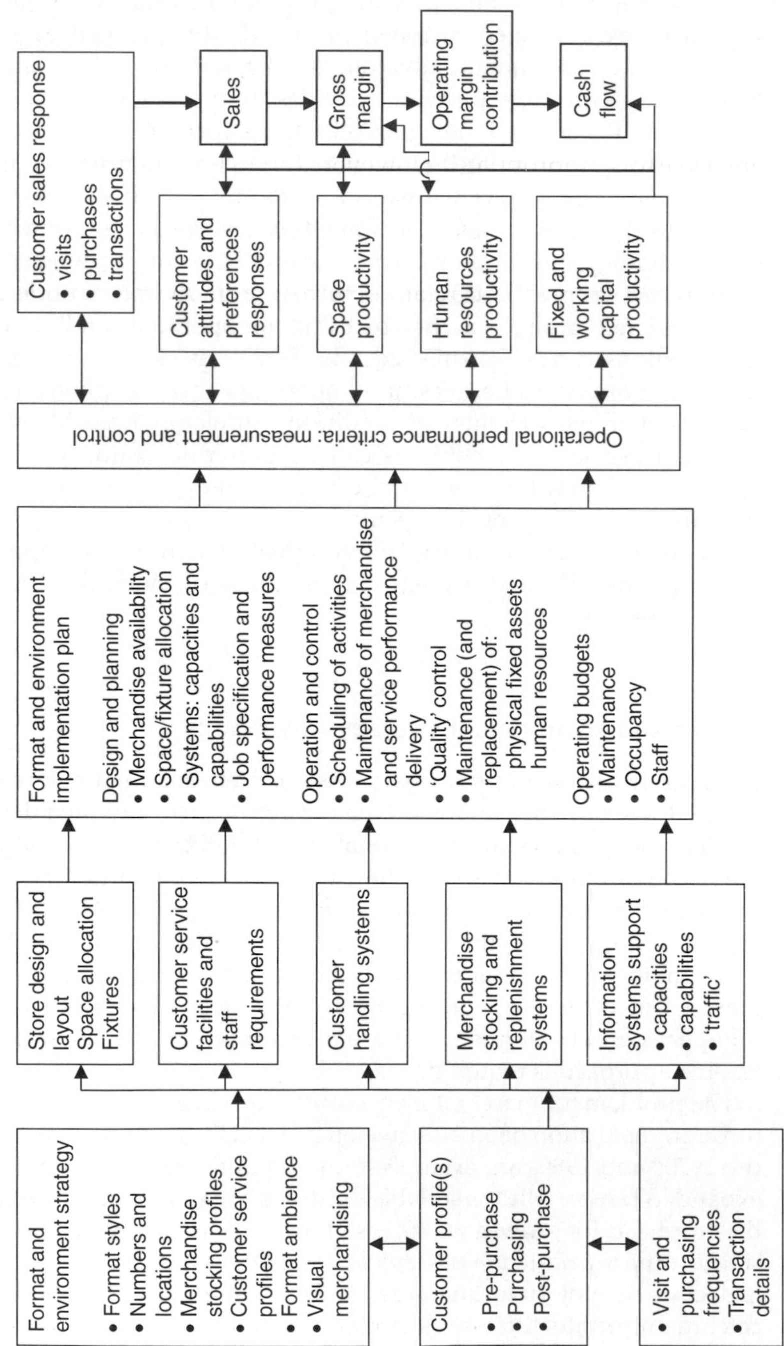

Figure 12.1 Implementing format and environment strategy decisions.

was ideal; however, the problem for Fine Fare was that because of narrow access to stores (most were located in small streets in the North of England) physical distribution became difficult and very expensive. It follows that if implementation is to be effective the issues of size of location(s) and a detailed catchment profile are essential.

The importance of these factors becomes very apparent when *merchandise stocking profiles* and *customer service profiles* are decided; blanket allocations are clearly inappropriate. However, there is a temptation to take this approach because buying discounts may benefit from volume increases. But the subsequent markdowns and inventory write-offs are usually larger than the assumed margin benefits. Furthermore, it is bad marketing. It suggests (and in fact there is) a lack of knowledge concerning customers and local markets. It is also inexcusable given the amount of information that is available or can be generated.

Format ambience is also closely related to the customer profile and to the *overall positioning* (see Chapter 10). Very clear examples of effective ambience decisions can be seen on an international basis. For example, in the USA both Nordstrom and Wal-Mart are very clear who it is they are appealing to. In the UK there are clear ambience differences between Marks & Spencer and Littlewoods (and BHS and Woolworth for that matter). In Australia there is a marked contrast between Target and Grace Brothers. Both offer similar merchandise categories (and both are part of the Coles Myer group), but the ambience differences make very clear who it is the offer is targeting. *Visual merchandising* decisions are clearly associated with store ambience decisions. Both are attempting to identify with the target customer group, to create an atmosphere in which the customer is comfortable and to which they respond. If the offer is strongly price-oriented the ambience should reflect this, with an emphasis on price rather than service. High merchandise density (narrow aisles, high fixture displays) displaying price offers is clearly 'expected' and 'accepted' by customer groups in this segment. By contrast, the Nordstrom, David Jones and Harrods customer would be repelled by such an approach.

The buying process and activities of customer groups are also necessary inputs. For example, a requirement for advice and product information when purchasing durables and computers on the part of customers should be reflected in both visual merchandising and the customer service profile. An important issue here is to be aware of both *changes* in consumer needs and *differences* in the needs between segments. The growth of domestic, personal computer sales illustrates this point. Initially doubt and uncertainty existed among consumers as the category was new. As consumer experience matured, and knowledge of products and applications increased, less advice was required. Thus the emphasis has shifted, and many computer sales outlets can (and do) put almost a commodity emphasis on the category, using price as a primary incentive. Consequently both ambience and visual merchandising decisions have seen changes in recent years.

The quantitative characteristics of customer behaviour are equally important in the implementation process. Frequent purchasing (either by the same customers or a very large customer base visiting infrequently) has implications for format decisions. Furthermore the nature of the merchandise has implications. For example, high-volume, low purchase value items such as newspapers and magazine sales require both adequate display area (particularly for magazine browsers) and rapid customer handling facilities (again requiring adequate space). By contrast, durables, apparel and similar expensive categories, for which the decision process may be considerably longer, requires a much different approach. Spector and McCarthy (1995) describe how Nordstrom has provided facilities for partners (comfortable seating, coffee and newspapers) in apparel areas. Experience has shown how important it is to consider the purchasing process as one in which there are both *active* and *passive* participants. Again the needs of different customer targets vary, as can be observed in multiple clothing chain outlets compared with specialists and department stores.

It is not understating the fact to suggest that a detailed format and environment strategy is much more effective if it contains details of the strategy, the target customer and behaviour profile *and* the rationale underlying the strategy.

Store design, layout, space allocation and fixtures

Given a detailed profile of the target customer group's purchasing activities and spends we can begin the process of store design. We will know from our research (and our objectives) the performance requirements necessary to make the format profitable. It follows that given a profile of customer:

- shopping visits, transactions and spends, range of purchases
- departments expected to be 'shopped'
- expectations and perceptions
- purchasing patterns and cycles
- use of services

and the company performance criteria:

- profitability
- productivity
- cash flow

It is possible to identify the operational performance criteria to be considered. These are:

- catchment penetration/ 'market' share volume and percentage
- sales/contribution/selling space
- sales/contribution/employees
- inventory turnover rates
- customer credit collection

- credit sales/sales
- cost/sales ratios
- staff hours worked/budgeted
- customer complaints incidence
- store contribution $/percentage
- return on assets managed

Given both sets of data the task then becomes one of ensuring:

- customer visit frequencies and spend per visit generate target revenues *and* contribution, and therefore,
- all departments/categories are 'shopped'
- customer loyalty is built, thereby ensuring an ongoing relationship with the customer.

The store design and layout must have two characteristics: it must be capable of meeting customer requirements *and* manage the customer flows cost efficiently. This requires a cost-effective design. To meet objectives a strategy must be *effective* and implemented *efficiently*.

For the design and layout to meet the objectives both should reflect the way in which the customer 'shops' the store. The *effective* component of the decision is to ensure that the merchandise and service requirements are met, i.e. that the relevant merchandise is available (width, depth and availability). The *efficient* component is the management of the costs of activities involved; this concerns the in-store merchandising costs and the costs involved in distribution. Basic components of the decision are:

- location within the store, and
- space allocation: sufficient space to provide variety, availability *and* credibility; both decisions contributing to
- confirmation of the positioning of the retail offer.

Location within the store has a number of considerations. There is the need to conform to a logic followed by the customer and a layout which is consistent and complementary. In the 1970s Woolworth (UK) appeared not to have a logic aimed at encouraging the customer to do much else than purchase the few items intended for purchase on that specific visit. By contrast, NEXT in the 1980s began to coordinate merchandise displays which provided the customer with ideas for both style and wardrobe coordination *and* increased the size of customer transactions. Cost efficiencies must also be considered. Fast-moving merchandise often requires replenishment during the hours of business (as 24 hour opening moves towards the rule rather than an exception this problem increases). It follows that location, space allocated, fixture systems and packaging merge in the decision process and the cost-efficient solutions to meeting customer expectations at budgeted costs often involve suppliers. By considering rate of sale, 'value' and logistics costs we now consider the trade-off possibilities among the major variables.

Another factor concerns the need to ensure that *all* of the store is visited. Considerable research is undertaken by retailers, monitoring in-store behaviour to ensure that store design and layout encourage customers to visit all departments. Failure to ensure such coverage may result in lower than planned transaction values, with a consequent impact on revenues and contribution.

Space allocation has similar considerations. Prior to the introduction of reliable mixing for paint colour choices, DIY retailers were obliged to make large allocations of space to ensure that choice was seen to be available (despite the fact that a Pareto effect resulted in two or three colours accounting for 70–80% of paint sales). The large displays also served to establish credibility as a supplier. Other considerations include the need to ensure that brand space allocation reflects customer choice preferences *and* contribution returns. Related to customer choice is the concern that the positioning message (and its continuity) is clearly in focus. For example, a food retail chain whose value/price offer is price/economy based should ensure that prominent display/space allocation is given to national manufacturer brands which reassure customers of the price competitiveness of the offer.

Customer service facilities

Customers are very clear in their views concerning their expectations for service facilities and staff requirements: Nordstrom has researched this aspect of its offer very closely. Spector and McCarthy (1995) comment:

> Comfort and ease are the guiding principles behind the design of Nordstrom's large, carpeted dressing rooms, fitting rooms, and customer lounges.... Fitting rooms in the stores' more fashionable ready-to-wear departments include tables, table lamps and telephones...
>
> Particular attention is given to the lighting of the mirrors in the dressing rooms. Nordstrom uses a combination of incandescent and fluorescent lights so that the customer can see the actual colours of the item she is purchasing.

And quoting the vice-president of store planning, David Lindsey:

> The whole point of everything we do is to make the customer happy for the long haul. If people are satisfied and excited about the experience of shopping at Nordstrom, they will come back. And if you haven't created that atmosphere, they won't come back....
>
> It's just that simple.

It is interesting to observe that Nordstrom sacrifices selling area to provide service facilities. Whereas Macy's devotes some 70% of its available store space to sales, Nordstrom by comparison uses some 50%.

Food and restaurant services are used to enhance the shopping environment *and profits*. Chapter 10 used Nordstrom's approach to illustrate the use of restaurant services as a means of extending customers' time spent in the stores, but at the same time reflecting the customers' differing needs and expectations. This aspect of strategy implementation is clearly seen in the refurbished Grace Brothers store in central Sydney.

Staff recruitment and training requirements

Staff involvement in the format and environment strategy is a major contribution. Employees are a means by which the positioning of the organization is communicated to customers. As such they represent a major asset or, if their contribution is neglected, a liability. Staff recruitment should be made with this in mind. A store environment reflecting a 'leading edge' approach should be staffed with people who reflect this strategy and whose product knowledge and service approach integrate with the positioning message, and whose appearance and approach to customers reinforce the design of the store environment. Consequently, staff training should extend to include an explanation of the rationale of the retail offer, its positioning and implementation, and their role in complementing the store environment.

In the 1970s Hornes, then a *very* traditional (UK) menswear chain, undertook a radical repositioning exercise. It attempted to move into a more casual/informal wear segment of the market in which competition was intense and well entrenched. The competitors understood the market well; in particular they had identified a need for their employees to reflect the appearance that their customers sought. This required the recruitment and training of empathetic employees, interested in clothing *and* the leisure interests of potential customers. Research at that time by one of the authors identified the success of those companies who gave attention to this detail. Hornes did not, and this omission to attend to such issues was one of a number of reasons why 'You Bring the Body We Have the Clothes' was an unsuccessful campaign.

The use of information technology can augment the service and staff inputs. The 'high-tech' approach can be adopted successfully by a range of formats. The application of CAD/CAM design packages by furniture/interior design companies is used in the USA and UK to augment skilled (and expensive) design staff.

Customer handling systems

In Chapter 11 we quoted the views of Kemper (*New York Times*) suggesting that consumer preferences for shopping environment options have changed. Spector and McCarthy also quoted Petrucci, a marketing consultant, who suggested:

> In the 1980s, it was the quest for trendy merchandise. In the 1990s, it's a mission: find it, buy it, and get out.

Customer handling systems should reflect customer expectations. Food retailers have responded to the requirements of young mothers, usually accompanied by their small children, with 'self-check-out systems' (Sainsbury and Safeway) and by minimizing check-out queues with 'One Ahead' campaigns (Tesco).

In other merchandise category areas information technology is used to offer product information and application data. The use of free video cassette material is commonplace, particularly in services retailing where holiday packages may be considered at home and the details of financial services can be explained in detail *without* the involvement of expensive sales staff.

Thus while operations management is tasked with achieving sales and profitability objectives from a prescribed merchandise mix and space and human resource inputs it is not always possible to do so. Increasingly, occupancy and staff costs/sales ratios force the high service content formats to identify more cost-efficient methods of delivering information and handling transactions.

Merchandise stocking and replenishment systems

The merchandise strategy will have established merchandise profiles for each format and will have considered the implications of size differences within each format category. The operational concerns of these decisions are to ensure that customer transactions are maximized at an optimal level of cost. It will be recalled that the basis of revenue and contribution forecasts are customer visits, frequency of visits and average transaction value per visit. Essentially, this is a sales productivity issue and the format and environment concerns are with ensuring the visibility and replenishment of merchandise, such that in-store choice and availability targets are met.

The productivity concern extends therefore to space allocation and utilization together with that of the logistics system. We shall devote a chapter to supply chain management, and at this point will mention only briefly some of the issues.

The merchandise stocking and replenishment decision will consider a number of factors. Clearly the positioning/retail offer made to the customer will require primary concern. The choice, availability and continuity by category and product group will decide not only the space requirements within stores, but also the replenishment cycles (and therefore systems required) to ensure the achievement of merchandise objectives and customer sales response. Clearly there are different issues and implications for different retail offers.

The discount food multiples (for example, the KwikSave and Aldi formats) require a replenishment system that ensures maximum availability of their (comparatively) limited width ranges. The *value* they deliver is a combination of availability, convenience and low prices across the assortment. Therefore, while it could be argued that having a restricted assortment is an advantage within the context of logistics activities, it must be remembered that to make the offer both effective and profitable, the targets for availability and low price put a large burden on logistics system efficiency and costs.

The problem is greater for retailers majoring on fresh produce ranges. European consumers' tastes for a wide range of fresh fruits and vegetables have been developed by retailers seeking to establish themselves as strong competitors in this merchandise category. While there may be advantages such as margins and customer appeal (i.e. visit frequencies and transactions), the supply chain tasks and costs pose a number of difficulties for management. Many of these difficulties can be relieved by the use of sophisticated information management.

Information systems support

Information management will be an entire chapter topic later in this text. However, it is useful to identify some important issues within this topic.

Increasingly, information management is assuming significance in retailing management decisions at both strategy and implementation levels. When used as a strategic and operational facilitator, information management can identify decision tasks, the accuracy required, and the timing of information flows relevant to decision making.

Given the two examples of the previous section the information support will differ in a number of respects. The discount organization will be able to establish a support system that ensures that its availability targets are met and which links outlets with replenishment sources. It is also essential for the discounter to be able to monitor activities and their costs in order to meet budgeted cost levels and, if possible, lower them and/or improve the efficiency levels of the activities involved in delivering customer value. An additional demand on its information system is to monitor sales patterns and trends. An important characteristic of competitive advantage for the discounter is to offer relevant merchandise; hence it is vital that not just rates of sale are monitored, but also merchandise items and categories.

The fresh produce retailer also requires a support system that monitors sales and links outlets with replenishment sources, but it is also essential to monitor inventory levels and stock turns on a daily (if not twice daily) basis. There are two reasons. First, if margins are to be maintained then rapid stock turns (consistent with the costs of replenishment) are necessary. Secondly, the market positioning will suffer damage if the 'freshness' is not maintained.

The store operations plan

The implementation of the format and environment strategy (and its success or failure) is in the hands of store operations: Chapter 3 dealt with operations management processes and activities in detail. Here our concern is to identify the role of a store operations activity in implementing a format and environment strategy.

Figure 12.1 identifies three components of an effective store operations plan. The purpose is to ensure the efficient acquisition, deployment and use of human and physical resources employed in delivering a prescribed level of value to meet customer expectations. Wild (1977) defined operations management as: 'the design and planning, operation and control of operating systems' and an operating system as: 'a configuration of resources combined for the provision of goods and services'.

Given the format and environment strategy, the operations repositioning is to undertake both *design and planning* and the *operation and control* activities *and* to produce a budget for financial control purposes. The detail of specific retailing operations activities will vary depending upon the nature of the business and its positioning. However, the tasks identified in Figure 12.1 are common to all forms of retailing.

The operating budget

To ensure the successful implementation of the format and environment strategy the operating budget details revenue expectations, resource requirements and expenditure levels necessary to realize the strategy.
As with other functions, specific budget items will vary. Using the performance measures identified earlier, the following topics are proposed:

Revenues

Sales	by:	• regions	by:	• sales area
Gross margin		• locations		• employee
Contribution margin		• formats		
		• 'seasons'		

Resource requirements
Dedicated staff
Dedicated capital equipment

Expenses
Staff
Leases and occupancy costs
Planned refurbishment costs
Design costs (internal and external)

Exhibit 12.1

Grace Brothers: implementing a format strategy
The new Grace Bros City Central store is built on a site which once housed seven separate buildings, among them the old Farmers

department store. The original Grace Bros – the company is 125 years old – was out along Broadway in a large pair of department stores. Farmers eventually became a Myer store, then that became another Grace Bros store. Grace Bros on Broadway closed at the beginning of this decade. The Grace Bros store is part of Myer Grace Bros, in turn owned by Coles Myer.

For nearly 20 years, questions of what to do with the city site have been raised: refurbish or rebuild.

The shop was a dog's breakfast of a place, so eventually the board bit the bullet and some years ago began plans for the rebuilding project. It seems to have gone on for years, as the old, antiquated and shabby building was progressively closed, rebuilt and reopened.

During the past couple of weeks the hoardings have been coming down and Grace Bros city store has been revealed as not only completely unlike any other department store in Sydney (OK, there's only one) but completely unlike its former self.

Six floors of retail swing from a light and airy ground floor up to the sixth, which Rick Lowry, general manager of retail operations for Myer Grace Bros, says is the biggest supplier of electrical appliances anywhere in Australia. 'Sorry, Gerry Harvey', he said with a smile.

He's proud of how this store turned out and happy to show it off from the bottom to the top. Along the way, he talks about the philosophies and the processes which informed the decisions reflected in this glossy market-place.

There is less reserve space, more stock on the floor, and a new computer system which can interface with those of suppliers on a daily basis so that orders can start to be built as soon as an item sells. The sales are made at large, hard-to-miss islands scattered around the floors, and the sales assistants on the ground floor stand in front of their products, but behind their counters. Lowry and the team circled the globe and brought back ideas to incorporate into the new store: there are touches of Bloomingdales' basement on the second floor, it's Barney-like on the third with the imported labels and women's wear, and there's a touch of Galleries Lafayette in the first floor.

It goes into Virgin Megastore territory with about 100,000 CDs on the fifth floor and a book department – around 300,000 titles – which looks like heaven with a leak in the ceiling. Walking past the drip, Lowry was quick: 'Those waterfalls cost a lot to install...'.

As well there's a dedicated floor for the 18-to-24s. 'You and I mightn't feel comfortable there', said Lowry, 'but it's designed to offer people in that age range – and beyond – everything they could want'. Then he suggests a tour of the dressing rooms, which are (as are the others in the store) twice the size of normal stores, offer 360° views and are painted a vibrant purple with a yellow dado. 'The painter told me he got a headache doing that!' (There is a focus on this sort of thing at David Jones as well – Don Grover recommended a visit to the third-floor ladies' room. He was right – it's great.) It's a sensation, this new Grace Bros – and even old retail hands are amazed by the result. Its statistics are mind-boggling, too: 35,000 square metres, 1000 staff, 17,500 light fittings, 16,000 square metres of timber flooring (some of it salvaged from Grace Bros on Broadway), 45,000 litres of paint.

There's a fragrance wall on the ground floor – 270 perfumes for men and women – positioned by alphabetical order. And the food outlets... so many of them. Why? Research told them so.

Grace Bros surveyed its customers to find out what they wanted from a retailer. A number of different places to sit down and eat or have a cup of coffee was one need.

And armed with information Lowry and the team refocused on their customers. 'It's fair to say we lost sight of who our customers are. We might have gone a little too far upmarket and forgot we serve middle Australia,' he said over a latte in the Cantinetta while another celebrity chef, Neil Perry, does a walk-by inspection of the antipasto.

'Our customers are mainstream. We say to ourselves as a business that whatever we do we have to be relevant to those customers.'

And the market has changed. Deregulation means we can shop seven days a week – and stores' records show that unit sales on Sunday are higher than at any other time during the week. As well, now only some 10% of the retail market belongs to department stores. The remaining 90% is sold through other retail outlets, including speciality stores, boutiques and warehouses.

Lowry's philosophy of retailing is pretty easy to grasp: 'Product, product, and product', he said at the top of the first-floor escalators, where product stretches from the windows on Pitt Street across to George.

Extract from Hogan, Christine (1998) Store wars: retail giants strike back. *The Sun Herald*, 15 November.

SUMMARY

The successful implementation of the format and environment strategy will ensure the marketing and financial objectives of the organization are met. Given a format strategy and design, the implementation should not simply reflect the positioning intention but should also meet customer expectations for merchandise choice and availability and service facilities and activities.

The role of store operations management is one of monitoring the customer offer *and* the cost of delivering the offer. Given a resources budget, the implementation activity should deliver no less, and certainly no more, than the 'promise' made by the overall retail offer. The purpose should be to respond to the customer with a format and environment that encourages frequent visits and transactions. It should be cost-effective in its implementation and cost-efficient in its operation.

QUESTIONS, ACTIVITIES AND CONSIDERATIONS

- Assume the role of a consultant who is given the task of resolving a difference of views concerning the implementation of the format and environment strategy for a furniture retail chain. The marketing director's proposals are for the design to reflect room settings familiar to the target customer group. The alternative proposal suggests that this is cost inefficient in the use of space and that because of the wide price offer being made the customer group would respond to a product group display which better reflects the company's strength. What are the issues? How can they be resolved?
- What are the likely problems that will confront a retailer who attempts to develop a standard format and environment offer?
- Develop a model which can be used to monitor operations activities and facilities.
- A number of automobile manufacturers have announced their intentions to move towards Internet selling and away from the traditional vehicle showroom facilities. What are the considerations that such an approach should identify and address?

REFERENCES

Hogan, C. (1998) Store wars: retail giants strike back. *The Sun Herald*, 15 November.
Spector, R. and McCarthy, P. D. (1995) *The Nordstrom Way*. John Wiley, New York.
Wild, R. (1977) *Concepts for Operations Management*. John Wiley Chichester.

13 DEVELOPING CUSTOMER COMMUNICATIONS STRATEGY

LEARNING OBJECTIVES

The role of customer communications is important for a number of reasons. First, it is an essential component in identifying strategic positioning with the consumer. Secondly, it has a major role in the processes of informing and persuading customers to form (or change) attitudes and change preferences and, subsequently, behaviour. Thirdly, customer communications are important in extending the lifespan of customer relationships with the business. An effective customer communications strategy requires management to understand the following:

- To be effective we must first profile or segment customers. Broad segmentation characteristics are helpful, but need to be augmented by adding relevant shopping characteristics.
- The state of readiness to make a purchase (or 'customer qualifications') is important. The reader is taken through a model which illustrates how customer communications may improve the confidence, interest, knowledge and readiness to make a purchase from a specific retailer.
- The role of communication in developing a strong positioning is considered by first discussing the concept of positioning and then introducing specific retail marketing dimensions.
- Given a desired strategic positioning the communications implications are considered. These include creative and media strategies together with time perspectives; a balance between long-term and short-term continuity requirements.
- A review of the role of customer loyalty programs and the increase in their importance as information technology and management makes database management more accessible and accurate.
- Non-personal communications have an important role. Visual merchandising is a powerful link between merchandise and communications strategies.
- The increasing role and effectiveness of public relations and corporate affairs in both strategic and operational aspects of retailing strategy decisions.

INTRODUCTION

Effective customer communications are based upon a two-way flow of information. A successful communications strategy has a number of essential components. *First* we need a detailed profile of customer characteristics; these should include demographic and socio-economic data *together with* information on their lifestyles, shopping-related lifestyles, 'qualifications' and typical shopping missions. The *second* requirement is to identify which customers identify closely with our positioning strategy, their perceptions of the company and the format, their specific attitudes towards the company, their expectations (if they are to continue to express favourable attitudes towards us), and the extent of, and reasons for, their loyalty. A *third* component concerns their perceptions, attitudes towards and patronization of competitive offers.

Customer communications in retailing can only be effective if it identifies with its target customer group and understands how a decision to use a particular retail offer is made and how specific purchases are also arrived at. Recent developments in information management have facilitated this task: information technology has provided the means by which we can monitor customer store selection and purchasing behaviour much more effectively than ever before.

This chapter considers the process of developing a communications strategy. Figure 13.1 suggests an approach. It identifies aspects of customer decision-making characteristics and behaviour and demonstrates how these may be used to identify the methods and media of customer information and persuasion.

ESTABLISHING A CUSTOMER PROFILE

Broad customer typology

Depending upon the nature of the retail business and its merchandise offer so the need for complex customer data will vary. For example, multiple food retailing could plan an adequate communications program with the data provided under this heading (broad customer typology) in Figure 13.2. Age, location, income and family size provide a useful input into communications planning. Given the nature of food expenditure patterns, local television and newspaper campaigns, targeting customers within a prescribed drive time from the point-of-sale, are capable of achieving sales from the typical weekly food shopper (the B1/C2, 25–44 year-old suburban dweller with 2.5 children etc.). The data required is readily available from government and commercial research sources. Typically it is low-cost and accurate. The communications component is not difficult to create and implement.

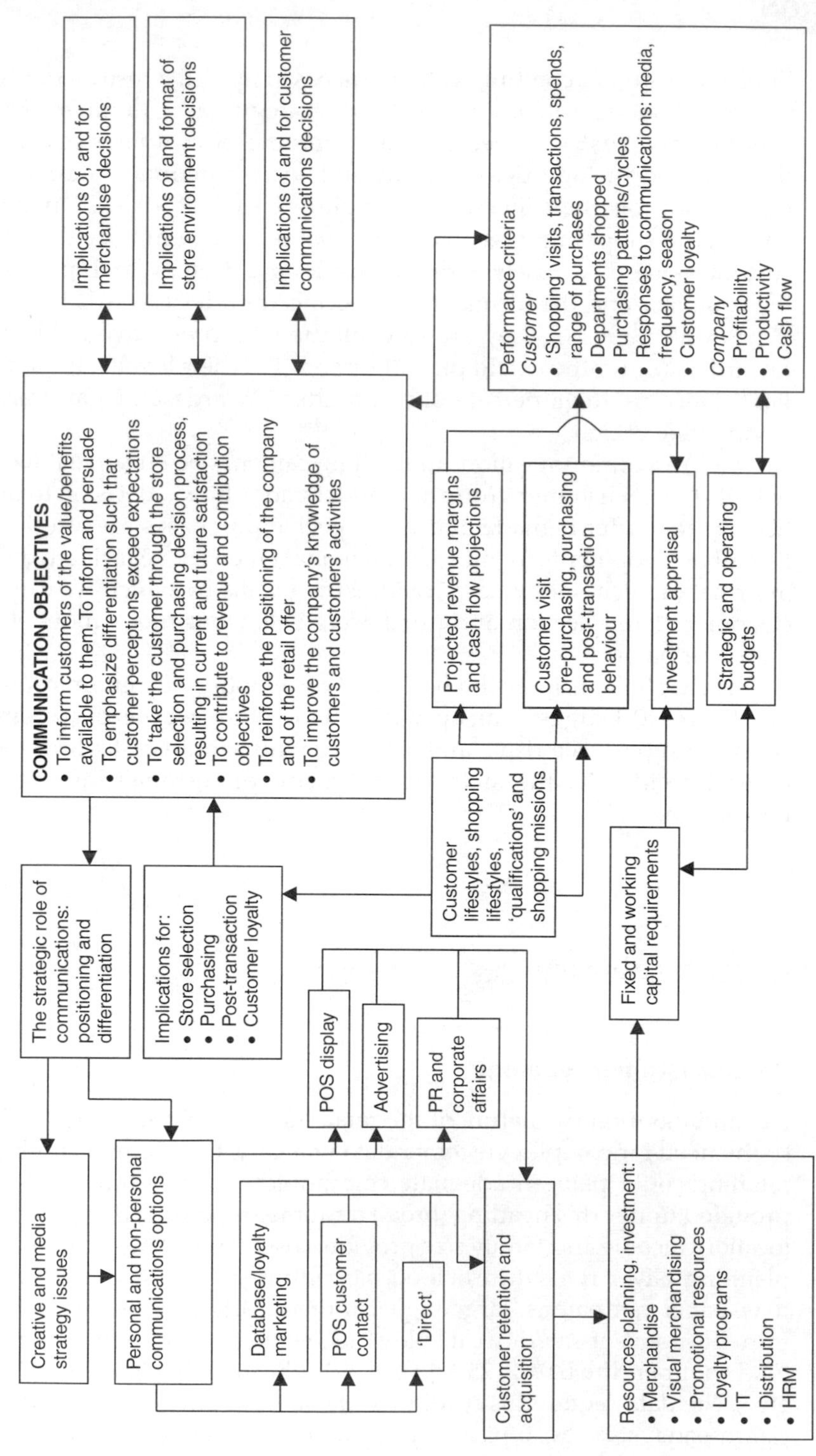

Figure 13.1 The customer communications strategy.

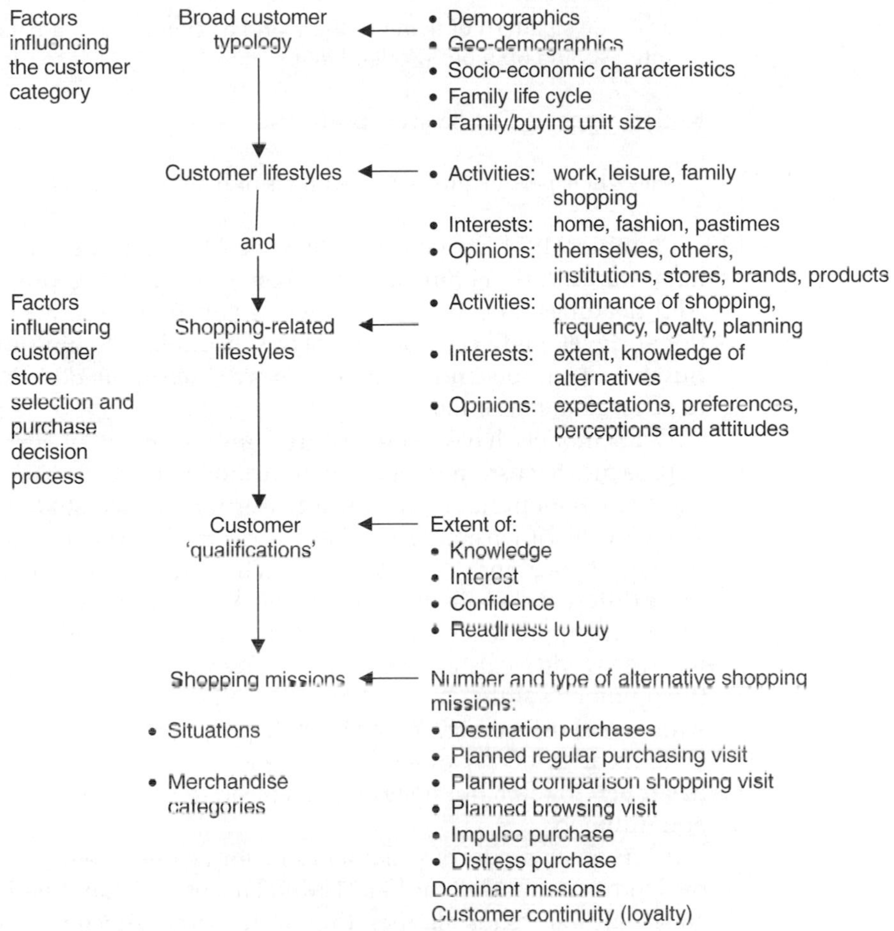

Figure 13.2 Profiling target customer groups.

A simple but effective approach is the overview of the family life cycle and buying behaviour proposed by Wells and Gubar (1966) and subsequently modified by Murphy and Staples (1979). The Wells and Gubar family life cycle proposed nine stages of the family life cycle, along with the expected financial situation and typical product interests of each group. Clearly the approach requires frequent updating to reflect social changes, but with such changes it is a useful planning guide for routine purchases in the FMCG and durable categories.

Customer lifestyles and shopping-related lifestyles

A criticism of the simple approaches outlined above is that people from the same culture, subculture, social class and occupational category quite often live very different types of lives. *Lifestyle* was coined to describe:

> a person's pattern of living in the world as expressed in a person's activities, interests and opinions (Kotler, 1986).

Kotler suggests that lifestyle portrays:

> the 'whole person' interacting with his or her environment.

Plummer (1974) proposed the lifestyle AIO (Attitudes, Interests and Opinions) framework. Figure 13.2 uses some of the topics proposed under the AIO headings. Subsequently, Mitchell (1983), a researcher at SRI International, developed a classification of the US public into nine lifestyle groups. A number of authors and researchers have since applied his VALS framework to other national situations.

VALS models have been featured in a number of texts as conceptual approaches to customer segmentation and in applications studies. The VALS 2 approach identifies eight consumer groups which share two dimensions. The vertical dimension represents consumers' resources, money, education, self-confidence and 'energy' levels. The horizontal dimension represents three different ways in which consumers see the world and reflects their attitudes and approaches. They may be principle-oriented (guided by views of how the world is or should be); status-oriented (their views are influenced by the opinions of others); or action-oriented (they share a desire for 'activity', variety and risk taking). When both dimensions are considered concurrently a matrix array of consumer typologies is developed. As an approach VALS 2 has much to offer, but it should be considered in the context of local issues and influences.

A European model of social standing and value orientation was developed by Homma and Ueltzhoffer (1990). The model identified eight common cross-cultural trends all operating in the same direction in the UK, France, Germany and Italy. They were classified as: consumer hedonism; individualism; nostalgia; environmentalism; opening-up and outward looking; anomie and social aggressiveness; focus on the body (health); and irrationalism. The authors used the model to identify differences in consumption behaviour. As with VALS the model offers a reference frame from which more specific categories can be developed. Adoption of the categories offered by any approach (not just VALS 2 and Homma and Ueltzhoffer's cross-cultural segmentation models) *without* modification may lead to serious errors; a cautious approach is therefore necessary.

Retailing interests in lifestyle are focused upon the activities, interests and opinions that relate to the store selection and purchasing decision; this facilitates the communications process. Thus, having identified a broad customer group using demographics or geo-demographics, we can focus on *their* lifestyle characteristics. It is using this approach that results in segmenting customer groups. For example, Tesco's range of outlets reflects the lifestyle differences of their customer mix. The large superstores have appeal to those with time and role tasks to include prolonged frequent shopping visits in the spectrum of their activities. By contrast the Metro store user is more likely to belong to a different demographic group, with a different socio-economic profile etc. *and* because of a quite different set of activities etc. have a considerably different lifestyle profile. Work and leisure will dominate *activities*; hobbies and other pursuits will be the primary *interests* and their *opinions* of themselves and of brands etc. will be based upon convenience and performance rather than price/value characteristics. Often the customer is the same person fulfilling different needs at different times.

Shopping-related lifestyles become more specific. The activities, interests and opinions relate to detailed purchasing situations and can be vital to the communications strategy. For example, shopping activity frequency (and specifically the day of the week) will dictate *when* advertising messages are sent; knowledge of the customer's loyalty to the store (or propensity for such schemes) can be used to reinforce the advertising message with direct marketing offers, and if their 'planning activities' can be identified the communications can be aligned to influence both store selection *and* the purchase decision process.

A knowledge of the *extent* of customer interests is helpful not only to merchandise decisions but to the communications strategy. For example, a US department store identified an interest in a group of its customers for creative involvement in home decorating. It developed a range of products and classes, and by using its database very quickly built an exclusive area in the home fashion sector.

Communications should be used to reinforce perceptions and attitudes. Research by a food multiple established a strong opinion that fresh products were important to competitive advantage and strategic positioning. A dominant feature of its communications program is reference to its strength as a 'fresh food' supplier.

Customer qualifications

The store selection and purchasing decision process for a number of high-priced and infrequently purchased items does require the customer to become 'qualified' to make the purchase. Customer qualifications characteristics are listed in Figure 13.2 and dealt with in detail in Figure 13.3. The proposition is that four characteristics influence customers' purchasing activities. To be 'qualified' to make a purchase they require positive readings on each of the four scales featured. It is not necessary that they become totally 'confident' or 'knowledgeable', but that they are sufficiently satisfied in their own minds that they have the information they require and confident they have evaluated the relevant decision alternatives. A level of interest (an identified need) is assumed, but this too may need to be exposed to the potential customer.

An example (a consumer durable purchase) is shown as Figure 13.4. In Figure 13.4(a) the subject is clearly not likely to consider a purchase. Figure 13.4(b) illustrates a 'qualified customer'. The levels of confidence, knowledge and interest have become sufficiently strong for a purchase to be made.

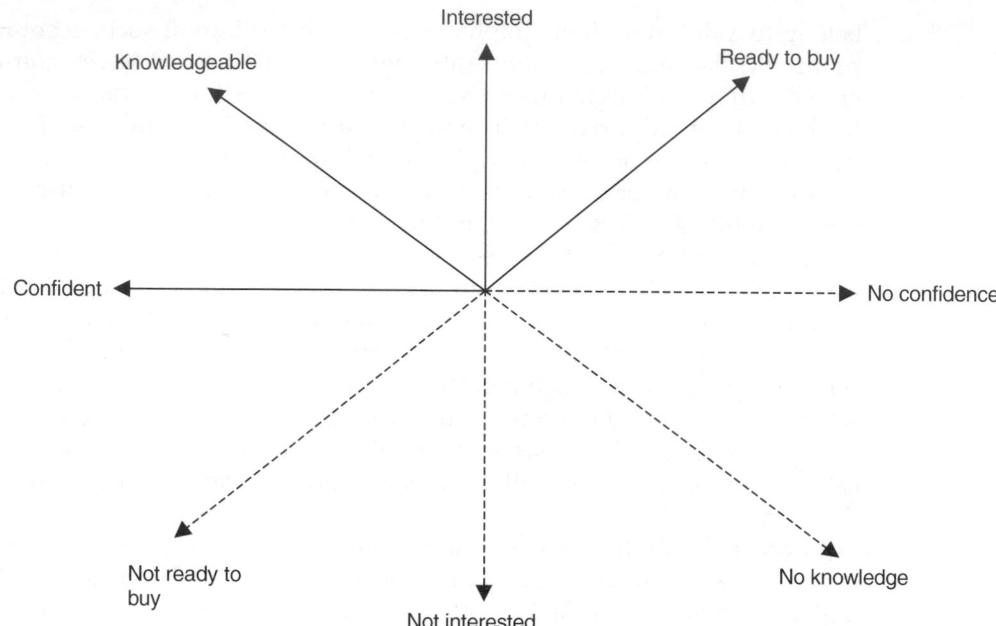

Figure 13.3 Customer qualifications map.

The role of customer communications is to develop customer qualifications such that *not only* is the purchase contemplated *but* it is made specifically *from one* retail outlet. The role of customer communications in the process is suggested by Figure 13.5. The structure of the model is changed a little to permit movement from negative values of interest, confidence, knowledge and readiness to buy towards positive values. Figure 13.5 contains examples of communications solutions assuming that initially negative views exist. The purpose of customer communications is to take an integrated approach by using those media (personal and non-personal, in-store and external) relevant to the store selection and purchase decision process that the target customer group will use in decision making.

Shopping missions

Returning to Figure 13.2, we complete the process of profiling customer groups. The role of shopping missions was discussed earlier. It was noted that they are important in determining format and environment decisions. They are equally important for the communications strategy. Again, there is a problem. Not all customer shopping missions are the same. However, for some retailers (for example the convenience store group Alldays) there is predominance of one or two shopping missions. As with the planning tasks for format and store environment, it is the frequency of occurrence of the shopping missions that is important. A predominance of one particular

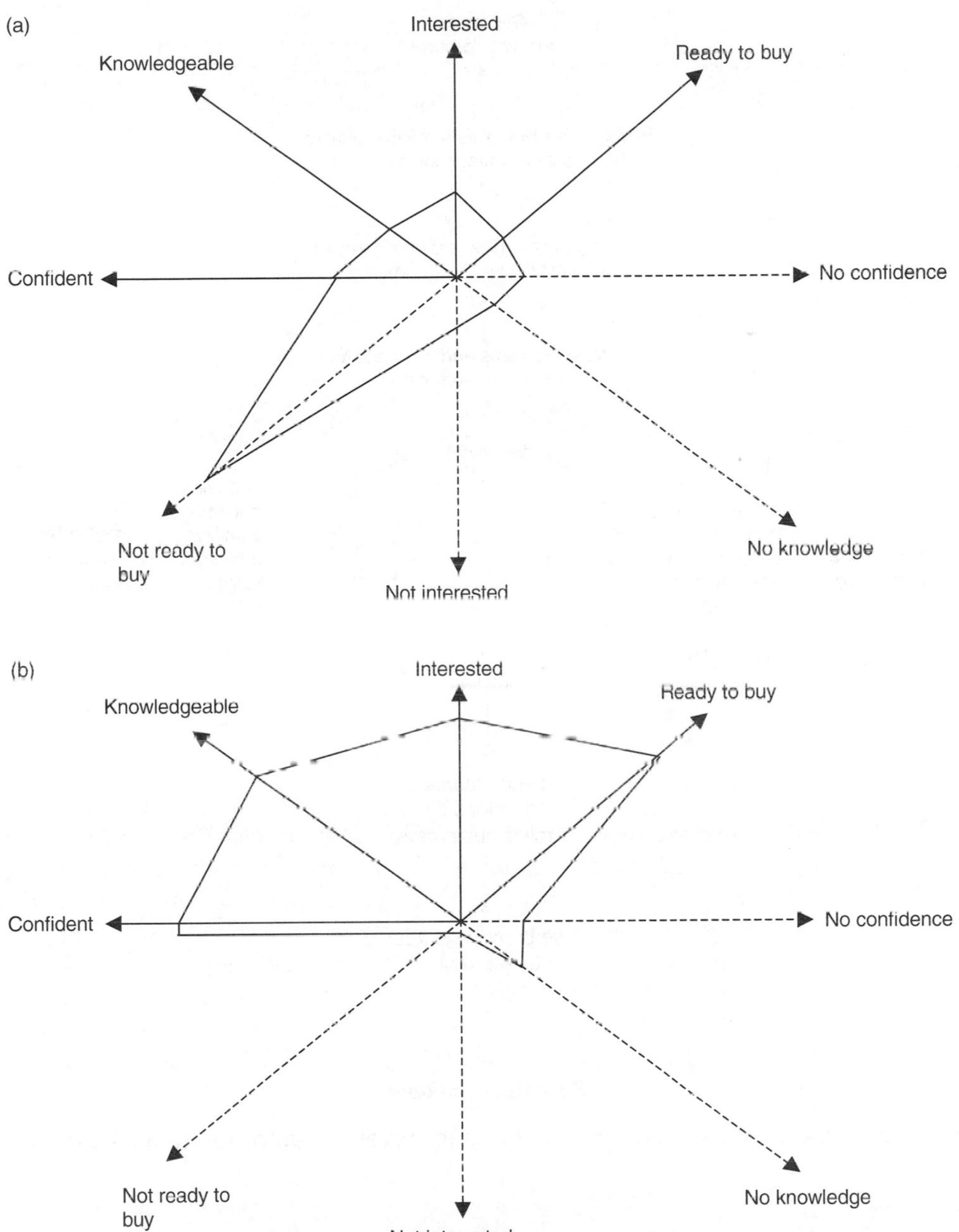

Figure 13.4 Customer qualifications map. (a) No purchase likely to occur; (b) qualifications developed into readiness to purchase.

shopping mission can be used to structure a communications theme. For example, a department store identified that a majority of its sales resulted from *planned comparison shopping visits*, this information was used to plan both the communication strategy and the format and environment of these

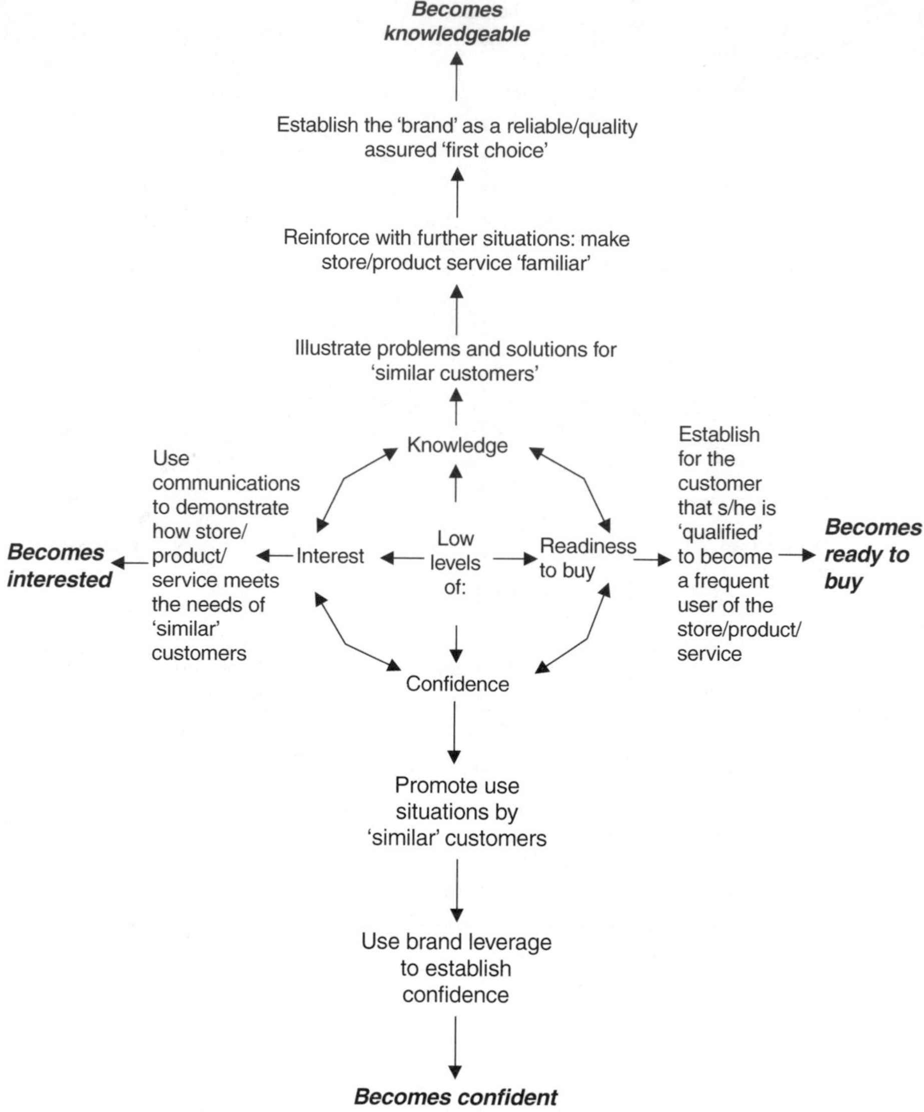

Figure 13.5 Using customer communications to develop customer 'qualifications'.

departments. The communications approach to customers comprised a direct marketing campaign and a press and television campaign featuring the wide range of international labels known to appeal to its target customer group. In-store visual merchandising reinforced the advertising with coordinated merchandise displays of the manufacturers featured in the advertising campaign. Sales showed a significant increase.

A convenience store group monitored its sales patterns on both daily and hourly bases. It found specific *destination purchase* patterns at specific times of the day and for days of the week. The result was a very successful campaign at weekends (using mail drops) promoting a video hire offer and a range of snack foods and convenience food items.

It has been found very helpful to identify communications needs across a range of shopping missions *and* through the store selection and purchasing decision process. Figure 13.6 is based upon observations and discussion. As the model suggests, a certain amount of flexibility must be available, but the observations suggested a certain consistency in the effectiveness of communications programs following the approach.

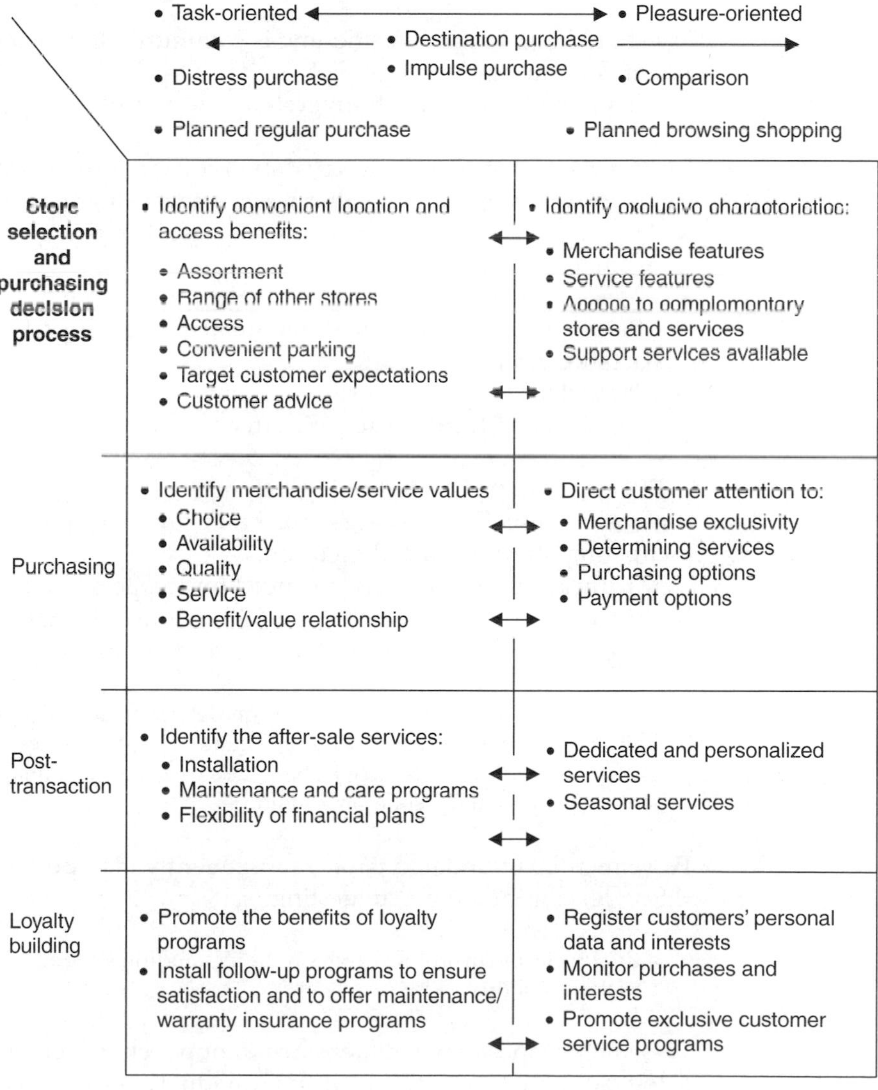

Figure 13.6 Taking the customer through the store selection and purchasing process.

POSITIONING AND DIFFERENTIATION

Positioning as a concept

We suggested (Chapter 2) that strategic positioning is:

> The long-term positioning sought by the organization as reflected by its decisions for customer value offer, product decisions, market decisions and shareholder value. Strategic positioning will be interpreted by its product positioning, market positioning and product–market positioning.

We should add to this: 'Positioning is communicated by a coordinated customer communications strategy'.

Urban and Hauser (1980) suggested four important aspects:

- *Perception*: identifies those key dimensions most relevant to the customer and how customers view alternative offers using these dimensions.
- *Preference*: identifies how consumers use the perceived dimensions to evaluate offers.
- *Segmentation*: determines whether the 'best' strategy is to maintain one offer for all customers or to differentiate offers, directing each to a specific customer group.
- *Choice*: determines what external events must be controlled to ensure that consumers preferring a specific offer actually purchase it.

Effective strategic positioning requires an understanding of the key dimensions used by the target customer group to perceive and compare competing offers on each dimension.

Martineau (1958) identified the need for retailers to establish a clear positioning which identifies what it is offering, how this *relates* to the needs of a specific group of customers and how it *differs* from its competitors' offers:

> Clearly there is a force operative in the determination of a store's customer body besides the obvious functional factors of location, price ranges and merchandise selection... this force is the store's personality or image – the way the store is defined in the shopper's mind.

Pessemier (in an undated paper) subsequently incorporated psychographic (lifestyle) considerations suggesting:

> a dual focus of current research on understanding shoppers *and* the stores in which they shop.

Pessemier proposed two dimensions, shopper characteristics and store characteristics, as a means by which an individual's relationship to a retail outlet might be described:

> *Shopper characteristics* comprise simple and complex *demographics* (age, sex, complex, life cycle and social class); *shopping-related lifestyle* (activities, interests and opinions); *shopping-related perceptions and preferences* (beliefs about stores, likes and dislikes about stores) and *shopping-related behaviour* (media exposure patterns, shopping patterns, purchasing patterns.

Pessemier suggests that the first two types of variable describe the personal qualities of individual shoppers and households. The other two describe the relationship of the individual to the store. Demographic and lifestyle variables tend to define fairly general needs and capacities of individuals and households, but rarely represent strong determinants of brands or store choices. Conversely, he suggests, perceptions and preferences are frequently closely linked to choice behaviour. For this reason these may be used to predict shopping behaviour while the demographic and life cycle variables may be used to profile or describe segments that display distinct modes of behaviour:

> *Store characteristics* comprise *customer mix* (demographic and lifestyle profiles of a store's customers); *life cycle position of store type* (store type life cycle position); *merchandise characteristics* (width, depth, availability); *merchandise mix* (fashion and staple items); *price points; brand profile* (national brands and labels, retail own brands); *convenience characteristics* (location and transactions); *promotional emphasis* (the 'benefit'/value offer); *integrity* (price guarantees; product returns etc.); *shopping pleasure* (ambience, services, staff response); *image strength and clarity* (a clear unambiguous statement of what it is and what it offers the target customer).

This inventory of characteristics is very helpful, not only to profile customers but to develop a communications platform. If we can identify shopper characteristics in detail we have 'someone to talk to', and knowledge of the *important aspects* of store characteristics can be used to formulate the retail offer *and* to promote it effectively. Constant monitoring of both shopper and store characteristics is essential. Failure to do so can result in preference shifts that are missed. For example, a number of retailers missed clues given by consumers in late 1998 and early 1999 concerning expenditure shifts (see Chapter 1), and as a result suffered very low (for some nil) year-on-year growth. Clearly a shift has occurred in store preferences: price has become important, as has a shift in expenditure towards service products.

The communications strategy can be used to respond to these and other changes. It requires a flexible approach and should ensure that the long-term strategic direction is maintained until there is very clear research evidence to the contrary.

CREATIVE AND MEDIA STRATEGIES

Given a strategic positioning and a communications strategy template constructed around the shopper's characteristics and store characteristics found to be dominant influences, the strategy can be carried on to the next stage:

that of deciding upon an appropriate creative approach and the media considered to be most effective for carrying the positioning message.

The lifestyle, perceptions and preferences and behaviour details will prove very useful. Earlier (see Figure 13.2 and the discussion on shopping-related lifestyles, shopping missions and customer qualifications) we considered the store selection and purchasing decision process in some detail. This data will identify the role required by the communications strategy in its task of reinforcing the long-term positioning/image proposition *and* the task of taking the customer through the store selection and purchasing process in the short and medium term. The way that both tasks are achieved in order that customer visits and transactions are built into long-term revenues and profits will be influenced by what messages are given, to which customers, how and when.

It is essential that the balance between long-term and short-term is maintained and continuity rather than confusion is established in the minds of the target customer group. An example may help. Sainsbury (the UK food multiple) has pursued a strategic positioning identifying exclusivity, quality and variety as key positioning characteristics for a number of years. The creative strategy has been built around Sainsbury's own-brand products. These have been selected to reinforce the strategic positioning message. The media selected to carry this message have been dominated by the 'upmarket' press, typically Sunday broadsheet colour supplements and magazines. However, the impact of competitive activities forced the company into responding with price/value advertising using a (predominantly) television campaign to future a price offer on fast-moving (competitive) merchandise items.

The opinion of financial and marketing writers appears unanimous in its verdict that it has not been particularly successful. These comments suggest that there may have been long-term damage to Sainsbury's strategic positioning. Drayton Bird (1998) comments:

> No wonder the staff were appalled when they saw their firm – in which I assume they feel a certain pride – represented by John Cleese, hideously dressed as a holiday camp comedian, bawling at us – obnoxious as usual, but not even vaguely funny. I suspect this campaign will alienate not only the staff but the customers – faster than you can say, 'Oh my God, what were we thinking when we did that?'

Bird was soon to be proven correct:

> Sainsbury's campaign starring John Cleese as a garishly clad loudmouth was been voted the most irritating TV ad of the year... seventeen percent of the sample (an NOP study) voted the campaign the most annoying of the year.... In October Sainsbury's staff complained that the ads portrayed them as gormless and stupid ... (Denny, 1998).

And eventually the financial press took note:

> The City cut its profits forecasts... estimates for the following year have been cut even further.... It's not a pretty picture. But Sainsbury insists that its

> fundamental approach – using its *value to shout about* campaign to persuade us that dear old Sainsbury is a pretty cheap place to do our shopping as well as being packed with stuff worthy of middle class dinner tables – can be made to work...
>
> ...Sainsbury's new approach appears to have persuaded shoppers that there are indeed bargains to be had... more people were drawn into the stores after the campaign was launched, but, canny lot that they were, customers spotted the opportunity to pop into Sainsbury's and buy only those items that were on special offer – typically offering two for the price of one or giving loads of extra reward card points. But they didn't hang around to do the rest of their (full-price) shopping (Laurance, 1999).

Clearly there are other potential reasons for the problems currently being experienced. Laurance continues to suggest that control is an issue and points to the capital ownership structure; nearly 40% of shares are owned by the family or trusts linked to the family. However, there remains a question concerning the compatibility of the two campaign messages.

PERSONAL AND NON-PERSONAL COMMUNICATIONS

Retailing is a customer contact business (although this may well not be the case within five to ten years). Personal contacts (by staff) and communications (by direct marketing/database) have a strong influence on customer perceptions. It follows that *personal communications* are important when a strategy is being formulated. Often customer perceptions of a company are formed by point-of-sale contact or through customer dealings with service departments, which result in long-term customer relationships.

Thus the conduct of staff and the content of 'messages' delivered by them and by direct marketing communication are important aspects of positioning. They can only be *developed* if all personnel share a philosophy that puts customer care uppermost in their minds and responses. It can be reinforced by training, but essentially staff must believe in, and share, an ethos of customer care. Recent trends have moved towards minimizing personal selling: the pressure on occupancy costs has influenced even the most service-minded retailers towards reducing staffing levels. However, there remain a number of retailers (Nordstrom for example) who continue to place an emphasis (and therefore resources) on staff development and training. Spector and McCarthy (1995) comment:

> The Nordstrom culture sets employees free. The company believes that people will work hard when they are given the freedom to do their job the way they think it should be done, and when they can treat customers the way *they* like to be treated.

To integrate staff into the communications program, training is helpful. It should be designed to include:

- *Customer buying behaviour (store selection and purchasing decision processes)*: a description of the processes and illustrations of how personal selling can help customers progress through the process.
- *Merchandise knowledge*: application, alternatives, sourcing and purchasing options, competitive offers, availability and location are all aspects that create strong customer relationships for the long term and revenue and profit in the short and medium terms.
- *Service support facilities*: maintenance of previous items purchased, storage, remodelling etc.
- *Customer contact*: approaches to customers, asking and using names, identifying their needs, demonstrating solutions and alternatives, asking for the order diplomatically but positively.
- *Customer follow up*: building the database which can be used for subsequent informed contact, to ensure satisfaction with purchases and to identify further needs.

Reverse customer communications is an essential feature of a communications strategy. Research shows that among 479 CEOs, only 8% of respondents believed that the opinion of the customer was well represented at board level within their own companies. A total of 41% thought that the customer was never, or rarely, represented at board level. The research also revealed that only 68% of boards included a marketing presence. Denny (1998) suggests:

> The core idea of board-level customer representation is related both to customer retention – that it is cheaper and more profitable to sell to your existing customers – and to customer acquisition. If the customer comes first, you will both acquire them and retain them'.

Denny provides an interesting case study. In 1996 Burger King was confronting problems. BSE was damaging its business. The company had stopped listening to its customers. Its pricing was wrong. Visit frequency was declining and prices were increased to maintain cash volume, which led to fewer visits. Burger King customers are calculated to be worth £3000+ over an 'average' lifespan. Fail to deliver value once and they may be lost. Research showed that customers were prepared to wait no more than three minutes for a meal – but 60% of customers were waiting longer. The solution was found by promoting management who were obsessive about customer service to listen to staff, customers and franchises. By the year-end June 1998 market share had risen by 1.5%, 'representing many millions of pounds worth of extra sales'.

Customer loyalty programs: a personal communications option

Effective communications is about relationship management. We saw earlier that the value of a customer over a lifespan amounts to a considerable sum. Customer loyalty programs are increasingly being used to manage the customer portfolio. The sophistication of many loyalty programs owes much to the application of information management/technology, so much so that increasing levels of resources are being applied to loyalty programs.

Gofton (1999) reports on a tracking research study conducted by Carlson Loyalty Monitor. As an initiative, loyalty programs have been very successful in the UK. Some 90% of the Carlson sample of 3000 are aware of loyalty programs and just under two-thirds actively participate. Women are bigger users than men, and their appeal is greater for the ABC1 social groups than it is for the C2s, Ds and Es. More than 40% of 16–34 year olds enrolled in loyalty programs say they 'are likely to spend more at those outlets.

The high-profile schemes (Tesco, Sainsbury, Boots and Safeway) mostly appeal (not surprisingly) to women. The Carlson data also shows that while the number of participants has not increased substantially over the past three years of the Carlson study, the number of schemes that consumers participate in has increased. Again this is not surprising; a number of companies/organizations have seen the obvious benefits of customer data *and* increased business. However, the enthusiasm of organizations is showing concern as the research suggests that the number of senior marketing management who considered them 'very effective' for building customer relationships has halved (to 13% from 29%). Similarly, the number of organizations considering introducing a loyalty scheme has also declined.

Supermarket company schemes revealed interesting facts. The appeal of these favours the more affluent: some 95% of ABs are aware of loyalty schemes and 77% are active participants. Of the DEs, 84% are aware and 50% participate. Data in Figure 13.7 reveal further interesting aspects. Participation in retailer schemes is high and the pattern of use suggests that the reward system *may* have an influence on the level of participation. The percentages of participants in the Tesco, Sainsbury, Safeway and Boots programs are much larger than for Somerfield. Each of the first four mentioned offer a reward system that is either a 'discount on future purchases' or 'offers' on those products in the range they otherwise would not purchase; whereas the Somerfield scheme is linked to a redemption program with Argos (a catalogue-based retailer).

A view of the effectiveness of the loyalty schemes is identified by responses to questions concerning the transfer of patronage should the retailer currently favoured end the scheme. Responses showed that 9% of Sainsbury's card users say they would transfer to another store; 7% at Safeway and Somerfield; and the lower number of 3% for Tesco. The Tesco response is interesting and places loyalty schemes in context. The Tesco marketing director Tim Mason commented:

> The willingness to switch may be to do with the nature of the scheme, but it is more likely to be a reflection of the whole offer... people would switch if they felt that, without a card (loyalty scheme), a particular retailer would be substandard....
>
> We've always felt in Tesco that a card can be the icing on the cake, but it can't be the cake itself. It can be a part of the plan, and can contribute to changing

attitudes but it would be over ambitious to expect to change attitudes on its own.

Fiona McAnena (managing director of the Added Value Company, a marketing agency) agrees, and suggests that loyalty schemes have a place if they can enhance or complement the core brand proposition.

David Perkins (Carlson Loyalty Monitor) sums up the progress of loyalty schemes:

Participants in supermarket scenarios: participants reporting 'a main or important influence' on use (per cent)

Year	Tesco	Sainsbury's	Safeway	Somerfield
1996	16	13	–	–
1997	21	20	15	13
1998	23	21	19	12

Awareness and participation of the larger schemes

Company	Awareness (%)	Participation (% of 'population')
Tesco	66	28
Sainsbury's	63	24
Safeway	51	16
Boots	51	17
Somerfield	31	7
W. H. Smith	29	6
Homebase	29	9
BP/Mobil	25	6
Shell	21	3

Users of loyalty schemes

Age/group	Awareness (%)	Active use (%)
Men	90	58
Women	91	69
16–24	92	57
25–34	93	63
35–44	96	73
45–54	94	71
55+	83	59
AB	95	77
C1	94	72
C2	90	63
DE	84	50

Figure 13.7 A profile of customer loyalty schemes.

> Real loyalty is about dialogue and a two-way relationship. In this respect the company database is a gold mine, and people need to start mining it, start using the data and interacting with their customers.
>
> People haven't taken that far enough, and that's the battle for tomorrow. Schemes which make the brand live at the individual level will have a potency that no existing programs have – and it is something that advertising cannot deliver.

Virtual marketing communications and Internet marketing (market-place and market-space)

A growth area in terms of interest and intentions, but to date the Internet share of business is very small. There is both optimism and pessimism expressed. Rayport and Sviokla (1994) consider recent developments in information sciences to have modified, even replaced the *market-place* (the interaction between *physical vendor* and *physical buyer*) with a *market-space* (a combination of information, context and infrastructure). In the market-space *information about* the product replaces the product; *context* is the series of information links which replace face-to-face selling and *infrastructure* is a combination of hardware and software communications which replace physical market locations. The suggestion is that the market-space is a structure of information defined transactions whereby value creation and consumption take place.

The authors provide two examples of market-space product–markets: bank ATMs and voicemail. Both examples identify a number of benefits:

- Replacing hardware and/or human resources with an information-based service
- A reduction of operating costs
- Lower maintenance costs
- Enhanced operating margins

Rayport and Sviokla suggest benefits unavailable in the market-place. Apart from cost benefits they argue that flexibility is available, together with new ways of adding value, new ways of delivering value (alliances and partnerships) and a rethinking of ownership issues. An example is America Online, which combines the contributions of a dozen national newspapers and permits readers to customize content to meet their own requirements. The production and delivery infrastructure becomes an electronic network as opposed to a printing plant and a logistics system.

It is difficult to envisage a totally virtual superstore. However, some of the aspects of its products and services may well become virtual. There are some interesting issues for both merchandise decisions and *communications*. Ghosh (1998) reminds us of the ability, through the Internet to *bypass* other members of the supply chain through the direct links the Internet offers. It offers the facility to develop new products and services and to customize both existing and new products and services. It also offers the ability to dominate the 'electronic channel', thereby controlling access to customers *and* to establish the terms of trade. Added value for the vendor (retailer) can be enhanced by offering additional information, transaction services, and by selling complementary products and services.

Evans and Wuster (1997) review a number of product markets that have felt the impact of information technology. One notable example is the success of the CD-ROM edition of the Encyclopedia Britannica at around $400 compared with the success of the hard copy version at $1500–$2000. The authors identify a number of aspects. Customers' (parents') attitudes towards the CD-ROM version were quite different: it was initially considered as a 'toy' rather than an educational aid.

A significant point made by Evans and Wuster concerns value communication and delivery. Information is seen as the vehicle that achieves both tasks:

> More fundamentally, information is the glue that holds together the structure of all businesses. A company's value chain consists of all the activities it performs to design, produce, market, deliver and support its product. The value chains of companies that supply and buy from one anther collectively and make up an industry's value chain, its particular configuration of competitors, suppliers, distribution channels and customers... we tend to visualise a linear flow of activities. But the value chain also includes all the information that flows within a company and its suppliers, its distributors, and its existing or potential customers. Supplier relationships, brand identity, process coordination, customer loyalty and switching costs all depend on various kinds of information... the value of customer relationships, for example... is the proprietary information that their customers have about the company and its products.

The authors expand their argument by suggesting that brands are essentially information that successful positioning has created for the customer by effective use of advertising and other communication media. The role of the Internet is becoming significant in this respect, as the growth of retailer Web sites and pages suggests.

Potter (1999) would have us consider the world beyond e-commerce:

> With new applications for mobile phones, e-commerce is already leading to m-commerce or mobile commerce... mobile phones will become computers and much else besides. The mobile phone will be for data communication too.

But a pessimistic view of developments should also be considered. Warner (1999) identifies investment problems. He points to Buy.com in the USA seeking to raise US$60 million. It has a unique selling proposition. It envisages a negative margin on everything it sells over the Net; the difference will be made up by advertising revenue. It 'hopes' that an attractive merchandise assortment will in turn attract more advertising!

Buy.com will attempt to compete with established Internet companies. Companies such as Amazon.com will be undercut over time, and the logical conclusion (proposes Warner) is:

> we'll end up with a situation where the intensity of competition on the Net will mean nobody is capable of making a profit.

Clearly this will not occur. But it does suggest low margins and caution being used when considering WWW applications. Despite this not illogical comment, the forecast is for phenomenal growth, constrained perhaps by the telephone costs of accessing the Net. However, a number of retailers have (or are considering) free Internet services (e.g. Dixons and Tesco) and access costs can be expected to be lowered still further. As Warner concludes:

> Nobody can reasonably object to competition and transparency, but many businessmen are beginning to think there are limits. Unfortunately the Internet doesn't recognize them.

And:

> Nobody has any doubt but that the Web is going to transform the way they do business, but they also worry about how they are ever going to make any money out of it. It may well be that the only the business beneficiaries are the Internet wholesalers and gate keepers, those able to offer a mechanism for searching the Web for the lowest possible prices.
>
> And as for established consumer goods producers, the outlook is only for more and more competition and keener and keener pricing.

Internet communications clearly offer benefits but they also offer problems. The integration of net and Web site applications should follow rigorous examination of costs and benefits.

NON PERSONAL COMMUNICATIONS

The growth of multiple retailing and the increase in specialist retailing has required the development of non-personal communications. The size of the largest multiples, together with their territorial and 'market' coverage, now ensures economies of scale in both press and electronic media.

Three elements of non-personal communications will be considered briefly here; the reader will be aware of each, and this review suffices to prevent omission. They are: merchandising/display advertising and public relations and corporate affairs.

Visual merchandising

The visual element is often considered part of the merchandise strategy or more usually the format and store environment. However, it is a powerful method of communicating the positioning statement of the company within the store and of persuasion at the point of sale.

By using merchandise displays to inform customers, arouse interest, encourage comparative shopping, visual merchandising moves a customer towards a purchasing decision. It is not difficult therefore to see its role within the communications strategy. Visual merchandising should coordinate the merchandise offer into an integrated message reflecting customer expectations. It should also classify merchandise into related categories, departments or end-use applications.

The visual merchandising role of the supporting strategy positioning is important. It should imply authority, credibility and advice. Visual merchandising should, therefore, be based upon identified shopping missions and levels of 'customer qualification'. An effective visual merchandising program will:

- Increase sales revenues by increasing customer visits and transaction value per visit
- Increase gross margins by directing customers towards higher margin merchandise, ensuring it is sold at 'full price' and influencing coordinated purchasing
- Contain costs by using visual merchandising as part of the customers' purchasing decision processes, thereby answering questions that would otherwise require sales assistance.
- Improving productivity by converting browsing missions into purchases, thereby increasing sales and contribution per employee and unit of space and increasing inventory turnover.
- Add value for the customer by offering 'advice' on style and colour coordination, product application and problem identification and resolution

Advertising

Advertising (press, television, radio, cinema and outdoor) has been, and remains, a major element in retail communications. The role of advertising in retailing has changed over recent years: from the somewhat stark stance of price and product availability to a *brand* proposition (see comments earlier in this chapter concerning Sainsbury's advertising). Because of the wide availability of media types and readership/viewing consumption it permits targeting and flexibility (such as that required for rapid response to product failure recalls *as well as* competitive responses on price etc.). Over time, the exclusivities of retailers have been eroded: the availability of most products is widespread and a communications role of all forms of advertising becomes the *differentiation of the equally acceptable* due to competitor intensification and uniform offers. Advertising should therefore:

- Emphasize the added value of the offer by adding emotional or theatrical values which, when reinforced by visual merchandising, can create preferential choice, regular choice and customer loyalty.
- Take customers through the store selection and purchase decision process.

- Establish the company as a store of first choice by identifying company/customer congruence in expectations and perceptions.
- Build credibility in category/merchandise classifications.
- Increase profitability, productivity and cash flow by building volume markets in selected merchandise areas, resulting in increased buying margins and enhanced/preferential positions with suppliers.

The purpose and application of advertising will vary according to the needs of the company. It is quite possible for two levels or time perspectives of advertising to be running concurrently. It is not unusual to observe a retailer conducting a corporate campaign aimed at reinforcing the features of its strategic positioning and at the same time addressing a short-term pricing issue. The important issue is to ensure that the short-term response advertising will not have an adverse impact on the ongoing long-term campaign.

Public relations and corporate affairs

There are two aspects of public relations to be considered: a public relations activity, which deals with *business development issues* (and uses press and television news journalism to feature the activity in some depth); and *corporate affairs* (the corporate concern for environmental issues (which uses similar media to publicize its activities in working on education, conservation, community aspects of employment etc.). Both require to be dealt with within a communications strategy. Care should be taken over areas of overlap. Specifically, any possibility of the inference of blatant commercialism within a corporate affairs campaign should be identified and eliminated or minimized.

Within the communications strategy, business development can benefit from a PR campaign which supports the advertising and visual merchandising activities. A recent development by a large food multiple announced an intention to add children's books to its assortment. The use of PR and the relevant journalists and media can add credibility to the decision. The issue is that there must be credibility in the activity, because the PR content is based upon objectivity. Thus the developments in these and other children's products should be discussed at the development stage with the editorial staff of the relevant media; often valuable contributions are made (and 'involvement' occurs). As and when the venture is launched there is an accompanying endorsement, resulting in invaluable publicity.

The role of corporate affairs is particularly relevant in the areas of community development (employment, education, health and consumer interests – pricing, product availability etc.). An objective perspective of the company's views and activities usually results in a favourable response from the financial press.

Public relations have been used to good effect by the major multiples. Gray (1998) reports on a number of PR activities:

- The Tesco/BBC documentary *Superstore* which was aimed at positioning the company as having an effective strategy with efficient implementation and an innovative and caring attitude towards customers and employees.
- The Asda campaign to oppose resale price maintenance on pharmaceutical products.
- Sainsbury's campaign to 'help' village shops, hit hard by competition from the large superstore operators, by allowing them to sell Sainsbury's own-label products.
- The Tesco campaign against over-priced branded products has involved the company in offering Adidas, Nike, Sony, Levi, Calvin Klein and Tommy Hilfiger products at discounted prices

Press Watch monitors and assesses articles written about more than 1000 UK leading companies. Reports are issued on a quarterly basis based upon an objective assessment of favourable and unfavourable comments. Over the 1997/98 period (five quarters) Tesco ranked second, first, third, sixth and third. These results reflect a planned approach to both public relations and corporate affairs. The Tesco corporate communications manager is quoted by Gray:

> It's about doing what's right for the customer.... It's about business strategy. It's not about positioning.

And from a PR consultancy who suggests that Tesco's PR is 'streets ahead' of its competitors because it is: '..."culturally driven" fired by a belief in what the company is doing'.

SUMMARY

This chapter has considered the role of customer communications within the retail strategy decision.

Communications objectives should contribute to the positioning strategy of the organization, together with informing customers of the comparative benefits offered by the company and persuading the customer to purchase, or continue purchasing, from the company. Effective communications campaigns are ongoing. They are based upon an understanding of the customer (customer demographics, lifestyles and 'qualifications') and of customer purchasing behaviour(s). The combination of shopping missions and store selection and purchasing decisions to identify communications tasks was discussed.

The elements of communications strategy decisions were approached by considering the role of creative and media strategies which are developed to meet communications objectives. The example of ensuring balance and congruence between long- and short-term objectives was explored using the Sainsbury (UK) case.

The efficacy of customer loyalty schemes was discussed. The chapter was concluded with a prospective view of virtual marketing and non-personal communications.

QUESTIONS, ACTIVITIES AND OBSERVATIONS

- Identify two retailing companies in the same product market with contrasting retail offers. What are the differences in their communications strategies?
- 'Long-term communications strategies should be directed towards developing customer loyalty. In the short term our objectives are to respond to competitive shifts and, if necessary, increase our volume.' Discuss this statement using an industry example.
- Using the model described by Figure 13.5, design a communications strategy for a consumer durables retailer that creates 'interest' and increases 'readiness' to buy among customers. Consider all aspects of media and creativity.
- How might the internet be developed to enhance customer loyalty in FMCG retailing?

REFERENCES

Bird, D. (1998) Has Sainsbury's gone crazy with its comic caper? *Marketing*, 5 November.

Denny, N. (1998) Listening to your customer is vital. *Marketing*, 19 November.

Denny, N. (1998) Sainsbury's tops 'irritating' poll. *Marketing*, 17 December.

Evans, P. B. and Wurster, T. S. (1997) Strategy and the new economics of information. *Harvard Business Review*, Sep/Oct.

Ghosh, S. (1998) Making business sense of the Internet. *Harvard Business Review*, Mar/Apr.

Gofton, K. (1999) Pinpointing loyalty. *Marketing*, 21 January.

Gray, R. (1998) PR: The new retail battle ground. *Marketing*, 3 September.

Homma, N. and Ueltzhoffer, J. (1990) The internationalization of everyday-life-research: markets and milieus. *Marketing and Research Today*, November.

Kotler, P. (1996) *Marketing Management: Analysis, Planning and Control*. Prentice Hall International, Englewood Cliffs, NJ.

Laurence, B. (1999) Nothing to shout about at crumbling Sainsbury's. *The Observer*, 7 February.

Martineau, P. (1958) The personality of the retail store. *Harvard Business Review*, Jan/Feb.

Mitchell, A. (1983) *The Nine American Life Styles*. Macmillan, New York.

Murphy, P. E. and Staples, W. A. (1979) A modernised family life cycle. *Journal of Consumer Research*, June.
Pessemier, E. A. Retail patronage behaviour. Undated working paper, Krannert Graduate School of Management, Purdue University.
Plummer, J. T. (1974) The concept and application of life-style segmentation. *Journal of Marketing*, January.
Potter, D. (1999) Never mind e-commerce. Say hello to m-commerce. *The Observer*, 7 February.
Rayport, J. F. and Sviokla, J. (1994) Managing the marketspace. *Harvard Business Review*, Nov/Dec.
Spector, R. and McCarthy, P. (1995) *The Nordstrom Way*. John Wiley, New York.
Urban, G. L. and Hauser, J. R. (1980) *Design and Marketing of New Products*. Prentice Hall, New York.
Warner, J. (1999) Net gain may be only for consumers. *The Independent*, 6 February.
Wells, W. D. and Gubar, G. (1966) Life cycle concepts in marketing research. *Journal of Marketing Research*, November.

14 IMPLEMENTING CUSTOMER COMMUNICATIONS STRATEGY

LEARNING OBJECTIVES

The previous chapter reviewed communications strategy alternatives. This chapter considers the important issues of implementation. A number of topics, necessary if the implementation task is to be successful, are identified:

- The relationship 'fit' between shopper and store characteristics.
- The importance of understanding 'value' sought by customers. The role of value in implementing an effective communications strategy.
- The components of the business definition and how communications activities support them in creating a theme for communicating value benefits.
- A detailed perspective of the communications issues and the store selection and purchasing decisions.
- How long-term and short-term communications tasks may be integrated.
- Developing market maps for communications implementation planning.
- Developing a 'communications mix' which considers tasks *and* resources.
- Determining a communications budget.

INTRODUCTION

Chapter 13 identified and discussed a number of concepts which influence the development of a communications strategy. This chapter develops the discussion further, adding additional concepts and discussion to add depth and to explore their role in implementing strategy.

The benefit/value equation is a major concern for communications. Successful communications are those which leave the target audience in no doubt concerning the components of the benefit/value offer. The implications of value in a retailing context and for communications is discussed at length.

The Martineau model of shopper and store characteristics is reintroduced in this chapter as a means by which both aspects may be analysed and used for communications planning. The proposition made is that by auditing the value proposition in its broadest context we can eliminate confusion in the customers' minds and reinforce the positioning offer. A time perspective is also proposed in which the positioning reflects both long- and short-term strategic intentions.

Communication seeks to influence a target audience. We wish to achieve a cognitive, affective or behavioural response within the target customer group. To do this effectively requires an understanding of customer response models *and* the store selection and purchasing decision process. These are combined, as are the shopper and store characteristics into an overall (generic) model which tracks tasks and processes over time. The purpose is to establish the need for an integrated time perspective on communications planning. A method by which we can quantify customer categories using *market maps* is discussed at this point.

A review of relevant activities among competitors discusses a number of issues. A major concern for management is the resource implications required to support a communications program. We consider there to be significant considerations in a number of related areas. This leads to the communications plan. The activities involved are identified and discussed. Some examples of retail communications activities conclude the chapter.

An overview of the process is given in Figure 14.1.

CUSTOMER COMMUNICATIONS: ISSUES FOR IMPLEMENTATION

Any communications process (manufacturer or retailer) has a number of objectives. In Chapter 13 we identified typical communications objectives for a retailing company. In this chapter we are considering how these might be realized. Clearly the ultimate response is for the communications process to build a relationship with the target customer group such that there is strong customer loyalty which is reflected by frequent visits, high spends (across the assortment) and a significant proportion of the customers' relevant disposable income spent with the organization.

However, this 'ultimate response' is the end of a long process of consumer decision making. The decision maker needs to know *how* to move the target customer group through the decision-making process. Furthermore, the process is complicated by the fact that the target audience is not necessarily at the same stage. To this end, the communications program should be designed to achieve a *cognitive*, *affective* or *behavioural* response: to create awareness or an attitude or to do something specific.

Chapter 13 reintroduced positioning and differentiation using contributions from Urban and Hauser and Martineau to explore issues relevant to communications. Clearly, before we implement a communications strategy the fit between *shopper and store characteristics* is strong, but we must also ensure that the value positioning of the entire retail offer fits the *perceptions*

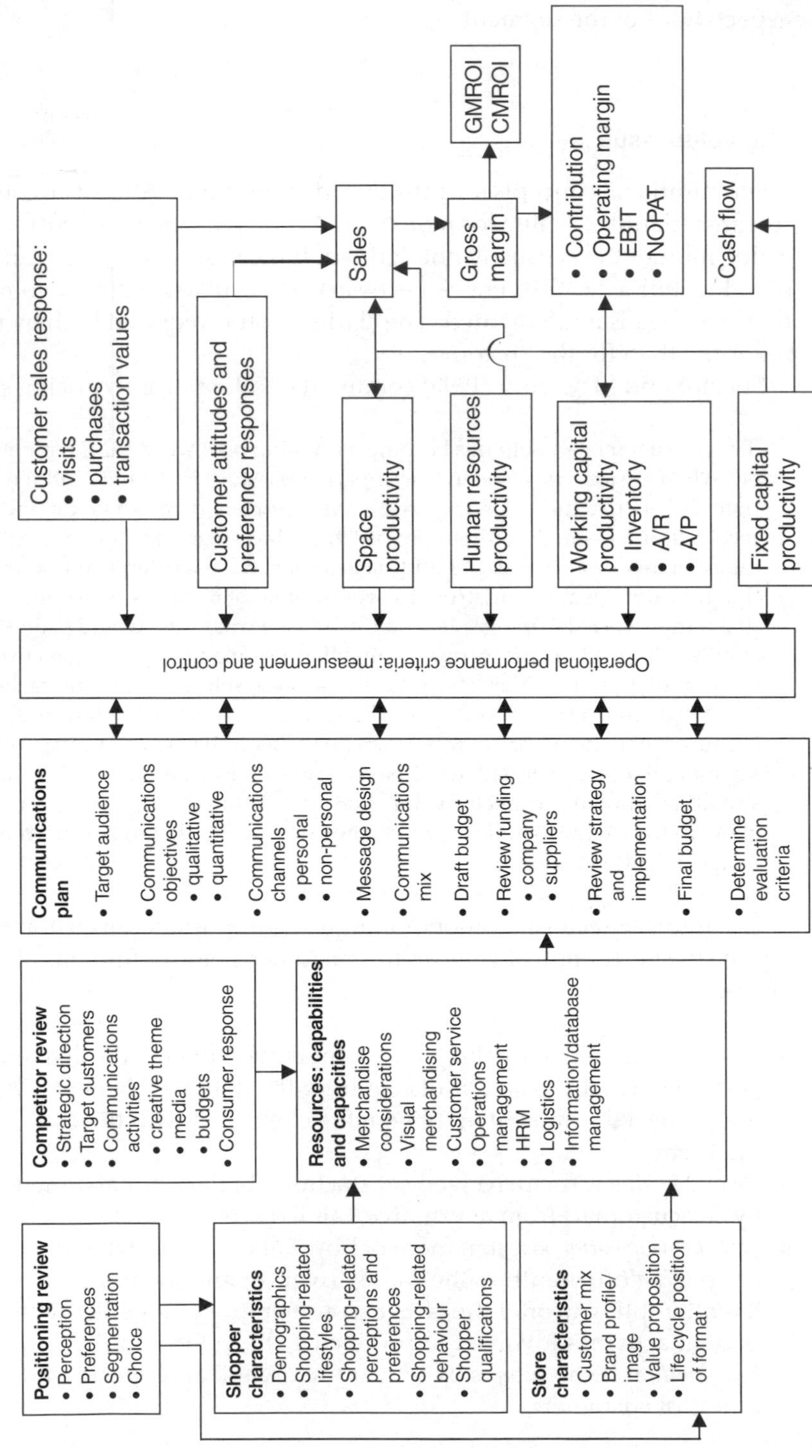

Figure 14.1 Implementing customer communications strategy.

and *preferences* of the *target segment* and that the value proposition meets the expectations of the segment.

The value issue

Some additional concepts are introduced at this point. Almost all commercial research identifies 'value for money' as a primary concern of customers. But 'value for money' is usually not defined. It is certain that price is an element of value, but a clearer view is necessary, particularly before a communications strategy is implemented. The clarification is required both by management *and* then for the customer.

Spector and McCarthy (1995) comment on Nordstrom's pricing strategy:

> 'Price/value' relationship has become a retailing buzzword for the nineties, an era when customers' allegiance to a particular store is strongly influenced by their belief that the price they are paying for an item is fair for the value received. Interestingly, although Nordstrom has stressed value in its advertising for many years, scores of faithful customers have written to the store to say that they don't want Nordstrom to overemphasize its prices. 'Customers tell us that if they were shopping solely on the basis of price they would shop at a discounter' (Cynthia Paur, corporate merchandise manager).... These customers say that they shop at Nordstrom for the service, selection, and the cachet that the Nordstrom gift box conveys. That attitude 'has been interesting for us because when the economy was down (in the early 1990s) we emphasized pricing more than we ever had in the past. Now we've balanced it back. I think we should be known for greater value, but I don't think our customers will ever allow us to be famous for low prices. They don't want that to be our prominent image' (Cynthia Paur).

Two important considerations emerge: the importance of customer targeting *and* the perception of value to the customer. Some definitions of value are offered:

- *Value* is determined by the utility combination of benefits delivered to the customer less the *total costs* of acquiring the delivered benefits. Value then is a preferred combination of benefits compared with the costs of acquiring them.
- *Relative value* is the perceived satisfaction obtained (or assumed available by the customer) from alternative value offers.
- A *value proposition* is a statement of how value is to be delivered to customers. *internally* it identifies the value drivers (components of the retail offer) it is attempting to offer the target customer group, together with the component activities involved in producing the value and their cost drivers. *Externally* it is the means by which the organization position itself in the minds of customers.

Webster (1994) suggests:

> The value proposition should be the firm's single most important organizing principle.

It follows that value positioning has implications for marketing strategy; it requires some fundamental decisions on segmentation, target customer profiles, profiles of prominent competitors and identification of value communications and delivery media and methods.

Webster again:

> The conclusion that market share *caused profitability* (has) proved simplistic.... Strategy must be based on analysis of the company, the competition, and the customer, identifying these opportunities for the firm to deliver superior value to customers based on its distinctive competencies. The firm's *value proposition* becomes the primary organizing force for the business.

It follows that unless our communications strategy is based upon a similar analysis and is seen by the customer to interpret both their expectations *and* perceptions it is very unlikely to achieve its purpose.

Nordstrom uses its own retail brands as a major component of its benefit/value offer. While they account for an average of 20% of the overall merchandise offer. They represent a small component of some departments' assortment and the foundation of others. Nordstrom's overall view is that for some categories *current* design/fashion trends are important, but over time these will change (a consumer aspect). However, the basic Nordstrom value offer of 'value, quality, exclusivity and size (range of sizes)' will retain significant benefit/value characteristics.

Positioning: customer and store perspectives

The relevance of Urban and Hauser (1980) and Martineau (1958) come into context. Unless we have a clear focus on the customers' perceptions and preferences and the aspects of store and merchandise/service that are required, together with strong congruence between shopper characteristics and store characteristics, it is unlikely that any *effective* communications strategy can be developed, and less likely that any communication with the customer will be *efficiently* delivered.

It follows that the strategy/implementation activities must be based not only on an understanding of the interrelationships between shopper and store but also upon a model which *integrates* both perspectives. This will avoid confusion, ambiguity and possibly contradiction in the communication process, and by seeking congruence will achieve greater success. To do this requires minor modifications to the original Martineau proposition; these are rearrangements rather than anything of major significance.

Therefore *shopper characteristics* become:

- *Demographics* (age, gender, geo-demographics, life cycle stage and socio-economics).

- *Lifestyles and shopping-related lifestyle*. ((*activities*: work, leisure, family, shopping; dominance of shopping, frequency and loyalties); (*interests*: home, fashion, past times; extent, knowledge of alternatives); (*opinions*: themselves, others, institutions, stores, brands, products; expectations, preferences, perceptions and attitudes)).
- *Shopping-related perceptions and preferences* (of stores, likes and dislikes, destination purchase stores).
- *Shopping-related behaviour* (dominant shopping missions, customer qualifications).
- *Store characteristics*.
- *Customer mix* (profile(s) of demographics, lifestyle, perceptions and preferences, and related behaviour patterns of dominant user group(s)).
- *Brand profile/image* (the role of branding; its application to the retail offer, to category groups etc.).
- *Value proposition* (the value/price offer and its interpretation for the assortment, merchandise characteristics, price points, 'convenience', ambience, integrity and credibility).
- *Life cycle position of format* (relative to the company, relative to competition, relative to consumer expectations and perceptions).

If we combine an analysis of both sets of characteristics we can evaluate their congruence and identify problems that may require to be addressed by a review of merchandise, service and format strategies. Very simply we are asking: is the positioning communicated to the target customer the one which is intended? Or because of *gaps* in the positioning component set, are we likely to create confusion in the customers' minds rather than reinforce the *value proposition* when the communications program is implemented? Essentially we are conducting an audit of the value proposition.

Positioning: time and strategic direction

In Chapter 13 we discussed the time perspectives of communications strategy and suggested that some thought be given to ensuring that no confusion between short-term and long-term messages occur. It is the role of senior management to ensure that clear long-term and short-term perspectives are provided. These may take the form of mission statements or perhaps use Abell's business definition model. Figure 14.2 illustrates this proposition with a hypothetical example. The short-term business definition describes the hypothetical business as it currently is. The diagram suggests two alternatives for long-term development. For alternative 1, management would introduce the notion of its long-term direction by emphasizing its innovative approach to consumer problem-solving with creative themes focusing upon a proactive customer full-service orientation. To pursue option 2 management should focus on its expertise in the specialist field. Having identified its strategic direction the short-term, operational communications program(s) can be developed around the long-term positioning communications

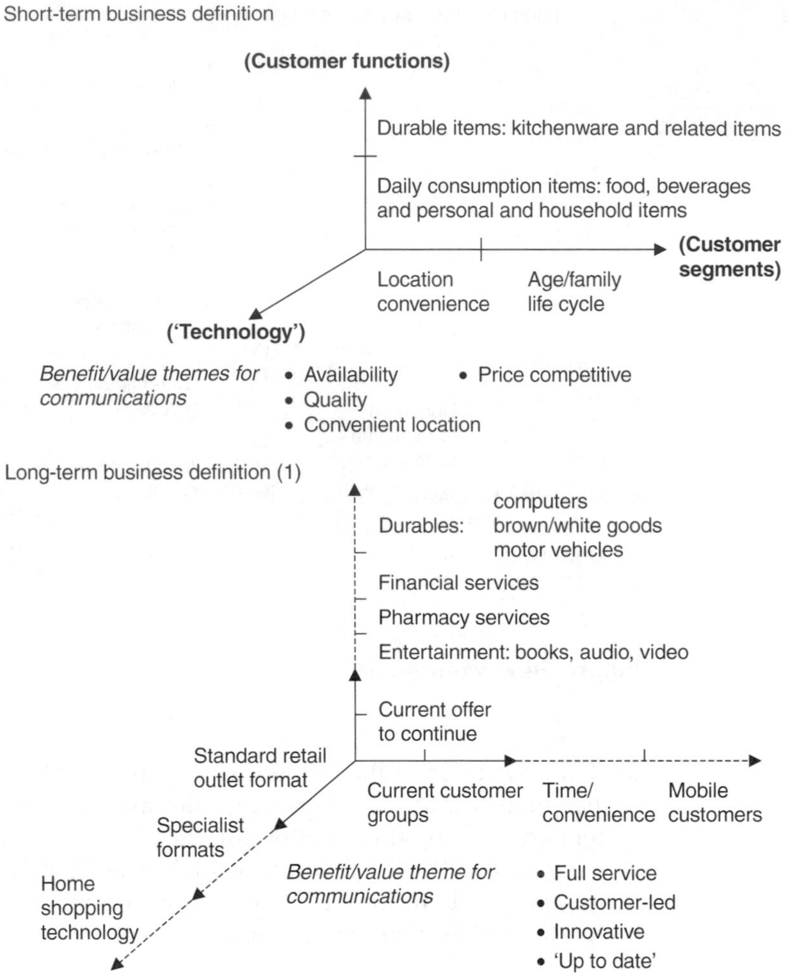

Figure 14.2 Define the time perspectives for communications *(continued overleaf)*.

objectives. This may require a different order in which the store and shopper characteristics are viewed. Figure 14.3 proposes a matrix format for approaching both long- and short-term communications decisions. In Figure 14.3 the long-term perspective shows an emphasis on *brand/image profile* and the *value proposition* whereas in the short-term *customer mix* and *value proposition* are likely to dominate the communications decision, but as the diagram suggests there is a clear link between the two strategies. The proportion of each axis allocated to each characteristic suggests the importance (and therefore the amount of management time and other resources that should be allocated) of each characteristic.

The importance of this, or some similar, approach was emphasized by the implications of a report by Smith (1999), in which he discusses long-term wealth trends. Smith forecasts an ever-increasingly wealthy middle class in

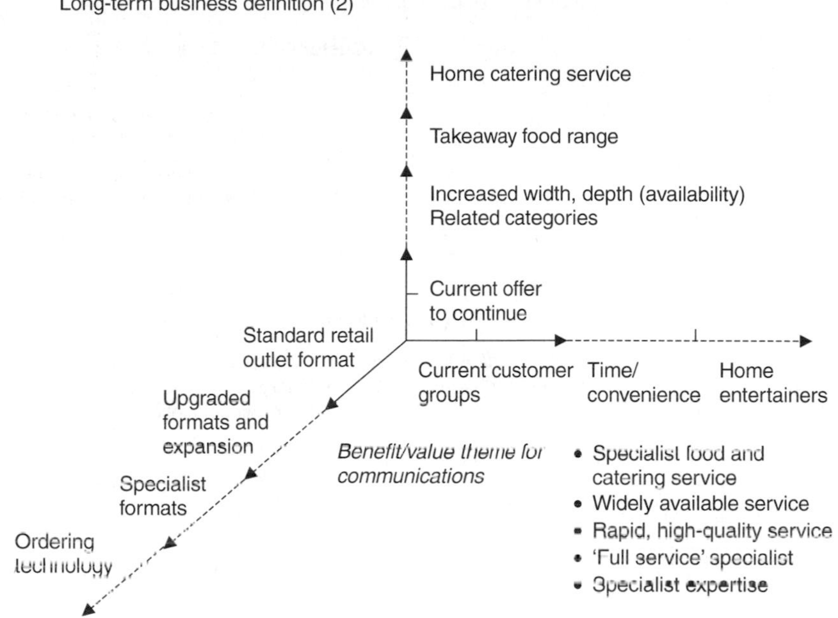

Figure 14.2 *(continued)*

the UK and discusses the influences responsible. He concludes that changes in income distribution, inherited wealth and the existing welfare payment system are creating this wealthy middle class sector. In retailing terms they are now, and will be in the future, a 'highly desirable' customer segment and for this reason both long-term and short-term communications should be integrated rather than seen as separate tasks.

Store selection and purchasing decisions: communications issues

Another concern for communications planning is the decision-making process. Chapter 13 introduced the store selection and purchasing decision process (i.e. store selection, purchasing, post-transaction and loyalty building); this needs to be related to a response hierarchy model. Whether we are seeking to communicate with the target audience in the long or short term, a response is sought. While the ultimate response may be a purchase, we are more interested in developing a long-term purchasing relationship. The issue for the communications strategy(ies) is to link the process with the outcome. Typically marketing communications seek a *cognitive*, *affective* or *behavioural* response. As Kotler suggests:

> the marketer may want to put something into the consumer's mind, change the consumer's attitude, or get the consumer to undertake a specific action.

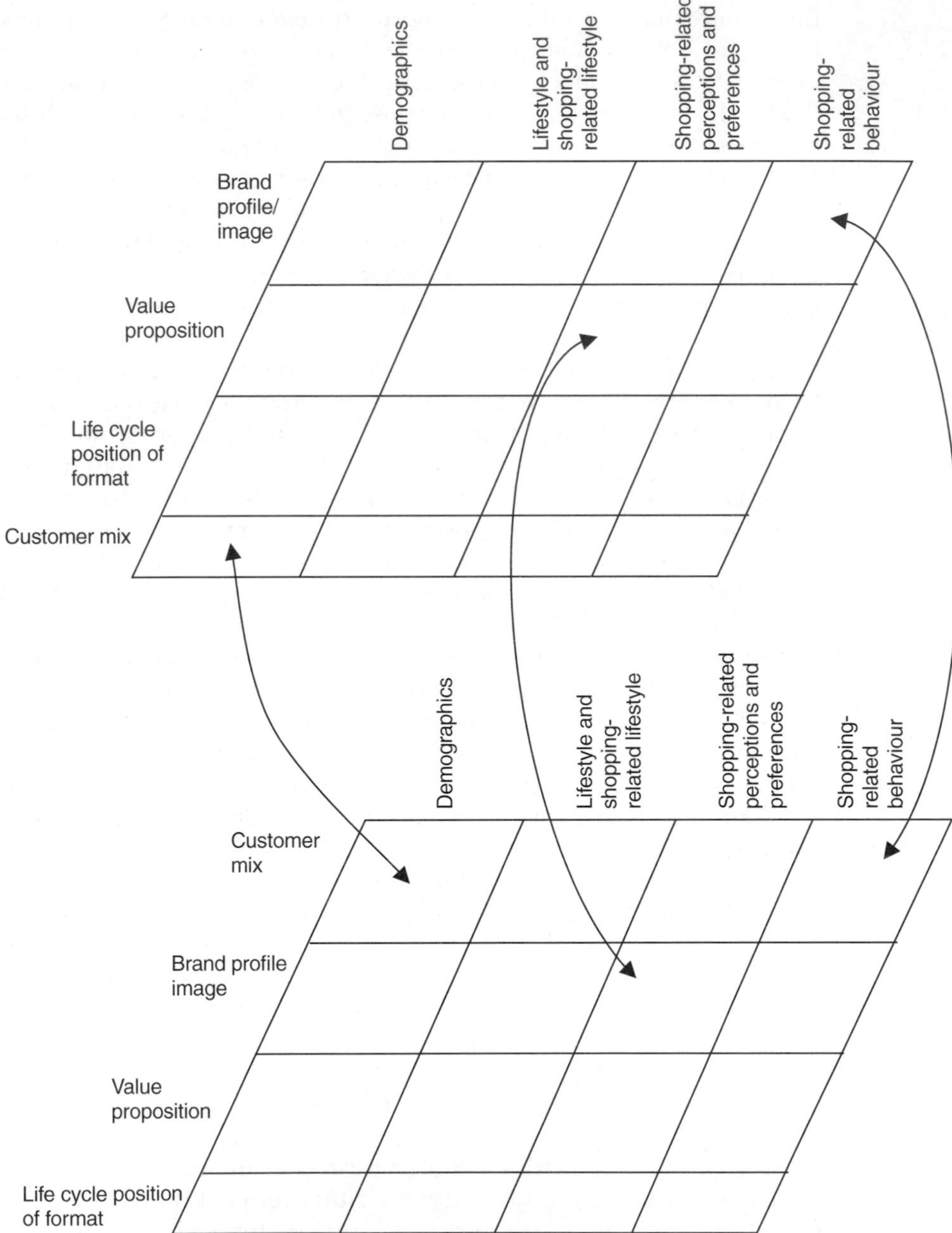

Figure 14.3 Relating long-term and short-term shopper and store characteristics to plan the implementation of communications strategy.

Kotler identifies a number of models of consumer-response stages. For our purposes the 'hierarchy of effects model' (proposed by Lavidge and Steiner (1961)) is most suitable. The model offers six buyer-readiness states: awareness, knowledge, liking, preference, conviction, and purchase. This meets

the requirements of long- and short-term communications horizons. The long-term objectives are to create *awareness* and impart *knowledge* (of the brand profile and value proposition). Over the long term the task is to identify for the target customer the purpose (mission) of the business. It seeks to establish in the minds of the consumer an identity for (in the terms of Figure 13.2) innovativeness, specialist expertise and of course reliability. The short-term task is to create *liking* and *preference* and *conviction* to *purchase*. If both long term and short term are combined we would suggest that it is against a background of awareness and knowledge of what it is the company is offering on an ongoing basis, and where it sees itself for the long term, that *regular* purchasing is developed.

An example may help. Asda (the UK food multiple) has an ongoing long term communications program that emphasizes a price/value-based positioning supported by width and depth in selected categories, one of which is non-food (apparel). Its short-term programmes are strongly oriented towards price/value offers on selected merchandise items. It has an extensive public relations program opposing resale price maintenance (price/value) and has featured 'singles nights', World Cup promotions and church services via its FM station. Asda's communications campaign is consistent and well integrated.

The Lavidge and Heiner model can be extended to include *customer retention*. In Figure 14.4 we propose a consumer-response model which accommodates long-run and short-run aspects of the process and identifies the relevant shopper and store characteristics appropriate to each stage. The shopper and store characteristics are broad indications of what (and where) emphasis is made; clearly the detailed implementation is the concern of the company.

Other issues are of concern. One very important issue is the nature of the target audience and the familiarity of the audience with the retailer and the value proposition. While it is dated, Ottesen (1977) developed a *market map* which identifies the characteristics of the market-place and indicates the extent of the task confronting the communications program. Ottesen's model compares the percentage of *awareness* of a product in a target market with the percentage of the target market that has *tried* the product. The model was used to set communications objectives for an FMCG brand – see Figure 14.5.

The model can be readily adapted for retail communications planning – see Figure 14.6. The groups that have either rejected the offer or have not tried it are researched as to their specific reasons for not having done so. Similarly, the group that is unaware of the offer will also be researched to establish reasons for the situation.

Our particular interests are in the loyal and occasional users. Our overall communications objective is to develop a core customer group of loyal users. By researching the loyal users we can identify their *benefit/value* (or value proposition preferences) together with the ways in which they use the store. Similarly, we would research the occasional users to identify preferences and behaviour patterns in order that we understand their reasons for their

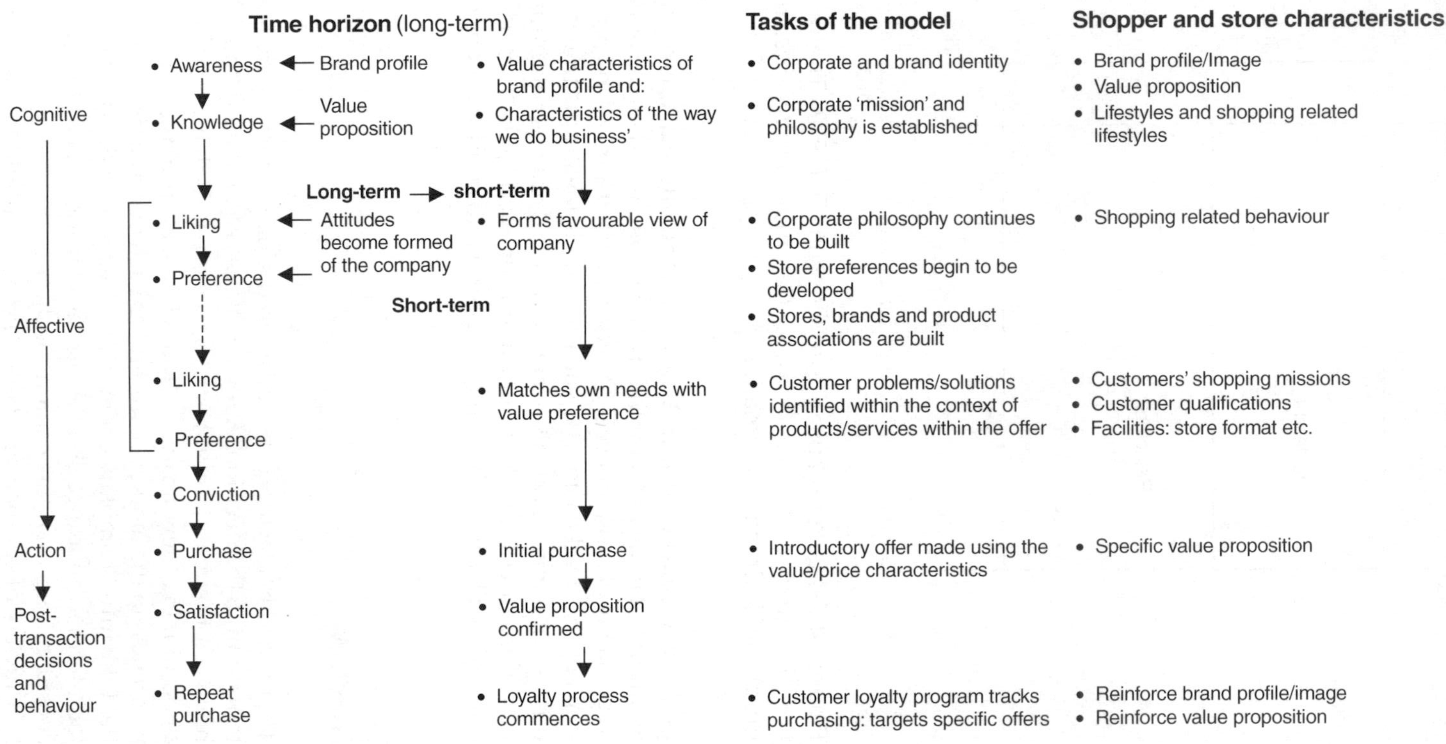

Figure 14.4 Long-term and short-term communications tasks are integrated.

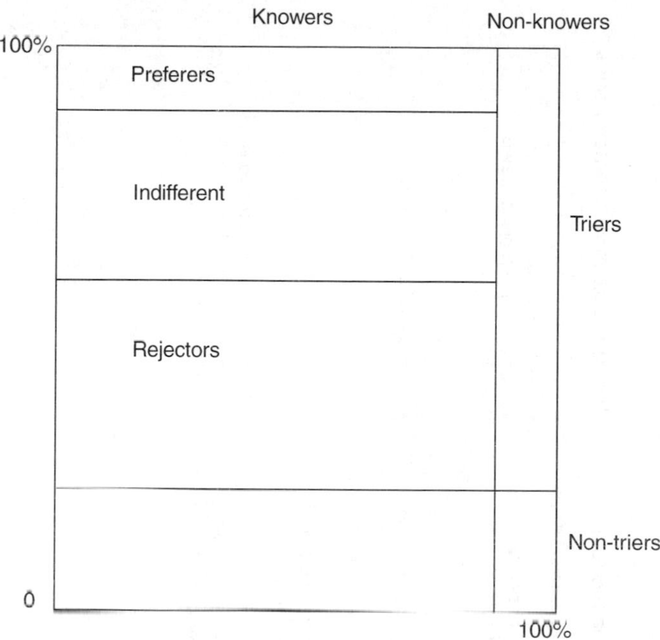

Figure 14.5 Market maps. (From Ottoson, O. (1977) The response function, in *Current Themes in Mass Communications Research* (ed. Mic Berg). GMT, Grenaa, Denmark.)

preferences and behaviour. Armed with this information we may now make an informed judgement on the creative content and media options available to persuade occasional users to become loyal users *and* to reinforce the decisions of the loyal customers such that their loyalty is strengthened. Given this information we can also begin to make decisions concerning the allocation of resources (the communications budget) to the characteristics of the offer that will achieve both the long-term and short-term objectives.

COMPETITOR REVIEW

There are other factors to be considered. Competitive activities are an important input to the decision. A review of *competitor strategy* should be ongoing; however, there are a number of specific issues that have direct relevance. Repositioning, new format introductions, even branch openings, all create awareness in the market-place, and as such may require some counter activities built into a company communications plan in the short term. Clearly, the long-term significance should also be considered, but this may have wider considerations than just communications.

A review of competitors' *target customers* should be taken. There may be shifts in competitors' ideal target customers (which may of course be towards

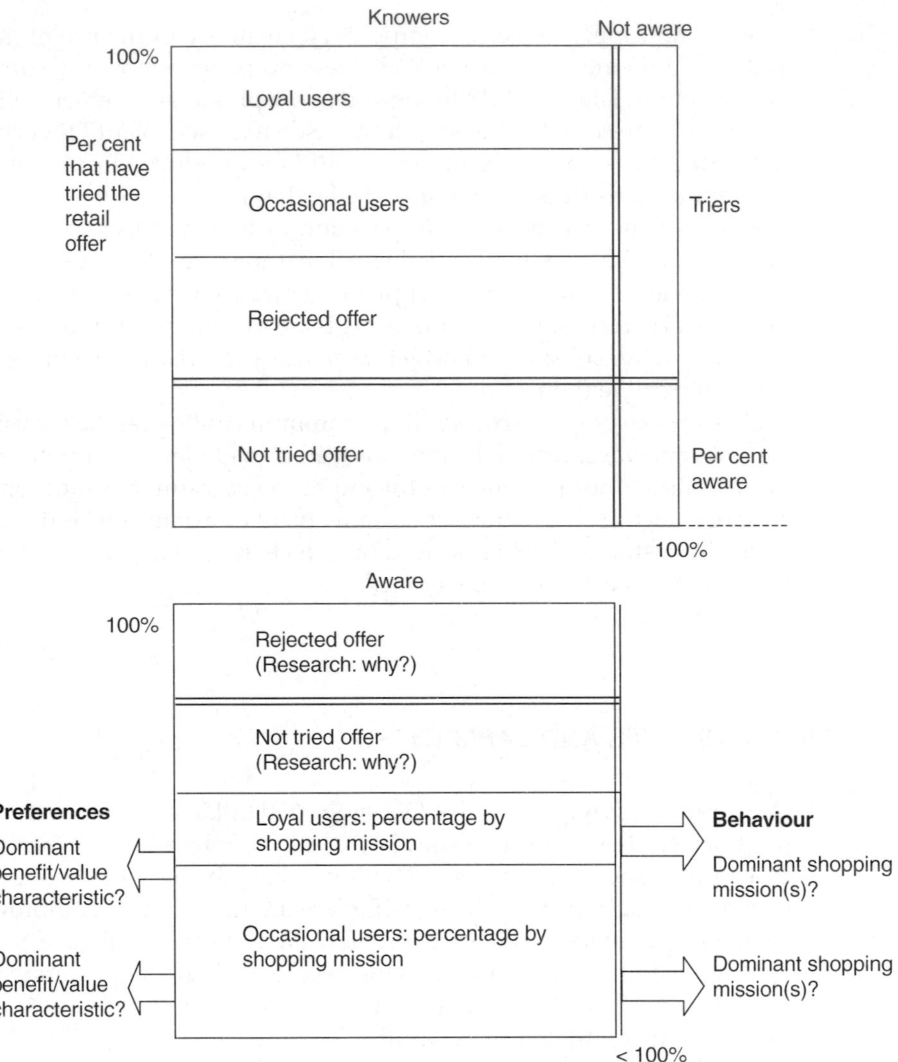

Figure 14.6 Using market maps to identify preferences and behaviour of a target audience. (Adapted from Ottesen, O. (1977) The response function, in *Current Themes in Mass Communications Research* (ed. Mic Berg). GMT, Grenaa, Denmark.)

the company's core customer group); whichever direction a move takes it is likely (almost certain) that competitor communications will intensify.

Competitors' *communications activities* should be reviewed on an ongoing basis. There are a number of reasons for doing so. One reason is the 'share of voice/share of market' aspect. For relatively stable markets (stable in the sense of food retailing, where change is neither radical nor rapid) an increase in communications activity is likely to result in volume shifts rather than generate primary demand increases. It follows that in such situations communications activities and *budgets* should be monitored.

A second aspect concerns competitors' creativity in the use of marketing and media themes. The use of Web sites and pages is now the rule and not the exception. The use of PR (reviewed in the previous chapter) is effective in the short term as well as the long term. Asda has used event PR very successfully. B&Q have announced their intention to produce 'documentary/soap' communications (this will be discussed below).

A third issue concerns the implication of merchandise assortment. The trade press in the UK has carried small features/reports suggesting that the major food multiples are contemplating entrance into automobile retailing. This has all sorts of ramifications. A big issue for communications to consider is the impact of subsidised budgets *as well as* the 'creative' changes that will occur to creative themes.

Consumer responses to competitors' communications can be informative in a number of ways. One is the obvious lead provided into competitor marketing activities. Another concerns the impact on consumers. Questions should be asked, such as: is this market reinforcement or expansion? Is it to attract or to retain customers? What long-term effects is it planned to have on customer spend, customer transfer etc.?

RESOURCES: CAPABILITIES AND CAPACITIES

In the previous chapter, Figure 13.1 suggested linkages between the communications strategy and the other key areas: merchandise, customer service and format and environment. These can be considered by reviewing the resources required for effective implementation of the communications strategy. The topics necessary for review are indicated in Figure 14.1.

Merchandise considerations are (with visual merchandising) among the most important factors. Part of a communications strategy message is the reinforcement given by the merchandise. Here we are concerned with in-store availability, variety (choice), quality (shelf-life, damage etc.) and performance. For each characteristic there is either an implied level of performance delivery or augmentation of the positioning statement. Failure to deliver on any of these characteristics will result in a failure to support the offer proposition of the communications strategy *and* disappointed customers.

Another important supporting activity is that of *visual merchandising*. We have discussed the topic in earlier chapters, and there is no need to repeat that discussion. However, it is necessary to emphasize the mutual support given by each to the other. Apparel retailers ensure that coordinated groups of merchandise appear *in the store* as they are featured in advertising and PR features. Failure to ensure this simple requirement may result in the lost revenue and profit opportunities. The cost-efficient use of merchandise, space *and* communications expenditures will be optimal only when they are coordinated.

Customer service offers must also match the offer made in communications. Customer services are increasingly used to improve a competitive position.

Simple detail is important, such as an informed response to an enquiry prompted by a communications campaign. The same obtains for service facilities, such as the Nordstrom example of carpeted dressing-rooms and customer lounges, which are essential components in their ready-to-wear departments. A moment's thought will identify the obvious need to provide adequate fitting room facilities for customers who are buying (rather than being sold) 'off-the-peg' items. They expect to be able to try a number of alternative garments, quickly, on their own and to reach a purchase decision promptly.

Operations management can make a number of significant contributions to support the communications program. Customer convenience, in terms of store opening hours, merchandise replenishment and transactions handling, is an important element of the overall offer. If the communications program is making promises, these have to be delivered at the point of sale, and efficient delivery is the task of operations management.

The role of communications, as we have seen, is to create awareness, impart knowledge, change or create attitudes and develop a profitable ongoing relationship with a selected group of customers. This can only be achieved if there is strong support from employees who reinforce the communications offer and are largely responsible for its delivery. It follows that *HRM* capacity (number of staff) and capabilities (training and development) are essential components. They also account for a major part of the resource budget.

Merchandise availability in-store and for delivery to customers, together with the support required on product recalls and re-deliveries when customers are not available to accept the initial deliveries, are all part of the support afforded by a *logistics system*. Increasingly, retailing is playing an important part in structuring and managing the retail supply chain. To be effective in this role requires planning. The planning can only be achieved if the implications of customer expectations of availability and delivery services are known. The logistics support concerns capacity, capability and 'time' management. A chapter follows which will discuss the role of supply chain management and its implications for the business.

A major drive of any retailing organization is information. An effective *information/database management system* tracks customer attitudes and behaviour and provides a forecasting input into resources planning. Information management is required for replenishment of inventories and to ensure that adequate labour is available if sales and profits targets are to be met. We devote a chapter to this topic and issues concerned with information management later. The connection with customer loyalty programs will also be discussed.

THE COMMUNICATIONS PLAN

Having collected and considered the data and given management's strategic intentions the detail of the communications plan can be written. Figure 14.1 proposes the topics that should ideally included.

The target audience

By now there is no doubt as to who comprises the target customer group. The research into shopper and store characteristics will have identified who the *current* target customer is and who is to be identified as an *ideal* target. If there is a planned shift from an existing customer base this will influence the communications message on *what* is to be said and to *whom*, *how* it is to be said, *when*, *where* and by *whom*.

Communications objectives

As we have discussed earlier in this chapter, objectives will be both qualitative and quantitative depending upon the expected response. Typically, cognitive and affective responses will be measured by qualitative objectives – awareness of the organization and attitudes towards the company and its market-place offer – which are responses which can be used to direct a long-term strategy. Behavioural responses are more likely to be set as objectives when we are seeking some specific action(s) from the target audience, for example a sales response to a promotional offer.

Communications channels

We have discussed personal and non–personal channels in Chapter 13. Examples were given of Nordstrom's approach towards employees, and we suggested that *personal communications* were very effective if staff were given (and trained for) a role in the communications process. Customer loyalty programs were also discussed in some detail and the emerging role of electronic commerce was also considered.

Non-personal communications were considered to be an important element of the communications process. Visual merchandising, advertising, and public relations and corporate affairs were also discussed.

The communications plan should comprise a combination of personal and non-personal elements. Typically we would expect to use a predominance of personal communications for products that are expensive, considered to be high risk (in the context of the financial commitment and time perspective involved) and purchased infrequently. By contrast, FMCG retailing is likely to feature a considerable level of non-personal communications: advertising, visual merchandising and sales promotion activities.

However, areas of grey exist. The sophistication of information management systems facilitates targeting database management to individual customers and has been very successful for retaining customers in multiple food retailing through customer loyalty programs. At the same time, the non-personal aspects of visual merchandising can be minimized and successfully directed towards selected small target customer groups.

Message design

The message *content* (what is to be said), its *structure* (the logic of the message), its *format* (the creativity of visual and copy) and its *source* (the media to be used) are all components of message design.

The communications plan should make explicit the details of each component. *Content* must have a response in mind. Consequently it proposes some benefit and motivates or identifies reasons why the target audience should think or do something. *Structure* is very important to effectiveness. Kotler (1998) recalls work completed by Hovland and Mandell (1952), an early attempt to show how communications effectiveness is influenced by a decision on whether or not to be *conclusive in the message* (or to leave the recipient to reach a conclusion); *to present one-or two sided arguments* (to mention only positive comment or both positive and negative); and the *order of presentation* (when the strongest arguments should be presented).

Format is used to attract attention, to differentiate the communication from others competing for the attention of the target audience. How this is achieved depends upon the media used and what competitors are doing. The message *source* is important because an audience is influenced by how it perceives the sender. Messages delivered by suitably credible sources (i.e. the source should have context) are more persuasive.

It follows that message design decisions should be made in the context of time perspectives, target audience characteristics and the communications channels to be used.

The communications mix

Communications mix decisions extend those made concerning communications channels. Whereas the communications channels suggest a *broad* perspective for resource allocation, the communications mix *details specific* communications tools. The communicator's task is to achieve an optimal mix: to design a cost-effective communications program which has reach and penetration, realizes objectives and does so at an affordable level of budget. At this stage the plan identifies an ideal program mix. The next task is to cost this ideal and, if necessary (and it usually is) to make compromises.

Draft budgets

At this stage in the planning process we are attempting to estimate two budget levels. One is an 'ideal' figure based upon the communications objectives, channels and mix. The other is a realistic budget, a combined estimate of what is required and what the company can afford. Typically we have a shortfall between these projections and some compromise is required.

Kotler (1998) has a useful review of budgeting approaches for communications and promotional decisions. The reader is recommended to refer to this source for details.

One option available when communications budget requirements exceed the funds available is to accept supplier 'involvement'. Supplier involvement is not without problems. If suppliers are to contribute funds to the communications budget there are constraints. These may be based upon volume increases, and here the retailer must estimate the probability of achieving the volume expectations. Other constraints may be more difficult to deal with. For example, an offer to contribute to the communications budget from a 'market-place number two' may restrict the acceptance of less funding from the market leader. There may also be constraints on creative and media strategies, which prove to be dysfunctional; this may be more significant.

Finally, the issue of overall positioning is to be considered. As we have discussed, many retailers use their communications activities to reinforce their positioning, and are reluctant to relax their control over decision making. Many suppliers understand the power of retail marketing and now contribute to their distributors' budgets on the understanding that the retailer is more knowledgeable and closer to the target customer.

Review strategy and implementation plan

Before making final commitments on production and media spends, a final review of the strategy and plan is conducted. Some simple questions should be asked to ensure that the communications plan does in fact address the tasks identified. We should, therefore, review:

- The target audience
  - core customers (existing and potential)
  - new customers (targeted and reasons)
- The long- and short-term marketing and therefore communications objectives
- The long- and short-term marketing and communications strategies
- The cohesiveness between objectives and strategies
- The logic of the communications channels and communications mix
- The realism of the communications budget:
  - will it achieve the expected results?
  - what will competitors' responses be?
- Pre-testing of any or all of the communications activities
- The performance measures to be established.

Set a final budget

Given that satisfactory conclusions are reached at each stage of the planning process a final budget can be agreed. A detailed budget statement should detail expenditures by:

- Creative expenses
- Media (all types)
- Internal expenditures
  - visual merchandising
  - operations expenditures (support)
  - customer service (support)
- Public relations and corporate affairs

In addition, an expenditures schedule should be published (together with a media schedule) detailing the range of activities and costs committed.

Finally, a 'sources and applications' statement of company, supplier and other sources of communications funds and their application over the planning period is a useful statement for senior management.

Determine evaluation criteria

The performance criteria will have evolved through the planning process. Clearly many of the original objectives may have been modified during the development processes and compromises that will have resulted.

Those that remain will form the basis of the evaluation of the communications program and expenditures. Figure 14.1 proposes a series of performance measures which are to be applied to each of the strategy areas. The quantitative objectives of visits, purchases and transaction values should not form the primary basis for performance appraisal; qualitative measures may have more significance, much depending upon the life cycle of the business.

The operating budget

To ensure the successful implementation of the customer communications strategy, the operating budget details revenue expectations, resource requirements and expenditure levels necessary.

As with other functions specific budget items will vary. Using the performance measures identified earlier, the following topics are suitable:

Revenues

Sales	by:	• regions	by:	• internal communication $
Gross margin		• locations		
Contribution margin		• formats		• external communication $
		• 'seasons'		

Resource requirements

Dedicated staff

Dedicated visual merchandising staff

Dedicated equipment

Expenses
Staff
Internal communications activities
External communications activities
- creative
- media
- promotional

EXAMPLES OF COMMUNICATIONS DECISIONS

Exploiting consumer interests

B&Q is the leading DIY retailer in the UK, with a 19.1% share of the market and 283 stores across the country (September 1998).

The company seeks to exploit the current consumer interest in home improvement fuelled by television programs encouraging the interest. B&Q have introduced a '...new family soap-opera-style advertising campaign', featuring a family's transformation of their home over a 10 week campaign period. Each week the characters are shown tackling a different task with the help and advice of B&Q staff. The tasks include laying an oak-laminated floor, tiling the bathroom fitting internal doors, building a shed and fitting kitchen units.

B&Q suggest:

> We wanted to do something different, and reinforce the idea that B&Q is an authority on DIY, and that customers can get the confidence to tackle DIY with B&Q.
>
> This is supposed to be light hearted yet educational, with a typical interfering mother-in-law.

Source: *Marketing*, 3 September 1998.

Using an alliance to launch nationwide home shopping

Iceland, a UK frozen food supermarket, announced a home shopping service via a link with BSkyB. Iceland became the first food retailer to launch a nationwide service.

> Iceland, a small but profitable multiple considers itself to be an innovator in the sector.

Source: Bainbridge, J. (1998) 1998 review of the year. *Marketing*, 17 December.

Switching from price to a price/value offer based on choice

Currys is part of the Dixons Stores Group, a dominant retailer in the UK durables market with a 20% market share. The total Dixons Store Group advertising spend is some £108 million in media. Currys accounted for £49 million in 1997.

Currys' agency commented:

> Our research shows that people have a clear understanding of the price proposition but are consistently surprised about the depth of range.... Here we've been trying to communicate choice to the consumer as strongly as possible... Press advertisements show a variety of products, but consumers have tended to assume that they (Currys) cover only the middle range.

The agency opted for a 'different look'. Instead of the usual shots of customers wandering through the store, there is a range of different types of people posing in front of a broad range of products.

Any cheaper price found elsewhere will be matched immediately (the advertisement proclaims). Other services such as delivery and in-store demonstration of hi-fi products are featured.

Source: McLuhan (1998) Currys TV ads stress choice. *Marketing*, 1 October.

Cable TV home shopping: Asda stores

Asda, the UK food multiple, has launched its own branded TV programs: a test series of seven five-minute programs to promote its apparel and its home and leisure range.

The programs are based on 'TV formats': a chat show, a current affairs slot and a *You've been Framed* theme. Characters wear George clothes (Asda label) and price appears on-screen. The programs will air on UK Living, a cable TV channel.

Consumers will be asked to phone a central call centre if they are interested in the products featured. They can be ordered at store price plus postage and packing. The programs were centred upon the end-of year festive season and ran for four weeks.

Source: *Marketing*, 12 November 1998.

Using humour successfully: Tesco

Tesco have used 'Dotty' (actor Prunella Scales of *Fawlty Towers*), to name just one, for four years. The latest series (October 1998), the sixteenth, continues a comedy approach which features 'the mother of all shoppers' whose demanding behaviour tests Tesco staff to the limits.

The campaign continues a customer-focused strategy aimed at building brand values. Tesco's advertising manager, Catherine Baxendale was quoted as saying:

> Our success is due to a set of factors which we've tried to combine and bring to life: low prices, a wide range of goods, and excellent quality...

> The heart of it is about doing the right thing for customers, and we want to communicate that.

Source: McLuhan, R. (1998) Dotty plot keeps Tesco top. *Marketing*, 15 October.

SUMMARY

We have considered the difficult decisions that accompany implementing communications strategy. Often these decisions become difficult because of management involvement (and often interference), and it is not unknown for seniority to be used to impose decisions. Furthermore, it should be said that for many situations there may be more than one implementation that would prove to be effective.

This chapter has presented an approach which evaluates objectives and strategies and has identified systematic methods for achieving an optimal solution. We suggest that the communications decision is no different from any other marketing-related decision. It is based upon an understanding of customers' expectations, their pre-purchase activities, their purchasing patterns and behaviour, and a need to develop a long-term relationship with the target customer group.

QUESTIONS, ACTIVITIES AND OBSERVATIONS

- For a multiple retailer of your choice, use Figure 14.2 to identify the relevant customer segments, functions and 'technology' characteristics of the organization, together with the value characteristics offered. How well does the company integrate its business definition with its value from a communications perspective?
- Construct a store selection and purchasing decision model for an FMCG retailer. Identify the communications tasks and the shopper and store characteristics for the company. Are they compatible?
- How would you advise a department store, seeking to add computers and related products to its merchandise range, on its communications activities? The communications objectives are: to create an awareness among existing and potential customers, to establish itself as an 'expert' and then to create volume sales.
- What are the advantages and disadvantages of the Internet in developing a customer communications implementation plan? What can it offer? What is it unable to offer?

REFERENCES

Hovland, C. I. and Mandell, W. (1952) An experimental comparison of conclusion-drawing by the communication and by the audience. *Journal of Abnormal and Social Psychology*, July.

Kotler, P. (1996) *Marketing Management: Analysis Planning and control*. Prentice Hall International, Englewood Cliffs, NJ.

Lavidge, R. J. and Steiner, G. A. (1961) A model for predictive measurements of advertising effectiveness. *Journal of Marketing*, October.

Martineau, P. (1958) The personality of the retail store. *Harvard Business Review*, Jan/Feb.

Ottesen, O. (1977) The response function, in *Current Themes in Mass Communications Research* (ed. Mic Berg). GMT, Grenaa, Denmark.

Smith, D. (1999) All aboard the money go round. *The Sunday Times*, 14 February.

Spector, R. and McCarthy, P. (1995) *The Nordstrom Way*. John Wiley, New York.

Urban, G. L. and Hauser, J. R. (1980) *Design and Marketing of New Products*. Prentice Hall, New York.

Webster, F. (1994) *Market Driven Management*. John Wiley, New York.

15 HUMAN RESOURCES DEVELOPMENT

LEARNING OBJECTIVES

Customer service and staff response to customers have been major concerns of retailing in recent years. The recession of the late 1980s/early 1990s caused considerable damage to consumer confidence, and this was reflected in the slow recovery of retail spending. Customers became selective and discerning and their 'value' expectations shifted such that the store selection and purchasing decision for major purchases assumed greater importance than it had prior to the event. This chapter considers the role of the employee in building a positive relationship with the customer by considering the implications of strategic decisions for human resources development.

Among the issues addressed are:

- The importance of understanding the relationship between customer *and* employee satisfaction.
- The variables of the relationship, such as: the strategic positioning (the format offer), the range of merchandise characteristics, cultural differences (an important consideration for international retailing), competitive perspectives of necessity vs. clear advantage benefits.
- The role of the relationship in developing customer loyalty.
- The implications of the relationship for human resource development decisions.
- An approach to evaluating the existing relationship between employee and customer satisfaction, the implications for profitability and indications of how it may be developed to *improve* profitability.
- An application of the employee–customer–profit chain by Sears, Roebuck and Company.

INTRODUCTION

Human resources management (HRM) has become a proactive consideration in strategy decisions, assuming a planning role in what has become human resources development (HRD). Human resources decisions are now

considered to be central to the strategy decision and its implementation. Questions are now raised at the strategy analysis and development stages relating to the implications of strategic direction decisions for human resources. Heskett *et al.* (1997) offers a series of questions which may be modified for use for HRD purposes.

An important issue for HR decision-makers concerns the relationship between customer and employee satisfaction. Heskett *et al.* argues that unless this satisfaction is 'mirrored' it is unlikely that HR policies are totally effective. Earlier, in Chapter 14, we discussed the role of communications in customer retention, and there it was suggested (not only by these authors) that customer retention is a significant issue. If customer loyalty can be built and long-term transaction relationships developed, considerable savings for communications costs can occur. It follows that for retailing the employee/customer relationship is (and will remain to be for some time) a major strategy consideration.

It also follows that at the strategy stage a number of questions should be asked in order that a role for human resources may be identified. If this is done successfully it will ensure that the type, number and job specifications required for successful implementation of the strategy will be established very early in the process. Further, it will identify development and training needs for the human resource team if customer satisfaction *and* employee satisfaction are to be achieved.

Questions needing to be addressed initially are:

- How strong is (should be) the relationship between customer and employee satisfaction?
- Are there variations depending upon, categories, formats, regions etc.?
- What are the implications for job specifications and development and training? What are the gaps in number, skills and development programs?
- Is the consistency of service offered by employees a problem? Could it be given new strategies?
- Does the current organization structure require review?

Additional questions aimed at amplifying the role of customer loyalty in the customer/employee satisfaction equation should be asked:

- How important is customer loyalty to business development?
- Has the organization developed a definition of customer loyalty and a means of measuring it?
- Does the organization monitor the customer satisfaction/customer loyalty relationship?
- Are a variety of complementary measures used to measure customer satisfaction, customer loyalty *and* employee satisfaction?
- How is the information collected, analysed and disseminated?
- Is customer satisfaction measured across customer segments and by 'degrees' of satisfaction? Is this analysed?

- Is there an employee reward system linked to customer satisfaction achievements?
- Is there a customer loyalty system? Are loyalty levels compared by significant variables?
- Is investment in customer satisfaction measured in a similar way as other investment?

And when developing an HRD perspective:

- What is the HR role in the overall strategy?
- How important is the input of employees?
- What are the expectations of customers of sales staff?
  - advice
  - product demonstration
  - insurance/risk reduction
- To what degree must services be customized at the point or time of purchase?
- How important is the consistency of service delivery?
- How important is employee empowerment?
- Can employee innovation improve customer and employee satisfaction?
- How important are incentives?
  - for customer loyalty
  - for employee performance *and* loyalty?
- How should employees be remunerated?
- What form of organization structure should be considered to make strategy effective?

And at an operational level:

- Can employee efficiency be increased by adding non-traditional techniques?
- Are sales employees selected on the basis of sales skills, attitudes to customer service and/or to the company? Should these be changed?
- Does (or will) training reflect the needs of the employee's job specification *and* the ongoing strategic positioning objectives of the organization?
- At the point of sale does the employee enjoy freedom to respond to customer problems?

Clearly if the human resource role is to take on strategic importance a shift of emphasis is necessary. In reaching answers to these questions an assumption is made concerning the proactive nature of HR decisions. Questions need to be asked concerning value delivery methods throughout the planning horizon, and these should be far-reaching. They should consider *all* options and, therefore, the implications for HRD decisions.

Exhibit 15.1

The employee–customer–profit chain at Sears

The dramatic turnround in market and financial performance at Sears, Roebuck and Company has been a source of case study material. Rucci *et al.* (1998) provide an excellent account of the work undertaken in analysing 'the logic and culture of the business'.

A three-year project was undertaken to rebuild the company around its customers:

> In the course of rethinking what Sears was and wanted to become, these managers developed a business model of the company that tracked success from management behaviour through employee attitudes to customer satisfaction and financial performance. Along with its measurement system, this *employee–customer–profit model* is rigorous enough to serve as an integral piece of the management information system and as a tool that every individual in the company can use for self-assessment and self-improvement.

The model builds on an intuitive understanding that retailing demonstrates a 'chain of cause and effect running from employee behaviour to customer behaviour to profits... and that behaviour depends primarily on attitude.

An important input is data reflecting 'attitudes' and 'satisfaction', neither of which are easy to capture, but Sears does, by means of a set of measures that show the company how well it is performing with respect to customers, employees and investors. The TPI (total performance indicators) work because of the time taken by Sears to understand the layers of factors that drive employee attitudes and how these affect employee retention, and how these in turn influence customer satisfaction and eventually how customer satisfaction affects financial performance.

Three critical components contribute to making the employee–customer–profit chain operational. The first is to create the model and define the measurement system. Secondly, build the management alignment around the model so that it is both an information system and decision support system, central to the business. Thirdly, use the model to build all understanding of the business among employees and to encourage and develop ownership. Sears' management both built the model *and* developed affiliation with it at the same time.

Rucci *et al.* recall the dramatic *turnaround* activity, and its success, undertaken during 1992/1993 by the new CEO, Arthur Martinez. The year 1992 was the worst in Sears' 111 years of trading. On sales of $52.3 billion a net loss of $3.9 billion occurred, of which $3 billion came from the merchandising group. In 1993 the merchandising

group reported a net income of $752 million, a sales increase in excess of 9% in existing stores, and market share gains in apparel, appliances and electronics. It proved to be one of its most profitable years. Total shareholder return for the year was 56%.

Management's concern was to ensure that the momentum would continue. It was time for *transformation*. The need was to turn the short-term success into a long-term future of prosperity. A number of concerns were identified. Employees were important, and their involvement was essential. Customer expectations (and their satisfaction) were equally important and management had both a leadership and a coordination role to undertake.

Space prevents recounting the detail that Rucci *et al.* record, but the essential steps are necessary to the understanding of the process.

Initially Martinez presented to senior management five new strategic priorities: core business growth; customer focus ('Make Sears a compelling place to shop'); cost reduction; responsiveness to local markets; and organizational and cultural renewal. The management team was tasked to fill in the detail. Progress meetings were held and difficulties discussed. A major problem was communicating the five priorities beyond the senior management levels, who themselves were not totally clear on some issues. A considerable amount of work was undertaken, resulting in four recurring themes: customers, employees, financial performance and innovation. Eventually a fifth was added: values.

Task groups were formed to explore and define *world class status* in each group *and* to identify ways and means of achieving it in Sears *and* of measuring it. The *financial* taskforce built a model of shareholder value components and drivers for a 20 year period, and concluded what Sears would need to do to be in the top 25% of the *Fortune* 500. The *innovation* group explored the nature of change and suggested generating ideas from employees. The *value* group identified six core values that Sears' employees felt strongly about: honesty, integrity, respect for the individual, teamwork, trust, and customer focus. The *customer* task force reviewed past customer surveys as well as conducting focus groups. Participants were asked why they shopped at Sears, what they wanted and expected, and what their dislikes were. The focus groups produced '...endless stories of how we failed to meet customers' expectations'. Despite the numerous negative comments, '...people basically liked Sears'.

During the period that task groups were gathering data an additional group was working on a *vision and values statement*. Not surprisingly, this initially '...came up with a set of values that sounded like the Boy Scout Oath'. External help from consultants failed to add much else. It was the management group that eventually resolved the stalemate and the result was:

Sears a compelling place to work, to shop and to invest.

It became known as 'the three compellings' (subsequently the three Cs) and it was combined with three shared values (the three Ps): 'passion for the customer, our people add value and performance leadership'. As Rucci *et al.* suggest, this simple but concise statement:

> amounted to a wonderfully concise version of the entire employee–customer–profit chain, from motivated employees to satisfied customers to pleased investors.

The result was a model linking employee, customer and investor interests:

$$\text{Work} \times \text{Shop} = \text{Invest}$$

with a number of components:

A compelling place to work

Objectives
- Environment for personal growth and development
- Support for ideas and innovation
- Empowered and involved teams and individuals

Measures
- Personal growth and development
- Empowered teams

A compelling place to shop

Objectives
- Great merchandise at great values
- Excellent customer service from the best people
- Fun place to shop
- Customer loyalty

Measures
- Customer needs met
- Customer satisfaction
- Customer retention

A compelling place to invest

Objectives
- Revenue growth
- Superior operating income growth
- Efficient asset management
- Productivity gains

Measures
- Revenue growth
- Sales per square foot
- Inventory turnover
- Operating income margin
- Return on assets

The next step by Sears took HRD into pioneering. An econometric model was built using the data assembled by the task forces and data generated previously. A consulting company used *causal pathway modelling* (as opposed to regression analysis) to identify connections along and across the data sets. Causal pathway modelling is a qualitative and quantitative technique which utilizes relational databases to identify the relationships between employee attitudes and activities, the customers' quantitative responses (frequency of shopping visits and the value of transactions) and their qualitative responses (such as their use of Sears as a destination purchase, their role as 'ambassadors' by referral and recommendation). Interesting relationships emerged. Sears could see how employee attitudes drove not just customer service but also employee turnover and the probability that employees would recommend Sears' merchandise to friends, family and customers. Among the many useful relationships, two are significant to HRD. A strong relationship between the employee's ability to see the connection between his or her work and the company's strategic objectives was a driver of positive behaviour. Also, two dimensions of employee satisfaction – attitude toward the job and toward the company – had a greater effect on employee loyalty and behaviour toward customers than all the other dimensions put together.

The result of the work, a model of the employee–customer–profit chain, is shown as Figure E15.1. As Rucci *et al.* comment at the beginning of their article:

> It goes without saying that you must be able to measure and manage the drivers of employee and customer satisfaction.

The employee–customer–profit chain has made this increasingly possible for Sears. An essential part of the exercise was its deployment. The implementation process (see Rucci *et al.* for details) involved a study which linked positive employee attitudes with an increase in the customer's understanding of their (the customers') role and value to Sears.

DEVELOPING A STRATEGIC APPROACH

Rucci *et al.* provide an excellent base from which an approach to HRD based upon a designed interaction between customers, employees and the organization can be developed. Figure 15.1 identifies the task of human resources development. The three important characters (customers, employees and the company) are featured at the apex points of the diagram. These, we have seen, are central to an effective approach to HR strategy. For each character a

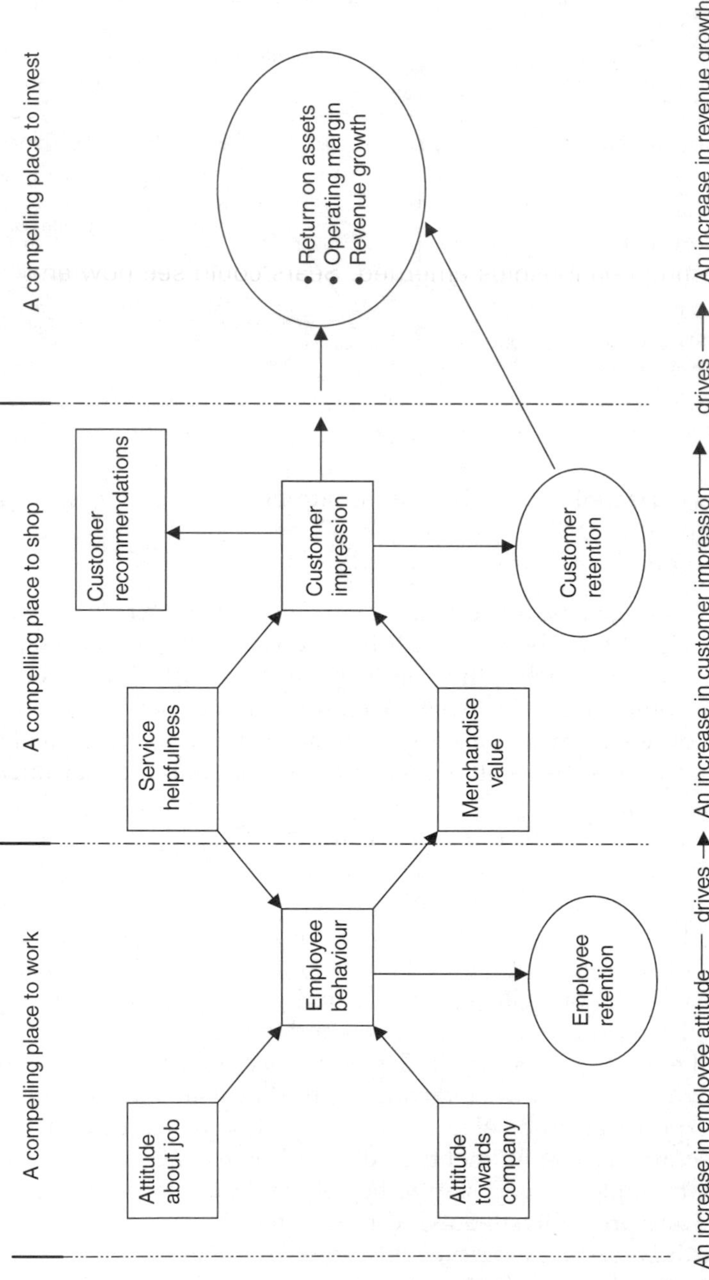

Figure E15.1 Sears' employee–customer–profit chain. (Adapted from: Rucci, A. J. Kirn, S. P. and Quinn, R. T. (1998) The employee–customer–profit chain. *Harvard Business Review* Jan/Feb.)

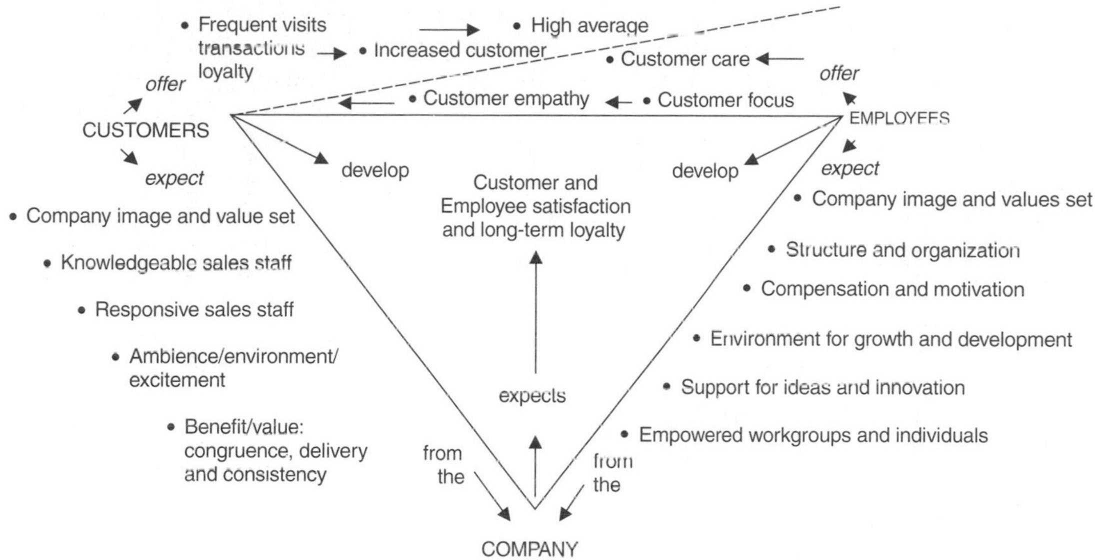

Figure 15.1 Deriving expectations and offer commitments of customers, employees and the retail organization.

number of generic features are listed. These are either *offered* or *expected*, and we suggest that the features listed are typical for most retailing organizations. Research such as that conducted by Sears will identify the expectations of customers and employees. We are assuming that the company expects employee and customer satisfaction and long term loyalty. However, these can only be as the result of meeting the expectations of both customers and employees.

A review of the features adds context to the proposal.

Company image and values set is important for both customers and employees. It refers to the honesty, integrity, commitment, respect for the individual etc. identified by Sears. It is important for customers because it offers the basis of 'a compelling place to shop' and equally for employees it identifies the basis of 'a compelling place to work'. Customers expect *knowledgeable sales staff*; that is, knowledge of products and their applications, prices and terms, and knowledge of services. *Responsive sales staff* are those who offer high levels of customer care and concern. In almost all forms of retailing customers expect staff to be able to make decisions which commit the company. These may be commitments to delivery times or to special prices. Increasingly customers expect staff to be able to deal with product repair, replacement and price adjustments, i.e. they expect *empowered managers and staff*. We have discussed *ambience/environment/excitement* in Chapters 11 and 12; here it is sufficient to comment that it is a component of 'a compelling place to shop'. Finally, the importance of meeting customers' *benefit/value expectations* consistently has been part of the thesis of this text. Clearly this is reflected in the development of human resources.

Employee expectations, in addition to *company image and values set* (which provides both a guide for their behaviour but also their expectations of how the company responds to its staff), require a clear and unambiguous *structure and organization* format which prescribes the 'compelling place to work': it offers process and order and systems and procedures. A fair and equitable *compensation and motivation* package is essential if the employee is to meet company performance criteria, as is an opportunity for personal development: an *environment for growth and development*. Equally, initiative should be encouraged; typically new ideas are better ideas if they come from the workforce rather than being presented to them by management. Thus *support for ideas and innovation* is expected. To meet the expectations of customers for staff that can make decisions when confronted with non-routine situations, employees expect to be *empowered work groups and individuals*.

In response to the company having met both customer and employee expectations, each will deliver activities that will move the company towards its own set of expectations of customer and employee satisfaction and loyalty. Customers deliver their commitment by adjusting/increasing the frequency of visits, the size of their purchases and their purchasing across the assortment of the company. Satisfied employees develop stronger customer focus, customer empathy and customer care. Figure 15.1 suggests that the expectations and offers bind customers, employees and the retail company together into a consensus of mutual understanding and cooperation from which the success formula *work* × *shop* = *invest* will emerge.

The 'compelling place to invest' dimension is added by Figure 15.2, which is in effect an application of Kaplan and Norton's balanced scorecard. Figure 15.2 was developed by Heskett *et al.* from Sweden's Swedbank. The bank's CEO and senior management first identified three clusters around which performance weaknesses existed and new initiatives could be structured. They were 'people value added', 'customer value added' and 'economic value added'. When applied at the branch level it was found that high-performance branches ranked highly on all three dimensions. Management concluded that not only could performance be enhanced but so too could the culture and designed sets of measures focusing on financial performance, customer satisfaction and employee satisfaction. The bank (like Sears in the exhibit) used all three to measure overall performance.

Both qualitative and quantitative performance criteria are identified in Figure 15.2. The concept of a 'balanced scorecard' is that no one performance measure is adequate. It is argued that by focusing on one aspect of performance a sub-optimal output may occur elsewhere – hence the notion of trade-offs between customer, employee and corporate financial performance. Some examples may explain the significance of this approach. An attempt to increase the EVA productivity performance of working capital may result in setting levels of inventory turnover that result in poor perceptions of service by customers. Similarly, a stringent limit on customer credit may have similar results. Both would be seen in customer attitude and performance responses. A lack of delegation (empowerment) to sales assistants may also have detrimental effects. The absence of the authority to reduce a

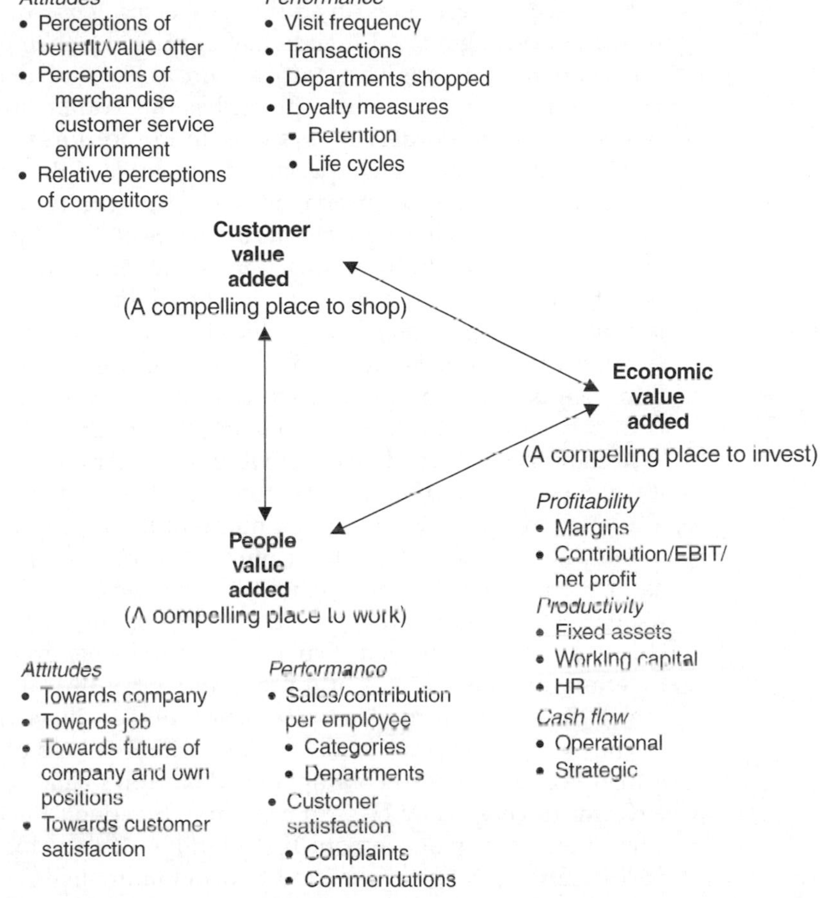

Figure 15.2 A 'balanced scorecard' approach. (Adapted from: Heskett, J. L., Sasser, W. E. Jr and Schlesinger, L. A. (1997) *The Service Profit Chain*. The Free Press, New York.)

price to meet competition can result in lost sales, as may the need to return a product to the supplier for comment or agreement to replacement.

The balanced scorecard approach does require some research input. The approach taken by Sears, and that suggested by Figure 15.1, provides the environment for performance to take place and must be understood before the response metrics for attitudes and performance are set.

Heskett *et al.* (1997) also identify the linkages between employee loyalty and satisfaction and between employee satisfaction and the internal quality of work life. They give a number of examples of service companies to demonstrate the linkage. The Heskett *et al.* service profit chain has been discussed earlier. An important component of their model is the identification of relationships between elements of the service profit chain. Using internal company studies they measured relationships between various features. Using a

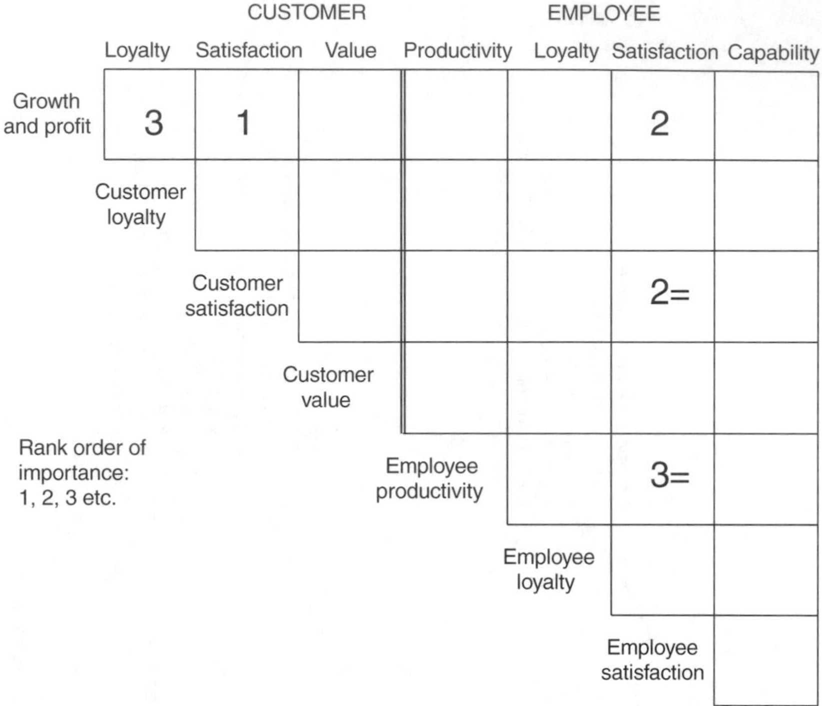

Figure 15.3 Relationships between elements of the service profit chain.

matrix (represented by Figure 15.3) they identified strong links between important factors.

A strong relationship was found between growth and profit and customer satisfaction, customer loyalty and employee satisfaction. Another significant linkage appeared between customer satisfaction and employee satisfaction, with less noticeable links for employee loyalty and capability. Employee loyalty correlated with employee satisfaction. The authors admit that evidence is not substantial; as yet not many companies have completed this or similar research. However, it offers a useful analytical tool. When considering the HR content of a strategic move an exercise similar to that of Sears in the exhibit may be conducted. Possibly more useful is to apply the matrix to existing situations. It is not difficult to envisage how it may be used. Focus groups among customers and employees will identify the criteria important to them. Furthermore we can, using a similar approach to that of Sears, identify ideal profiles (and linkages) which when costed can add a quantitative dimension to Figure 15.3.

In the context of the Kaplan and Norton model introduced (and modified) in Chapter 5 (Figures 5.4 and 5A.1) we can emphasize the HR content. Figure 15.4 considers the broad balanced scorecard approach and adds detail to the objectives to facilitate planning and control decisions.

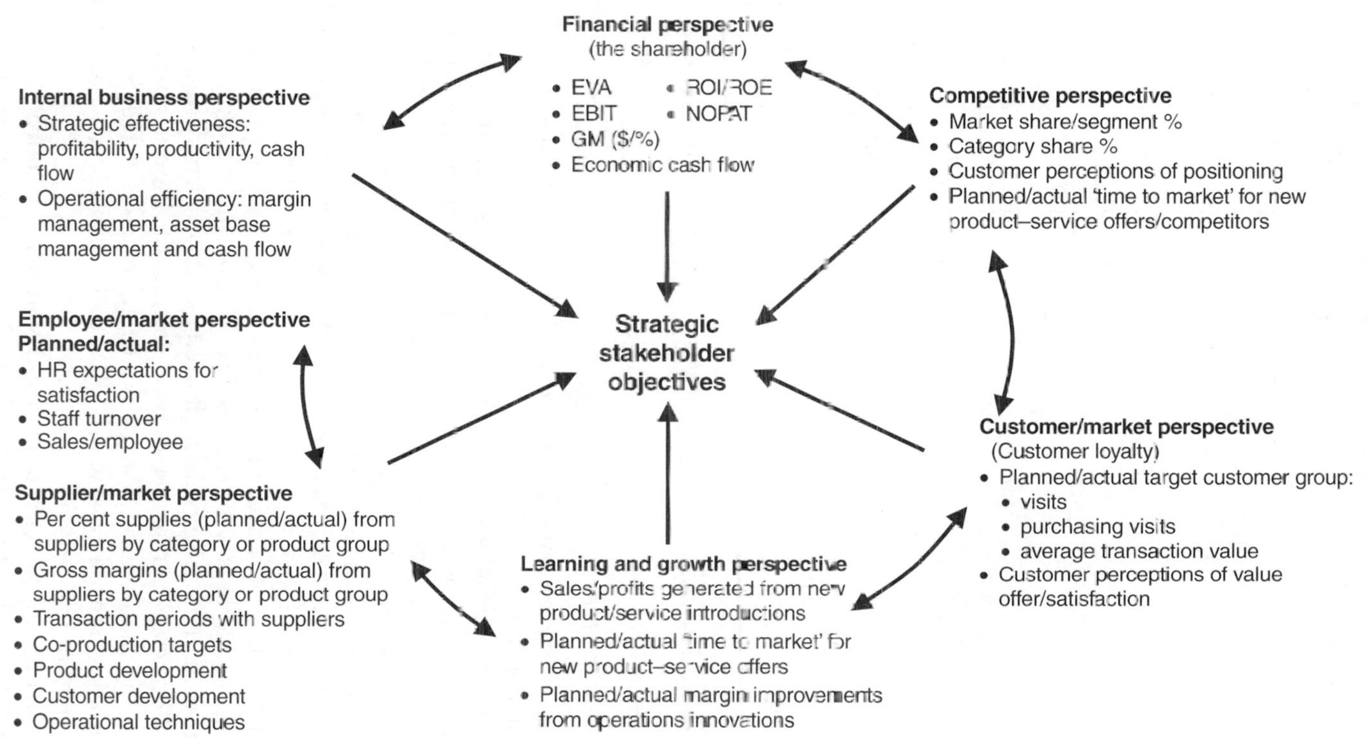

Figure 15.4 Developing stakeholder objectives introducing an HR perspective.

AN OPERATIONAL PERSPECIVE

In previous chapters we considered strategy and implementation decisions. Given that the human resources decisions have been made at a strategic level, the deployment of staff in terms of roles and tasks is made within the context of those decisions.

Figure 15.5 considers how this may be achieved such that support is available within the communications strategy and implementation. Human resources play an important role in retailing to ensure that the objectives for 'a compelling place to shop' and a compelling place to invest' are realized. For this to be effective the role of staff in customer communication is important and requires some careful thought. A review of format and communications implementation activities will identify opportunities.

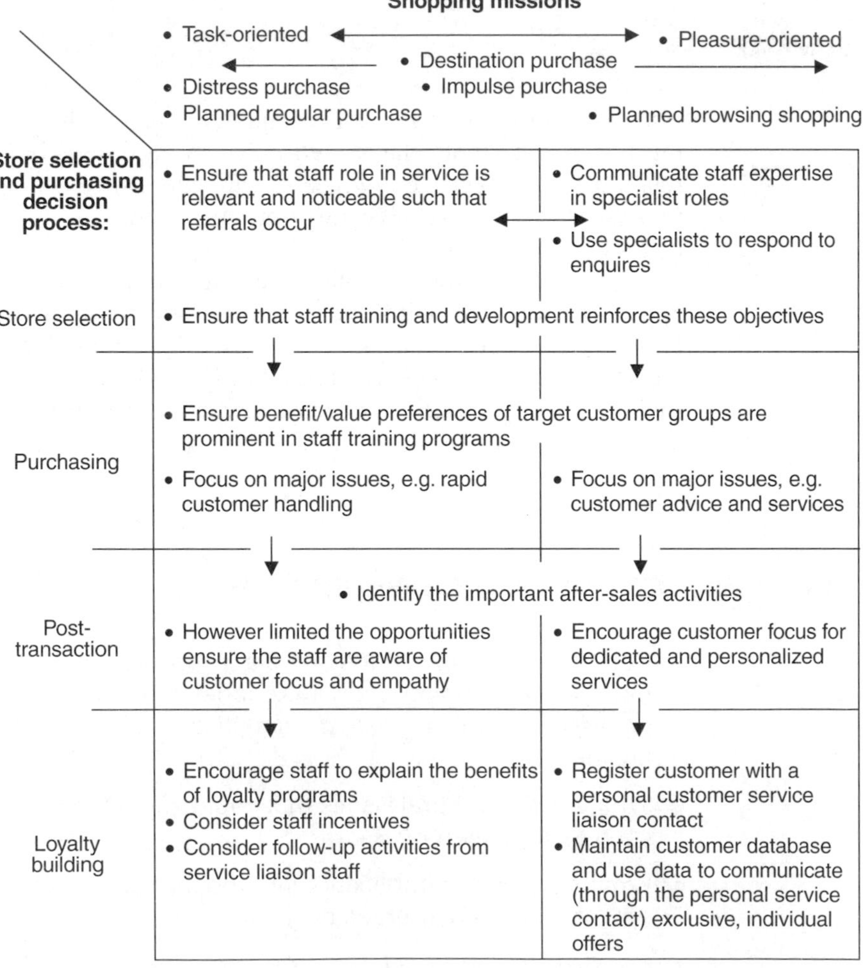

Figure 15.5 Using shopping missions and the store selection and purchasing decision process to identify key roles and activities for sales staff.

Clearly the role played by human resources will vary by type of retail offer. Figure 15.5 follows the approach used for format and communications decisions. The opportunity for demonstrating customer focus, empathy and care will vary considerably. For superstore/supermarket activities, concern should be directed towards meeting the desire of most customers for rapid and accurate transaction handling. While customer/employee contact time is limited, the overall objectives of customer satisfaction and customer loyalty do not change. Indeed, it could be argued that it is essential that they are more important for small transactions and low-margin retail situations.

Management's task, having identified the criteria for customer and employee satisfaction, is to design the operational tasks such that work × shop = investment, whatever the situation.

SUMMARY

The role of human resources in retailing has always been important. It is significant to note that retailers who place a high level of importance on the relationship between employee satisfaction and customer satisfaction are those who typically survive the impact of downturns in aggregate consumer confidence and expenditure.

The Sears example identifies the importance of this linkage and their approach, together with the service profit chain model (developed by Heskett *et al.*) offer retailers a way of identifying HRD issues that should be incorporated into strategies. If built into performance reviews, it can ensure the relationship continues to be monitored for its impact on ultimate profitability and productivity.

QUESTIONS, ACTIVITIES AND CONSIDERATIONS

- Consider the implications of the approach taken by Sears for an FMCG multiple. Would you apply the model in a similar way, or are changes necessary which reflect significant differences between the businesses?
- What are the cultural issues that could affect the results of an approach such as that used by Sears?
- What may be the implications of the increased application of technology on human resources decisions?
- Construct an approach for comparing the *relative* effectiveness of customer value added, people value added, and economic value added that could be used for competitive analysis purposes.

REFERENCES

Heskett, J. L., Sasser, W. E. Jr and Schlesinger, L. A. (1997) *The Service Profit Chain*. The Free Press, New York.

Kaplan, R. S. and Norton, D. P. (1992) The balanced scorecard – measures that drive performance. *Harvard Business Review*, Jan/Feb.

Rucci, A. J. Kirn, S. P. and Quinn, R. T. (1998) The employee–customer–profit chain. *Harvard Business Review* Jan/Feb.

16

MANAGING THE SUPPLY CHAIN

LEARNING OBJECTIVES

Managerial efficiency, the management of operations, has accounted for significant increases in the profitability of the major multiple retailers throughout the world; Tesco, Wal-Mart, and Ahold are notable examples. The supply chain has been one function in which these retailers have focussed considerable time and cost in developing efficient systems which support strategic decisions. In this chapter we identify:

- The major areas of development which are largely responsible for transforming supply chain management.
- The infrastructure of supply chain management techniques, the philosophies, business processes and technological developments that have emerged as major influences.
- The role of information systems and technology.
- The retail value chain which extends supply chain thinking into demand chain thinking.
- The relationships between performance and 'value chain facilitators' in the value chain.

INTRODUCTION

Supply chain management has become an important feature of retail operations. Increasingly, as the potential for cost savings within buying and merchandising and the operations functions become difficult to achieve, the focus is on the internal supply chain function within retail businesses and the external supply chain between the retail company and its suppliers. Focusing on the overall supply chain offers two potential benefits. The first is further cost savings. These may accrue from economies of scale and scope that occur when the retail supply chain moves closer towards that of major suppliers. The second benefit is related to increased competitive advantage, which is based upon enhanced control of the replenishment processes which facilitate the effective implementation of the merchandise and customer

service components of a positioning strategy. A retail offer based upon exclusivity, choice and availability may be unprofitable without exercising control of a highly integrated supply chain.

During the last ten years three major development areas have largely been responsible for transforming retailing supply chain management. These are: improved supplier/retailer relationships (in which mutual trust and cooperation have replaced conflict); developments in information systems (technology and applications); and the development of supply chain management techniques which improved efficiency throughout the supply chain.

McKinnon (1996) identifies six trends which he suggests are 'closely inter-related and in most cases, mutually reinforcing'. These are:

- The increase in control of secondary distribution by retailers. An increasing proportion of their merchandise supplies pass through their distribution centres. This, together with the accompanying investment in IT, is extensive, but has resulted in significant decreases in inventory holding *and* an increase in control.
- Restructuring of logistics systems to enhance the inventory reduction and efficiencies through 'composite distribution', centralization of slow-moving inventory and, in mixed businesses (e.g. department stores, multiple variety stores), the establishment of 'common stock rooms'.
- The adoption of 'Quick Response' (QR) has resulted in reducing inventory levels by the reduction of order lead times and utilizing more frequent deliveries of smaller consignments throughout the supply chain. A number of 'facilitators' are responsible for making this possible. Electronic data interchange (EDI) and electronic point of sale (EPOS) data systems driving sales-based ordering are notable here.
- Rationalization of primary distribution (from supplier to retailer warehouse) is in effect an extension of the retailer control of the total supply chain. McKinnon reports that many retailers are seeking to improve asset productivity by integrating secondary and primary distribution operations.
- An introduction of supply chain management (SCM) and efficient consumer response (ECR) (both described in some detail below) have had two benefits: they have improved supplier/distributor relationships *and* the overall efficiency.
- The acknowledgment of the role 'reverse logistics' has to play in environmental conservation *and* the potential for developing 'reuseable containers' and management systems.

We suggest one other factor that is noticeable in the larger retailing company:

- The development of a strategic role for supply chain management that enables the retailer to add value to the retail offer and create competitive advantage, e.g. the management of materials flows into supplier manufacturing facilities and the management of the co-production relationship between retailer and customer. The IKEA example referred to in Chapter 2 is an example!

RECENT DEVELOPMENTS

Before we discuss the specific needs that should be considered in constructing a retail supply chain, developments in the area are reviewed. We shall consider these under three areas: relationship management, techniques and information systems.

Fernie (1998) offers a thorough review of recent developments. He reminds us that relationship management has two aspects. Strong links with customers which result in increased levels of expenditure and the benefits of accurate, timely data which facilitate accurate forecasts of demand (by SKU at store level) which benefits replenishment processes and stock levels. Strong links with suppliers result in more efficient operations by a better understanding of mutual issues. Fernie's review of the relevant literature identifies that research suggests: 'a more confrontational picture than is often portrayed in the trade publications'. The inference is that while there have been improvements in supplier/distributor relationships they have moved towards a rational professionalism and a tendency for retailers to gain more of the benefits.

RELATIONSHIP MANAGEMENT

Of the recent developments in *relationship management* two are of significance to our discussion. The benefits of reducing the number of suppliers and moving towards *preferred supplier* status have resulted in more than cost reductions and increased buying discounts. It has resulted in guaranteed exclusivity of manufacturing facilities and more rapid product development and introduction and, as Kumar (1996) suggests (quoted by Fernie), advantageous terms and service from *all* major suppliers.

Whiteoak (1998), in Fernie and Sparks, discusses *supply chain integration* and offers some interesting perspectives. He suggests integration has two dimensions: one is the optimization of the supply chain (an efficiency issue), while the other may be a means of increasing the control exercised by one of the partners. Whiteoak continues by suggesting that much of the literature (specifically concerning ECR, efficient consumer response) is focussed *along* the supply chain (i.e. between manufacturer and retailer). Few examples have been given of *across* the chain integration. He points to the fact that multi-supply situations are commonplace, that supply chains are *networks*:

> So far, improvements in efficiency have come from the application of techniques, none of which is universally beneficial. Integration *across* the network will help overall *optimization*.

Whiteoak implies that the application of techniques, of which there are an increasing number available, enhances *across* the chain integration.

A study by GEA Consulenti Associata di gestione aziendale (GEA) on behalf of the Coca-Cola Retailing Research Group-Europe explored the notion of *supplier–retailer collaboration* (SRC). GEA defined SRC as:

> Supplier/Retailer Collaboration (SRC) is when both retailers and suppliers share proprietary internal or external data, and/or share policies and processes used in decision making with the clear objective of sharing the benefits.

The report by GEA suggests that cooperation between suppliers and retailers becomes real collaboration when sales and cost data are exchanged. As the type of data becomes increasingly market-oriented the possibilities of strategic collaboration also increase. They found, in a study involving 175 companies in five different European locations, two types of SRC. The first focuses on reducing costs in operations with a majority of benefits accruing to retailers due to their wider span of activities within the supply chain. The second focuses on developing synergies in the marketing mix by means of improved assortments, joint product innovation and lower cost promotion. The second is more strategic.

Some interesting findings are offered.

Collaboration is usually retailer-led and is based upon their determination to reduce costs and focus more closely on their customers. This results in greater customer loyalty and value/price differentiation *not* based on bargain prices. Large retailers have developed strategic power *and* the human and financial resources required to set up the systems and manage the decision-making processes. Centralization of information and product flows through Regional Distribution Centres and the overall resulting productivity are critical success factors. Suppliers play an important role. Their focus on product categories helps shape collaboration by several means, such as cost cutting or forming strategic alliances (between powerful counterparts or by 'virtual integration', defined by GEA as collaboration between a strong leader and a facilitator partner).

Adoption is a function of time and critical mass. Retailers require a minimum number of partners willing to share information and adopt new operating standards. This initial phase results in a transparency of costs and, in the medium term, a move towards sharing the reductions. Collaboration in marketing does not require a critical mass for the benefits to be realized, and GEA suggests that eventually these are shared with consumers.

Organization is an important consideration. Typically collaboration is a commitment by top management, but the ability to integrate functions is essential. For retailers the integration of purchasing, distribution, marketing and merchandising is important. For suppliers it is selling, marketing and logistics. The growth of *category management* (discussed below) offers a useful framework. Trust, long-term relationships, employee skills, incentives and positive attitudes towards change are key organizational strengths required for success.

Collaboration changes the routine of marketing and buying activities, resulting in the downsizing of selling and purchasing personnel together with a reshaping of skills.

Customer/consumer needs and purchasing information exchange between suppliers and retailers are the essence of collaboration, as is the flow of product data. GEA found that information exchange transforms traditionally independent data sets into 'one integrated vision'.

Information technology (EDI, EPOS) is a major key to collaboration. Interestingly, GEA suggests that national facilities for common standards, transmission codes and third party data management companies 'greatly facilitate the development of collaboration'.

Implementation involves a number of critical steps *internally*:

- top management support
- willingness to share information
- training functional experts (marketing and logistics) to communicate ways and means of designing and managing the evolving supply chain
- developing a category management focus
- a review of processes involved in planning and control.

External concerns are:

- choosing the partner (trust and affinity are important basic criteria)
- selecting the right products
- careful and open evaluation of benefits
- setting standards for key activities (data management) to ensure critical mass is achieved and to increase the benefits
- building an organization and mechanism which promotes industry interest and commitment to expand the collaboration *and* the benefits.

SUPPLY CHAIN MANAGEMENT TECHNIQUES

Developments in *supply chain management techniques* have been numerous. While we are considering these individually, they are often applied together and typically require collaboration between trading partners and across networks.

Quick response (QR) techniques are designed to reduce inventory levels by reducing order lead times and moving to more frequent deliveries of smaller consignments. (McKinnon (1996) suggests QR as being one of the important trends in the development of retail logistics). QR, if it is to be successful, requires a number of changes to the 'logistics' structure and philosophy. First, the technique requires the implementation of 'cross-docking' (product is unloaded from the inbound vehicle and moved 'across the dock' to be marshalled with other goods for onward dispatch *without* being put into storage). QR also requires rapid (electronic) data transfer if it is to be effective (discussed below), and clearly this, together with the changes to facility structures, requires considerable capital investment. It follows that size and

volume throughput are also essential for success. Whiteoak (1998) identifies two types of cross-docking; full pallet and case level. Both require accurate and timely deliveries. He identifies a number of benefits. Working capital is lowered because of the need for less inventory in the system. Fixed assets are affected. Space is created by reducing the amount of racking and static stock positions. Less labour is required for stock transfer into (and out of) storage. Both represent a considerable proportion of operating costs. The released space can be used for assortment growth (new categories, wider and deeper assortments etc.). Furthermore, the application of electronic data systems results in sales-based ordering (SBO), offering greater accuracy and availability.

Efficient consumer response (ECR) has had a major impact on fast-moving consumer goods manufacturers and retailers on a worldwide basis. Whiteoak comments:

> The vision of ECR Europe, working together to fulfil consumer wishes better, faster and at less cost is driving a unique initiative by suppliers, distributors and retailers that claims to provide European consumers with the best possible value, service and variety of products through a collaborative approach to improving the supply chain.

However, as Whiteoak suggests in a quote from Stern (1996), ECR is not a long-term solution:

> ECR is a short-term survival tactic, a mandatory set of tactics which may allow the business to buy time... it does not ask the question 'How do people really want to shop for food? Rather it assumes that the answer is the existing supermarket... and then goes on from there to address value chain logistics.

He also had some cynical words for the notion of collaboration:

> partnership as it's practised today is manipulation... we'll be partners if it benefits me.

At the same time there is little evidence to suggest that experiments in 'home shopping', particularly for food products, are likely to become mainstream. The current value delivery system in food retailing is likely to remain dominant for many years. The pattern of investment by retailers and the expansion of companies such as Wal-Mart suggests a long-term perspective.

ECR was initially concerned with efficient product replenishment in the USA. A European perspective added two other benefits: margin and cash flow improvements. The addition of margin management and cash flow considerations puts pressure on supplier/distributor relationships and leans heavily on collaboration. Whiteoak identifies a number of components within the process of efficient replenishment which he describes as:

> a smooth, continual flow of product, matched to consumption and supported by a timely, accurate and paperless information flow.

Continuous replenishment programs have a number of variants. *Vendor-managed inventory* (VMI) uses daily sales data for reordering processes. Typically driven by data generated at the point of sale, it enables the manufacturer to 'control' both the production/replenishment process *and* the in-store availability of an item. Its other benefits are load planning (economies of scale), 'market data' (although this may be insufficient for planning purposes) and (potentially) the opportunity to become a 'preferred' supplier. *Co-managed inventory* (CMI) systems differ in that retailers share information about promotional activities of *all* suppliers in a category with participating suppliers. Both VMI and CMI systems use either fixed order quantity (FOQ) or fixed order cycle (FOC) processes. Whiteoak tells us that FOC is an approach which is used to service smaller outlets who are without the sophisticated inventory systems of larger organizations. He also makes a comment concerning UK multiple food retailers who run CRP processes in which they retain control of replenishment volumes, frequencies and timetables.

Cross-docking was discussed earlier. Clearly the role of cross-docking in ECR systems is essential if inventory levels are to be kept at minimum levels consonant with availability targets *and* CRP systems involving short lead time (QR) responses.

Manufacturing production cycles are matched with retail sales by using *synchronized production*. As Whiteoak suggests, it is difficult to the point of being impossible in most FMCG situations. Typically batch production systems run in cycles and customers are serviced from inventory. To improve on such situations and to move towards a 'make to order' process, not only is POS data required but so too are detailed customers' marketing plans from which sales forecasts may be developed and monitored. *Reliable operations* (the operations equivalent of the marketing/distribution ideal: right product, right place at the right time) and is described as the ability to produce the planned product, in the planned volumes, at a planned quality at the relevant time, is an essential adjunct to successful implementation of *synchronized production*.

Broader perspectives of ECR should be considered; for example, the influence that ECR has on *financial management* in terms of increasing profitability (either through volume increases or cost decreases), the influence on asset base productivity (in terms of inventory management and improving the use of production and logistics assets) and the impact on cash flow (through more accurate and rapid transfer of invoices and payment via electronic networks such as EDI). Similarly, the influence on marketing management should be considered. Improved information, better control of product offers at the point of sale, and coordinated promotional activities are a few of the benefits available.

Category management is closely related to ECR, and many practitioners consider it to be integral with ECR in an attempt to improve the response to customer demand. In a corporate context category management is arguably a means by which strategic positioning is made manifest. The process of market segmentation, customer profiling and targeting should result in a definition of the ideal merchandise assortment offer. Categories comprise a

collection of products (or product groups) which may be considered by a customer when planning an end-use outcome. For example, a category such as *breakfast* would include those products likely to be considered as components of that meal and would include cereal alternatives, a range of bread options and other items (possibly ethnically defined). Category management has the following component processes:

- *Category definition*: determines the products that make up the category from the consumer's perspective.
- *Category role*: to develop and assign a role for the category such that it delivers the customer perspective *and* reinforces the retail offer. Key considerations are the importance of the category to the customer, its importance to the retailer, its importance to competitors and the growth potential that the category offers

  Category roles reflect strategic intentions of the organization for the category. A *destination role* reflects some intended aspect of competitive advantage, e.g. to be a first-choice provider or to reinforce an innovatory role. *Routine roles* are support functions which reinforce the competitive advantage feature. *Occasional/seasonal roles* play secondary roles in reinforcing an image. A *convenience role* again may reinforce aspects of image but also play an important role in profit margin management.
- *Category assessment*: an analysis of customer, market, distributor and supplier perspectives and activities. Within an ECR structure this assumes a 'total cost' approach which includes acquisition and storage and handling costs, and also reviews inventory turnover and service levels.
- *Category performance indicators* are established. These may include sales, market share for a destination category and a minimum contribution margin for a convenience category.

INFORMATIONS SYSTEMS AND TECHNOLOGY

As with supply chain management developments, *information systems* (and technology) have been equally numerous. The previous chapter discussed these in some depth; our focus here is on their application to supply chain management issues.

EDI (electronic data interchange) is one of the more important *enabling technologies* recently to have made an impact on the supply chain. Ghosh (1998) referred to information as being the 'glue' that combined enterprises into effective systems. EDI is the means by which this notion becomes effective by facilitating the flow of structured data through the supply chain. Mitchell (1997), reporting views of supply chain managers, suggests that one view is that a number of companies are involved in excessive flows of electronic information. ECR Europe recommends the database should include:

- *item numbers* (EAN, retail and manufacturers' item number)
- *item information* (name, description, dimension)
- *pricing information* (regular list prices, bracket prices)
- *promotion pricing and conditions* (promotion cards, promotion type, effective dates, performance requirements)
- logistics information (case quantities, inner pack quantities, pallet configuration details, truck loading information)

There are a number of examples of successful applications of EDI. Benetton (Fernie, 1998; Christopher, 1997) give detached accounts of the benefits that have accrued to the company from its long-term investment in logistics systems resulting in the fastest replenishment cycles in its industry together with a major reduction in working capital.

Christopher and Peck (1998) describe the application of EDI in The Limited (the US apparel retailer) and Bhs (the UK-based variety store group). The Limited identified the financial benefits of accurate and rapid information flows, and very rapidly minimized working capital requirements throughout their organization. They have used EDI to gain marketing advantage by using the technology to transmit design details to Far Eastern suppliers for manufacturing and order assembly to be forwarded to Ohio. The process can be completed in three to five weeks.

Bhs (British Home Stores) was an early IT pioneer in the UK. The company was one of the first British retailers to use EPOS in its stores (1980s), and this innovation resulted in improving the effectiveness of the buying operation in terms of availability and inventory holding. Relationships with suppliers also showed significant improvements.

A review of the logistics system (part of an overall analysis of operations) resulted in a decision to concentrate on its core retailing competences and to outsource all other activities. The effectiveness of EDI can be seen by Christopher and Peck's comments.

> The costly bulging stock rooms rapidly gave way to a system where almost all stock is held by suppliers, the majority of whom are EDI linked to Bhs. By August 1991 (some 15 months), an estimated 85 percent of Bhs' merchandise was called through the replenishment system by EDI. Plans were in place to raise the figure to 100 percent. The EDI links gave Bhs' suppliers access to data on how their own lines were selling in the stores, allowing them to detect emerging sales trends and anticipate replenishment orders.... The use of EDI all but eliminated order handling time, improving time-to-serve, as did the appointment of a single specialist contractor, Excel Logistics, to handle all Bhs' distribution.

Performance improvements of replenishment cycles are impressive. Sixty per cent of all orders arrive by the following day and are completed within 48 hours. Daily deliveries have reduced storage space requirements from 20% to 10% during the last ten years; further reductions are planned.

Both cases give examples of EDI investment increasing the productivity of fixed assets (selling space and warehouse facilities) and working capital

(inventory holding). Cash flow throughout the supply chain will be improved, as will margins because of the reduced markdowns.

EPOS (electronic point of sale) systems have been making an impact on retailing productivity for some time. Christopher and Peck comment on the introduction of EPOS by Bhs in the early 1980s. More recently the impact of EPOS has been in the wealth of customer information that has enabled companies such as Tesco, Sainsbury and B&Q to develop vast databases of information on customer behaviour in-store, responses to promotions etc. Tesco (1998) reported over 10 million loyalty card holders who collectively received over £340 million in Clubcard vouchers and product coupons. Tesco also suggests that Clubcard allows a response to much smaller groups of customers. The data generated by the card provide the company with a detailed understanding of customer shopping and purchasing behaviour. By monitoring purchasing trends they (Tesco) identify new needs and are able to direct customers to them – as well as offering price incentives.

EFT (electronic funds transfer) was initially viewed with suspicion by retailing. It was seen as benefiting the banks, with few benefits for the retailer. However, EFT systems have had a major impact on cash management and handling costs between customer and retailer, and similarly, via the EDI link between retailer and supplier, supply chain cash flow has been increased. While some financial managers may disagree that this is an 'improvement', because it decreases the time available to use suppliers' funds, the costs of payment management have undoubtedly decreased.

Non-store shopping via the Internet and other means is one other aspect of technology to be considered. A number of systems now operate, and most offer proprietary links. *Peapod*, developed in the USA, enables 'home shoppers' who own a personal computer and modem to access a base store. Using the Peapod system customers can 'shop' in a number of ways. They can roam the aisles as they might do on actual visits or, alternatively, look for items by categories. Within categories, products are listed in a number of ways, such as by price or alphabetically. Peapod maintains a memory of the customer's frequent purchases. Price changes are made as and when they occur and promotional prices are featured. Quality issues are the concern of the 'store'; an employee responds to a very detailed shopping list.

Peapod (and similar systems) provides information on store performance (out-of-stocks, rates of sale etc.) and customer response behaviour to out-of-stock situations. Peapod permits directions concerning acceptable product substitutions, and this data is generated on both merchandise and customer performances.

RETAIL VALUE CHAIN

Retailers, in one way or another, are face to face with the consumer. Some consumers become lasting (or loyal) customers; others, having sampled the

retail offer, move on. The satisfied core customer group becomes a focus for the retailer, who monitors their expectations, behaviour and perceptions closely to ensure that the maximum value is delivered to these customers. Financial (as well as market) viability is essential. It follows that the value chain (i.e. the customer value delivery) must be a component of the retail strategy. It is based upon identifying both customer value and cost criteria and responding to these with a *benefit/value* offer that *maintains* customer loyalty. Figure 16.1 illustrates the retail value chain.

Customer value criteria are likely to differ by the type of shopping mission and the category sought within that mission. Some examples of value and cost criteria are detailed below:

Security: use-by dates, 100% available items
Performance: 'full' service; returns, warranties *and* loan/replacement items
Aesthetics: style/design to meet *their* lifestyle (this includes product-services as well as tangible product design)
Convenience: easy access (minimum drive time, easy parking, creche facilities etc.)
Economy: a benefit/value equation in which price is an influence but not necessarily the dominant feature
Reliability: a retail or manufacturer brand in which the customer has confidence

Customer cost criteria:
Specification: identifying a brand, range of choice, quality etc.
Search: the extent to which time and effort is expended acquiring information
Transaction: the alternative payment and financing options
Installation: delivery, installation and instructions on use, removal of replaced item(s) if necessary
Operations: follow up calls to ensure that effective use is being made of the purchase and 'value' being delivered
Maintenance: the availability of a maintenance program to ensure full use and lifespan of the item purchased

As Figure 16.1 suggests, the components of the customer value equation should be identified and monitored for change; this ensures that the value delivered is relevant to customer needs *and* continues the customer/retailer relationship.

Value delivery is a function of service and cost drivers. These are identified in Figure 16.1. Service drivers are the organization's response to customer value expectations. The term *demand chain management* has begun to be used in the literature. Lamey (1997) suggests that the term 'supply chain management' has come into question as the emphasis of the supply chain is switched to customer satisfaction, and Slywotzky and Morrison (1997)

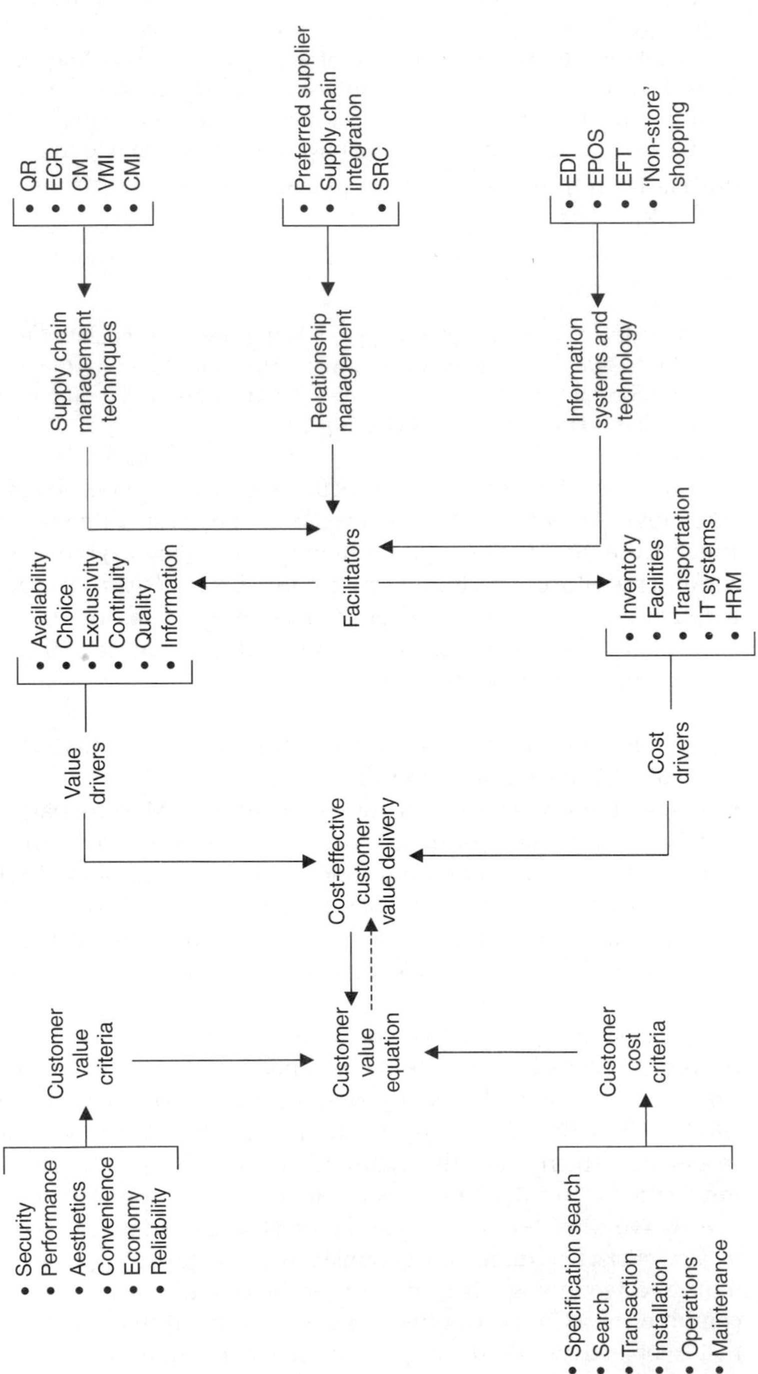

Figure 16.1 The retail value chain.

discuss the value chain in the context of 'customer-centric' thinking which reverses the approach:

> everything else is driven by the customer. Managers should think of: (1) what their customers' needs and priorities are; (2) what channels can satisfy those needs and priorities; (3) the service and products best suited to flow through those channels; (4) the inputs and raw materials required to create the products and services; and (5) the assets and core competencies essential to the inputs and raw materials:

and:

> The value of any product or service is the result of its ability to meet a customer's priorities. Customer priorities are, in simple terms, the things that are so important to customers that they will pay a premium for them or when they can't get them they will switch suppliers

In some ways this explains the focus on core competencies of retailing and the move to outsource non-core, non-specialist value adding activities. Indeed, the thrust of ECR (and category management) is more about achieving and monitoring customer satisfaction. *Demand chain management* suggests a demand-pull emphasis rather than a supply-push orientation.

A retail value chain can be constructed if we understand the customer. Lamey suggests three important steps:

- Understand who your customers are. Retailer loyalty schemes provide invaluable information in this context.
- Understand what your customers want. Wal-Mart managers spend time talking to customers in the store. Others use focus groups and other market research techniques. Such data when combined with POS data results in customer driven merchandise and service decisions.
- Understand where and when your customers want the merchandise. Again EPOS data provides data on variety, volume and timing.

By focusing on customer-generated data and apply its findings to supply decisions results in the supply chain becoming a value chain. It is demand driven rather than driven by manufacturers' production and inventory levels. Thus the *supply drivers* in Figure 16.1 become customer-driven responses which meet the customer value criteria. Clearly there are cost implications, and the *cost drivers* influence the supply driver activities.

Here we consider the ways and means of value delivery. Figure 16.1 refers to *facilitators*: techniques, relationships management and information systems and technology. It is the task of the operations management group to combine these in a cost-effective way to ensure that customer satisfaction meets objectives set through customer consultation. It is suggested that activity-based costing or attribute costing methods are used to determine a cost-effective benefit/value combination. Activity-based costing (ABC)

techniques with specific application to supply/value chain topics and retailing can be found in Gattorna and Walters (1996) and Walters and Laffy (1996).

Finally, we consider the impact of cost-effective delivery of customer value. Chapters 4 and 5 discussed the concept of shareholder value and concluded that unless shareholder expectations for share price appreciation, dividend growth and positive economic cash flow were met, or a positive EVA achieved, their dissatisfaction would result in their divestment of the company's shares. We also suggested that management's influence on shareholder value was through the effective management of profitability, productivity and cash flow. In Figure 16.2 we suggest how this may be realized. By reaching a mix of facilitators which meets customer value expectations at acceptable levels of resource utilization and costs we will achieve customer satisfaction objectives *and* meet shareholder expectations.

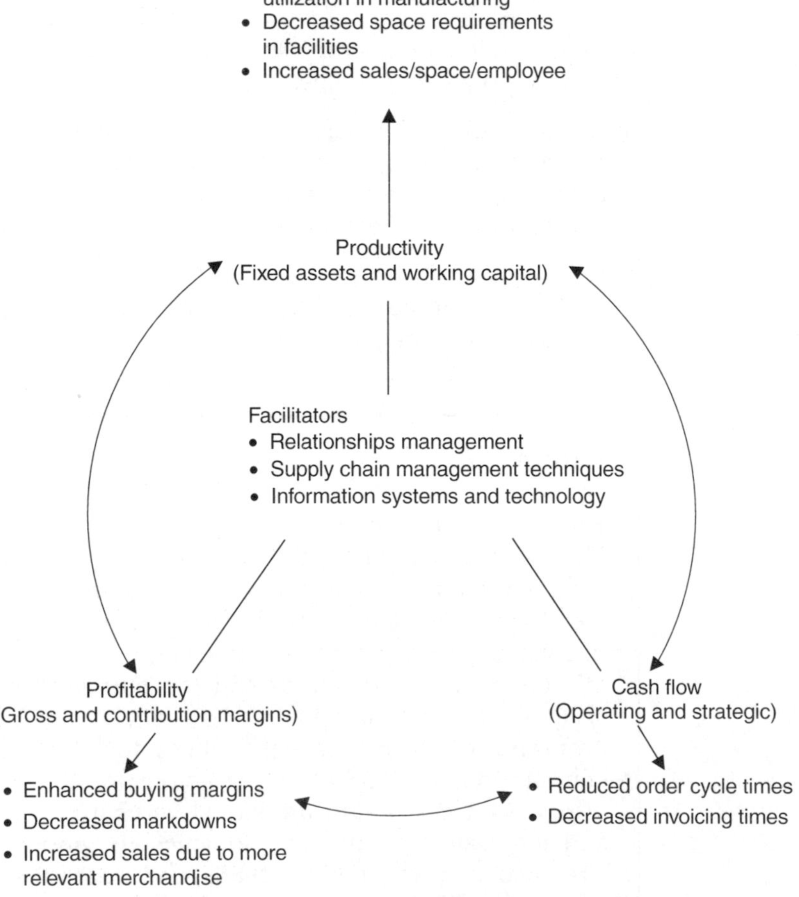

Figure 16.2 The impact of value chain facilitators on corporate/financial performance.

SUMMARY

The supply chain has been seen as the link between the retailers' value offer and delivery for some years. However, recently that perspective has changed; the supply chain has assumed a more direct role within the operations management of the progressive companies. It reflects more the demand chain approach, in which customer expectations of the organization assume a product *and* service perspective. It has become more of a value chain in which the retailer manages customer and corporate performance expectations through the management of three important facilitating agents: relationships management, supply chain management techniques and information systems and technology.

QUESTIONS, ACTIVITIES AND CONSIDERATIONS

- Research the annual reports of the major retail multiples and construct their supply/value chains.
- Consider the role of relationships management in developing supply/value chain management. If retailers continue to focus on their core activities, how can they ensure that performance and costs continue to be controlled and produce profit enhancement?
- A significant increase in e-commerce and e-retailing is forecast to occur over the next 5–10 years. What are the implications for supply/value chain management.

Exhibit 16.1

The Ahold value chain

The value chain concept (in which demand management replaces supply management) is being embraced by major retailers. Mitchell (1997) provides an example of how Ahold, the Dutch grocery retailer, is approaching the transition. Ahold accepted that ECR offered an opportunity to reverse the 'supplier/retailer push' emphasis to one of 'customer pull'. In 1993 it began its *Today For Tomorrow* program, in which the responsibility for store replenishment was centralized and EPOS/EDI systems ensure daily replenishment.

In 1994 it eliminated traditional vertical departmental structures and integrated buying and logistics (buying and marketing had already been merged in the 1980s) and created seven *category manager* posts. The categories are structured around customer applications/occasions such as 'breakfast' or 'main meal' rather than

logistics criteria (such as fresh, chilled or ambient) or manufacturer criteria based on product categories. Category managers are responsible for every category items and activity and are rewarded on the category's net profit rather than gross margin.

The Today For Tomorrow concept was then expanded to include large suppliers to exploit sales-led just-in-time replenishment. Ahold saw a number of advantages:

- It minimizes negotiation time with suppliers.
- It creates system efficiencies and the system 'runs by itself'.
- There are fewer stockouts.
- It releases up to 10% sales space (because of the short lead times and rapid movement of inventory through the system).
- Delivery appointments ensure increased labour productivity (resulting in less labour being employed).

Using activity-based costing to evaluate category costs a classification system in which categories are identified as 'losers', 'commodity', 'premium' or 'starts', based upon their respective contribution. The *value chain* concept is being brought a step closer by Ahold seeking to transform its relationship with suppliers by seeking to integrate them into the *cost-effective customer value delivery* process.

REFERENCES

Fernie, J. (1998) Relationships in the supply chain, in *Logistics and Retail Management* (ed. Fernie, J. and Sparks, L.). Kogan Page, London.

GEA (1994) *Supplier–Retailer Collaboration in Supply Chain Management*. GEA Consulenti Associata di gestione aziendale, Italy.

Ghosh, S. (1998) Making business sense of the Internet. *Harvard Business Review*, Mar/Apr.

Kumar, N. (1996) The power of trust in manufacture – retailer relationships. *Harvard Business Review*, Nov/Dec.

Lamey, J. (1997) *Supply Chain Management*. Financial Times Retail and Consumer Publishing, London.

McKinnon, A. (1996) The development of retail logistics in the UK: a position paper. Paper prepared for Technology Foresight: http://www.21stcentury-retailing.org.UK/Ukretail.htm.

Mitchell, A. (1997) *Efficient Consumer Response: A New Paradigm for the European f.m.c.g. Sector*. Financial Times Retail and Consumer Publishing, London.

Slywotzky, A. J. and Morrison, D. J. (1997) *The Profit Zone*. John Wiley, New York.

Stern, L. (1996) 39th CIES Annual Executive Congress, Paris, June.

Tesco (1998) *Annual Report*.

Walters, D. W. and Laffy, D. (1996) *Productivity and Profitability in Retailing*. Macmillan, Basingstoke.

Whiteoak, P. (1988) Rethinking efficient replenishment in the grocery sector, in *Logistics and Retail Management* (ed. Fernie, J. and Sparks, L.). Kogan Page, London.

17 MANAGING INFORMATION IN THE RETAIL VALUE CHAIN

LEARNING OBJECTIVES

The role of information in retail management is assuming increasing importance. This chapter assumes the value chain perspective developed in Chapter 16. It identifies some important issues central to the development of customer-led information systems. Specific issues include:

- An exploration of value in a context of retail demand management.
- Consideration of the features of a customer-led value chain: the view that it is customer expectations that are the value drivers, not the functions of the business.
- The development of an information strategy based upon organizational decision making, key success factors and organizational structure.
- A discussion on the overall role of key success factors within an organization and as important influences within the construction of an information system.
- Consideration of the role of net technology in the construction of both the value chain and its information infrastructure.
- A review of the basic aspects of information technology upon the developments of the economics of information.
- Specification of an information-led retail value chain model with database, category management models and performance metrics.

INTRODUCTION

There is an interesting issue emerging in distribution which has implications for information management. Much of the distribution systems thinking that has been or is being developed is customer-oriented. We discussed ECR, Category Management and a number of other 'customer-centric' techniques and applications in the previous chapter. Lamey (1997) suggests:

> 'The customer is king' is a well-worn phase in the retailing world but ECR initiatives bring the achievement of this concept closer. Customer measures are

> gaining more importance including regular measures of customer satisfaction and retention rates. Numerous research projects have shown the savings that can be gained in all sectors by maintaining existing customers... customer satisfaction has become a key criterion for retailers and is playing a greater role in the supply chain.

This, as we commented in the previous chapter, leads to the question: should we be focusing on a supply chain or perhaps a restructured view of the value chain. Lamey (1997) comments that the term 'supply chain management' which was coined in the 1970s but is associated with a 'producer-driven approach'. From a manufacturer point of view this is a reversal of the practice of manufacturing to stock rather than to meet customer orders. The notion of 'supply push' is being replaced by the concept of 'demand chain management'. Information technology has played an important role. EPOS systems (discussed in the previous chapter) have made it possible to reduce replenishment times and for some categories actually to manufacture to order (e.g. Benetton). Initiatives such as ECR, QR and JIT are shifting managements' focus to a demand-driven supply chain.

Vollman and Cordon (1999) offer a similar conclusion:

> A fundamental shift in thinking is to replace the term 'supply chain' with 'demand chain'. The critical difference is that demand chain thinking starts with the customers and works backwards. This breaks out of parochial approaches that focus solely on reducing transport costs. It supports a 'mass customization' view point, in which bundles of goods and services are offered in ways that support customers' individual objectives.

They continue to suggest that service aspects often require differentiation such as, transaction handling, deliveries and other parts of the commercial relationship.

THE VALUE CHAIN

The notion of the value chain has moved some considerable distance since Porter's first proposal (1985). One approach is shown in Figure 17.1, in which Anterasian and Phillips (1988) identify three value creating activities. This in itself is helpful but is incomplete because it does not identify fully the role of distribution nor does it identify the role and tasks of information.

What is value?

Value is determined by the utility combination of benefits delivered to the customer *less* the total costs of acquiring the delivered benefits. Value, then, is a preferred combination of benefits compared with acquisition costs. In some respects value is a combination of expectations, perceptions, acquisition *and*

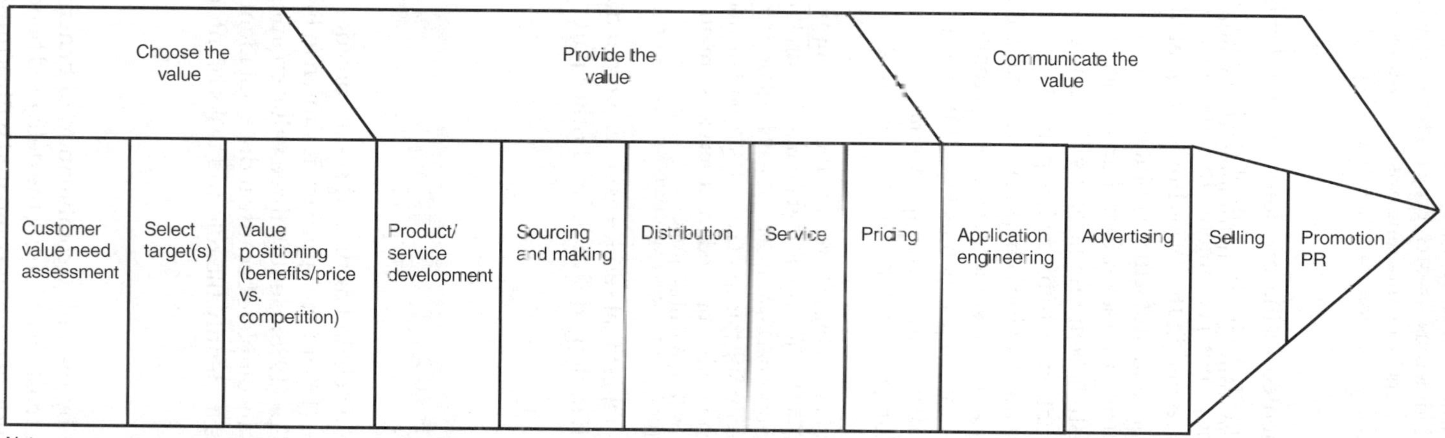

Choose the value

Provide the value

Communicate the value

Customer value need assessment

Select target(s)

Value positioning (benefits/price vs. competition)

Product/ service development

Sourcing and making

Distribution

Service

Pricing

Application engineering

Advertising

Selling

Promotion PR

Notes:
Value = Benefit – price.
Benefit = Attribute(s) desirable to customer (in customer's eyes).
Price = Total costs to customer (as perceived by customer).
Superior perceived value = Customer believes buying/using the product or service gives a net value superior (more positive) than alternative's value.

Figure 17.1 The marketing value chain. (Adapted from: Anterasian, C. and Phillips, L. W. (1988) *Discontinuities, Value Delivery, and the Share-Returns Association: A re-examination of the 'Share-Causes-Profits' Controversy*. Research Program Monograph, Report No. 88-109. The Marketing Science Institute, Cambridge, MA.)

opportunity costs. Opportunity costs should be included because the individual's perception of value will be influenced by the cost of alternatives forgone in acquiring the value.

Relative value is the perceived satisfaction obtained (or assumed available by the customer) from alternative value offers. A *value proposition* is a statement of how value is to be delivered to customers. It is important both internally and externally. Externally it is the means by which the organization positions itself in the minds of customers: the value to be delivered. Internally it identifies the value drivers and the cost drivers which are involved in producing and delivering customer value.

Value and retail demand management

Vollman and Cordan (1999) explain the derivation of demand management in a logistics context:

> Essentially, a company has a 'pipeline' of capacity which is filled in the short run with customer orders and in the long-run with forecasts of demand. The point is that order entry consumes the forecast, and demand management explicitly integrates both of these processes.

They suggest a more current view to be one that includes a band of 'knowledge', and expand on this to suggest that in a manufacturing context 'knowledge' is an understanding of precise requirements. This approach is unrealistic for retailing management. However, there is a basis for developing an argument concerning a retail demand-based value chain. Some relevant interesting issues were raised in the previous chapter. The GEA study explored supplier/retailer collaboration and suggested that 'real' collaboration occurred when sales and cost data are exchanged. Furthermore, such collaboration is usually retailer-led and is based upon their determination to reduce costs and to focus more closely on their customers. This results in greater customer loyalty and benefit/value differentiation *not* based on price alone. Chapter 16 concluded by describing the retail value chain (Figure 16.1).

A customer-led value chain

Contemporary views of the value chain start with the organization and its industry, on to which customer interests are grafted. While they now include the role of outsourcing to achieve effective value delivery, it could be argued that the value chain concept would be more effective if in fact it is *created around* customer value expectations.

Scott (1998) takes a strategic management view. He uses the value chain concept to identify the tasks necessary to deliver a product or service to the market. Scott's approach is to combine segmentation and value chain analysis and suggests a number of questions:

- In which areas of the value chain does the firm have to be outstanding to succeed in each customer segment?
- What skills or competencies are necessary to deliver an outstanding result in those areas of the value chain?
- Are they the same for each segment or do they differ radically?

Scott argues:

> All firms, whether industrial or services, have a value chain.... Each part of the value chain requires a strategy to ensure that it drives value creation for the firm overall. For a piece of the value chain to have a strategy means that the individual managing it is clear about what capabilities the firm requires to deliver effective market impact.

It follows that the firm may not have the relevant competencies to match opportunities. Three final questions follow:

- Is the structure of the organization relevant and are its managers competent? Or:
- Can the organization compete effectively by forming a partnership/alliance with other firm(s)?
- But most important, does the organization have the information required to make both customer and supplier decisions.

The core elements of Scott's value chain comprise seven areas:

- Operations strategy
- Marketing, sales and service strategy
- Innovation strategy
- Financial strategy
- Human resource strategy
- Information technology strategy
- Lobbying position with government.

Coordination across the value chain is essential, and Scott identifies the fact that traditionally this did not occur.

Slywotzky and Morrison (1997) discuss the value chain in the context of 'customer-centric' thinking. They suggest that the *traditional value chain*, which begins with the company's core competencies, its assets, then moves to other inputs and raw materials, to a product offer, through marketing channels and finally to the customer, should be reversed. In customer-centric thinking the *modern value chain* reverses the approach. The customer becomes the first link and everything else follows:

> everything else is driven by the customer. Managers should think of: (1) what their customers' needs and priorities are; (2) what channels can satisfy those needs and priorities; (3) the service and products best suited to flow through

> those channels; (4) the inputs and raw materials required to create the products and services; and, (5) the assets and core competencies essential to the inputs and raw materials.

and:

> The value of any product or service is the result of its ability to meet a customer's priorities. Customer priorities are, in simple terms, the things that are so important to customers that they will pay a premium for them or, when they can't get them, they will switch suppliers.

Slywotzky and Morrison suggest that *value* opportunities are identified by understanding customers' priorities and monitoring priorities for change. They give a number of examples: Nicolas Hayek (Swatch) understood that a growing segment of consumers would buy watches based upon taste, emotion and fashion rather than on prestige. Jack Welch (GE) identified that customers saw less value in the product and more value in the services and financing.

This suggests a broad perspective of value, well beyond direct benefits, and one which encompasses the nuances of basic criteria. Figure 17.2 interprets this suggestion. Basic value criteria are seen to be broad characteristics, such as security, performance, aesthetics, convenience, economy and reliability. However, at a detailed level these may prove to be a wide range of criteria.

The approach suggested by these authors changes the traditional value chain such that it takes on a customer-driven perspective. Slywotzky and Morrison go further:

> In the old economic order, the focus was on the immediate customer. Today, business no longer has the luxury of thinking about just the immediate customer. To find and keep customers, our perspective has to be radically

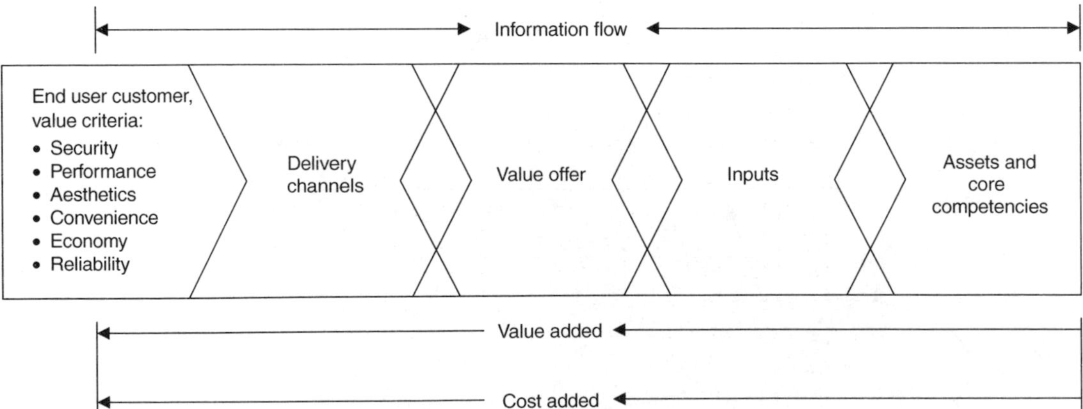

Figure 17.2 A customer-centric value chain. (Based on Slywotzky, A. J. and Morrison, D. J. (1977) *The Profit Zone*. John Wiley, New York.)

> expanded. In a value migration world, our vision must include two, three, or even four customers along the value chain. So, for example, a component supplier must understand the economic motivations of the manufacturer who buys the components, the distributor who takes the manufacturer's products to sell, and the end-use consumer.

The organization's value chain becomes merged with those of other value chain members. Figure 17.3 takes an industry perspective of the value chain. An important feature is the role of information management which provides a coordinating activity.

Other authors have made contributions. Of particular interest is that of Normann and Ramirez (1993). They suggest:

> Strategy is the art of creating value... is the way a company defines its business and links together with the only two resources that really matter in today's economy: knowledge and relationships on an organization's competencies and customers.

They see the value chain as an analytical tool which facilitates strategy:

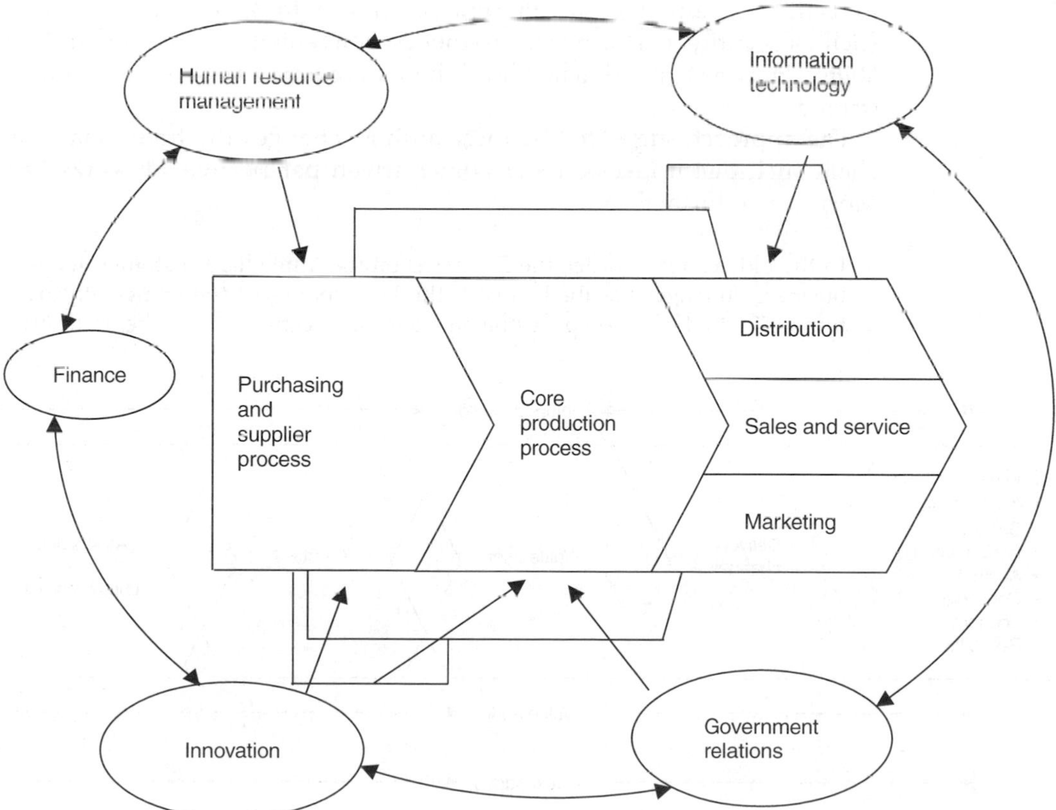

Figure 17.3 An alternative view of the value chain. (Adapted from Scott (1998).)

> strategy is primarily the art of positioning a company in the right place on the value chain – the right business, the right products and market segments, the right value-adding activities.

and add:

> Their [an example using IKEA] focus of strategic analysis is not the company or even the industry but the *value creating system* itself, within which different economic actors – suppliers, business partners, allies, customers – work together to *co-produce* value. Their key strategic task is the *reconfiguration* of roles and relationships among this constellation of actors in order to mobilise the creation of value in new forms and by new players... their underlying strategic goal is to create an ever improving fit between competencies and customers...

The value chain has an expanded role. It becomes an integral component in the strategy process: the evaluation of the company's core competence and its fit in the *overall creation of value*. The questions to be asked are:

- What is the combination of value criteria required by the target customer group?
- What are the implications for differentiation decisions?
- What are the implications for costs: do economies of scale or scope exist?
- Are there opportunities for trade-offs to occur between the value creation system partners?
- What are the information requirements?

Knox and Maklan (1998) argue that:

> the value of IT no longer lies in its ability to crunch numbers quickly. IT creates value in the organization when it helps it to develop a profound understanding of the capabilities of information technology and of all that is required to exploit its potential. In the best companies, IT is often a catalyst for reinventing customer value, business process improvement and improving organization structures. The appropriate measures of performance should help IT explore electronic commerce, align information systems to the goals of the business, and achieve the right balance between business benefit and technology investment.

This suggests three components that, when integrated, combine to move towards successful information strategy. They are related to organizational issues. They also reflect a chronological application of information sciences to management. Figure 17.4 illustrates these. *Automate* identifies the early application of IT. Its purpose was to control repetitive decision making in production and subsequently procurement activities. Customer response applications were basic: monitoring orders received and despatched and accounts receivable details.

The *informate* application expanded the scope of employee knowledge of activities, events and situations that were both internal and external to the

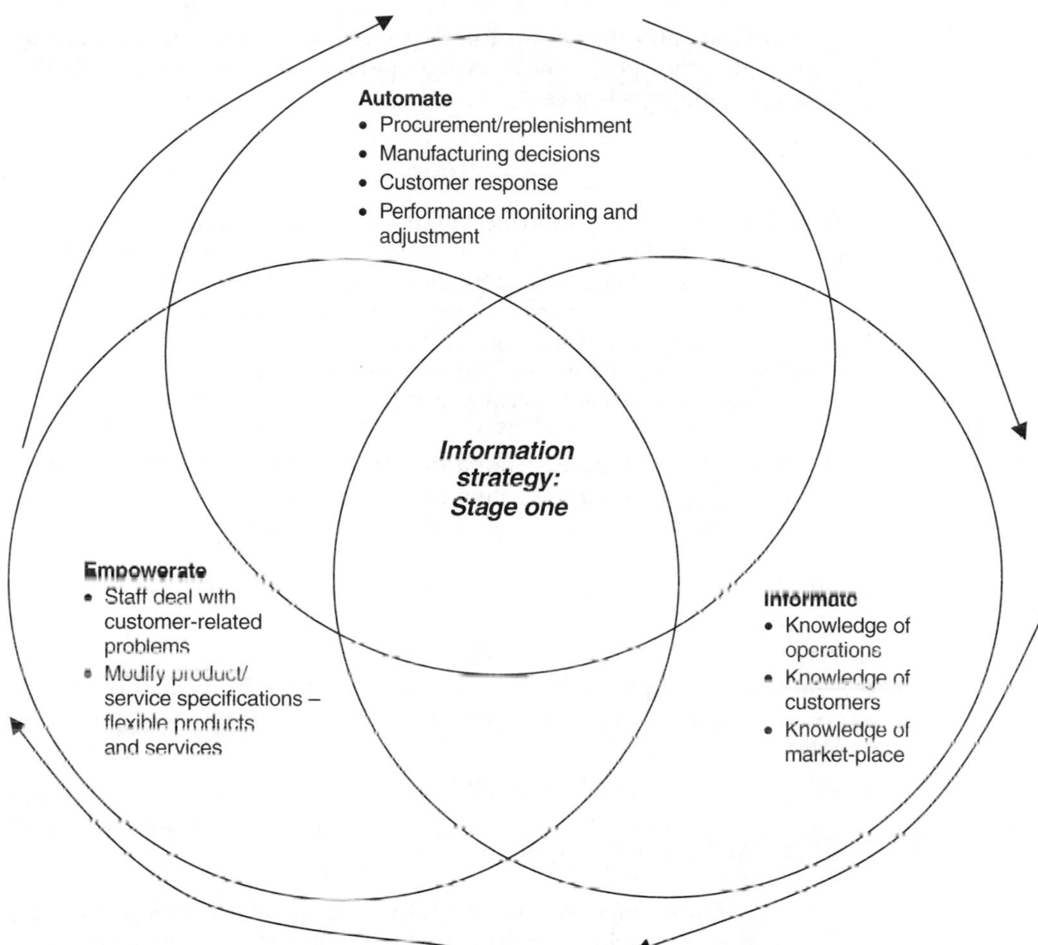

Figure 17.4 Components of an intermediate move towards developing an information strategy.

firm. The development of MIS (management information systems) and their all-embracing application within the value chain (linking information inputs and outputs between and among partners) was, and remains for some firms, a major step. Possibly the largest impact came from laser-based point-of-sale applications, where the 'culture' of FMCG distribution was revolutionized in order to benefit fully from the technology. Information exchange and flows had the ability to improve operating efficiencies, lower costs and improve customer service. It changed supplier/retailer relationships in ways once assumed impossible.

Delegated decision making arrived, with technology to *empowerate* employees. Empowered staff are able to resolve customer service related problems as they occur. Database management identifies customer records (and customer loyalty) as well as apprising staff of current events and

situations. Empowerment has been responsible for major changes in organization structures: the typical organizational pyramid has been inverted by a number of companies, Pepsi-Cola being one of the largest. They argue that if effective decisions are to be made, they should be actioned by the company employee on the spot. Referral of problems up a chain of command results in delays, distortion and dissatisfaction.

Effective use of information requires changes in organization structure which often are unacceptable or resisted. It is late 20th century Luddism, and remains a problem for many organizations, particularly those in traditional industries.

Moreton and Chester (1997) discuss these issues:

> Apart from the pioneering businesses studied for this book, we are aware of relatively few instances where the design, development and implementation of IS has been carried out in a manner that was fully co-ordinated with the organization design and implementation.

They stress:

> the importance of ensuring that the systems and organization developments are, *and remain*, aligned with the business vision.

and:

> to ensure that this objective is achieved, there should be a management process that actively monitors the design process for alignment, commitment and competence.

Typically, many organizations attempt to install information strategies based upon the assumption that to do so will relieve management of decision making. Clearly this is not so. Wigand (1995) made this point. See Figure 17.5 and refer to the earlier discussion).

Dow Europe used an approach similar to that proposed by Wigand. Dow used a combination of process analysis and critical (key) success factor analysis. After considerable debate nine business processes were identified. By matching the KSFs against the processes, management was able to determine the priorities for action. The next step for Dow was to determine the changes needed and separately identify those processes that could benefit from IT support.

The application of KSF analysis to strategy issues was developed from the work of Hofer and Schendel (1978) and Rockart (1979) who used it as a means to encourage managers to '...organize and articulate their needs with reference to the factors which were essential or critical to their businesses'. It used an intervening and analysis method that concentrates on a limited number of areas in which satisfactory results will ensure successful competitive performance.

A formal approach will use interviews as a preliminary step leading to a management workshop. At the workshop senior managers review and

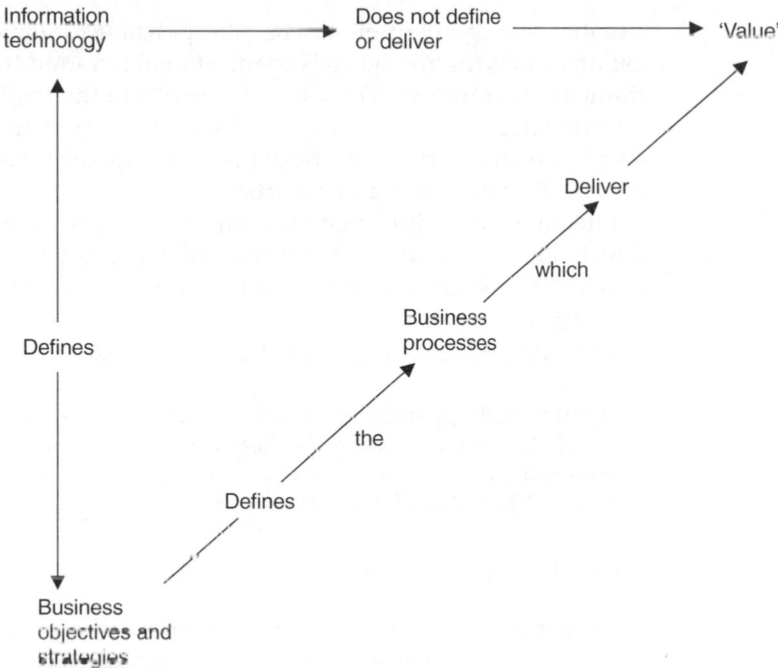

Figure 17.5 IT can only add value within a structure designed for organizational fit (from Wigand, 1995).

refine the KSFs, eventually arriving at a consensus on the organization's KSFs. With these resolved the contribution that IT can make towards achieving (and implementing) the KSFs is determined. Figure 17.6 illustrates a generalized example of the approach and was developed by Earl (1989). A strength of the method is that it focuses on major issues for the business, rather than on those that are merely necessary, *and* it avoids becoming

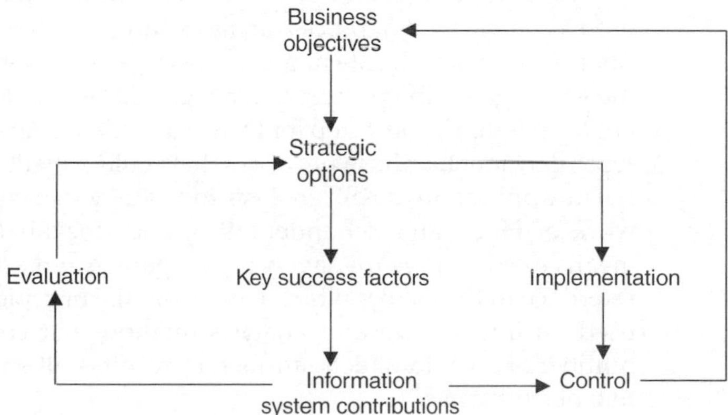

Figure 17.6 Using strategic direction to develop key success factors and information requirements.

bogged down in methods of implementation. In effect it identifies the KSFs responsible for creating competitive advantage rather than just those which offer competitive necessity. We discuss KSFs in more detail in the following section.

A final step is to consider how the organization may use information to take a commanding lead in the market-place (or indeed the market-space). By using decision support systems and simulation it is possible to model strategic options and evaluate their impact upon the firm, the value chain and the end-user. Figure 17.7 illustrates the addition of a facility to *innovate* and thus completes the information strategy model.

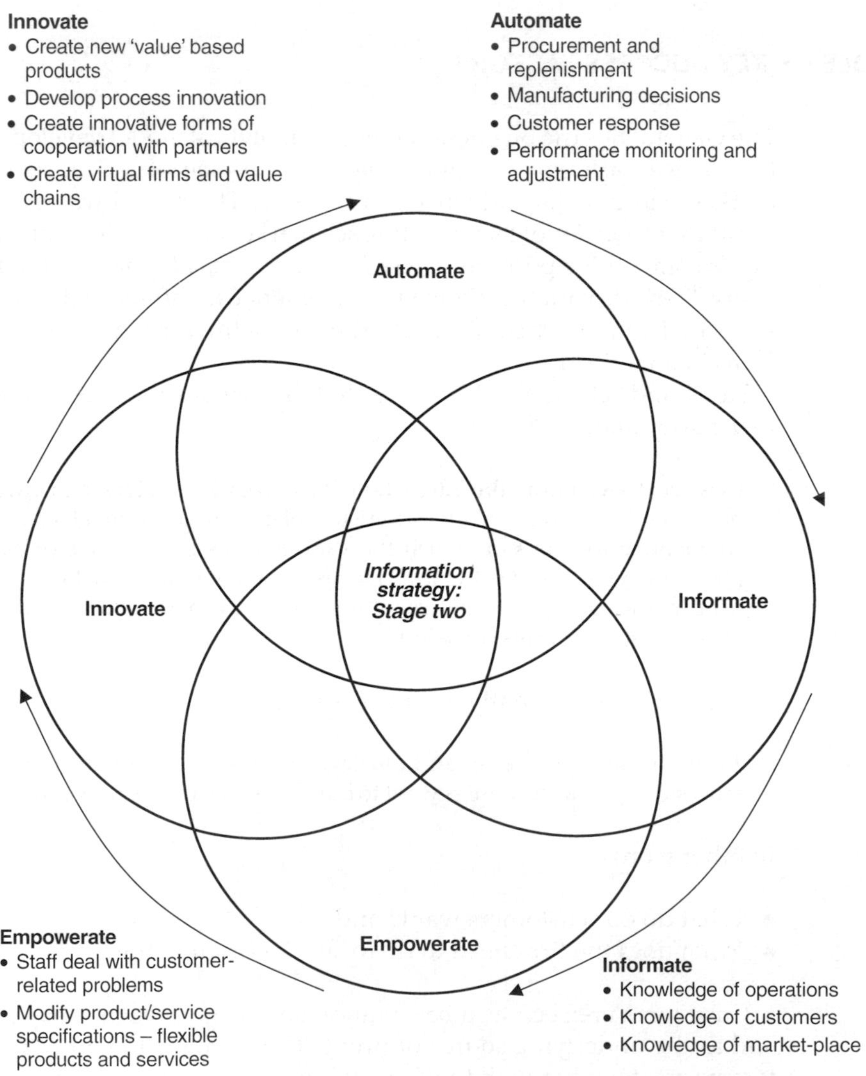

Figure 17.7 The use of information to facilitate innovation completes the information strategy model.

Finally, Figure 17.8 suggests how, ideally, the firm approaches strategic decision making.

Given a clear and agreed set of objectives concerning the stakeholder interests the three elements of strategy can be developed. In Figure 17.8 there is a proposition that each element (or component) plays a contributory role in the process. By using a process similar to that of Dow Europe (see earlier) each strategy element influences the others in arriving at a balanced approach. The point made is that unless each of the components in this process play an interactive role the strategy cannot be optimal.

THE ROLE OF KEY SUCCESS FACTORS

The General Electric Business Screen, an analytical model developed to identify *industry attractiveness* and *competitive position* of a firm in a specified market, was a major influence in the 1970s. The model was based upon a thesis that a *number* of factors influence market performance outcomes and a firm's competitive position. These *key success factors* typically differ between firms. They are variables which management can influence through its decisions that can affect significantly the competitive positions of the various firms in an industry.

Hofer and Schendel (1978) suggested that usually they vary from industry to industry and:

> they are derived from the interaction of two sets of variables, namely, the economic and technological characteristics of the industry involved... and the competitive weapons on which the various firms in the industry have built their strategies. Normally, such factors are known quite well to the various firms participating in an industry, although they may not always be clear to outsiders such as firms considering entry into the industry.

Grant (1995) subsequently used the concept:

> To survive and prosper in an industry, a firm must meet two criteria: first it must supply what customers want to buy; second, it must survive competition.

In other words:

- What do our customers want? and
- What does the firm need to do to survive competition?

Customers are seen as a basic rationale for the existence of the industry and as the underlying source of profit. The firm must identify who its customers are, together with their needs, and then establish the basis on which they select the offer of one supplier in preference to those of another. Secondly the firm must identify the basis of industry competition. This requires

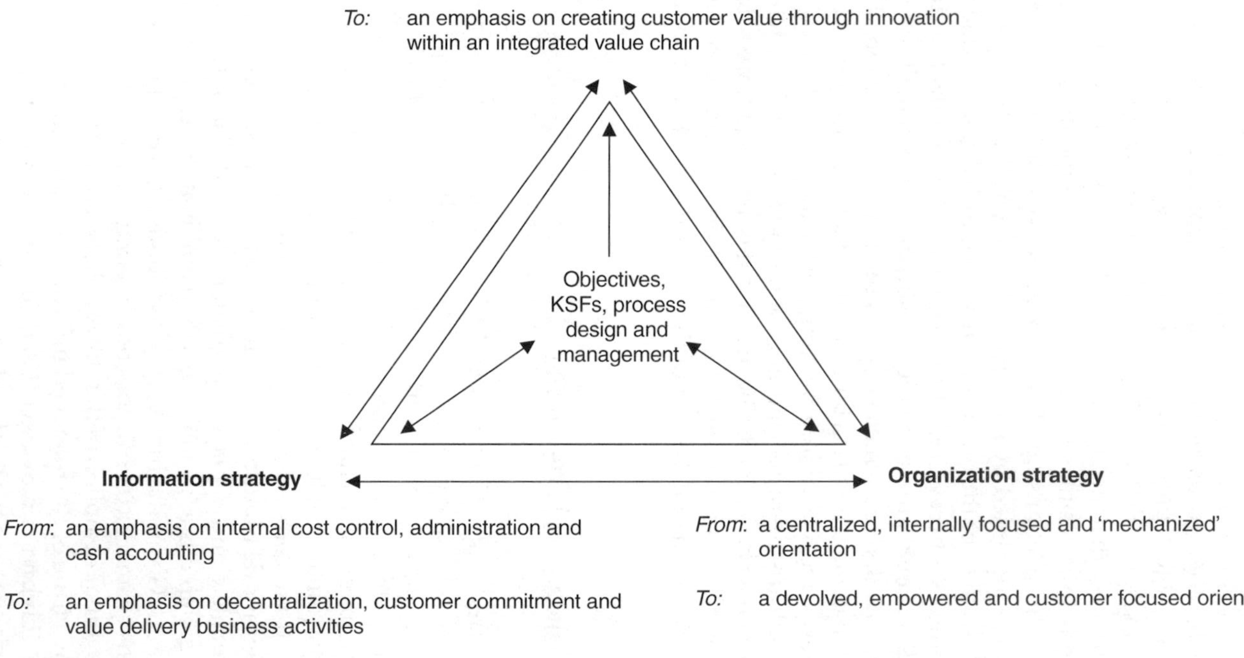
Business strategy
From: an emphasis on costs reduction and efficient administration
To: an emphasis on creating customer value through innovation within an integrated value chain
Objectives, KSFs, process design and management
Information strategy
From: an emphasis on internal cost control, administration and cash accounting
To: an emphasis on decentralization, customer commitment and value delivery business activities
Organization strategy
From: a centralized, internally focused and 'mechanized' orientation
To: a devolved, empowered and customer focused orientation

Figure 17.8 Business strategy/organization strategy and information strategy: the well-balanced firm.

a knowledge of the *basis* of competition, and its *key dimensions*. Grant suggests:

> At a more formal level, identifying key success factors can also be derived from efforts to the model the determinants of firm profit within an industry.

In other words the *value drivers* responsible for delivering profitability and, we suggest, productivity and cash flow.

In Figure 17.9, adapted from Grant, we identify key success factors (value drivers) that influence profitability, productivity and cash flow in three industries, using customer needs and competitive characteristics.

The relationships between objectives, strategy and key success factors were identified by Earl (1986). He suggests a three-stage process. First, the objectives of the organization are identified. Second, the tasks, activities and processes necessary if the objectives of the organization are to be realized are determined; these are the key success factors. Finally an operations strategy can be derived which supports the key success factors. The role of information management becomes a fourth factor. It monitors activities related to the key success factor of reporting performance levels.

Clearly there are a number of methods available by which key success factors may be derived. The important issue is that unless they are used to plan an information strategy, i.e. information coverage, frequency, accuracy and delivery, the full benefit of the exercise cannot be obtained.

AN INFORMATION-LED VALUE CHAIN

Porter's value chain model (1985) focused on cost drivers and differentiation, and subsequent proposals have largely been supply-led. We referred to Lamey's comments earlier concerning the producer-driven perspective of the supply chain model, which is essentially a construction of industry member value chains *linked* by information flows to ensure a cost-effective coordinated delivery of end-user value.

If we consider Lamey's view to be representative of an informed view within distribution ('customer satisfaction has become a key criterion for retailers and is playing a greater role in the supply chain') then the value delivered is a 'product–service' combination response to customer expectations. Given the numerous contributions, we can consider the retailer to be the primary conduit for coordinating resources to meet customer requirements. The notion of the supply chain as a demand chain is further extended by virtue of the managed information flows into a value chain.

Rayport and Sviokla (1994) consider recent developments in information sciences to have modified and even replaced the *market-place* (the interaction between *physical vendor* and *physical buyer*) with a *market-space* (a combination of information, context and infrastructure). In the market-space information *about* the product replaces the product; *context* is the series of information

	What do customers want? (Analysis of demand)	+	How does a firm survive? (Analysis of competition)	=	Key success factors
Steel	• Large customers • Price sensitive customers • Product consistency and reliability of supply are essential • Specific technical specifications required for special steels		• Competition is price based • Declining demand is intensifying competition • High fixed costs require volume throughput • Low cost imports • Entry and exit barriers are high • Strong unions • High transport costs • Scale economies are important		• Cost efficiency through scale efficient plants • Low cost location • Flexibility – adjustment of capacity to output – scope for differentiation of product specification, etc. • Low labour costs • Minimum of labour stoppages
Fashion retailing	• Demand fragmented by garment, style, quality, colour. • Customers willing to pay price premium for style, quality and exclusivity • Retailers seek reliability and speed of supply		• Low entry barriers • Low seller concentration • Few scale economies • Medium/high retailer concentration • Retail buying power strong • Price and non-price competition strong		• Need to combine selective differentiation with low cost operations • Key differentiation variables are rapid response to style and fashion change • Strong customer franchise • Low overhead and labour costs except in less price-sensitive segments
Superstore activities: • food • home improvement	• Low prices • convenient location • Wide range of products		• Local dense catchments • Customers are price sensitive: price competitiveness a requirement • Uses bargaining power to influence merchandise and other input costs		• Low-cost operation requires operational efficiency, scale efficient stores • Large purchasing volumes to maximize buying power • Wide merchandise ranges • Large sales areas • Convenient access (drive time) • Easy parking

Figure 17.9 Identifying key success factors from an analysis of demand and competition. (Adapted from Grant (1995).)

links which replace face-to-face selling and *infrastructure* is a combination of hardware and software communications which replace physical market locations. The suggestion is that the market-space is a structure of information-defined transactions whereby value creation and consumption take place.

The authors provide two examples of market-space product markets: bank ATMs and voicemail. Both examples identify market-space benefits which they suggest are:

- Replacing hardware and/or human resources with an information based service
- A reduction of operating costs
- Lower maintenance costs
- Enhanced operating margins

The authors also suggest (somewhat boldly) that managing in the market-space offers benefits not available in the market-place. Apart from cost benefits they argue that flexibility is available. The market-place requires some structure in which the product market's content, context and delivery infrastructure are aggregated to create a *brand*. However, in a market-space context they may be disaggregated, offering additional benefits to those already outlined; these are:

- New ways of adding value
- New partnerships and alliances
- A rethinking of ownership issues

Their argument is that in the market-place content, context and infrastructure are managed through the marketing mix to create brand equity through an aggregation of the three components. The market-space approach can, through disaggregation, add these benefits. They give as an example the Internet service provider America Online, which combines the contributions of a dozen national newspapers and permits readers to customize content to meet their own requirements. The production and delivery infrastructure becomes an electronic network as opposed to printing plant and a physical distribution system. Rayport and Sviokla suggest that America Online's value proposition, 'AOL's "brand" – must centre on a unique context in which a variety of contents may be consumed'.

The Internet as a *channel* for commerce

> The internet is fast becoming an important new channel for commerce in a range of businesses... established businesses that over decades have carefully built brands and physical distribution relationships risk damaging all they have created when they pursue commerce in cyberspace (Ghosh, 1998).

Ghosh (1998) suggests that the newness of Internet commerce causes concern for both new and old companies. To identify opportunities (and threats) a structured approach is essential if the opportunities are to be understood.

The Internet offers *direct* links with customers, suppliers and distributors and therefore facilitates transaction processes and information transfer. It also enables companies to *bypass* others in the value chain. A third feature is the facility to *develop new products and services* for existing and new customers. It also offers the ability to *dominate* the 'electronic channel' and thereby control access to customers and set the terms of trade.

The Internet channel influences the service offer of users. Ghosh suggests that the level of service afforded to customers is much the same through the Internet as it is from a sales force. Customer loyalty can be enhanced by personalizing customer–supplier interactions, and new information-based services are provided inexpensively. The electronic channel permits an organization to provide customers with a range of value criteria (convenience, information, personalization and interactivity), each of which can create competitive advantage characteristics difficult to emulate without information technology to contain costs.

However, opportunities can quite easily become threats. 'Value chain pirates', suggests Ghosh, can eliminate layers of costs that are built into the value chain simply by; consolidating parts of the chain, eliminating transaction participants, developing exclusive skills and preempting other companies' competitive views. Ghosh makes the point that competition often emerges from outwith current transaction/physical distribution channels, citing an example in which a distribution company (United Parcels) offer its Web site facilities to 'merchants'. Once the transaction is completed UPS effects delivery.

Added value can be achieved by offering additional information, transactions services or possibly by selling complementary products/services. Ghosh suggests such 'leveraging of digital assets' as a means of avoiding a position of competitive disadvantage. *Customer magnets* can soon replace category destinations. The Internet removes physical distance between customers as a major problem and can offer rapid growth and segmentation opportunities. *Product magnets* are areas of product specialization in which *services* are created to offer not only product range width and depth but also extensive services such as information and new product availability, as well as transactions. Other 'magnet' possibilities include *customer segments* (targeting specific customer profile groups); *industry magnets* (in which an extensive range of suppliers is collected under one 'virtual' roof); and *business model magnets* (in which 'market-spaces' are created to manage supplier/customer exchange interactions). The concept also encourages the development of partnerships in which companies that provide complementary services to a common customer base could offer 'packaged' product–services to meet generic needs such as house purchase or travel.

Developing the virtual value chain

Porter's (1996) view of managers' focus having been concentrated on operational efficiencies rather than strategic effectiveness has been endorsed by other authors. Evans and Wurster (1997) suggest:

> Over the past decade, managers have focussed on adapting their operating processes to new information technologies. Dramatic as those *operating* changes have been, a more profound transformation of the business landscape lies ahead. Executives – and not just those in high-tech or information companies – will be forced to rethink the *strategic* fundamentals of their businesses. Over the next decade, the new economics of information will precipitate changes in the structure of entire industries and in the ways companies compete.

The authors discuss the impact of information technology on the value delivered by a number of products. The success of the CD-ROM edition of the *Encyclopedia Britannica* at around $400, compared with the success of the 'hard' copy of $1500–$2000, was difficult for Britannica's management to comprehend. Evans and Wurster suggest that they (the management) had not fully understood parents' view of the product. The CD-ROM application was a toy version of something parents bought to 'do the right thing' by their children. They argue that today 'the right thing' is a computer and it is in fact the way in which value is delivered (the computer) which was the competitive threat. An interesting fact to emerge from the Britannica case study is that the editorial content constituted only some 5% of total costs. The sales force accounted for a major part of costs, and this was the basis of Britannica's vulnerability. Hence value delivery is an integral component of the value chain. As Evans and Wurster suggest:

> More fundamentally, information is the glue that holds together the structure of all businesses. A company's value chain consists of all the activities it performs to design, produce, market, deliver and support its product. The value chain of companies that supply and buy from one another collectively and make up an industry's value chain, its particular configuration of competitors, suppliers, distribution channels and customers... we tend to visualise a linear flow of activities. But the value chain also includes all the information that flows within a company and its suppliers, its distributors, and its existing or potential customers. Supplier relationships, brand identity, process coordination customer loyalty, and switching costs all depend on various kinds of information... the value of customer relationships, for example,... is the proprietary information that their customers have about the company and its products.

The authors expand their argument by suggesting that brands are essentially information that successful positioning has created for the customer by effective use of advertising and other communication media. In a similar manner, information defines supplier relationships; two companies with established communications:

> (built) around personal acquaintance, mutual understanding, shared standards (EDI), electronic data interchange systems or synchronized production systems.

Information and its delivery mechanisms are, therefore, suggested as the means by which corporate and industry structures are stabilized and which underlie competitive advantage. But as Evans and Wurster suggest:

> the informational components of value are so deeply embedded in the physical value chain (the supply chain) that, in some cases, we are just beginning to acknowledge their separate existence.

The authors also suggest that information conducted by physical means (sales persons, direct mail etc.) restricts the flow of information to the linear flow of the physical value chain. The revolutionary aspect of the 'explosion in connectivity is the possibility it offers to unbundle information from its physical carrier'.

A basic aspect of the economics of information is developed by Evans and Wurster: the trade-off between *reach* and *richness*. Reach comprises the number of people exchanging information. Richness is defined as the *amount* of information that can be transmitted from sender to receiver; the extent of its *customization*; and the extent to which *interaction* (dialogue) is possible. Figure 17.10 is used to describe the traditional economics of information with the suggested trade-off which occurred between reach and richness. Evans and Wurster suggest:

> This pervasive trade-off has shaped how companies communicate, collaborate, and conduct transactions internally and with customers, suppliers and distributors.

Marketing resource allocation decisions are managed within this trade-off. A sales message may be 'sent' within an advertisement or a targeted letter, or through a personal sales visit. The richness increases as reach decreases. The

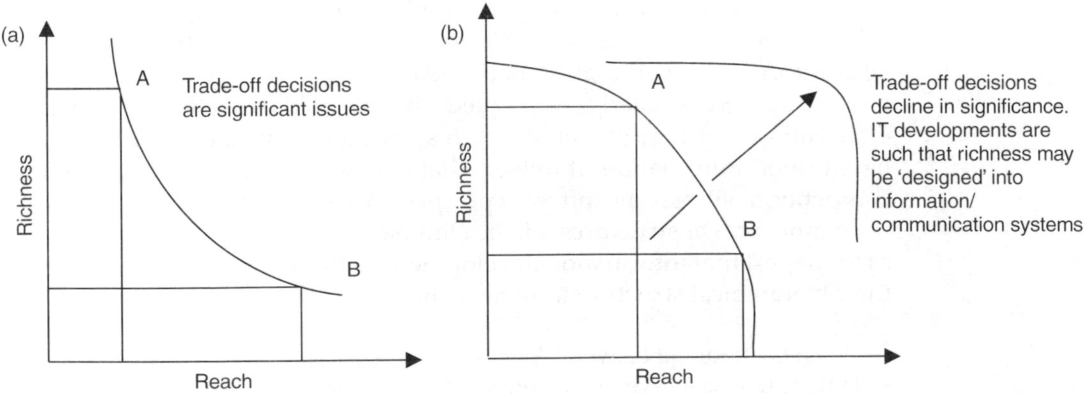

Figure 17.10 The economics of information.

authors refer to transaction cost economics and the work of Coase (1937) and Williamson (1985) as an example of how the model works. *Communications boundaries* for organizations are set by the economies of information exchange; further, it could be argued that it prescribed the 'whole set of premises about how the business world works. And it is precisely this trade-off that is now being blown up'.

The development of information technology is delivering concurrent increases in both reach and richness and decreases in capital and operating costs. However, we would argue that IT developments are changing this relationship. Figure 17.10 presents the Evans and Wurster view of the trade-off situation between reach and richness. Figure 17.10(a) presents options A and B. Management must choose between high-quality/content information with limited dialogue (A) or the facility to contact much larger numbers with limited content and two-way contact (B). In Figure 17.10(b) we show the impact of IT developments. The trade-off situation is reduced in significance due to the increase in cost-effectiveness of IT developments. While trade-off situations do exist, the convex shape of the relationship presents a more favourable choice as A and B move closer together. Furthermore, emerging technology offers an improved mix of reach and richness. Figure 17.10(b) also suggests that the direction of future developments will continue the trend. Porter's argument concerning operational effectiveness, together with our comment concerning its focus by management towards a cost-effective use of operational technology, is applicable here.

As cost-effectiveness increases (see Figure 17.11) we can expect the contact costs of both richness and reach to decline and for management to be offered the facility of customizing or targeting information flows. The Net technologies are making this possible.

The impact of Net technologies with:

> their open standards for exchanging information over intranets fosters cross-functional teams and accelerates the demise of hierarchical structures and their proprietary information systems (Evans and Wurster, 1997).

The point made by the authors is simply that the changing economics of information now threatens established value chains. If, as the authors suggest 'information is the glue that holds together the structure of all businesses', it may similarly be argued that it holds together channels of distribution and that power structures within channels of distribution are based upon information. It follows that conflict, cooperation, coercion and competition will assume different perspectives: perhaps the negative aspects of channel power structures will be eliminated. Evans and Wurster go so far as to suggest that information developments will end channel structures and their hierarchical structure to replace them with *hyperarchy*:

> When the trade-off between richness and reach is eliminated, channels are no longer necessary: everyone communicates richly with everyone else on the basis of shared standards'.

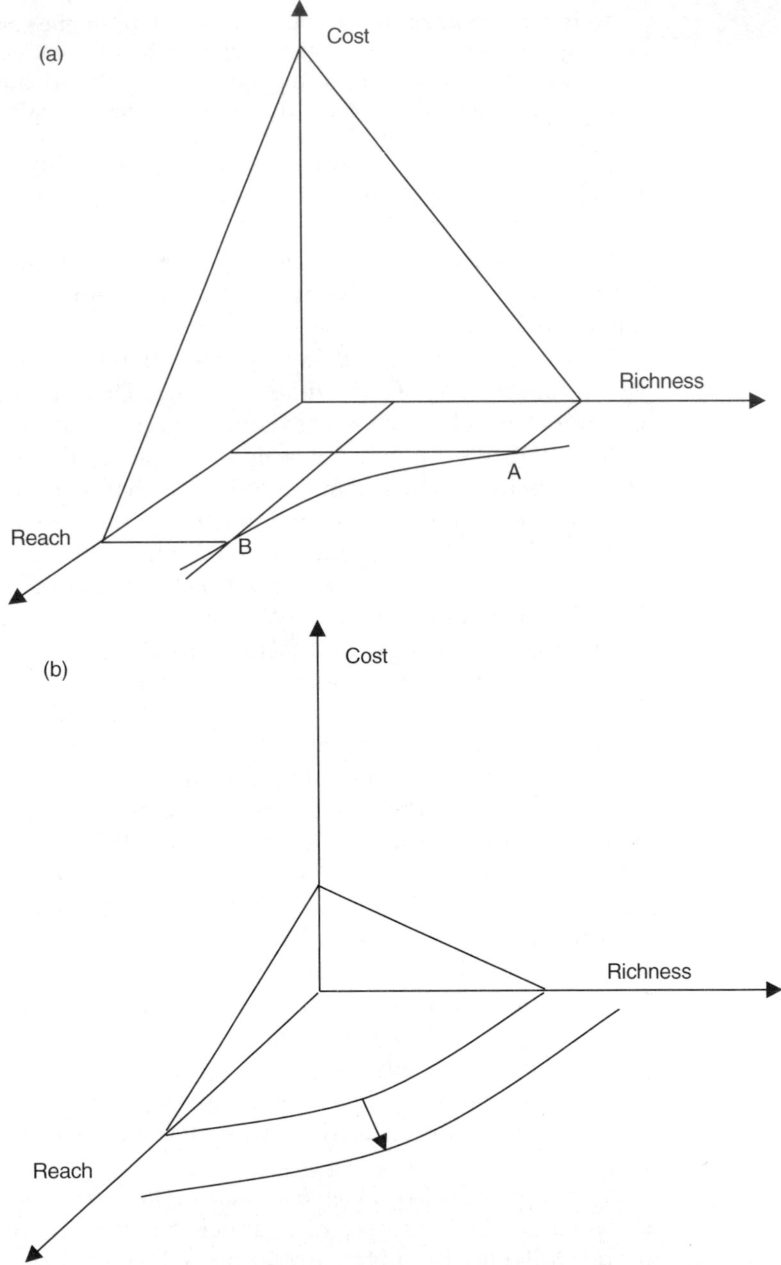

Figure 17.11 The impact of information technology developments on the economics of information.

It is conceivable that power will then be with the consumer!

Furthermore, the impact on hard-earned, hitherto critical, success factors such as brand and store loyalty will make them increasingly less valuable:

> As it becomes easier for customers to switch from one supplier to another, the competitive value of one-stop shopping and established relationships will drop. Cross-selling will become more difficult. Information about customers' needs or behaviour will be harder for companies to obtain. Competitive advantage will be determined product by product, and therefore providers with broad product lines will lose ground to focused specialists... distribution will be done by the phone company, statements by financial management software...

The authors suggest that the new economics of information will alter the sources of competitive advantage. These may appear as pending threats, but equally they may be perceived as opportunities.

Existing value chains will fragment into multiple businesses, each of which will have its own sources of competitive advantage. The argument made here is that existing channel structures are combinations of individual businesses, each with differing economies of scale or scope resulting in sub-optimal value chain structures. The argument offered is that by removing the information link that combines many manufacturer/intermediary(ies) structures the result and model would differ markedly from that currently in place.

Some new businesses will benefit from network economies of scale, which can give rise to monopolies. Evans and Wurster suggest that Net technologies may expand to offer services and facilities to small channel members. They cite the GE example of a networked procurement system which when opened to other buyers of industrial goods easily reached critical mass *and* changed the nature of its own sourcing activity into a *market-making business*.

As value chains fragment and reconfigure, new opportunities will arise for purely physical businesses. Physical distribution efficiencies are often compromised by the requirement to deliver information. It is argued that the need to be effective in both physical distribution *and* information delivery results in sub-optimization. The example of Amazon (book distributors) is given to support an argument that having no physical stocks but access to 2.5 million books through two wholesalers maximizes the effectiveness of both activities. Instant delivery, physical browsing and other features of the traditional bookstore are replaced by choice, superior information (Web-based book reviews) and lower physical costs. An interesting characteristic of the format is its vulnerability. As Evans and Wurster suggest, the wholesalers could create the lowest-cost distribution system in the industry by filling orders directly.

When a company focuses on different activities, the value proposition underlying its brand identity will change. Channel structure changes will require new brand strategies. Brands once offering exclusivity may find a need to re-think this aspect of value as information developments extend access and availability. These may be aspects of value that are not expected by the brand loyal customer.

New branding opportunities will emerge for third parties that are information based: 'Navigator' or 'agent brands' are not new. However, a network navigator or guide for specific products or specialist attributes of products within generic product groups may be required as networked markets proliferate.

Bargaining power will shift as a result of a significant reduction in the ability to monopolize the control of information. Often market power and control of important information are strongly positively correlated. Retailers have managed to use this fact to 'manage' brand loyalty. As richness and reach are extended, this control will be eroded. Buyers will be as knowledgeable of prices and availabilities as their suppliers. New dimensions for loyalty will be necessary if brand loyalty is to be maintained. Extensive price comparative data may provide an opportunity for this.

Customers' sustaining costs will decline, requiring the customer loyalty benefits to be refocused. The Web is already being used to address this problem. Customer convenience is being extended by Net-based home shopping facilities (Woolworth in Australia, Tesco in the UK). Commercial linkages have existed for some time: proprietary EDI systems have 'locked in' industrial and commercial buyers. Evans and Wurster report on the US auto industry's extranet, which will link auto manufacturers with several thousand automotive suppliers. When operational it is anticipated that ordering and billing errors will be reduced and information flows accelerated.

DESIGNING AN INFORMATION-LED RETAIL VALUE CHAIN

Clearly information has a vital and an intriguing role in adding value, and the retail value chain has become both information- *and* demand management-led. Figure 17.12 suggests how the retail value chain is emerging. Based upon *customer value criteria* the retailer identifies the *key success factors* necessary for a relevant *value offer* to be coordinated by the value chain members. An understanding of what is necessary to create expected value is an essential task to be undertaken by the value chain coordinator, and this is based on

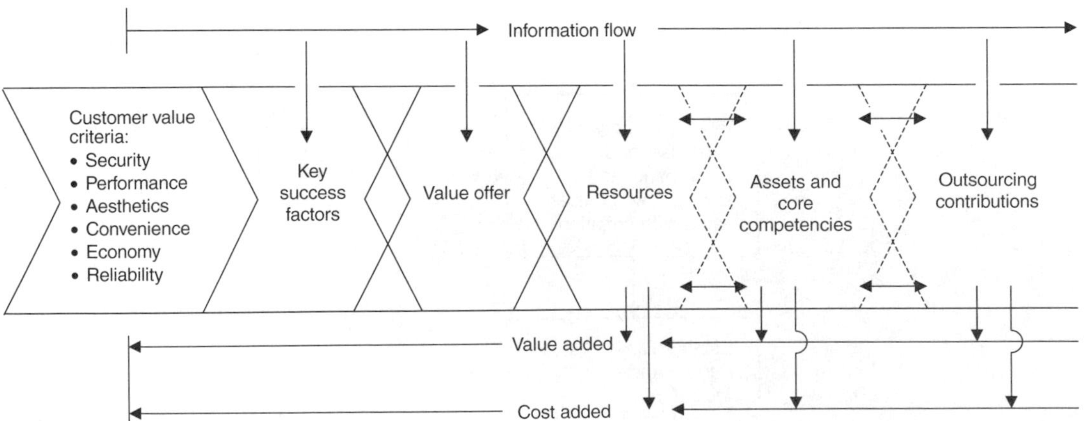

Figure 17.12 The retail value chain: an information- and demand-led response to customer satisfaction.

expert knowledge of the customer. *Resources, assets and core competencies* and *outsourcing contributions* are part of an integrated resource allocation process.

The emphasis on demand management has resulted in the retailer becoming the channel captain or value chain coordinator. In turn this has resulted in significant changes in the structure of individual value chains; for example, the decision by many retailers to use information to coordinate the logistics activities component of the value chain. This has resulted in a review of core competencies and the decision to outsource activities other than logistics. The definition of value has expanded and includes merchandise, elements of service *and* information. As we have seen above, value comprises additional information and transaction services and often includes complementary services. The offer by Dixons (audio-visual, photographic and computer retailer) of free Internet connection to customers is an example of this development.

Clearly, if a demand-led value chain is to be constructed a considerable amount of information is required. Furthermore, a structured approach is necessary. In Figure 17.13 we suggest such an approach. Our major concern

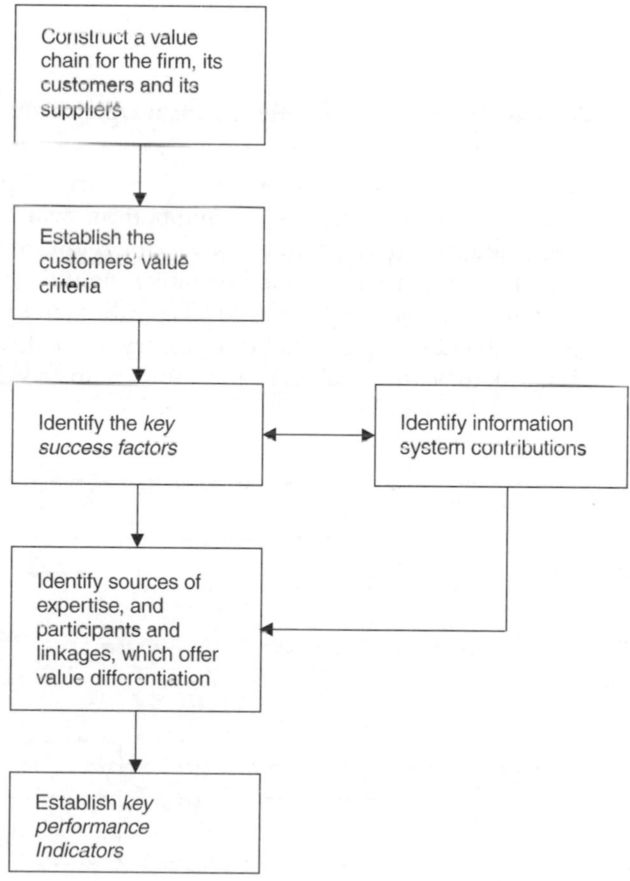

Figure 17.13 Using information to enhance strategic and operational value delivery decisions.

(the topic of this chapter) is the use of information to structure the value chain. Information is usually collected, analysed and then distributed via a control database. Figure 17.14 depicts a typical database. Information on customers, competitors and suppliers is usual; for a large retailing company we may choose to emphasize territorial data. The reason for choosing to do so is to identify customer differences that may require alternative service arrangements or even category structures. Significant differences may offer more cost-efficient servicing alternatives, which, as we have seen in the earlier discussion within this chapter, may be dealt with in an increasing number of ways. Given that a few retailers have become international brands (e.g. Harrods, Hamleys, Harvey Nichols), these options can include Net-based communications facilities.

Chapter 16 (the retail supply chain) discussed *category management* at some length, and it offers some interesting possibilities for delivering differentiated customer value. As a management technique it requires additional

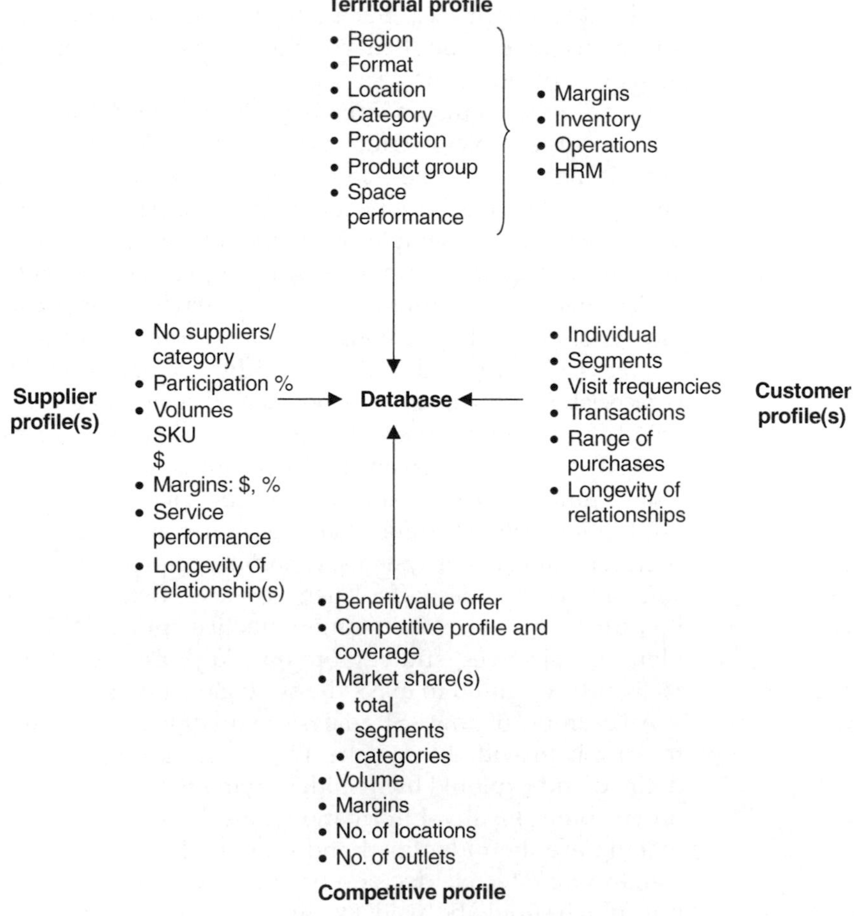

Figure 17.14 Understanding the business environment.

information if it is to be managed effectively. Figure 17.15 represents a *category profile* for a typical FMCG retailer. We have identified seven categories, and there are probably others. However, the point to be made concerns the *structure* of the information. If the concept is to be made to work effectively information flows both *horizontally* and *vertically*. Horizontal flows of information have two levels. At a *macro level* it is essential that management ensures an offer congruence *across* categories. In other words, it is essential that the same benefit/value offer is made by each category and has in mind the same target customer. At a *micro level* the information assumes more of a *relationship perspective*. The information looks for assortment items that may be required in two or more categories. It is not surprising that this should occur, and the concern is for consistency and also for logistics purposes (i.e. to ensure that similar 'brands', pack sizes, flavours etc. are stocked). As and where this does occur it offers an opportunity to maximize economies of procurement and of logistics (particularly storage and transportation). *Vertical information* is necessary if the value chain design is to be made effective. The data will identify volumes, rates of sale, locations, and time periods of heavy, medium and light sales. Such information offers the opportunity to investigate alternative value chain configurations which deliver the required value at a lower overall cost.

Any process requires a series of performance metrics, qualitative and quantitative, if the implementation is to be successful. Figure 17.16 proposes some generic metrics. The role of information in developing an effective value chain strategy is shown as a number of *information system contributions*. The linkages are quite clear. For example, to ensure optimal supplier selection, information systems management can develop a supplier performance evaluation model which reviews the customer appeal of merchandise, supplier terms and service. Cost-efficient operations are more readily achieved if a financial control model is in place and is supported by an operating productivity analysis (space, labour and inventory) model. And customer loyalty (their expenditure patterns, retention, loyalty etc.) may be enhanced by a central customer database supported by detailed customer transaction analysis.

It is unlikely that an information format can be designed for universal application. What is more likely is that components may be transferable between value chain systems. A number of processes, planning and control software companies offer such services. Before undertaking significant investments in systems, common practice appears to be for management to identify objectives, strategy options, key success factors and the systems facilitators required to make the strategies successful.

An example of how KSF analysis may contribute towards strategy decision making is provided by Figure 17.17. The strategy topic, *customer loyalty*, is defined and explored by first identifying the KSFs which have an influence on customer loyalty. Information contributions that can facilitate decision making are then identified and examined from a benefit/cost perspective: can a more effective decision be made with this information, and if it can, how much should be 'paid' for the information? In other words, when investigating the benefits of customer loyalty for the company, what information

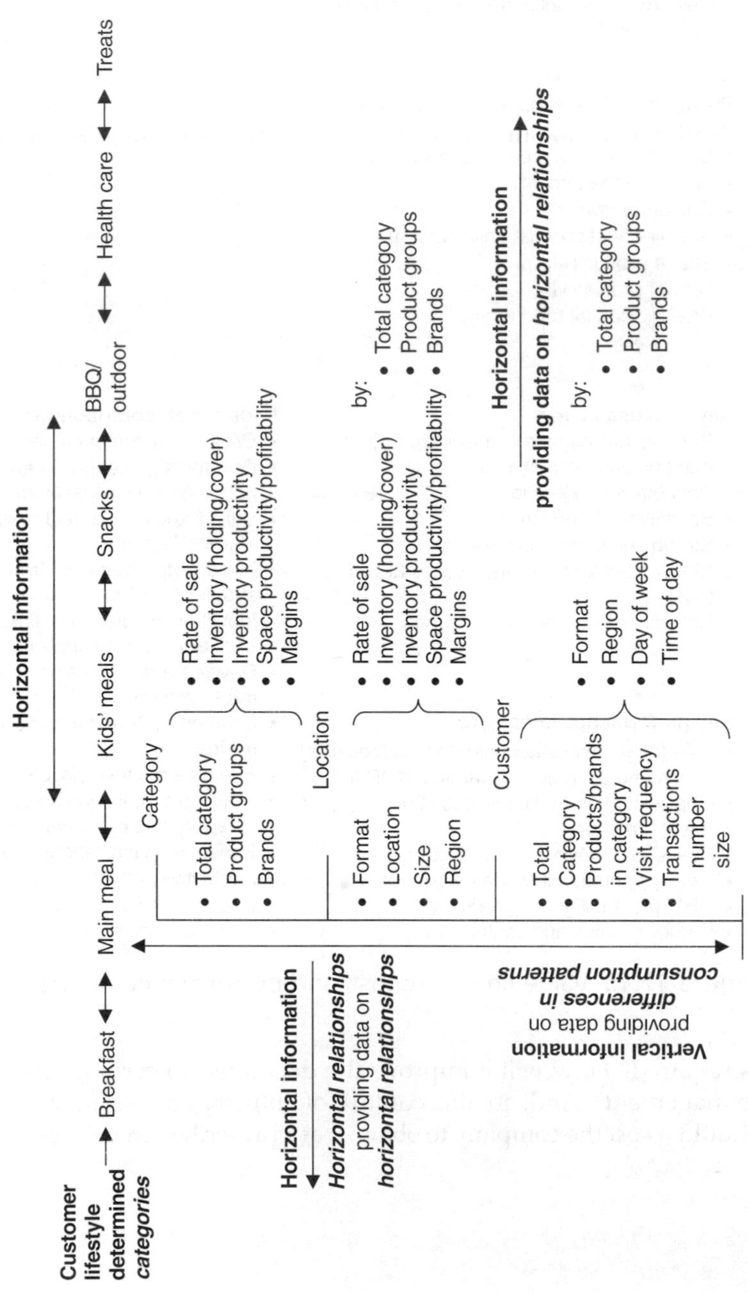

Figure 17.15 Effective information for category management.

Objectives
- Profitability
- Productivity
- Cash flows
- Customer satisfaction/value expectations

Strategies which enhance customer value expectations:
- Category development and management
- Margin management
- Customer loyalty
- Supplier relationships development
- Space productivity
- Labour productivity
- Working capital productivity

Key success factors
- Purchasing volumes to maximize buying margins and influence
- Cost efficient operations
- Selective differentiation
- Strong customer franchise
- 'Convenient location' and access (travel time)
- Relevant merchandise categories

Key performance indicators
- EVA (or suitable shareholder value measure)
- Gross and contribution margins, NOPAT
- Operational and strategic cash flow
- Asset turnover
- Space profitability and productivity
- Inventory profitability and productivity
- HRM profitability and productivity
- Category sales and contribution

Information contributions
- Develop customer database
- Develop supplier price/service/sales performance evaluation model
- Build flexibility into retail value chain 'delivery' system
- Investigate on/line electronic links with suppliers and with customers
- Install online/electronic links with ancillary service suppliers
- Develop a retail version of 'track and trace' system
- Develop customer transactions analysis system
- Enhance the financial control system
- Develop contribution analysis model; category and customer based
- Enhance space, labour and inventory productivity analysis
- Subscribe to catchment survey analysis
- Develop competitor data base

Figure 17.16 Value chain process and performance metrics.

is required? How will it improve the decisions concerning customer loyalty management? And, in the context of information economics, how much should it cost the company to obtain it at a prescribed frequency and content?

SUMMARY

The developments in information sciences seem limitless and are likely to lead the expectations of management for the future developments and applications.

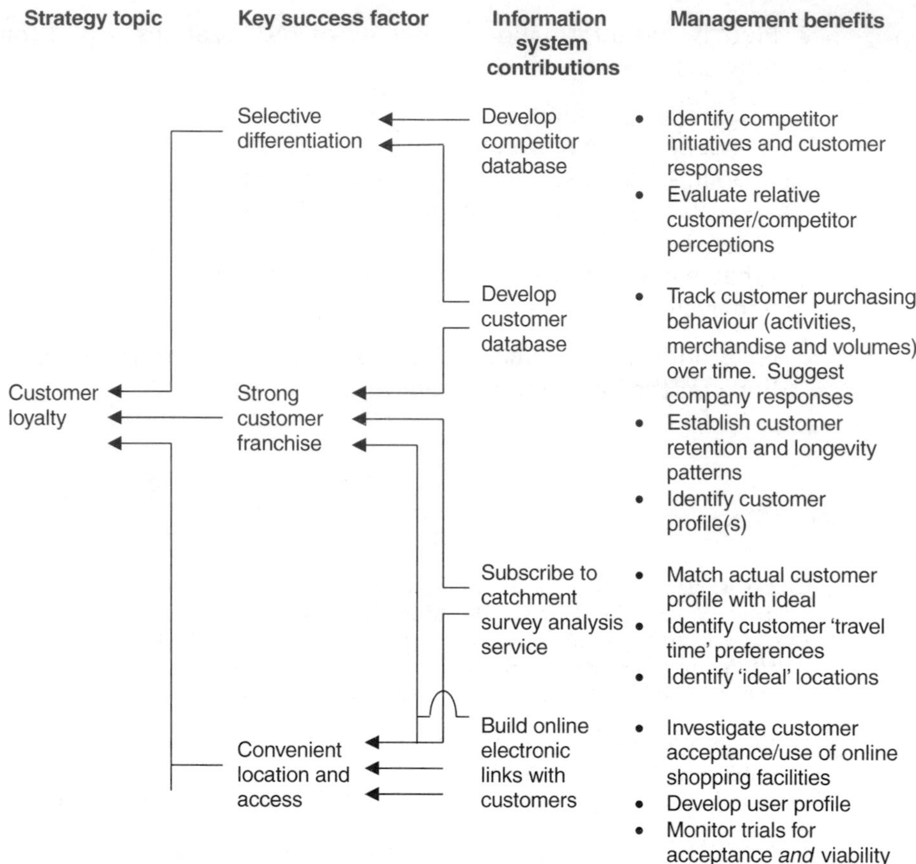

Figure 17.17 Using KSFs and information system contributions in the strategy process.

A value chain approach focuses management attention on the need for an information system which identifies the customer as an important component, and from which other data requirements flow, assuming customer satisfaction to be the primary consideration of the organization.

Information provides a means of creating competitive advantage. Increasingly this is realized by extending the information base of the organization into supplier organizations by creating competitor profiles and using qualitative and quantitative sources of information.

QUESTIONS, ACTIVITIES AND CONSIDERATIONS

- From Chapter 16, the first task is to develop an information system designed to make the supply/value chain an effective decision-making vehicle.

- Identify the information strategies of organizations in the following retail categories:
  - an FMCG multiple
  - a department store group
  - an Internet-based book and music vendor
  - a retail service company such as a dry-cleaning multiple operation

  Are there differences? Are these significant? Why?
- What is the role of key success factor analysis in developing information systems?
- If retail format life cycles are becoming shorter, what are the implications for the design of retail information systems?

REFERENCES

Coase, R. H. (1937) The nature of the firm. *Economica* 4(1), 386. Reprinted in *The Economic Nature of the Firm* (ed. Louis Putterman).

Evans, P. B. and Wurster, T. S. (1997) Strategy and the new economics of information. *Harvard Business Review*, Sep/Oct.

Ghosh, S. (1998) Making business sense of the Internet. *Harvard Business Review*, Mar/Apr.

Hofer, C. W. and Schendel, D. (1978) *Strategy Formulation: Analytical Concepts*. West Publishing Company, New York.

Lamey, J. (1997) *Supply Chain Management*. FT Retail and Consumer Publishing, London.

Lawrence, P. J. and Lorsch, J. W. (1967) *Organization and Environment: Managing Differentiation and Integration*. Irwin, Homewood, IL.

Mintzberg, H. (1979) *The Structuring of Organizations*. Prentice Hall, Englewood Cliffs, NJ.

Moreton, R. and Chester, M. (1997) *Transforming the Business: The IT Contribution* McGraw-Hill, London.

Murray, J. A. and O'Driscoll, A. (1996) *Strategy and Process in Marketing*. Prentice Hall, Hemel Hempstead.

Porter, M. E. (1996) What is strategy? *Harvard Business Review*, Nov/Dec.

Rayport, J. F. and Sviokla, J. (1994) Managing in the marketspace, *Harvard Business Review*, Nov/Dec.

Vollman, T. and Cordon, C. (1999) Building a smarter demand chain, in Mastering information management, Pt 4. *Financial Times*, 22 February.

Williamson, O. (1985) *The Economic Institutions of Capitalism*. The Free Press, New York.

FREEDOM FURNITURE: DECIDING UPON A FUTURE DIRECTION

FREEDOM FURNITURE LTD: STRATEGY DECISIONS

INTRODUCTION

In July 1997 the board of Freedom Furniture initiated a strategy review exercise with the assistance of a consulting company. The purpose of the review was to identify strategic alternatives for the company.

Freedom opened its first store in 1981 and now has 42 retail outlets. Twenty-two are company-owned and 20 are operated by franchisees in Australia and New Zealand. Sales and profit growth have exceeded the forecast made in the prospectus issued prior to the company being floated on the Australian Stock Exchange in 1996. Sales for the year ended September 1997 are planned to exceed A$250 million, with profits estimated to exceed $9 million. Market share of the Australian furniture market increased from 5% in 1991 to 8.9% in 1991 and EBIT (earnings before interest and tax) increased from 4% in 1993 to over 6% in 1996. Other significant financial performance revealed:

- For 1995/1996 a RONA of 12.9% which compared with a WACC of 11.1%.
- Performance during the 1997 fiscal year showed an increasing RONA to more than 20%.

To support its retail activities, Freedom Furniture owns an importing operation in Sydney as well as manufacturing operations in Sydney and Brisbane and a 50% interest in a manufacturing operation in New Zealand. These operations, combined with the company's buying power and established relationships with suppliers provide Freedom Furniture with significant competitive and cost advantages.

The strength of Freedom Furniture's operations is derived from a number of factors including:

- An established brand name and an extensive store network in the major population centres of Australia.
- A reputation as a quality retailer of furniture and homewares and as a leader in product innovation.
- A distinctive market positioning and image founded on the key attributes of style and value.

- A vertically integrated supply chain in key product categories.
- A focused management team with a considerable depth of retail experience.
- Tight controls based on advanced business information systems.
- Strong operating cash flows.

INDUSTRY OVERVIEW AND COMPETITIVE POSITION

For the year ended 30 September 1995, Freedom Furniture estimates that it had a share of approximately 8.9% of the A$2.4 billion Australian retail furniture market.

The Australian retail furniture market is made up of a number of retail formats, varying in size and presentation, from traditional and discount department stores such as David Jones, Myer-Grace Bros and Harvey Norman, through to large speciality retailers such as Freedom Furniture and IKEA and small single-store specialists. The major participants account for approximately 50% of the national market, with the balance being serviced by over 3000 smaller operators. The large specialty retailers have enjoyed significant market share growth over the past four years, in line with this trend in other retail product markets.

Freedom Furniture, like most other retailers, is affected by general economic conditions including the level of interest rates, household disposable incomes and consumer sentiment. As a retailer of home furnishings, Freedom Furniture's sales also tend to be influenced by the level of housing activity.

Despite the recent slowdown in the domestic economy and competitive conditions in the retail furniture market, Freedom Furniture has increased its market share and profitability, reflecting, among other things, the strength of the brand name and the benefits of the capital expenditure and efficiency programs implemented over the last five years.

Freedom Furniture is well positioned to benefit from an anticipated improvement in the domestic economy and housing activity.

Management has identified significant growth opportunities for the company, through the opening of new stores in Australia and New Zealand and potential expansion into Asia. Growth is also expected from new retail formats which the company is developing, such as Freedom Kitchens.

STORES

Location

Freedom Furniture has 35 stores in major population centres throughout Australia and has recently opened two stores in New Zealand. Of the 37

stores, 21 are company-owned with the remaining 16 being franchise stores. In general, the company-owned stores are concentrated in and around major capital cities, with franchise stores existing primarily in regional areas.

Freedom Furniture has continued to develop its store location strategy to meet changing demographics and to take advantage of new market opportunities. The main criteria considered when identifying locations for new stores under the current retailing format are:

- A minimum population catchment area of approximately 100,000 people.
- Proximity to complementary stores.
- Major road access with prominent store and signage visibility.
- Sufficient parking, customer pick up and truck docking facilities.
- Minimal impact on sales of existing Freedom Furniture stores.

A feature of Freedom Furniture's store location strategy is its flexibility in size and presentation. The showrooms vary in size (from approximately 750 to 3300 square metres) and in presentation, such that Freedom Furniture can adapt to upmarket shopping areas such as South Yarra, bulky goods centres such as Blacktown and Moore Park, suburban shopping malls such as Westfield Miranda, or large regional centres such as Cairns and Newcastle.

Franchise arrangements

Franchise stores account for the majority of stores opened in recent years and the new store openings planned for 1996, 1997 and thereafter.

Freedom Furniture generally prefers single-store franchises, but will consider multiple store franchises where economies can be achieved by one franchisee operating multiple stores. In New Zealand, all stores will be operated by a single franchisee, Farmers Trading Company (a subsidiary of Farmers Deka Limited, a major New Zealand retailer).

Under franchise agreements, franchisees are conferred the right to utilize Freedom Furniture's name and logo as well as its business systems, including its merchandising and store operating procedures, during the franchise period. Franchise agreements are generally for a period of 10 years, although Freedom Furniture will consider longer or shorter terms in appropriate circumstances. Only one franchise agreement is scheduled to expire during the forecast period; however, negotiations have commenced which may result in the extension of this agreement. Freedom Furniture also offers an intensive franchisee training program and closely monitors the performance of franchise stores.

Franchisees pay an upfront fee upon entering into a franchise agreement with Freedom Furniture in addition to an ongoing franchise fee. Except on the two occasions where Freedom Furniture has provided start-up financing to ex-employees, franchisees are required to meet all pre-opening expenses and capital requirements associated with their stores, including the purchase of stock and fit-out costs.

New retail formats

The company is also investigating the introduction of new retail formats as a means of expanding the Freedom Furniture business in Australia.

New formats will allow the company to continue to broaden its target market demographically and geographically. The new formats being developed include Freedom Kitchens (in both existing and standalone stores), Freedom Homewares (in shopping malls) and Freedom Galleries (focusing on individual segments of the product range in more upmarket, established areas).

The fragmented nature of the retail furniture market presents an opportunity for a strongly branded retailer like Freedom Furniture to gain a larger market share than other retailers currently hold.

Some of the new retail formats, such as Freedom Kitchens, are planned to be implemented on a franchise or concession basis.

PRODUCT

Range

Freedom Furniture stores offer a comprehensive range of furniture and homewares, including:

- *Furniture*: fabric and leather sofas, dining suites, chairs, tables, beds, ensembles, entertainment units, bookcases, wall units desks, office furnishings and folding chairs and tables.
- *Homewares*: blinds, curtains, lighting, cushions, rugs, kitchenware, decorations, dinnerware, storage and bathroom accessories.

Freedom Furniture designs or commissions approximately 90% of its products. Virtually all products are sold under the Freedom Furniture brand name.

Freedom Furniture has built on its core product, furniture, by expanding into homewares and other complementary products in recent years. The proportion of total sales represented by homewares has increased from 22% in 1991 to 29% currently. In addition to diversifying Freedom Furniture's sales base, increasing the proportion of homewares in the product mix has the benefits of increasing customer flow into the stores and improving gross margins.

Buying practices and distribution

To ensure that Freedom Furniture is at the forefront of product development in the industry, the company's buyers are continually identifying and

analysing emerging trends in furniture and homewares, both locally and internationally. Freedom Furniture sources its products from a number of suppliers both in Australia and overseas.

Freedom Furniture has developed long-term relationships with its local and overseas suppliers. Approximately 80% of Freedom Furniture's product is currently sourced from 18 main suppliers. Two of these suppliers are wholly owned divisions, Freedom Manufacturing and Freedom Imports.

The majority of the company's large furniture items are delivered through distribution centres operated by Freedom Furniture throughout Australia, from where they are delivered directly to customers.

In recent years, Freedom Furniture has devoted considerable capital and management resources to re-engineering the supply chain – improving the management of the process from raw material supply to delivery into the customer's home to ensure that it is as efficient as possible.

The capital invested in information systems in the areas of merchandise planning and distribution has facilitated reductions in overall inventory levels and lower stock markdowns and shrinkage. Management believe there are opportunities to further improve the company's performance in these areas.

Freedom Furniture's buying power and established relationships with its suppliers provide the company with leverage to further improve operating efficiencies. In this regard, Freedom Furniture is currently working towards further integrating each of its main suppliers into its supply channel.

Freedom manufacturing and imports

To support its Australian retail activities in its largest selling product category, sofas, Freedom Furniture owns manufacturing operations in Lidcombe, NSW, and Geebung, Queensland, which together produce approximately 50% of its sofas. Freedom Manufacturing is a low-cost efficient manufacturer which competes effectively with Freedom Furniture's external suppliers. With relative certainty of demand Freedom Manufacturing can confidently invest in new technology, further widening the gap between the company and its competitors.

Freedom Furniture also operates a chair assembly and finishing plant at Lidcombe, NSW. The plant assembles metal and wooden chairs from imported components, enabling the company to control the supply and quality of these products as well as make significant savings in transportation costs.

In order to support its international expansion, Freedom Furniture also manufactures sofas in New Zealand through a joint venture company equally owned by Freedom Furniture and Farmers Trading Company. The manufacturing operation supplies sofas to Freedom Furniture's New Zealand stores and plans to supply direct to Farmers Trading Company as well.

Freedom Furniture owns and runs an import warehouse operation which currently supplies 22% of the company's product. Freedom Furniture's

buying power allows it to purchase directly from overseas manufacturers in bulk and bypass the agents and wholesalers used by most retailers. Aside from the price and margin advantage, this provides the company with exclusivity in many products. In the future, Freedom Imports will assist the company in developing an infrastructure to support its international requirements and in expanding the number and variety of products sourced directly from overseas manufacturers.

Vertical integration is a key competitive advantage for Freedom Furniture. It provides the company with the opportunity to improve margins through:

- Greater flexibility to respond to fashion trends and changes in consumer demand, by operating just-in-time manufacturing practices.
- An efficient, low cost, integrated channel from the supply of raw material through to delivery of furniture into the customer's home.
- Best practice sourcing of components throughout the world with local furniture assembly.

MARKETING

Freedom Furniture's distinctive market positioning and image are founded on the key attributes of style and value. This has been maintained by the execution of an integrated marketing strategy covering all aspects from advertising to in store display.

Freedom Furniture is unique in its product range and focus on lifestyle designs. The attention paid to the design of both furniture and homewares has achieved a coordinated look. The range of design styles offers the customer a comprehensive selection from which to choose.

The customer benefits not only from the creative ideas offered by the display of merchandise, but also from the one-stop shopping opportunity that the lifestyle focus provides.

Freedom Furniture has traditionally been successful in attracting customers in the younger age groupings who are in the first home market. In addition to reinforcing Freedom Furniture's strength in this market segment, the company is extending its appeal to other target markets. The mature home market, the retirement market and the second home market, all offer good potential for both higher sales and gross margins.

Visual merchandising

One of Freedom Furniture's key competitive advantages is the unique look of its stores. The customer experiences how the furniture and accessories look and feel in a room. Clear pricing tickets and other important information are provided with each item on display, further assisting the customer and reinforcing the value component of the brand.

The company's merchandising team is continually developing new concepts to improve the presentation of its stores and merchandise. Freedom Furniture's management maintains close control over visual merchandising in each of its stores (including franchise stores), while at the same time allowing local creativity and appeal to the local market.

ADVERTISING AND PROMOTION

Freedom Furniture's main form of advertising is its catalogue, which is currently published twice yearly, in summer and winter. The catalogue has proven to be a key element in attracting potential customers to the stores. It is highly regarded and is often retained as a reference, long after its publication date.

Television, magazines, radio, cinema and outdoor media are also utilized to encourage customers to visit the stores and to maintain the brand image and awareness across a broader audience. The selection of media is tailored to the competitive environment.

Freedom Furniture prefers to hold only two clearances and one interest-free promotion each year, giving these events credibility with the customer and reinforcing the brand positioning of value.

A pilot customer loyalty program 'Freedom First' is currently being trialed in Adelaide and Canberra. The program, designed to reward good customers and encourage further sales, includes special offers, previews and information. The program will also provide valuable information on purchase patterns, specific sub-segment profiles and an opportunity for ongoing customer feedback.

INFORMATION TECHNOLOGY

Freedom Furniture is committed to the use of information technology in all aspects of the business. Over the last three years Freedom Furniture has implemented the major part of its information technology plan, which is scheduled for completion by the end of 1997. This has involved the replacement of what was essentially a manual system with modern, open systems at a total investment to date of A$4.5 million. This excludes the A$2.8 million write-off of systems which were not considered appropriate to meet the future needs of the business.

Some of the key systems implemented include:

- A point of sale (POS) system which operates in each company store and most franchise stores. In addition to increasing productivity through more efficient processing of transactions, the POS system provides

extensive sales information which facilitates improved understanding of customer preferences, margins and salespersons' performance.

- A stock system which enables efficient inventory management. The system provides information for merchandise planning purposes, which in turn allows for buying efficiencies, shorter lead times, and lower stock obsolescence and markdowns.
- A distribution system which consolidates and manages large furniture orders for delivery to customers. Economies are achieved by removing this function for the stores enabling them to focus on customer service and generating sales.

The information systems implemented to date represent the major technology infrastructure necessary to operate the business. The next key task is the integration of all systems. This will involve additional capital investment of approximately A$1.5 million, bringing total project investment to A$6.0 million.

Beyond 1997, Freedom Furniture intends to continue developing and upgrading its systems to provide further operational efficiencies and better information to support decision making.

MANAGEMENT AND STAFF

The directors believe that the quality, enthusiasm and energy of its staff and management are a strength of the business and have contributed significantly to the success and growth of Freedom Furniture.

The management and organizational structure of Freedom Furniture have matured and developed in conjunction with its growth. The management team has considerable retail experience and has been responsible for overseeing the expansion of the business and the operational improvements implemented in recent years.

Staff

Freedom Furniture currently employs 971 full-time, part-time and casual employees, of which over 65% are store staff.

Other employment conditions are also set out in that agreement. Freedom Furniture also has specific incentive programs to reward staff for outstanding performance.

Freedom Furniture has negotiated a new Certified Agreement that covers all company store and distribution centre staff (other than location management who are on individual contracts). The agreement has received strong employee and union support and was ratified by the Industrial Relations Commission on 14 June 1996 to take effect from 1 July 1996. There have been no significant industrial disputes in the last 10 years.

Training and customer service

Freedom Furniture places great emphasis on staff training and the future development of its people. The company is continually conducting in-store training programs as well as off-site management development programs. On-the-job staff training covers a number of areas including sales, customer service, store presentation and merchandising techniques and product knowledge.

Freedom Furniture has recently introduced a 5-star Service Program to all stores (including franchise stores) and distribution warehouses in order to continue to promote and instil a customer service attitude throughout the entire organization. This program was launched at the company's 1995 National Conference and has received very positive support. The program is reinforced during monthly training sessions at all locations throughout the company.

BUSINESS RISKS

There are a number of factors, both specific to the company and external, which may impact on the operating and financial performance of Freedom Furniture and the achievability of the forecasts discussed on pp. 385–91. These are described below.

Dependence on general economic conditions

Freedom Furniture, like most other retailers, is affected by general economic conditions including the level of interest rates and consumer spending. As a retailer of home furnishings, Freedom Furniture's sales also tend to be influenced by the level of housing activity.

The recent slowdown in the Australian economy has coincided with a downturn in housing activity. The subdued economic conditions are reflected by the decline in the size of the retail furniture market (as measured by the Australian Bureau of Statistics). The directors believe that Freedom Furniture is well positioned to benefit from an anticipated improvement in the economy, the level of housing activity and a rebound in the retail furniture market. However, any prolonged economic slowdown and continued decline in the retail furniture market could be expected to have an adverse effect on the company's business.

Freedom Furniture's results could also be affected by any changes in government fiscal, monetary and regulatory policies. These factors apply to both the Australian and New Zealand markets.

Competition

The Australian retail market for furniture is highly fragmented and competitive. Freedom Furniture has demonstrated the ability to compete effectively

with a variety of different furniture retailers, including traditional department stores and speciality retailers. However, there can be no assurance that the competitive environment will not change adversely for Freedom Furniture due to actions of competitors or customer preferences.

Expansion plans

The continued growth of the company is to a large degree dependent upon its ability to open and operate new stores on a profitable basis.

The company has already signed lease agreements in respect of four of the eight new store openings planned for the remainder of the forecast period. Lease terms for two of the other new stores planned have been agreed, subject to documentation. Sites for the remaining two stores have been identified and negotiations have commenced with the property owners. Freedom Furniture expects that all but one of the new stores planned for the remainder of the forecast period will be opened on a franchise basis. Franchise agreements in respect of four of these seven stores have been signed and franchise agreements for the remaining three stores are in advanced states of negotiation.

The company's ability to open new stores on schedule will in part depend on the availability of suitable sites the ability to negotiate attractive lease terms and in respect of franchise stores, the ability to attract qualified franchisees. As a result, there can be no assurance that management will be able to open the new stores on a timely basis.

Similarly, there can be no assurance that the opening of new stores will not adversely impact on the sales of existing stores, although management aims to minimize any impact by opening new stores in markets not serviced by existing stores.

FREEDOM STORE PORTFOLIO

The stores vary in size. Some small stores are only 500 m^2 and the largest is 2900 m^2. The company has an 'ideal' size of 2000 m^2. Typically the stores contain 50 'lifestyle' room settings. They are ideally located in catchments of no fewer than 100,000 persons, close to complementary stores with easy access, and are highly visible. Free and ample parking is essential.

The merchandise range follows a 'casual style' theme which is developed through a number of lifestyle categories. These change with the researched changes in consumer style attitudes but are aimed at reflecting emerging trends and existing popular styles. For each style, a coordinated range of seating, dining and tableware products are developed. Bedroom furniture is augmented with a complementary range of bed linens, towels and accessories. Auxiliary ranges are offered for kitchens, bathrooms and home offices.

Room settings are an important aspect of the Freedom offer. The company considers 'ideas' to be a primary service component and strong visual merchandising in the stores is continued within the catalogue, which is produced twice yearly.

THE MARKET

The Australian furniture market has an estimated value of A$7 billion at RSP (retail selling prices). Freedom estimates an 'attainable' (i.e. a realistic market sector considering Freedom's positioning and core competencies) market of A$4.6 billion. Freedom's target market is:

> Mainly women with a 'taste and attitude' for stylish and value oriented furniture and homewares. Typically they are aged between 27 to 46 years old with an annual household income of $30,000. Freedom has identified this as the 'Lifestyle Segment' of the total market.

Competition is increasing at the bottom end of the lifestyle segment in the form of OZ Design and Fantastic Furniture. Other competitors include IKEA, David Jones, Myer-Grace Bros and Harvey Norman.

FREEDOM'S STRENGTHS

Freedom Furniture management believe that the company's major strengths are:

- established strong brand name and image
- distinctive market position based on coordinated style and value
- established retail store network in major population centres
- vertically integrated supply chain for major product categories
- continuous focus on reducing supply chain and all other costs
- strong and consistent cash flow
- focused and experienced retail management team
- continual investment in new IT systems, staff training, inventory management and merchandising systems
- management also believes that further sales and improved profits will be derived from:
  - opening new retail stores in the current format
  - increasing sales in the current stores by leveraging off the existing skills and infrastructure
- further improvements in inventory management, merchandising and staff training

- developing innovative new retail store formats
- maximizing Freedom Furniture's competitive advantage provided by the company's buying power, international sourcing, product exclusivity, distribution skills and vertical integration
- improvements in Australian economy, consumer confidence and an increase in housing construction through lower interest rates
- possible further international expansion.

FREEDOM'S CORE COMPETENCIES

Senior management considers the company to possess a number of core competencies which offer Freedom competitive advantage:

- idea generation/commercialization of trends and styles/new product development (furniture/sofas)
- management and staff having a 'can do' culture (not product group specific)
- sourcing of local and international products (furniture and homewares)
- information technology – management information for retail stores, and general management, inventory management (not product group-specific)
- in-store merchandising (not product group-specific)
- franchise relationship management (not product group-specific)

Competencies in which Freedom is only 'par for the course' are:

- store location/'roll out'
- time to market for new products
- marketing/brand building/communications/catalogue development
- consumer offtake/delivered in full and on time (DIFOT)
- retail operations/training

These core competencies will have a significant influence on the eventual direction of the company's strategy.

FREEDOM'S STRATEGIC OPTIONS

Strategic alternatives discussed by the board were:

- category dominance
- a 'new' superior customer proposition (e.g. assured delivery in seven days)
- new categories/formats
- brand expansion and/or acquisition

- international expansion
- expanding manufacturing

These alternatives were cross-referenced with Freedom's core competencies. Figure 1 was developed to identify the relative ease (or difficulty) with which Freedom may address these options.

STRATEGIC ANALYSIS

At this juncture the company decided to review its external and internal environment. Two sources of information were considered. The first (Appendix 1) was an overview of retail trends in Australia and the other (Appendix 2) was a series of issues concerning the company that were developed from a senior management workshop. Appendix 3 is a review of major competitors and their respective positioning.

FREEDOM'S BROAD STRATEGIC OPTIONS

- Continue to improve the operational performance of the company owned and franchised retail stores while expanding the Freedom Furniture brand franchise (in its current retail format) by 'stretching' it to cover an increased product range. It should be noted that the extent of product range expansion will be limited by Freedom Furniture's core competencies.
- As above, plus continue to develop the skills and competencies (and gather the necessary market and consumer intelligence) required to expand into international markets.
- Use its base of core competencies to move into new target markets in Australia. This will involve Freedom Furniture increasing its market share by either acquiring or building a new retail brand in Australia.
- Establish a standalone business out of the manufacturing and importing divisions. Such a business would sell to third parties as well as the Freedom Furniture network.

The selection of a preferred strategic option will be determined by the option(s) market attractiveness, the core competencies required to implement.

EXPANDING THE STRATEGIC OPTIONS

The following options were developed during a workshop held by senior management and the consultants:

	Competencies	Category dominance	New customer proposition	New categories/ formats	New brand development acquisition	International expansion	Expand manufacturing
Better than competitors	Idea generation/commercialization*		✓✓✓	✓✓✓			
	'Can do' culture	✓✓✓	✓✓✓	✓✓✓	✓✓✓	✓✓✓	✓✓✓
	Local/international sourcing	✓✓✓			✓✓		✓✓
	IT	✓✓✓	✓✓✓	✓✓✓	✓✓✓	✓✓✓	✓✓✓
	In-store merchandising	✓✓	✓✓	✓✓	✓✓	✓✓	✓✓
	Franchise management (depends on expansion strategy)						
No significant advantage	Store location/'roll out'	✓✓	✓✓	✓✓		✓✓	
	Time to market	✓✓					✓✓
	Marketing/brand building		✓✓	✓✓	✓✓		
	Consumer offtake/DIFOT		✓✓				
	Retail operations	✓✓	✓✓	✓✓	✓✓	✓✓	

* Specific to furniture/homewares
✓✓✓ Must have
✓✓ Not critical but important

Figure 1 The match of competencies to strategic alternatives guides option selection.

0. Base case
1. Additional space
2. Additional stores
3. Homeware stores
4. Store 30s
5. Freedom classics
6. Expand manufacturing/importing

Essentially Options 1, 2 and 6 are modifications to the existing business, and Options 3, 4 and 5 are new categories/formats.

The impact on shareholder value of these options is summarized on pp. 390–1.

Base case: growth from existing assets

The base case assumes business continues as it, with modest growth

Assumptions

- No new stores
- Growth 5% pa
  - volume 2%
  - price 3%
- Product mix does not change
- Present margins continue
- Capital expenditure for maintenance only (equal to depreciation)

Results

Measure	1997 ($m)	2000 ($m)
Sales	251.4	291.5
NOPAT	9.9	15.0
Funds	57.5	60.5
EVA	3.5	7.9

Option 1: extra space

This option makes use of the extra space at the back of existing stores to generate additional sales

Assumptions

Base case, together with:

- Additional sales area is 230 m^2, a 9% increase
- Additional sales of 6%
- Fitout cost is $220/$m^2$
- Half stores converted in 1998, other half in 1999

Results

Measure	1997 ($m)	2000 ($m)
Sales	251.4	304.8
NOPAT	9.9	16.6
Funds	57.5	62.7
EVA	3.5	9.3

Option 2: additional stores

This option assumes six additional stores are opened.

Assumptions
Base case, together with:

- Six additional stores
  - two company stores (1998, 1999)
  - four franchise stores (1999, 2000)
- Capital expenditure $450k per company store
- Sales per store
  - company: $100k/week first year
  - $120k/week later years
  - franchise: $70/week first year
    $80k/week later years
- Product mix and sourcing unchanged

Results

Measure	1997 ($m)	2000 ($m)
Sales	251.4	325.3
NOPAT	9.9	17.5
Funds	57.5	62.8
EVA	3.5	10.1

Option 3: homeware stores

This option involves 50 new stores selling homewares only. (Homeware stores are specialist stores stocking tableware, kitchenware, glassware, gifts and household line etc.) The planned size was to be 250 m^2.

Assumptions
Base case, together with:

- 50 new homeware stores
  - 5 company stores (1998)
  - 45 franchise stores (5 in 1998, 10 in each of 1999–2002)
- Capital expenditure $202k for each company store (250 m^2)

- Sales $27k per week each store
- Franchise fee 3% plus $50k per store upfront payment
- Sourcing as for present homewares

Results

Measure	1997 ($m)	2000 ($m)
Sales	251.4	337.4
NOPAT	9.9	17.5
Funds	57.5	61.7
EVA	3.5	10.2

Option 4: Store 30s

This option involves 50 new smaller stores with breakeven sales of $30k/week

Assumptions
Base case, together with:

- 50 new smaller stores
  - 5 company stores (1998)
  - 45 franchise stores (5 in 1998, 10 in each of 1999–2002)
- Share area 900 m^2
- Capital expenditure $200k per company store
- Sales $35k/week each store
- Franchise fee 3% of sales
- Product mix and sourcing as for existing stores

Results

Measure	1997 ($m)	2000 ($m)
Sales	251.4	356.7
NOPAT	9.9	18.0
Funds	57.5	63.1
EVA	3.5	10.6

Option 5: Freedom Classics

This option involves 10 new stores selling an upmarket product range.

Assumptions
Base case, together with:

- 10 new stores
  - 2 company stores (1999)
  - 8 franchise stores (2 in 2000, 3 in each of 2001, 2002)

- Capital expenditure of $400k each company store
- Sales $60k/week each store
- Franchise fee 5% sales

Results

Measure	1997 ($m)	2000 ($m)
Sales	251.4	306.6
NOPAT	9.9	16.0
Funds	57.5	62.0
EVA	3.5	9.0

Option 6: increased manufacturing and importing

This option involves increasing the output of FF's manufactured and imported products to provide a greater share of FF's retail requirements

Assumptions
Base case, together with:

- Manufacturing sales to retail increase from present $25m to $80m in 2002 (compared with $33m in base case)
- Importing sales to retail increase from present $32m to $80m in 2002 (compared with $41m in base case)
- Manufacturing requires additional space of 5000m^2 and additional plant – total cost $5m
- Importing requires additional space of 5000m^2 and associated fittings – total cost $2.5m

Results

Measure	1997 ($m)	2000 ($m)
Sales	251.4	291.5
NOPAT	9.9	17.9
Funds	57.5	80.3
EVA	3.5	9.0

Evaluation of options

All options considered are financially desirable and increase shareholder value.

- The base case option creates significant value each year, which results in a shareholder value of $1.81 per share
- Each of the other options creates additional value, with corresponding increases in shareholder value ranging from $0.19 to $0.47

- Subsequent consideration of Option 4 at the Phase 4 workshop led to its elimination on practical grounds
- Each of the other options subject to management resources could be implemented, and their benefits would be additive

Option		EVA 2000 $m	Shareholder value $/share	Increase $/share
0.	Base case	7.9	1.81	
1.	Extra space	9.3	2.00	0.19
2.	Additional stores	10.1	2.11	0.30
3.	Homeware stores	10.2	2.17	0.36
4.	Store 30s	10.6	2.28	0.47
5.	Freedom Classics	9.0	2.03	0.22
6.	Expand mfg/imp	9.0	2.25	0.44

SELECTING FUTURE DIRECTION

Some development was occurring during the strategy process. Freedom was moving on three fronts:

- Optimizing the existing offer through the addition of new products, opening additional stores and working on shortening the production/ logistics activities within the supply chain.
- Opening a range of standalone homeware stores.
- Expanding its manufacturing and importing capabilities

ISSUES FOR DISCUSSION

Given the research date in the appendices which of the options would appear to offer Freedom Furniture an optimal expansion strategy?

Are there alternatives?

Given a strategy how should it be implemented?

APPENDIX 1

OVERVIEW OF RETAIL TRENDS IN AUSTRALIA

The Australian retail sector today

- Increasingly competitive
- Increasing costs
- More demanding consumers
- New local and international entrants
- Emerging new forms of retailing, i.e. Internet
- Profitability and ROI under pressure

Economic realities

- Low inflation
- Economic growth – slow
- High unemployment
- Lack of consumer confidence
- Farm/rural sector not performing

Regulatory changes

- Trading hours
- Employment laws

Emerging consumer and demographic trends – demographic

- Decreasing migration levels
- Slow population growth
- Population mobility
- Increase in 'have's and have nots'
- Reduction in retail share of disposal income
- Increasing number of working women and mothers
- Aging population

Emerging consumer and demographic trends – consumer trends

- Poverty of time
- Convenience
- Increased spending on recreation and lifestyle
- Changing shopping patterns
- Level of consumer sophistication and confidence
- Advertising and marketing will need to change
- Consumers want immediate satisfaction

Emerging consumer and demographic trends – consumer trends

- Environmental and ethical considerations
- Safety and security
- Increase use of service providers
- Increased spending on new activities, i.e. mobile phones, computers, gambling
- Technology is empowering the consumer, and providing options to shopping

Consumers are now demanding.

- Benefit value equation
  - Consumers' benefit value equation has changed
  - Value now means good quality products which can be purchased quickly, at anytime, stress free and at a competitive price

APPENDIX 2

FINDINGS FROM FREEDOM SENIOR MANAGEMENT/CONSULTING WORKSHOP

What business is Freedom Furniture in?

The manufacturing, importing and retailing of a wide choice of stylish, value-oriented furniture and homewares to a broad range of house-proud customers, encompassing first serious home owners/renters, young growing families and empty nesters.

Competitive strengths – consistent views across freedom furniture

- Merchandising
- IT systems
- In-store presentation
- Vertical integration
- FF's people – management and staff
- Culture of continuous improvement

Freedom furniture's weaknesses/impediments to growth – wide range of views

- Product quality
- Deployment of leading edge practices across retail network
- Maintaining product differentiation
- Unprofitable regional stores
- Lack of prioritization of opportunities
- Supplier management
- Forecasting and product planning
- Training
- Combatting price competition
- Product range – homewares
- Role of marketing in FF
- Quality store managers as FF expands
- Complex fashion product database

- Staff turnover
- Poor advertising quality and quantity

Opportunities for Freedom Furniture

	No. of times rated
Homewares stores	7
Other new retail formats (e.g. bedding, galleries, garden/outdoor, superstores	6
International expansion	6
Improve/expand current range	8
Improve/expand vertical integration	3

The vision – Freedom Furniture in the year 2000

- Leading international retailer and manufacturer of lifestyle products
- \$300–\$600m turnover, with excellent financial returns
- Increased reliance on vertical integration
- Expanded retail concepts, e.g. homewares
- Micromarketing in stores with tailored offerings

Key issues for the future:
- Focus and planning
- New CEO
- New product development:
  - innovative ideas
  - lead times
  - buyer accountability and measurement
  - product selection and planning
  - reliable supplier/manufacturing base to support expansion
- Improved market and customer understanding
- Improved internal communication
- Improved quality control
- Faster IT development and improved input by line management
- Improved regional franchisee performance
- Improved inventory planning and forecasting systems

Freedom Furniture's present position and prospects

Overview

Freedom Furniture – a great success story... but are we staying '6 inches ahead of the duck?'... nevertheless we have a firm base from which to build... but what should be our priorities?

Freedom Furniture – a great success story
- Significant growth in share price since listing
- Creation of shareholder value
- Profit growth
- Market share growth
- Unique value proposition
- Culture of continuous improvement

Culture of continuous improvement
- 'Can do' attitude
- Passion for company
- Youthful employees
- Progressive
- Executive team lead by example
- Continual cost reduction focus
- Supply chain improvement
- Sales and profit driven

Have we grown beyond our original value proposition?
- Areas where we may not be consistently providing and communicating desired value:
  - planning and follow-through
  - product innovation
  - micromarketing the range
  - catalogues and advertising
  - store locations
  - price
  - finance
  - product quality
  - in-store maintenance

Variable customer service
- Product quality problems and market perceptions
- Product availability issues:
  - lead times not meeting customer requirements
  - unsuccessful deliveries
  - unsophisticated forecasting and replenishment systems

Nevertheless we have a firm base from which to build.
- Presentation excellence
- Combination of co-ordinated style, choice and value positioning
- Inherent ability to commercialize emerging trends
- Integrated computer systems
- Integrated supply chain
- Continuous improvement culture
- High brand awareness and differentiation

Strategic options and priorities

But what should be our priorities?
- More of the same
- Optimizing existing business
- 6 more destination stores
- Establishing Homeware Stores
- Establishing Store 30s
- Expanding Freedom Furniture's manufacturing base
- Establishing other retail formats (specific options to be agreed)
- International expansion

Other new retail format options that may be considered
- Gardens/outdooor furniture stores
- Decorator stores
- Galleria stores
- Bed and bath stores
- Kitchen stores
- Superstores
- Other

APPENDIX 3

FREEDOM FURNITURE MAJOR COMPETITORS

David Jones Pty Ltd

David Jones has 26 full line department stores across all states of Australia. It positions itself at the premium end of the market. The positioning has altered over the years with consumers reacting to these changes negatively. Marketing of late has focused on positioning the brand more appropriately and frequency has been high. David Jones is in the middle of a turnaround strategy with more emphasis on quality and style.

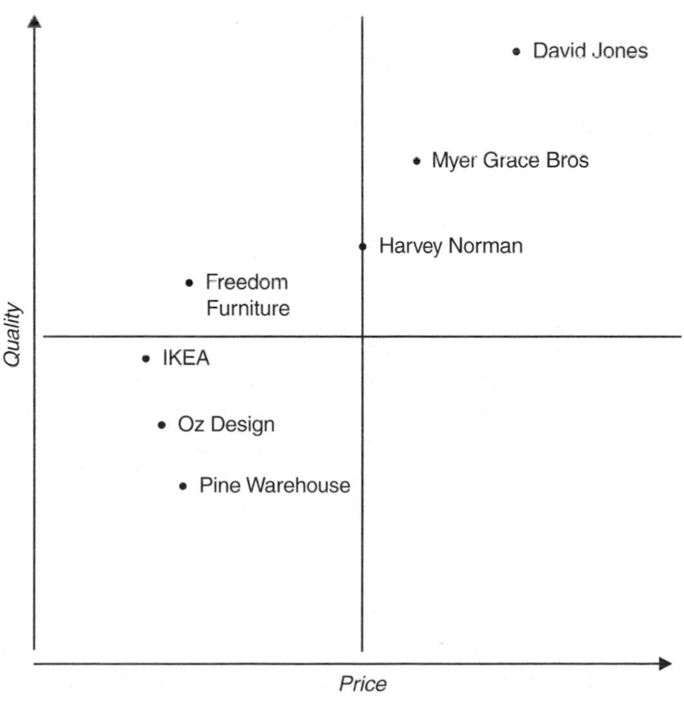

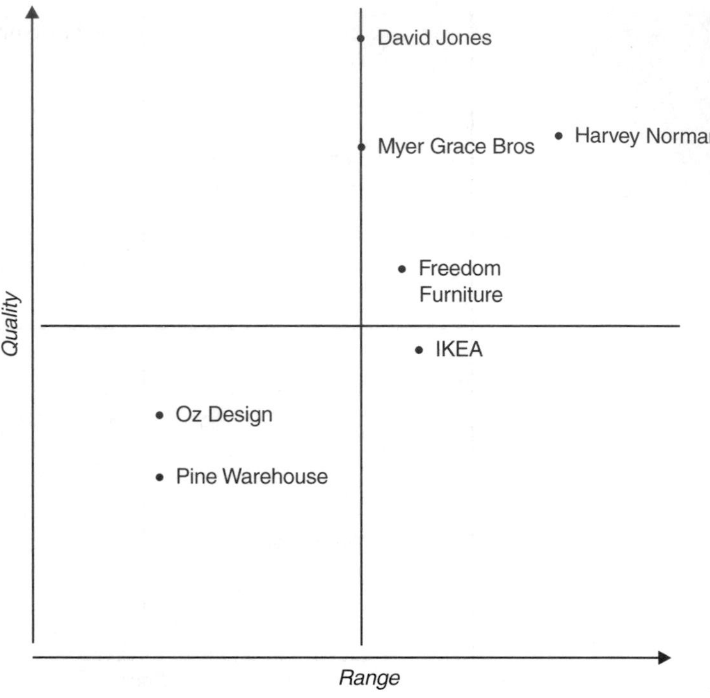

Myer Grace Bros Pty Ltd

A subsidiary of the largest retailer publicly listed Coles Myer, with a head office located in Melbourne, Victoria. Is over 80 years old with 69 stores nationally. It is a full line department store with a selection of stores not carrying furniture. Myer Grace positions itself in the middle to upper quartile. Little advertising has occurred recently except to promote sale time. The range has recently moved to a more modern style.

Harvey Norman Pty Ltd

The fastest growing retailer in Australia, Harvey Norman has stores in all states of Australia selling homemaker products (white and brown goods, furniture and computers). The major growth has come from computers; however, furniture turnover is important to the group. The company franchises departments within a store. As a result salesmanship is excellent. They have a traditional product range of furniture. Advertising is very heavy and as a result Harvey Norman has the largest share of the furniture market.

OZ Design Pty Ltd

Twenty-two franchised stores located on the eastern seaboard. The range of furniture and homewares has a modern style.

APPENDIX 3

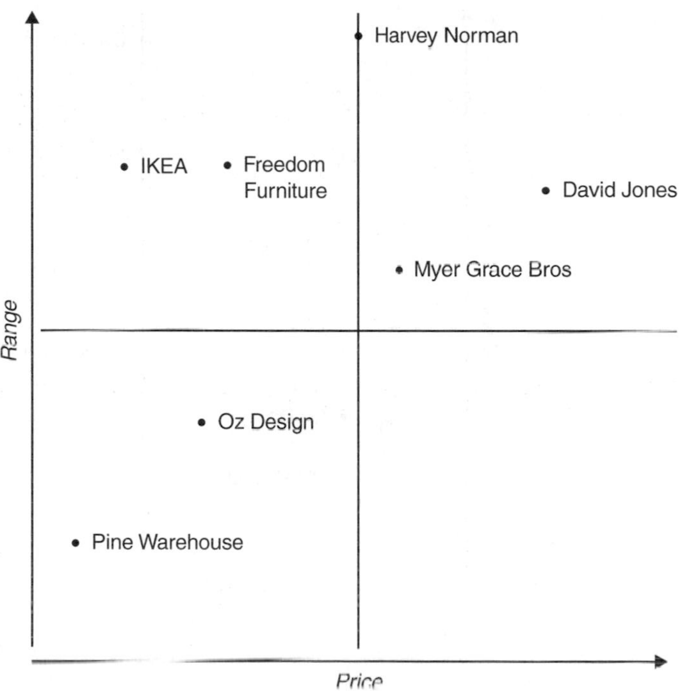

IKEA Pty Ltd

IKEA open their first store in 1975 in Australia. At present they have 10 stores across Australia. IKEA offers a wide range of furniture and home furnishings. IKEA offers furniture in pre-packed boxes for consumer assembly. All marketing is based on the IKEA business idea: 'We shall offer a wide range of home furnishings items of good design and function, at prices so low, that the majority of people can afford to buy them'. There are about 12,000 products in the total IKEA product range. Each store carries a selection of these 12,000 products.

FREEDOM FURNITURE: MERCHANDISE RANGE REVIEW AND DECISIONS

MERCHANDISE STRATEGY AND IMPLEMENTATION AT FREEDOM FURNITURE

Introduction

The merchandise offer is a principal component of a retail positioning statement. It represents an interpretation of customer expectations as well as expressing the creative personality of the organization Freedom Furniture considers it has developed a *culture* within which merchandise decisions may be made effective. The Freedom culture is one in which innovation and creativity are encouraged, decisions can be made rapidly, in which 'science' has limited influence and one which operates well within a loose structure.

The range of merchandise comprises some 13,000 SKUs, of which 40% changes each year. The range covers three merchandise areas. A *basics* component is a functional range of cookware, linen, tableware and glass. It is priced competitively and comprises 25% of the range. The *smart casual* component reflects the lifestyle theme that Freedom uses as its positioning platform: some 50% of the range is covered by this category. *Seasonal themes* are the remaining 25% of the range and it is here where much of the 40% of merchandise change occurs.

Merchandise reviews take place twice yearly for the winter and summer 'catalogues', the central communication media for customers, franchise operators and the company itself.

Merchandise organization

The merchandise director has three accountable activities. The *buyers* are essentially product managers. Their tasks are essentially creative, they work within the structure of an agreed theme (which reflects the Freedom positioning strategy); they manage sourcing and suppliers. Their responsibilities include sales, supplier support and gross margins (and therefore pricing). Their performance is reflected by customer response (i.e. purchases at planned prices and margin yield) and supplier performance (i.e. lead times, availability and delivery reliability). Buyers are essentially working in qualitative aspects of the business concerned with design and coordinating the

implementation of design decisions. *Planners* are quantitative managers. They are responsible for forecasting, stock replenishment and the 'logistics'. Their task is to ensure an in-stock position at all times. *Visual merchandisers* have the responsibility for designing the coordinated interpretation of Freedom's positioning strategy by using the merchandise and the sales area space to create persuasive and informative displays. This is an important role because the visual merchandising role also influences the twice yearly catalogue. Furthermore the task is complicated by the need to design displays that take account of a range of store size *and* displays that franchisees will accept and implement.

Merchandise planning: departmental reviews

An important part of merchandise planning is the monitoring of the range. Reviews take place as nearest possible to the next buying period. The spring/summer review commences as the previous season ends. A number of stages are involved.

A *departmental sales analysis* examines the overall performance of the department compared with total sales achievement; both volume change and share of the total sales are examined. Discussions are held with manufacturers and suppliers to obtain market performance characteristics. If increases have occurred and Freedom has not experienced similar growth patterns, a detailed analysis follows. This occurred in office products, a small but significant product group for Freedom, in 1997/98. The review undertook an examination of causes and changes that should be made to rectify the situation.

Classes within the department are examined closely. In the office products group it was found that bookcases (responsible for a third of department sales) had decreased by some 15%. The decline was noticeable in all but one model/style. Reasons for the decline are thought to be due to a less than competitive offer or a lack of alignment with the rest of the range.

Desks and returns sales increased by over 9% (these represent 51% of sales), and the increase is attributed to increases in functional office products such as computer workstations.

Office chair sales increased by almost 20%, reflecting the changes that were released in August 1997. The class has a balanced selection of price points and options. Office storage had increased by 18%, accounting for almost 6% of total business.

Price groups within the department: in this product category Freedom operates three price groups. The *entry* group accounts for 28% of sales, the *mid level* accounts for 49% and the *upper* price group accounts for 23% of sales.

Sales performance by product (within each price group) is examined and reasons for increases/decreases are determined. Typically the reasons for changes occurring are internal. For example, a complementary product (e.g. a desk) may have been discontinued, or often new products have been introduced and compete for sales. Other reasons include additional fabric colours

and choices (or their reduction) and the level of promotional spend. Often poor sales may reflect that a design is 'tired' and that a replacement should be required; that the product does not 'fit' within the specific range; or that a recent price increase has not proved to be successful.

A *product assortment review* follows. An overview of the current range is undertaken. This component of the review seeks to identify reasons for success (or the lack of it). Essentially it is looking for evidence of balance in terms of alignment and the strength of a 'merchandise story'. Freedom considers this an important issue. A range lacking coherence can result in both customer and sales staff confusion and does not take advantage of the 'easy selling concept' that is an integral part of Freedom. Examples of the lack of alignment and strength of offer include a lack of logical 'step up' within a range; offers that are incomplete (planned 'links' between product classes, e.g. within office products, between shelving and desks, and between desks and chairs, can result in increases in sales for both classes); specific products may not be offered (e.g. corner desking is a growing subclass for students and small-spaced environments); or specific emerging designs may not be offered.

Proposed assortment changes follow. Given the outcome of the overview, specific actions result. Typically a rework of the current ranges into a more consistent and aligned offer is seen as an opportunity for increasing sales and, at the same time, creating a strong merchandisable offer that is easy to understand and to sell. A balanced offer includes the following elements:

- Clearly defined range offers that incorporate different product requirements.
- An appropriate choice of sizes and functions within each range offer.
- Products that are functionally linked to price level and theme.

Decisions are taken to rework the range such that these criteria are met. Examples include merging individual products into a focused range at a specific price point; quality improvements; the revision of colour offer and the colour becoming a range; the addition of functional features to a product to meet increasing customer demands (or to match competitive moves); the provision of 'linkages' between product groups; a reduction of slow-selling item prices to reduce stockholding; and restructuring existing product items into a new range.

From both review activities a *proposed assortment plan* emerges. This plan itemizes changes recommended by price point group (i.e. entry, mid-level and upper).

Merchandising is an important element of the Departmental Review. Merchandising decisions are based upon a view concerning the impact the product group needs to make if sales targets are to be realized. Freedom uses a concept of modules, or room settings, and decides upon the number of modules necessary to meet objectives for each range within the product group. Allowances are made for the variation in store sizes.

Marketing and point of sales considerations follow, and specific purchasing considerations are taken into account. For example, functions and sizes are important considerations in the purchase of office products and these features are used in displays and brochure design. For these specific product groups a decision to simplify and reduce the cost of brochures by using line drawings is being developed.

Action plans follow. These detail responsibility, timing and specific actions to be undertaken for each change to be made. In addition to the detail of the required changes five other activities are included. These are: competitor analysis (product ranges and prices), merchandising SWOT analysis, an SKU review (numbers and sales activities) and the development of a promotional plan.

IMPLEMENTING MERCHANDISE DECISIONS

Another important task for the merchandise activity at Freedom Furniture is the *development* of the twice-yearly catalogue. The catalogue objectives and content are communicated to managers for its implementation in an *information pack* for each product group (e.g. office products). There are two sections, one for the marketing team and another for the merchandise team.

The *marketing team section* details actions required by them under specific activity headings. *Timing* details the actions to be taken to launch the catalogue in terms of where, when and how the launch will proceed. For example, the March 1999 catalogue was launched in-store, a TV commercial supported the launch, and POS material was designed to reinforce the launch. The *format* of the catalogue (page numbers, page sizes, etc.) and details of content are described. For a retailer dependent on style and design *theming* detail is essential. The marketing team receives details on coverage (categories included), emphasis (such as core ranges and colour) and the catalogue's direction. The March 1999 catalogue contained a strong emphasis on value, price, quality and decorator services, as well as identifying the four main lifestyle categories reflecting emerging trends and existing popular styles.

The *merchandise team section* contains detailed content on rationale. *Product selection* identifies the style themes and their origin and interpretation. The March 1999 catalogue introduced three new style themes (East West, Casbah Bazaar, Traditional Romantic) together with the smart casual theme used by Freedom in its positioning stance. For each theme an outline of the basis of the offer is given together with the interpretation of the themes in homewares (a specialist offer being expanded) and for store presentation.

For each product group an 'update' details changes made for the forthcoming catalogue. Updates provide a summary of the findings of the *range review*:

- The contribution by the product group to the overall business and the views of suppliers.
- Problems of balance and alignment and story strength within the range.
- Proposed changes to the range to make a more consistent and aligned offer. Typically these would include changes that would include the following key elements:
  - clearly defined range offers that incorporate different product requirements
  - an appropriate choice of sizes and functions within each range offer
  - products that are functionally linked to price level and theme
- The assortment plan and product development requirements to provide the missing links in the range at each price level.
- A merchandising plan for small, medium and large stores by product/style group. For each style, the number of modules together with the products (including colours and sizes) are given. Recommended floor stocks are also given.

A *summary of important dates* is the first component in the information pack. This details actions (and their completion dates) required for successful implementation of tasks required prior to the launch of the catalogue.

FREEDOM FURNITURE: CUSTOMER SERVICE DECISIONS

CUSTOMER SERVICE RESEARCH AT FREEDOM FURNITURE

INTRODUCTION

The benefits that a customer derives from a product can be in the form of economic benefits, perceptions of product performance, brand reputation or service quality. Service quality has both qualitative and quantitative aspects. Qualitative aspects of service relate to perceptions of customer care and concern when customer enquiries and problems arise. Quantitative aspects of service are reflections of levels of satisfaction of service delivery. An important service feature of concern to furniture retailers is the delivery of an order in full and on time. Service failures on these characteristics are major problems for furniture retailers internationally.

Freedom Furniture has always been conscious of the need to perform well on these service criteria; consequently, customer perceptions of the Freedom Furniture service offer are sought on an ongoing basis.

The company undertakes customer service research through a specialist consultancy. The approach used, which is similar to the concept of customer service discussed earlier (see Chapters 9 and 10) is based on *quality* (success in the market-place) which is the result of *performance* (the perceptions of customers of the performance delivered) less *expectations* (the customers' perceptions of actual customer service delivered). The study used by Freedom Furniture (as implemented by the consultants) produces a service quality index based upon the computations of quality, which is weighted to reflect the importance of the service factors used in the customer service research (see Figure 1).

Research process

The objectives agreed for the research are:

- To identify customer needs
- To measure customer expectations
- To measure performance

	Factor weight	Customer expectations of an attribute	Mean score of customers' perceptions of performance	Gap: mathematical gap between performance and expectations
Factors and attributes ↓				

Figure 1 The research structure.

- To benchmark performance against customer expectations
- To benchmark competitors' performance against customer expectations

The process used is to identify customer service factors, together with their importance, from preliminary work with focus groups structured to represent Freedom's customer base. The research identifies two aspects of service. *Content quality* is concerned with visible, tangible features, while *process quality* is far less visible; it is intangible and 'soft' in nature, but is nevertheless very important in contributing to the value proposition.

Content quality

- Product expectations
- 'Making it easy' (staff, store, catalogue and product availability)
- Store layout
- Purchase decision

Process quality

- After-sale follow-up
- Delivery
- Caring attitude
- Store activities
- Time sensitivity

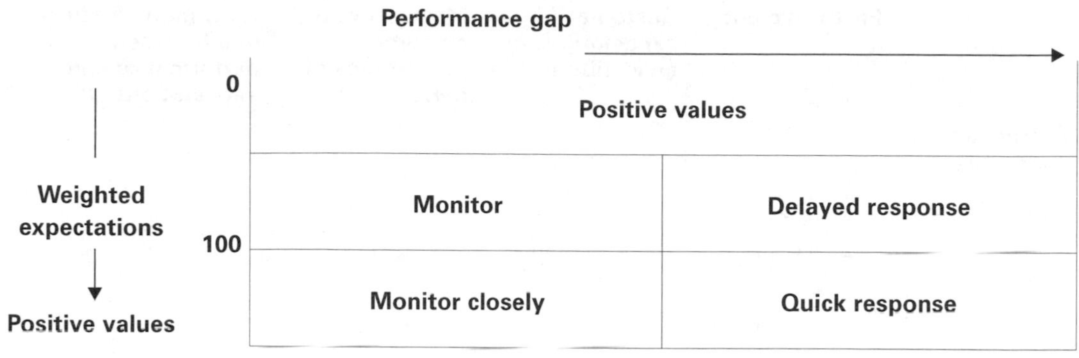

Figure 2 Customer service priorities matrix.

The research outcome is displayed using two forms of presentation. An index is calculated which shows factors (and detailed factor attributes), the importance (i.e. factor weights) and the performance scores (the gap between expectations and actual performance). The other display is a matrix presentation which prioritizes responses by comparing the performance scores against the attribute weights. The result is four categories of *priority issues* (see Figure 2).

Quick response: the issues requiring immediate attention as they have the largest negative performance gaps and largest factor weights – *your weaknesses*.

Delayed response: these are issues with large negative performance gaps but are *not* listed as particularly important by customers – *annoyances*.

Monitor closely: these are issues whose factor weights are large but which have received negative performance ratings but are not excessive – *nice to have*.

Monitor: low factor weight issues with negative performance ratings; they may have significance if not reviewed occasionally – *your strengths*.

Survey sample

A sample of 965 was selected. The sample structure was:

Demographics

- Male 31%
- Female 69%

- 18–24 yrs 13%
- 25–34 yrs 34%
- 34–44 yrs 30%

- 45–54 yrs 14%
- 55 yrs 8%

- married 66%
- separated 3%
- divorced 3%
- widowed 2%
- de facto 7%
- never married 18%

- with children 50%
- no children 50%

- Freedom customers 98%
- Competitors' customers 2%

SURVEY VALIDITY 97%

Competitors	**Number of customers**
A Mart	11
David Jones	48
Fantastic Furniture	7
Grace Bros	47
Harvey Norman	62
IKEA	33
Myer	37
Oz Design	6
Target	6
K-Mart	5
Town & Country	7

Customer characteristics

Recency of purchase	**Per cent**
4–12 months	33
1–3 months	35
Last month	32
	100

Amount spent	**Per cent**
$1000+	75
$500–$999	14
$100–$499	9
Under $100	2
	100

Amount spent at last visit by main store	Per cent
$1000+	46
$500–$999	21
$250–$499	14
$100–$249	9
Under $100	10
	100

THE SURVEY RESULTS

Key findings

Overall Freedom satisfaction	Per cent
Very satisfied	41
Quite satisfied	48
Quite dissatisfied	8
Very dissatisfied	3
No comment	0

Customers want

- Value for money products
  - undamaged goods on delivery
  - guarantees
  - easy exchange
  - good instructions
  - fair delivery charges
- Stores to 'make it easy' for them
  - knowledgeable staff
  - good labelling
  - neat and clean surrounds
  - catalogue items available as promised

Good after-sale follow-up

  - no 'run around'
  - proactive communication if problem(s) arise
  - willingness to help them
  - returns to their calls
- Reasonable delivery arrangements
  - arranged time

  - realistic date set
  - flexibility
- Caring, empathetic staff
- Challenges facing the industry and Freedom are similar
- David Jones and Myers provide industry role models
- 'Best in class' competitor varies by attribute

Content quality issues

- Availability of product is a big issue to customers
- Product-related issues provide the greatest leverage
- Issues perceived to be important by Freedom have less impact on customer satisfaction than anticipated

Process quality issues

- Improvement in after-sales service will have the largest process quality impact on customer satisfaction
- Addressing 'soft' issues soon will achieve a 'profitable' result rapidly
- Industry outperforms Freedom on most attributes

Market perceived quality profiles

FREEDOM – CONTENT QUALITY

Factors	**Importance weights**	**Performance**	**Total competitor performance**	**Scores ratio**	**Weight times ratio**	**Performance indicator**
Product expectations	39	79.2	83.6	0.95	36.95	–2.05
Making it easy	28	78.9	77.8	1.01	28.39	0.30
Store layout	18	57.7	49.0	1.18	21.20	3.20
Purchase decision	15	57.7	56.4	1.02	15.35	0.35
Customer satisfaction index	100	72	71.6		101.89	1.89

FREEDOM – PROCESS QUALITY

Factors	Importance weights	Performance	Total competitor performance	Scores ratio	Weight times ratio	Performance indicator
After-sale follow-up	30	72.7	79.0	0.92	27.61	–2.39
Delivery	22	76.3	81.9	0.93	20.50	–1.5
Caring attitude	21	68.8	72.5	0.95	19.94	–1.06
Store	14	70.7	67.6	1.04	14.62	0.62
Time-sensitive	13	68.8	78.3	0.88	11.43	–1.57
Customer satisfaction index	100	71.9	76.6		94.11	–5.89

Detailed findings

Given the key findings management now needed to explore their implications by reviewing the specific issues. This was conducted by first of all obtaining a perspective of industry performance and comparing this, by attribute, for Freedom's operations and those of their major competitors. From this analysis the company considered specific Freedom performance features and from these developed customer service *matrices* for both *content* and *process* qualities. These data are presented below.

Content quality

Table 1: Priority attributes:	*content* quality critical issues
Table 2: Priority attributes:	*content* quality best and worse in class
Table 3: Content quality index:	Freedom Furniture and homeware buyer – total performance
Table 4: Content quality index matrix:	Freedom Furniture and homeware buyers

Process quality

Table 5: Priority attributes:	*process* quality critical issues
Table 6: Priority attributes:	*process* quality best and worse in class
Table 7: Process quality index:	Freedom Furniture and homeware buyers – total performance
Table 8: Process quality index matrix:	Freedom Furniture and homeware buyers

Given the results of the research some questions arise:

- What are the major competitive issues for customer service?
- Should Freedom Furniture develop specific aspects of service, if so which?
- How should the company monitor customer service in order to obtain constant feedback?

Table 1 Priority attributes: content quality critical issues.

Performance gaps

Order No.	Att. No.	Attribute	Industry expectation	Industry performance	Freedom (NSW & QLD)	NSW	QLD
1	33	Item(s) are delivered complete and undamaged	97.7	–13.2	–14.7	–14.9	–14.2
2	44	Provides guarantees on furniture	94.3	–10.6	–12.6	–12.6	12.7
3	31	Allows easy exchange/return of faulty goods	93.8	–13.4	**–16.0**	**–18.1**	–10.9
4	34	Offers you the best value for money	92.6	–12.3	–13.2	–12.8	–14.0
5	38	Self-assembly products come with clear instructions	92.4	–12.3	–12.6	–13.4	–10.6
6	18	Delivery charges are reasonable	87.2	–11.9	–14.0	–14.4	–13.2
7	4	Has knowledgeable staff	88.2	–9.3	–9.4	–10.8	–6.3
8	21	Products are adequately labelled with important information	87.6	–8.5	–8.2	–9.3	–5.7
9	37	The store is always neat and clean	86.1	3.6	4.4	3.8	5.6
10	29	Items in the catalogue are available when you go to the store	85.1	–25.3	**–20.6**	**–30.0**	**–27.1**
11	3	Provides a comprehensive and attractive brochure to preview its products	73.8	10.6	16.5	16.6	10.7

Order No.	Att. No.	Attribute	Franchisees	Company-managed stores	David Jones	Grace Bros	Harvey Norman	IKEA
1	33	Item(s) are delivered complete and undamaged	–11.6	–14.3	–6.1	–9.1	–14.6	–11.2
2	44	Provides guarantees on furniture	–11.2	–10.6	0.5	–6.9	–8.3	**–21.9**
3	31	Allows easy exchange/return of faulty goods	–12.9	–14.0	–2.1	–8.0	**–18.9**	–10.7
4	34	Offers you the best value for money	–11.8	–12.6	–8.1	–14.3	–13.0	–14.8
5	38	Self-assembly products come with clear instructions	–10.5	–13.5	–7.7	–10.7	–13.1	–13.6
6	18	Delivery charges are reasonable	–10.8	–12.8	–4.8	–8.5	–10.5	**–17.1**
7	4	Has knowledgeable staff	–6.8	–10.5	–5.4	**–16.8**	–6.1	**–16.3**
8	21	Products are adequately labelled with important information	–7.6	–9.2	–4.3	–12.4	–7.2	–12.5
9	37	The store is always neat and clean	4.7	2.9	3.2	2.5	–1.2	2.1
10	29	Items in the catalogue are available when you go to the store	**–22.3**	**–27.3**	–11.1	**–15.9**	**–20.8**	**–25.0**
11	3	Provides a comprehensive and attractive brochure to preview its products	13.0	9.3	–1.6	–1.2	3.3	18.2

Table 2 Priority attributes:content quality best and worse in class.

Performance gaps

Order No.	Att. No.	Attribute	Industry expectation	Industry performance	Freedom (NSW & QLD)	NSW	QLD
1	33	Item(s) are delivered complete and undamaged	97.7	–13.2	–14.7	–14.9	–14.2
2	44	Provides guarantees on furniture	94.3	–10.6	–12.6	–12.6	–12.7
3	31	Allows easy exchange/return of faulty goods	93.8	–13.4	–16.0	–18.1	–10.9
4	34	Offers you the best value for money	92.6	–12.3	–13.2	–12.8	–14.0
5	38	Self-assembly products come with clear instructions	92.4	–12.3	–12.6	–13.4	–10.6
6	18	Delivery charges are reasonable	87.2	–11.9	–14.0	–14.4	–13.2
7	4	Has knowledgeable staff	88.2	–9.3	–9.4	–10.8	–6.3
8	21	Products are adequately labelled with important information	87.6	–8.5	–8.2	–9.3	–5.7
9	37	The store is always neat and clean	86.1	–3.6	4.4	3.8	5.6
10	29	Items in the catalogue are available when you go to the store	85.1	–25.3	–29.5	–30.6	–27.1
11	3	Provides a comprehensive and attractive brochure to preview its products	73.8	10.6	16.5	15.6	**18.7**

Order No.	Att. No.	Attribute	Franchisees	Company-managed stores	David Jones	Grace Bros	Harvey Norman	IKEA
1	33	Item(s) are delivered complete and undamaged	–11.6	–14.3	–6.1	–9.1	–14.6	–11.2
2	44	Provides guarantees on furniture	–11.2	–10.6	**0.5**	–6.9	–8.3	**–21.9**
3	31	Allows easy exchange/return of faulty goods	–12.9	–14.0	–2.1	–8.0	–18.9	–10.7
4	34	Offers you the best value for money	–11.8	–12.6	–8.1	–14.3	–13.0	–14.8
5	38	Self-assembly products come with clear instructions	–10.5	–13.5	–7.7	–10.7	–13.1	–13.6
6	18	Delivery charges are reasonable	–10.8	–12.8	–4.8	–8.5	–10.5	–17.1
7	4	Has knowledgeable staff	–6.8	–10.5	–5.4	–16.8	–6.1	–16.3
8	21	Products are adequately labelled with important information	–7.6	–9.2	–4.3	–12.4	–7.2	–12.5
9	37	The store is always neat and clean	4.7	2.9	3.2	2.5	–1.2	2.1
10	29	Items in the catalogue are available when you go to the store	–22.3	–27.3	–11.1	–15.9	–20.8	–25.0
11	3	Provides a comprehensive and attractive brochure to preview its products	13.0	9.3	–1.6	–1.2	3.3	18.2

Table 3 Content quality index: Freedom Furniture and homeware buyers – total performance.

Furniture/homeware buyers		Factor weight (%)	Total EXP	*N*	Total performance PERF	*N*	GAP
Content quality index			**77.16**		**71.88**		**–5.28**
1	**Product expectations**	**39**	**92.99**		**80.72**		**–12.28**
2	**Making it easy**	**28**	**84.15**		**78.37**		**–5.78**
3	**Store layout**	**18**	**52.30**		**54.71**		**2.41**
4	**Purchase decision**	**15**	**54.54**		**57.26**		**4.72**
1	**Product expectations**	**39**	**92.99**		**80.72**		**–12.28**
33	Item(s) are delivered complete and undamaged	39	97.68	964	84.53	876	–13.16
44	Provides guarantees on furniture	39	94.33	962	83.69	803	–10.64
31	Allows easy exchange/return of faulty goods	39	93.79	964	80.43	707	–13.35
34	Offers you the best value for money	39	92.57	965	80.32	950	–12.26
38	Self-assembly products come with clear instructions	39	92.40	960	80.07	766	–12.33
18	Delivery charges are reasonable	39	87.20	959	75.28	840	–11.92
2	**Making it easy**	**28**	**84.15**		**78.37**		**–5.78**
4	Has knowledgeable staff	28	88.22	965	78.88	954	–9.34
21	Products are adequately labelled with important information	28	87.55	965	79.09	930	–8.46
37	The store is always neat and clean	28	86.12	964	89.72	961	3.60
29	Items in the catalogue are available when you go to the store	28	85.07	961			
3	Provides a comprehensive and attractive brochure to preview its products	28	73.78	965			
3	**Store layout**	**18**	**52.30**		**54.71**		**2.41**
42	The store layout is convenient for prams/strollers	18	62.04	936	69.99	826	7.84
5	Has a child play room which is enjoyable and safe	18	49.88	936	54.61	683	4.73
12	Has a babies change room/parents room	18	44.99	922	39.05	498	–5.34
4	**Purchase decision**	**15**	**52.54**		**57.26**		**4.72**
32	No deposit and delayed payment terms is a way to buy new furniture	15	57.58	954	63.60	656	6.02
30	In store credit card offers better purchasing	15	56.01	939	65.53	618	9.53
26	Allows you to order directly from the catalogue on a 008 number	15	52.54	950	55.39	539	2.85
24	Has a café to give you time to relax/consider your purchase	15	44.04	959	44.53	805	0.49

Table 4 Content quality index matrix: Freedom Furniture and homeware buyers.

		QUICK RESPONSE			MONITOR
10	29	Items in the catalogue are available when you go to the store	12	42	The store layout is convenient for prams/strollers
		DELAYED RESPONSE	13	32	No deposit and delayed payment terms is a way to buy new furniture
		MONITOR CLOSELY	14	30	In store credit card offers better purchasing options
1	33	Item(s) are delivered complete and undamaged	15	5	Has a child play room which is enjoyable and safe
2	44	Provides guarantees on furniture	16	26	Allows you to order directly from the catalogue on a 008 number
3	31	Allows easy exchange/return of faulty goods	14	12	Has a babies change room/parents room
4	34	Offers you the best value for money	18	24	Has a café to give you time to relax/consider your purchase
5	38	Self-assembly products come with clear instructions			
6	18	Delivery charges are reasonable			
7	4	Has knowledgeable staff			
8	21	Products are adequately labelled with important information			
9	37	The store is always neat and clean			
11	3	Provides a comprehensive and attractive brochure to preview its products			

Table 5 Priority attributes: process quality critical issues.

Performance gaps

Order No.	Att. No.	Attribute	Industry expectation	Industry performance	Freedom (NSW & QLD)	NSW	QLD
1	7	Gives you what you expected	94.3	–10.2	–11.0	–11.2	–10.4
2	17	You don't get the 'run around' trying to sort out problems	92.3	–17.1	**–19.9**	**–20.3**	**–18.9**
3	1	Rings you to advise your furniture order will not arrive on time	92.3	–22.7	**–26.9**	**–25.9**	**–29.1**
4	6	Is willing to help solve any problem you may have, once you have purchased furniture/homewares from them	91.0	–15.5	**–17.2**	**–18.5**	–14.1
5	19	Rings you to advise when your furniture order will	90.9	–14.9	**–17.3**	**–16.4**	**–19.4**
6	20	Returns your calls promptly	90.8	–17.4	**–19.6**	**–20.0**	**–18.8**
7	14	Coordinates delivery with you	89.4	–11.1	–13.3	–14.7	10.0
8	28	Staff are around when you need them	[illegible]	–14.8	**–15.2**	–14.2	**–17.5**
9	23	The after-sale process was well managed	85.3	–14.8	**–17.7**	**–17.7**	**–17.7**
10	22	Deliverers arrive at the arranged time	92.9	–15.1	**16.6**	**–18.2**	–12.8
11	36	Gives you a realistic and acceptable date once you have bought an item	90.6	–15.1	**–18.4**	**–17.7**	**–19.9**
12	43	Delivery times are flexible, to suit your availability	80.2	–14.3	**–15.7**	**–18.0**	–10.2
13	41	Deliverers place your furniture where you ask	84.5	0.0	–1.1	–2.0	1.2
14	39	Sales staff understand your needs	83.9	–7.0	–8.5	–9.5	–6.3
15	15	Staff give you their total attention	83.6	–9.5	–10.7	–11.4	–9.0
16	13	Sales staff are genuine and caring about your needs	80.4	–9.2	–10.9	–12.2	–7.9

(Continues...)

Table 5 *(continued)*

Order No.	Att. No.	Attribute	Franchisees	Company-managed stores	David Jones	Grace Bros	Harvey Norman	IKEA
1	7	Gives you what you expected	–9.2	–10.9	–6.8	–13.7	–10.6	–11.8
2	17	You don't get the 'run around' trying to sort out problems	–13.2	**–19.7**	–8.8	**–19.5**	**–16.1**	**–17.2**
3	1	Rings you to advise your furniture order will not arrive on time	–20.0	**–24.3**	–8.6	**–18.9**	**–19.5**	**–17.1**
4	6	Is willing to help solve any problem you may have, once you have purchased furniture/homewares from them	–12.8	**–17.0**	–8.7	**–20.1**	**–17.7**	**–17.1**
5	19	Rings you to advise when your furniture order will	–11.5	**–17.0**	–6.1	**–15.0**	**–15.7**	**–15.1**
6	20	Returns your calls promptly	–13.6	**–19.9**	–10.7	**–20.8**	**–18.8**	**–20.3**
7	14	Coordinates delivery with you	–9.4	–12.5	–2.0	–8.4	–11.6	–14.4
8	28	Staff are around when you need them	–11.2	**–16.9**	–14.2	**–23.8**	**–16.8**	**–18.5**
9	23	The after-sale process was well managed	–13.5	**–15.9**	–3.8	**–17.0**	–12.4	–14.1
10	22	Deliverers arrive at the arranged time	–14.6	**–15.5**	–6.0	**–19.6**	–13.4	–11.6
11	36	Gives you a realistic and acceptable date once you have bought an item	–13.5	**–16.4**	–1.6–1.18	–12.7	–14.2	–12.2
12	43	Delivery times are flexible, to suit your availability	–12.7	**–15.4**	–6.6	–11.7	**–18.4**	–7.9
13	41	Deliverers place your furniture where you ask	–0.1	0.1	7.3	0.1	–2.7	0.1
14	39	Sales staff understand your needs	–5.7	–7.8	–7.0	–6.8	–4.5	–9.1
15	15	Staff give you their total attention	–6.4	–11.4	–8.2	–13.4	–9.6	**–17.3**
16	13	Sales staff are genuine and caring about your needs	–6.8	–10.5	–1.9	–8.9	–8.6	–14.4

Table 6 Priority attributes: process best and worse in class.

Performance gaps

Order No.	Att. No.	Attribute	Industry expectation	Industry performance	Freedom (NSW & QLD)	NSW	QLD
1	7	Gives you what you expected	94.3	−10.2	−11.0	−11.2	−10.4
2	17	You don't get the 'run around' trying to sort out problems	92.3	−17.1	−19.9	−20.3	−18.9
3	1	Rings you to advise your furniture order will not arrive on time	92.3	−22.7	−26.9	−25.9	**−29.1**
4	6	Is willing to help solve any problem you may have, once you have purchased furniture/homewares from them	91.0	−15.5	−17.2	−18.5	−14.1
5	19	Rings you to advise when your furniture order will	90.9	−14.9	−17.3	−16.4	−19.4
6	20	Returns your calls promptly	90.8	−17.4	−19.6	−20.0	−18.8
7	14	Coordinates delivery with you	89.4	−11.1	−13.3	−14.7	−10.0
8	28	Staff are around when you need them	86.2	−14.8	−15.2	−14.2	−17.5
9	23	The after-sale process was well managed	[illegible]	14.0	17.7	−17.7	−17.7
10	22	Deliverers arrive at the arranged time	92.9	−15.1	−16.6	−18.2	−12.8
11	36	Gives you a realistic and acceptable date once you have bought an item	90.5	−15.1	−18.4	−17.7	10.9
12	43	Delivery times are flexible, to suit your availability	89.2	−14.3	−15.7	−18.0	10.2
13	41	Deliverers place your furniture where you ask	84.5	0.0	−1.1	−2.0	1.2
14	39	Sales staff understand your needs	83.9	−7.0	−8.5	−9.5	−6.3
15	15	Staff give you their total attention	83.6	−9.5	−10.7	−11.4	−9.0
16	13	Sales staff are genuine and caring about your needs	80.4	−9.2	−10.9	−12.2	−7.9

(Continues...)

Table 6 *(continued)*

Order No.	Att. No.	Attribute	Franchisees	Company-managed stores	David Jones	Grace Bros	Harvey Norman	IKEA
1	7	Gives you what you expected	–9.2	–10.9	–6.8	–13.7	–10.6	–11.8
2	17	You don't get the 'run around' trying to sort out problems	–13.2	–19.7	–8.8	–19.5	–16.1	–17.2
3	1	Rings you to advise your furniture order will not arrive on time	–20.0	–24.3	–8.6	–18.9	–19.5	–17.1
4	6	Is willing to help solve any problem you may have, once you have purchased furniture/homewares from them	–12.8	–17.0	–8.7	–20.1	–17.7	–17.1
5	19	Rings you to advise when your furniture order will	–11.5	–17.0	–6.1	–15.0	–15.7	–15.1
6	20	Returns your calls promptly	–13.6	–19.9	–10.7	–20.8	–18.8	–20.3
7	14	Coordinates delivery with you	–9.4	–12.5	–2.0	–8.4	–11.6	–14.4
8	28	Staff are around when you need them	–11.2	–16.9	–14.2	–23.8	–16.8	–18.5
9	23	The after-sale process was well managed	–13.5	–15.9	–3.8	–17.0	–12.4	–14.1
10	22	Deliverers arrive at the arranged time	–14.6	–15.5	–6.0	–19.6	–13.4	–11.6
11	36	Gives you a realistic and acceptable date once you have bought an item	–13.5	–16.4	–1.6–1.18	–12.7	–14.2	–12.2
12	43	Delivery times are flexible, to suit your availability	–12.7	–15.4	–6.6	–11.7	–18.4	–7.9
13	41	Deliverers place your furniture where you ask	–0.1	0.1	7.3	0.1	–2.7	0.1
14	39	Sales staff understand your needs	–5.7	–7.8	–7.0	–6.8	–4.5	–9.1
15	15	Staff give you their total attention	–6.4	–11.4	–8.2	–13.4	–9.6	–17.3
16	13	Sales staff are genuine and caring about your needs	–6.8	–10.5	–1.9	–8.9	–8.6	–14.4

Table 7 Process quality index: Freedom Furniture and homeware buyers – total performance.

Furniture/homeware buyers		Factor weight (%)	Total		Total performance		
			EXP	*N*	PERF	*N*	GAP
Process quality index			**83.54**		**73.42**		**–10.12**
1	**After-sale follow-up**	**30**	**90.27**		**74.88**		**–15.39**
2	**Delivery**	**22**	**89.25**		**78.10**		**–11.15**
3	**Caring attitude**	**21**	**76.20**		**69.98**		**–6.22**
4	**Store**	**14**	**71.65**		**69.42**		**–2.23**
5	**Time-sensitive**	**13**	**83.28**		**72.15**		**–11.14**
1	**After-sale follow-up**	**30**	**90.27**		**74.88**		**–15.39**
7	Gives you what you expected	30					
17	You don't get the 'run around' trying to sort out problem(s)	30					
1	Rings you to advise your furniture order will not arrive on time	30					
6	Is willing to help solve any problem you may have, once you have purchased furniture/homewares from them	30					
19	Rings you to advise when your furniture order will arrive	30					
20	Returns your calls promptly	30					
14	Coordinates delivery with you	30					
28	Staff are around when you need them	30					
23	The after-sale process was well managed	30					
2	**Delivery**	**22**	**89.25**		**78.10**		**–11.15**
22	Deliverers arrive at the arranged time	22					
36	Gives you a realistic and acceptable date once you have bought an item	22					
43	Delivery times are flexible, to suit your availability	22					
41	Deliverers place your furniture where you ask	22					
3	**Caring attitude**	**21**	**76.20**		**69.98**		**–6.22**
39	Sales staff understand your needs	21	83.86	965	76.85	954	
15	Staff give you their total attention	21	83.62	965	74.07	903	
13	Sales staff are genuine	21	80.38	964	71.15	957	
10	Staff make you feel important	21	68.79	965	67.33	941	
16	Furniture made to order makes you feel special	21	64.37	950	60.52	701	
4	**Store**	**14**	**71.65**		**69.42**		**–2.23**
25	The purchase is well coordinated in the store	14	78.74	961	78.93	953	0.19
40	When staff are in uniform it is easy to identify them when you need help	14	77.73	965	80.92	917	3.18
2	Has a store layout which gives you ideas and options about home decorating	14	76.07	964	80.72	954	4.65
35	Staff collect around information/sales counters	14	71.64	961	71.59	946	–0.05
27	Follows up after the sale by phone or letter	14	54.08	963	34.95	853	–19.13
5	**Time-sensitive**	**13**	**83.28**		**72.15**		**–11.14**
9	Delivers the furniture item on the promised date	13	92.34	963	76.23	845	–16.11
8	Staff do not hassle you while you are browsing	13	82.43	965	85.77	963	3.34
11	Items are available immediately	13	75.08	965	54.45	952	–20.64

Table 8 Process quality index matrix: Freedom Furniture and homeware buyers.

QUICK RESPONSE		
2	18	You don't get the 'run around' trying to sort out problem(s)
3	1	Rings you to advise your furniture order will not arrive on time
4	6	Is willing to help solve any problem you may have once you have purchased furniture/homewares from the store
6	20	Returns your calls promptly
10	22	Deliverers arrive at the arranged time
11	36	Gives you a realistic and acceptable date once you have bought an item
DELAYED RESPONSE		
17	9	Delivers the furniture item on the promised date
24	11	Items are available immediately
26	27	Follows up after the sale by phone or letter
MONITOR CLOSELY		
1	7	Gives you what you expected
5	19	Rings you to advise when your furniture order will arrive
7	14	Co-ordinates delivery with you
8	28	Staff are around when you need them
9	23	The after sale process was well managed
12	43	Delivery times are flexible to suit your availability
13	41	Deliverers place your furniture where you ask
14	39	Sales staff understand your needs
15	15	Staff give you their total attention
16	13	Sales staff are genuine and caring about your needs
MONITOR		
18	10	Staff make you feel important
19	16	Furniture made-to-order makes you feel special
20	8	Has a child play room which is enjoyable and safe
21	25	Staff do not hassle you while you are browsing
22	40	The purchase is well coordinated in the store
23	2	Has a store layout which gives you ideas and option about home decorating
25	35	Staff collect around information/sales counters

FREEDOM MAKES AN ACQUISITION

INTRODUCTION: CONSIDERING THE OPTIONS

During 1998 and early 1999 the Freedom Executive took stock of its position and of the market. For some three or four years the market would offer little growth. Options for new sites were decreasing. The company had brought forward its planned growth of store expansion. In an economic environment that encouraged consumer spending Freedom had opened 14 company-owned stores in the space of a year.

The market-place was encouraging for Freedom. Figure 1 illustrates the shift of consumer preferences from traditional styling towards contemporary, modem designs. Added to this was an increase in consumer confidence resulting in increased expenditure patterns. The problem confronting Freedom Furniture was how the company should take advantage of this buoyant situation.

OPTIONS FOR GROWTH

It was clear to Freedom that if the momentum of the company was to be maintained opportunities for growth should be sought. The Executive was clear on a number of important issues:

- Any growth opportunity pursued should be within the scope of Freedom's core competencies
- It should reflect the mission or business scope of the business with respect to customer segments, customers' product expectations and its 'delivery' structure.

In addition the board were agreed that any expansion option they decided upon *should not have* a negative impact on the existing business and *should have* a positive impact on shareholder value.

A number of options were available to Freedom but these needed to be evaluated against a set of criteria that would ensure objective analysis. A brainstorming session developed these. The starting point was an analysis of Freedom's history and its evolution into the business it currently is. This

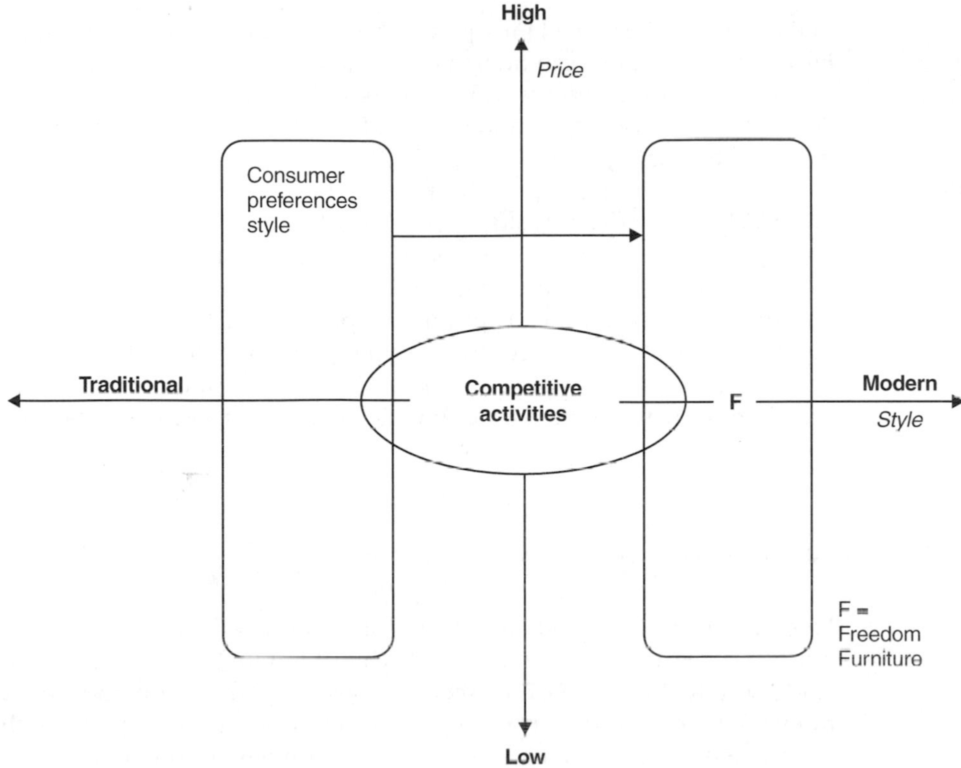

Figure 1 The Australian furniture market: 1998/99 – changes in customer preferences and style.

process identified a number of corporate characteristics. These included capital structure and constraints, its effective management and the systems developed to date, and the fact that it was a listed company.

The options were similarly identified. During the analysis an extensive range of alternatives emerged, these included:

- Do nothing
- Import a franchise
- Explore peripheral product markets
- Backward vertical integration
- Broaden the offer
- Dominate the middle and upper segments of the market
- Brand extensions
- International expansion
- Introduce the 'Big Box' concept
- Make an acquisition which offered the basis of profitable expansion

Not all of the options were exclusive, nor were they possibilities that could be undertaken immediately. Each was evaluated against the criteria determined earlier. Of all the options the acquisition route had most appeal. Furthermore an ideal candidate was available.

Guest and Anderson was a Victoria-based company. It had a turnover of $65 million, was profitable and was positioned in the middle and upper segments of the market.

The Guests Group operated 18 stores: 13 were Guests (a mainstream offer) and five were Andersons stores, positioned in the upmarket segment. The group operated in Victoria, Queensland and Western Australia. Being a family-owned business the group, if it were to grow, would have either to 'list' the company or find an appropriate partner. Bill Guest (current managing director, and who will continue as managing director of the Guests Division within the new expanded Freedom Group), commented: 'I believe with Freedom we have found a partner which shares our vision for the Group'.

ACQUISITION VS. ORGANIC GROWTH

Potential acquisition candidates were listed and evaluated. Some were ideal but expensive; others were not worthwhile. Despite the fact that Guests and Andersons had attraction, the Executive considered that a comparison exercise to evaluate the acquisition vs. organic growth was necessary. A number of advantages and disadvantages could be seen for either option. An acquisition brought with it a number of locations, customer acceptance, management and systems, and, in this instance, a record of profitability. An acquisition candidate which is rejected remains a competitor. Furthermore, an attempt to stretch the Freedom brand would be accompanied by risk. An advantage, therefore, is the fact that an acquisition would not impede the growth of the Freedom format provided that financially it remained a viable option.

Clearly the decision required objective analysis. A model was constructed in which revenue and cost projections were explored. A number of positioning options around the existing Freedom Furniture position were evaluated, using revenues and costs for both the acquisition and the organic growth options. Based upon the results the decision to proceed with the acquisition was made.

NEGOTIATING THE ACQUISITION

A number of considerations were made and these are worth examination. Guests and Andersons insisted that their names should continue and not be absorbed, and the Guests directors were concerned for the employees' job security. This matched well with Freedom's growth direction. They sought to expand as a group by further penetration of the medium/high price/contemporary/modern furniture sector. The Guests and Andersons acquisition offered Freedom this opportunity. In many respects they had achieved more than they could have hoped for: the acquisition of a profitable company; an opportunity to position two additional offers or retail brands in a sector they understood very well, and at the same time benefit from some obvious synergies.

The acquisition was financed by a combination of two thirds shares and the remainder in cash. Late in 1998 Freedom had entered the 'market' in a 7% share buy-back exercise aimed at increasing shareholder value by increasing share prices. They purchased the shares at $1.18; the shares were issued to Guests at $1.80; this represented 10.6% of the issued capital of the company. The total price paid by Freedom was $16.2 million in shares and $6.2 million in cash.

A NEED TO REVIEW STRUCTURE

Organization

Freedom Furniture was now the Freedom Group. It had three clearly separate brands, each with its own distinctive offer and customer group. A decision was taken to establish a Brands Director whose responsibility it would be to position the two new brands, Guests *and* Andersons in 'market-space' that made most of the opportunities identified for each of them *and* did not conflict with the existing Freedom positioning.

The structure that evolved was for three general managers, one for each of Freedom, Guests and Andersons with their own HRD functions to ensure that the separate corporate cultures necessary to reflect customer differences were maintained. Separate operations managers report into a Group Retail Director. There were other benefits in this, the largest being the opportunities for employees to progress within the Group. Prior to the acquisition concern was growing within the Executive that the existing Freedom structure was limiting the progress of able employees and that some might move on, not because of dissatisfaction but because of lack of opportunity. Now this was resolved. The ideal structure emerged: three separate companies with centralized services.

Some opportunity for synergy was clearly possible. The distribution function became centralized. The centralization of the finance function resulted in a number of efficiencies and savings. Most notable was the integration of accounts payable. The centralization of services has resulted in a review of cost allocation based upon sales levels as a proportion of the Group sales.

Finance

The acquisition also led to the restructuring of Freedom's finances. Management was concerned to avoid unnecessary gearing and to ensure that this

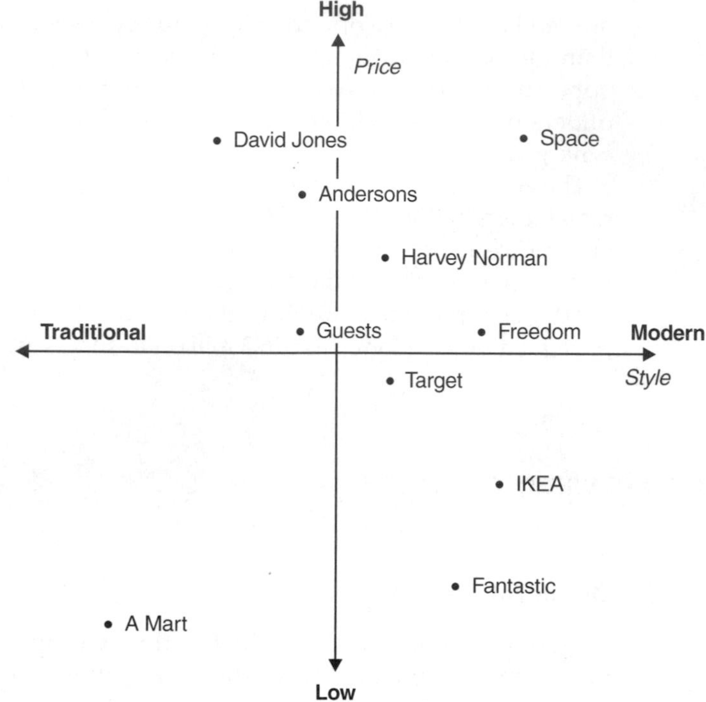

Figure 2 Positioning strategy – post acquisition.

policy was implemented, so the company negotiated a sale and lease back arrangement on its warehousing facility (This realized A$23.5 million). The result was that subsequent to the acquisition the gearing was significantly reduced.

Marketing

The market positioning decisions taken by the Executive are shown as Figure 2. Andersons has been positioned in a location that had been seen as offering opportunity for some time. Currently, Andersons' customer profile is quite close to this position and the changes to be made will be to reflect more emphasis than currently exists. Guests will be positioned in the competitive 'middle area' of the market. Both leave the Freedom brand clear to continue its growth unimpeded.

INDEX